W9-AYF-551

MEASUREMENT AND EVALUATION IN PSYCHOLOGY AND EDUCATION

SIXTH EDITION

Ch 3- 51- 70

Robert M. Thorndike
Western Washington University

Merrill,
an imprint of Prentice Hall
Upper Saddle River, New Jersey   *Columbus, Ohio*

Library of Congress Cataloging-in-Publication Data

Thorndike, Robert M.
    Measurement and evaluation in psychology and education / Robert M.
Thorndike.—6th ed.
      p.   cm.
    Rev. ed. of: Measurement and evaluation in psychology and
education / Robert M. Thorndike . . . [et al.]. 5th ed. c1991.
    Includes bibliographical references and index.
    ISBN 0-13-254178-5
    1. Educational tests and measurements.   2. Psychological tests.
I. Title
LB1131.M433   1997
371.'6—dc20

[371.2'6]   96-33590
                                             CIP

Cover art: © Diana Ong/SuperStock
Acquisitions Editor: Kevin Davis
Production Editor: Mary M. Irvin
Production Manager: Patricia A. Tonneman
Cover Designer: Russ Maselli
Design Coordinator: Julia Zonneveld Van Hook
Director of Marketing: Kevin Flanagan
Advertising/Marketing Coordinator: Julie Shough
Editorial Production Supervision: WordCrafters Editorial Services, Inc.

This book was set in Garamond by The Clarinda Company and was printed and bound by
R. R. Donnelley & Sons. The cover was printed by Phoenix Color Corp.

© 1997 by Prentice-Hall, Inc.
Simon & Schuster/A Viacom Company
Upper Saddle River, New Jersey 07458

All rights reserved. No part of this book may be reproduced, in any form or by any means,
without permission in writing from the publisher.

Earlier edition, © 1991, by Macmillan Publishing Company.

Printed in the United States of America

10 9 8 7 6 5 4 3

ISBN: 0-13-254178-5

Prentice-Hall International (UK) Limited, *London*
Prentice-Hall of Australia Pty. Limited, *Sydney*
Prentice-Hall of Canada, Inc., *Toronto*
Prentice-Hall Hispanoamericana, S. A., *Mexico*
Prentice-Hall of India Private Limited, *New Delhi*
Prentice-Hall of Japan, Inc., *Tokyo*
Simon & Schuster Asia Pte. Ltd., *Singapore*
Editora Prentice-Hall do Brasil, Ltda., *Rio de Janeiro*

Preface

When the first edition of this book was published in 1955, I was 11 years old and made minimal contribution. The second and third editions were also published without any input from me, but I started using the third edition for my own classes in measurement in 1970. My father, Robert L. Thorndike, and I discussed many measurement issues once I became psychometrically literate, so my reactions to the third edition had some indirect influence on the fourth, which was published just after my father retired. With the fifth edition I took over many of my father's responsibilities, although he continued to influence the revisions. Throughout these five versions of the book, Elizabeth Hagen provided a healthy dose of applied educational material, although much of her role was played by George Cunningham in the fifth edition. As this sixth edition goes to press, my father has been dead for six years, but his influence is still clearly present, both in parts of the text that retain his unique flair for language and in the profound influence he has had on my own thinking and professional development. Thanks, Pop.

During the four decades since the first edition, there have been major changes in educational theory and practice. Concern for the rights of all individuals without regard to color, gender, disability, or any number of other characteristics has become a central issue that has led to attempts to provide optimal educational experiences for all children. Society at large has been pressured to assure that everyone is given equal opportunity for access to higher education and to desirable employment. But even with these changes (and perhaps because of them), the need for objective, dependable information as the basis for making decisions remains. Tests provided much of that information in 1955, and they still remain an important source of information.

The first five editions of this book have helped almost three generations of educators and psychologists develop the skills to use test information; this sixth edition is intended to continue providing that service. To that end, four specialists in various areas of measurement theory and application were asked to prepare revisions of five chapters. One, my daughter Tracy Thorndike-Christ, an educational psychologist, has become the third generation to work on this book by revising the chapters on

Tests and Educational Decisions (Chapter 7) and Performance and Product Evaluation (Chapter 10). Max and Arleen Lewis, both clinical/counseling psychologists, prepared the revision of Chapter 11 on Personality, Interests, and Adjustment. Rick Ittenbach, a school psychologist, contributed revisions of Chapter 13, Testing in Special Situations, and Chapter 14, Professional and Legal Issues in Assessment.

This sixth edition continues our tradition of treating tests as sources of information that aid in decision making. We emphasize that tests exist to help people make decisions and that the quality of those decisions depends on a knowledgeable use of test information. Many of the problems that have been attributed to tests are as much as consequence of improper test use as of poorly constructed tests. Our purpose is to provide users with the information and skills needed to avoid making mistakes in using and interpreting test information.

CHANGES IN THE SIXTH EDITION

Reorganization

The first five editions of this book had a fairly strong emphasis on teacher-made tests. With this edition we are shifting the focus more toward the use of tests to support educational and counseling practitioners. The reason for this change is twofold. First, there is a decreasing role for the formal teacher-made test as more publishers are including assessment tools with their books. The kinds of assessment materials teachers construct are more likely to be performance evaluations and product assessments than formal tests. Second, the role of counseling professionals, both in the schools and in the community at large, has increased dramatically in recent years. It is important that counselors, school psychologists, and others in helping roles have a reasonable grounding in testing if they are to use tests effectively in practice.

We have reorganized the book into three parts. The first part, Chapters 1 through 6, provides a general overview of the issues in testing with which any user of test information should be familiar. It includes a chapter setting out our basic theme, followed by a chapter on necessary quantitative concepts, one on frames of reference (normative, ipsative, and criterion), moves on to chapters on reliability and validity of measurement procedures, and concludes with a chapter on practical issues, including a discussion of where to get information on specific tests. The validity chapter, in particular, has been expanded with greater emphasis on content definition as a critical element of test validity and coverage of multitrait-multimethod analysis of the convergent and discriminant validity aspects of construct validity.

The second part of the book, Chapters 7 through 12, provides material on measurement procedures for specific applications. Chapter 7 covers the kinds of decisions that must be made in educational settings and what kinds of test results are appropriate for each kind of decision. Chapter 8, Measures of General Cognitive Abilities, has been expanded to include a discussion of the major theories of cognitive abilities. The specific tests are then arranged by the underlying theory. Chapter 9, Standardized Achievement Tests, has been expanded to include information on individually administered tests. Chapter 10, Performance and Product Evaluation, introduces scoring rubrics and other methods for appraising behavior "on the fly" in nonstandardized settings. Chapter 11 introduces the major instruments for measuring interests, adjustment, and personality. Finally, Chapter 12 presents methods for measuring attitudes and for constructing rating scales and checklists.

The third part of the book has four chapters. The first is on testing exceptional children and includes a discussion of the historical legal issues as well as various practical issues in such assessment. Chapter 14 presents the legal and ethical responsibilities of test users. Chapter 15 discusses the process of standardized test construction with a primary focus on ability measurement. Guidelines for writing test items and procedures of item analysis form the major portion of the chapter. The last chapter covers a number of special topics in testing, including introductions to item response theory and meta analysis. The major addition to this chapter is a brief introduction to the process and interpretation of factor analysis.

Pedagogical Aids

Each chapter begins with a listing of topics to be covered and ends with a summary statement. The topic listings help students by giving them a brief overview of the material they will encounter; the summaries allow them to review and remember key points. All chapters are also followed by suggested readings, which can provide alternate perspectives on the issues covered in the chapter or present the material in greater depth, and by study questions, which allow students to test their understanding of concepts. A complete reference list appears at the end of the book.

Updated Sources for Tests

We have continued our practice of including a chapter that gives detailed information on where to get information about tests. We have placed this material earlier in the book (Chapter 6) and revised its references to the major electronic data bases as well as the more traditional sources. We have also continued to include extensive appendices providing annotated lists of various kinds of tests, a list of major test publishers, and computational details for certain statistics.

Supplementary Materials

An *Instructor's Manual,* available free to professors who adopt the text, provides chapter outlines, additional study questions for students, lists of major topics, and over 400 test items. These test items are available in *computerized form* for use with IBM-PCs and compatibles and Macintosh computers.

ACKNOWLEDGMENTS

I would like to than the following reviewers for their insightful comments: Susan M. Brookhart, Duquesne University; Sonya L. Blixt, Kent State University; Yi-Ming Hsu, West Chester University; Edward Neukrug, Old Dominion University; and Ruth N. Oliver, Troy State University. I am grateful to all of them, as well as to my wife, Elva, who has now been put through the process of authorship and production five times, and who continues to offer support and understanding.

Robert M. Thorndike

CONTENTS

CHAPTER 4

Qualities Desired in Any Measurement Procedure: Reliability   95

CHAPTER 5

Qualities Desired in Any Measurement Procedure: Validity   129

CHAPTER 6

Practical Issues Relating to Testing   169

CHAPTER 7

Assessment and Educational Decisions   193

Prepared by Tracy Thorndike-Christ

CHAPTER 8

Aptitude Tests   217

CHAPTER 9

Standardized Achievement Tests   263

Prepared by Tracy Thorndike-Christ

CHAPTER 10

Performance and Product Evaluation   287

CHAPTER 11

Interests, Personality, and Adjustment   307

Prepared by Arleen Lewis and Max Lewis

CHAPTER 12

Attitudes and Rating Scales   351

CHAPTER 13

Assessment and Exceptional Children   393

Prepared by Richard F. Ittenbach

CHAPTER 14

Ethics and Issues in Assessment   419

Prepared by Richard F. Ittenbach

CHAPTER 15

Principles of Objective Test Development   443

CHAPTER 16

Special Topics in Test Development and Use   487

References   521

APPENDIX 1

Calculating the Mean, Standard Deviation, and Correlation Coefficient   533

APPENDIX 2

Percent of Cases Falling Below Selected Values on the Normal Curve   539

APPENDIX 3

Sources for Educational and Psychological Tests   541

APPENDIX 4

CHAPTER 1

Fundamental Issues in Measurement

INTRODUCTION

Societies and individuals have always had to make decisions. Making decisions is a requirement of daily life for everyone. We all decide when to get up in the morning, what to have for breakfast, and what to wear; we make so many personal decisions with such regularity that we hardly think about the process.

Some decisions that must be made less frequently require careful thought and analysis: Which college should I attend? What should I major in? Should I accept a job with XYZ Enterprises? Decisions of this kind are best made based on information about the alternative choices and their consequences: Am I interested in a particular college? What job prospects will it open for me? What are the chances that I will succeed? What are the benefits and working conditions at XYZ Enterprises?

Other decisions are made by individuals acting for the larger society. Daily, teachers must make decisions about the best educational experiences to provide for students, based on an assessment of their current knowledge and abilities. A school psychologist may have to decide whether to recommend a special educational experience for a child who is having difficulty in reading or mathematics. School, district, and state educational administrators must make decisions about educational policy and may have to produce evidence for state and local school boards on the achievement of students. Employers must decide which job applicants to hire and which positions they should fill. A college counselor must decide what action to take with a student who is having difficulty adjusting to the personal freedom that a college environment provides. The list of decisions that people must make is as long as the list of human interactions.

We generally assume that the more people know about the factors involved in their decisions, the better their decisions are likely to be. That is, more and better information is likely to lead to better decisions. Of course, merely having information is no guarantee that it will be used to the best advantage. The decision maker must also know how to use the information and what inferences it does and does not support. Our purpose in this book is to present some of the basic concepts, practices, and methods that have been developed in education and psychology to aid in the decision-making process. With these methods, the potential decision maker will be better prepared to obtain and use the information needed to make sound decisions.

A LITTLE HISTORY

Although educational measurement has gained considerable prominence in recent decades, the formal evaluation of educational achievement and the use of this information to make decisions has been going on for centuries. As far back as the dawn of the Christian era, the Chinese used competitive examinations to select mandarins for civil service (DuBois, 1970; R. M. Thorndike, 1990a). Over the centuries, they developed an elaborate system of checks and controls to eliminate possible bias in their testing—procedures that in many ways resembled the best of modern practice. For example, examinees were isolated to prevent possible cheating, compositions were copied by trained scribes to eliminate the chance that differences in penmanship might affect scores, and each examination was evaluated by a pair of graders, differences being resolved by a third judge. In a number of ways, Chinese practice served as a model for developing civil service examinations in western Europe and America during the 1800s.

Formal measurement procedures began to appear in Western educational practice during the 19th century. For several centuries, secondary schools and universities had been using essay and oral examinations to evaluate student achievement, but in 1897, Joseph M. Rice used some of the first uniform written examinations to test spelling achievement of students in the public schools of Boston. Rice wanted the schools to make room in the curriculum for teaching science and argued that some of the time spent on spelling drills could be used for that purpose. He demonstrated that the amount of time devoted to spelling drills was not related to achievement in spelling and concluded that this time could be reduced, thus making time to teach science. His study represents one of the first times tests were used to evaluate curriculum and to make a curriculum decision.

Throughout the latter half of the 19th century, pioneering work in the infant science of psychology involved developing new ways to measure human behavior and experience. Many of the measurement advances of the time came from laboratory studies such as those of Hermann Ebbinghaus, who in 1896 introduced the completion test (fill in the blanks) as a way to measure mental fatigue in students. Other important advances, such as the development of the correlation coefficient by Sir Francis Galton and Karl Pearson, were made in the service of research on the distribution and causes of human differences. The late 1800s have been characterized by DuBois (1970) as the *laboratory period* in the history of psychological measurement.

Increasing interest in human differences in the second half of the 19th century can be traced to the need to make decisions in three contexts. First, there was the growing demand for objectivity and accountability in assessing student performance in the public schools, which resulted from the enactment of mandatory school attendance laws. These laws brought into the schools for the first time a large number of students who were of middle or lower socioeconomic background and unfamiliar with formal education. Many of these children performed poorly and were considered by many educators of the time to be "feebleminded" and unable to learn. The development of accurate measurement methods and instruments was seen as a way to differentiate children with true mental handicaps from those who suffered from disadvantaged backgrounds. Second, the medical community was in the process of refining its ideas about abnormal behavior. Behavioral measurements were seen as a way to classify and diagnose patients. Third, all sorts of government agencies began to replace patronage systems for granting employment with examination of the prospective employees' abilities. Tests began to be used as the basis of employee selection.

Not until the first years of the 20th century did well-developed prototypes of modern educational and psychological measurements begin to appear. Although it is difficult to identify a single event that started it all, the 1905 publication of the Binet-Simon scales of mental ability is often taken as the beginning of the modern era in behavioral measurement. These scales, originally published in French but soon translated into English, represented the first successful attempt to measure complex mental processes with a standard set of tasks of graded complexity. The Binet-Simon scales were designed to aid educators in identifying students whose mental ability was insufficient for them to benefit from standard public education. On the basis of the mental measurement, a decision was then made whether to place these students in special classes. Subsequent editions of the scales, published in 1908 and 1911, contained tasks that spanned the full range of abilities for school-age children and could be used to identify students at either extreme of the ability continuum.

At the same time that Binet and Simon were developing the first measures of intelligence, E. L. Thorndike and his students at Teachers College of Columbia University were tackling problems related to measuring school abilities. Their work ranged from theoretical developments on the nature of the measurement process to the creation of scales to assess classroom learning of reading and arithmetic, and level of skill development in tasks such as handwriting.

It is convenient to divide the history of mental testing in the 20th century into five periods: an early period, a boom period, a first period of criticism, a battery period, and a second period of criticism.

The Early Period

The *early period,* which comprises the years before American entry into World War I, was a period of tentative exploration and theory development. The Binet-Simon scales were revised twice by Binet and were brought to the United States by several pioneers in measurement. The most influential of these was Lewis Terman of Stanford University. In 1916, Terman published the first version of a test that in its fourth edition is still one of the standards by which measures of intelligence are judged: the Stanford-Binet Intelligence Scale. Working with Terman at this time, Arthur Otis began to explore the possibility of testing the mental ability of children and adults in groups. In Australia, S. D. Porteus prepared a maze test of intelligence for use with people with hearing or language handicaps.

During the time Binet was developing the first modern test of intelligence, Charles Spearman published two important theories relating to the measurement of human abilities. The first was a statistical theory that proposed to describe and account for the inconsistency in measurements of human behavior. The second theory claimed to account for the fact that different measures of cognitive ability showed substantial consistency in the ways that they ranked people. The statistical theory to describe inconsistency has developed into the concept of reliability that we will discuss in Chapter 4. Spearman's second theory, that there is a single dimension of ability underlying most human performance, played a major role in determining the direction that measures of ability took for many years. Spearman proposed that the consistency of people's performance on different ability measures was the result of the level of general intelligence that they possessed. We discuss modern descendants of this theory and the tests that have been developed to measure intelligence in Chapter 8.

The Boom Period

American involvement in World War I brought a need to expand the army very quickly. For the first time, the new science of psychology was called on to play a part in a military situation. This event started a 15-year *boom period* during which there were many advances and innovations in the field of testing and measurement. As part of the war effort, a group of psychologists expanded Otis' work to develop and implement the first large-scale group testing of ability with the Army Alpha (a verbal test) and the Army Beta (a test using mazes and puzzles similar to Porteus' that required no spoken or written language). The Army Alpha was the first widely distributed test to use the multiple-choice item form. The first objective measure of personality, the Woodworth Personal Data Sheet, was also developed for the army to help identify those emotionally unfit for military service. The Alpha and Beta were used to select officer trainees and to remove the intellectually handicapped from military service.

In the 12 years following the war, the variety of behaviors that were subjected to measurement continued to expand rapidly. E. K. Strong and his students began to measure vocational interests to help college students choose majors and careers consistent with their interests. Measurements of personality and ability were developed and refined, and the use of standardized tests for educational decisions became more widespread. In 1929, L. L. Thurstone proposed ways to scale and measure attitudes and values. Many people considered it only a matter of time before accurate measurement and prediction of all types of human behavior would be achieved.

The First Period of Criticism

The 1930s saw a crash not only in the stock market but also in the expectations for mental measurement. This time covered the *period of criticism* and *consolidation.* To be sure, new tests were published, most notably the original Kuder scales of vocational interests, the Minnesota Multiphasic Personality Inventory, and the first serious competitor for the Stanford-Binet, the Wechsler-Bellevue Intelligence Scale. Major advances were also made in the mathematical theory underlying tests, particularly L. L. Thurstone's refinements of a statistical procedure known as factor analysis. However, it was becoming clear that the problems of measuring human behavior had not all been solved and were much more difficult than they had appeared to be in the heady years of the 1920s.

The Battery Period

In the 1940s, psychological measurement was once again called on for use in the military service. As part of the war effort, batteries of tests were developed that measured several different abilities. Based on the theory developed by Thurstone and others that there were several distinct types or dimensions of abilities, these test batteries were used to place military recruits in the positions for which they were best suited. The success of this approach in reducing failure rates in various military training programs led the measurement field into a period of emphasis on test batteries and factor analysis. For 25 years, until about 1965, efforts were directed toward analyzing the dimensions of human behavior by developing an increasing variety of tests of ability and personality. Taxonomies of ability, such as those of Bloom (1956) and Guilford (1959, 1985), were offered to describe the range of mental functioning.

During the 1950s, educational and psychological testing grew to become big business. The use of nationally normed, commercially prepared tests to assess student progress became a common feature of school life. Business, industry, and the civil service system made increasing use of measurements of attitudes and personality, as well as ability, in hiring and promotion decisions. Patients in mental institutions were routinely assessed through a variety of measures of personality and adjustment. The widespread use and misuse of tests brought about a wave of protests.

The Second Period of Criticism

The beginning of a *second period of criticism* was signaled in 1965 by a series of congressional hearings on testing as an invasion of privacy. Since that time, there has been a continuing debate over the use of ability and personality testing in public education and employment. A major concern has been the possible use of tests to discriminate, intentionally or otherwise, against women and/or members of minority groups in education and employment. As a result of this concern, the tests themselves have been very carefully scrutinized for biased content, certain types of testing practices have been eliminated or changed, and much more attention is given to the rights of individuals. The testing industry has responded vigorously to making tests fair to all who take them, but this has not been sufficient to forestall both legislation and administrative and court decisions restricting the use of tests. This situation is unfortunate because it deprives decision makers of some of the best information on which to base their actions. In effect, we may have thrown out the baby with the bath water in our efforts to eliminate bias from the practice of testing. In Chapter 14 we will take a closer look at the controversies surrounding educational and psychological uses of tests.

TYPES OF DECISIONS

Educational and psychological evaluation and measurement have evolved to help people make decisions related to people, individually or in groups. Teachers, counselors, school administrators, and psychologists in business and industry, for example, are continuously involved in making decisions about people or in helping people make decisions for and about themselves. The role of measurement procedures is to provide information that will permit these decisions to be informed and appropriate.

Some decisions are *instructional;* many decisions made by teachers and school psychologists are of this sort. A decision may relate to a class as a whole: For example, should class time be spent reviewing "carrying" in addition? Or does most of the class have adequate competency in this skill? Other decisions relate to specific students: For example, what reading materials are likely to be suitable for Mary, in view of her interests and level of reading skill? If such decisions are to be made wisely, it is important to know, in the first case, the overall level of skill of the class in "carrying" and, in the second, how competent a reader Mary is.

Some decisions are *curricular.* A school may be considering a curricular change such as introducing computer-assisted instruction to teach the principles of multiplying fractions. Should the change be made? A wise decision hinges on finding out how well students are found to progress in learning to multiply fractions using this approach rather than the conventional one. The evidence of progress can only be as good as the measures of mathematics competence we use to assess the outcomes of the two alternative instructional programs.

Some decisions are *selection* ones made by an employer or a decision maker in an educational institution. A popular college must decide which applicants to admit to its freshman class. Criteria for admission are likely to be complex, but one criterion will usually be that the admitted student is likely to be able to complete successfully the academic work that the college requires. Selection decisions also arise in employment. The employer, seeking to identify the potentially more effective employees, may find that performance in a controlled testing situation provides information that can improve the accuracy and objectivity of hiring decisions, resulting in improved productivity and greater employee satisfaction.

Sometimes decisions are *placement,* or *classification,* decisions. A high school may have to decide whether a senior should be put in the advanced placement section in mathematics, or in the regular section. An army personnel technician may have to decide whether a recruit should be assigned to the school for electronic technicians or the school for cooks and bakers. A family doctor makes a classification decision when he or she diagnoses a backache to be the result of muscle strain or a pinched nerve. For placement decisions, the decision maker needs information to help predict how much the individual will learn from or how successful the candidate will be in each of the alternative programs. Information helps the person making a classification, or placement, decision to identify the group to which the individual most likely belongs.

Finally, many decisions can best be called *personal* decisions. They are choices that each individual makes at the many crossroads of life. Should I plan to go on for a master's degree or to some other type of post-college training? Or should I seek a job at the end of college? If a job, what kind of job? In light of this decision, what sort of program should I take in college? The more information people have about their own interests and abilities, the more informed decisions they can make on questions like these.

MEASUREMENT AND DECISIONS

Educational and psychological measurement techniques can help people make better decisions by providing more and better information. Throughout this book, we will identify and describe properties that measurement devices must have if they are to help people make sound decisions. We will show the form in which test results should be presented if they are to be most helpful to the decision maker. As we look at each type of assessment technique, we will ask for what types of decisions the particular technique can contribute valuable information. We will be concerned with a variety of factors, including poor motivation, emotional upset, inadequate schooling, or atypical cultural background, all of which can distort the information provided by a test, questionnaire, or other assessment procedure. We will also consider precautions that need to be observed in using the information in decision making.

The Role of Values in Decision Making

Measurement procedures do not make decisions; *people* make decisions. At most, measurement procedures can provide information on some of the factors that are relevant to the decision. A scholastic aptitude test can provide an indication of how well Grace is likely to do in college-level work. Combined with information about how academically demanding the engineering program is at Siwash University, the test score can be used to make a specific estimate of how well Grace is likely to do in that program. However, only Grace can decide whether she should go to Siwash and whether she should study engineering. Is she interested in engineering? Does she have a personal reason for wanting to go to Siwash rather than to some other university? Are there economic factors? In what role does Grace aspire to serve? Maybe she has no interest in further education and would rather be a beachcomber.

This example should make it clear that decisions about courses of action to take involve values as well as facts. A scholastic aptitude test produces a score that is a *fact,* and that fact may lead to a prediction that Grace has five chances in six of being admitted to Siwash and only one chance in six of being admitted to Harvard. But, if she considers Harvard 10 times more desirable than Siwash, it still might be a sensible decision for her to apply to Harvard despite her radically lower chance of being admitted. The test provides no information about the domain of values. This information must be supplied from other sources before Grace can make a sensible decision.

The issue of *values* affects institutional decision makers as well as individuals. An aptitude test may permit an estimate of the probability of success for a Black or a Hispanic student, in comparison with the probability of success for a White student, in some types of professional training. However, an admission decision would have to include, explicitly or implicitly, some judgment on the relative value to society of adding more White individuals to the profession in comparison with the value of having increased African American or Hispanic representation.

Issues of value are always complex and often controversial, but they are frequently deeply involved in decision making. Very few decisions are value-neutral. It is important that this fact be recognized, and it is also important that assessment procedures that can supply better information not be blamed for the ambiguities or conflicts that may be found in our value system. We should not kill the messenger who brings us news we do not want to hear. Rather, we should consider policies and procedures that might change the unwelcome facts.

As we suggested at the beginning of this chapter, all aspects of human behavior involve decisions. We *must* make decisions. Even taking no action in a situation is a decision. In most cases, people weigh the evidence on the likelihood of various outcomes and the positive and negative consequences of each possible outcome. The role of educational and psychological assessment procedures can be no more than to provide some of the information on which certain kinds of decisions may be based. The evidence suggests that, when properly used, these procedures can provide useful information that is more accurate than that provided by alternate approaches. The study of educational and psychological assessment should yield an understanding of the tools and techniques available for obtaining the kinds of information about people that these measures can yield. Beyond that, such study should provide criteria for evaluating the information that these tools offer, for judging the degree of confidence that can be placed in the information, and for sensing the limitations inherent in that information.

So far, we have considered practical decisions leading to action. Measurement is also important in providing information to guide theoretical decisions. In these cases, the desired result is not action but, instead, understanding. Do girls read better than boys do? A reading test is needed to obtain the information on which to base a decision. Do students who are anxious about tests do worse on them than students who are not anxious? A questionnaire on "test anxiety" and a test of academic achievement could be used to obtain information helpful in reaching a decision on this issue. Measurement is fundamental to answering nearly all the questions that science asks, not only in the physical sciences but also in the behavioral and biological sciences.

STEPS IN THE MEASUREMENT PROCESS

In this book, we discuss the measurement of human abilities, interests, and personality traits. We need to pause for a moment to look at what is implied by measurement and what requirements must be met if we are legitimately to discuss measurement. We also need to ask how well the techniques for measuring the human characteristics of interest do in fact meet these requirements.

Measurement in any field involves three common steps: (1) identifying and defining the quality or the attribute that is to be measured, (2) determining the set of operations by which the attribute may be isolated and displayed for observation, and (3) establishing a set of procedures or definitions for translating our observations into quantitative statements of degree or amount. An understanding of these steps and of the difficulties that each presents provides a sound foundation for understanding the procedures and problems of measurement in psychology and education.

Identifying and Defining the Attribute

We never measure a thing or a person. We always measure a *quality* or an *attribute* of the thing or person. We measure, for example, the *length* of a table, the *temperature* of a blast furnace, the *durability* of an automobile tire, the *flavor* of a soft drink, the *intelligence* of a school child, or the *emotional maturity* of an adolescent. Psychologists and educators frequently use the term *construct* to refer to the more abstract and difficult-to-observe properties of people, such as their intelligence or personality.

When we deal with simple physical attributes, such as length, it rarely occurs to us to wonder about the meaning or definition of the attribute. A clear meaning for length was established long ago in the history of both the species and the individual. The units for expressing length and the operations for making the property manifest have changed over the years; however, the underlying concepts have not. Although mastery of the concepts of *long* and *short* may represent significant accomplishments in the life of a preschool child, the concepts are automatic in adult society. We all know what we mean by *length.* The construct of length is one about which there is little disagreement, and the operations by which length can be determined are well known.

However, this level of agreement and clarity of definition do not exist for all physical attributes. What do we mean by durability in an automobile tire? Do we mean resistance to wear and abrasion from contact with the road? Do we mean resistance to puncture by pointed objects? Do we mean resistance to deterioration and decay with the passage of time and exposure to the elements? Or do we mean some combination of these three and possibly other factors? Until we can reach some agreement on what we mean by durability, we can make no progress toward measuring it. To the extent that we disagree on what durability means (i.e., on a definition of the construct), we will disagree on what procedures are appropriate for measuring it. If we use different procedures, we are likely to get different results from our measurements, and we will disagree on the value that we obtain to represent the durability of a particular brand of tire.

The problem of agreeing on what a given construct means is even more acute when we start to consider those attributes of concern to the psychologist or educator. What do we mean by intelligence? What kinds of behavior shall we characterize as intelligent? Shall we define the construct primarily in terms of dealing with ideas and abstract concepts? Or will it include dealing with things—with concrete objects? Will it refer primarily to behavior in novel situations? Or will it include responses in familiar and habitual settings? Will it refer to speed and fluency of response, or to level of complexity of reaction without regard to time? Will it include skill in social interactions? What kinds of products result from the exercise of intelligence: a theory about atomic structures, a ballet, or a snowman? We all have a general idea of what we mean when we characterize behavior as intelligent, but there are many specific points on which we may disagree as we try to make our definition precise. This problem of precisely defining the attribute is true for almost all psychological constructs—more for some than for others. And the first problem that psychologists or educators face as they try to measure attributes is arriving at clear, precise, and generally accepted definitions of those attributes.

Of course, there is another question that we must answer before we face the problem of defining the attribute. We must decide which attributes are relevant and important to measure if our description is to be useful. A description may fail to be useful for the need at hand because the chosen features are irrelevant. For example, in describing a painting, we might report its height, breadth, and weight. We might report these attributes with great precision and reach high agreement about the amount of each property the painting possesses. If our concern were to crate the picture for shipment, these might be just the items of information that we would need. However, if our purpose were to characterize the painting as a work of art, our description would be useless; the attributes of the painting we just described would be irrelevant to its quality as a work of art.

Similarly, a description of a person may be of little value for our purpose if we choose the wrong things to describe. A company selecting employees to become truck drivers might test their verbal comprehension and ability to solve quantitative problems, getting very accurate measures of these functions. It is likely, however, that information on these factors would be of little help in identifying people who have low accident records and would be steady and dependable on the job. Other factors, such as eye-hand coordination, depth perception, and freedom from uncontrolled aggressive impulses might prove much more relevant to the tasks and pressures that a truck driver faces.

Consider a high school music teacher who thoroughly tested the pupils' knowledge of such facts as who wrote the "Emperor Concerto" and whether andante is faster than allegro. The teacher would obtain a dependable appraisal of their knowledge about music and musicians without presenting them with a single note of actual music, a single theme or melody, a single interpretation or appraisal of living music. As an appraisal of musical appreciation, such a test seems almost worthless because it uses bits of factual knowledge *about* music and composers in place of information that would indicate progress in appreciation of the music itself. It is important to measure traits that are relevant to the decisions to be made rather than merely to measure traits that are easy to assess. We will discuss the issue of relevance again when we cover validity in Chapter 5.

Determining Operations to Isolate and Display the Attribute

The second aspect of measurement is finding or inventing a set of operations that will isolate the attribute of interest and display it. The operations for measuring the length of an object such as a table have been essentially unchanged for many years. We convey them to the child early in elementary school. The ruler, the meter stick, and the tape measure are uniformly accepted as appropriate instruments, and laying one of them along an object is an appropriate procedure for displaying to the eye the length of the table, desk, or other object. But the operations for measuring length, or distance, are not always so simple. By what operations do we measure the distance from New York to Chicago? From the earth to the sun? From our solar system to the giant spiral galaxy in Andromeda? How shall we measure the length of a tuberculosis bacillus or the diameter of a neutron? Physical science has progressed by developing both instruments that extend the capabilities of our senses and indirect procedures that make accessible to us amounts too great or too small for the simple, direct approach of laying a measuring stick along the object. The operations for measuring length, or distance, have become indirect, elaborate, and increasingly precise. These less intuitive methods (such as the shift of certain wavelengths of light toward the red end of the spectrum) are accepted because they give results that are consistent, verifiable, and useful.

Returning to the example of the durability of the automobile tire, we can see that the operations for eliciting or displaying that attribute will depend on and interact with the definition that we have accepted for it. If our definition is in terms of resistance to abrasion, we need to develop some standard and uniform procedure for applying an abrasive force to a specimen and gauging the rate at which the rubber wears away, that is, a standardized simulated road test. If we have indicated puncture resistance as the central concept, we need a way of applying graduated puncturing forces. If our definition is in terms of resistance to deterioration from sun, oil, and other destructive agents, our procedure must expose the samples to these agents and provide some index of the resulting loss of strength or resilience. A definition that incorporates more than one aspect will require an assessment of each, with appropriate weight, and combine the aspects in an appropriate way; that is, if our definition of durability, for example, includes resistance to abrasion, punctures, and deterioration, then a measure of durability must assess all of these properties and combine them in some way to give a single index of durability.

The definition of an attribute and the operations for eliciting it interact. On the one hand, the definition we have set up determines what we will accept as relevant and reasonable operations. Conversely, the operations that we can devise to elicit or display the attribute constitute in a very practical sense the definition of that attribute. An attribute defined in this way is said to have an *operational definition.* The set of procedures we are willing (or forced by our lack of ingenuity) to accept as showing the durability of an automobile tire become the operational definition of durability for us and may limit what we can say about it.

The history of psychological and educational measurement during the 20th century has largely been the history of the invention of instruments and procedures for eliciting, in a standard way and under uniform conditions, the behaviors that serve as indicators of the relevant attributes of people. The series of tasks devised by Binet and his successors constitute operations for eliciting behavior that is indicative of intelligence, and the Stanford-Binet and other tests have come to provide operational definitions of intelligence. The fact that there is no single universally accepted test and that different tests vary somewhat in the tasks they include and the order in which they rank people are evidence that we do not have complete consensus on what intelligence is or on what the appropriate procedures are for eliciting it. This lack of consensus is generally characteristic of the state of the art in psychological and educational measurement. There is enough ambiguity in our definitions and enough variety in the instruments we have devised to elicit the relevant behaviors that different measures of what is alleged to be the same trait may rank people quite differently. This fact requires that we be very careful not to overgeneralize the results of our measurements.

The problem of developing an operational definition for the attribute, or characteristic, of interest is also present in the classroom. Teachers regularly face the problem of assessing student performance, but what we will call performance is closely linked with the way we assess it. Only to the extent that teachers agree on their operational definitions of student achievement will their assessments have comparable meaning. If one teacher emphasizes quick recall of facts in his assessments and another looks for application of principles in hers, they are, to some undetermined extent, evaluating different behaviors, and the grades they give their students will mean different things. Here, we do not suggest that this difference in emphasis is inappropriate, only that it is a fact of which educators should be aware. This variability in definitions also provides a major impetus for standardized achievement tests, because such tests are seen as providing a common definition of the attribute to be measured and the method of measurement. The definition provided by the test may not exactly represent what either teacher means by achievement in Subject X, but such definitions usually are developed to provide an adequate fit to the definitions most teachers espouse.

Quantifying the Attribute

The third step in the measurement process, once we have accepted a set of operations for eliciting an attribute, is to express the result of those operations in quantitative terms. *Measurement involves assigning numbers to objects or people;* the numbers represent how much of the attribute is present in the person or thing. Using numbers has several advantages, two of which concern us. First, quantification makes communication more efficient and precise. We know much more from the statement that Ralph is 6 ft tall and weighs 175 lbs than we could learn from an attempt to describe Ralph's size in nonquantitative terms. We will see in Chapter 3 that much of the meaning that numbers have comes from the context in which the measurements are made, but, given that context, information in quantitative form is more compact, more easily understood, and generally more accurate than is the same information in other forms, such as verbal descriptions or photographs. In fact, we are so accustomed to communicating some types of information, such as temperature or age, in quantitative terms that we would have difficulty using another framework.

A second major advantage of quantification is that we can apply the power of mathematics to our observations to reveal broader levels of meaning. Consider, for example, trying to describe the performance of a class on a reading test or the accomplishments of a batter in baseball. In either case, we are accustomed to using the average as a summary of several individual performances. For many purposes, it is useful to be able to add, subtract, multiply, or divide to bring out the full meaning that a set of information may have. Some of the mathematical operations that are useful to educators and psychologists in summarizing their quantitative information are described in Chapter 2.

The critical initial step in quantification is to use a set of rules for assigning numbers so that we may answer the question, how many or how much? Such a set of rules is called a *scale*. In the case of the length of a table the question becomes, how many inches? The inch, or the meter, represents the basic unit, and the set of rules includes the measuring instrument itself and the act of laying the instrument along the object to be measured.

We can demonstrate that any inch equals any other inch by laying two inch-long objects side by side and seeing their equality. Such a demonstration is direct and straightforward proof of equality that is sufficient for some of the simplest physical measures. For measuring devices such as the thermometer, equality of units rests on a *definition*. Thus, we define equal increases in temperature to correspond to equal amounts of expansion of a volume of mercury. One degree Centigrade is defined as 1/100 of the difference between the freezing and boiling points of water. Long experience with this definition has shown it to be useful because it gives results that relate in an orderly and meaningful way to many other physical measures. (Beyond a certain point—the boiling point of mercury—this particular definition breaks down. However, other procedures that can be used outside this range can be shown to yield results equal to those of the mercury thermometer. The same principle allows educators to use a graded series of tests to assess student progress over several years.)

None of our psychological attributes have units whose equality can be demonstrated by direct comparison in the way that the equality of inches or pounds can, at least not by any currently available definition or measurement procedure. How will we demonstrate that arithmetic Problem X is equal, in amount of arithmetic ability that it represents, to arithmetic Problem Y? How can we show that one symptom of anxiety is equal to another anxiety indicator? For the qualities of concern to the psychologist or educator, we always have to fall back on some definition to provide units and quantification. Most frequently, we call one task successfully completed—a word defined, an arithmetic problem solved, an analogy completed, or an endorsement of an attitude statement—equal to any other task in the series and then use the total number of successes for an individual as the value representing the person on the particular attribute. This count of tasks successfully completed, or of choices of a certain type, provides a plausible and manageable definition of amount, but we have no adequate evidence of the equivalence of different test tasks or different questionnaire responses. By what right or evidence do we treat a number series item such as *1, 3, 6, 10, 15,* __?__, __?__ as showing the same amount of intellectual ability as, for example, a verbal analogies item like *Hot is to cold as wet is to* __?__ ?

The definition of equivalent tasks and, consequently, of units for psychological tests is shaky at best. When we have to deal with a teacher's rating of a student's cooperativeness or a supervisor's evaluation of an employee's initiative, for example, where a set of categories such as "superior," "very good," "good," "satisfactory," and "unsatisfactory" is used, the meaningfulness of the units in which these ratings are expressed is even more suspect.

Problems Relating to the Measurement Process

In psychological and educational measurement, we encounter problems in relation to each of the three steps just described.

First, we have problems in selecting the attributes of concern and in defining them clearly, unequivocally, and in mutually agreeable terms. Even for something as straightforward as reading ability, we can get a range of interpretations. To what extent should a definition include each of the following abilities?

1. Read quickly
2. Convert visual symbols to sounds
3. Obtain direct literal meanings from the text
4. Draw inferences that go beyond what is directly stated
5. Be aware of the author's bias or point of view

As we deal with more complex and intangible concepts such as cooperativeness, anxiety, adjustment, or rigidity, we may expect even more diversity in definition.

Second, we encounter problems in devising procedures to elicit the relevant attributes. For some psychological attributes, we have been fairly successful in setting up operations that call on the individual to display the attribute and permit us to observe it under uniform and standardized conditions. We have had this success primarily in the domain of abilities, where standardized tests have been assembled in which the examinee is called on, for instance, to read with understanding, to perceive quantitative relationships, or to identify correct forms of expression. However, there are many attributes with which we clearly have been less successful. By what standard operations can we elicit, in a form in which we can assess it, a potential employee's initiative, a client's anxiety, or a soldier's suitability for combat duty? With continued research and with more ingenuity, we may hope to devise improved operations for making certain of these attributes or qualities manifest, but identifying suitable measurement operations for many psychological attributes will remain a problem.

Finally, even our best psychological units of measure leave much to be desired. Units are set equal by definition; the definition may have a certain plausibility, but the equality of units cannot be established in any fundamental sense. For this reason, the addition, subtraction, and comparison of scores will always be somewhat suspect. Furthermore, the precision with which the attribute is assessed—the consistency from one occasion to another or from one appraiser to another—is often discouragingly low.

In spite of the problems involved in developing educational and psychological measuring devices, the task has proved to be worthwhile. The procedures now available have developed a record of usefulness in helping individuals make decisions in a wide variety of human contexts. Efficiency of education and equality of opportunity are enhanced by the proper use and interpretation of tests. Use of interest and personality inventories has led to people having greater self-understanding and reduced psychological discomfort. Measures of human abilities have been used to provide access to educational and occupational positions without regard to ethnic or racial background. Critics of testing are quick to point out that inequalities in test performance still exist, but, in the last 25 years, the users of tests have become much more cautious in their interpretations and much more sensitive to the rights of the test taker. Generally, the information provided by tests is more accurate than that available from other sources. When we acknowledge that decisions *must* be made and that accurate information coupled with a clear understanding of our values generally leads to the best decisions, we will find continuing growth in the importance of measurement and assessment processes in psychology and education.

SOME CURRENT ISSUES IN MEASUREMENT

Educational and psychological assessments are far from perfect. Since the earliest attempts were made to develop measurement techniques in a systematic way, the procedures have been a target for a wide spectrum of critics. Much of this criticism has been a justified response to the naive enthusiasm of measurement proponents and some of their ill-conceived applications and interpretations of measurement results. In subsequent chapters in our discussion of test interpretation and use, we will try to be sensitive to earlier criticisms and to the more technical questions that arise concerning the reliability and validity of test results. At this point, however, we will identify and comment briefly on some of the issues that recently have been of special concern.

Testing Minority Individuals

For many years, the use and interpretation of tests within minority and other groups whose experiences and cultures differ from that typical of the general population have received a great deal of attention. There are, of course, all sorts of subgroups in our society, differing from one another in a variety of ways. Ethnic and linguistic minorities are probably the most clear-cut of these; they are the ones for whom the appropriateness of tests and questionnaires designed to reflect the values and experiences of the typical middle-class, White American are most open to question. Additionally, feminist groups complain that test material is often male oriented. Major test publishers now go to considerable lengths to ensure that their test items do not present an unfair challenge to females or to members of ethnic or linguistic minority groups.

   Some questions arise concerning achievement tests that attempt to assess what a student *has learned* to do. In part, these questions center on the degree to which the same educational objectives hold for groups from minority cultures. Is the ability to read standard English with understanding an important goal for African American, Hispanic, or Native American children? Is knowledge about the U.S. Constitution as relevant for these groups as for the middle-class, White eighth grader? One senses that as far as the basic skills of dealing with language and numbers are concerned, many of the same objectives would apply but that as one moves into the content areas of history and literature there might be more divergence.

In part, the questions focus on the specific materials through which basic skills are exhibited. Is the same reading passage about the life of the Zulu appropriate in a reading test for a Hispanic and a Native American youngster? Or should test materials be specifically tailored to the life and experiences of each? We know too little about the importance of factors of specific content on performance in areas such as reading comprehension and need to do further research to make informed decisions.

The motivation of minority groups to do well on tests in school is also an issue. Some minority groups, such as recent immigrants from Southeast Asia, place great emphasis on individual academic achievement. Others, such as some Native American groups, place much more value on communal accomplishments and group identity. In many cases of academic difficulty, we must ask whether unfortunate experiences with testing in school have soured students on the whole enterprise, so that they withdraw from the task and do not try. It is perhaps a challenge to the whole pattern of education, not just to the choice of testing instruments, to provide a reasonable mixture of satisfying and success-enhancing experiences in school with all types of school tasks. Tasks and tests must be adapted to the present capabilities and concerns of the individual student.

Many more questions—perhaps more serious ones—are raised when tests are used as a basis for deciding what an individual *can learn to do,* that is, as aptitude measures. An inference from a test score obtained at Time 1 concerning what a person can learn to do by Time 2 is clearly a more questionable inference than an inference that merely states what that person can do at Time 1. There are many intervening events that can throw the prediction off. And there are correspondingly more possibilities of biasing factors coming in to distort systematically the prediction for minority group members. Present facts that imply one prediction for the majority group may imply a different prediction for a minority group member whose experiences before testing were far from typical.

The problem is to learn what types of inferences *can* appropriately be made for individuals with differing backgrounds and what types of adjustments or modifications need to be built into the system to permit the most accurate and equitable inferences and decisions for all people.

Invasion of Privacy

A second concern often expressed involves invasion of privacy. What kind of information is it reasonable to require individuals to give about themselves, and under what circumstances? This issue arises not only in relation to testing, but also in relation to all types of information from and about a person. What types of records should appropriately be kept? And to whom should they be made available? At one end of the spectrum are tests of job knowledge or skill, such as clerical tests, to which few would object when the skill is clearly and directly relevant to the position for which the person is applying. At the other end of the spectrum are self-descriptive instruments that lead to inferences about emotional stability or a scattering of tests that try to assess honesty under temptation to lie or steal; in these latter tests, individuals are led to give information about themselves without being aware of what information they are giving or how it will be interpreted. The use of these instruments seems most open to question. In between are instruments that involve varying degrees of self-revelation and that appear to have varying degrees of immediate relevance to a decision.

The issue is not only what information is being obtained, but also the purpose for which it is being obtained. Is the information being obtained at the individual's request to provide help with personal or vocational problems or for use in a counseling relationship? The fact that the person has come for help implies a willingness on his or her part to provide the information needed for help to be given; here, invasion of privacy becomes a matter of relatively minor concern. However, when the information is obtained to further institutional objectives—that is, those of an employer, of an educational institution, or of "science"—then concern for the individual's right to privacy mounts, and some equitable balance must be struck between individual values and rights, and social ones. For example, more students were willing to allow the use of a questionnaire to verify the emotional stability of an airline pilot, who is responsible for many lives, than to verify that of a bank clerk (75% vs. 34%). The rights of the individual are not absolute, but the feeling is often expressed that these rights have received too little consideration in the past.

To an increasing extent, the courts are taking a role in deciding what information is allowable. Several court cases have required a demonstration of the validity or relevance of test scores or personality profiles to job performance before such instruments could be used for employee selection. These court decisions have affected the type of information that may be collected and who may have access to that information.

The Use of Normative Comparisons

A somewhat different type of issue has been raised concerning the emphasis, in test interpretation, on comparing the performance of one person with norms representing the typical performance of a national, or sometimes a local, sample of people. The point being made with increasing fervor is that many of the decisions for which tests are used, especially instructional ones, do not call for—and are only confused by—comparisons with other people. The essential information is whether the person can perform a specified task; this information should guide decisions on what should be taught or what tasks should be undertaken next. Of course, there are settings in which comparison with others is essential to sound judgment and decision: Is the latest applicant at the personnel office a good keyboard operator? How do we define "good keyboard operator" except in terms of the performance of other job applicants? A rate of 60 words per minute with two errors per minute is meaningless unless we know that the average graduate from a commercial school can enter about 70 words per minute with perhaps one error per minute. The employer wants an employee who comes up to a standard of typical performance, and that standard is set by the performance of others. In the same way, a school system trying to evaluate the reading achievement of its sixth graders as "good," "satisfactory," or "needing improvement" needs some benchmark against which to compare its own performance. No absolute standard of reading performance exists. Whether it is reasonable to expect the sixth graders in Centerville to read and understand a particular article in *Reader's Digest* can only be judged by knowing whether representative groups of sixth graders nationwide are able to read and understand the same article.

In the past, normative comparisons with an outside reference group have often been used to guide decisions for which they had little or no relevance. Greater emphasis is now being given to criterion-referenced and mastery tests and to performance assessments. These procedures have an important place in making some sorts of decisions, but not all. We need to know which type of comparison is useful for which situation. When should we ask if a student can satisfactorily perform a specific task? And when should we ask how that student compares in relation to other students? This issue is discussed in more detail in Chapter 3.

Other Factors That Influence Scores

An issue that has concerned measurement professionals and consumers for many years is the effect of extraneous factors on performance. One such factor that has received considerable study is the effect of anxiety. Does anxiety raise or lower performance on achievement tests? If it does have a systematic effect, what can or should the teacher or examiner do to minimize the effect?

Other factors, such as the nutritional status of students or their ability to concentrate on the tasks at hand, may also affect scores. Two particular factors that have received considerable theoretical attention are (1) the racial, ethnic, and gender relationship between examiner and examinee and (2) the effect of coaching on test performance. Although the effects of these extraneous factors are not clear, public concern over their possible effects has prompted increasing attention to them among educators and measurement professionals.

Professional Standards in Testing

To promote the responsible and ethical use of tests in education and psychology, the American Psychological Association, the American Educational Research Association, and the National Council on Measurement in Education (1985) have published a series of standards for the development and use of tests. The most recent edition of the *Standards for Educational and Psychological Testing* was published in 1985 and a revision is currently being considered. From time to time, we will refer to specific sections of these standards as they apply to the topic being discussed. All regular users of tests should be familiar with these standards.

SUMMARY

The objective of this book is to improve the knowledge and understanding of decision makers by giving them a better basis for evaluating different measurement procedures and for knowing what each signifies and how much confidence can be placed in each. To this end, we will describe the process of preparing test exercises, develop the general criteria of validity and reliability by which all types of measures are evaluated, provide a familiarity with the different ways of reporting test scores, and describe and evaluate a number of the techniques and instruments commonly used for appraising human characteristics. Our success will be measured by the extent to which our readers use measurement results with wisdom and restraint in their decision making.

QUESTIONS AND EXERCISES

1. List some instances, preferably recent, of decisions you made about yourself or others made about you in which results from some kind of educational or psychological measurement played a part. Classify each decision as (1) instructional, (2) selection, (3) placement or classification, or (4) personal.

2. Describe one or more instances from your personal experience of a decision made, for which an educational or psychological measurement could have been helpful but was unavailable. On what basis was the decision actually made?

3. What are some alternatives to educational or psychological measurements as guides for each of the following decisions?

    a. How much time should be spent on phonics in the first-grade reading program?

    b. Which 5 of 15 applicants should be hired as computer programmers?

    c. Should Charles Turner be encouraged to realize his desire to go to college and law school and to become a lawyer?

4. What are the advantages of the alternatives you proposed in Question 3, in comparison with some type of test or questionnaire? What are the disadvantages?

5. To what extent and in what way might *values* be involved in each of the decisions stated in Question 3?

6. Give an example of each of the following types of tests:

    a. A criterion-referenced achievement test

    b. A norm-referenced achievement test

    c. An aptitude test

    d. A measure of likes and preferences

    e. A measure of personality or adjustment

    f. A measure of a trait or construct

7. For one of the attributes listed here, describe how you might (1) define the attribute, (2) set up procedures to make that attribute observable, and (3) quantify the attribute.

    a. Critical thinking

    b. Friendliness

    c. "Good citizenship" in an elementary school pupil

    d. Competence as an automobile driver

8. The usefulness of tests for decisions involving minority group members depends on the type of decision involved. For what sorts of decisions would a standardized test be most defensible? For what sorts would one be most questionable?

9. Which of the following practices would you consider acceptable? Which would you consider to be an invasion of privacy? What factors influenced your opinion?

    a. Requiring medical school applicants (1) to take an achievement test in chemistry, (2) to fill out a questionnaire designed to assess emotional stability, or (3) to take a scale of attitudes toward socialized medicine.

    b. Requiring applicants for a secretarial job (1) to take a test of general intelligence, (2) to take a test of keyboarding speed and accuracy, or (3) to fill out a questionnaire designed to appraise dependability.

    c. Giving a 10-year-old boy whose reading achievement is at the 8-year-old level (1) a nonverbal test of intellectual ability, (2) an interview focused on the conditions in his home, or (3) a series of diagnostic tests of specific reading skills.

10. Why is it important for test users to know and adhere to professional recommendations for appropriate test use?

SUGGESTED READINGS

Aiken, L. R. (1991). *Psychological testing and assessment* (7th ed.). Boston: Allyn and Bacon.

Alexander, L., & James, H. T. (1987). *The nation's report card: Improving the assessment of student achievement.* Washington, DC: National Academy of Education.

American Psychological Association, American Educational Research Association, & National Council on Measurement in Education. (1985). *Standards for educational and psychological testing.* Washington, DC: American Psychological Association.

Anastasi, A. (1988). *Psychological testing* (6th ed.). New York: Macmillan.

Cronbach, L. J. (1975). Five decades of public controversy over mental testing. *American Psychologist, 30,* 1–14.

DuBois, P. H. (1970). *A history of psychological testing.* Boston: Allyn and Bacon.

Gottfredson, L. S., & Scharf, J. C. (1988). *Fairness in employment testing: A special issue of the Journal of Vocational Behavior, 33(3).* Duluth, MN: Academic Press.

Gronlund, N. E., & Linn, R. L. (1990). *Measurement and evaluation in teaching* (6th ed.). New York: Macmillan.

Haney, W. (1981). Validity, vaudeville, and values: A short history of social concerns over standardized testing. *American Psychologist, 36,* 1021–1034.

Hartigan, J. A., & Wigdor, A. K. (Eds.). (1989). *Fairness in employment testing: Validity generalization, minority issues, and the General Aptitude Test Battery.* Washington, DC: National Academy Press.

Hopkins, K. D., Stanley, J. C., & Hopkins, B. R. (1990). *Educational and psychological measurement and evaluation* (7th ed.). Englewood Cliffs, NJ: Prentice-Hall.

Howard, G. S. (1985). The role of values in the science of psychology. *American Psychologist, 40,* 255–265.

Jones, L. V. (1971). The nature of measurement. In R. L. Thorndike (Ed.), *Educational measurement* (2nd ed., pp. 335–355). Washington, DC: American Council on Education.

Linn, R. L. (1989). Current perspectives and future directions. In R. L. Linn (Ed.), *Educational measurement* (3rd ed., pp. 1–12). New York: Macmillan.

Rogers, T. B. (1995). *The psychological testing enterprise.* Pacific Grove, CA: Brooks/Cole.

Thorndike, R. M. (1990). *A century of ability testing.* Chicago: Riverside Publishing.

Vold, D. J. (1985). The roots of teacher testing in America. *Educational Measurement: Issues and Practice, 4*(3), 5–8.

Wigdor, A. K., & Garner, W. R. (Eds.). (1982). *Ability testing: Uses, consequences, and controversies: Pt. 1. Report of the committee.* Washington, DC: National Academy Press.

CHAPTER 2

Measurement and Numbers

QUESTIONS TO ASK ABOUT TEST SCORES

Catherine Johnson and Peter Cordero wanted to gather information about achievement levels in their two sixth-grade classes. They gave their students a reading test provided in their current reading series, a review test from the mathematics book, and a dictation spelling test based on the words their classes had been studying over the past 6 weeks. They marked the papers, counted the number of correct answers on each, and recorded the scores. Then they made up a joint class list that showed the three scores for each student. With three scores for each of 44 students, they wondered what they should do with all those numbers.

Tests *do* produce scores, and scores *are* numbers. So, if we are to think about and use test scores, we must be prepared to think with and work with numbers. The numbers that represent test scores can be organized to provide the answers to a range of questions, but first we must know what kinds of questions to ask. Once we have the questions in mind, we can begin to ask how the numbers can be arranged to provide the answers.

Look at the numbers (scores) shown in Table 2.1 for the sixth graders in the two classes. What kinds of questions might the two teachers ask about this set of numbers? What questions can *you* ask? Before reading further, study the sets of scores and jot down the questions that come to your mind in connection with these scores. See how many of the question types you can anticipate.

A first, rather general type of question that we might ask is, what is the basic pattern of the set of scores? How do they "run"? What do they "look like"? How can we get a picture of the set of reading scores, for example, so that we can get an impression of the group as a whole? To answer this type of question, we will need to consider simple ways of tabulating and graphing a set of scores.

A second type of question that will almost certainly arise is, what is this group like, on the average? In general, have they done as well on the test as some other sixth-grade group? What is the typical level of performance in the group? All these questions call for some single number to represent the group as a whole, some measure of where the *middle* of the group lies. To answer this type of question, we will need to become acquainted with statistics developed to represent the average, or typical, score.

Third, to describe the group we might feel a need to describe the extent to which the scores spread out away from the average value. Have all the children in the group made about the same progress, or do they show a wide range of achievement? How does this group compare with other classes, with respect to the *spread* of scores? This type of question calls for a study of measures of variability.

Fourth, we might ask how a particular individual stands on one of the tests. We might want to know whether James A. did well or poorly on the mathematics test. And if we decide that his score is a good one, we might want some way of saying just how good it is. We might ask whether James A. did better in reading or in mathematics. To answer this question, we will need a *common yardstick* on which to express performance in two quite different areas. One need, then, is for some uniform way of expressing and interpreting the performance of an individual, independent of the particular test. How does this person stand relative to the group?

A fifth query is of the following type: To what extent do those who excel in reading also excel in mathematics? To what extent do these two abilities go together in

Table 2.1
Scores for Two Sixth-Grade Classes at School X

Name	Test Scores		
	Reading	Mathematics	Spelling
Carol A.	32	3	27
James A.	36	29	33
Mary B.	27	27	26
Albert B.	21	16	13
Ruby C.	31	9	23
Donald C.	27	7	24
Alice D.	36	18	32
Peter D.	37	29	31
Theresa E.	47	21	38
Samuel E.	46	36	37
Ida F.	42	34	38
George F.	33	10	31
Vivian G.	22	4	13
Roger G.	17	14	14
Grace H.	50	42	46
Newton H.	35	18	30
Opal I.	20	18	12
Karl I.	30	12	25
Ursula J.	37	2	36
Isidore J.	22	30	17
Beatrice K.	25	10	21
John K.	43	9	37
Karen L.	37	13	30
Benjamin L.	31	15	29
Susan M.	28	20	18
Theodore M.	50	38	48
Jane N.	34	15	32
Michael N.	34	20	27
Dorothy O.	31	19	28
Herman O.	30	15	29
Frances P.	21	2	17
Charles P.	52	39	47
Elizabeth Q.	35	48	30
Patrick Q.	40	33	33
Pearl R.	59	41	54
William R.	42	6	33
Joan S.	44	41	39
Martin S.	17	26	17
Nancy T.	32	40	28
Frank T.	32	20	23
Judith U.	56	24	54
Ralph U.	38	20	30
Edith V.	38	24	37
Thomas V.	29	29	33

Note: Maximum score = 60. Number of correct answers are given.

the same individuals? Is the individual who is superior in one area likely to be superior in the other? To express this *association* between two measurements, we will need to become acquainted with indices of correlation.

Many other questions may arise with respect to a set of scores. The most important ones concern the drawing of general conclusions from data on a limited group. For example, the 22 girls in this group have an average reading score of 35.6, and the 22 boys have an average score of 33.7. These are *descriptive* facts of this testing of these particular girls and boys. But these children might be considered to represent a larger population, such as all students in this school district. From the results in these two classes, we might want to make an estimate or best guess of the average level of reading achievement in the larger group. We also might want to know whether we can safely conclude that the total population of girls from which this sample is drawn would surpass the total population of boys on this same test. These problems are of *inference*. Problems of statistical inference make up the bulk of advanced statistical work, but, in this book, we are only concerned with them in a few specialized situations. They do not enter into the basic interpretation of test scores for an individual or a group.

The routines developed for organizing numbers to answer these and other questions constitute the field called *statistics*. This name and, in fact, the very prospect of working with numbers seem a bit scary to some people. Fortunately, much of the mechanics of working with numbers can now be performed on a pocket calculator or personal computer; so we can concentrate on the questions to ask and on the ways in which the numbers are arranged to answer them, rather than worry about computational details.

Although we present the answers to the above questions as though we had only a pencil and paper, in practice, almost all statistical work is now done on calculators and computers. For analyses of any size, hand calculation is rarely used, and the skill of calculating the basic statistics described here is becoming somewhat obsolete, just as mathematics in the home is. In a time when most people have pocket calculators on hand to check their income tax returns or the per pound price of groceries in the supermarket and many schools and individuals have their own microcomputers that easily compute statistical indices, it may seem unnecessary to learn hand procedures for calculating basic statistics. However, experience has shown that the best way to come to understand a statistical procedure and what the results of a statistical analysis mean is to "get your hands dirty" by doing some of the calculations by hand. After you have mastered the ideas, you can leave the daily calculations to a machine; however, there may even be situations in which no computer or calculator is available. For these reasons, we continue to display some of the long-established computational routines.

In Table 2.1, we showed a record sheet on which test scores for 44 sixth graders were recorded. Let us look at the scores in the Reading column and consider how they can be rearranged to give a clearer picture of how the pupils have performed on the reading test.

The simplest rearrangement is merely to list the scores in order from highest to lowest, as follows:

59	40	34	28
56	38	33	27
52	38	32	27
50	37	32	25
50	37	32	22
47	37	31	22
46	36	31	21
44	36	31	21
43	35	30	20
42	35	30	17
42	34	29	17

This arrangement gives a somewhat better picture of the way the scores fall than does Table 2.1. We can see the highest (59) and lowest (17) scores at a glance. It is also easy to see that the middle person in the group falls somewhere in the mid-30s. We can see by inspection that roughly half of the scores fall between 30 and 40. But this simple rearrangement of scores still has too much detail for us to see the general pattern clearly. We need to condense the data into a more compact form.

PREPARATION OF A FREQUENCY DISTRIBUTION

Often, the first step in organizing scores for presentation is to prepare a display called a *frequency distribution*, a table that shows how often each score has occurred. Each score value is listed, and the number of times it occurs is shown. A portion of the frequency distribution for the reading test is shown in Table 2.2. However, Table 2.2 is still not a very good form for reporting the facts. The table is too long and spread out. We have shown only part of it: the whole table would take 43 lines, almost as many as the original listing of scores. It would have a number of zero entries, and there would be marked variations in the Frequency column from one score to the next.

Grouped Frequency Distributions

Scores are often *grouped* into broader categories to further improve the form of presentation. We discard some detail in the data to make it easier to grasp the picture presented by the entire set of scores. In our example, we have grouped three adjacent scores, so that each grouping *interval* includes three points of score. When this is done, the set of scores is represented as shown in Table 2.3, a fairly compact table illustrating how many people there are in each *score interval*. Thus, for example, we have six people in interval 34–36. We do not know how many of them got 34s, 35s, or 36s; we have lost this information in the grouping. We assume that they are evenly spread throughout the interval. In most cases, there is no reason to believe that one score will occur more often than any other, and this assumption is a sound one, so the gains in compactness and convenience of presentation more than make up for

Table 2.2
Frequency Distribution of Reading Scores (Ungrouped Data)

Test Score	Frequency
59	1
58	0
57	0
56	1
55	0
54	0
53	0
52	1
51	0
50	2
.	.
.	.
.	.
20	1
19	0
18	0
17	2

any slight inaccuracy introduced by the groupings. (In some special applications, such as reports of family income, certain values are more likely than others, for example, $10,000, $18,000, $25,000. Special precautions are required when grouping material of this type. An effort should be made to get the most popular values near the middle of an interval to reduce distortion.)

Table 2.3
Frequency Distribution of Reading Scores (Grouped Data)

Score Interval	Tallies	Frequency
58–60	/	1
55–57	/	1
52–54	/	1
49–51	//	2
46–48	//	2
43–45	//	2
40–42	///	3
37–39	////	5
34–36	⧌ /	6
31–33	⧌//	7
28–30	⧌	4
25–27	///	3
22–24	//	2
19–21	///	3
16–18	//	2

In practical situations, we always face the problem of deciding how broad the groupings should be, that is, whether to group by 3, 5, 10, or some other number of points of score. The decision is a compromise between (1) losing detail from our data and (2) obtaining a convenient, compact, and smooth representation of the results. A broader interval loses more detail but condenses the data into a more compact picture. A practical rule of thumb is to choose an interval that will divide the total score range into roughly 15 groups. In our example, the highest score is 59, and the lowest is 17. The range of scores is 59 to 17, giving a range of 42 points. Dividing 42 by 15, we get 2.8. The nearest whole number is 3; so we group the data by 3s. In addition to the "rule of 15," we also find that intervals of 5, 10, and multiples of 10 make convenient groupings. Because the purpose of grouping scores is to make a convenient and clear representation, factors of convenience enter as a major consideration.

In cases where graphs are going to be prepared using the scores in their grouped form, it is also convenient to use an interval that includes an odd number of score points, for example, 3, 5, or 7, because it is sometimes necessary to use the midpoint of the score interval. If there is an even number of scores in the interval, this point will be halfway between two actual scores, but if an odd number is used for the interval width, the midpoint will be a whole score value, making for a more attractive graph and easier subsequent computations.

It also should be noted that sometimes there is no need to group the data into broader categories. If the original scores cover a range of no more than about 20 points, grouping may not be required. Also, with modern computing equipment, it is usually easier to compute the statistical indices, described later in the chapter, from the original set of scores unless a large number of scores are being analyzed. In this latter case, it is highly likely that some central agency would be doing the computing and you would only need to interpret the results correctly.

In practice, when we tabulate a set of data, deciding on the size of the score interval is the first step. Next is setting up the score intervals, as shown in the left-hand column of Table 2.3. Each individual is then represented by a tally mark, as shown in the middle column. (It is easier to keep track of the tallies if every fifth tally is a diagonal line across the preceding four.) The entries in the Frequency column are obtained by counting the number of tallies in each score interval.

Cumulative Frequency Distributions

We often want to know how many people got scores below some particular value. The most direct way to answer this question is with a *cumulative frequency distribution,* which lists each score or interval and the number of scores falling *in or below* the interval. A cumulative frequency distribution is easily prepared from the frequency distribution, as shown in Table 2.4, which presents the *cumulative frequency,* as well as the frequency in each interval. Each entry in the column labeled "Cumulative Frequency" shows the total number of individuals having a score equal to or less than the highest score in that interval; that is, there are $(2 + 3) = 5$ cases

Table 2.4
Frequency Distribution and Cumulative Frequencies
for Reading Scores

Score Interval	Frequency	Cumulative Frequency
58–60	1	44
55–57	1	43
52–54	1	42
49–51	2	41
46–48	2	39
43–45	2	37
40–42	3	35
37–39	5	32
34–36	6	27
31–33	7	21
28–30	4	14
25–27	3	10
22–24	2	7
19–21	3	5
16–18	2	2

scoring at or below 21, $(2 + 3 + 2) = (5 + 2) = 7$ scoring at or below 24, 10 scoring at or below 27, and so forth. The cumulative frequency distribution is especially useful for determining some expressions of relative position.

GRAPHIC REPRESENTATION

It is often helpful to translate the facts of a table like Table 2.3 into a pictorial representation. A common type of graphic representation, called a *histogram,* is shown in Figure 2.1. This type of graph can be thought of, somewhat grimly, as "piling up the bodies." The score intervals for the reading test scores are shown along the base line (the *abscissa*), and the vertical height of the pile (the *ordinate*) represents the number of people whose scores fall in that interval. The diagram shows that there are two "bodies" piled up in interval 16–18, three in interval 19–21, and so forth. This figure gives a clear picture of how the scores pile up, with most of them in the 30s and a long, low "tail" running up to the high scores.

Another way of picturing the same data is by preparing a *frequency polygon,* such as that shown in Figure 2.2. Here, we have plotted a point at the *midpoint* of each of the score intervals. (Note that because we used an interval width of 3, these midpoints are whole numbers.) The height at which we have plotted the point corresponds to the number of cases, or frequency, *(f),* in the interval. These points have been connected, and the jagged line provides a slightly different picture of the same set of data illustrated in Figure 2.1. The frequency polygon displays the data more clearly when two different groups are included in the same chart. Otherwise, the choice between the two is a matter of personal preference because they are inter-

Figure 2.1
Histogram of 44 reading scores.

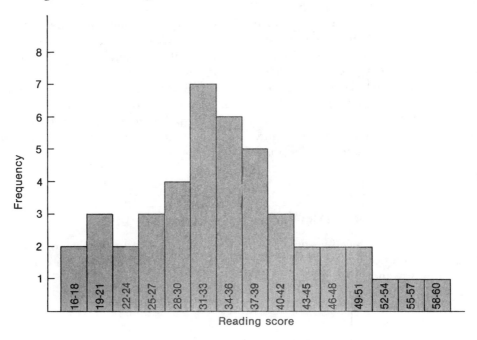

Figure 2.2
Frequency polygon of 44 reading scores.

changeable ways of showing the same facts. Many computer programs that can prepare frequency distributions can also plot graphs of those distributions, using any interval width you select.

The histogram and the frequency polygon provide alternative ways to display the information in the frequency distribution. We can use a similar procedure to provide a graphic representation of the cumulative frequency distribution. This graph, known as the *cumulative frequency curve* (also sometimes called an *ogive*) is prepared by placing values of the cumulative frequency on the ordinate, and scores or interval midpoints on the abscissa. A point representing the cumulative frequency for each interval is then plotted, and the points are connected, forming a graph such as the one shown in Figure 2.3. Note that the cumulative frequency curve never drops back toward the abscissa.

MEASURES OF CENTRAL TENDENCY

We often need a statistic to represent the typical, or average or middle, score of a group of scores. We present three, each of which defines the center in a different way and conveys slightly different information.

Figure 2.3
Cumulative frequency curve of 44 reading scores.

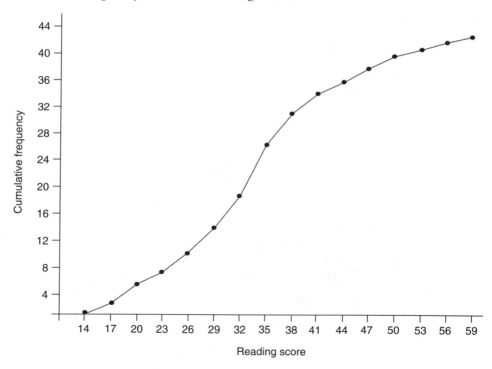

The Mode

A very simple way of identifying the typical score is to pick the one that occurs most frequently. This score is called the *mode* and corresponds to the highest point in the frequency polygon. If you examine the array of scores in the tabulation that follows Table 2.1, you will find that the scores 37, 32, and 31 each occur three times. A unique value for the mode does not exist with these data. If one of the students who scored 38 had instead scored 37, the mode would be 37. If one of the 30s had been a 31, then 31 would have been the mode. The mode is sensitive to such minor changes in the data and is therefore a crude and not very useful indicator of the typical score. In Table 2.3, where we have the grouped frequency distribution, the *modal interval* is 31–33. When the scores are grouped in this way, we can call the midpoint of the modal interval, 32, the *mode.*

The Median

A much more useful way of representing the typical, or average, score is to find the value on the score scale that separates the top half of the group from the bottom half. This value is called the *median.* In our example, with 44 cases, this means separating the top 22 people from the bottom 22. The required value can be estimated from the scores shown in Table 2.4. Starting with the lowest score, we count up until we have the necessary 22 cases. As was indicated, we want to identify the point below which 50% of the cases fall. Because 50% of 44 is 22, we must identify the point below which 22 pupils fall.

Table 2.4 shows that 21 individuals have scores of 33 or below. We need to include 1 more case to obtain the required 22 cases. Note that in the next score interval (34–36), there are six individuals. We require only one-sixth of these individuals. Now how shall we think of these cases being spread out over the score interval 34–36? As noted earlier in this chapter, a reasonable assumption is that they are spread out evenly over the interval. Then to include one-sixth of the scores, we would have to go one-sixth of the way from the bottom of the interval toward the top.

At this point, we must define what we mean by a score of 34. First, let us note that although test scores go by jumps (or discrete increments) of one unit (34, 35, and 36), we consider the underlying ability that the test measures to have a continuous distribution that takes in all the intermediate values between two scores. We might liken the situation to a digital clock. Although time is continuous, the recording instrument runs by jumps, with one jump every time the basic unit of 1 minute is passed.

Figure 2.4 illustrates this point. The heavy line represents the continuum of ability. We define *34* as the interval on the continuum that is closer to the point 34 than to either 33 or 35. Thus, in Figure 2.4, 34 is represented as a slice extending from 33.5 to 34.5. Although somewhat arbitrary, this definition of a score is a reasonable one and is accepted by most authorities. The score interval 34–36 is really to be

Figure 2.4
Relation between scores and ability continuum.

thought of as extending from 33.5 to 36.5 on the underlying continuum, as is shown in the figure. We do not get scores lying *between* 33 and 34—not because those levels of ability do not exist, but just because our measuring instrument does not register any values between 33 and 34.

Because we require one-sixth of the cases in interval 34–36, we must go one-sixth of the way from 33.5 to 36.5; that is, we have

$$(1/6)(36.5 - 33.5) = (1/6) \times 3 = 3/6 = 0.5$$

We must add 0.5 to the value 33.5, which is the lower limit of the score interval that contains the median. The median for this set of scores is $33.5 + 0.5 = 34.0$. Note that the median need not be a whole score value. Had there been 45 students, we would have needed 22.5 people to make up half of the group. We would then have taken $1.5/6 = 1/4$ of the interval and obtained a median of 34.25.

Steps in Computing the Median.   These are the steps used to compute the median from a frequency distribution:

1. Calculate the number of cases that represents 50% of the total group ($0.5 \times N$, where N is the number of people in the total sample).
2. Starting with the lowest score interval, add the scores up through each interval, to get the cumulative frequencies.
3. Find the interval for which the cumulative frequency is just less than the required number of cases. The next interval, which contains the median, is called the median interval.
4. Find the score distance to be added to the bottom of the median interval to include the required number of cases, by the following operation:

$$\frac{\text{No. of added cases needed}}{\text{No. of cases in median interval}} \times \text{No. of points in an interval}$$

5. Add this amount to the lower limit of the median interval, to give the median.

In our example, we compute the median as follows, using the listed steps:

1. $0.5 \times 44 = 22$.
2. The cumulative frequencies, as shown in Table 2.4, are 2, 5, 7, 10, 14, and so on.
3. The cumulative frequency through interval 31–33 is 21.
4. $(1/6)(3) = 0.5$.
5. $33.5 + 0.5 = 34.0$.

Some computer programs take a slightly different approach to defining the median. In these programs, the median is defined as the score obtained by the middle person, regardless of how many people got the same score. Such programs work on the original set of scores, as shown in Table 2.1, rather than on the frequency distribution. In our example, the two middle people have identical scores of 34, so the program would report a median equal to the one we found using the traditional procedure, but this will not usually be the case. Because the differences found in computing the median by these two approaches are usually small, the differences are not likely to be important to test users.

Percentiles

The same steps used to compute the median may be used to find the score below which any other percentage of the group falls. These values are called *percentiles*. The median is the 50th percentile, that is, the score below which 50% of the individuals fall. If we want to find the 25th percentile, we must find the score below which 25% of the cases fall, 25% of 44 is 11. Eleven cases take us through interval 25–27, and include one of the four cases in interval 28–30. So, the 25th percentile is located in the interval 28–30 and is computed to be $27.5 + (1/4)3 = 27.5 + 0.75 = 28.25$.

As another illustration, consider the 85th percentile. We have $(0.85)(44) = 37.4$ people making up the bottom 85% of our group. Because 37 cases carry us to the top of interval 43–45, and there are 2 cases in the next interval, for the 85th percentile, we have

$$45.5 + [(37.4 - 37)/2](3) = 46.1$$

Other percentiles can be found in the same way. Percentiles have many uses, especially in connection with test norms and the interpretation of scores. We will encounter them again in Chapter 3.

The Arithmetic Mean

Another frequently used statistic for representing the middle of a group is the familiar average of everyday experience. Because statisticians speak of all measures of central tendency as averages, they identify this one as the *arithmetic mean (M)*. It is computed as the sum of a series of scores divided by the total number of scores. Thus, the arithmetic mean of the scores 4, 6, and 7 is

$$(4 + 6 + 7)/3 = 17/3 = 5.67$$

In our example, we can add the scores of all 44 individuals in the group, giving us 1,526. Dividing by 44, we get 34.68 for the average, or arithmetic mean, for this group.

Steps in Computing the Arithmetic Mean.   These are the steps used to compute the arithmetic mean:

1. Add all of the scores.
2. Divide this total by the total number of scores.

Like the median, the mean can be computed from data in the form of a grouped frequency distribution. Procedures for computing the mean and the standard deviation *(SD)* from a grouped frequency distribution are illustrated in Appendix 1, as are the procedures for computing the correlation coefficient *(r)*.

Central Tendency and the Shape of the Distribution

The mode, arithmetic mean, and median seldom correspond exactly, but usually they do not differ greatly. In our example, the values are 32, 34.68, and 34.0, respectively. They will differ substantially only when the set of scores is *skewed* greatly, that is, when there is a piling up of scores at one end and a long, thin tail at the other. Figure 2.5 shows three distributions that differ in the amount and direction of skewness. The top figure is positively skewed; that is, it has a tail running up to the high scores. We might get a distribution like this for income in the United States, because there are many people with small and moderate incomes and only a few with very large incomes. The center figure is negatively skewed. A distribution like this would result if a class were given a very easy test that resulted in a piling up of perfect and near-perfect scores. The bottom figure is symmetrical and is not skewed in either direction. Many psychological and educational variables give such a symmetrical distribution.

In the distributions that are approximately symmetrical, either the mean or the median will represent the average of the group equally well, but with skewed distributions, the median generally seems preferable because it is affected less by a few cases out in the long tail. The mean is more often used when the distribution is symmetrical, for reasons that will become clear later in this chapter, when we discuss the normal distribution. The mode is used less often because, although it is easy to obtain, it is less stable than the mean and median. Also, the mode is not related to other statistics we may wish to obtain.

Figure 2.5
Frequency distributions
differing in skewness.
(a) Positively skewed;
(b) negatively skewed;
(c) symmetrical.

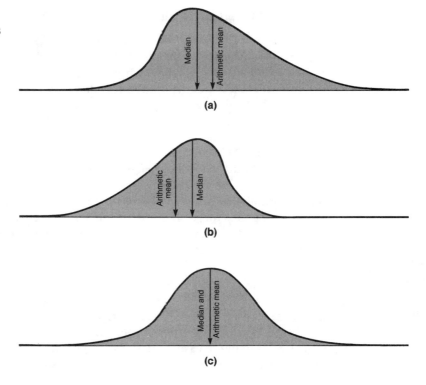

MEASURES OF VARIABILITY

It is often significant, when describing a set of scores, to report how *variable* the scores are—that is, how much they spread out from high to low. For example, two groups of children, each with a median age of 10 years, would represent quite different educational situations if one group had a spread of ages from 9 to 11 and the other ranged from 6 to 14. A measure of this spread is an important statistic for describing a group.

The Range

A simple measure of variability is the *range* of scores in the group, which is simply the difference between the highest and the lowest scores. In our reading test example, the spread of scores is from 59 to 17, giving a range of 42 points. However, the range depends only on the two extreme cases in the total group. This fact makes the range quite undependable because it can be changed quite a bit by the addition or omission of a single extreme case.

The Semi-Interquartile Range

A better measure of variability is the range of scores that includes a specified part of the total group—usually the middle 50%. The middle 50% of the cases in the group are the cases lying between the 25th and the 75th percentiles. We can compute these two percentiles, following the procedures outlined earlier. For our example, the 25th percentile was computed to be 28.25. If you calculate the 75th percentile, you will find that it is 40.5. The distance between the 25th and 75th percentiles is thus 12.25 points of score.

The 25th and 75th percentiles are called the *quartiles,* because they cut off the bottom quarter and the top quarter of the group, respectively. The score distance between them is called the *interquartile range.* A statistic that is often reported as a measure of variability is the *semi-interquartile range (Q),* which is half of the interquartile range. It is the average distance from the median to the two quartiles; that is, it tells how far the quartile points lie from the median on the average. In our example, the semi-interquartile range is

$$Q = (40.5 - 28.25)/2 = 12.25/2 = 6.125$$

If the scores spread out twice as far, Q would be twice as large; if they spread out only half as far, Q would be half as large. Two distributions that have the same mean, the same total number of cases, and the same general form and that differ only in that one has a variability twice as large as the other are shown in Figure 2.6.

The Standard Deviation

The semi-interquartile range belongs to the same family of statistics as the median. Its computation is based on percentiles. There are also measures of variability that belong to the family of the arithmetic mean and are based on score deviations from the mean. Suppose we had four scores: 4, 5, 6, and 7. Adding these scores and dividing by the total number of scores, we find the arithmetic mean to be

$$(4 + 5 + 6 + 7)/4 = 22/4 = 5.5$$

But now we ask how widely these scores spread out around that mean value. Suppose we find the difference between each score and the mean; that is, we subtract 5.5 from each score. We then have -1.5, -0.5, 0.5, and 1.5. These represent *deviations* of the scores from the mean. The bigger the deviations, the more widely the set of scores spreads out around the mean. What we require is some type of average of these deviations to give us an overall measure of the variability, or spread, present in the data.

If we simply add the four deviation values in the preceding paragraph, we find that they add up to zero. The positive deviations exactly balance the negative ones. This outcome will always be true because one of the definitions of the arithmetic

Figure 2.6
Two distributions differing
only in variability. *(a)* Large
variability; *(b)* small
variability.

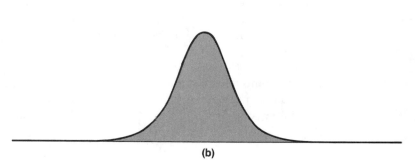

mean is that it is the point around which the sum of deviations is zero. We will have to do something else to get an index of the amount of spread. The procedure that statisticians have devised for handling the plus (positive) and the minus (negative) signs is to square all the deviations, thus getting only positive values. (A minus times a minus is a plus.) An average of these squared deviations is obtained by adding them up and dividing by the total number of cases. This value is called the *variance* and is widely used in more advanced statistical procedures. The variance is defined as the *mean* of the *squared* deviations from the mean.

To compensate for having squared the individual deviations, we must then compute the square root of this average value. The resulting statistic is called the *standard deviation (SD)*. It is the square root of the average of the squared deviations from the mean or variance. (With most calculators, you need only press the designated key to get the square root of a number.) For the scores used in the preceding example, calculations are as follows:

$$SD = \sqrt{[(-1.5)^2 + (-0.5)^2 + (0.5)^2 + (1.5)^2]/4}$$
$$= \sqrt{[2.25 + 0.25 + 0.25 + 2.25]/4} = \sqrt{5.00/4}$$
$$= \sqrt{1.25} = 1.12$$

The variance is 1.25; the standard deviation is 1.12.

Computing the Standard Deviation.   Most calculators and all computer spreadsheet and statistics packages include a program that will calculate the standard deviation for a set of data. Because the exact procedures vary from one brand of calculator or program to another, here we outline the general steps in the process. Your computing equipment will probably carry out these steps automatically, but it is useful to know what the machine is "thinking," that is, how it computes the standard deviation.

The first step in the process is to square each person's score. Carol A.'s reading score of 32 becomes 1,024 when squared, Mary B.'s 27 yields 729, and so forth. The second step is to add all of the squared scores. A statistician would express the first two steps in the process with the symbols ΣX^2. The symbol Σ means to "take the sum of," and X^2 stands for the square of each person's raw, or original, score. Thus, the expression ΣX^2 tells you to add up the squares of the people's raw scores. Next, we divide the quantity ΣX^2 by N, the number of people in the group. From this quantity, we subtract the *square of the group's mean,* and, finally, we take the square root of the result.

Although this procedure may sound more complicated than the first method used to compute the standard deviation, it is really much easier because we do not have to find a deviation, which is usually a decimal number, for each person. For the set of four scores (4, 5, 6, and 7) we find the standard deviation with the following steps:

$$\Sigma X^2 = 4^2 + 5^2 + 6^2 + 7^2 = 126$$

and

$$SD = \sqrt{\Sigma X^2/N - M^2}$$
$$= \sqrt{126/4 - (5.5)^2} = \sqrt{31.5 - 30.25}$$
$$= \sqrt{1.25} = 1.12$$

The two ways of doing it yield the same answer. (Procedures for computing the standard deviation from a grouped frequency distribution are given in Appendix 1.) To compute the standard deviation for the set of reading scores in Table 2.1, we first find $\Sigma X^2 = 57,288$. The mean for all 44 students was 34.68, and

$$SD = \sqrt{57,288/44 - (34.68)^2} = \sqrt{1302 - 1,202.7}$$
$$= \sqrt{99.3} = 9.96$$

There is one factor in computing the standard deviation that may cause your calculator to give results that are different from the ones presented here or that are obtained by a classmate when you are both working with the same set of data. Earlier in the chapter, we mentioned that statistical inference was the term applied when using the data from a sample to estimate a characteristic of a larger group (called a population). This distinction does not affect the mean (the same value serves as a description of the sample and as an estimate for the population), but it does affect the standard deviation. In the standard deviation that is used to describe the variability of the sample, the sum of the squared deviations from the mean is divided by the number of members of the sample. The best estimate (from the sample data) of the standard deviation of the population is found by dividing the sum of squared deviations from the sample mean by $N - 1$ rather than N. Using $N - 1$ in the denominator has the effect of making the population estimate slightly larger than the sample value. The difference is not of practical importance for most measurement applications, but it can cause some confusion when people compare their answers to a problem. You may want to check the manual for your calculator to see which version it uses so that you will not get frustrated if you obtain slightly different answers from the ones we provide.

INTERPRETING THE STANDARD DEVIATION

It is almost impossible to say in simple terms what the standard deviation is or what it corresponds to in pictorial or geometric terms. Primarily, it is a statistic that characterizes the spread of a distribution of scores. It increases in direct proportion to the scores spreading out more widely. The larger the standard deviation, the greater the variability among the individuals. A student sometimes asks, but what is a small standard deviation? What is a large one? There is really no answer to either question. Suppose that for some group the standard deviation of weights is 10. Is this value large or small? It depends on whether we are talking about ounces, pounds, or kilograms and on whether we are dealing with the weights of mice, men, or mammoths.

The standard deviation gets its most clear-cut meaning for one type of distribution of scores, the *normal distribution,* or *normal curve.* This distribution is defined by a particular mathematical equation, but to the everyday user, it is defined approximately by its pictorial qualities. The normal curve is a symmetrical curve having a bell-like shape. In fact, it is sometimes called the bell curve. Most of the cases pile up in the middle score values; going away from the middle in either direction, the pile drops off, first slowly and then more rapidly and then slowly again as the cases trail out into relatively long tails at each end. An illustration of a typical normal curve is shown in Figure 2.7. This curve is the normal curve that best fits the reading test data taken from Table

Figure 2.7

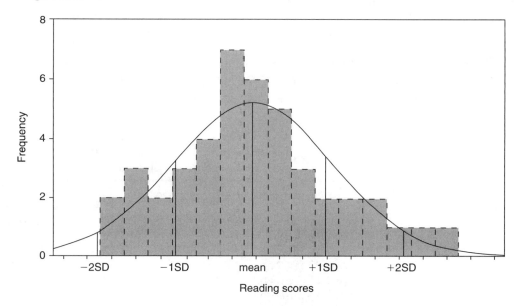

2.1. It has the same mean, standard deviation, and total area (number of cases) as the reading test data. The histogram of reading test scores (Figure 2.1) appears in the dotted lines and reveals how closely the curve fits the actual test scores.

For the normal curve, there is an exact mathematical relationship between the standard deviation and the proportion of cases. The same proportion of cases will always be found within the same standard deviation limits. This relationship is shown in Table 2.5. From this table, we can see that in any normal curve about two thirds (68.2%) of the cases fall in the range between +1.0 and −1.0 SD from the mean. Thus, if the mean is 50 and the standard deviation is 10, about 68% of the cases will fall in the range from a score of 40 to a score of 60 (34% between 40 and 50 and 34% between 50 and 60). Approximately 95% (actually, 95.4%) will fall between +2.0 and −2.0 SD from the mean, and nearly all the cases will fall between +3.0 and −3.0 SD from the mean. Because of this constant relationship between the standard deviation and the proportion of cases, we know that in a normal distribution, an individual who gets a score one SD above the mean will surpass 84% of the group—the 50% who fall below the mean and the 34% who fall between the mean and +1.0 standard deviation.

This unvarying relationship of the standard deviation unit to the arrangement of scores in the normal distribution gives the standard deviation a type of *standard* meaning as a unit of score. It becomes a yardstick in terms of which groups may be compared or the status of a given individual on different traits expressed. For example, if John's score in reading is one SD above the mean and his score in mathematics is two SDs above the mean, then his performance in mathematics is better than his performance in reading. (The use of the standard deviation and the normal distribution for expressing relative performance is discussed in Chapter 3.) Although the relationship of the standard deviation unit to the score distribution does not hold *exactly* in distributions other than the theoretical normal distribution, frequently the distributions of test scores and other measures approach the normal distribution closely enough for the standard deviation to continue to have nearly the same meaning.

In summary, the statistics most used to describe the variability of a set of scores are the semi-interquartile range and the standard deviation. The semi-interquartile

Table 2.5

Proportion of Cases Falling Within Certain Specified Standard Deviation *(SD)* Limits for a Normal Distribution

Limits Within Which Cases Lie	% of Cases
Between the mean and *either* +1.0 SD or −1.0 SD	34.1
Between the mean and *either* +2.0 SD or −2.0 SD	47.7
Between the mean and *either* +3.0 SD or −3.0 SD	49.9
Between +1.0 SD and −1.0 SD	68.2
Between +2.0 SD and −2.0 SD	95.4
Between +3.0 SD and −3.0 SD	99.8

range is based on percentiles—specifically, the 25th and 75th percentiles—and is commonly used when the median is being used as a measure of the middle of the group. The standard deviation is a measure of variability that goes with the arithmetic mean. It is useful in the field of testing primarily because it provides a standard unit of measure having comparable meaning from one test to another.

INTERPRETING THE SCORE OF AN INDIVIDUAL

The problems of interpreting the score of an individual are treated more fully in Chapter 3, where we turn to test norms and units of measure. It will suffice now to indicate that the two sorts of measures we have just been considering—percentiles and standard deviation units—give a framework in which we can view the performance of a specific person. Both provide a way to view the person's performance relative to a specific reference group. Percentile information tells us what point in the score distribution just exceeds a specified fraction of the scores for the group; the standard deviation provides a common unit of distance from the mean of the group. The individual's score can then be expressed as a distance above or below the mean in these common units. In this way it is possible to give a meaningful answer to questions such as, Are you taller than you are heavy?

MEASURES OF RELATIONSHIP

We look now for a statistic to express the relationship between two sets of scores. For example, in Table 2.1, for each pupil we have scores for reading and mathematics, as well as spelling. To what extent did those pupils who scored well in mathematics also score well on the reading test? In this case, we have two scores for each individual. We can picture these scores by a plot in two dimensions, one for each test. Such a plot is shown in Figure 2.8. The first person listed in Table 2.1, Carol A., had a reading test score of 32 and a mathematics test score of 3. Her scores are represented by the X in Figure 2.8, plotted at 32 on the vertical, or reading, scale and at 3 on the horizontal, or mathematics, scale. There is a dot in the figure to represent each of the other 43 pupils' scores.

When a person who does well in reading also does well in mathematics, the dot representing those two scores falls in the upper right-hand part of the figure. The dot for one who does poorly on both tests falls in the lower left. Where a good score on one test is paired with a poor score on the other, we find the points falling in the other corners, that is, the upper left and the lower right. Children who score in the middle on both tests are represented by points in the center of the plot. Inspection of Figure 2.8 reveals some tendency for the scores to scatter in the lower left to the upper right direction, from low reading and low mathematics to high reading and high mathematics, but there are many exceptions. The relationship is far from perfect; it is a matter of degree. We need some index to express this degree of relationship.

As an index of degree of relationship, a statistic known as the *correlation coefficient* can be computed. (The symbol r is used to designate this coefficient.) This

Figure 2.8

Scatter plot of reading and mathematics scores.

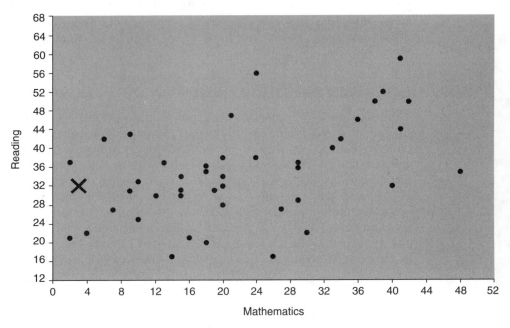

coefficient can take values ranging from +1.0 through zero to −1.0. A correlation of +1.0 signifies a perfect positive relationship between the two variables. It means that the person with the highest score on one test also had the highest score on the other, the next highest on one was the second highest on the other, and so forth, exactly parallel through the whole group. A correlation of −1.0 means that the scores on one test go in exactly the reverse direction from the scores on the other. The person highest on one test is the lowest on the other, the second highest on one is the second lowest on the other, and so forth. A zero correlation represents a complete lack of relationship; that is, there is no tendency for people who score high on one test to be either above or below average on the other. The pattern is essentially random. In-between values of the correlation coefficient represent tendencies for a relationship to exist, but with discrepancies.

Every correlation coefficient contains two pieces of information. One is the *sign* of the correlation, which tells whether the two variables tend to rank people in the same order (plus) or in the reverse order (minus). The second piece of information is the *magnitude* of the correlation, which tells how strong the relationship is. The correlations +.50 and −.50 indicate the same strength of relationship, but the first reveals that there is some tendency for people to be in the same rank order on both variables; the second shows some tendency for people with the highest scores on one variable to have the lowest scores on the other.

Figure 2.9 illustrates four different levels of relationships. In Figure 2.9a, the correlation is zero, and the points scatter in a pattern that is almost circular. All combinations are found—high-high, low-low, high-low, and low-high. Figure 2.9b corresponds to a correlation of +.30. You can see a slight trend for the points to group in the low-low and high-high direction. This tendency is more marked in Figure 2.9c, which represents a correlation of +.60. In Figure 2.9d, which portrays a correlation of +.90, the trend is much more pronounced. Note that when the correlation is −.60 (Figure 2.9e) or −.90 (Figure 2.9f), the scattering of the points is the same, but the swarm of dots falls along the opposite diagonal from that of Figures 2.9c and 2.9d—from the upper left-hand corner to the lower right-hand corner. But even with as high a correlation as +.90, the scores spread out quite a bit and do not all lie directly on the line from low-low to high-high. The scores plotted in Figure 2.8 correspond to a correlation coefficient of +.48. Procedures for computing the correlation coefficient are outlined in Appendix 1 for readers who wish to carry out the calculations with a numerical example. In this appendix, we also show how to compute the mean and standard deviation for data from a frequency distribution rather than for data in their raw form. As is the case for the standard deviation, many modern pocket calculators include a program to compute the correlation coefficient. Likewise, spreadsheet and statistics packages will always have programs to compute correlations, although they may be listed under the heading of *regression*, a closely related topic we discuss briefly in Chapter 5.

You will encounter correlation coefficients in connection with testing and measurement in three important settings. The first situation is one in which we are trying to determine how precise and consistent a measurement procedure is. Thus, if we want to know how consistent a measure of speed we can expect to get from a 50-meter dash, we can have each person run the distance twice, perhaps on successive days. Correlating the two sets of scores will give information on the stability, or *reliability*, of this measure of running speed. The second situation is one in which we are studying the relationship between two different measures to evaluate one as a *predictor* of the other. Thus, we might want to study a scholastic aptitude test as a predictor of college grades. The correlation of the test with grades would give an indication of the test's usefulness as a predictor. These two uses of the correlation coefficient are described more fully in Chapters 4 and 5.

The third situation in which we encounter correlation coefficients is more purely descriptive. We often are interested in the relationships between variables, simply to understand better how behavior is organized. What correlations do we find between measures of verbal and quantitative abilities? How close is the relationship between interest in mechanical jobs and comprehension of mechanical devices? Is rate of physical development related to rate of intellectual development? Many research problems in human behavior can only, or perhaps best, be studied by observing relationships as they develop in a natural setting, and these relationships are expressed with correlation coefficients.

We face the problem, in each case, of evaluating the correlation we obtain. Suppose the two sets of 50-meter dash scores yield a correlation of .80. Is this

Figure 2.9
Distribution of scores for representative values of correlation coefficient:
(a) correlation of 0.00; *(b)* correlation of +.30; *(c)* correlation of +.60;
(d) correlation of +.90; *(e)* correlation of −.60; *(f)* correlation of −.90.

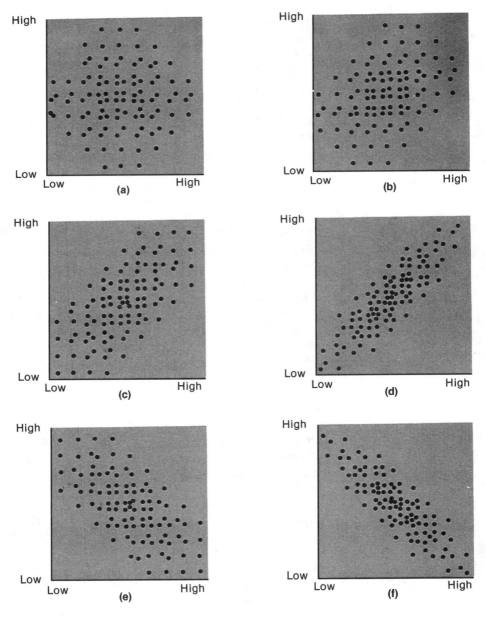

satisfactory? Suppose the aptitude test correlates .60 with college grades. Should we be pleased or discouraged? (The wording of this question implies that we want correlations to be high. When a correlation expresses the reliability, or consistency, of a test, or its accuracy in predicting an outcome of interest to us, it is certainly true that the higher the correlation, the more pleased we are. In other contexts, however, "bigness" does not necessarily correspond to "goodness," and we may not have a preference on the size of a correlation—or may even prefer a low one.)

The answer to the last question lies in part in the plots in Figure 2.9. Clearly, the higher the correlation, the more closely one variable goes with the other. If we think of discrepancies away from the diagonal line, from low-low to high-high, as "errors," the errors become smaller as the correlation becomes larger. But these discrepancies are still discouragingly large for even rather substantial correlation coefficients, for example, Figure 2.9c. We must always be aware of these discrepancies and realize that with a correlation such as $+.60$ between an aptitude test and school grades (which is about as high as correlations between these measures usually get), there will be a number of children whose school performance differs a good deal from what we have predicted from the tests.

However, everything is relative, and any given correlation coefficient must be interpreted in comparison with values that are commonly obtained. Table 2.6 contains a number of correlations that have been reported for different types of variables. The nature of the scores being correlated is described, and the coefficient is reported. An examination of this table will provide some initial background for interpreting correlation coefficients. The coefficient will gradually take on added

Table 2.6
Correlations Between Selected Variables

Variable	Correlation Coefficient
Heights of identical twins	.95
Intelligence test scores of identical twins	.88
Reading test scores in Grade 3 versus Grade 6	.80
Rank in high school class versus teacher's rating of work habits	.73
Height versus weight in 10-year-olds	.60
Arithmetic computation test score versus nonverbal intelligence test (Grade 8)	.54
Height of brothers (adjusted for age)	.50
Intelligence test score versus parents' occupational level	.30
Strength of grip versus running speed	.16
Height versus intelligence test score	.06
Ratio of head length to width versus intelligence test score	.01
Armed Forces Qualification Test scores of recruits versus number of school grades repeated	−.27
Artist interest score vesus banker interest score	−.64

meaning as you encounter coefficients of different sizes in your reading and as you work with tests.

SUMMARY

All measurements produce numbers. It is usually desirable to summarize the numbers that result from measurements so that we can both answer specific questions about the people we have measured and draw general conclusions. We have focused on five basic types of questions.

1. *What does the general array of numbers "look like"? Or how do they arrange themselves?*
   The answer to this question involves sorting the scores into a frequency distribution (Table 2.2) or a grouped frequency distribution (Table 2.3). Plotting histograms (Figure 2.1) or frequency polygons (Figure 2.2) can also give a picture of the data.

2. *What does the typical individual look like? Or where is the middle of the group?*
   The mode, median (or 50th percentile), and mean are indices of where the middle of the group falls. The mean, or arithmetic average, is the most commonly used measure of the center of the group.

3. *How widely do the scores spread out around their center? Or what is their spread?*
   The spread of scores can be represented by the range, the semi-interquartile range (half the distance between the 25th and the 75th percentiles), and the standard deviation, which is a measure of how far scores deviate, on the average, from the mean.

4. *How should we interpret the score of any individual?*
   We will discuss this topic in Chapter 3.

5. *To what extent do the scores from two measurements "go together"? Or what is the degree of relationship between the two sets of scores?*
   Generally, the most useful measurement of relationships is the correlation coefficient. This index runs from +1.00, indicating a perfect positive relationship or exact agreement, through zero, indicating no association between the sets of scores, to −1.00, indicating a perfect negative relationship, or exact disagreement, on the order of individuals on the two traits. The correlation coefficient is important as an index of stability of measurement and as a measure of how well one trait can be predicted from another.

QUESTIONS AND EXERCISES

1. For each of the following sets of scores, select the most suitable score interval and set up a form for tallying the scores:

Test	Number of Cases	Range of Scores
Mathematics	103	15–65
Reading Comprehension	60	60–140
Interest Inventory	582	65–248

2. In each of the following distributions, indicate the size of the score interval, the midpoints of the intervals shown, and the real limits of the intervals (i.e., the dividing points between them):

a.	b.	c.
4–7	17–19	60–69
8–11	20–22	70–79
12–15	23–25	80–89
.	.	.
.	.	.
.	.	.

3. Using the spelling scores given in Table 2.1, make a frequency distribution and a histogram. Compute the median and the upper and lower quartiles. Also, compute the arithmetic mean and the standard deviation from the original scores and from the frequency distribution.

4. The Bureau of Census uses the median in reporting average income. Why is this index used rather than the mean?

5. A 50-item mathematics test was given to the 150 students in five classes at Sunnyside School. Scores ranged from 16 to 50, with 93 of the students getting scores above 40. What would this score distribution look like? What could you say about the suitability of this test for this group? What measures of central tendency and variability would be most suitable? Why?

6. A high school teacher gave two sections of a biology class the same test. The results were as follows:

	Section A	Section B
Median	74.6	74.3
Mean	75.0	73.2
75th percentile	79.0	80.0
25th percentile	71.0	64.4
Standard deviation	6.0	10.5

From these data, what can you say about these two classes? What implications do the test results have for teaching the two groups?

7. A test in history given to 2,500 10th-grade students had a mean of 52 and a standard deviation of 10.5. How many standard deviations above or below the mean would the following students fall?

Heather	48	Rob	60	Marc	31
Krista	56	Tina	36	Bill	84

8. If the distribution in Question 7 was approximately normal, what percentage of the group would Heather, Krista, Rob, Tina, Marc, and Bill each surpass?

9. Assuming that a set of scores is normally distributed with a mean of 82 and a standard deviation of 12, what percent of the distribution would each of the following scores exceed?

   a. 74

   b. 85

   c. 99

10. Explain the meaning of each of the following correlation coefficients:

  a. The correlation between scores on a reading test and scores on a group test of general intellectual ability is +0.78.

  b. Ratings of students on good citizenship and on aggressiveness show a correlation of −0.56.

  c. The correlation between weight and sociability is +0.02.

SUGGESTED READINGS

Bluman, A. G. (1995). *Elementary statistics* (2nd ed.). Dubuque, IA: Wm. C. Brown.

Lehman, R. C. (1995). *Statistics in the behavioral sciences*. Pacific Grove, CA: Brooks/Cole.

Moore, D. S., & McCabe, G. P. (1993). *Introduction to the practice of statistics*. New York: Freeman.

Witte, R. S. (1993). *Statistics* (4th ed.). Fort Worth, TX: Harcourt Brace.

CHAPTER 3

Giving Meaning to Scores

THE NATURE OF A SCORE

Johnny got a score of 15 on his spelling test. What does this score mean, and how should we interpret it?

Standing alone, the number has no meaning at all and is completely uninterpretable. At the most superficial level, we do not even know whether this number represents a perfect score of 15 out of 15 or a very low percentage of the possible score, such as 15 out of 50. Even if we do know that the score is 15 out of 20, or 75%, what then?

Consider the two 20-word spelling tests in Table 3.1. A score of 15 on Test A would have a vastly different meaning from the same score on Test B. A person who gets only 15 correct on Test A would not be outstanding in a second- or third-grade class. Have a few friends or classmates take Test B. You will probably find that not many of them can spell 15 of these words correctly. When this test was given to a class of graduate students, only 22% spelled 15 or more of the words correctly. A score of 15 on Test B is a good score among graduate students of education or psychology.

As it stands, then, a score of 15 words correct, or even of 75%, has no direct meaning or significance. The score has meaning only when we have some standard with which to compare it.

Table 3.1
Two 20-word Spelling Tests

Test A	Test B
bar	baroque
cat	catarrh
form	formaldehyde
jar	jardiniere
nap	naphtha
dish	discernible
fat	fatiguing
sack	sacrilegious
rich	ricochet
sit	citrus
feet	feasible
act	accommodation
rate	inaugurate
inch	insignia
rent	deterrent
lip	eucalyptus
air	questionnaire
rim	rhythm
must	ignoramus
red	accrued

Frames of Reference

The way that we derive meaning from a test score depends on the context or frame of reference in which we wish to interpret it. This frame of reference may be described using three basic dimensions. First, there is what we might call a temporal dimension: Is the focus of our concern what a person can do now or what that person is likely to do in the future? Are we interested in describing the current state or in forecasting the future?

A second dimension involves the contrast between what people *can* do and what they would *like* to do or would normally do. When we assess a person's capacity, we determine *maximum performance,* and when we ask about a person's preferences or habits, we assess *typical performance.* Maximum performance implies a set of tasks that can be judged for correctness; there is a "right" answer. With typical performance there is not a right answer, but we may ask whether one individual's responses are like those of most people or are unusual in some way.

A third dimension is the nature of the standard against which we compare a person's behavior. In some cases, the test itself may provide the standard; in some cases, it is the person's own behavior in other situations or on other tests that provides the standard; and in still other instances, it is the person's behavior in comparison with that of other people. Thus, a given measurement is interpreted as being either oriented in the present or oriented in the future; as measuring either maximum or typical performance; and as relating the person's performance to a standard defined by the test itself, to the person's own scores on this or other measures, or to the performance of other people.

Many instructional decisions in schools call for information about what a student or group of students can do now. Walter is making a good many mistakes in his oral reading. To develop an instructional strategy that will help him overcome this difficulty, we need to determine the cause of his problem. One question we might ask is whether he can match words with their initial consonant sounds. A brief test focused on this specific skill, perhaps presented by the teacher to Walter individually while the other students work on other tasks, can help to determine whether a deficiency in this particular skill is part of Walter's problem. How many children in Walter's class have mastery of the rule on capitalizing proper nouns? A focused test such as the one in Table 3.2 can provide evidence to guide a decision on whether further teaching of this skill is needed. At a broader level, we may ask whether the current program in mathematics in Centerville is producing satisfactory achievement. A survey mathematics test with national or regional norms can permit a comparison of Centerville's students with students in the rest of the country, and this comparison can be combined with other information about Centerville's students and its schools to make a decision on whether progress is satisfactory.

Whenever we ask questions about how much a person can do, there is also the issue of the purpose of our evaluation. There are two fundamental purposes for evaluating capacity in an educational context. One is to reach a summary statement of the person's accomplishments to date, such as teachers do at the end of each marking period. Evaluation for this purpose is called *summative evaluation.* It provides a summary of student achievement. By contrast, teachers are often interested in using

Table 3.2
A Focused Test

Test on Capitalizing Proper Nouns

Directions: Read the paragraph. The punctuation is correct, and the words that begin a sentence have been capitalized. No other words have been capitalized. Some need to be. Draw a line under *each word* that should begin with a capital.

We saw mary yesterday. She said she had gone to chicago, illinois, to see her aunt

helen. Her aunt took her for a drive along the shore of lake michigan. On the way they

passed the conrad hilton hotel, where mary's uncle joseph works. Mary said she had

enjoyed the trip, but she was glad to be back home with her own friends.

---

tests to determine their students' strengths and weaknesses, the areas where they are doing well and those where they are doing poorly. Assessment for this purpose, to guide future instruction, is called *formative evaluation.* Test results are used to inform or to shape the course of instruction.

The type of maximum performance test that describes what a person *has learned to do* is called an *achievement test.* The oral reading test given to Walter, the capitalization test in Table 3.2, and the mathematics test given to the students in Centerville are illustrations of sharply contrasting types of achievement tests. The test on initial consonant sounds is concerned with mastery of one specific skill by one student, and no question is raised as to whether Walter's skill in this area is better or worse than that of any other student. The only question is, can he perform this task well enough so that we can rule out this skill as a cause of his difficulty with oral reading?

Similarly, Walter's teacher is concerned with the level of mastery, *within* this class, of a specific skill in English usage. Tests concerned with level of mastery of such defined skills are often called *domain-referenced* or *criterion-referenced* tests because the focus is solely on reaching a standard of performance on a specific skill called for by the test exercises. The test itself and the domain of content it represents provide the standard. Many, perhaps most, assessments needed for instructional decisions are of this sort.

We may contrast these tests with the mathematics survey test given to appraise mathematics achievement in Centerville. Here, the concern is whether Centerville's students are showing satisfactory achievement *when compared with the students in other towns and school systems like Centerville.* Performance is evaluated not in relation to the set of tasks per se, but in relation to the performance of some more general reference group. A test used in this way is spoken of as a *norm-referenced* test, because the quality of the performance is defined by comparison with the behavior of others. A norm-referenced test may appropriately be used in many situations calling for curricular, guidance, or research decisions. Occasionally throughout this book, we will compare and contrast criterion-referenced and norm-referenced achievement tests with respect to their construction, desired characteristics, and use.

Some decisions that we need to make require information on what a person *can learn to do.* Will Helen be able to master the techniques of computer programming? How readily will Richard assimilate calculus? Selection and placement decisions typically involve predictions about future learning or performance, based on present characteristics of the individual. A test that is used in this way as a predictor of future learning is called an *aptitude test.* Aptitude tests are usually norm referenced.

There are also situations where our decision calls for an estimate of what a person *is likely to do.* The selection of bus drivers, police officers, and candidates for many other jobs is best made with an eye to aspects of the person's personality or temperament. We would not want to select someone with a high level of aggression to be driving a large vehicle on confined city streets. Nor would we want people who have difficulty controlling their tempers serving as keepers of the peace. A measure of typical performance can serve as a useful aid in such situations, and these measures usually are also norm referenced.

Note that some of the most effective predictors of future learning are measures of past learning. Thus, for both computer programming and calculus, an effective predictor might be a test measuring competence in high school algebra. Such a test would measure previously learned knowledge and skill, but we would be using that achievement measure to predict future learning. Any test, whatever it is called, assesses a person's present characteristics. We cannot directly measure a person's hypothetical "native" or "inborn" qualities. All we can measure is what that person is able and willing to do in the here and now. That information may then be used to evaluate past learning, as when an algebra test is used to decide whether Roxanne should get an A in her algebra course, or to predict future learning, as when a counselor must decide whether Roxanne has a reasonable probability of successfully completing calculus. The distinction between an aptitude and an achievement test often lies more in the purpose for which the test results are used than in the nature or content of the test itself.

Domains in Criterion- and Norm-Referenced Tests

It is important to realize that all achievement tests relate to a specified domain of content. The mathematics survey test covers a fairly broad array of topics, while the test on the rules for capitalization is restricted to a narrowly defined set of behaviors. Thus, it is not really appropriate to differentiate between criterion-referenced and norm-referenced tests by saying that the former derive their meaning from a precisely specified domain, while the latter do not. A well-constructed, norm-referenced test will represent a very carefully defined domain, but the domain is generally more diverse than that of a criterion-referenced test, and has only a small number of items covering a given topic or instructional objective. The criterion-referenced test will represent a narrowly defined domain and will therefore cover its referent content more thoroughly than will a norm-referenced test of the same length.

There is a second dimension to using information from an achievement test. In addition to the traditional distinction between criterion-referenced and norm-referenced tests on the breadth of the domain they cover, another dimension relates to the way that the level, or altitude, of performance is represented or used in reaching decisions. A test score from either type of test gets its content meaning from the domain of content that the test represents, but the kind of inference that a teacher or counselor draws from the score can be either absolute or relative. The teacher makes a judgment on the basis of the test score. If the judgment is that when a student or group of students have gained a particular level of proficiency with respect to that content they have mastered the material, then the judgment is an absolute, *mastery/nonmastery* one. The decision reached is either that the students have mastered the material or that they have not; degree of mastery is not an issue. Decisions of this type are called *mastery* decisions. The usual definition of a criterion-referenced test is a test that covers a narrow domain and is used for mastery decisions.

By contrast, teachers can also use tests to judge relative achievement of objectives. Relative mastery involves estimating the percentage of the domain that students have mastered. For example, the teacher may decide that students have mastered an objective relating to spelling when they can spell correctly 19 out of 20 words from the domain. But the same teacher might use the information that the average student got a score of 14 on the spelling test to indicate that the students had achieved about 70% mastery of the domain. We refer to decisions of this kind as *relative achievement* decisions, but the frame of reference is still the domain of content without regard to the performance of anyone other than the current examinees.

The typical norm-referenced test uses neither of these ways to represent the level of performance. Rather, level is referenced to a larger group called a *norm group,* or norm sample. A normative interpretation of a score could lead to the conclusion that the individual was performing at a very high level compared with an appropriate reference group, but the same performance might fall far below mastery from the criterion-referenced perspective. Conversely, a ninth grader who has achieved mastery of multiplication facts at the level of 95% accuracy ordinarily would not show a high level of performance when compared with other ninth graders.

CRITERION-REFERENCED EVALUATION

We can approach the problem of a frame of reference for interpreting test results from the two rather different points of view mentioned earlier. One, criterion-referenced evaluation, discussed here, focuses on the tasks themselves, and the other, norm-referenced testing, on the performance of typical people. Consider the 20 spelling words in Test A of Table 3.1. If we knew that these had been chosen from the words taught in a third-grade spelling program and if we had agreed on some grounds (at this point unspecified) that 80% correct represented an acceptable standard for performance in spelling when words are presented by dictation, with illustrative sentences, then we could interpret Ellen's score of 18 correct on the test as indicating that she had reached the criterion of mastery of the words taught in third-grade spelling and Peter's score of 12 correct as indicating that he had not.

Here, we have test content selected from a narrowly defined domain and we have a mastery test interpretation. The test is criterion referenced in that (1) the tasks are drawn from and related to a specific instructional domain, (2) the form of presentation of the tasks and the response to them is set in accordance with the defined objective, and (3) a level of performance acceptable for mastery, with which the performance of each student is compared, is defined in advance. That is, criterion-referenced tests relate to a carefully defined domain of content, they focus on achievement of behavioral objectives, and the results are often (but not necessarily) used for mastery judgments.

The "mastery" frame of reference is an appropriate one for some types of educational decisions. For example, decisions on what materials and methods should be used for additional instruction in spelling with Ellen and Peter might revolve around the question of whether they had reached the specified criterion of mastery of the third-grade spelling words. More crucially, in a sequential subject such as mathematics, the decision on whether to begin a unit involving borrowing in subtraction might depend on whether students had reached a criterion of mastery on a test of two-place subtraction that did not require borrowing.

By contrast, teachers also use tests to judge the relative achievement of objectives. Relative mastery may involve estimating the percentage of a domain that the students have mastered.

Although the two topics of domain referencing of test content and a mastery/nonmastery decision about achievement historically have been linked, it is important to realize that they are quite different and independent ideas that have recently come to be treated together. It is also important to realize that both exist in a sociopolitical context that invests them with normative meaning. What, for example, should a third grader be expected to know about multiplication? The answer to this question depends on what is expected of second and fourth graders, and these expectations put norm-referenced boundaries on what is taught in the third grade. Professional judgment and many years of experience combine to define the reasonable domain of content. A test is then constructed to represent this content.

Given a test that is designed to represent a particular domain of content, the scores from that test may be interpreted strictly with respect to that content, or they may be interpreted in a normative framework by comparing one person's performance with that of others. Domain-referenced interpretation means that the degree of achievement is assessed relative to the test itself and the instructional objectives that gave rise to the test. The evaluation may result in a dichotomous judgment that the person has mastered the material and is ready for further instruction, for certification or licensure, or for whatever decision is the object of the measurement. Or, the evaluation may result in a judgment of degree of mastery. The latter approximates what teachers do when they assign grades, while the former is similar to a pass/fail decision or a decision to begin new material.

For the group of tests that are typically called criterion referenced, the standard, then, is provided by the definition of the specific objectives that the test is designed to measure. When the type of decision to be made is a mastery decision, this description of the content, together with the level of performance that the teacher, school, or school system has agreed on as representing an acceptable level of mastery of that objective, provide an absolute standard. Thus, the illustrative content-referenced test of capitalization of proper nouns in Table 3.2 is presumed to provide a representative sample of tasks calling for this specific competence. If we accept the sample of tasks as representative and if we agree that 80% accuracy in performing this task is the minimum acceptable performance, then a score of 10 out of 13 words correctly underlined defines the standard in an absolute sense.

Even the dichotomous or mastery judgment is made in a sociopolitical, hence normative, context. The teacher or school has to decide what constitutes mastery, and there are some not-so-subtle social pressures that affect such decisions. Most teachers define the level of achievement necessary for mastery in such a way that an "appropriate" number of students are identified as masters. In practice, this means that over a period of time the teacher develops a fairly accurate idea of how typical students will perform on his or her tests covering a course of instruction. The tests, grading practices, or passing standards are adjusted so that, in the long run, the right number of students pass, which makes the setting of passing standards basically a normative decision! (See Shepard [1984] for a discussion of setting standards in criterion-referenced testing.)

In the usual classroom test used for summative evaluation, such a standard operates indirectly and imperfectly, partly through the teacher's choice of tasks to make up the test and partly through his or her standards for evaluating the responses. Thus, to make up their tests, teachers pick tasks that they consider appropriate to represent the learnings of their students. No conscientious teacher would give spelling Test A to an ordinary high school group or Test B to third graders. When the responses vary in quality, as in essay examinations, teachers set standards for grading that correspond to what they consider is reasonable to expect from students like theirs. Quite different answers to the question "What were the causes of the War of 1812?" would be expected from a ninth grader and from a college history major.

However, the inner standard of the individual teacher tends to be subjective and unstable. Furthermore, it provides no basis for comparing different classes or different areas of ability. Such a yardstick can give no answers to such questions as, Are the children in School A better in reading than those in School B? Is Mary better in reading than in mathematics? Is Johnny doing as well in algebra as most ninth graders? We need some broader, more uniform, objective, and stable standard of reference if we are to be able to interpret those psychological and educational measurements that undertake to appraise some trait or to survey competence in some broad area of the school curriculum. Most of this chapter is devoted to describing and evaluating several normative reference frames that have been used to give a standard meaning to test scores.

NORM-REFERENCED EVALUATION

The other frame of reference for interpreting test performance is based not on a somewhat arbitrary standard defined by a particular selection of content and interpreted as representing mastery of that content domain but rather is based on the performance of other people. This represents a norm-referenced interpretation. Thus, the scores of Ellen and Peter can be viewed in relation to the performance of a large reference group of typical third graders or of students in different school grades. Their performance is viewed not in terms of mastery versus nonmastery or in terms of relative mastery of the subject matter, but instead as above average, average, or below average; ways are sought to refine that scale of relative performance so that all degrees of excellence can be expressed in quantitative terms.

In seeking a scale to represent degrees of excellence, we would like to report results in units that have the following properties:

1. Uniform meaning from test to test, so that a basis of comparison is provided through which we may compare different tests—for example, different reading tests, a reading test with an arithmetic test, or an achievement test with a scholastic aptitude test
2. Units of uniform size, so that a gain of 10 points on one part of the scale signifies the same thing as a gain of 10 points on any other part of the scale
3. A true-zero point of *just none of* the quality in question, so that we can legitimately think of scores as representing *twice as much as* or *two-thirds as much as*

The different types of norm-referenced scales that have been developed for tests represent marked progress toward the first two of these objectives. The third can probably never be reached for the traits with which we are concerned in psychological and educational measurement. We can put five 1-lb loaves of bread on one side of a pair of scales, and they will balance the contents of one 5-lb bag of flour placed on the other side. "No weight" is *truly* "no weight," and units of weight can be added so that 2 lb is twice 1 lb. But we do not have that type of zero point or that type of adding in the case of educational and psychological measurement. If you put together two below-average students, you will not get a genius, and a pair of bad spellers cannot jointly win a spelling bee. In some cases, this deficit is the result of the particular way we have chosen to measure the trait, but for many psychological and educational traits, the deficit is a result of how we conceptualize the trait itself.

Basically, a raw point score on a test is given normative meaning only by referring it to some type of group or groups. A score on the typical test is not high or low or good or bad in any absolute sense; it is higher or lower or better or worse than other scores. There are two general ways that we may relate one person's score to a more general framework. One way is to compare the person with a graded series of groups and see which one he or she matches. Each group in the series usually represents a particular school grade or a particular chronological age. The other way is to find where in a particular group the person falls in terms of the percentage of the group surpassed or in terms of position relative to the group's mean and standard deviation. Thus, we find four main patterns for interpreting the score of an individual. These are shown schematically in Table 3.3. We shall consider each in turn, evaluating its advantages and disadvantages.

Table 3.3
Main Types of Norms for Educational and Psychological Tests

Type of Norm	Type of Comparison	Type of Group
Grade norms	Individual matched to group whose performance he or she equals	Successive grade groups
Age norms	Same as above	Successive age groups
Percentile norms	Percentage of group surpassed by individual	Single age or grade group to which individual belongs
Standard score norms	Number of standard deviations individual falls above or below average of group	Same as above

Grade Norms

For any trait that shows a progressive and relatively uniform increase from one school grade to the next, we can prepare a set of grade norms. The norm for any grade, in this sense, is the average score obtained by individuals in that grade. Because school participation and the related cognitive growth are both more or less continuous, grade norms typically are expressed with one decimal place. The whole number gives the grade, and the decimal is the month within grade. Thus, a grade equivalent of 5.4 is read as performance corresponding to that of the average child in the fourth month of fifth grade.

In simplest outline, the process of establishing grade norms involves giving the test to a representative sample of pupils in each of a number of consecutive grades, calculating the average score at each level, and then establishing *grade equivalents* for the in-between scores. Thus, a reading comprehension test, such as that from the Iowa Tests of Basic Skills (ITBS)—Form J, Level 9, might be given in November to pupils in grades 2, 3, 4, and 5, with the following results.

Grade Level	Average Raw Score
2.3	13
3.3	22
4.3	31
5.3	37

The testing establishes grade equivalents for raw scores of 13, 22, 31, and 37. However, grade equivalents are also needed for the in-between scores. These are usually determined arithmetically by interpolation, although sometimes intermediate points may be established by actually testing at other times during the school year. After interpolation, we have the following table.*

Note: Copyright © 1993 by The University of Iowa. Reproduced from *Iowa Tests of Basic Skills. Interpretive Guide for Teachers and Counselors, Form J.* Reproduced by permission of the publisher, The Riverside Publishing Company, 425 Springlake Drive, Itasca, IL 60143.

Raw Score	Grade Equivalent	Raw Score	Grade Equivalent
10	1.9	24	3.5
11	2.0	25	3.6
12	2.2	26	3.7
13	2.3	27	3.8
14	2.5	28	3.9
15	2.6	29	4.0
16	2.8	30	4.1
17	2.9	31	4.3
18	3.0	32	4.4
19	3.1	33	4.5
20	3.2	34	4.7
21	3.2	35	4.9
22	3.3	36	5.1
23	3.4	37	5.3

Because raw scores on this particular test can range from 0 to 49, some way is needed to establish grade equivalents for the more extreme scores. Establishing such grade equivalents is often done by equating scores on the level of the test on which we are working with scores from lower and higher levels of the same test series, forms that have been given to earlier and later grades. In this way, grade equivalents may be extended down as low as the first month of kindergarten (denoted K.1) and up as high as the end of the first year in college (denoted 13.9), and a complete table to translate raw scores to grade equivalents can be prepared. (The reading test of this particular edition of the ITBS actually is a multilevel test that uses six overlapping sets of passages and items in a single booklet. In this way, some of the same items are used for three different levels of the test, and the projection of grade equivalents is simplified and made more accurate.)

If Jennifer got a raw score of 28 on this test, it would give her a grade equivalent of 3.9, and this score could be translated as "performing as well as the average child who has completed 9 months of third grade." Such an interpretation has the advantage of connecting the test score to familiar milestones of educational development. However, this seductively simple interpretation of a child's performance has a number of drawbacks as well.

A first major question about grade norms is whether we can think of them as providing precisely or even approximately equal units. In what sense is the growth in ability in paragraph reading from grade 3.2 to 4.2 equal to the growth from grade 6.2 to 7.2? Grounds for assuming equality are clearly tenuous. When the skill is one that has been taught throughout the school years, there may be some reason to expect a year's learning at one level to be about equal to a year's learning at some other. And there is evidence that during elementary school (and possibly junior high), grade-score units are near enough to equal to be serviceable. However, even in this range and for areas where instruction has been continuous, the equality is only approximate. If, on the other hand, we are concerned with a subject like Spanish, in which instruction typically does not begin until secondary school, or in something like biology, for which instruction is concentrated in a single grade, grade equivalents become almost completely meaningless. In addition, instruction in many skills, such as the basic skills in reading and in arithmetic computation, tapers off and largely stops by high school, so grade units have little or no meaning at this level. For this reason many achievement batteries show a grade equivalent of 10.0+ or 11.0+ as representing the whole upper range of scores. When grade equivalents such as 12.5 are reported, these do not really represent the average performance of students tested in the middle of the 12th grade, but rather, they are an artificial and fictitious extrapolation of the score scale, used to provide some converted score to be reported for the most capable eighth and ninth graders.

A further note of caution must be introduced with respect to the interpretation of grade norms. Consider a bright and educationally advanced child in the third grade. Suppose we find that on a standardized mathematics test this child gets a score with the grade equivalent of 5.9. This score does *not* mean that this child has a mastery of the mathematics taught in the fifth grade. The *score* is as high as that earned by the average child at the end of fifth grade, but this higher score almost certainly has been obtained in part by superior mastery of third-grade work. The average child falls well short of a perfect score on the topics that have been taught at his or her own grade level. The able child can get a number of additional points (and consequently a higher grade equivalent) merely by complete mastery of this "at-grade" material. This warning is worth remembering. The fact that a child has a grade equivalent of 5.9 need not mean that the child is ready to move ahead into sixth-grade work. The grade equivalent is only the reflection of a score and does not tell in what way that score was obtained. Reference to the content of the questions the child answered correctly would be needed to reach a judgment that the child had sufficient mastery of fifth-grade material to be able to move into the sixth grade. Thus, grade equivalents should not be used to make mastery decisions.

Finally, there is reason to question the comparability of grade equivalents from one school subject to another. Does being a year ahead (or behind) one's grade level in language usage represent the same amount of advancement (or retardation) as the same deviation in arithmetic concepts? A good deal of evidence exists, which we consider later in this chapter, that it does not. Growth in different school subjects proceeds at different rates, depending on in-school emphasis and out-of-school learning. For this reason, the glib comparison of a pupil's grade equivalent in different school subjects can result in quite misleading conclusions.

To summarize, grade norms, which relate the performance of an individual to that of the average child at each grade level, are useful primarily in providing a framework for interpreting the academic accomplishment of children in the elementary school. For this purpose, they are relatively convenient and meaningful, even though we cannot place great confidence in the equality of grade units or their exact equivalence from one subject to another.

Grade norms are relatively easy to determine because they are based on the administrative groups already established in the school organization. In the directly academic areas of achievement, the concept of grade level is perhaps more meaningful than is age level, for it is in relation to grade placement that a child's performance is likely to be interpreted and acted on. Outside the school setting, grade norms have little meaning.

Developmental Standard Scores

We have noted several problems with grade equivalents as normative representations of a child's performance, particularly that there is an implicit assumption that the amount of growth in the ability being tested is equal from one year to the next. Because this assumption clearly is violated for many abilities, test publishers have developed a type of score scale that is anchored to school grades but provides a better approximation to an equal interval scale, the *Developmental Standard Score Scale.*

Developmental standard scores (DSSs) are based on normalized score distributions within each grade (see the discussion of normalizing transformations later in this chapter). Scale values for two grades are chosen arbitrarily to define the scale metric, and the within-grade means and standard deviations are then used to locate other grade equivalents on this scale. For example, the Iowa Tests of Basic Skills authors have chosen to fix a scale value of 200 as equivalent to the median performance of fourth graders and a value of 250 for eighth graders tested in the spring. The relationship between grade equivalents and DSSs reported in the test manual is as follows:

Grade	K	1	2	3	4	5	6	7	8	9	10
DSS	130	150	168	185	200	214	227	239	250	260	268

One fact is quite clear from comparing grade equivalents and DSSs, equal changes in grade equivalents do not correspond to equal changes in DSS. The DSS scale is constructed to have equal intervals (a 10-unit change has the same meaning everywhere on the scale). The comparison shows that there is a bigger change from year to year during the early years of school than there is in later years, 18 points from first to second grade, 10 points from eighth to ninth.

The main drawback of DSSs is that, unlike grade equivalents, they have no inherent meaning. The values chosen for the anchor points are quite arbitrary. Meaning is given only by their relationship to the grade equivalent scale. It would be appropriate, for example, to say that a student who received a DSS of 255 was performing at the level of students in about December of their ninth-grade year. Because of their complexity and lack of obvious meaning, developmental standard scores are hard to interpret correctly and should be used with caution, even though they are reported by many test publishers.

Age Norms

If a trait is one that may be expected to show continuous and relatively uniform growth with age, it may be appropriate to convert the score into an *age score,* or *age equivalent,* as a type of common score scale. During childhood we can observe continuous growth in height and weight, in various indices of anatomical maturity, and in a wide range of perceptual, motor, and cognitive performances. It makes a crude type of sense to describe an 8-year-old as being as tall as the average 10-year-old and having the strength of grip of the average 9-year-old, as well as the speaking vocabulary of the average 6-year-old. In the early development of intelligence and aptitude tests, raw scores were typically converted into age equivalents, and the term "mental age" was added to the vocabulary of the mental tester and the general public alike, with occasionally unfortunate results.

An age equivalent is, of course, the average score earned by individuals of a given age and is obtained by testing representative samples of 8-year-olds, 9-year-olds, 10-year-olds, and so forth. In this respect, it parallels the grade equivalent described in the previous section. And, as in the case of grade equivalents, a major issue is whether we can reasonably think of a year's growth as representing a standard and uniform unit. Is growth from age 5 to age 6 equal to growth from age 10 to age 11? And is growth in any 1 year equivalent to growth in any other year on our scale? As we move up the age scale, we soon reach a point where we see that the year's growth unit is clearly not appropriate. There comes a point, some time in the teens or early 20s, when growth in almost any trait that we can measure slows down and finally stops. In Figure 3.1, which illustrates the normal growth of height for girls, the slowdown takes place quite abruptly after age 14. A year's growth after 14 seems clearly to be much less than a year's growth earlier on the scale. At about age 14 or 15, the concept of height-age ceases to have any meaning. The same problem of a flattening growth curve is found, varying only in the age at which it occurs—and in abruptness, for any trait that we can measure.

The problem introduced by the flattening growth curve is most apparent when we consider the individual who falls far above average. What age equivalent shall we

Figure 3.1
Girls' age norms for height.

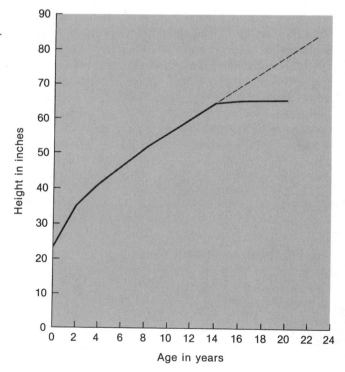

assign to a girl who is 5 ft 10 in. (70 in.) tall? The average woman *never* gets that tall at any age. If we are to assign any age value, we must invent some hypothetical extension of our growth curve, such as the dashed line in Figure 3.1. This line assumes that growth after 14 continues at about the same rate that was typical up to age 14. On this extrapolated curve, the height of 5 ft 10 in. would be assigned a height-age of about 16 years and 6 months. But this is a completely artificial and arbitrary age equivalent. It does *not* correspond to the average height of 16 1/2-year-olds. It does not correspond to the average height at *any* age. It merely signifies "taller than average." Unfortunately, there is no cue to be gotten from these extrapolated age equivalents that suggests their arbitrary nature.

Age norms, which are based on the characteristics of the average person at each age level, provide a readily comprehended framework for interpreting the status of a particular individual. However, the equality of age units is open to serious question, and as one goes up to adolescence and adulthood, age ceases to have any meaning as a unit in which to express level of performance. Age norms are most appropriate for infancy and childhood and for characteristics that grow as a part of the general development of the individual, such as height, weight, or dentition. General mental development, such as the cognitive characteristics embodied in the concept of mental age, show a sufficiently universal pattern to be useful normative indicators of status, but, in general, age norms should not be used for cognitive characteristics beyond the elementary school years, because the patterns of growth of these functions depend too heavily on formal school experiences or have not been found to show the pattern of growth necessary for age norms to be appropriate.

Percentile Norms

We have just seen that in the case of age and grade norms, meaning is given to the individual's score by determining the age or grade group in which the person would be exactly average. But, often such a comparison group is inappropriate or some other group would be more useful. For example, we are frequently concerned with the performance of people who are no longer in the elementary grades where grade norms have meaning. Or, we may be interested in personality or attitude characteristics for which age or grade norms are wholly unusable. Or, the type of information that we seek may require that we specify the group of interest more narrowly than is practical for age or grade norms. For example, we may be interested in people who are all the same age or are all in the same grade.

Each individual belongs to many different groups. An individual who is 18 years old belongs to some of the following groups, but not to others: all 18-year-olds, 18-year-olds in the 12th grade, 18-year-olds applying to college, 18-year-olds not applying to college, 18-year-olds applying to Ivy League colleges, 18-year-olds attending public (or parochial) schools, and 18-year-olds attending school in California. For some purposes it is desirable or necessary to define the comparison group more narrowly than is possible with grade or age norms. One universally applicable system of norms is the percentile norm system.

The typical percentile norm, or *percentile rank,* uses the same information that we used to compute percentiles in Chapter 2, but the procedure is slightly different. *Percentile ranks are calculated to correspond to obtainable score values.* If a test has 10 items, it can yield 11 different raw scores, the whole scores from zero to 10. There are only 11 possible values that percentile ranks could assume for this test, one for each obtainable score, but it would still be possible to calculate any number of percentiles. For example, one could compute, using the procedures described in Chapter 2, the 67.4th percentile as well as the 67th and 68th. But only the 11 obtainable scores would have corresponding percentile ranks. The normative interpretation of test scores more often uses percentile ranks than percentiles, because test results come in a limited number of whole score units.

The procedure for determining percentile ranks starts with a frequency distribution such as the one shown in Table 3.4. We assume, as we did for percentiles, that the underlying trait that the test measures is continuous, that each observable score falls at the midpoint of an interval on this continuum, and that the people who obtained a given raw score are spread throughout the interval. Because each raw score falls at the middle of an interval, half of the people in the interval are considered to be below the midpoint and half above. Even if only one person falls in a particular interval, we assume that half of that person falls above the midpoint of the interval and half falls below.

To find the percentile rank of a raw score, we count the number of people who are below the score and divide by the total number of people. The number of people below a raw score value includes all of the people who obtained lower scores plus half of the people who received the score in question (the latter group because they are assumed to be in the bottom half of the interval and, therefore, below the raw score). For example, to calculate the percentile rank of a raw score of 4 in Table 3.4, we would take the eight people who got scores below 4 and half of the seven people at 4. The result is $(8 + 3.5)/60 = 11.5/60 = 0.1917$. In reporting percentile ranks it

Table 3.4
Determining Percentile Ranks for a 10-Item Test

Raw Score	Frequency	Cumulative Frequency	Percentile Rank
10	1	60	99
9	3	59	96
8	5	56	89
7	12	51	75
6	15	39	52
5	9	24	32
4	7	15	19
3	4	8	10
2	2	4	5
1	1	2	2
0	1	1	1

is conventional to round the answer to two places and multiply by 100 to remove the decimal point except at the extremes of the scale. The percentile rank that corresponds to a raw score of 4 is therefore 19.

The major procedural difference between calculating percentiles such as the median and percentile ranks such as those in Table 3.4 is where one starts. To calculate percentiles, we specify a percent of interest, such as the 25th or 60th, and determine the answer, a point on the score scale, by the procedures described in Chapter 2. The values that correspond to these percentages need not be, and seldom are, whole points of score. When calculating percentile ranks, we start with a point on the score scale, an obtainable score value, and find as the answer the percentage of the group that falls below the chosen point of score.

Percentile norms are very widely adaptable and applicable. They can be used wherever an appropriate normative group can be obtained to serve as a yardstick. They are appropriate for young and old and for educational and industrial situations. To surpass 90% of a reference comparison group signifies a comparable degree of excellence whether the function being measured is how rapidly one can solve simultaneous equations or how far one can spit. Percentile norms are widely used and their meaning is readily understood. Were it not for the two points we next consider, they would provide a framework very nearly ideal for interpreting test scores.

The first issue that faces us in the case of percentile norms is specifying the norming group. On what type of group should the norms be based? Clearly, we will need different norm groups for different ages and grades in the population. A 9-year-old must be evaluated in terms of 9-year-old norms; a sixth grader, in terms of sixth-grade norms; an applicant for a job as real estate agent, in terms of norms for real estate agent applicants. The appropriate norm group is in every case the relevant group to which the individual belongs and in terms of which his or her status is to be evaluated. It makes no sense, for example, to evaluate the performance of medical school applicants on a biology test by comparing their scores with norms based on high school seniors. If the test is to be used by a medical school, the user must find or develop norms for medical school applicants.

Hence, If percentile norms are to be used, multiple sets of norms are usually needed. There must be norms appropriate for each distinct type of group or situation in which the test is to be used. This requirement is recognized by the better test publishers, and they provide norms not only for age and grade groups but also for special types of educational or occupational populations. However, there are limits to the number of distinct populations for which a test publisher can produce norms, so published percentile norms will often need to be supplemented by the test user, who can build up norm groups particularly suited to local needs. Thus, a given school system will often find it valuable to develop local percentile norms for its own pupils. (Most test publishers will assist school districts with the development of local norms.) Such norms will permit scores for individual pupils to be interpreted in relation to the local group, a comparison that may be more significant for local decisions than is comparison with national, regional, or state norms. Likewise, an employer who uses a test with a particular category of job applicant may well find it useful to accumulate results over a period of time and prepare norms for this particular group of people. These strictly local norms will greatly facilitate evaluating a new applicant.

Thus, the possibility of specifying many different norm groups for different uses of a test constitutes both a problem, in the sense of greater complexity, and a strength, in that more accurate comparisons can be made.

The second percentile-norm issue relates to the question of equality of units. Can we think of five percentile points as representing the same amount of the trait throughout the percentile scale? Is the difference between the 50th and 55th percentile equivalent to the difference between the 90th and 95th? To answer this question, we must notice the way in which the test scores for a group of people usually pile up. We saw one histogram of scores in Figure 2.1 of Chapter 2. This picture is fairly representative of the way the scores fall in many situations. Cases pile up around the middle score values and tail off at either end. The ideal model of this type of score distribution, the normal curve, was also considered in connection with the standard deviation in Chapter 2 (see Table 2.5 and Figure 2.7) and is shown in Figure 3.2. The exact normal curve is an idealized mathematical model, but many types of test results distribute themselves in a manner that approximates a normal curve. You will notice the piling up of most cases in the middle, the tailing off at both ends, and the generally symmetrical pattern.

In Figure 3.2, four points have been marked: the 50th, 55th, 90th, and 95th percentiles. The baseline represents a trait that has been measured in a scale with equal units. The units could be items correct on a test. Note that near the median, 5% of the cases (the 5% lying between the 50th and 55th percentiles) fall in a tall narrow pile. Toward the tail of the distribution, 5% of cases (the 5% between the 90th and 95th percentiles) make a relatively broad low bar. In the second instance, 5% of the cases spread out over a considerably wider range of the trait than in the first. The same number of percentile points corresponds to about three times as much of the score scale when we are around the 90–95th percentiles as when we are near the median. The farther out in the tail we go, the more extreme the situation becomes.

Thus, percentile units are typically and systematically unequal, relative to the raw score units. The difference between being first or second in a group of 100 is many times as great as the difference between being 50th and 51st. Equal percentile differences do not, in general, represent equal differences in amount of the trait in question. Any interpretation of percentile ranks must take into account the fact that such a scale has been pulled out at both ends and squeezed in the middle. Mary, who falls at the 50th percentile in arithmetic and at the 55th in reading, shows a trivial difference in these two abilities, whereas Alice, with respective percentiles of 90 and 95, shows a larger difference, one that may be important for decision making.

Figure 3.2
Normal curve, showing
selected percentile points.

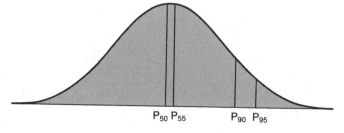

One of the consequences of this inequality of units in the percentile scale is that percentiles cannot be treated with many of the procedures of mathematics. For example, we cannot add two percentile ranks together and get a meaningful result. The sum or average of the percentiles of two raw scores will not yield the same result as determining the percentile rank of the sum or average of the two raw scores directly. A separate table of percentile equivalents would be needed for every combination of raw scores that we might wish to use.

Standard Scores

Because the units of a score system based on percentile ranks are so clearly unequal, we are led to look for some other unit that does have the same meaning throughout its whole range of values. *Standard-score scales* have been developed to serve this purpose.

In Chapter 2 we became acquainted with the standard deviation *(SD)* as a measure of the spread, or scatter, of a group of scores. The standard deviation is a function of the deviations of individual scores away from the mean. Any score may be expressed in terms of the number of standard deviations it is away from the mean. The mean *mathematics* score for ninth graders on the Tests of Achievement and Proficiency is 24.1 and the standard deviation is 9.8, so a person who gets a score of 30 falls

$$30 - 24.1/9.8 = 0.60$$

SD units above the mean. A score of 15 would be 0.93 *SD* units *below* the mean. In standard deviation units, we would call these scores +0.60 and −0.93, respectively.

Scores that are reported as deviations away from the group mean in standard deviation units are called *standard scores,* or *z* scores. A *z* score can be found in any score distribution by first subtracting the group mean *(M)* from the raw score *(X)* of interest and then dividing this deviation by the standard deviation:

$$z = (X - M)/SD$$

If this is done for every score in the original distribution, the new distribution of *z* scores will have a mean of zero, and the standard deviation of the new distribution will be 1.0. About half of the *z* scores will be negative, indicating that the people with these scores fell below the mean. Most of the *z* scores (about 99%) will fall between −3.0 and +3.0.

Suppose we have given the Tests of Achievement and Proficiency—Form G during the fall to the pupils in a ninth-grade class, and two pupils have the following scores on mathematics and reading comprehension.

Pupil	Mathematics	Reading Comprehension
Henry	30	48
Joe	37	42

Let us see how we can use standard scores to compare performance of an individual on two tests or the performance of the two individuals on a single test.

The mean and standard deviation for mathematics and reading comprehension are as follows:

	Mathematics	Reading Comprehension
Mean	22.7	33.8
SD	9.4	11.1

On mathematics, Henry is 7.3 points above the mean. His z score is $7.3/9.4 = +0.78$. On reading comprehension, he is 14.2 points above the mean, or $z = 14.2/11.1 = +1.28$. Henry is about one-half of a standard deviation better in reading comprehension than in mathematics. For Joe, the corresponding calculations for mathematics give

$$(37 - 22.7)/9.4 = +1.52$$

and for reading comprehension give

$$(42 - 33.8)/11.1 = +0.74$$

Thus, Henry has done about as well on mathematics as Joe has done on reading comprehension, while Joe's mathematics score is about one-quarter of a standard deviation better than Henry's score on reading comprehension.

Each pupil's level of excellence is expressed as a number of standard deviation units above or below the mean of the comparison group. The z scores provide a standard unit of measure having essentially the same meaning from one test to another. For aid in interpreting the degree of excellence represented by a standard score, see Table 2.5.

Converted Standard Scores

In all, z scores are quite satisfactory except for two matters of convenience: (1) They require use of plus and minus signs, which may be miscopied or overlooked, and (2) they get us involved with decimal points, which may be misplaced. Also, people do not generally like to think of themselves as negative or fractional quantities. We can get rid of the need to use decimal points by multiplying every z score by some constant, such as 10. We can get rid of minus signs by adding a convenient constant amount, such as 50. Then, for Henry's scores on mathematics and reading comprehension we would have

	Mathematics	Reading Comprehension
Mean of distribution of scores	22.7	33.8
SD of distribution	9.4	11.1

Henry's raw score	30	48
Henry's z score	+0.78	+1.28
z score $\times$ 10	8	13
Plus a constant amount (50)	58	63

(It is conventional to round such converted scores to the nearest whole number, consistent with the objective of making them easy to use.)

Converted standard scores are based on a simple equation that changes the size of the units and the location of the mean. In symbolic form, the equation for the above transformation is

$$C = 10(z) + 50$$

where z is the standard score defined earlier and C is the converted standard score.

The use of 50 and 10 for the mean and the standard deviation, respectively, of a linear transformation is an arbitrary decision. We could have used values other than 50 and 10 in setting up the conversion into convenient standard scores. The army has used a standard score scale with a mean of 100 and a standard deviation of 20 for reporting its test results. The College Entrance Examination Board has long used a scale with a mean of 500 and a standard deviation of 100 for reporting scores on the Scholastic Aptitude Test, the Graduate Record Examination, and other tests produced under its auspices. The navy has used the 50 and 10 system; many intelligence tests use a mean of 100 and a standard deviation of 15 or 16.

The scale of scores following a conversion such as this one is stretched out or squeezed together (depending on whether the original standard deviation is smaller or larger than the new one), but the stretching is uniform all along the scale. The *size* of the units is changed, but it is changed uniformly throughout the score scale. If the raw score scale represented equal units to begin with, the new scale still does, but nothing has been done to make unequal units more nearly equal. Because the above equation is an equation for a straight line, this type of transformation of scores is called a *linear conversion,* or a *linear transformation.* (It is necessary here to add a note on terminology. We use the symbol z to stand for standard scores in their original form and C to stand for *any* linear transformation of a z score. Some authors use the symbol T for the special case of a linear transformation using a mean of 50 and a standard deviation of 10. While details of notation are a matter of personal preference, this use of the symbol T is historically incorrect. The symbol T was first used by William McCall in 1922 to stand for the special kind of *nonlinear transformation* described in the next section. Only relatively recently has the distinction been lost, and it seems useful to reinstate the traditional notation to make the important distinction between scores that have been normalized and those that have not.)

Normalizing Transformations

Frequently, standard score scales are developed by combining the percentile ranks corresponding to the raw scores with a linear transformation of the z scores that are associated with those percentile ranks in the normal distribution, making the assumption that the trait being measured has a normal distribution. (This is called an *area conversion* of scores. Because the complete transformation cannot be expressed by a straight line, or linear equation, it is also called a nonlinear transformation.) Thus, in the mathematics test, we might find that 35% of ninth-grade boys fall below a score of 17. In the table of the normal distribution (provided as Appendix 2), the z score below which 35% of the cases fall is -0.39. Consequently, we would *assign* to a raw score of 17 a standard score of -0.39. Expressing this result on a scale in which the standard deviation is to be 10 and the mean 50, we have

$$T = 10 \, (-0.39) + 50 = -4 + 50 = 46$$

As discussed earlier, the designation of T score and the symbol T have often been used to identify this particular type of normalized standard score scale.

The complete process of preparing a normalized standard score scale by the area conversion method involves finding the percentile rank for each obtainable raw score. The z score below which the specified percentage of the normal distribution falls is then substituted for the raw score, resulting in a set of z scores that yield a normal distribution for the group on which we have obtained our data. These z scores are then subjected to a linear transformation using whatever mean and standard deviation are desired (50 and 10, respectively, for T scores).

Normal Curve Equivalents

A second type of normalized standard score gaining popularity in education is the scale of normal curve equivalents, or NCE scale. This scale is developed using the same procedures and mean as the T scale uses, but the standard deviation is set at 21.06 rather than at 10. The reason for choosing this particular standard deviation is that it gives a scale in which a score of 1 corresponds to a percentile rank of 1 and a score of 99 corresponds to a percentile rank of 99. The relationship between NCEs and percentile ranks is shown in Table 3.5. Most major publishers of educational achievement tests provide tables of NCE scores, thus allowing for comparison of relative performance on different tests. As these publishers note, however, the tests differ in content, so a common score scale does not imply that one test could be substituted for another.

We have now identified two ways to develop standard score scales based on an arbitrary mean and standard deviation. In one, the linear transformation method, z scores are *computed* from the observed mean and standard deviation and the resulting z scores may be further transformed by first being multiplied by an arbitrary new standard deviation and then added to an arbitrary new mean. This method does not change the relative distances between scores and leaves the shape of the score distribution unchanged. In the other method, the area or normalizing transformation, percentile ranks are used to *assign z* scores to raw scores, based on the percentage of the normal distribution that falls below the z score. These assigned z scores are then transformed with an arbitrary standard deviation and mean to a desired scale. The re-

Table 3.5
Relationship Between Normal Curve Equivalents, Percentile Ranks, and Stanines

NCE	PR	Stanine	PR
99	99	9	≥96+
90	97	8	89–95
80	92	7	77–88
70	83	6	60–76
60	65	5	40–59
50	50	4	23–39
40	32	3	11–22
30	17	2	4–10
20	8	1	3≤
10	3		
1	1		

sulting scores will form a normal distribution, regardless of the shape of the distribution of the raw scores.

Normalized standard scores make sense whenever it seems likely that the group is a complete one that has not been curtailed by systematic selection at the upper or lower ends. Furthermore, they make sense whenever it seems likely that the original raw score scale does not represent a scale of equal units but the underlying trait could reasonably be assumed to have a normal distribution. Many test makers systematically plan to include in their tests many items of medium difficulty and few easy or hard items. The effect of this practice is to produce tests that spread out and make fine discriminations among the middle 80% or 90% of test takers, while making coarser discriminations at the extremes. That is, the raw score units in the middle of the distribution correspond to smaller true increments in the ability being measured than do raw score units at the extremes. The "true" distribution of ability is pulled out into a flat-topped distribution of scores. The operation of normalizing the distribution reverses this process.

Stanines

A type of normalized standard score that has become quite popular for educational tests is the *stanine* (a condensation of the phrase *standard nine-point scale*) score. The stanine scale has a mean of five, and stanine units each represent half of a standard deviation on the basic trait dimension. Stanines tend to play down small differences in score and to express performance in broader categories, so that attention tends to be focused on differences that are large enough to matter. The relationship between the stanine scale and the percentile rank scale is shown in Table 3.5.

The relationships between a number of the different standard score scales (after normalization) and the relationship of each to percentiles and to the normal distribution are shown in Figure 3.3. This figure presents the model of the normal curve, and beneath the normal curve are a scale of percentiles and several of the common standard score scales. This figure illustrates the equivalence of scores in the different systems. Thus, a College Board standard score of 600 would represent the same level of excellence (in relation to some common reference group) as an army standard score of 120, a Navy standard score (or *T* score) of 60, a stanine score of 7, a percentile rank of 84, an NCE of 71, or a Wechsler IQ of 115. The particular choice of score scale is arbitrary and a matter of convenience. It is unfortunate that all testing agencies have not been able to agree on a common score unit. However, the important thing is that the same score scale and comparable norming groups be used for all tests in a given organization, so that results from different tests may be directly comparable.

Earlier, we discussed the importance of identifying an appropriate norm group, to allow interpretation of a raw score using percentile norms. The same requirement applies with equal force when we wish to express a person's characteristics within a standard score framework. The conversion from raw to standard score must be based on a relevant group of which the individual with whom we are concerned can be considered a member. It makes no more sense to determine an engineering graduate student's standard score on norm data obtained from high school physics students than it does to express the same comparison in percentiles.

In summary, standard scores, like percentile ranks, base the interpretation of the individual's score on his or her performance in relation to a particular reference group. They differ from percentiles in that they are expressed in units that are presumed to be equal. The basic unit is the standard deviation of the reference group, and the individual's score is expressed as a number of standard deviation units above or below the mean of the group. Standard score scales may be based on either a linear or an area (normalizing) conversion of the original scores. Different numerical standard score scales have been used by different testing agencies. Standard score scales share with percentile ranks the problem of defining an appropriate reference group.

INTERCHANGEABILITY OF DIFFERENT TYPES OF NORMS

Whichever type of normative scale is used, a table of norms will be prepared by the test publisher. This table will show the different possible raw scores on the test, together with the corresponding score equivalents in the system of norms being used. Many publishers provide tables giving more than one type of score equivalent. Table 3.6 gives an example, which shows the norms for the vocabulary test of the ITBS—Form J, Level 9. Four types of norms are shown. The percentiles are based on a group tested early in the third-grade. The NCE score scale assigns a mean of 50 and a standard deviation of 21.06 to an early third-grade group. Thus, a boy with a raw score of 21 can be characterized as follows:

1.   Having a grade equivalent of 3.9
2.   Falling at the 74th percentile in the third-grade group

Figure 3.3

Various types of standard score scales in relation to percentiles and the normal curve.

(Differential Aptitude Tests—4th Edition. Copyright © 1982, 1972, by The Psychological Corporation. Reproduced and adapted by permission. All rights reserved.)

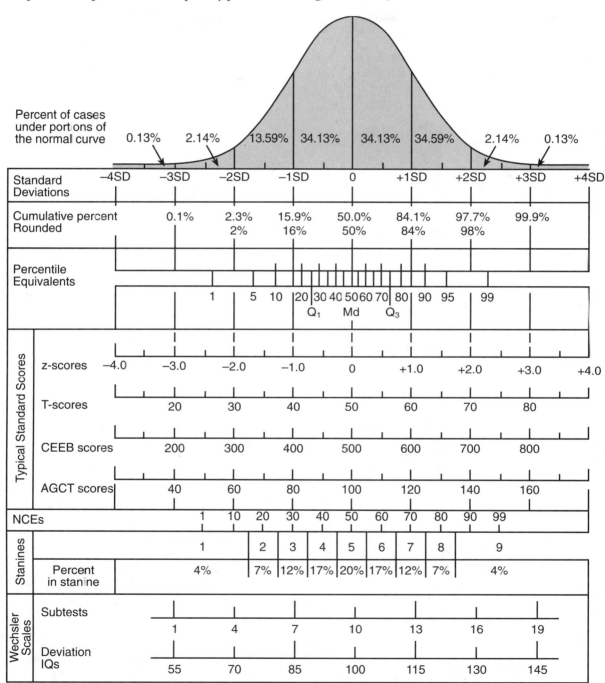

Table 3.6
Vocabulary Norms for the Iowa Tests of Basic Skills—Form J,
Level 9

Raw Score	Grade Equivalent	Percentile Rank	Normal Curve Equivalent	Stanine
1	K.3	1	1	1
2	K.5	1	1	1
3	K.8	1	1	1
4	1.1	2	7	1
5	1.3	4	13	1
6	1.6	8	20	2
7	1.8	11	24	2
8	2.0	15	28	3
9	2.3	21	33	3
10	2.5	26	36	4
11	2.7	31	40	4
12	2.8	35	42	4
13	2.9	39	44	4
14	3.0	43	46	5
15	3.1	47	48	5
16	3.2	51	51	5
17	3.3	55	53	5
18	3.4	58	54	5
19	3.6	65	58	6
20	3.8	72	62	6
21	3.9	74	64	6
22	4.0	77	66	7
23	4.2	82	69	7
24	4.4	86	73	7
25	4.6	89	76	8
26	4.8	92	80	8
27	5.1	95	85	8
28	5.5	98	93	9
29	6.0	98	93	9
30	6.8	99	99	9

Source: Copyright © 1993 by The University of Iowa. Reproduced from *Iowa Tests of Basic Skills, Interpretive Guide for Teachers and Counselors, Form J.* Reproduced by permission of the publisher, The Riverside Publishing Company.

3.   Receiving an NCE of 64
4.   Receiving a stanine of 6

From Table 3.6, it is easy to see that the different systems of norms are different ways of expressing the same thing. We can translate from one to another, moving back and forth. Thus, a child who falls at the 66th percentile in the third-grade group tested in October has a grade equivalent of 4.0. A grade equivalent of 4.0 corresponds to a percentile rank of 77 and a stanine of 7. The different systems of interpretation support one another for different purposes.

However, the different norm systems are not entirely consistent as we shift from one school subject or trait to another. This inconsistency occurs because some functions mature or change more rapidly from one year to the next, relative to the spread of scores at a given age or grade level.

This can be seen most dramatically by comparing reading comprehension and mathematics. The phenomenon is illustrated by the pairs of scores shown in Table 3.7, based on the ITBS. It is assumed that the three boys were tested at the end of 2 months in the fifth grade. John received scores on both tests that were just average. His grade equivalent was 5.2, and he was close to the 50th percentile for pupils tested after 2 months in the fifth grade. Henry shows superior performance, but how does he compare in the two subjects? From one point of view, he does equally well in both; he is just 1 full year ahead in grade placement. But in terms of percentiles he is better in mathematics than in reading, that is, at the 84th percentile compared with the 74th percentile. Will, on the other hand, falls at just the same percentile in both reading and mathematics. However, in his case the grade equivalent for reading is 7.2, and for mathematics, it is 6.6.

The discrepancies that appear in this example result from the differences in the variability of performance and rate of growth in reading and mathematics. Reading shows a *wide* spread within a single grade group, relative to the mean change from grade to grade. Some fifth graders read better than the average eighth or ninth grader, so a reading grade equivalent of 8.0 or even 9.0 is not unheard of for fifth graders. In fact, a grade equivalent of 8.0 corresponds to the 95th percentile for pupils at grade 5.2 in this particular test series. By contrast, a fifth grader almost never does as well in mathematics as an eighth or ninth grader—in part because the fifth grader has not encountered or been taught many of the topics that will be presented in the sixth, seventh, and eighth grades and included in a test for those grade levels. All the basic skills that are involved in reading usually have been developed by fifth grade, so changes in reading performance result largely from greater mastery of those processes. With mathematics the case is quite different. Eighth graders are not doing better the same things fifth graders do; eighth graders are doing different things. For example, fifth graders are likely to be working with whole numbers and relatively simple fractions, while eighth graders will be studying decimals, complex fractions, and geometry. A fifth grader might well be able to read and understand an

Table 3.7

Comparison of Grade Equivalents and Percentiles

Type of Score	Reading Composite			Mathematics Composite		
	John	Henry	Will	John	Henry	Will
Raw score	27	36	44	156	186	198
Grade equivalent	5.2	6.2	7.2	5.2	6.2	6.6
Grade 5.2 percentile rank	50	74	90	53	84	90

eighth-grade history book, but very few could do eighth-grade mathematics. Thus, fifth graders are more homogeneous with respect to mathematics than to reading skills.

The preceding point must always be kept in mind, particularly when comparing grade equivalents for different subjects. A bright child will often appear most advanced in reading and language and least so in mathematics and spelling, when the results are reported in grade equivalents. This difference may result, in whole or in part, simply from the differences in the growth functions for the subjects and need not imply a genuinely uneven pattern of progress for the child. For this reason most testing specialists are quite critical of grade equivalents and express a strong preference for percentile ranks or some type of standard score. However, because they appear to have a simple and direct meaning in the school context, grade equivalents continue to be popular with school personnel and are provided by most test publishers.

QUOTIENTS

In the early days of mental testing, after age norms had been used for a few years, it became apparent that there was a need to convert the age score into an index that would express rate of progress. The 8-year-old who had an age equivalent of 10 1/2 years was obviously better than average, but how much better? Some index was needed to take account of chronological age (actual time lived), as well as the age equivalent on the test (score level reached).

One response to the need was the expedient of dividing the test age by the chronological age to yield a quotient. This procedure was applied most extensively with tests of intelligence, where the age equivalent on the test was called a *mental age* and the corresponding quotient was an *intelligence quotient* (IQ). In the 1920s it became common practice to multiply this fraction by 100 (to eliminate decimals), thus giving rise to the general form of the scale that is now so well known in education and psychology (see Chapter 8).

The notion of the IQ is deeply embedded in the history of the testing movement and, in fact, in contemporary American language and culture. The expression "IQ test" has become part of our common speech. We are probably stuck with the term. But the way that the IQ is defined has changed. IQs have become, in almost every case, standard scores with a mean of 100 and a standard deviation of about 15, and we should think of them and use them in this way.

In a number of recent tests of intelligence, the scores that are reported are, in fact, normalized standard scores, based on the type of normalizing area transformation discussed earlier in this chapter. These are sometimes referred to as deviation intelligence quotients, or deviation IQs because they are basically standard scores expressed as a deviation above or below a mean of 100. The latest revision of the Stanford-Binet Intelligence Scale has substituted the term *standard age score* for IQ to reflect more accurately the true nature of the scores.

Unfortunately, the score scale for reporting IQs does not have *exactly* the same meaning from test to test. The Wechsler test series is based on a mean of 100 and a standard deviation of 15, while the Stanford-Binet and several group tests use a mean of 100 and a standard deviation of 16. Furthermore, tests are normed at different points in time and use different sampling procedures. These differences in procedure also lead to some variation in the norms and, consequently, in the distribution of IQs they yield for any given school or community. A study by Flynn (1984) also suggests that there has been a long-term rise in IQs in the United States, dating at least to the mid-1930s, which would mean that norms that are 20 to 30 years old are probably not appropriate for use today. Such a change in mean performance makes it difficult to compare results over time or between successive test forms. We discuss issues related to intelligence and tests used to measure it in Chapter 8.

PROFILES

The various types of normative frames of reference we have been considering provide a way of expressing scores from quite different tests in common units, so that the scores can be meaningfully compared. No direct way of comparing a score of 30 words correctly spelled with a score of 20 arithmetic problems solved exists. But, if both are expressed in terms of the grade level to which they correspond or in terms of the percentage of some defined common group that gets scores below that point, then a meaningful comparison is possible. A set of different test scores for an individual, expressed in a common unit of measure, is called a *score profile*. The separate scores may be presented for comparison in tabular form by listing the converted score values. A record showing such converted scores for several pupils is given in Figure 3.4. The comparison of different subareas of performance is made pictorially clearer by a graphic presentation of the profile. Two ways of plotting profiles are shown in Figures 3.5 and 3.6.

Figures 3.4 and 3.5 show part of a class record form and an individual profile chart for the ITBS, respectively. The class record illustrates the form in which the data are reported back to the schools by the test publisher's computerized test scoring service. (The precise form that the report of results takes differs from one scoring service to another.) There are four norm-referenced scores reported for each pupil on each test (see Figure 3.4). The first row of the report for each student contains developmental standard scores (called *SS*s in this publisher's materials) for the 13 subtests and six composites. The second row of scores are grade equivalents, and because the tests were given after the pupils had spent 7 months in the fourth grade, the norm for the country as a whole would be 4.7. The last two rows for each student contain normal curve equivalents and percentile ranks based on the spring 1992 national norm group. Looking at the scores for Lannet Marquez, we can see that the four score systems give an essentially equivalent picture of her performance. Her grade equivalent of 4.8 is slightly above average, and this is reflected in her NCE and PR scores of 52 and 53. The standard scale score of 200 is also consistent with average performance in the spring of fourth grade. Note that all four reference systems show her to be well above average in capitalization and punctuation.

Figure 3.5 shows data for testings of a student in two successive years. The so-called "developmental scale" referred to toward the left is actually a scale of grade

Figure 3.4

List report of pupil scores.

(Copyright © 1993 by The University of Iowa. Reproduced from *Iowa Tests of Basic Skills, Interpretive Guide for Teachers and Counselors, Forms K and L.* Reproduced by permission of the publisher, The Riverside Publishing Company.

Iowa Tests of Basic Skills

Service 9:
List Report of Student Scores

Class/Group: NESS WEBER
Building:
Building Code: 304
System: DALEN COMMUNITY
Norms: SPRING 1992
Order No.: 000-A33-76044-00-001

Grade: 4
Form: K
Test Date: 03/93
Page: 38

Student (Level/Sex)		READING VOCAB	READING COMPRE	READING TOTAL	LANG SPELL	LANG CAPITAL	LANG PUNC	LANG USAGE/EXPRESS	LANG TOTAL	MATH CONCEPTS/ESTIM	MATH PROBS/DATA INTERP	MATH TOTAL	CORE TOTAL	SOCIAL STUDIES	SCIENCE	SRC MAPS & DIAGRAMS	SRC REF MAT'LS	SRC TOTAL	COMPOSITE	MATH COMPUTATION
MARQUEZ, LANNET 10/82 10-05 Level 10 (F)	SS	176	192	184	200	255	231	200	222	218	196	207	204	211	215	205	228	216	209	210
	GE	3.2	4.2	3.7	4.8	9.2	7.3	4.8	6.4	6.2	4.6	5.4	5.0	5.6	5.8	5.1	6.9	5.9	5.4	5.6
	NCE	30	45	38	52	77	67	51	65	68	48	57	53	59	61	55	72	63	58	63
	NPR	17	40	28	53	90	79	51	77	65	46	64	56	67	70	60	85	73	64	72
NICOLA, STEPHANIE 09/82 10-06 Level 10 (F)	SS	201	237	219	254	255	240	208	239	199	200	200	219	211	210	205	238	222	217	207
	GE	4.8	7.6	6.1	9.2	9.2	8.0	5.4	7.7	4.7	4.8	4.8	6.2	5.6	5.4	5.1	7.7	6.2	5.9	5.4
	NCE	52	74	66	89	77	71	56	76	51	51	51	66	59	59	55	79	66	64	59
	NPR	55	88	78	97	90	84	62	89	51	53	53	77	67	65	60	92	78	75	67
PICKERING, AMANDA 01/83 10-02 Level 10 (M)	SS	194	183	188	200	255	231	197	221	199	173	186	198	203	247	179	204	192	206	210
	GE	4.4	3.6	4.0	4.8	9.2	7.3	4.6	6.3	4.7	3.1	3.8	4.6	5.0	8.6	3.3	5.0	4.1	5.2	5.6
	NCE	46	38	41	52	77	67	49	65	51	29	39	48	54	79	34	55	44	55	63
	NPR	43	29	33	53	90	79	48	76	51	16	30	47	57	92	22	59	39	59	72
POWERS, SCOTT 03/83 10-00 Level 10 (M)	SS	199	218	208	207	269	250	273	250	211	243	227	228	239	269	258	214	236	238	207
	GE	4.8	6.0	5.4	5.3	11.0	8.8	11.5	8.7	5.6	8.2	6.8	6.9	7.8	11.0	9.6	5.8	7.5	7.6	5.4
	NCE	51	63	58	58	85	75	90	84	62	79	73	74	80	74	86	62	76	84	59
	NPR	51	73	64	65	95	89	97	95	72	92	86	87	93	99	96	72	89	95	67
RIZZIO, NATHAN 08/83 09-07 Level 10 (M)	SS	187	198	192	222	196	276	208	226	215	211	213	210	191	196	205	208	206	204	218
	GE	4.0	4.6	4.3	6.5	4.6	12.0	5.4	6.6	6.1	5.6	5.7	5.5	4.0	4.5	5.1	5.3	5.2	5.0	6.3
	NCE	40	50	44	70	48	92	56	68	66	59	62	58	43	48	55	58	55	53	70
	NPR	31	49	39	82	47	98	62	80	77	67	72	65	37	46	60	65	60	56	83
SU, TAO 07/83 09-08 Level 10 (M)	SS	204	213	208	222	240	240	241	236	225	200	212	219	216	210	211	220	216	216	203
	GE	5.0	5.8	5.4	6.5	8.0	8.0	8.2	7.5	6.7	4.8	5.7	6.2	5.9	5.4	5.5	6.1	5.9	5.8	5.2
	NCE	55	60	58	70	71	71	71	74	75	51	61	66	63	58	59	66	63	63	55
	NPR	60	68	64	82	84	84	84	87	89	53	70	77	73	65	66	78	73	73	60

SS=Standard Score, GE=Grade Equivalent, NCE=Normal Curve Equivalent, NPR=Nat'l %ile Rank

Figure 3.5
Pupil profile chart.

(Copyright © 1993 by The University of Iowa. Reproduced from *Iowa Tests of Basic Skills, Interpretive Guide for Teachers and Counselors, Forms K and L*. Reproduced by permission of the publisher, The Riverside Publishing Company.)

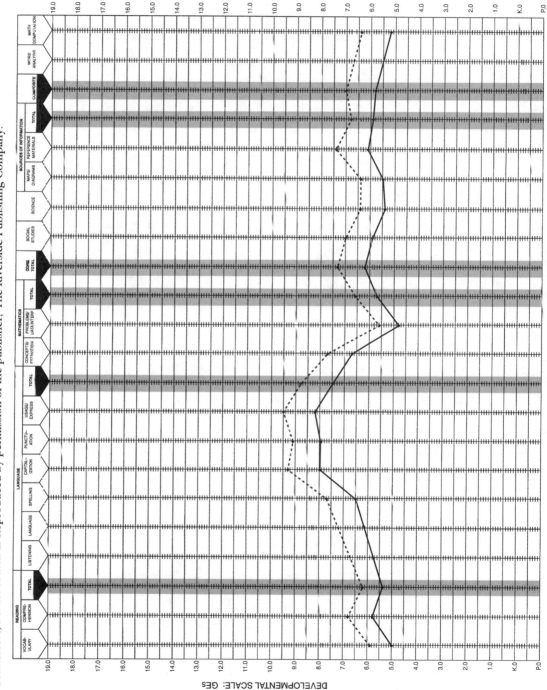

equivalents (GEs). Thus, this pupil had a vocabulary grade equivalent of 5.0 when she was tested the first time. By the next year her grade equivalent on this test was 5.9. Similar growth of approximately one GE is shown for each of the other subtests, although the level of performance in either year shows considerable variation from one subject to another.

The results show her scores generally to have been above the national average. An examination of her profile for the fourth-grade test indicates that she was strongest in capitalization, punctuation, and language usage skills and weakest in mathematics problems. Some of the hazards of paying a great deal of attention to small ups and downs in a profile can be seen in a comparison of her performance on successive testings. Although the profile shows a relatively consistent pattern of highs and lows over the years, relative superiority changes somewhat from one year to the next.

Figure 3.6 shows a second type of profile chart for the ITBS. Here, the scores for one of the students in the class list (see Figure 3.4) are shown for each of the separate subtests of the battery. Note that in this case the different tests are represented by separate bars rather than by points connected by a line. The scale used in this case is a percentile scale, but in plotting percentile values, appropriate adjustments in the scale have been made to compensate for the inequality of percentile units. That is, the percentile points have been spaced in the same way that they are in a normal curve, being more widely spaced at the upper and lower extremes than in the middle range. This percentile scale corresponds to the scale called percentile equivalents in Figure 3.3. By this adjustment, the percentile values for an individual are plotted on an equal unit scale. A given linear distance can reasonably be thought to represent the same difference in amount of ability, whether it lies high in the scale, low in the scale, or near the middle of the scale. By the same token, the same distance can be considered equivalent from one test to another.

In the profile in Figure 3.6, the middle 50% is shaded to indicate a band of average performance for the norm group. The scores of this student have been plotted as bars that extend from the left side of the chart. For this type of norm, the average of the group constitutes the anchor point of the scale, and the individual scores can be referred to this base level. This type of figure brings out the individual's strengths and weaknesses quite clearly. Note also that the numerical values for this student's percentile ranks in the national norm group are given to the left of the profile. In addition, this particular test publisher's scoring service provides a narrative interpretation of the profile. Such an interpretation can also help draw the attention of teachers and parents to noteworthy features of the student's performance.

The profile chart is a very effective way of representing an individual's scores, but profiles must be interpreted with caution. First, procedures for plotting profiles assume that the norms for the tests are comparable. For this to be true, age, grade, or percentile scores must be based on equivalent groups for all the tests. We usually find this to be the case for the subtests of a test battery. Norms for all the subtests are established at the same time, on the basis of testing the same group. This guarantee of comparability of norms for the different component tests is one of the most attractive features of an integrated test battery. If separately developed tests are plotted in a profile, we can usually only hope that the groups on which the norms were established were

Figure 3.6
Profile narrative report—Parent copy.

(Copyright © 1993 by The University of Iowa. Reproduced from *Iowa Tests of Basic Skills, Interpretive Guide for Teachers and Counselors, Forms K and L.* Reproduced by permission of the publisher, The Riverside Publishing Company.

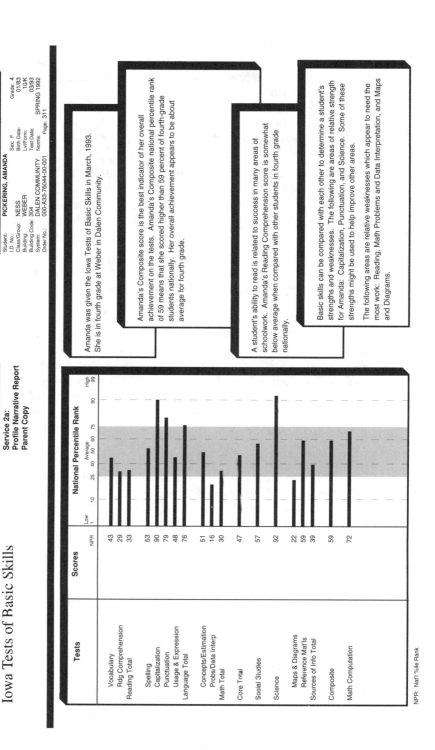

NPR: Nat'l %ile Rank

comparable and that the profile is an unbiased picture of relative achievement in different fields. When it is necessary to use tests from several different sources, one way to be sure of having equivalent norm groups is to develop local norms on a common population and to plot individual profiles in terms of those local norms.

A second problem in interpreting profiles is that of deciding how much attention to pay to the ups and downs in the profile. Not all the differences that appear in a profile are meaningful, either in a statistical or in a practical sense. We must decide which of the differences deserve some attention on our part and which do not. This problem arises because no test score is completely exact. No magic size exists at which a score difference suddenly becomes worthy of attention, and any rule of thumb is at best a rough guide. But, differences must be big enough so that we can be reasonably sure (1) that they would still be there if the person were tested again and (2) that they make a practical difference, before we start to interpret them and base action on them. We will return to this topic during our discussion of reliability in Chapter 4.

CRITERION-REFERENCED REPORTS

Interest in criterion-referenced interpretations of test scores has led test publishers to produce a profile of student performance based on specific item content. A well-designed test will include items that tap various aspects of skill or knowledge development. Modern test scoring and computer technology have made it possible to report a student's performance on subsets of items that are homogeneous with respect to a particular kind of content. An example of such a report for the ITBS is shown in Figure 3.7.

The report presented in Figure 3.7 lists each subtopic for each test of the ITBS, along with the number of items assessing that skill. The number of items the student attempted, the number and percentage of items correct for the student, and the percentages correct for the class and nation are also given. This report allows the teacher to identify specific strengths and weaknesses at a more fine-grained level than is possible with the ordinary norm-referenced report. For example, this student seems to have particular problems with math estimation, although her overall mathematics performance is average, and she shows relative strength in math concepts. Although each subskill is measured by too few items to yield a very reliable assessment, the information can be valuable to the classroom teacher in designing the instructional program for the individual student. Skills marked with a (+) represent areas of relative strength for the student, while those marked (−) are areas of relative weakness.

An even more detailed description of this student's performance can be provided in an individual item analysis such as that shown in Figure 3.8, which shows part of the class results for reading comprehension. Each column represents a student and each row corresponds to an item. The item numbers are given, organized by the skill they measure, and the student's response to the item is indicated if it was incorrect (a blank indicates the student got the item correct and an O indicates an omission). From the information on this chart the teacher can see that eight students got item 37 correct, six students omitted the item, six chose alternative B, three chose alternative C, and one chose alternative D. By looking for commonly made errors, the teacher can diagnose particular skill areas where the students need extra work.

Figure 3.7

Student criterion-referenced skills analysis.

(Copyright © 1993 by The University of Iowa. Reproduced from *Iowa Tests of Basic Skills, Interpretive Guide for Teachers and Counselors, Forms K and L.* Reproduced by permission of the publisher, The Riverside Publishing Company.

Iowa Tests of Basic Skills

Service 1: Student Criterion-Referenced Skills Analysis

	READING			LANGUAGE					MATHEMATICS			CORE TOTAL	SOCIAL STUDIES	SCIENCE	SOURCES OF INFO.			COMPOSITE	MATH COMPUTATION
	VOCABULARY	COMPRE-HENSION	TOTAL	SPELLING	CAPITAL-IZATION	PUNC-TUATION	USAGE/EXPRESS	TOTAL	CON-CEPTS/ESTIM.	PROBS/DATA INTERP	TOTAL				MAPS & DIAGRAMS	REF. MATLS	TOTAL		
Standard Score	194	183	188	200	255	231	197	221	199	173	186	198	203	247	179	204	192	206	210
Grade Equivalent	4.4	3.6	4.0	4.8		7.3	4.6	6.3	4.7	3.1	3.8	4.6	5.0	8.6	3.3	5.0	3.3	5.2	5.6
Normal Curve Equivalent	46	38	41	52	77	67	49	65	51	29	39	48	54	79	34	55	44	55	63
Nat'l %ile Rank	43	29	33	53	90	79	48	76	51	16	30	47	57	92	22	59	39	59	72

Student: PICKERING, AMANDA   Sex: F
Birth Date: 01/83
Age: 10 Yrs 2 Mos
Norms: SPRING 1992

Class/Group: NESS
Building: WEBER
Building Code: 304
System: DALEN COMMUNITY
Order No.: 000-A33-76044-00-001

Grade: 4
Level: 10
Form: K
Test Date: 03/93
Page: 302

Skills

Skills	(Class N)	Number of Items	Number Attempted	Number Correct Student	Percent Correct this Student	Average Percent Correct Class	Average Percent Correct Nation
Vocabulary	(24)	34	34	20	59	70	63
Comprehension	(24)						
Factual Meaning		38	38	16	42	71	55
Inferential Meaning		12	12	4	33	77	55
Evaluative Meaning		20	20	9	45	70	56
Spelling	(24)						
Root Words		31	31	22	71	80	68
Words w/Affixes		20	20	15	75	82	68
Correct Spelling		6	6	4	67	87	57
		5	5	5	60	73	81
Capitalization	(24)						
Names & Titles		27	27	24	89	09	66
Dates & Holidays		3	3	2		100	78
Place Names		3	3	2		96	67
Organizations/Groups		3	3	3	100	83	80
Ling/Lit Conventions		8	8	5		88	66
Overcap/Correct Use		5	5	5	100	78	68
Punctuation	(24)						
Terminal Punctuation		27	27	19	70	78	53
Comma		10	10	6	60	82	56
Other Punctuation Marks		6	6	5	83	81	55
Overuse/Correct Use		6	6	4	80	83	44
Usage & Expression	(24)						
Usage		36	36	20	56	71	56
Verb Forms		19	19	11	58	71	55
Pronouns; modifiers		8	8	3		81	48
Other Conventions		5	5	3	60	78	54
Correct Usage		3	3	3	100	65	68
Expression		17	17	9	53	69	57
Concise & Clear		6	6	3		67	51
Appropriate Lang.		3	3	3		65	56
Organization		8	8	3		80	63
Math Concepts & Estimation	(24)						
Concepts		40	40	24	60	76	63
+ Number/Operations		24	24	19		86	70
Geometry		8	8	5		87	72
+ Measurement		5	5	2		79	64
Fract/Dec/%.		3	3	1		65	65
Probability/Stat.		1	1	1	100	88	61
Equations/Inequal.		4	4			94	75
Estimation		16	16	7		60	60
Standard Rounding		7	7	3	43	72	60
− Order of Magnitude		4	4	1	25	66	64
[−] Compensation		5	5	1	20	38	37

Skills	(Class N)	Number of Items	Number Attempted	Number Correct Student	Percent Correct this Student	Average Percent Correct Class	Average Percent Correct Nation
Problems & Data Interp.	(24)						
Problem Solving		27	27	10	37	72	61
+ Single-step: +/−		16	16	6		79	66
Single-step: x/÷		5	5	3	60	93	76
Multiple-step		4	4	1		65	62
Prob-Solv Strategy		4	4	1	25	63	58
Data Interpretation							
Read Amounts		11	11	4	36	81	65
Compare Quantities		6	6	3	33	53	65
Interpret Relationships		2	2	1	50	56	49
Social Studies	(24)						
History		35	35	22	63	72	66
Geography		17	17	12	71	75	62
Economics		9	9	5	56	78	60
Political Science		4	4	2	50	71	59
Sociology & Anthropology		2	2	1	50	44	53
Science	(24)						
Nature of Science		35	35	28	80	73	59
Life Science		7	7	6	86	72	59
Earth & Space		10	10	8	80	60	49
Physical Science		10	10	8	90	78	59
Maps & Diagrams	(24)						
Map Reading		26	26	11	42	74	56
Locate & Describe		13	13	6	46	76	64
Determine Direction		6	6	2	33	78	71
Determine Distance		1	1	1	100	71	49
Behavior and Living Conditions		3	3	1	33	60	52
Diagrams & Charts		13	13	5	38	90	67
Locate Information		5	5	3	20	74	62
+ Explain Relationships		3	3	2	67	74	61
Infer Processes		5	5	2	40	70	58
Reference Materials	(24)						
Alphabetizing		30	30	23	77	88	63
Table of Contents		4	4	4	100	98	67
Dictionary		6	6	5	83	81	63
− Card catalog: Locate		4	4	4	83	92	73
Encyclopedia		4	4	1	75	78	67
General Ref. Materials		6	6	5	83	96	74
Math Computation	(24)						
Add Whole Numbers		37	37	30	81	83	67
Subtract Whole Numbers		9	9	9	100	90	74
Multiply Whole Numbers		11	11	8	89	86	68
− Divide Whole Numbers		8	8	3	38	79	57
Thinking Skills	(24)						
Focus/Info-Gathering		26	26	14	52	80	66
Remembering		26	26	20	77	86	66
Organizing		69	69	40	58	75	60
Analyzing		136	136	92	68	78	60
Generating		64	64	37	58	69	58
Integrate/Evaluate		30	30	16	53	74	60

Figure 3.8
Individual item analysis.

(Copyright © 1993 by The University of Iowa. Reproduced from *Iowa Tests of Basic Skills, Interpretive Guide for Teachers and Counselors, Forms K and L.* Reproduced by permission of the publisher, The Riverside Publishing Company.)

Iowa Tests of Basic Skills

Service 23:
Class Item Response Record

Class/Group: NESS WEBER	Grade: 4
Bldg. Code: 304	Level: 10
System: DALEN COMMUNITY	Form: K
Norms: SPRING 1992	Test Date: 03/93
Order No: 000-A33-76044-00-001	Class N: 24
	Page: 225

Legend:
%C = Percent Correct
A–N = incorrect response
O = omit
* = multiple responses
blank = correct response

Item summary (%C = Percent Correct)

Item	Description	No. Items	%C Nation	%C System	%C Class
	Reading Comprehension	38	55	59	71
	Factual Meaning	12			
5	Factual information		69	73	92
7	Factual information		73	82	92
10	Factual information		80	89	96
21	Factual information		64	70	88
22	Factual information		49	57	79
27	Factual information		50	55	79
30	Factual information		57	69	92
32	Factual information		41	54	71
	Literal Meanings				
33	Factual information		57	63	79
34	Factual information		48	56	75
35	Factual information		37	40	46
37	Literal Meanings		29	31	33
	Inferential/Interpretive	20	55	58	70
1	Conclusions, inferences, deduct.		82	79	96
2	Traits, feelings, or motivations		71	75	92
3	Conclusions, inferences, deduct.		64	67	83
4	Traits, feelings, or motivations		83	88	96
6	Traits, feelings, or motivations		75	73	83
8	Conclusions, inferences, deduct.		31	32	54
9	Conclusions, inferences, deduct.		57	65	75
14	Apply information		24	24	75
16	Traits, feelings, or motivations		60	66	88
17	Traits, feelings, or motivations		71	75	96
18	Traits, feelings, or motivations		36	42	46
19	Traits, feelings, or motivations		63	61	83
20	Traits, feelings, or motivations		67	70	92
23	Traits, feelings, or motivations		58	65	88
24	Apply information		47	52	58
26	Conclusions, inferences, deduct.		54	53	88
28	Conclusions, inferences, deduct.		42	45	46
31	Conclusions, inferences, deduct.		44	47	50
36	Conclusions, inferences, deduct.		50	55	58
38	Conclusions, inferences, deduct.		25	22	21

Student roster and %C

Student	Reading Comp %C	(row 2)	Inferential %C
ABBOTT, BRITTON B	66	67	70
ARNDT, MATTHEW B	63	75	60
BAINBRIDGE, ANGELA	55	67	45
BJERKE, KERRI	76	58	80
CATALANO, ANTHONY	76	75	80
DONAHUE, MICHAEL	87	92	85
FONG, YI-AN CHANG	84	92	95
FRIEDMAN, JASON	87	92	85
HARRINGTON, AMY	79	100	70
KOHTZ, NICOLE	63	58	65
MAINS, RONNIE	55	75	50
MARQUEN, LANNETTE	50	50	45
NICOLA, STEPHANIE	79	83	80
PICKERING, AMANDA	42	33	45
POWERS, SCOTT	68	83	70
PINNO, NATHAN	55	67	45
SU, TAO	66	83	65
SUTHERLAND, GARRETT	71	83	65
SWANSON, MARY LYNN	74	67	75
SWIFT, VALHERIE	66	75	65
TAYLOR, CATHRYN	92	100	90
WASTA, JEAN	74	83	80
WELTER, SEAN	92	100	90
YOUNGBLOOD, JON	89	83	90

(Response grid: for each item, cells contain a letter indicating an incorrect response chosen, "O" for omit, or blank for a correct response, per the legend above.)

Figure 3.8 gives student-by-student detail, but for examining the strengths and weaknesses of the class as a whole, information such as that provided in Figure 3.9 may be more useful. This report compares the performance of this class with that of the national norm group. The results, shown item by item in terms of percent correct, are displayed both numerically and graphically. The shaded area indicates when the difference is less than 10% and, therefore, probably too small to be of interest. The results for this class show a broad pattern of performance above the norm group (note that the table would continue similar information about items covering other skills and knowledge areas).

Figure 3.7 illustrates quite clearly the way content-based and norm-based frames of reference can coexist in the same test and can supplement each other in score interpretation. The report shows this student's performance, by content area, with reference to the number of items covering that content, the average performance of her class, and the average performance of the grade-equivalent national norm group. Additional reports are available that show, for example, the performance of the class on each item relative to national, system, and building norms (school performance) or that summarize the individual information in Figure 3.7 for the entire class. The publisher's catalog for this test lists over 30 forms of reports that are available. However, it is important to keep in mind that criterion-referenced interpretations of standardized tests are based on very small numbers of items (one or two in some cases) for each content area or objective. Therefore, any conclusions based on such data must be tentative and should be confirmed using other sources of information.

NORMS FOR SCHOOL AVERAGES

Up to this point, we have asked how we can interpret an individual's standing on a test. Sometimes a question arises about the relative performance of a class, a school, a school district, or even the schools of a whole state. The recent emphasis on accountability in education provides ample reason for educators to be concerned about evaluating the performance of students taken as groups. When evaluating the achievement of a school in relation to other schools, it is necessary to have norms for school averages.

It should be clear that the variation from school to school in average ability or achievement is much less than the variation from pupil to pupil. No school average comes even close to reaching the level of its ablest student, and no average drops anywhere near the performance of the least able. Thus, a single pupil at the beginning of fifth grade who gets a reading grade equivalent of 6.2 might fall at the 75th percentile, whereas a school whose *average* reading grade equivalent of beginning fifth graders is 6.2 might fall at about the 94th percentile of schools. The relationship between norms for individuals and groups is illustrated more fully in Table 3.8.

The two distributions center at about the same point, but the greater variation among individuals quickly becomes apparent. On this test, an individual grade equivalent of 6.0 ranks at the 60th percentile, but a school in which the average performance is a grade equivalent of 6.0 is at the 85th percentile. The same effect is found for performances that are below average.

Figure 3.9

Group item analysis.

(Copyright © 1993 by The University of Iowa. Reproduced from *Iowa Tests of Basic Skills, Interpretive Guide for Teachers and Counselors, Forms K and L.* Reproduced by permission of the publisher, The Riverside Publishing Company.)

Iowa Tests of Basic Skills

Service 6:
Group Item Analysis
Class Report: Diff=Class Minus National
All Diffs Are Printed

Class/Group: NESS	Grade: 4
Building: WEBER	Level: 10
Building Code: 304	Form: K
System: DALEN COMMUNITY	Test Date: 03/93
Norms: SPRING 1992	Page: 128
Order No.: 000-A33-76044-00-001	

MATH CONCEPTS & ESTIMATION

Item No.	Skill	Item Count	Class Avg %C N=24	Building Avg %C N=116	System Avg %C N=238	Nat'l Avg %C	Diff Class Minus Nat'l
	NUMERATION & OPERATIONS	8					
1	Place value & write numbers		87	79	76	73	+14
4	Properties		100	92	89	85	+15
5	Properties		96	83	79	75	+21
10	Performing operations		87	76	76	82	+5
12	Compare & order		88	90	85	85	+3
14	Place value & write numbers		92	84	85	73	+19
20	Classify by divisibility		88	75	71	65	+23
22	Place value & write numbers		79	63	59	49	+30
	Compare & order		63	65	67	59	+4
	GEOMETRIC OPERATIONS & PROCEDURES	5					
2	Geometric shapes		94	78	77	70	+24
9	Geometric shapes		83	72	73	64	+19
11	Perimeter, area, and volume		100	85	87	86	+14
16	Properties, patterns & relationships		96	89	82	71	+29
18	Perimeter, area, and volume		96	85	73	61	+35
	Geometric shapes		92	69	71	67	+25
	MEASUREMENT	3					
3	Appropriate unit of measurement		82	76	72	64	+18
21	Time		100	89	85	83	+17
24	Estimate measurement		92	55	55	48	+8
	FRACTIONS, DECIMALS & PERCENTS	3					
7	Create & interpret representations		65	69	68	65	0
13	Compare & order		67	70	69	68	-1
23	Create & interpret representations		79	81	78	71	+8
			50	55	57	56	-6
	PROBABILITY & STATISTICS	1					
19	Explain meaning of chance		88	71	68	61	+27
			88	71	68	61	+27
	EQUATIONS, INEQUALITIES & NUMBER SENTENCES	4					
6	Solve equations		94	85	82	75	+19
8	Use variables & number sentences		100	93	93	91	+9
15	Solve equations		96	85	85	66	+26
17	Use & interpret symbols		83	71	68	59	+24
	ESTIMATE USING STANDARD ROUNDING	7					
25	In context		72	66	64	60	+12
27	In context		79	61	65	61	+18
30	In context		83	74	65	66	+11
32	In context		58	55	52	51	+7
33	In context		58	68	61	63	+7
34	Without context		75	68	61	62	+12
38	In context		63	55	53	49	+14
	ESTIMATE USING ORDER OF MAGNITUDE	4					
26	Without context		66	62	63	64	+2
28	Without context		88	81	64	80	+8
35	In context		67	65	64	65	+2
36	Without context		42	44	40	47	-5

MATH CONCEPTS & ESTIMATION (CONTINUED)

Item No.	Skill	Item Count	Class Avg %C N=24	Building Avg %C N=116	System Avg %C N=238	Nat'l Avg %C	Diff Class Minus Nat'l
	OTHER ESTIMATION METHODS	5					
29	Without context		38	38	39	37	+1
31	Without context		67	70	68	65	+2
37	Without context		29	30	32	31	-2
39	Without context		38	40	39	36	+2
40	In context		29	27	31	28	+1
			25	22	26	26	-1
	MATHEMATICS PROBLEM SOLVING & DATA INTERPRETATION						
	SINGLE-STEP w/: +/-	5					
1	Whole numbers		93	87	83	76	+17
7	Whole numbers		96	92	85	84	+12
10	Whole numbers		100	92	81	84	+16
10	Whole numbers		92	85	85	72	+20
13	Whole numbers		83	84	79	70	+22
						70	+13
	SINGLE-STEP w/: x/÷	3					
4	Whole numbers		65	59	57	62	+3
8	Fractions		50	84	80	85	+8
12	Whole numbers		54	39	41	42	+8
				55	51	59	-5
	MULTIPLE-STEP	4					
5	Whole numbers		63	62	60	58	+5
6	Whole numbers		79	82	79	74	+5
14	Whole numbers		79	75	73	68	+1
15	Whole numbers		67	64	65	66	+1
			25	26	24	25	0
	PROBLEM-SOLVING STRATEGIES	4					
3	Insufficient information		85	71	69	65	+20
9	Insufficient information		92	80	75	84	+8
11	Method of solution		96	77	71	71	+25
16	Insufficient information		63	56	53	61	+19
			88	72	69	61	+27
	READ AMOUNTS	3					
19	Bar and line graphs		81	64	62	65	+16
21	Circle graph		63	42	45	44	+19
24	Bar and line graphs		96	82	77	80	+16
	Bar and line graphs		89	69	65	65	+13
	COMPARE QUANTITIES	6					
17	Ranks		53	46	47	48	+5
18	Sums and differences		63	54	51	51	+12
22	Ratios		67	61	63	64	+3
25	Sums and differences		63	56	63	62	+1
26	Sums and differences		58	42	45	46	+12
27	Ratios		42	37	35	38	+4
	Ratios		25	27	31	29	-4
	INTERPRET RELATIONSHIPS	2					
20	Conclusions		56	48	45	49	+7
23	Underlying relationships		42	35	25	30	+12
			71	61	65	68	+3

Table 3.8
Individual and School Average Norms for the Iowa Tests of Basic
Skills Vocabulary Test (Grade 5)

Grade Equivalent	Individual Percentile Rank	Percentile Rank for School Averages
8.6	99	99
7.0	87	99
6.7	83	98
6.5	79	96
6.0	60	85
5.5	57	65
5.2	50	52
5.0	46	43
4.5	34	23
4.0	24	9
3.5	16	2
3.4	14	1
2.5	5	1
1.7	1	1

When a school principal or an administrator in a central office is concerned with interpreting the average performance in a school, norms for school averages are the appropriate ones to use, and it is reasonable to expect the test publisher to provide them. The better test publishers will also provide item analyses and criterion-referenced reports at the level of the class, building, district, and state.

CAUTIONS IN USING NORMS

For a test that assesses standing on some trait or competence in some area of knowledge, norms provide a basis for interpreting the scores of an individual or a group. Converting the score for any test taken singly into an age or grade equivalent, percentile rank, or standard score permits an interpretation of the level at which the individual is functioning on that particular test. Bringing together the set of scores for an individual in a common unit of measure, and perhaps expressing these scores in a profile, brings out the relative level of performance of the individual in different areas.

The average performance for a class, a grade group in a school, or the children in the same grade throughout a school system may be reported similarly. We can then see the average level of performance within the group on some single function or the relative performance of the group in each of several areas. Norms provide a frame of reference within which the picture may be viewed and bring all parts of the picture into a common frame. Now, what does the picture mean, and what should we do about it?

Obviously, it is not possible, in a few pages, to provide a ready-made interpretation for each set of scores that may be obtained in a practical testing situation. However, we can lay out a few general guidelines and principles that may help to forestall some unwise interpretations of test results.

The most general point to keep in mind is that test results, presented in any normative scale, are a *description of what is,* not a *prescription of what should be.* The results make it possible to compare an individual or a class with other individuals and classes with respect to one or more aspects of accomplishment or personality, but they do not in any absolute sense tell us whether the individual is doing "well" or "poorly." They do not provide this information for several reasons.

Normative Scores Give Relative Rather Than Absolute Information. They tell whether an individual pupil's achievement is as high as that of other pupils or whether a class scores as high as other classes. But they do not tell us whether the basic concepts of numbers are being mastered or whether the pupils read well enough to comprehend the instructions for filling out an income tax return. Furthermore, they give us little guidance on how much improvement we might expect from *all* pupils if our educational system operated throughout at higher efficiency.

Remember that by the very nature of relative scores, there will be as many people below average as above. When "the norm" means the average of a reference group, it is a statistical necessity that about half of the group be, to a greater or lesser degree, below average. There has been an enormous amount of foolishness—both in single schools and in statewide legislation—about bringing all pupils "up to the grade norm." This might conceivably be done temporarily if we had a sudden and enormous improvement in educational effectiveness; however, the next time new norms were established for the test it would take a higher absolute level of performance to, say, read at the sixth-grade level. So we would be back again with half of the pupils falling at or below average. And if the effectiveness of the schools were to return to the former level, we would be faced with the unhappy prospect of more than half of the students testing "below grade level."

The relative nature of norms has been recognized in the criterion-referenced test movement. When a teacher or a school is concerned with appraising mastery of some *specific* instructional objective, it may be more useful to develop test exercises that appraise that objective, to agree on some standard as representing an acceptable level of mastery, and to determine which students do and which do not have mastery of that specific objective than it would be to know how the students from this school perform relative to those from other schools. In the context described, it is possible for all students to achieve mastery, but some will get there faster than others. Even in a criterion-referenced framework there will still be differences among individuals in their levels of accomplishment.

Output Must Be Evaluated Relative to Input. Test results typically give a picture of output—of the individual or of the group as it exists at the time of testing, after a period of exposure to educational effort. But what of the input? Where did the group start?

The notion of input is a complex and rather subtle one. Our conception of input should include not only earlier status on the particular ability being measured and individual potential for learning, as far as we are able to appraise this, but also the familial circumstances and environmental supports that make it easier for some children to learn than for others. Parental aspirations for the child, parental skills at teaching and guidance of learning, parental discipline and control, linguistic patterns, and cultural resources in the home are part of the input just as truly as are the biological characteristics of the young organism. Furthermore, peer group and community attitudes are an additional real, though possibly modifiable, part of the input as far as the prospects for learning for a given child are concerned. We must recognize that the adequate appraisal of input is no simple matter, and that, correspondingly, the appraisal of output as "satisfactory" or "unsatisfactory" is something we can do with only modest confidence.

Output Must Be Evaluated Relative to Objectives.   The design, content, and norms for published standardized tests are based on their authors' perception of common national curricular objectives. The topics included, their relative emphasis, and the levels at which they are introduced reflect that perceived general national pattern. To the extent, then, that a given school system deviates in its objectives and curricular emphases from the national pattern, as interpreted by the test maker, its output at a given grade level can be expected to deviate from the national norms. If computational skills receive little emphasis, it is reasonable to find that computational facility will be underdeveloped. If map reading has been delayed beyond the grade level at which it is introduced into the test, it is reasonable to find that relative standing on that part of the test will suffer. Unevenness of the local profile, in relation to national norms, should always lead one to inquire whether the low spots represent failures of the local program to achieve its objectives or a planned deviation of emphasis from what is more typical of schools nationally. Low performance that results from conscious curricular decisions would be much less cause for alarm than a similar level of performance would be in an area of curricular emphasis. Which of these conditions obtains will no doubt influence what is done with the finding.

To the extent that individual states have uniform objectives for all districts within their boundaries, well-designed standardized tests measuring achievement of these objectives often are available through contract arrangements with test publishers. Several states now contract with organizations that specialize in test development to have tests constructed according to specifications provided by the state board of education. Such tests usually are intended to be used at particular points in the educational program, such as the transitions from elementary school to middle school, middle school to high school, and near the end of high school.

If these considerations and some of the caveats discussed in the next two chapters are borne in mind, the teacher, principal, superintendent, or school board will be interpreting the reported test results with increased wisdom and restraint.

SUMMARY

A raw score, taken by itself, rarely has meaning. A score may be given meaning by a consideration of the domain of instructional content that the test items represent. The performance of individuals or groups may then be assessed either in terms of the percentage of the domain they have mastered or relative to a standard of performance set before the test is administered. These methods of giving meaning to a raw score are called criterion-referenced interpretations. They are appropriate for tests that focus on one or a small number of carefully defined objectives and for which standards of performance can be either empirically or logically derived.

Because many tests are designed to appraise several objectives, and because meaningful absolute standards of performance are not available for most tests, a raw score is generally given meaning by comparison with some reference group or groups. This method of giving a raw score meaning is called norm-referenced interpretation. The comparison may be with

1. A series of grade groups (grade norms)
2. A series of age groups (age norms)
3. A single group, in which performance is indicated by what percentage of that group the score surpassed (percentile norms)
4. A single group, in which performance is indicated by the number of standard deviations the score is above or below the group mean (standard score norms). (Norms of this type may be subjected to a linear conversion to eliminate decimal points and negative values or to nonlinear transformations to normalize the score distribution.)

Each alternative has certain advantages and certain limitations.

Quotients such as the IQ were developed to get a single index to express the degree to which individuals deviated from their age group. Because of their various limitations, quotients have been replaced by standard scores, and the term IQ is no longer technically appropriate.

If the norms available for a number of different tests are of the same kind and are based on comparable groups, all the tests can be expressed in comparable terms. The results can then be shown pictorially in the form of a profile. Profiles emphasize score differences within the individual. When profiles are used, we must take care not to overinterpret their minor ups and downs.

Norms represent a descriptive framework for interpreting the score of an individual, a class group, or some larger aggregation. However, before a judgment can be made on whether an individual or group is doing well or poorly, allowance must be made for ability level, cultural background, and curricular emphases. The norm is merely an average and not a straitjacket into which everyone can be forced to fit. It describes the person's current performance, relative to some specified comparison group.

QUESTIONS AND EXERCISES

1. Why does the frame of reference used to interpret a test score make a difference?

2. Can the same test be interpreted in both a criterion-referenced and a norm-referenced manner? If so, how would the two interpretations differ?

3. A pupil in the sixth grade received a raw score of 25 on the Level 12 Reading Test (Form J) of the Iowa Tests of Basic Skills. What additional information would be needed to interpret this score?

4. Why do standardized tests designed for use with high school students almost never use age or grade norms?

5. What limitations would national norms have for use by a county school system in rural West Virginia? What might the local school system do about the limitations?

6. What assumptions lie behind developing and using age norms? Grade norms? Normalized standard scores?

7. In Figure 3.3, why are the standard scores evenly spaced, while the percentile scores are unevenly spaced?

8. State A gives a battery of achievement tests each May in the 4th, 8th, and 11th grades. The median grade level in each subject in each district in the state is reported to the State Board of Education. Should these results be reported? If so, what else should be included in the report? In what ways might the board use the results to promote better education? What uses should the board avoid?

9. Ms. P takes pride in the fact that each year she has gotten at least 85% of her fourth-grade class "up to the norm" in each subject. How desirable is this as an educational objective? What limitations or dangers do you see in it?

10. School F has a policy of assigning transfer students to a grade on the basis of their average grade equivalent on an achievement battery. Thus, a boy with an average grade equivalent of 5.3 would be assigned to the fifth grade, no matter what his age or his grade in his previous school. What are the values and limitations of such a practice?

11. The superintendent of schools in Riverview, Iowa, noted that Springdale Elementary School fell consistently about a half grade below national norms on an achievement battery. He was distressed because this performance was the lowest of any school in the city. How justified is his dissatisfaction? Do you need other information to answer this question? If so, what?

12. The Board of Education in East Centerville noted that the fourth and fifth grades in their community fell substantially below national norms in mathematics, although they scored at or above average in all other subjects. They propose to study this situation further. What additional information do they need?

13. The third-grade teachers in Bigcity school district have prepared a 30-item test to assess mastery of the basic multiplication facts. What score should they accept as demonstrating "mastery" of these facts? How should such a score be determined?

14. What are the advantages of reporting test performance in terms of stanines? In terms of normal curve equivalents? What problems arise from using each of these forms of normative report?

15. Obtain the manual for some test, and study the information given about norms.

    a. How adequate is the norming population? Is sufficient information given for you to make a judgment?

    b. Calculate the chance score (i.e., the score to be expected from blind guessing) for the test, and note its grade equivalent. What limitations does this suggest for using the test?

    c. What limitations are there on the usefulness of the test at the upper end of its range?

    d. How many raw score points correspond to 1 full year on the grade-equivalent scale? Is this number of points of score the same throughout the range of the test?

SUGGESTED READINGS

Angoff, W. H. (1971). Scales, norms, and equivalent scores. In R. L. Thorndike (Ed.), *Educational measurement* (2nd ed., pp. 508–600). Washington, DC: American Council on Education.

Holland, P. W., & Rubin, D. B. (Eds.). (1982). *Test equating.* New York: Academic Press.

Hoover, H. D. (1984). The most appropriate scores for measuring educational development in the elementary schools: GE's. *Educational Measurement: Issues and Practices, 3,* 8–14.

Kolen, M. J. (1988). Defining score scales in relation to measurement error. *Journal of Educational Measurement, 25,* 97–110.

Livingston, S. A., & Zieky, M. J. (1982). *Passing scores: A manual for setting standards of performance on educational and occupational tests.* Princeton, NJ: Educational Testing Service.

Michell, J. (1986). Measurement scales and statistics: A clash of paradigms. *Psychological Bulletin, 3,* 398–407.

Nitko, A. J. (1984). Defining "criterion-referenced test." In R. A. Berk (Ed.), *A guide to criterion-referenced test construction* (pp. 8–28). Baltimore: Johns Hopkins University Press.

Petersen, N. S., Kolen, M. J., & Hoover, H. D. (1989). Scaling, norming, and equating. In R. L. Linn (Ed.), *Educational measurement* (3rd ed., pp. 221–262). New York: Macmillan.

Shepard, L. A. (1984). Setting performance standards. In R. A. Berk (Ed.), *A guide to criterion-referenced test construction* (pp. 169–198). Baltimore: Johns Hopkins University Press.

Thorndike, R. L. (1982). *Applied psychometrics.* Boston: Houghton Mifflin.

Yen, W. M. (1986). The choice of scale for educational measurement: An IRT perspective. *Journal of Educational Measurement, 23,* 299–325.

CHAPTER 4

Qualities Desired in Any Measurement Procedure: Reliability

INTRODUCTION

Whenever we would like to use a test or other measurement procedure to provide information to help in some decision, we face the problem of which test or procedure to use or whether there is any instrument that will really help in the decision. There are usually several tests that have been designed to help or that seem at least to have the possibility of helping with the decision. We would like to know whether any tests will indeed provide useful information. And if any will, which is the best one to use? (For simplicity, we use the term *test* throughout this chapter and the next, but the issues we present apply to all forms of measurement and all sources of information. Where special concerns arise, they will be addressed in the chapter dealing with that assessment procedure.)

Many specific factors enter into the evaluation of a test, but we will consider them under two main headings: reliability and validity. *Reliability* refers to the accuracy and precision of a measurement procedure. Indices of reliability give an indication of the extent to which the scores produced by a particular measurement procedure are consistent and reproducible. *Validity* has to do with the degree to which the test scores provide information that is relevant to the inferences that are to be made from them. Thus, a judgment of validity is always in relation to a specific decision or use, and evidence that test scores are appropriate for one purpose does not necessarily mean that the scores are appropriate for another. A third consideration, *practicality,* is concerned with a wide range of factors of economy, convenience, and interpretability that determine whether a test is realistically employable for our purpose. Issues of practicality are presented in Chapter 6.

Reliability and validity are both required of any test that we would choose, regardless of how practical it is to use. Validity of test scores for their intended use is the absolutely essential quality for a test to have, but in a sense, reliability is a necessary precondition for validity. Test scores must be at least moderately reliable before they can have any validity, but a reliable test may be devoid of validity for the application we have in mind. Although the true bottom line in selecting a test is the test's validity for our proposed use, we discuss reliability first as a necessary condition for validity to exist. Validity is discussed in Chapter 5.

RELIABILITY AS CONSISTENCY

When we ask about a test's reliability, we are asking not what the test measures but, instead, how accurately it measures whatever it does measure. What is the precision of the resulting score? How accurately will the score be reproduced if we measure the individual again?

Some degree of inconsistency is present in all measurement procedures. Consider the experience of your author who bought a new, digital electronic bathroom scale because he did not trust the old spring-operated one he had been using for 20 years. When I took the new scale home and tried it out, the first reading seemed reasonable. Then, just to show myself that the new scale was an improvement, I tried it again. The reading was 7 lbs lower! Not believing that a diet could work that fast, I took a third reading and then a fourth. After 10 minutes of testing the scale, I decided to return it because the readings had spread over a range of 15 lbs.

This little experience illustrates the central issue in reliability. My actual weight was, for all practical purposes, constant throughout the series of measurements, but my scores differed from one testing to the next. If we call my real, constant weight my *true score (T)*, then each observation or *measurement (X)* includes this true score plus some *error of measurement (e)*. That is,

$$X = T + e.$$

Any difference between an observation and the true score is an error of measurement.

On the bathroom scale, and indeed in all measurements, many errors of measurement appear to be random; sometimes they are positive, making the score too high, and sometimes they are negative, making the score too low. Most of them are fairly small, but some can be quite large. Their distribution often looks like the normal distribution that was discussed in Chapter 2.

There are other errors of measurement that remain constant from one measurement to another. The scale could have read 10 lbs too high on every repetition. Errors of this kind cannot be detected just by repeating the measurement; the instrument must be compared to another one in which the error is not present. However, constant errors do not lead to inconsistency, so they do not affect the reliability of the measuring instrument.

The bathroom scale offers a unique opportunity to observe random errors of measurement in action, but that situation is far removed from the environment in which educational or psychological measurements are made. Measurements of human behavior are particularly susceptible to inconsistency.

Let us consider a second example that is also somewhat artificial but more nearly approximates a testing context. Suppose we were to test all the girls in a class one day and again the next day to see how far each could throw a football. We might mark a starting line on the field, give each girl one of the old footballs that the physical education department has for team practice, send an assistant out to mark where the ball hit, and tell each girl to throw the ball as far as she could. With a steel tape, we would measure the distance from the starting line to where the assistant marked the fall of the ball. On each day, we would have each girl make one throw, with each attempt giving us one measurement of that girl's ability to throw a football.

In comparing the two scores for an individual, we would find that they are seldom exactly the same. In these tests, most of the differences will be fairly small, but some will be moderately large. The differences show that one throw is not perfectly reliable as a measure of a person's throwing ability. Results are, to some degree, inconsistent from one day's throw to the next.

Sources of Inconsistency

We can identify three classes of reasons for inconsistency between a throw one day and a throw the next day.

1. *The person may actually have changed* from one testing to the next. On one day, a girl may have been more rested than she was on the other. On one day, she could have been motivated to try harder on the task, or she could even have gotten some special coaching from a parent between the two testings. If the interval between the two tests happened to be months rather than days, there could have been real physical growth, differing from girl to girl, that affected the two testings. This example has involved changes affecting physical performance, but it is easy to think of similar categories of change that would apply to a test of mental ability or to a self-report inventory dealing with mood or with interests.

2. *The task could have been different* for the two measurements. For example, the ball Betty used one day could have been tightly inflated, whereas the one she had on the next day could have been a squashy one that permitted a somewhat different grip. Or, one day the examiner may have permitted the girls to take a run up to the release line, whereas on the second day the examiner may have allowed only one or two steps. Environmental factors such as the presence of a head wind could also have been present on one day and not on another. Any of these variations could have helped some girls more than others. In paper-and-pencil tests we often use one form of the test on one occasion and a second, parallel form on the second occasion. The specific items are different, and some pupils may happen to be better able to handle one sampling of tasks, while others are better at the other sampling.

3. *The limited sample of behavior* could have resulted in an unstable and undependable score. Even if we had each girl make two throws with the same ball and the same instructions, with only a 5-minute rest in between, the two distances would rarely come out the same. A single throw, like a single test item, is a meager sample of behavior. That sample and the evaluation of it are subject to all sorts of chance influences. Maybe Betty's finger slipped. Maybe she got mixed up in the coordination of her legs and her arm. Or maybe the ball was held a little too far forward or a little too far back, the scorer was looking the other way when the ball landed, or there was a gust of wind just as Betty threw. Maybe any of a hundred things occurred—some favorable, some unfavorable. The effect of such unknown random influences on an observed performance is that a small sample of behavior does not provide a stable and dependable characterization of an individual—whether the sample be of footballs thrown for distance or of sentences read for understanding. The average of 100 throws of the football would provide a much more stable index of this ability than would the result of a single throw, and performance on 100 reading comprehension items would likewise provide a more stable assessment of that ability.

TWO WAYS TO EXPRESS RELIABILTIY

There are two ways to express the reliability, or precision, of a set of measurements or, from the reverse point of view, the variation within the set. One approach directly addresses the amount of variation to be expected within a set of repeated measurements of a single individual. If we were to take 200 readings of the bathroom scale or if it were possible to have Betty throw the football 200 times (assuming for the present that this could be done without introducing effects of practice or fatigue), we could produce a frequency distribution of weights or of distances thrown. This frequency distribution has an average value which we can think of as approximating a person's "true" weight or the "true" distance that Betty can throw a football. The distribution also has a standard deviation describing the spread, or scatter, of the measurements around their mean. Because the scatter results from errors of measurement, we will call this variation the *standard error of measurement.* It is the standard deviation of the distribution of "errors" of measuring football-throwing ability or the weight of a person.

With psychological or educational data, we usually cannot make a whole series of measurements on each individual. There *are* practice and fatigue effects; besides, time does not permit giving 200 reading tests or 200 interest inventories. Often, we are fortunate if we can get *two* scores for each individual. But, if we have a pair of measurements for each individual, we can make an estimate (see Interpretation of Reliability Data later in this chapter) of what the scattering of scores would have been for the average person if we had made the measurements again and again.

Reliable measurement also implies that each individual stays in about the same place in the group on each testing. The girl who scores highest on the football throwing test the first time should also be one of the highest the next time, and each person in the group should stay in about the same relative position on successive occasions. The correlation coefficient provides a statistical index of the extent to which two measurements tend to agree or to place each person in the same relative position, high with high and low with low. If the two things we are correlating happen to be two applications of the same measure, the resulting correlation provides an indicator of reliability. We can designate it a *reliability coefficient.* We have already seen the characteristics of the correlation coefficient in Chapter 2. But the relationship now before us is that of two measurements with the same or an equivalent measuring instrument. The more nearly individuals are ranked in the same order the second time as the first, the higher the correlation and the more reliable the test.

WAYS TO ASSESS RELIABILITY

A measure is reliable, then, to the extent that an individual remains nearly the same on repeated measurements—that is, nearly the same, as represented by a low standard error of measurement (low variation in the person's performance over repeated measurements) or by a high reliability coefficient (consistent ranking of individuals within the group from one measurement to another). But what exact type of data do we need to get an appropriate estimate of this degree of stability or precision of measurement? We will consider three distinct possibilities, noting their similarities and differences and evaluating the advantages and disadvantages of each:

1. Repeating the same test or measure (retest)
2. Administering a second "equivalent" form of the test (also called parallel or alternate test forms)
3. Subdividing the test into two or more equivalent fractions from a single administration (single-administration methods)

Retesting with the Same Test

If we wish to find out how reliably we can evaluate an individual's football throw, we can test the person twice. It may be a reasonable precaution to have the two measures taken independently by two testers. We do not want the examiner's recollection of the first score to affect perception of the second. It may be desirable to have the two testings done on different days, depending on what we are interested in. If we want to know how accurately a single throw (or possibly a single set of throws) characterizes a person at a specific point in time, the two measurements should be carried out one immediately after the other. Then, we know that the *person* has stayed the same and that the only source of variation or "error" is in the measuring operation. If we want to know how precisely a given measurement characterizes a person from day to day—how closely we can predict an individual's score next week from what he or she does today—it would be appropriate to measure the person on two separate occasions. In this second case, we are interested in *variation of the individual from time to time,* as well as *variation due to the operation of measurement.*

Sometimes we are interested in variation in the individual from day to day; sometimes we are not. We may ask, how accurately does our measurement characterize Sam at this moment? Or we may ask, how accurately does our measurement of Sam describe him as he will be tomorrow, or next week, or next month? Each is a sensible question. But the questions are not the same. The data we must collect to answer one are different from the data we need to answer the other.

Repetition of the measurement is a straightforward and satisfactory operation for studying the reliability of measurement of such a physical characteristic as weight or height of a person. The reading of a bathroom scale on one occasion is not affected by the reading it gave on a previous weighing. Use of simple repetition of the measurement also seems satisfactory and applicable with some simple aspects of behavior, such as speed of reaction or the type of motor skill exemplified by the football throw. Suppose, however, that we are interested in the reliability of a measure of reading comprehension. Let us assume that the test is made up of six reading passages with five questions on each. We administer the test once and then immediately administer it again. What happens? Certainly the people taking the test are not going to have to reread all of the material that they have just read. They may do so in part, but to a considerable extent, their answers the second time will involve merely remembering what answers they had chosen the first time and marking them again. Those who had not been able to finish the first time will now be able to work ahead and spend most of their time on new material. These same effects hold true to some degree even over longer periods of time. Clearly, a test like this one given a second time does not present the same task that it did the first time.

A second consideration enters into the repetition of a test such as a reading comprehension test. Suppose that one of the six passages in the test was about baseball and that a particular girl was an expert on baseball. The passage would then be especially easy for her, and she would, in effect, get a bonus of several points. This portion of the test would overestimate her general level of reading ability. But note that it would do so consistently on both testings if the material remained the same. The error of measurement for this individual would be a *constant error* in the two testings. Because the error would affect both her scores in the same way, it would make the test look reliable rather than unreliable.

In an area of ability such as reading, we must recognize the possibility that an individual does not perform uniformly well throughout the whole area. Specific interests, experiences, and backgrounds give individuals different strengths and weaknesses. A particular test is *one sample* from the whole domain of behavior. How well an individual does on the test, relative to other people, is likely to depend to some degree on the particular sample of tasks chosen to represent the particular domain of ability or personality we are trying to appraise. If the sample remains the same for both measurements, the person's behavior will stay more nearly the same than if the sample of tasks is varied between measurements.

So far we have identified three main sources of performance variation that will tend to reduce the consistency, or stability, of a particular score as a description of an individual:

1. Variation from trial to trial in the individual's response to the task at a particular moment
2. Variation in the individual from one time to another
3. Variation arising out of the particular sample of tasks chosen to represent a domain of behavior

Retesting the individual with an identical test can reflect the first two sources of "error," but this procedure cannot evaluate the effects of the third type. In addition, there may be memory or practice effects such as those referred to above.

Testing with Parallel Forms

Concern about variation resulting from the particular sample of tasks chosen to represent a domain of behavior leads us to another set of procedures for evaluating reliability. If the sampling of items may be a significant source of "error" and if, as is usually the case, we want to know with what accuracy we can generalize from the specific score based on one sample of tasks to the broader domain that the sample is supposed to represent, we must develop some procedures that take into account the variation resulting from the sample of tasks. We may do this by correlating scores from two alternate, parallel or equivalent forms of a test.

Alternate forms of a test should be thought of as forms built according to the same specifications but composed of separate samples from the defined behavior domain. Thus, two parallel reading tests should contain reading passages and questions of the same difficulty. The same sorts of questions should be asked; for example, there should be a balance of specific-fact and general-idea questions. The same types of passages should be represented, such as expository, argumentative, and aesthetic. But the specific passage topics and questions should be different.

If we have two forms of a test, we may give each pupil first one form and then the other. The tests may follow each other immediately if we are not interested in stability over time, or they may be separated by an interval if we are interested in stability. The correlation between the two forms will provide an appropriate reliability coefficient. If a time interval has been allowed between the testings, all three sources of variation will have a chance to get in their effects—variation arising from the measurement itself, variation in the individual over time, and variation resulting from the sample of tasks.

To ask that a test yield consistent results under the conditions of parallel tests separated by a time interval is the most rigorous standard that can be set for it, because all three sources of variation can affect the scores. And, if we want to use test results to generalize about what Johnny will do on other tasks of this general sort next week or next month, then this standard is the appropriate one by which to evaluate a test. For most educational situations, this procedure *is* the way we want to use test results, so evidence based on equivalent test forms with a time interval between administrations should usually be given the most weight in evaluating the reliability of a test.

The use of two parallel test forms does provide a sound basis for estimating the precision of a psychological or educational test. This procedure, however, also raises some practical problems. It demands that two parallel forms of the test be available and that time be allowed for testing each person twice. Often, no second form of the test exists or could reasonably be constructed, or no time can be found for a second testing. To administer a second test is often likely to represent a somewhat burdensome demand on available resources. These practical considerations of convenience and expediency have made test makers receptive to procedures that extract an estimate of reliability from one administration of one form of a test. However, such procedures are a compromise at best. The correlation between two parallel forms, usually administered after a lapse of several days or weeks, in most applications represents the preferred procedure for estimating reliability.

Single-Administration Methods

Internal Consistency Reliability.   Practical considerations often dictate that a reliability estimate be obtained from a single administration of the test. Although several procedures for obtaining such estimates have been developed, the ones that are now most widely used are based on the idea that each item in a test can be considered to be a one-item test. The total test of *n* items is then seen as a set of *n* parallel, but very short, tests. (Here, *n* is the number of test items.) An estimate of the reliability of the total test is developed from an analysis of the statistics of the individual items.

The procedure for estimating the reliability of a test from a single administration of a single form depends on the consistency of the individual's performance from item to item and is based on the standard deviation of the test and the standard deviations of the separate items. In its most general form, this procedure is called *coefficient alpha* and is given by the following equation:

$$\alpha = \left(\frac{n}{n-1}\right)\left(\frac{SD_t^2 - \Sigma SD_i^2}{SD_t^2}\right) \tag{4.1}$$

Cronbach's Alpha

where α is the estimate of reliability,

$\quad$ n is the number of items in the test,

$\quad$ SD_t is the standard deviation of the test scores,

$\quad$ Σ means "take the sum of" and covers the n items, and

$\quad$ SD_i is the standard deviation of the scores from a

group of individuals on an item. There are n values of

$\quad$ SD_i which are summed to give the second term in the

$\quad$ numerator.

When each item is scored as either 1 or 0, that is, as either passed or failed,

$$SD_i{}^2 = p_i q_i$$

where p_i is the proportion passing the item and

$\quad$ q_i is the proportion failing the item.

Equation 4.1 then becomes

$$r_{11} = \left(\frac{n}{n-1}\right)\left(\frac{SD_t{}^2 - \Sigma p_i q_i}{SD_t{}^2}\right) \tag{4.2}$$

where r_{11} is the estimated reliability of the full-length test. This equation, called Kuder-Richardson Formula 20 (KR-20) after its originators and the numbering in their original article, is a special form of coefficient alpha that applies when the items are scored right or wrong. Both coefficient alpha and KR-20 provide an estimate of what is called the *internal consistency* of a test, that is, the degree to which all of the items measure a common characteristic of the person. When the test is homogeneous, in the sense that every item measures the same general trait of ability or personality as every other item, coefficient alpha and KR-20 estimates can reasonably be interpreted as reflecting the reliability of the test.

$\quad$ A formula involving simpler calculations and based on an assumption that all items are of the same difficulty is called Kuder-Richardson Formula 21 (KR-21). This formula substitutes $M_t (1 - M_t/n)$, where M_t is the mean score on the test, for $\Sigma p_i q_i$ in Equation 4.2 and yields a close, but conservative, approximation to KR-20. KR-21 can be useful for teachers who would like to estimate the reliability of the tests they use in their classes, because it can be easily calculated from the mean and standard deviation of the distribution of test scores. However, the assumption that all items are of equal difficulty is quite restrictive and seldom true in practice. This fact, coupled with the availability of computers to do the extra work required by the KR-20 and coefficient alpha formulas suggests that KR-21 should seldom be used.

$\quad$ The appealing convenience of the internal consistency procedures has led to their wide use. Many test manuals will be found to report this type of reliability coefficient and no other. Unfortunately, KR-20, KR-21, and coefficient alpha have several types of limitations.

$\quad$ First, because all of the item responses have occurred during a single testing, they all necessarily represent the individual as he or she is at a single moment in time.

Even events lasting only a few minutes will affect many items about equally. In other words, variation in the individual from day to day cannot be reflected in this type of reliability coefficient. It can only give evidence on the precision with which we can appraise the person at a specific moment.

A second factor will sometimes make item sets more alike than would be true of separate parallel forms. If the test includes groups of items based on common reference material, such as reading items based on a single passage or science items all referring to a single described experiment, performance on all of these items will depend to some extent on the common act of comprehending the reference materials. Thus, the examinee who succeeds on one item of the set is more likely to succeed on the others than would be the case for truly independent items.

For some situations, the assumption that all items on a particular test measure a single trait may be too restrictive. An achievement test in general science might include items on biology, chemistry, and geology. To the extent that there is a single trait of general science knowledge, the items should show consistent performance, but if there are separate, only moderately correlated, traits of biology knowledge, chemistry knowledge, and geology knowledge, we should find three clusters of items, each cluster showing high internal consistency. It would be inappropriate for a test like this to show high internal consistency across the whole test.

Finally, an internal consistency reliability coefficient becomes meaningless when a test is highly speeded. Suppose we had a test of simple arithmetic made up of 100 problems like $3 + 5 = \underline{\quad?\quad}$, and that the test was being used with adults, with a 2-minute time limit. People would differ widely in scores on such a test, but the differences would be primarily differences in speed. Computation errors would be a minor factor. The person who got a score of 50 would very probably have attempted just 50 items. The position of an item in the test then determines almost completely whether an individual attempts the item. Because almost everyone who attempts an item gets the item correct, the values of p and q for the item are determined by its placement in the test, and this fact will greatly inflate the apparent consistency of performance.

Few tests depend as completely on speed as does the one chosen to illustrate the point; however, many tests involve some degree of speeding. This speed factor tends to inflate estimates of reliability based on internal consistency procedures. The amount of overestimation depends on the degree to which the test is speeded, being greater for those tests in which speed plays a greater role. But speed enters in sufficiently general a manner that internal consistency estimates of reliability should usually be discounted somewhat.

Subdivided Tests.   A procedure that has been widely used in the past for obtaining a reliability estimate from a single administration of a test divides the test into two presumably equivalent halves. The half-tests may be assembled on the basis of a careful examination of the content and difficulty of each item, making a systematic effort to balance out the content and difficulty level of the two halves. In essence, this is the same as constructing two, short, parallel tests and then combining them for a single administration. After testing, the two forms are separated for scoring. This approach solves the problem of tests that measure more than one trait because items measuring each trait are present in each half-test.

A simpler procedure, often relied on to give equivalent halves, is to put alternate items into the two half-tests, that is, to put the odd-numbered items into one half-test and the even-numbered items in the other half. This procedure is usually a sensible one because items of similar form, content, or difficulty are likely to be grouped together in the test. For a reasonably long test, 60 items or more, splitting the test in this way will tend to balance out factors of item form, content covered, and difficulty level. The two half-tests will have a good probability of being "equivalent" tests.

These procedures divide the test in half only for scoring, not for administration. That is, a single test is given with a single time limit at a single sitting. However, two separate scores are derived—one by scoring one half, or the odd-numbered items, and one by scoring the other half, or the even-numbered items. The correlation between these two scores, called an odd-even reliability coefficient or, more generally, a *split-half reliability,* provides a measure of the accuracy with which the test is measuring the individual at this point in time. Split-half reliability coefficients provide an estimate of what the correlation would be between two equivalent tests given at the same time.

However, it must be noted that the computed correlation is between two half-length tests. This value is not directly applicable to the full-length test, which is the actual instrument prepared for use. In general, the larger a sample of a person's behavior we have, the more reliable the measure will be. That is, the more behavior we record, the less our measure will depend on chance elements in the behavior of the individual or in the particular sampling of tasks. Single, lucky answers or momentary lapses in attention will be more nearly evened out.

Where the halves of the test that gave the scores actually correlated are equivalent, we can get an unbiased estimate of the total-test reliability from the correlation between the two half-tests. The estimate is given by the following equation:

$$r_{11} = \frac{2r_{1/2\ 1/2}}{1 + r_{1/2\ 1/2}} \qquad (4.3)$$

where r_{11} is the estimated reliability of the full-length test and
$r_{1/2\ 1/2}$ is the actual correlation between the two half-tests.

Thus, if the correlation between the halves of a test is 0.60, Equation 4.3 would give

$$r_{11} = 2(0.60)/(1 + 0.60) = 1.20/1.60 = 0.75$$

as our best estimate of the reliability of scores on the total test. This equation, referred to generally as the Spearman-Brown Prophecy Formula from its function and the names of its originators, makes it possible to compute an estimate of reliability from a single administration of a single test. It has the advantage over the internal consistency methods that it does not assume homogeneous content across all items, only between the two halves, but it is still a single-administration method.

However, the split-half method is sensitive to the equivalence of the two halves. If the split does not produce equivalent tests, the correlation between them will underestimate the reliability of the full-length test. The use of any particular split of the test is somewhat arbitrary, and different splits will produce different estimates of the test's reliability. Internal consistency methods were developed in part to overcome this problem. The value given by coefficient alpha is the average of all possible Spearman-Brown–corrected half-test correlations, so it evens out the possible effects of an inappropriate split.

Comparison of Methods

A summary comparison of the different procedures for estimating reliability is given in Table 4.1. The table shows the four factors (sources of variation) we have discussed that may make a single test score an inaccurate picture of the individual's usual performance and which sources of error are reflected in score variation in each of the procedures for estimating reliability. In general, the different procedures are not equivalent; the more Xs there are in a column, the more conservative (i.e., lower) the estimate of a test's reliability. Only administration of parallel test forms with a time interval between testings permits all sources of instability to have their effects. Each of the other methods masks some source of variation that may be signifi-

Table 4.1
Sources of Variation Represented in Different Procedures for Estimating Reliability

Sources of Variation	Experimental Procedure for Estimating Reliability				
	Immediate Retest, Same Test	Retest After Interval, Same Test	Parallel Test Form Without Interval	Parallel Test Form with Interval	Single-Administration Methods[a]
Variation arising within the measurement procedure itself	X	X	X	X	X
Changes in the person from day to day		X		X	
Changes in the specific sample of tasks			X	X	X
Changes in the individual's speed of work	X	X	X	X	

Note: X indicates that this source of variation can affect reliability from this method of testing.

[a]The single-administration methods are Kuder-Richardson Formulas 20 and 21, coefficient alpha, and split-half.

cant in the actual use of the test. Retesting with an identical test neglects variation arising out of the sampling of items. Whenever all testing is done at one time, day-to-day variation in the individual is omitted. When the testing is done as a single unit with a single time limit, variation in speed of responding is neglected. The facts brought out in this table should be borne in mind in evaluating reliability data found in a test manual or in the report of a research study. Test users should demand that commercial publishers provide estimates based on parallel forms of the test and on retesting after a delay, whenever possible, so that a reasonable estimate of the effects of the sources of unreliability can be assessed.

INTERPRETATION OF RELIABILITY DATA

Suppose that analysis of data obtained from an elementary school test of academic aptitude has yielded a reliability coefficient of 0.90. How should we interpret this result? What does it mean concerning the precision of an individual's score? Should we be pleased or dissatisfied to get a coefficient of this size?

One interpretation of test reliability is found in the relationship between the reliability coefficient and the standard error of measurement. Remember that *the standard error of measurement is the standard deviation that would be obtained for a series of measurements of the same individual.* (It is assumed that the individual is not changed by being measured.) The standard error of measurement can be estimated from the reliability coefficient by the following equation:

$$SD_m = SD_t \sqrt{(1 - r_{tt})} \tag{4.4}$$

where SD_m is the standard error of measurement and
$\quad$ r_{tt} is the reliability of the test determined by one of the methods presented earlier.

Suppose that the test with a reliability of 0.90 has a standard deviation of 15 points. Then, we have

$$SD_m = 15 \sqrt{(1 - 0.90)} = 15 \sqrt{0.10} = 15(0.316) = 4.7$$

In this instance, a set of repeated measures of some one person (such as that obtained for my weight) would be expected to have a standard deviation (i.e., a standard error of measurement) of 4.7 points. Remember that in a normal distribution a fairly uniform proportion of observations falls within any given number of standard deviation units of the mean; about 32% of cases, or about one in three, differ from the mean by more than 1 standard deviation; 4.6%, by more than 2 standard deviations. This situation is illustrated for the present example in Figure 4.1.

Applying this to a case in which the standard deviation is 4.7 points, one could say that there is about one chance in three that an individual's observed score differs from his or her "true" score (falls outside the 68% band in Figure 4.1) by as much as 4.7 points in either direction. There is about 1 chance in 20 that it differs by as much

Figure 4.1
The standard error of measurement (SD_m) can be used to determine a range for
estimating an individual's true score.

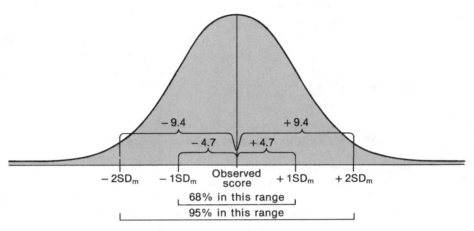

as 9.4 points (2 standard errors of measurement). A little less than one-third of the
scores from such a measurement are likely to be in error by about five points or
more, while about 1 in 25 will be in error by 10 or more points.

Another way to view the standard error of measurement is as an indication of
how much a person's score might change on retesting. Each person's score on the
first testing includes some amount of error. Most of the errors will be fairly small, but
some will be quite large. About half of the errors will be positive (make the observed
score too high) and about half will be negative (make the observed score too low).
But we see only the observed score and have no way of knowing how large the error
of measurement is for any individual—or in what direction.

The numerical values of .90 for the reliability and 15 for the standard deviation
are fairly representative of what might be found for standard scores from one of the
commercially distributed academic aptitude tests for children in the upper elementary grades. Note that even with this relatively high reliability coefficient, appreciable errors of measurement are possible in at least a minority of cases. With a standard
deviation of 15 or 16, shifts of 5 or 10 points from one testing to another can be expected fairly frequently, just because of errors of measurement. Anyone who is impressed by—and tries to interpret—a score difference of five points between two
people or between two testings of the same person on a test such as this has been
fooled into thinking that the test has a precision that it simply does not possess. Further testing could reverse the result. Any interpretation of test scores must be made
with acute awareness of the standard error of measurement.

The manner in which the standard error of measurement is related to the reliability coefficient is shown in Table 4.2. Column one contains selected values for the
reliability, column two gives the value of the expression $(SD_t) \sqrt{1 - r_{tt}}$, and column
three gives the value of SD_m when SD_t is 15. Note that the magnitude of errors

Table 4.2
Standard Error of Measurement for Different Values
of Reliability Coefficient

	Standard Error of Measurement	
Reliability Coefficient	General Expression[a]	When $SD_t = 15$
.50	$.71SD_t$	10.6
.60	$.63SD_t$	9.5
.70	$.55SD_t$	8.2
.80	$.45SD_t$	6.7
.85	$.39SD_t$	5.8
.90	$.32SD_t$	4.7
.95	$.22SD_t$	3.4
.98	$.14SD_t$	2.1

Note: SD_t signifies the standard deviation of the test.
[a] $\sqrt{1 - r_{tt}}\ (SD_t)$.

decreases as the reliability coefficient increases, but also that errors of appreciable size can still be found with reliability coefficients of 0.90 or 0.95. It is the standard error of measurement that must be kept in mind in interpreting the score of an individual. A range extending from 2 standard errors of measurement above the obtained score to 2 below will produce a band which we can be reasonably sure (19 chances in 20) includes the individual's true score. Thus, in the case of the aptitude test described in this section, we can think of a test standard score of 90 as meaning rather surely a score lying between about 80 and 100. If we think in these terms, we will be much more discreet in interpreting and using test results.

It is desirable when interpreting the test score of an individual to think in terms of the standard error of measurement and a band of uncertainty, and to be somewhat humble and tentative in drawing conclusions from that test score. But for making comparisons between tests and for a number of types of test analyses, the reliability coefficient will be more useful. Where measures are expressed in different units, as height in inches and weight in pounds, the reliability coefficient provides the only possible basis for comparing precision of measurement. Because the competing tests in a given field, such as reading comprehension, are likely to use types of scores that are not directly comparable, the reliability coefficient will usually represent the only satisfactory basis for test comparison. *Other things being equal,* the test with the higher reliability coefficient, that is, the test that provides a more consistent ranking of the individuals within their group, should be preferred.

The other things that may not be equal are primarily considerations of validity and practicality. Validity, insofar as we can appraise it, is the crucial requirement for a measurement procedure. Reliability is important only as a necessary condition for a measure to have validity. The ceiling for the possible validity of a test is set by its reliability. A test must measure *something* before it can measure what we want to measure. A measuring device with a reliability of zero is reflecting nothing but chance factors. It does not correlate with itself and cannot correlate with anything else.

The theoretical ceiling for the correlation between any two measures is the square root of the product of their reliabilities:

$$r_{12} \leqq \sqrt{r_{11}r_{22}}$$

Thus, if a selection test has a reliability of .80 and a set of supervisory ratings has a reliability of .50, the theoretical maximum for the correlation between the two is

$$(.80)(.50) = .40 = .63.$$

Often there is not too much we can do about the reliability of the criterion variable except to get information about it, but we can take steps to assure reasonable reliability in our predictor tests.

The converse of the relationship we have just presented does not follow. A test may measure with the greatest precision and still have no validity for our purposes. For example, we can measure head size with a good deal of accuracy, but this measure is still practically useless as an indicator of intelligence. Validity is something beyond mere accuracy of measurement, and we consider it in Chapter 5.

Considerations of cost, convenience, and so on may also sometimes lead to a decision to use a less reliable test. We may accept a less reliable, 40-minute test in preference to a more reliable, 3-hour one, because 3 hours of testing time is too much of a burden in view of the purpose that the test is designed to serve.

FACTORS AFFECTING RELIABILITY

Within the limitations discussed in the preceding paragraphs, we prefer the more reliable test. There are several factors that must be taken into account, however, before we can fairly compare the reliability coefficients of two or more different tests:

1. Variability of the group on the trait the test measures
2. Level of the group on the trait the test measures
3. Length of the test
4. Operations used for estimating the reliability

Variability of the Group

The reliability coefficient indicates how consistently a test places each individual relative to others in the group. When there is little shifting from test to retest or from Form A to Form B, the reliability coefficient is high. But the extent to which individuals will switch places depends on how similar they are. It does not take very accurate testing to differentiate the reading ability of second graders from that of seventh graders. But to place each second grader accurately within a second-grade class is much more demanding.

If the scores of children from several different grades are pooled together, we may expect a much higher reliability coefficient. For example, the manual for the Otis Quick-Scoring Mental Ability Test—Beta once reported alternate-form reliabilities for single grade groups that ranged from .65 to .87, with an average value of .78. But for a pooling of the complete range of grades (4–9), the reliability coefficient was reported as .96. These data are all for the same testing with the same test. They are the same set of scores, just grouped differently. They reflect the same precision. Yet the coefficient for the combined groups is strikingly higher simply as a function of the greater range of individual differences in the combined group.

In evaluating the reported reliability coefficient, we must take into account the range of ability of the group tested. A reliability coefficient based on a combination of age or grade groups must usually be discounted. But, even in less extreme cases, we must still take into account variability of the group on the trait. Reliability coefficients for age groups will tend to be somewhat higher than for grade groups, because a group of children of the same age will usually contain a greater spread of talent than will the students in a single grade. A sample made up of children from a wide range of socioeconomic levels will tend to yield higher reliability coefficients than a very homogeneous sample. In comparing different tests, we must take account of the type of sample on which the reliability data were based, insofar as this can be determined from the reported facts, and judge more critically the test whose estimated reliability is based on data from a more heterogeneous group.

Level of the Group on the Trait

Precision of measurement of a test may be related to the ability level of the people being measured; however, no simple rule can be formulated for stating the nature of this relationship. The nature of the relationship depends on the way the test was built. For those people for whom the test is very hard, such that they are doing a large amount of guessing, accuracy is likely to be low. At the other extreme, if the test is very easy for the group, such that all of them can do most of the items very easily, that test may be expected to be ineffective in discriminating among the group members. When most of the items are easy for the group being tested, it is as if the test were shortened, because all differentiation is based on just those harder items that some can do and some cannot. This factor of most of the pupils getting extreme scores is a particular concern in mastery testing, which is given special consideration in this chapter under Reliability of Criterion-Referenced Tests.

Also, the test may vary in accuracy at different intermediate difficulty levels. The meticulous test constructor will report the standard error of measurement for the test at different score levels. When separate values of the standard error of measurement are reported in the manual, they provide a basis for evaluating the precision of the test for different types of groups and permit a more appropriate estimate of the accuracy of a particular individual's score. Each individual's score can be interpreted in

Table 4.3
Iowa Tests of Basic Skills Standard Error
of Measurement for the Vocabulary Test

Grade Equivalent Interval	Standard Error of Measurement in Grade Equivalent Units		
	Grade 4	Grade 6	Grade 8
20–29	5.4		
30–39	3.8		
40–49	3.1	9.0	
50–59	3.6	6.3	10.1
60–69	4.0	4.5	8.1
70–79	4.9	3.8	6.8
80–89		5.3	5.9
90–99		7.6	5.5
100–109			5.3
110–119			5.7
120–129			6.1
Total distribution	4.5	5.5	6.6

relation to the standard error of measurement for scores of that level. For example, the Iowa Tests of Basic Skills—Form G/H, which reports scores in grade equivalents, reported the standard error of measurement at different score intervals for the vocabulary test shown in Table 4.3.

This test measures somewhat more accurately those pupils who score near the center of the distribution than those who succeed with only a few items or with almost all. The test authors produced this result intentionally by including many items of moderate difficulty, which discriminate degrees of ability in the middle range, and relatively few very hard or very easy items. In effect, a longer test is operating for pupils in the middle range rather than at the extremes, and the result is a more accurate measurement of this large, middle group.

Length of the Test

As we saw earlier in discussing the split-half reliability coefficient, test reliability depends on the length of the test. If we can assume that the quality of the test items, the traits measured by those items, and the nature of the examinees remain the same, then the relationship of reliability to length can be expressed by the following equation:

$$r_{kk} = \frac{kr_{tt}}{1 + (k - 1) \, r_{tt}} \qquad (4.5)$$

where r_{kk} is the reliability of the test k times as long as the original test,
    r_{tt} is the reliability of the original test, and
    k is the factor by which the length of the test is changed.

This is a more general form of Equation 4.3.

Suppose we have a spelling test made up of 20 items that has a reliability of .50. We want to know how reliable the test will be if it is lengthened to contain 100 items comparable to the original 20. The answer is

$$r_{nn} = \frac{5(.50)}{1 + 4(.50)} = 2.5/3.0 = .83$$

As the length of the test is increased, the chance errors of measurement more or less cancel out, the score comes to depend more and more completely on the characteristics of the person being measured, and a more accurate appraisal of the individual is obtained.

Of course, how much we can lengthen a test is limited by a number of practical considerations. It is limited by the amount of time available for testing, by factors of fatigue and boredom on the part of examinees, and is sometimes limited by our inability to construct more equally good test items. But within these limits, reliability can be increased as needed by lengthening the test, subject only to the constraint that each item measures with some reliability other than zero.

We should note, however, that there is a point of diminishing returns in lengthening a test. When the reliability is already moderately high, it takes a considerable increase in test length to accomplish a modest increase in reliability. Quintupling the length of our 20-item spelling test would yield a substantial increase in its reliability (from .50 to .83). But, doubling the length again to 200 items would produce only a modest increase, from .83 to .91. Adding 200 more items would bring the reliability to .95, a rise that is hardly worth the increase in testing time.

One special type of lengthening is represented by increasing the number of raters who rate a person or a product the person has produced. To the extent that the unreliability of an assessment results from the inconsistency with which a sample of behavior is judged, this source of unreliability can usually be reduced by increasing the number of judges, or raters. If several raters are available who have equal competence with the materials to be rated, or equal familiarity with the ratee if the ratings are of a person, then a pooling of their ratings will produce a composite that is more reliable; the increase to be expected is described approximately by Equation 4.5. For example, if a typical pair of judges evaluating samples of writing show a correlation of .40, then the pooled ratings of three judges could be expected to correlate with three others, as follows:

$$\frac{3(.40)}{1 + 2(.40)} = 1.2/1.8 = .67$$

It is also possible to estimate the loss in reliability that would occur if a measurement procedure is shortened. Suppose we have a 100-item spelling test that has a reliability of .90, and we wish to estimate the reliability of a 40-item test made up of a sample of items from the longer test. The length of the new test is $40/100 = .40$ times the length of the original one, so our estimate of the reliability of the shorter test is

$$r_{kk} = \frac{.40(.90)}{1 + (.40 - 1.00)\,(.90)} = \frac{.36}{1 + (-.60)(.90)} = .36/.46 = .78$$

This procedure is quite useful for judging whether the shortened test would have sufficient reliability for our purposes.

Operations Used for Estimating the Reliability

How high a value will be obtained for the reliability coefficient depends also on which of the several sets of experimental operations is used to estimate the reliability. We saw in Table 4.1 that the different procedures treat different sources of variation in different ways and that it is only the use of parallel forms of a test with a period intervening that includes all four possible sources of instability as "error." That is, this procedure of estimating reliability represents a more exacting definition of the test's ability to reproduce the same score. The individual must then show consistency both from one sample of tasks to another and from one day to another. In Table 4.4, we have gathered a few examples that show reliability coefficients for the same test when the coefficients have been computed by different procedures and with different time intervals.

The procedures compared in Table 4.4 are test-retest correlations with an interval of 8, 24, or 48 months, correlations between equivalent forms with a very short interval, and KR-20 internal consistency reliabilities. Note that the test-retest correlation is as low as, or lower than, the other coefficients in every case and is lower for longer intervals than for shorter ones. The differences between the procedures vary, but in every case, it is necessary to discount the internal consistency estimate. Had the alternate forms of these tests been administered with an interval of 8 months, we would expect the correlations between different forms of the test on different occasions to be lower than the test-retest coefficients.

Practical versus Theoretical Reliability

The APA Standards require test publishers to report reliability and standard error of measurement information for tests offered for public use. Because the potential users of tests will examine the reliability evidence presented by the publisher closely, it is to the publisher's advantage to report the highest values possible. We have reviewed several factors that can influence the apparent reliability of a test, the most potent of which in most cases will be group variability and test length. An additional source of

Table 4.4

Comparison of Reliability Coefficients Obtained from Test-Retest
and Kuder-Richardson Formula 20 (KR-20) and Equivalent Forms

Test	Test-Retest (Months)			KR-20	Equivalent Forms[b]
	8	24[a]	48[a]		
Cognitive Abilities Test, Level C					
Verbal	.91	.85	.83	.93	
Quantitative	.87	.82	.79	.91	
Nonverbal	.86	.75	.73	.93	
Iowa Tests of Basic Skills, Grade 5					
Mathematics composite	.85	.84	.64	.94	.88
Language composite	.88	.89	.75	.96	.91
Gates-MacGintie Reading Test, Survey D					
Vocabulary, Grade 4	.87			.91	.89
Comprehension, Grade 4	.82			.91	.82

[a]24- and 48-month retests were not available for the Gates-MacGintie Reading Test.

[b]Equivalent forms correlations were not available for the Cognitive Abilities Test.

error variance, and hence unreliability, in test scores is examiner/scorer inconsistency. For machine-scored tests this source is limited to errors in test administration and should be essentially zero, but for essay tests, product ratings, and many of the assessments made in clinical and educational practice, the potential for errors from this source is very real.

The reliability of a test score depends on the context in which the particular measurement was made. If the conditions that obtain in test use are different from those during standardization, the reliability of the scores will be different. For example, a test publisher may base estimates of the reliability of a test on test protocols that have been scored by two or more carefully trained raters who are also monitored for the consistency of their scoring, thus eliminating most scorer variability. This was the case for the scoring of the Wechsler Intelligence Scale for Children, Third Edition (Wechsler, 1991). Reliability estimates obtained under these conditions approximate the maximum or theoretical reliability of the test. When the test is used in practice, the real or practical reliability of the scores will be lower than that estimated during standardization to an unknown degree, because practitioners may not be as highly trained and certainly are not subject to the same level of scoring verification. Kaufman (1990), for example, documents the high number of scoring errors made, even by experienced clinicians, in administering and scoring the Wechsler scales. Consequently, the standard error of measurement will be higher when the test is used "in the field." There is no single value that represents the correct reliability of a test. The most appropriate estimate depends on how the scores will be obtained and used.

When estimating the reliability of a test, the design for data collection should allow for all sources of error variation that are likely to occur in the application of the test to be present in the reliability study. Only then can the test user know how much confidence to place in the test scores.

MINIMUM LEVEL OF RELIABILITY

Obviously, other things being equal, the more reliable a measuring procedure, the better satisfied we are with it. A question that is often raised is, what is the *minimum* reliability that is acceptable? If we *must* make some decision or take some course of action with respect to an individual, we will do so in terms of the best information we have—however unreliable it may be—provided only that the reliability is better than zero, in which case we have *no* information. (Of course here, as always, the crucial consideration is the validity of the measure.) The appraisal of any new procedure must always be in terms of other procedures with which it is in competition. Thus, a high school mathematics test with a reliability coefficient of .80 would look relatively unattractive if tests with reliabilities of .85 or .90 were readily available at similar cost. On the other hand, a procedure for judging "leadership" that had a reliability of no more than .60 might look very attractive if the alternative was a set of ratings having a reliability of .45 or .50.

Although we cannot set an absolute minimum for the reliability of a measurement procedure, we can indicate the level of reliability that is required to enable us to achieve specified levels of accuracy in describing an individual or a group. Suppose that we have given a test to two individuals and that Individual A fell at the 75th percentile of the group while Individual B fell at the 50th percentile. What is the probability that Individual B would surpass Individual A if they were tested again? In Table 4.5, the probability of such a reversal is shown for different values of the reliability of the test. Thus, where the reliability is zero, there is exactly a 50-50 chance that the order of the two individuals will be reversed because both measurements represent completely random error. When the reliability is .50, the probability of a reversal still is more than 1 in 3. For a correlation of .90, there remains 1 chance in 12 that we will get a reversal on repetition of the testing. To have 4 chances in 5 that our difference will stay in the same direction, we must have a reliability of .80.

Table 4.5 also shows the percentage of expected reversals of two *groups*—groups of 25 and of 100. For example, if in Class A of 25 pupils, the average fell at the 75th percentile of some larger reference group and in Class B, also of 25 pupils, the average fell at the 50th percentile, what is the probability that we would get a reversal if the testing were repeated? Here, we still have a 50-50 chance in the extreme case in which the reliability coefficient is zero. However, the security of our conclusion increases much more rapidly with groups than with individuals, as the reliability of the test becomes greater. With a reliability of .50, the probability of a reversal is already down to 1 in 20 for groups of 25, to 1 in 2,500 for groups of 100. With a correlation of .70, the probability of a reversal is only 1 in 1,000 for groups of 25 and is vanishingly small for groups of 100. Thus, a test with relatively low reliability will permit us to make useful studies of and draw dependable conclusions about groups,

Table 4.5

Percentage of Times Direction of Difference Will be Reversed in Subsequent Testing for Scores Falling at 75th and 50th Percentiles

Reliability Coefficient	Percentage of Reversals with Repeated Testings		
	Scores of Single Individuals	Means of Groups of 25	Means of Groups of 100
.00	50.0	50.0	50.0
.40	40.3	10.9	.7
.50	36.8	4.6	.04
.60	32.5	1.2	
.70	27.1	.1	
.80	19.7		
.90	8.7		
.95	2.2		
.98	.05		

especially groups of substantial size, but quite high reliability is required if we are to speak with confidence about individuals.

RELIABILITY OF DIFFERENCE SCORES

Sometimes we are less interested in single scores than we are in the relationship between scores taken in pairs. We may be concerned with the differences between scholastic aptitude and reading achievement in a group of pupils, or we may wish to study gains in reading from an initial test given in October to a later test given the following May. In these illustrations, the significant fact for each individual is the difference between two scores. We must inquire how reliable our estimates of these differences are, knowing the characteristics of the two component tests.

It is unfortunately true that the appraisal of the difference between two test scores usually has substantially lower reliability than the reliabilities of the two tests taken separately. This lower reliability is due to two factors: (1) the errors of measurement in both separate tests accumulate in the difference score, and (2) whatever is common to the two tests is canceled out in the difference score. We can illustrate the situation by a diagram such as that in Figure 4.2.

Each bar in Figure 4.2 represents performance (more precisely, variance in performance) on a test, broken up into a number of parts to represent the factors producing this performance. The first bar represents a reading test, and the second, a scholastic aptitude test. Notice that we have divided reading performance into three parts. One part, labeled "common factors," is a complex of general intellectual abilities and test-taking skills that operate in both the reading and the scholastic aptitude tests. We may view this component as what causes the correlation between the two tests. Another part, labeled "specific reading factors," includes abilities that appear only in the reading test. These are reliable individual differences, but

Figure 4.2
Nature of a difference
score.

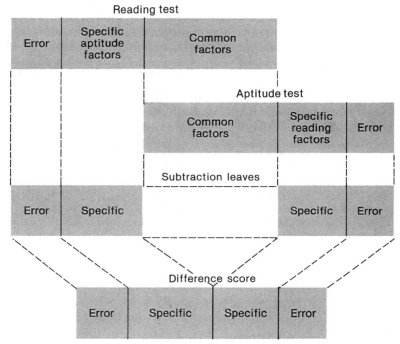

due to factors not shared with the scholastic aptitude test. The third part, labeled "error," is the chance error of measurement that is represented by the standard error of measurement for the test. Three similar parts are indicated for the aptitude test. The reliability of each test reflects the combination of its common and specific factors.

Now examine the third bar (and the fourth, which shows the third with blank space removed). The third and fourth bars represent the difference score—that is, the reading score expressed in some type of standard score units minus the aptitude test score expressed in those same units. In this bar, the common factors have disappeared. They appeared with a positive sign in the reading test and a negative sign (due to the subtraction) in the aptitude test and thus canceled out. Only the specific factors and errors of measurement remain. The specific factors are the factors that determine the difference score. The errors of measurement make up a much larger proportion of this fourth bar, showing that the reliability of the difference scores will be lower than that of either of the original tests. For example, if error made up 25% of each test, and specific factors made up another 25% of each test, the difference score would contain 50% error and 50% specific factors. Thus, the difference score would be much less reliable than either of the original tests. If the two tests measured exactly the same abilities so that there were only common and error factors, only the errors of measurement would remain in the difference scores, and these scores would have exactly zero reliability. This problem is particularly acute in attempts to assess educational gains by retesting with the same or a parallel test, because in such a case the common factors are at a maximum.

The reliability of the difference between two measures expressed in standard scores can be obtained by the following fairly simple equation:

$$r_{diff} = \frac{1/2(r_{AA} + r_{BB}) - r_{AB}}{1 - r_{AB}}$$

where r_{diff} is the reliability of the difference score,
   r_{AA} is the reliability of Test A,
   r_{BB} is the reliability of Test B, and
   r_{AB} is the correlation between the two tests.

Thus, if the reliability of Test A is 0.80, the reliability of Test B is 0.90, and the correlation between Tests A and B is 0.60, for the reliability of the difference score, we get

$$r_{diff} = \frac{1/2(0.80 + 0.90) - 0.60}{1 - 0.60} = 0.25/0.40 = 0.62$$

In Table 4.6, the value of r_{diff} is shown for various combinations of values of $1/2(r_{AA} + r_{BB})$ and r_{AB}. If the average of the two reliabilities is 0.80, the reliability of the difference score is 0.80 when the two tests are exactly uncorrelated and is zero when the correlation is 0.80. It is clear that as soon as the correlation between the two tests begins to approach the average of their separate reliabilities, the reliability of the difference score drops very rapidly.

The low reliability that tends to characterize difference scores is something to which the psychologist and educator must always be sensitive. Lower reliability becomes a problem whenever we wish to use test patterns for diagnosis. Thus, the judgment that Herbert's reading lags behind his scholastic aptitude is a judgment that must be made a good deal more tentatively than a judgment about either his

Table 4.6
Reliability of a Difference Score

Correlation Between Two Tests (r_{AB})	Average of Reliability of Two Tests ($1/2(r_{AA} + r_{BB})$)					
	.50	.60	.70	.80	.90	.95
.00	.50	.60	.70	.80	.90	.95
.40	.17	.33	.50	.67	.83	.92
.50	.00	.20	.40	.60	.80	.90
.60		.00	.25	.50	.75	.88
.70			.00	.33	.67	.83
.80				.00	.50	.75
.90					.00	.50
.95						.00

scholastic aptitude or his reading taken separately. The conclusion that Mary has improved in reading more than Jane must be a more tentative judgment than that Mary is now a better (or poorer) reader than Jane. Any difference needs to be interpreted in the light of the standard error of measurement of that difference, which will be about 1.4 times as large as the average of the two standard errors of measurement of the two tests. This caveat applies with particular force to the practice of assigning grades to students based on an assessment of their improvement or growth.

Many differences will be found to be quite small relative to their standard error and, consequently, quite undependable. This caution especially applies for the interpretation of profiles and of gain scores. (Recent work on patterns of growth suggests that some of the problems with measures of change may be overcome by using measurements at more than two points in time. However, the problems with interpreting differences between scores in a profile remain. See Willett (1988) for a review. Also, Kaufman (1990) shows how the distribution of difference scores in a standardization sample can be used to improve the interpretation of profiles.)

EFFECTS OF UNRELIABILITY ON CORRELATION BETWEEN VARIABLES

There is one further effect of unreliability that merits brief attention here because it affects our interpretation of the correlations between different measures. Let us think of a measure of reading comprehension and one of mathematical reasoning. In each of these tests, the individual differences in score result in part from true differences in ability and in part from chance errors of measurement. But, if the errors of measurement are really chance matters, the reading test errors and the mathematical reasoning test errors are uncorrelated. These uncorrelated errors are part of the total or observed score for each individual, which means that they must dilute any correlation that exists between the true scores on reading and the true scores on mathematical reasoning. That is, because the observed scores are a combination of true scores and errors of measurement, the correlation between observed scores is a compromise between the correlation that exists between the underlying true scores and the zero correlation between the errors of measurement on the two tests.

We would often like to extract an estimate of the correlation between the underlying true scores from our obtained data to understand better how much the functions involved have in common. Fortunately, we can do this quite simply. The process is called correcting for attenuation due to unreliability. The estimate is provided by the following equation:

$$r_{1T,2T} = \frac{r_{12}}{r_{11}r_{22}}$$

where $r_{1T,2T}$ is the correlation of the underlying true scores,

r_{12} is the correlation of the observed scores, and

r_{11} and r_{22} are the reliabilities of the two measures.

If, for example, the correlation between the reading test and the mathematical reasoning test was found to be .56 and the reliabilities of the two tests were .71 and .90, respectively, we would have

$$r_{1T,2T} = .56/ (.71)(.90) = .70$$

Our estimate of the correlation between error-free measures of mathematics and reading would be .70. In thinking of these two *functions,* it would be appropriate to think in terms of the correlation as .70 rather than .56, though the *tests* correlate only .56.

RELIABILITY OF CRITERION-REFERENCED TESTS

Our discussion of reliability up to this point has assumed that our tests are continuous variables that have no upper limit, or "ceiling," which is usually the case for tests that are developed for use within a normative frame of reference. We have excluded the idea that a large number of examinees would achieve perfect or near-perfect scores. However, criterion-referenced tests are generally designed to be sharply focused on a limited range of behavior that is being taught in a program of instruction. For tests of this type, it is reasonable to expect that a substantial proportion of the examinees may get perfect or near-perfect scores on the test. Traditional measures of reliability do not work well for tests of this type because there is little variability in the set of scores and, as we saw earlier, this lack of variability tends to yield a low reliability coefficient.

Criterion-referenced test scores are interpreted in three basic ways. The first of these is mastery/nonmastery of the particular skill or body of knowledge being tested. Individuals are classified as masters (as having achieved the requisite level of performance with this material) if their test scores surpass a preset cutoff, and as nonmasters if their scores fail to reach this level. There is no middle ground, and all masters are considered equal.

Second, criterion-referenced test scores are interpreted as reflecting the degree of mastery. In this approach, each person's score is again compared to a preset standard, but people whose scores greatly exceed the cutoff are considered to be more complete masters than are those who just barely surpass the cutoff. Likewise, people whose scores fall far short of the cutoff are considered farther from mastery than are those who just missed the cutoff.

The third interpretation of criterion-referenced tests is based on the idea that the test items sample a domain of content. The examinee's score on the test is seen as an estimate of the *domain score,* the score he or she would have gotten on a test that included every item in the domain. The question becomes one of how accurately the domain score is estimated.

There has been considerable progress in the estimation of reliability for criterion-referenced tests. Although somewhat different approaches are required for each interpretation of a criterion-referenced test, all approaches share the notion of consistency of information. We will examine in detail the issue of consistency as it applies to mastery/nonmastery decisions and then mention briefly some of the issues for the other interpretations. Systematic reviews of the available methods for all three interpretations are provided by Berk (1984), Brennan (1984), and Subkoviak (1984).

The mastery/nonmastery approach requires that examinees be classified into one of two categories. Reliability for this interpretation is assessed by evaluating the consistency with which classifications are made either by the same test administered on two occasions or by alternate forms of the test (there are also single-test methods analogous to KR-20). As an example, consider a test that was designed for use with foreign students studying English, to assess their mastery of certain specific English constructions. In one such test, Blatchford (1970) assessed mastery of each of 10 English constructions, using four items for each construction. Two forms of the test were developed and administered to groups of students with an interval of about 1 week between testings. Students were required to choose the construction that was correct English usage. Multiple-choice items illustrating two of the constructions are shown in Figure 4.3. Each item is followed by a table showing the percentage of students getting zero, one, two, three, or four items correct on each of the testings. For example, the entry in the top row and first column for Set 6 shows that 2% of the group got zero correct on Form A and four correct on Form B.

Let us look first at Set 6 in Figure 4.3. Note that 36% of the students got perfect scores of four on *both* testings and 21% got zero scores on *both* testings. For this 57% of the group, the little four-item test gave perfectly consistent and unequivocal information. One group appeared to have completely mastered the correct usage, and the other group appeared to be completely in the dark or to possess misinformation. The other 43% showed some inconsistency within a test or between the two tests. How shall we express this degree of inconsistency or unreliability?

The important thing to remember is that a test such as this is being used to decide whether each student has mastery of a specific skill. We might set a severe standard and accept only a perfect performance—four correct out of four—as indicating mastery. Or we might be willing to accept a more relaxed standard of three out of four as satisfactory performance, recognizing that lowered vigilance or some extraneous factor might have been responsible for a single error. Whichever standard is adopted, the question we ask is, how often would the decision have been reversed on the other testing? Or how often would we have switched from "pass" to "fail" or the reverse?

The results from Set 6 are shown here for the two standards.

	Severe Standard (All Four Correct) Form A			Lenient Standard (Three Out of Four Correct) Form A	
Form B	Fail	Pass	Form B	Fail	Pass
Pass	11	36	Pass	8	53
Fail	43	10	Fail	33	6

Figure 4.3
Two samples from a mastery test of English constructions. Asterisk indicates the correct answer. (Numbers in the table are percents.)

Set 6. The use of "but" after an "although" clause.
  (1) Because he was late, he still attended the meeting.
*(2) Although he was late, he still attended the meeting.
  (3) Although he was late, but he still attended the meeting.
  (4) Because he was late, but he still attended the meeting.

Number Correct—Form B	Number Correct—Form A					Total
	0	1	2	3	4	
4	2	1	2	6	36	47
3	1	1	1	4	7	14
2	1	1	1	1	1	5
1	3	1	1	1	1	7
0	21	3	1	1	1	27
Total	28	7	6	13	46	

Set 10. The use of "most" with plural nouns.
  (1) The most of the students must study three hours every night.
*(2) Most students must study three hours every night.
  (3) Most student must study three hours every night.
  (4) Most of student must study three hours every night.

Number Correct—Form B	Number Correct—Form A					Total
	0	1	2	3	4	
4	1	3	4	12	18	38
3	1	2	3	5	5	16
2	2	2	1	3	2	10
1	4	4	1	1	1	11
0	15	5	1	3	1	25
Total	23	16	10	24	27	

Using the severe standard, we would reach the same decision for both forms for 79% of students and opposite decisions for 21%. With the more relaxed standard, the corresponding percentages are 86% and 14%.

The decisions for Set 10 can be expressed in the same way.

	Severe Standard (All Four Correct) Form A		Lenient Standard (Three Out of Four Correct) Form A	
Form B	Fail	Pass	Form B	Fail	Pass
Pass	20	18	Pass	14	40
Fail	53	9	Fail	35	11

Clearly, the percentage of reversals is greater for Set 10 than for Set 6. There are 29% and 25% reversals by the severe and lenient standards, respectively. This set provides a less reliable basis for the central decision: Has the student mastered the skill?

For a test that is being used for the single "go-no go" decision of mastery versus nonmastery, the percentage of consistent decisions seems to be a reasonable index of reliability. Unfortunately, this index is a function of the characteristics of the group as well as of the test. If many students are close to the threshold of mastery—having learned a certain skill, but just barely having learned it—there are likely to be numerous reversals from one testing to another. If, on the other hand, there are many who have considerably overlearned the skill or many who have never learned it at all, reversals will be relatively infrequent. Also, if the consistency of the decisions is assessed during a period of active instruction in the skill, students may be changing from nonmasters to masters in the interval between administrations, giving the appearance of unreliable assessment. It will be important, therefore, to evaluate the reliability of a test that is intended for mastery decisions by using groups of students who have reached just about the same degree of assurance in their mastery of the skill as those with whom the test will eventually be used. It is also important to conduct the reliability study when active instruction is not taking place.

We now need some way to decide what percentage of consistent decisions represents a satisfactory test. At one extreme, with two choices (i.e., master or nonmaster), pure chance would produce agreement 50% of the time. If the test yields no more consistent results than flipping a coin, it is obviously worthless. At the other extreme, if there were 100% agreement between the two forms in the decision to which they led, the reliability of that decision is clearly perfect. It is the intermediate percentages, which almost always occur, that require evaluation. Are the agreements of 79%, 86%, 71%, and 75% that were found for the two four-item tests by two standards of mastery good, just tolerable, or unsatisfactory?

It is hard to give a general answer to the above question. The answer depends on the length of the test on the one hand, and on the seriousness and irreversibility of the decision on the other. The shorter the test, the more reversals we can expect. The less crucial the decision, the more reversals we can tolerate. Considering that the tests that we have analyzed were composed of only four items, consistencies ranging from 70% to 85% are probably as good as can be expected. If the test results were to be used merely to guide review and remedial instruction, this level of consistency might be quite tolerable because errors in the initial decision would usually be corrected in later testing.

The illustration that we have discussed used data from alternate test forms given about 1 week apart. Of course, it would be possible to subdivide a test and get two scores from a single testing. These scores could be tabulated to determine the frequency of reversals of the decision of mastery. However, it seems likely that with students who are just on the threshold of mastery, changes from one testing to another will be much more common than those from one subscore to another at a single point in time. Blatchford (1970) found median reliability coefficients for a four-item test at a single time to be .80, while the median correlation between forms given 1 week apart was only .61. Such a result suggests that two very short tests given on different days may provide a good deal more conservative, and probably a sounder, basis for a decision on mastery than a longer test at one time if the students are still in a period of instruction on the skill.

Methods for estimating the reliability of degree of mastery measurements, as well as methods for assessing the accuracy of estimates of domain scores, require a more complex statistical methodology than we can cover thoroughly in this book. Detailed reviews of available methods are given by Berk (1984) and Brennan (1984). We will, however, describe the logical processes that underlie these methods.

The basic feature of methods for estimating reliability in these cases is the use of *variance components*. As we noted in Chapter 2, variances are squares of standard deviations. (More accurately, they are what you have before you take the square root to get the standard deviation.) The size of the variance of any set of scores depends on how many sources of variability go into the scores. For example, the scores of a group of White, middle-class, 10-year-old girls from a farming community in Kansas could be expected to show a much smaller variance on a test measuring knowledge of the geography of the American Great Plains than would the scores from a group of the same size drawn at random from the general American population on a test of general American geography. The reason for the difference is that the scores on the test in the latter case might be affected by variation in racial or ethnic background (race, socioeconomic status, and geographic factors), gender, age, and the greater diversity of the test items themselves.

It is possible to estimate the effect of each of these factors (and many others that might be of interest) on the variance in a set of test scores by systematically controlling the other sources of variability. For example, the difference in reliability using the test-retest procedure and that obtained from a procedure with parallel forms provides a simple estimate of the variance that can be attributed to the sampling of items, because in the first case the items remain constant, and in the second they vary. The impact of gender, age, and many other variables can be estimated by comparing the variances of scores when these characteristics are held constant with the variances from groups where they vary.

The procedures for assessing the reliability of estimates of domain scores and of degree of mastery measures require variance components that reflect both the variability among all examinees across all items in the test and the inconsistency of each person's performance from item to item across the test. Different variance components are used, depending on which type of consistency is being assessed. The resulting ratios indicate the proportion of variance in test scores that can be attributed to different sources, some of which represent reliable aspects of performance. A detailed discussion of this issue and other advanced issues in reliability estimation is provided by Feldt and Brennan (1989).

SUMMARY

Reliability, or consistency, is a necessary property for any measurement procedure to have. The differences in individuals revealed by the measuring instrument should represent, to the greatest extent possible, real differences on the characteristic of interest. Because any measurement is made with some error, reliability may be viewed as the instrument's relative freedom from error.

There is not a single value that is the correct reliability for any instrument. The observed reliability is a function of the properties of the underlying trait, the test itself, the group being tested, and the situation in which the information about reliability is obtained. All of these factors must be considered when evaluating the reliability of a test.

How reliable a test must be depends on the purpose of the testing. If the decisions to be made from the test scores are relatively unmodifiable, we would want to be quite certain of the accuracy of our information and would require the highest possible reliability. If, on the other hand, the instrument is being used for short-range decisions that are easily changed, a considerably lower level of reliability may be satisfactory. Also, the intended use of the scores affects the type of reliability needed. If we are concerned with assessing current levels of performance, a reliability coefficient that reflects the internal consistency of the test or its short-term stability will yield the necessary information. By contrast, if the use for the scores involves forecasting future levels of achievement, a reliability index that shows the stability of those scores over an equivalent time span is needed. In either case, when we are concerned with describing the performance of individuals, the standard error of measurement derived from the appropriate design is the best index of the consistency we can expect for individual scores. The better test publishers provide several types of reliability information for their products so the user can make an informed decision.

QUESTIONS AND EXERCISES

1. Look at the evidence presented on reliability in the manuals of two or three tests. How adequate is the evidence? What are its shortcomings? For what types of test use is it appropriate? What sources of variability does each type of evidence permit?

2. List two situations in which the standard error of measurement would be needed as an index of stability of performance.

3. The publishers of Test X suggest that it can be used to assess current levels of achievement in reading and to predict reading achievement after an additional year of instruction. What

evidence of reliability should you expect the publisher to provide to support each test use?

4. The manual for Test T presents reliability data based on (1) retesting with the same test form 2 weeks later, (2) alpha coefficients, and (3) correlating Form A with Form B, the two forms having been taken 2 weeks apart. Which procedure would you expect to yield the lowest coefficient? Why? Which one should yield the most useful estimate of reliability? What additional information do you need to give an answer?

5. For each of the following situations, indicate whether the change would raise or lower the reliability:

   a. Reliability is determined for scores from all elementary grades combined, rather than within each grade.

   b. A test with 25 items is used in place of a 100-item test.

   c. The ratings of four judges are averaged, instead of using a single judge.

   d. Reliability is determined using Kuder-Richardson Formula 20 rather than correlating scores on equivalent forms.

6. A student has been given a Wechsler Intelligence Scale for Children four times during her school career, and her cumulative record shows the following global intelligence quotients: 98, 107, 101, and 95. What significance should be attached to these fluctuations in scores?

7. A school plans to give Form R of a reading test in September and Form S in May to study individual differences in improvement during the year. The reliability of each form of the test is known to be about .85 for a grade group. The correlation between the two forms on the two occasions turned out to be .80. How much confidence can be placed in individual differences in amount gained? What factors other than real differences in learning can account for individual differences in gain?

SUGGESTED READINGS

American Psychological Association, American Educational Research Association, & National Council on Measurement in Education. (1985). *Standards for educational and psychological testing*. Washington, DC: American Psychological Association.

Blixt, S. L., & Shama, D. B. (1986). An empirical investigation of the standard error of measurement at different ability levels. *Educational and Psychological Measurement, 45,* 545–550.

Brennan, R. L. (1984). Estimating the dependability of the scores. In R. A. Berk (Ed.), *A guide to criterion-referenced test construction* (pp. 292–334). Baltimore: Johns Hopkins University Press.

Feldt, L. S., & Brennan, R. L. (1989). Reliability. In R. L. Linn (Ed.), *Educational measurement* (3rd ed., pp. 105–146). New York: Macmillan.

Jarjoura, D. (1985). Tolerance intervals for true scores. *Journal of Educational Measurement, 10,* 1–17.

Kane, M. T., & Wilson, J. (1984). Errors of measurement and standard setting in mastery testing. *Applied Psychological Measurement, 4,* 107–115.

Lord, F. M. (1984). Standard errors of measurement at different score levels. *Journal of Educational Measurement, 21,* 239–243.

Lord, F. M., & Novick, M. R. (1968). *Statistical theories of mental test scores.* Reading, MA: Addison-Wesley.

Rogosa, D. R., & Willett, J. B. (1983). Demonstrating the reliability of the difference score in the measurement of change. *Journal of Educational Measurement, 20,* 335–343.

Thorndike, R. L., & Thorndike, R. M. (1994). Reliability in educational and psychological measurement. In T. Husen & N. Postlethwaite (Eds.), *International encyclopedia of education,* (2nd ed., pp. 4981–4995). New York: Pergamon Press.

Thorndike, R. M. (1987). Reliability. In B. Bolton (Ed.), *Handbook of measurement and evaluation in rehabilitation* (2nd ed., pp. 21–36). Baltimore: Paul Brookes.

CHAPTER 5

Qualities Desired in Any Measurement Procedure: Validity

INTRODUCTION

Although reliability is a necessary feature that a test must have to be useful for decision making, it is not the most important characteristic. A test may be highly reliable and still bear no relationship to the property we wish to assess. Who, for example, would suggest that head circumference, which can be measured quite reliably, provides a measure of reading achievement? In education and psychology, as elsewhere, the foremost question to be asked with respect to any measurement procedure is, how *valid* is it? When we ask this question, we are inquiring whether the test measures what we want to measure, all of what we want to measure, and nothing but what we want to measure. In words from the *Standards for Educational and Psychological Testing,* "the concept [of validity] refers to the appropriateness, meaningfulness, and usefulness of the specific inferences made from test scores. Test validation is the process of accumulating evidence to support such inferences" (American Psychological Association, American Educational Research Association, & National Council on Measurement in Education, 1985, p. 9). Thus, a test does not have validity in any absolute sense. Rather, the test scores are valid for some uses and not valid for others.

When we place a steel tape measure on the top of a desk to determine its length, we have no doubt that the tape does in fact measure the length of the desk and that it will give information directly related to our decision, which may be to decide whether we can put the desk between two windows in our room. Long-time experience with this type of measuring instrument has confirmed beyond a shadow of a doubt its validity as a tool for measuring length.

Now suppose we give a test of reading achievement to a group of children. This test requires the children to select certain answers to a series of questions based on reading passages and to make pencil marks on an answer sheet to indicate their choices. We count the number of pencil marks made in the predetermined correct places and give the children as scores the number of correct answers each one marked. We call these scores measures of their reading comprehension. But a score by itself is not the comprehension. It is the *record* of a *sample* of behavior taken at a particular point in time. Any judgment regarding comprehension is an inference from this number of allegedly correct answers. The validity of the score interpretation is not self-evident but is something we must establish on the basis of adequate evidence.

Consider also the typical personality inventory that endeavors to provide an appraisal of "emotional adjustment." In this type of inventory, the respondents mark a series of statements about feelings or behaviors as being characteristic of or not characteristic of themselves. On the basis of this type of procedure, certain responses are keyed as indicative of emotional maladjustment. A score is obtained by seeing how many of these responses an individual selects. But making certain marks on a piece of paper is a good many steps removed from actually exhibiting emotional disturbance. We must find some way of establishing the extent to which the performance on the test actually corresponds to the quality of the behavior in which we are directly interested. Our problem is to determine the validity of such a measurement procedure.

These three instances of measurement, the steel tape, the reading comprehension test, and the personality inventory, all require evidence that the numbers they produce are useful for their intended purpose. The measurements differ from each other in two important respects: the length of the chain of inference between the measuring act and the interpretation of the resulting number, and the social consequences that may follow from the measurement. With the steel tape the chain of inference is short and the social consequences generally are negligible (although not so if the tape is being used to lay out a site for a toxic waste dump). With the psychological measurements both issues are more problematic. The relationship between reading comprehension test items and an inference about a person's level on the trait requires a careful consideration of the content of the behavior domain, but this analysis is reasonably direct. Likewise, the use that will be made of the test score usually will relate fairly directly and in a socially positive way to the education of the child. But if the test is used inappropriately, as, for example, with a child for whom English is a second language, then the score, although accurately representing the child's reading comprehension *in English,* may result in a decision that has adverse consequences for the child. The consequences of the decision are part of the use that is made of the test score and, therefore, are inextricably bound up with the issue of validity. Examples of this type of test misuse are becoming more rare, but test users must always be aware of the consequences that decisions will have. Of course, with the personality inventory the chain of inference is longer and the consequences for the test taker can also be adverse.

Types of Evidence of Validity

A test may be thought of as corresponding to some aspect of human behavior in any one of three senses. The terms that have been adopted to designate these senses are (1) content-related validity, (2) criterion-related validity, and (3) construct-related validity. We will examine each of these senses so that we may understand clearly what is involved in each case and for what kinds of tests and testing situations each is relevant.

CONTENT-RELATED EVIDENCE OF VALIDITY

Consider a test that has been designed to measure competence in using the English language. How can we tell whether the test does in fact measure that achievement? First, we must reach some agreement as to the skills and knowledge that comprise correct and effective use of English. If the test is to be used to appraise the effects of classroom instruction, we must specify the subset of skills and knowledge that have been the objectives of that instruction. Then we must examine the test to see what skills, knowledge, and understanding it calls for. Finally, we must match the analysis of *test content* with the analysis of *course content* and instructional objectives to see how well the former represents the latter. To the extent that our objectives, which we have accepted as goals for our course, are represented in the test, the test appears valid for use in our school.

Because the analysis is essentially a rational and judgmental one, this process has sometimes been spoken of as *rational* or *logical validity.* The term *content validity* has also been used widely because the analysis is largely in terms of test content. However, we should not think of content too narrowly because we may be interested in *process* as much as in simple content. In the field of English expression, for example, we might be concerned on the one hand with such content elements as the rules and principles for capitalization, use of commas, or spelling words with *ei* and *ie* combinations. But we might also be interested in such process skills as arranging ideas in a logical order, writing sentences that present a single unified thought, or picking the most appropriate word to convey the desired meaning. In a sense, *content* is what the pupil works with; *process* is what the pupil does with the content. The term content-related validity refers to an assessment of whether a test contains appropriate content *and* requires that appropriate processes be applied to that content.

To either assess the content validity of an existing test or construct a test that measures a particular set of contents and processes requires that we specify the contents and processes to be measured explicitly. This explicit statement of what a test is intended to measure is called a *test blueprint*. The correspondence between the test blueprint and the definition of the trait to be measured *is* the content validity of the test.

Preparing a Test Blueprint

A *test blueprint* (also called a table of specifications for the test) is an explicit plan that guides test construction. The basic components of a test blueprint are the specifications of cognitive processes and the description of content to be covered by the test. These two dimensions need to be matched to show which process relates to each segment of content and to provide a framework for the development of the test. It is useful for the test constructor, in planning the evaluation of a unit, to make a test blueprint that includes not only the cognitive processes and the content but also the method or methods to be used in evaluating student progress toward achieving each objective. The illustrations we use in this section are couched in terms of guidelines that an individual teacher or test constructor would use to produce a good achievement test for local use. Standardized achievement test construction applies the same procedures, but to more broadly specified curricula. When evaluating a test for content validity you would use the same steps of domain definition, but the validity question would relate to whether the test matches your domain rather than to serve as a guide for item writing. In Chapter 15 we cover the principles of item writing and analysis that experts use to produce content-valid measures of educational achievement.

A blueprint for an examination in health for an eighth-grade class is provided in Table 5.1. The test will use a short-answer, or objective, format and contain 60 items. This test is the type for which a formal blueprint is most useful, but the kind of thinking that goes into formulating a blueprint is useful even in constructing an essay test with five or six items. The issues that are involved in the decision about the type of test item to use are considered later.

The cognitive processes to be assessed by the test are listed in the left-hand column of the table. The titles of each of three content units have been entered as column headings. Each box, or cell, under the unit headings contains content entries that relate to the cognitive process on the same line with the cell. The complete blueprint specifies the content deemed important and how it will be measured. Most standardized achievement tests would cover a broader array of content than is shown here, but content definition and test construction would proceed in the same way.

In some states, test blueprints for most subject matter and courses are prepared centrally. These serve as guides for commercial test producers. Preparing a two-dimensional outline for a test is an exacting and time-consuming task, but once such a complete blueprint has been prepared, it can be used until the curriculum or teaching emphasis is changed.

An examination of the blueprint should make it clear to you that tests are just samples of student behavior—for four reasons.

1. Only those objectives suitable for appraisal with a paper-and-pencil test are included in the blueprint. (Procedures for assessing other objectives are discussed briefly in Chapter 10.)
2. The entries in the cells under each area of content are examples that illustrate, but do not exhaust, the total content.
3. There are an unlimited number of items that could be written for the material that is included in the blueprint.
4. The time available for testing is limited, and, therefore, the test can include only a small sample from the domain of all possible items.

If a test is to reflect local goals, you must carefully choose the items to include on your tests or select carefully a test that measures those goals. The following four issues should guide your construction or evaluation of the test.

1. What emphasis should each of the content areas and cognitive processes receive on the test? In other words, what proportion of all the items on the test should be written for each content area and for each cognitive process within each content area?
2. What type or types of items should be included on the test?
3. How long should the test be? How many questions or items should the total test contain? How many items should be written for each cell of the blueprint?
4. How difficult should the items be?

Relative Emphasis of Content Areas and Process Objectives. The proportion of test items allocated to each content area and to each cognitive process should correspond to the instructional emphasis and importance of the topic. The decision-making process involved is subjective, but the test user should ensure that the test has maintained an appropriate balance in emphasis for both content and mental processes. Allocating a different number of items to each topic and cognitive process is the most obvious way of weighting topics and processes on the test.

The initial weighting of the content areas and cognitive processes requires the assignment of percentages to each content area and cognitive process such that the total for both is 100%. In the blueprint shown in Table 5.1, the test maker decided that Topic A, nutrition, should receive a weight of 40%; Topic B, communicable diseases,

Table 5.1

Blueprint for Final Examination in Health in Eighth Grade

Process Objectives	Content Areas
	A. Nutrition, 40%
1. Recognizes terms and vocabulary 20%	Nutrients Incomplete protein Vitamins Complete protein Enzymes Amino acids Metabolism Glycogen Oxidation Carbohydrate 4 or 5 items
2. Identifies specific facts 30%	Nutrients essential to health Good sources of food nutrients Parts of digestive system Process of digestion of each nutrient Sources of information about foods and nutrition 7 or 8 items
3. Identifies principles, concepts, and generalizations 30%	Bases of well-balanced diet Enzyme reactions Transfer of materials between cells Cell metabolism Functions of nutrients in body 7 or 8 items
4. Evaluates health information and advertisements 10%	Analyzes food and diet advertisements Interprets labels on foods Identifies good sources of information about foods and diets 2 or 3 items
5. Applies principles and generalizations to novel situations 10%	Identifies well-balanced diet Computes calories needed for weight-gaining or weight-losing diet Predicts consequences of changes in enzymes on digestive system Identifies services and protection provided by the Federal Food and Drug Act 2 or 3 items
No. of items	24
Total time for test—90 minutes	

Content Areas		No. of Items
B. Communicable Diseases, 40%	C. Noncommunicable Diseases, 20%	
Immunity Epidemic Virus Pathogenic Carrier Endemic Antibodies Protozoa Incubation period 4 or 5 items	Goiter Deficiency diseases Diabetes Cardiovascular diseases Caries 2 or 3 items	12
Common communicable diseases Incidence of various diseases Methods of spreading disease Types of immunization Symptoms of common communicable diseases 7 or 8 items	Specific diseases caused by lack of vitamins Specific disorders resulting from imbalance in hormones Incidence of noncommunicable diseases Common noncommunicable diseases of adolescents and young adults 3 or 4 items	18
Basic principles underlying control of disease Actions of antibiotics Body defenses against disease Immune reactions in body 7 or 8 items	Pressure within cardiovascular system Control of diabetes Inheritance of abnormal conditions Abnormal growth of cells 3 or 4 items	18
Distinguishes between adequate and inadequate evidence for medicines Identifies misleading advertisements for medications 2 or 3 items	Identifies errors or misleading information in health material Identifies appropriate source of information for health problems 1 or 2 items	6
Recognizes conditions likely to result in increase of communicable disease Identifies appropriate methods for sterilizing objects Gives appropriate reasons for regulations, processes, or treatments 2 or 3 items	Predicts consequences of changes in secretion of certain hormones Predicts probability of inheriting abnormal conditions 1 or 2 items	6
24	12	60
	Total number of items—60	

should also receive a weight of 40%; and Topic C, noncommunicable diseases, should receive a weight of 20%. If the curriculum guide calls for five weeks of instructional time to be spent on Topic A and also on Topic B, and only 2 weeks on Topic C, the allocation of weights corresponds roughly to teaching time.

For the cognitive processes in Table 5.1, the test maker decided that 20% of all the items should be allocated to Process 1, 30% each to Processes 2 and 3, and 10% each to Processes 4 and 5. These allocations imply that the curriculum has emphasized remembering or recalling terms, specific facts, principles, concepts, and generalizations. In other words, the course was primarily focused on increasing the students' fund of knowledge, with less attention given to improving their ability to use the information in novel situations. If the allocation of items to the cognitive processes truly reflects the emphasis in the curriculum, then the allocation is appropriate. We might take issue with the emphasis, but, given that emphasis, we cannot say that the allocation of test items is inappropriate.

Types of Items To Be Used.   The types of items that can be used on a test can be classified into two categories: (1) those for which examinees produce their own answers, which are sometimes labeled *supply-response,* or *constructed-response* items, and (2) those for which students select their own answers from several choices, which are labeled *select-response* items. Examples of supply response items are the essay item requiring an extended answer from the student, the short-answer item requiring no more than one or two sentences for an answer, and the completion item requiring only a word or a phrase for an answer. Examples of selection type items are true-false, multiple-choice, and matching. The decision about which type of item to use will depend on the cognitive process to be measured, the strengths and weaknesses of each item type for the process and content to be measured, and the way the test will be used and scored.

Total Number of Items for the Test.   If the decision is made to use an essay type of test, there will be time for only a few questions. The more elaborate the answers required, the fewer the number of questions that it is possible to include. For example, a 40-minute test in high school might have three or four questions requiring extended answers of a page each. Select-response and short-answer tests can involve a much larger number of items.

The total number of items included in a test should be large enough to provide an adequate sample of student performance across content areas and across cognitive processes. The greater the number of content areas and cognitive processes to be measured by a test, the longer the test needs to be.

The time available for testing is also a factor that limits the number of items on a test. Most achievement tests should be power tests, not speed tests, meaning that there should be enough time for at least 80% of the students to attempt to answer every item. There are few subject areas in which speed of answering is a relevant aspect of achievement. The number of test items that can be asked in a given amount of time depends on the following factors:

1. *The type of item used on the test.* A short-answer item for which a student has to write his or her answer is likely to require more time than a true-false

or multiple-choice item for which a student is only required to choose an answer from among several choices. Of course, items that call for more extended written responses will take even more time.

2. *The age and educational level of the student.* Students in the primary grades whose reading and writing skills are just beginning to develop require more time per test item than older students do. Young children cannot attend to the same task for a long period of time. Testing time for them must be shorter, further reducing the number of items. With younger children, achievement testing is often distributed in short blocks over several days.

3. *The ability level of students.* Compared to lower ability students, high-ability students have better-developed reading and writing skills. They also have a better command of the subject matter and better problem-solving skills. As a rule, high-ability students can answer more questions per unit of testing time than low-ability students of the same age and grade can. Thus, a test for an advanced class could be longer, and a test for a slower-learning class should be shorter than a test for students of average ability.

4. *The length and complexity of the items.* If test items are based on reading passages, tabular materials, maps, or graphs, time must be provided for reading and examining the stimulus material. The more stimulus material of this type that is used on a test, the fewer the number of items that can be included on it.

5. *The type of process objective being tested.* Items that require only the recall of knowledge can be answered more quickly than those that require the application of knowledge to a new situation. Thus, tests intended to assess higher cognitive processes should include fewer items for a given amount of testing time.

6. *The amount of computation or quantitative thinking required by the item.* Most individuals work more slowly when dealing with quantitative materials than when dealing with verbal materials; therefore, if the items require mathematical computations, the time allotted per item must be longer than that for purely verbal items.

Conclusions on Total Number of Test Items.   It is impossible to give hard-and-fast rules about the number of items to be included in a test for a given amount of testing time. As a rule, the typical student will require from 30 to 45 seconds to read and answer a simple, factual-type multiple-choice or true-false item and from 75 to 100 seconds to read and answer a fairly complex, multiple-choice item requiring problem solving.

Keep in mind that there is a great deal of variation among students regarding the number of items that each student can complete in a given amount of time and that this variation is not always related to reading ability or knowledge of the content being assessed. This characteristic is also related to individual learning styles. The total amount of time required for a number of items sufficient to provide adequate coverage of the blueprint may, in some cases, be more than is available in a single class period. The most satisfactory solution to this problem is to divide the test into two or more separate subtests that can be given on successive days. As we will see in Chapter 9, this is the usual procedure for standardized achievement test batteries.

Determining Item Distribution.   For the examination in eighth-grade health (see Table 5.1), the test maker decided to have 60 items. The blueprint is used to determine how many items to write for each cell. The first step is to determine the total number of items for each content area and cognitive process. The blueprint in Table 5.1 specifies that 40% of the items, or 24 items (0.40×60), should be on Topic A; 24 items (0.40×60) on Topic B, and 12 items (0.20×60) on Topic C. These numbers are entered in the row labeled "No. of Items." The percentage assigned to each cognitive process is likewise multiplied by the total number of items to determine the number of items that should be written to measure each process. When this is done, we get the numbers entered in the extreme right-hand column of the blueprint.

To determine the number of items in each cell of the blueprint, we multiply the total number of items in a content area by the percentage assigned to the cognitive process in each row. For example, to determine the number of items for the first cell under Topic A, recognizing nutrition terms and vocabulary, we multiply 24 by 0.2 (20%), which gives 4.8 items. Because the number 4.8 is between 4 and 5, we can note that we should have either 4 or 5 items covering this content and this process. The other cells in the blueprint are filled in in the same way. It must be recognized that some process outcomes are related primarily to certain aspects of content. For instance, on a social studies examination, an objective related to map reading might be testable primarily in a content unit on natural resources rather than in one on human resources. Cell entries may need to be modified to make the content and process congruent. Furthermore, it is probably desirable to indicate a range of items for each cell, as our example does, to provide flexibility.

Appropriate Level of Difficulty of the Items.   *Difficulty* implies something different for an essay than it does for a short-answer or objective test item. An item that is of appropriate difficulty for an essay test is one for which each member of the class can produce a credible answer and which elicits responses varying in completeness, thoughtfulness, and quality of organization of ideas.

Difficulty can be thought of in terms of individual items or of the whole test. The difficulty of an item is determined by dividing the number of students getting the item correct by the total number of students attempting the item. (Usually we assume that all students have the opportunity to attempt all items.) The difficulty of the entire test is determined by dividing the mean of the test by the total number of items on the test, and it can be thought of as the average difficulty for all of the items on the test. For example, if a particular item on a test is answered correctly by 40% of all the students who take the test, we say the item has a 40% or .40 difficulty. An item that 75% of the students get correct would have a difficulty of .75. (This system can be confusing because the larger the difficulty index the easier the item. The value used could more logically be called the "easiness" of a test.) The difficulty of the whole test is the average of the individual item difficulties.

The appropriate average difficulty and spread of item difficulties differs for norm- and criterion-referenced tests. In general, criterion-referenced tests are easier than norm-referenced tests. On a diagnostic test intended to locate isolated individuals who are having special difficulty, it is reasonable to expect a large number of perfect or near-perfect scores and very few relatively low scores. On the other hand, if we administer a test to find out how much students already know before beginning instruction on a new topic, we should not be surprised to get a large number of near-zero scores, because the material has not yet been taught.

On criterion-referenced tests, diagnostic tests, or pretests administered prior to instruction, we are not concerned about maximizing variability. Even if everyone gets a perfect score or if everyone gets a zero score, we are obtaining the information that we were seeking. On the other hand, when the purpose of the test is to discriminate levels of achievement among different members of the class or group, then we want the test to yield a spread of scores. We want to be able to separate the really high achiever from the next highest achiever and the really low achiever from the next lowest achiever. Ideally, we would like to have every student get a different score on the test because that would increase variability and facilitate ranking. It is undesirable for anyone (or more than one person) to get a perfect score on such a test because that would decrease variability and make ranking more difficult. It would also mean that the test lacked sufficient ceiling to allow the really able students to demonstrate the limits of their knowledge. On the other hand, we would not want to get a zero or chance-level score, indicating that the student could not successfully answer any items, because then we would not have gotten down to his or her level. On such a test, we would not want an item that everyone got correct or an item that everyone got incorrect, simply because neither of these items contributes to making discriminations among students according to their levels of achievement.

As a rough rule of thumb, the difficulty of a test should be about halfway between the number of items a student could get correct by guessing and 100%. Because the effect of guessing adds chance variability to test scores, it is generally better to have the test be slightly easier than this guideline would suggest rather than more difficult. For a multiple-choice test with four options, the preferred level of difficulty would be about 0.65; for a true-false test, the optimum difficulty level would be about .75 to .80. Because the probability of getting an item right by chance is 1 divided by the number of answer choices, this rule leads to the conclusion that the average difficulty for items with five alternatives should be about .60. (Chance variability is 20%, and halfway between chance variability and a perfect score is .60.)

Continuing with our example (Table 5.1), suppose the 60 items on the health test were all completion items. We would want the average score for the class to be about 30 items correct (.50 × 60) because the probability of guessing the correct answer to a supply response item is assumed to be zero. If the 60 items had been five-alternative multiple-choice items, we would have wanted the average score to be about 36 items correct (.60 × 60).

Difficulties as low as this sometimes bother teachers and students who are accustomed to thinking of "passing" or "failing" scores in terms of the percentage of the items that a student gets correct on a test. The above suggestions have nothing to do with passing or failing; a decision based on any assessment device, including assigning marks or grades to students, is an entirely different problem that should be kept separate from the proportion of items correctly answered. The percentages that are suggested here will tend to yield a set of scores that will be maximally useful to test users who want to discriminate levels of achievement among examinees. It is for this reason that people who construct standardized achievement tests tend to use items with the properties outlined here.

In the process of achieving the desired average level of difficulty, the teacher is likely to produce some difficult items that are passed by as few as 30% or 40% of the students (assuming a four-choice multiple-choice item) and some easy ones that are passed by 80% to 90% of the students. We would hope that many of the items would approach the desired average level of about 65%, and they should be written with that goal in mind. However, achieving optimum difficulty levels is less important than ensuring that the items provide a good coverage of content and that each one is answered correctly more often by able than by less-able students. Ensuring proper content establishes content validity.

The problem of appraising content-related validity is closely parallel to the problem of preparing the blueprint for a test and then building a test to match the blueprint. A teacher's own test has content validity to the extent that a wise and thoughtful analysis of course objectives has been made in the blueprint and that care, skill, and ingenuity have been exercised in building test items to match the blueprint. A standardized test may be shown to have validity for a particular school or a particular curriculum insofar as the content of that test corresponds to and represents the objectives accepted in that school or that curriculum.

It should be clear that rational or content validity evidence is of primary importance for measures of achievement. In particular, validity of a formative test concerned with mastery of one or more specific educational objectives, the type of test that has been called content- or criterion-referenced, will be judged on how well the test tasks represent the defined objectives. But for the summative, norm-referenced achievement test (such as a standardized, end-of-course test), as well, the primary concern will be with how well the test represents what the best and most expert judgment would consider to be important knowledge and skill for the academic environment. If the correspondence is good, the test will be judged to have high validity for this application; if poor, the validity must be deemed low.

Responsible makers of tests for publication and widespread use go to considerable pains to determine the widely accepted goals of instruction in the fields in which their tests are to be developed and used. Test constructors may, and often do, resort to many sources, including the following:

1. The more widely used textbooks in the field
2. Recent courses of study for the large school units, such as state, county, and city school systems
3. Reports of special study groups that often appear in yearbooks of one or another of the educational societies
4. Groups of teachers who give instruction on the topic
5. Specialists in university, city, and state departments concerned with the training or supervision of teachers in the field

Gathering information from these sources, the test maker develops a blueprint for the test, and the test items are prepared in terms of this blueprint. Because of variations from community to community, no test published for national distribution can be made to exactly fit the content or objectives of every local course of study. In this sense, a test developed on a national basis is always less valid than an equally well-developed test tailored specifically to the local objectives. However, the well-made commercial test can take the common components that appear repeatedly in different textbooks and courses of study and build a test around these components. Such a test represents the common core that is central to the different specific local patterns. In addition, commercial tests are prepared by people who are testing specialists. The items are written by experienced and well-trained item writers and the tests are subjected to a thorough review both for style and for possible bias in either phrasing or content. Thus, the items are likely to be of high quality, which may be a reasonable trade-off for the poorer fit to local instructional objectives.

It should be clear from the previous paragraphs that the relationship between teaching and testing is typically intimate. Test content is drawn from what has been taught or what is proposed to be taught. An instructional program is the original source of achievement test materials. Sometimes the specification of test content may precede the curricular objectives underlying a local course of study, as when specialists have been brought together to design a test corresponding to some emerging trend in education. Sometimes the test may lag behind, as when the test is based on the relatively conventional objectives emphasized in established textbooks. But usually, test content and classroom instruction are closely related to each other, and the test may be appraised by how faithfully it corresponds to the significant goals of instruction.

For appraising the validity of test scores as representing the degree of achievement of curricular objectives, there is no substitute for a careful and detailed examination of the actual test tasks. A test may be labeled "mathematical concepts," but call for nothing except knowledge of definitions of terms. A test of "reading comprehension" may only call for answers to questions concerning specific details that appear in the passages. It is the tasks presented by the items that really define what the test is measuring, and one who would judge a test's content validity for a specific curriculum must take a hard look at the individual items.

Content Validity for Measures of Aptitude and Typical Performance

The need for content validity and how to evaluate it is fairly straightforward with achievement tests, but it is also an issue for measures of aptitudes and for instruments designed to measure personality or interests. In both of these latter cases, however, the definition of the domain is rather more complicated and indirect. Suppose we wish to construct a test that measures a person's general level of cognitive functioning, what we typically call a general intelligence, or IQ, test. How shall we decide what is the appropriate domain of content? The answer to this question is inextricably bound up with what we consider general intelligence to be, and that implies a theory about the nature of intelligence. Our theory defines both what intelligence is *for us* and what behaviors can be used as indicators of it. Our theory comes to occupy the place of the curriculum plan for an achievement test. Once we have specified our theory, we can proceed to construct and evaluate test items to measure the content and cognitive processes specified by the theory. We cover several major current theories of intelligence and the tests designed to fit those theories in Chapter 8.

Content validity can also be an issue for measures of typical performance, but here the relationship is seldom direct because the behaviors associated with personality constructs can seldom be listed exhaustively. Thus, one may be able to judge whether a given test item is an exemplar of the trait "sociability," but it would be practically impossible to list all of the contexts in which sociable behavior might occur and all the forms it might take. For this reason, and because there is little general agreement about which personality or interest constructs are most useful, the assessment of content validity for these instruments is much more an individual matter of whether the items included in the scale conform to the theory espoused by the test user. As we shall see later in this chapter, the fit of test items to a theory about behavior is an integral part of what has come to be called construct validity.

CRITERION-RELATED EVIDENCE OF VALIDITY

Frequently, we are interested in using a test in connection with a decision that implies predicting some specific future outcome. We give a scholastic aptitude test to predict how likely a high school student is to be successful in College X, where success is represented at least approximately by grade-point average. We give an employment test to select machine operators who are likely to be successful employees, as represented by some such criterion as high production with low spoilage and low personnel turnover. For this purpose, we care very little what a test looks like. We are interested almost entirely in the degree to which it correlates with some chosen criterion measure of job or academic success. Some other measure (often, but not necessarily, one that becomes available later) is taken as the criterion of "success," and we judge a test in terms of its relationship to that criterion measure. The higher the correlation, the better the test.

Face Validity

The statement that we do not care what a test looks like is not entirely true. What a test "looks like" may be of importance in determining its acceptability and reasonableness to those who will be tested. A group of would-be pilots may be more ready to accept a mathematics test dealing with wind drift and fuel consumption than they would be to accept a test with the same essential problems phrased in terms of costs of crops or recipes for baking cakes. This appearance of reasonableness is sometimes called *face validity*, and although it is never a sufficient condition for the use of a test, it can be considered a necessary condition whenever the voluntary coop-eration of the examinees is important. Unless the test looks like it could be used for the purpose the examinees have been told it will be used for, they may give less than their maximum effort or may not provide sincere responses.

Empirical Validity

Evaluation of a test as a predictor is primarily an empirical and statistical evaluation, and the collection of evidence bearing on this aspect of validity has sometimes been spoken of as *empirical* or *statistical validity*. The basic procedure is to give the test to a group that is entering some job or training program, to follow them up later, to get for each one a specified criterion measure of success on the job or in the training program, and then to compute the correlation between the test scores and the crite-rion measures of success. The higher the correlation, the more effective the test is as a predictor and the higher is its criterion-related validity.

There are really two broad classes of criterion-related validity, with the differen-tiation depending on the time relationship between collecting the test information and the criterion information. If the test information is to be used to forecast future criterion performance, as is the case in all selection decisions, then we speak of *pre-dictive validity*. On the other hand, there are also cases where we would like to be able to substitute a test for another more complex or expensive procedure. This might be the case when we use a group test of intelligence in place of an individually administered one. The question then is whether the two different sources of infor-mation have a strong enough relationship that the less expensive one can be used in place of the more expensive one. If this is our concern, we would want to know that scores on one test predict scores obtained concurrently on the other. When scores on the test and the criterion are obtained at essentially the same time, we speak of *concurrent validity*. The two names, predictive and concurrent, have more to do with the purpose of the study than with the time relationship between the assess-ments, but these are the names that have evolved. Because predictive validity is the more widespread concern, we will use that term in the discussion to follow, but the procedures and issues are the same for both types of empirical validity.

We can picture the relationship between a predictor and a criterion in various ways. For example, the bar chart in Figure 5.1 shows the percentage of candidates passing air force pilot training at each of nine score levels on a test battery designed to assess aptitude for flight training. The chart shows a steady increase in the per-centage passing as we go from low to high scores, so successful completion of train-ing is related to aptitude level. A similar chart could be produced to show the rela-tionship between scores on a college admissions test and subsequent grades in college or between clerical aptitude scores and success in clerical training. The rela-tionship pictured in the chart corresponds to a correlation coefficient of 0.49. A higher correlation would result in a greater difference in success rates for increasing levels of aptitude score.

Figure 5.1
Percent of cadets
completing pilot training at
each aptitude level. The
correlation coefficient is
0.49.

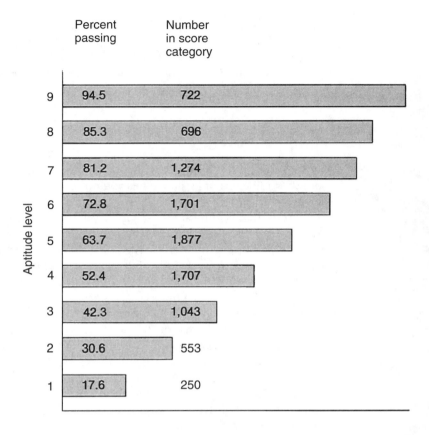

Aptitude level	Percent passing	Number in score category
9	94.5	722
8	85.3	696
7	81.2	1,274
6	72.8	1,701
5	63.7	1,877
4	52.4	1,707
3	42.3	1,043
2	30.6	553
1	17.6	250

The Problem of the Criterion.   We have said that empirical validity can be estimated by determining the correlation between test scores and a suitable criterion
measure of success on the job or in the classroom. The joker here is the phrase "suitable criterion measure." One of the most difficult problems that the investigator of selection tests faces is that of locating or creating a satisfactory measure of success to
be used as a criterion measure for test validation. This problem is most serious in employment settings but is also quite troublesome in the academic environment. It
might appear that it should be a simple matter to decide on some measure of rate of
production or some type of rating by superiors to serve as a criterion measure. It
might also seem that this measure, once decided on, should be obtainable in a simple
and straightforward fashion. Unfortunately, identifying a satisfactory criterion measure is not so easy. Finding or developing acceptable criterion measures usually involves the tests-and-measurements research worker in a host of problems.

Each possible type of criterion measure presents its own problems. A record of
actual performance has a good deal of appeal—number of widgets made, freedom
from errors as a cashier, or amount of insurance sold, for example. But there are

many jobs or positions, such as physician, teacher, secretary, or receptionist, that yield no objective record of performance or production. And, when such records do exist, the production is often influenced by an array of factors that are outside the worker's control. The production record of a weaver may depend not only on personal skill in threading and adjusting the loom, but also on the condition of the equipment, adequacy of the lighting in the work environment, or the color of thread being woven. The sales of an insurance agent are a function not only of individual effectiveness as a seller, but also of the territory to be covered and the supervision and assistance the agent receives.

Because of the absence or the shortcomings of performance records, the personnel psychologist has often depended on some type of rating by a supervisor as a criterion measure. Such ratings may exist as a routine part of the personnel procedures in a company, as when each employee receives a semiannual efficiency report, or the ratings may have to be gathered especially for the selection study. In either event, the ratings will typically be found to depend as much on the person giving them as on the person being rated. Ratings tend to be erratic and influenced by many factors other than performance. The problems in using rating procedures to describe and evaluate people are discussed in Chapter 12.

There are always many criterion measures that might be obtained and used for validating a selection test. In addition to using quantitative performance records and subjective ratings, we might also use later tests of proficiency. This type of procedure is involved when a college entrance mathematics test is validated in terms of its ability to predict later performance on a comprehensive examination on college mathematics. Here, the comprehensive examination serves as the criterion measure. Another common type of criterion measure is the average of grades in some type of educational or training program. Tests for the selection of engineers, for example, may be validated against course grades in engineering school.

All criterion measures are partial in the sense that they measure only a part of success on the job or only the preliminaries to actual job or academic performance. This last point is true of the engineering school grades just mentioned, which represent a relatively immediate—but partial—criterion of success as an engineer. The ultimate criterion would be some appraisal of lifetime success in a profession. In the very nature of things, such an ultimate criterion is inaccessible, and the investigator must be satisfied with substitutes for it. These substitutes are never completely satisfactory. The problem is always to choose the most satisfactory measure or combination of measures from among those that it appears feasible to obtain. The investigator is faced, then, with the problem of deciding which of the criterion measures is most satisfactory. How is that decided?

Qualities Desired in a Criterion Measure. There are four qualities desired in a criterion measure. In order of their importance, they are (1) relevance, (2) freedom from bias, (3) reliability, and (4) availability.

We judge a criterion measure to be relevant to the extent that standing on the criterion measure corresponds to, or exemplifies, success on the job. In appraising the relevance of a criterion, we must revert to rational considerations. There is no empirical evidence that will tell how relevant freshman grade-point average is, for example, as an indicator of someone having achieved the objectives of Supercolossal University. For achievement tests, therefore, it is necessary to rely on the best available professional judgment to determine whether the content of a test accurately represents our educational objectives. In the same way, with respect to a criterion measure, it is necessary to rely on professional judgment to provide an appraisal of the degree to which some available criterion measure can serve as an indicator of what we would really like to predict. We could even say that relevance corresponds to the content validity of the criterion measure. A relevant criterion corresponds closely to the behaviors of ultimate interest.

The second most important factor in the criterion measure is freedom from bias. By this, we mean that the measure should be one on which each person has the same opportunity to make a good score or, more specifically, one on which each equally capable person obtains the same score (except for errors of measurement), regardless of the group to which he or she belongs. Examples of biasing factors are such things as variation in wealth from one district to another for our previous example of the insurance agent, variation in the quality of equipment and conditions of work for a factory worker, variation in "generosity" of the bosses who are rating private secretaries, or variation in the quality of teaching received by students in different classes. To the extent that the criterion score depends on factors in the conditions of work, in the evaluation of work, or in the personal characteristics of the individual, rather than on competence in the job, there is no real meaning to the correlation between test results and a criterion score. A criterion measure that contains substantial bias cannot at the same time reveal relevant differences among people on the trait of interest.

The third factor is reliability, as it applies to criterion scores. A measure of success on the job must be stable or reproducible if it is to be predicted by any type of test device. If the criterion score is one that jumps around in an unpredictable way from day to day, so that the person who shows high job performance one week may show low job performance the next, or the person who receives a high rating from one supervisor gets a low rating from another, there is no possibility of finding a test that will predict that score. A measure that is completely unstable itself cannot be predicted by anything else.

Finally, in choosing a criterion measure, we always encounter practical problems of convenience and availability. How long will we have to wait to get a criterion score for each individual? How much is it going to cost—in dollars or in disruption of normal activities? Though a personnel research program can often afford to spend a substantial part of its effort getting good criterion data, there is always a practical limit. Any choice of a criterion measure must take this practical limit into account.

Interpretation of Validity Coefficients.   Suppose that we have gathered test and criterion scores for a group of individuals and computed the correlation between them. Perhaps the predictor is a scholastic aptitude test, and the criterion is an average of college freshman grades. How will we decide whether the test is a good predictor?

Obviously, other things being equal, the higher the correlation, the better. In one sense, our basis for evaluating any one predictor is in relation to other possible prediction procedures. Does Peter's Perfect Personnel Predictor yield a higher or lower validity coefficient than other tests that are available? Does it yield a higher or lower validity coefficient than other types of information, such as high school grades or ratings by the school principal? We will look with favor on any measure whose validity for a particular criterion is higher than that of measures previously available, even though the measure may fall far short of perfection.

A few representative validity coefficients are exhibited in Table 5.2. These give some picture of the size of correlation that has been obtained in previous work of different kinds. The investigator concerned with a particular course of study or a particular job will, of course, need to become familiar with the validities that the tests being considered have been found to have for the criterion measure to be used.

The usefulness of a test as a predictor depends not only on how well it correlates with a criterion measure but also on how much *new* information it gives. For example, the social studies subtest of the Tests of Achievement and Proficiency (TAP) was found to correlate on the average .51 with ninth-grade social studies grades, and the reading comprehension subtest to correlate .51 with the same grades. But, the two tests have an intercorrelation of .77. They overlap and, in part at least, the information either test provides is the same as that provided by the other test. The net result is that pooling information from the two tests can give a validity coefficient of no

Table 5.2

Validity of Selected Tests as Predictors of Certain Educational and Vocational Criteria

Predictor Test[a]	Criterion Variable[b]	Validity Coefficient
CogAT	TAP reading (Grade 12)	.79
Verbal	TAP social studies (Grade 12)	.78
Quantitative	TAP mathematics (Grade 12)	.79
ITED composite (Grade 9)	Cumulative high school GPA	.49
	College freshman GPA	.41
	SAT total	.84
ITBS composite (Grade 6)	Final college GPA	.44
Seashore Tonal Memory Test	Performance test on stringed instrument	.28
Short Employment Test		
Word knowledge score	Production index—bookkeeping machine operators	.10
	Job grade—stenographers	.53
Arithmetic score	Production index—Bookkeeping machine operators	.26
	Job grade—stenographers	.60

[a]CogAT = Cognitive Abilities Test; ITED = Iowa Tests of Educational Development; ITBS = Iowa Tests of Basic Skills.

[b]TAP = Tests of Achievement and Proficiency; GPA = grade-point average; SAT = Scholastic Aptitude Test.

more than .53. If the two tests had been uncorrelated, each giving evidence completely independent of the other, the combination of the two would have provided a validity coefficient of .70. Statistical procedures have been developed that enable us to determine the best weighting to give to two or more predictors and to calculate the correlation that results from this combination. (The procedures for computing the weights for the predictor tests *[regression weights]* and the correlation *[multiple correlation]* resulting from the combination are beyond the scope of this discussion. Presentation of these methods is found in intermediate statistics texts such as those of Cohen & Cohen [1983], Darlington [1990], and McClendon [1994].)

Clearly, the higher the correlation between a test or other predictor and a criterion measure, the better. But, in addition to this relative standard, we should like some absolute one. How high must the validity coefficient be for the test to be useful? What is a "satisfactory" validity? This last question is a little like asking, how high is up? However, we can try to give some sort of answer.

To an organization using a test as a basis for deciding whether to hire a particular job applicant or to admit a particular student, the significant question is, how much more often will we make the right decision on whom to hire or to admit if we use this test than if we operate on a purely chance basis or on the basis of some already available but less valid measure? The answer to this question depends in considerable measure on the proportion of individuals who must (or can) be accepted, called the *selection ratio.* A selection procedure can do much more for us if we can accept only the individual who appears to be the best 1 in every 10 applicants than if we must accept 9 out of 10. However, to provide a specific example, let us assume that we will accept half of the applicants. Let us examine Table 5.3.

The model is set up to show 200 people in all, 100 in each half on the test and 100 in each half on the job. If there were absolutely no relationship between the test and job performance, there would be 50 people in each of the four cells of the table. Defining "success" as being in the top half on the job, the success rate would be 50 in 100 for those accepted and also for those rejected. There would be no difference between the two, and the correlation between the selection test and job performance would be zero.

Table 5.3
Two-by-Two Table of Test and Job Success

		Performance on the Job		
		Bottom Half— "Failures"	Top Half— "Successes"	Total
Score on Selection Test	Top half (accepted)			100
	Bottom half (rejected)			100
	Total	100	100	200

Table 5.4
Percentage of Correct Assignments When 50%
of Group Must Be Selected

Validity Coefficient	Percentage of Correct Choices
.00	50.0
.20	56.4
.40	63.1
.50	66.7
.60	70.5
.70	74.7
.80	79.5
.90	85.6

Table 5.4 shows, for correlations of different sizes, the percentage of correct choices (i.e., "successes") among the 50% we accept. A similar percentage of correct rejections occurs in the 50% who are not accepted. The improvement in our "batting average" as the correlation goes up is shown in the table. Thus, for a correlation of .40, we will select correctly 63.1% of the time and be in error 36.9% of the time; with a correlation of .80 the percentage of correct decisions will be 79.5, and so forth.

The table shows not only the accuracy for any given correlation but also the gain in accuracy if we improve the validity of the predictor. If we were able to replace a predictor with a validity of .40 by one with a validity of .60, we would increase the percentage of correct decisions from 63.1 to 70.5. The percentages in Table 5.4 refer, of course, to the ground rules set above, that is, that we are selecting the top 50% of the group on the prediction test and that 50% of the complete group of 200 candidates would be successful. However, Table 5.4 gives a fairly representative basis for understanding the effects of a selection program from the point of view of the employing or certifying agency.

In many selection situations, the gain from greater validity can be crudely translated into a dollars-and-cents saving. If it costs a company $500 to employ and train a new employee to the point of useful productivity, a selection procedure that raises the percentage of successes from 56.4 to 63.1 would yield a saving in wasted training expenses alone of $3,350 per 100 new employees. This computation of benefits takes no account of the possibility that the test-selected workers might also be *better* workers after they had completed their training. The dollar saving would be balanced, of course, against any increase in cost in applying the new selection procedure. A selection procedure which cost $5,000 per candidate to administer would hardly be worthwhile for such modest savings.

Another way of appraising the practical significance of a correlation coefficient—and one that is perhaps more meaningful, from the point of view of the person being tested—is shown in Table 5.5. The rows in the tabulations represent the fourths of a group of applicants, potential students or employees, with respect to a

Table 5.5
Accuracy of Prediction for Different Values of the Correlation Coefficient (r).

$r = .00$						$r = .60$				
	Quarter on Criterion						Quarter on Criterion			
Quarter on Predictor	4th	3rd	2nd	1st		Quarter on Predictor	4th	3rd	2nd	1st
1st	250	250	250	**250**		1st	45	141	277	**537**
2nd	250	250	**250**	250		2nd	141	264	**318**	277
3rd	250	**250**	258	250		3rd	277	**318**	264	141
4th	**250**	250	250	250		4th	**537**	277	141	45

$r = .40$						$r = .70$				
	Quarter on Criterion						Quarter on Criterion			
Quarter on Predictor	4th	3rd	2nd	1st		Quarter on Predictor	4th	3rd	2nd	1st
1st	104	191	277	**428**		1st	22	107	270	**601**
2nd	191	255	**277**	277		2nd	107	270	**353**	270
3rd	277	**277**	255	191		3rd	270	**353**	270	107
4th	**428**	277	191	104		4th	**601**	270	107	22

$r = .50$						$r = .80$				
	Quarter on Criterion						Quarter on Criterion			
Quarter on Predictor	4th	3rd	2nd	1st		Quarter on Predictor	4th	3rd	2nd	1st
1st	73	168	279	**480**		1st	6	66	253	**675**
2nd	168	258	**295**	279		2nd	66	271	**410**	253
3rd	279	**295**	258	168		3rd	253	**410**	271	66
4th	**480**	279	168	73		4th	**675**	253	66	6

Note: There are 1,000 cases in each row and column.

predictor test. The columns indicate the number of cases falling in each quarter on the criterion measure. Look at the tabulation in Table 5.5 corresponding to a validity coefficient of .50. Note that of those who fall in the lowest quarter on the predictor, 480 out of 1,000 (48.0%) fall in the lowest quarter in terms of the criterion score, 27.9% in the next lowest quarter, 16.8% in the next to highest quarter, and 7.3% in the highest quarter. Another way to view this relationship is in terms of our previous example, which defined successful performance as being in the top half on the criterion. Only about one person in four who scored in the lowest quarter on the predictor test (168 + 73 = 241 out of 1,000) would prove to be a "successful" employee. The diagonal entries in boldface print represent cases that fall in the same fourth on both the predictor and the criterion. The farther we get from the diagonal, the greater the discrepancy between prediction and performance. Cases on or near the

Table 5.6

Probabilities of Scoring Within Specified Ranges on the Verbal Test of the Scholastic Aptitude Test (SAT), Given Scores on the Reading Comprehension Test of the Tests of Achievement and Proficiency (TAP)

TAP Standard Score Range	SAT Verbal Score Range					
	200–250	251–350	351–450	451–550	551–650	651+
251+			10	40	40	10
241–250		6	19	44	25	6
231–240		4	11	53	28	4
221–230			20	44	28	8
211–220			31	48	21	
201–210		11	36	40	3	
191–200	3	14	43	40		
181–190	3	20	56	21		
171–180	11	22	61	3	3	
Below 171	23	54	19		4	

Note: The data in this table represent a correlation of 0.61 between the reading comprehension test of TAP and the verbal test of the SAT.

diagonal represent cases where the predictor has been right; cases falling far from the diagonal represent cases in which the predictor has been decidedly wrong.

As an empirical example of the spread of criterion performance that one may find for people with the same predictor score, consider Table 5.6. This table shows the distribution of scores on the Scholastic Aptitude Test (SAT) earned by 260 11th-grade students with different levels of performance on the reading comprehension test of the TAP. It is clear from the table that as TAP scores go up, SAT scores also tend to go up, but it is equally clear that some students with TAP scores of 200 earn higher SAT scores than do some of the students with TAP scores of 250.

Tables 5.5 and 5.6 emphasize not so much the gain from using the predictor as they do the variation in criterion performance still remaining for those who are similar in predictor scores. From the point of view of schools or employers, the important thing is to improve the percentage of correct decisions (see Table 5.4). In dealing with large numbers, they can count on gaining from any predictor that is more valid than the procedure currently in use. From the point of view of the single individual, the marked discrepancies between predicted and actual success shown in Tables 5.5 and 5.6 may seem at least as important. Applicants who have done poorly on the test may be less impressed by the fact that the *probability* is that they will be below average on the job or in the training program than by the fact that they *may* still do very well. Each individual may be the exception.

Base Rates and Prediction.   We noted in introducing Table 5.3 that a selection procedure is most helpful if we need to accept only a small number of candidates. Although this principle is true, the facts in Tables 5.5 and 5.6 reveal that we would miss many potentially successful candidates if we took only those in the top 10% to 20% on the predictor. The overall value of a selection procedure depends on several factors, including (1) how we define success, (2) the selection rule that we use, (3) the "value" of a correctly identified success, (4) the "cost" of accepting someone who subsequently fails, and (5) the "cost" of missing a candidate who would have succeeded.

The proportion of a group of applicants who would have succeeded if all were admitted is called the *base rate* for success. The selection rule imposed is known as the *cutting score.* If being in the top half on the criterion is considered success, then the base rate is 50%.

When we use any particular cutting score, some of our decisions will be correct and some will not. At one extreme, if we admit all candidates, we will correctly identify all potentially successful individuals, but at the cost of admitting the 50% who will be failures. At the other extreme, if we reject all candidates, we will admit no failures, but at the cost of missing all of the potentially successful candidates. The proportion of correct decisions that result from our selection strategy—the proportion of correctly identified successes plus the proportion of correctly rejected failures—is known as the *hit rate* for the cutting score. Each cutting score has a hit rate that depends on the base rate of success in the population and the correlation between the predictor and the criterion. The values in Table 5.4 show the hit rates for a base rate of 50% and a cutting score that admits the top half of the applicants on the predictor variable.

As the base rate departs from 50% (either higher or lower), the hit rate for the selection procedure diminishes. If we define success as being in the top 25% on the criterion (i.e., the base rate is 0.25) and consider the results of using a predictor that has a correlation of 0.60 with this criterion, the results from using four cutting scores are as follows:

Cutting Score	Hit Rate
Admit all	.25
Admit top 75%	.37
Admit top 50%	.66
Admit top 25%	.77

The hit rate of 0.66 for a cutting score that admits the top 50% is slightly lower than the value in Table 5.4, and the drop results from the change in base rate. The decrease in overall gain from using the predictor becomes much more marked in situations with more extreme base rates. The greatest total gains from using a selection procedure occur in those situations where the rate of successful criterion performance in the population is close to 50%.

Making Predictions.   We have seen that the correlation coefficient tells us the degree of association between two variables and the direction of that relationship. We can use this information, along with the means and standard deviations of the predictor and criterion variables, to make the best possible prediction about criterion performance for each person, based on their score on the predictor. To do this we use what is called a *regression equation*. The regression equation for predicting a person's score on criterion variable Y from their score on predictor variable X is

$$\hat{Y} = \frac{SD_{crit}}{SD_X} r_{xy} X + (M_Y - \frac{SD_{crit}}{SD_X} r_{xy} M_X) \tag{5.1}$$

where $\hat{Y}$ is the predicted score on Y,
  SD_{crit} is the standard deviation of the criterion variable,
  SD_X is the standard deviation of the predictor variable,
  r_{xy} is the predictor-criterion correlation,
  X is the person's score on the predictor,
  M_Y is the mean of the criterion distribution, and
  M_X is the mean of the predictor distribution.

The predicted value that results from this equation is the mean criterion score for all people who had a predictor score equal to the value of X. Consider, for example, the two variables in Table 5.6. If the mean score on the TAP is 210 with an SD of 30, the mean score on the SAT is 500 with an SD of 100, and the correlation between them is .60 (all these values are approximate because of the grouping of the data that has taken place), then we can determine the predicted SAT score for any TAP score. Suppose Mark got a TAP score of 195. What is our best guess as to his SAT score? Using Equation 5.1 we get

$$\hat{Y} = \frac{100}{30} (.60)(195) + (500 - \frac{100}{30}(.60)(210))$$
$$= (3.33)(.60)(195) + (500 - 3.33(.60)(210))$$
$$= 2(195) + (500 - 2(210)) = 390 + 80 = 470$$

This value, 470, is the prediction we would make of SAT score for all people who earned a score of 195 on the TAP.

Standard Error of Estimate.   We have seen that when the relationship between a predictor and a criterion is less than perfect, there will be some variability in criterion performance for people who all have the same predictor score. Not all people who fall in a given quarter of the predictor test distribution will fall in the same quarter of the criterion distribution. There will be an average criterion performance for people with a particular predictor score, and there will be variation around that average. Regression procedures, which were mentioned earlier, are used to find the mean criterion performance for all people scoring at the same level on the predictor. The spread of actual criterion performances around that mean is reflected by the *standard error of estimate*. The standard error of estimate is the standard deviation of the distribution of actual criterion performances around predicted performance. Another way to say the same thing is to say that *the standard error of estimate is the standard deviation of criterion scores for people who all got the same score on the predictor variable.*

Figure 5.2

Predicted score on the criterion variable (Scholastic Aptitude Test [SAT]) is the mean of criterion scores earned by those at a chosen level of predictor (Tests of Achievement and Proficiency [TAP]). Standard error of estimate is the standard deviation of observed scores around that mean.

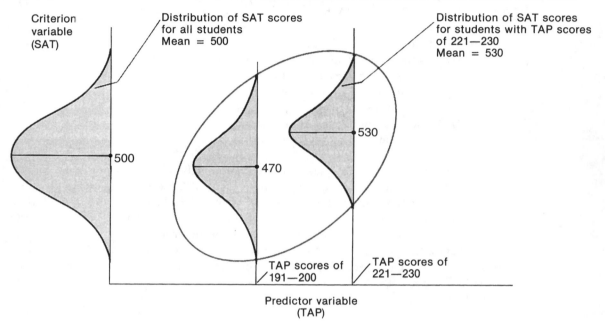

This principle is illustrated schematically in Figure 5.2 for the data in Table 5.6. The large normal distribution on the left in the figure is the distribution of all SAT scores. It has a mean of 500 and a standard deviation of 100. The ellipse is the scatter plot of SAT and TAP scores, and the two smaller normal distributions to the right are the distributions of SAT scores for those individuals who earned TAP scores between 191 and 200 and 221 and 230, respectively. The mean of the first distribution is 470, and this mean is the SAT score that we would predict for this group of individuals. The mean of the second distribution, 530, is the SAT score we would predict for individuals with TAP scores of 221 to 230. The standard deviations of these distributions are the standard errors of estimate for predicting SAT scores from TAP scores.

Two things are important to note in the figure. First, because there is a moderate positive correlation ($r = .60$) between the two variables, the predicted score is higher in the right-hand group than in the one to the left. People with higher TAP scores are predicted to earn higher SAT scores. Second, the predictions are in error by some small amount for most people and by a considerable amount for some. The standard deviation of observed scores around the predicted score is the standard error of estimate.

An overall value for the standard error of estimate can be obtained from the following equation:

$$SD_e = SD_{crit} \sqrt{(1 - r_{xy}^2)} \qquad (5.2)$$

where SD_e is the standard error of estimate,

SD_{crit} is the standard deviation of the *entire* distribution of criterion scores, and

r_{xy}^2 is the squared validity coefficient of the predictor test for predicting this criterion.

Notice that this formula looks quite similar to Equation 4.4 (Chapter 4) for the standard error of measurement. The standard error of measurement is an index of instability of performances on a test. It uses the test reliability to provide a way of estimating how much an individual's score might change from one testing to another. The standard error of estimate is an index of the error that may be made in forecasting performance on one measure from performance on another. It uses the correlation between the test and some criterion to provide an estimate of how much a predicted score might be in error as an estimate of a person's actual performance on the criterion. Both the standard error of measurement and the standard error of estimate are important, but for criterion-related validity, the standard error of measurement is a property that can be determined by the test publisher as characterizing the predictor test, while the standard error of estimate is unique to each criterion measure and must therefore be determined locally.

Let us look again at predicting SAT performance from scores on the TAP. We found (in Table 5.6) a correlation of .61 between the test and the criterion measure, and the standard deviation of SAT scores is 100. Using Equation 5.2, we find

$$SD_e = 100 \sqrt{(1 - .61^2)} = 100 \sqrt{0.63} = 79$$

The standard error of estimate is 79.

We may use standard error of estimate to place a band of uncertainty or a confidence interval around our prediction for a person in the same way that we used standard error of measurement to produce a band of uncertainty for the person's true score. If we assume that the errors of prediction have a normal distribution, about two out of three students will earn SAT scores within 1 standard of error of estimate of the score that was predicted for them and 95% will get SAT scores within the 2 standard-error-of-estimate band. In the example shown in Figure 5.3, 68% of the students for whom a prediction of 530 was made will actually earn SAT scores between 450 and 610 (SAT scores are reported only in multiples of 10), while about 95% will have criterion performances between 370 and 690.

The standard error of estimate is a sobering index because it illustrates clearly the limitations we face in predicting human behavior. *Even with the best measures available, predictions in psychology and education are approximate.* The regression techniques that are used to make predictions yield point estimates such as the predicted SAT score of 530 in Figure 5.3. By considering the standard error of esti-

Figure 5.3
Two people out of three will have criterion scores within 1 standard error of estimate (SD_e) of their predicted scores on the Scholastic Aptitude Test (SAT). Nineteen in 20 will be within 2 SD_e.

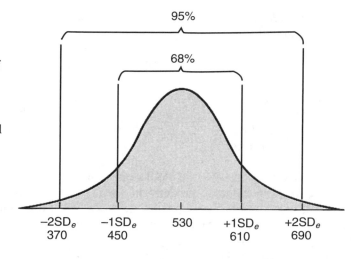

mate, teachers, counselors, and personnel workers get an appropriately pessimistic view of our present ability to predict human performance. This is not to say that we should stop trying to predict or that tests are often seriously wrong. On the contrary, predictions made from test scores are, *on the average,* correct. But, healthy skepticism is required to keep from overinterpreting test scores, particularly when, as is usually the case, we are making predictions about individuals.

Two other factors tend to distort validity coefficients and complicate their interpretation. The first is unreliability of the predictor and of the criterion that is being predicted. This attenuation effect was discussed in Chapter 4. The second is restriction of the range of ability in the group by some type of preselection. Low reliability on the one hand or preselection on the other will tend to lower the values that are obtained for validity coefficients, so that "true validities" are typically higher than the values obtained in validation studies.

An example of the effect that restricting the range in the predictor can have on the apparent validity of a predictor comes from a recent experience at a public university where there was dramatic growth in its pool of applicants. With over three times as many applicants as could be accommodated, the school changed from what had been a first-come, first-served admissions policy to one in which students were admitted on the basis of a combination of high school grades and aptitude test scores. The correlation of college grades with high school grades in the last class admitted under the old rules was 0.61. When the new admissions criteria were applied and only those students who would have been admitted under the new rules were included, the correlation dropped to 0.47. This change in the apparent validity of high school grades as a predictor of college grades occurred solely as a result of the smaller range of talent among the selected students.

Let us emphasize one additional point. Validity is fairly specific to a particular curriculum or a particular job. Although the concept of validity generalization, discussed in Chapter 16, indicates that certain tests may be valid across a range of jobs, when an author or publisher claims that a test is valid, it is always appropriate to ask, valid for what? For example, an achievement test in social studies that accurately represents the content and objectives of one program of instruction may be quite inappropriate for the program in a different community. An achievement test must always be evaluated against the objectives of a specific program of instruction. An aptitude test battery that is quite valid for picking department store sales clerks who will be pleasant to customers, informed about their stock, and accurate in financial transactions may be entirely useless in identifying insurance agents who will be effective in going out and finding or creating new business. Validity must always be evaluated in relation to a situation as similar as possible to the one in which the measure is to be used.

Criterion-related validity is most important for a test that is to be used to predict outcomes that are represented by clear-cut criterion measures. There are two key elements in this statement—prediction and clear-cut criterion measures. The main limitation to using criterion-related validity within the prediction context usually lies in the limited adequacy of the available criterion measures. The more readily we can identify a performance criterion that unquestionably represents the results that we are interested in, the more we will be prepared to rely on the evidence from correlations between a test and measures of that criterion to guide our decision on whether to use the test.

CONSTRUCT-RELATED EVIDENCE OF VALIDITY

Sometimes, with respect to an educational or psychological test, we ask neither *How well does this test predict future performance?* nor *How well does this test represent our curriculum?* but, instead, *What do scores on this test* mean *or* signify? What does the score tell us about an individual? Does it correspond to some meaningful trait or construct that will help us to understand the person? For this last question, the term *construct validity* has been used. (The term *construct* is used in psychology to refer to something that is not observable but is literally *constructed* by the investigator to summarize or account for the regularities or relationships in observed behavior. Thus, most names of traits refer to constructs. We speak of a person's "sociability" as a way of summarizing observed consistency in past behavior in relation to people and of organizing a prediction of how the individual will act on future occasions. The construct is derived from observations, but constructs may actually predict what we would observe in new situations. Such is the case in the research program described next.)

Let us examine a classic case of one specific testing procedure and see how its validity as a measure of a useful psychological quality or construct was studied. Mc-Clelland, Atkinson, Clark, and Lowell (1953) developed a testing procedure to appraise an individual's need or motivation to achieve—to succeed and do well. The test used pictures of people in various ambiguous situations. The individual was called on to make up a story about each picture, telling what was happening and how it turned out. A scoring system was developed for these stories, based on counting the frequency with which themes of accomplishment, mastery, success, and achievement appeared in the story material. In this way, each individual received a score representing the strength of his motivation to achieve (all subjects were male). The question posed by construct validity is whether this measure has validity in the sense of truthfully describing a meaningful aspect of the individual's makeup. Mc-Clelland and his coworkers proceeded as described here.

In essence, the investigators began by asking, to what should a measure of achievement motivation, as we have conceived of it, be related? They made a series of predictions, some of which follow:

1. Those students scoring high on achievement motivation should do well in college in relation to their scholastic aptitude. That is, their college grades should be higher than would be predicted from their SAT scores.
2. Achievement motivation should be higher for students just after they have taken tests described to them as measuring their intelligence.
3. Those students scoring high on achievement motivation should complete more items on a speeded test where the students are motivated to perform well.
4. Achievement motivation should be higher for children of families emphasizing early independence.

Each of these predictions was based on a sort of "theory of human behavior." For example, academic achievement is seen as a combination of ability and effort. Presumably, those with higher motivation to achieve will exert more effort and therefore will, ability being equal, achieve higher grades. A similar chain of reasoning lies behind each prediction.

In general, McClelland et al. (1953) found that most of their predictions were supported by the experimental results. The fact that the test scores were related to a number of other events in the way that had been predicted from a rational analysis of the trait that the test was presumably measuring lent support to the validity of the test procedure as measuring a meaningful trait or construct. The essential characteristics of the trait are fairly well summarized by the label "achievement motivation." When a series of studies supports the construct validity of a measure, the validity of the theory that gave rise to the construct is also supported.

A great many psychological tests and, to a lesser extent, some educational tests are intended to measure general traits or qualities of the individual. General intelligence, verbal reasoning, spatial visualization, sociability, introversion, and mechanical interest are all designations of traits or constructs. Tests of these functions have construct validity insofar as they behave in the way that such a trait should reasonably be expected to behave in light of the theory that gave rise to the construct.

A theory about a trait will lead to predictions of the following types, all of which can be tested to see if they hold up.

Predictions About Correlations

The nature of the trait, and therefore of valid measures of it, will indicate that it should be positively related to certain other measures and, perhaps, unrelated or negatively related to still others. These other measures might be already accepted measures of the function in question. Many subsequent group intelligence tests, for example, have been validated in part by their correlations with earlier tests, especially the Stanford-Binet. Also, the other measures may be ones with which the trait should logically be related. Thus, intelligence tests have been validated, in part, through their correlation with success in school and measures of mechanical aptitude by their correlation with rated proficiency in mechanical jobs.

One way of studying the constructs or traits that a test measures is to study jointly the intercorrelations of this test and a number of others. The patterning of these correlations makes it possible to see which tests are measuring some common dimension or factor. An examination of the tests clustering in a single factor may clarify the nature and meaning of the factor and of the tests that measure it. This means of studying the constructs that underly performance on a test is known as factor analysis. This widely used procedure is described in Chapter 16. However, this internal or *factorial validity* still needs evidence of a relationship to life events outside the tests themselves if the factors are to have much substance, vitality, and scientific or educational utility.

It may also be appropriate to predict that the measure of Construct X will show low or zero correlations with measures of certain other attributes, that is, that the construct is different from what the other tests measure. A test designed to measure mechanical comprehension should show only a modest correlation with a test of verbal ability. A measure of sociability should not show too high a correlation with a measure of assertiveness, if the two assess genuinely different constructs. High correlations between measures of supposedly unrelated constructs are evidence against either the validity of the instruments as measures of the constructs, the validity of the constructs as separate dimensions of human functioning, or both.

Multitrait, Multimethod Analysis.   An explicit method for studying the patterns of high and low correlations among a set of measures was suggested by Campbell and Fiske (1959). Their procedure, which they called the analysis of a multitrait, multimethod matrix, requires that several different methods be used to measure each of several different traits. Figure 5.4 provides an illustration of a multitrait, multimethod (MTMM for short) matrix. The entries in the matrix in Figure 5.4 are given as letters, although the results of an actual study would produce numerical values.

As is shown in Figure 5.4, we might measure each of three traits, ascendance, sociability, and trustworthiness, in each of three ways, self-report, ratings by friends, and observations in a controlled setting. Thus, we have nine scores for each person, and the MTMM matrix contains the correlations among these nine variables. The essence of the MTMM method for assessing construct validity is that scores resulting from different ways of measuring of the same trait should correlate more highly with each other than they do with scores for other traits measured by the same method.

The cells of the matrix that contain the letter *a* are known as *reliability diagonals*. They represent the correlation between two assessments of the same trait using the same measurement method (remember that we characterized reliability as being the correlation of a test with itself). We would want these values to be as high as possible, and they should be the highest values in the matrix. In the parlance of MTMM analyses, these are *monotrait, monomethod* correlations.

Figure 5.4
The multitrait, multimethod (MTMM) matrix.

		Self Rating			Friend Rating			Observation		
		A	S	T	A	S	T	A	S	T
Self	Ascendance	a								
	Sociability	b	a							
	Trustworth	b	b	a						
Friend	Ascendance	c	d	d	a					
	Sociability	d	c	d	b	a				
	Trustworth	d	d	c	b	b	a			
Observe	Ascendance	c	d	d	c	d	d	a		
	Sociability	d	c	d	d	c	d	b	a	
	Trustworth	d	d	c	d	d	c	b	b	a

A = Ascendance

S = Sociability

T = Trustworthiness

The values in the cells labeled *b* are the correlations between different traits assessed by the same measurement method (*heterotrait, monomethod* correlations). These correlations represent similarities due to both the natural relationships between the constructs and the fact that they have been measured by the same method. They should be substantially smaller than the reliabilities.

As far as construct validity is concerned, interest usually focuses on the values in the *c* cells. These are the correlations between different ways of assessing the same trait (*monotrait, heteromethod* correlations). If we have two or three good ways of measuring ascendance, then they should agree with each other, even though they use different methods. In a sense, this is a little like the question of parallel forms reliability; do different selections of items produce the same measurement. For well-defined measures of a well-defined construct, the answer should be *yes*. To the extent that different ways of measuring the same trait yield high correlations, the construct and its measures are said to demonstrate *convergent validity*. The different methods of measurement converge on the trait.

Finally, we come to the *d* cells. These are the correlations between different traits measured by different methods (*heterotrait, heteromethod* correlations). They represent the purest index of the association between the different traits, and they should be the smallest values in the matrix because they include only trait correlations.

To the extent that the values in the *b* cells are larger than those in the *d* cells, we say that *method variance* is present. That is, there are individual differences in scores that result not only from status on the trait but also from the way the trait was assessed. The presence of method variance reduces the construct validity of the measure because scores on the instrument include something else in addition to the person's status on the trait of interest. The extent to which measurements are free of method variance is called *discriminant validity*. Note, however, that the traits need not have near-zero correlations to demonstrate evidence of convergent and discriminant validity. A test of reading comprehension and one of general cognitive ability should be quite highly correlated because the traits seem to be highly correlated in the natural world, but the cross-trait correlations should be consistently lower than the within-trait correlations. The main issue is whether the different kinds of correlations show the pattern predicted by MTMM methodology.

Predictions About Group Differences

A theory will often suggest that certain kinds of groups should possess an especially high or low amount of a trait and, consequently, should score exceptionally high or low on a test of that trait. It seems reasonable that a group of successful salespeople should be high on a measure of ascendance, or assertiveness, and that a group of librarians should be low. We would probably predict that children of professional and business parents would be more ascendant than those whose parents were in clerical or semiskilled occupations. For any given trait, our general knowledge of our society and the groups within it will suggest an array of group differences that seem to make sense. Applying a test to these groups, the investigator finds out how consistently the predictions are borne out. Of course, the predictions could fail because, on the one hand, the test is not a valid measure of the characteristic or, on the other, because the world is not consistent with the theory that gave rise to the predictions. Failure of our predictions does not tell us which of these conditions exists (or is correct).

Predictions About Response to Experimental Treatments or Interventions

A theory may imply that the expression of a human characteristic will be modified as a result of certain experimental conditions or treatments. For example, one could reasonably predict that anxiety would increase just before a person was to undergo a minor operation. Rate of flicker fusion has been proposed as an indicator of anxiety level. (The *rate of flicker fusion* is the rate at which alternation of black-and-white stimulation fuses into a steady gray.) In one study (Buhler, 1953), it was found that, as predicted, the flicker fusion threshold was lower before the operation than after it, when anxiety had presumably relaxed. Other studies using anxiety-arousing stimuli such as dental chairs have found similar results, lending credence to the construct of anxiety and to certain measures of it.

For any test that presumes to measure a trait or quality, we can formulate a network of theory, leading to definite predictions which can be tested. Insofar as the predictions are borne out, the validity of the test as a measure of the trait or construct is supported. Insofar as the predictions fail to be verified, we are led to doubt either the validity of the test, our theorizing, or both.

THE UNIFIED VIEW OF VALIDITY

Construct validity, as Messick (1989) has pointed out, is really the central concept underlying test validation, because the validity of a test concerns what the test scores mean—that is, what kinds of inferences they support. The meaning may be couched in terms of relationships either with a defined body of subject matter (which we have called rational or content validity) or with other observations of human variation (criteria). Both of these sources are used to build the meaning of the test's scores as indicators of traits in the network of a behavioral theory.

Messick (1989) also points out that what is validated is not the test itself but interpretations of the test scores for particular purposes or uses. If we collect some test scores and lock them away in a vault, validation is not an issue. But, once we take the scores from the vault and use them for a purpose—any purpose—we must ask about the appropriateness of the scores for that use. The evidence to justify the use is, as we have seen, partly rational and partly empirical. Rational consideration of what is measured takes center stage when we are considering an end product—either a test that describes an individual's past learning or some indicator that we are accepting as a criterion measure. Such is the case when we use scores on an achievement test to represent the amount of material a student has learned from a course of instruction. It is also the case when we use grade point average (which may well result from an averaging of scores on several such tests) as an overall measure of learning, or supervisor ratings as an indicator of job performance. The elaboration of a theory by which we decide how to test the validity of a measure of a psychological construct is also a rational exercise. By contrast, when we use a test as a selection device to predict some accepted criterion measure, validation becomes primarily statistical. Checking the theory that we have developed for a measure of some construct is also an empirical undertaking. Judgment and evidence join in the validation enterprise.

Messick (1989) has also pointed out that using a test may have unintended consequences and these side effects must be included in validity considerations. In essence, current test theorists such as Shepard (1993) and Messick are arguing that test validation is a never-ending process of collecting and evaluating evidence that supports the use of the test scores for making particular decisions. Each decision or action based on the test scores has consequences, and these must be elaborated, considered, and found acceptable before the test can be used for the decision at hand. What are the consequences of using tests for referral for special education services? Are there differential impacts on different groups of students? Are the beneficial effects of referral greater than the social consequences, and are referrals made using the test preferable to referrals made by some other method? All of these questions and many others need to be considered and answered as part of the validation process before the test scores can appropriately be used to make decisions such as special education referral. As we shall see in Chapter 14, professional testing ethics require the test user to make a convincing argument for each use to which test scores will be put.

OVERLAP OF RELIABILITY AND VALIDITY

One way of thinking about the usefulness of a test is to ask to what extent one might safely generalize from a test score. If two forms of the test are given on the same day, the correlation between them tells us with what degree of confidence we can generalize from one set of test tasks to another set built to the same specifications and, by implication, with what degree of confidence we can generalize from the score to the whole domain of tasks sampled by the test. If the testing is conducted on different days, we gather evidence over a domain of occasions. And, if the testing on different days is also with different test forms, we gather evidence on the degree of generalizability over both tasks and occasions. If two different but similar tests are given, each intended by its author to measure the same trait or construct, we get evidence of generalizability from test to test. We are now considering a still broader domain that includes not merely samples of tasks chosen according to a common blueprint or design but also a range of blueprints or designs prepared by different authors. We are moving beyond what is ordinarily thought of as reliability into the realm of validity. And, of course, it is possible to consider generalizability from a test to other indicators of the same attribute, such as self-description or ratings by peers, supervisors, or teachers. Do the test scores allow us to draw inferences about what those ratings would be?

The notion of generalizability encompasses both reliability and validity, indicating that the two concepts differ only in the breadth of the domain to which generalization is undertaken. The concept of generalizability may eventually come to replace the several types of reliability and validity that we have discussed in this and the preceding chapter. Figure 5.5 provides an illustration of the notion of generalizability. We can view the situation as resembling the layers of an onion and can ask concerning any test how well it enables us to generalize our conclusions to situations at successive levels of remoteness from the central core.

VALIDITY FOR CRITERION-REFERENCED TESTS

Criterion-referenced tests are concerned with the measurement of particular, narrowly defined instructional objectives. For this reason, the critical concern in assess-

Figure 5.5
Layers of generalization
from a test score.

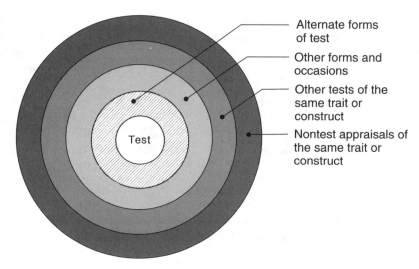

Alternate forms
of test

Other forms and
occasions

Other tests of the
same trait or
construct

Nontest appraisals of
the same trait or
construct

ing the validity of criterion-referenced tests is *content validity.* An instructional ob-jective includes two elements: the information content of the domain and what the student should be able to do with that content. Both of these elements must be pre-sent in the item in the form called for by the objective if the item is to be considered a valid indicator of achievement of that objective.

An often overlooked part of the content of a test is the conditions under which the examinees exhibit their performance. If the time allowed for testing is too short to enable most of the examinees to attempt all of the items, then speed of perfor-mance becomes a part of the content of the test. If the administration conditions are poor, these conditions become part of the test content *for these examinees.* To the extent that factors such as these vary from one group of examinees to another, the content of the test also varies. Content validity relates to the test score and all of the factors that affect it, including clarity of directions and adequacy of scoring proce-dures. When the content is critical to the use of the test scores, careful attention must be paid to all factors that make up the test's content.

Content validity, as we have seen, is primarily a matter of professional judg-ment on the part of teachers and subject-matter experts. There is, however, a use-ful type of empirical or statistical evidence that can be used to appraise the validity of criterion-referenced tests. This type of procedure is based on the point, made by Berk (1980), that a criterion-referenced test should maximize differences between groups that have achieved mastery of the objectives and those that have not achieved mastery, while it should minimize differences within the groups. That is, the ideal mastery-oriented test should divide the examinees into two homo-geneous groups of individuals: those who have achieved mastery and those who have not.

The problem, of course, is how to define mastery. One commonly used ap-proach is to have teachers identify those pupils who they are certain have mastered the objective and those who they are certain have not mastered it. This method can yield two widely separated groups, but the middle pupils must be omitted. A second approach is to compare those who have received instruction on the objective with those who have not yet had such instruction. Still another approach is to compare the performance of students before instruction with their performance following a period of instruction. Each of these approaches has certain limitations, and all are affected by the problem of the unreliability of difference, or change, scores. But any one of the approaches provides some evidence of the joint validity of the instructional activities aimed at the objectives, and the test as a measure of mastery of those objectives.

The validation procedure is similar to the item analysis methods discussed in Chapter 15. The examinees are divided into two groups—masters versus nonmasters or instructed versus uninstructed. The proportion in each group who answered each item correctly is then determined. The valid items are those for which the success rate in the master or instructed group is substantially higher than the success rate in the nonmaster or uninstructed group. In the extreme case, the success rate on each item for masters should be 100%, while the nonmasters should experience a chance rate of success. The total test should divide the examinees into masters, all of whom achieve perfect or near-perfect scores, and nonmasters, all of whom score at about the chance level. In the ideal test, there should be no misclassifications.

Mastery of an instructional objective is seldom an all-or-none thing. In any class, there will be varying degrees of mastery. In fact, one problem with the mastery concept in testing is deciding on an acceptable definition of mastery. The advantage of the criterion-referenced mastery philosophy of evaluation is that we know, in theory, what the students who have gained mastery can do—that is, what classes of problems or tasks they can solve. This type of knowledge is an essential part of formative evaluation. But, there are many situations, both in the school setting and elsewhere, where the question asked is one of relative position. Summative evaluations often call for norm-referenced tests that focus explicitly on relative performance.

META-ANALYSIS AND VALIDITY GENERALIZATION

In psychology and education, studies are often carried out with rather small samples of cases, and, partly as a consequence of this fact, different studies have often given quite inconsistent results. In the past two decades, researchers have sought better ways of distilling an essence of truth from a mass of seemingly contradictory results. The term *meta-analysis* was coined (Glass, 1977) to apply to the systematic pooling and integration of results from many different studies of the same phenomenon.

A specific example of meta-analysis is the integration of test validity data for different groups and from different sources. As soon as ability tests became available, researchers started to collect data on the validity of those tests for both educational and vocational criteria. For any given test or type of test, validity coefficients were found to vary rather substantially for the same school subject or for what appeared to be the same job. For example, the validity coefficient for English grades on the verbal reasoning test of the Differential Aptitude Tests (DAT) ranged, in different groups, from .07 to .76.

People came to accept the doctrine, especially in relation to vocational prediction, that validity must be established in each specific location. However, more recently, Schmidt and associates (Schmidt, 1988a, 1988b; Schmidt & Hunter, 1981; Schmidt, Hunter, Pearlman, & Hirsh, 1985) have demonstrated that much of the variation in results from one study to another can be attributed to a variety of statistical artifacts—sampling errors in small samples, criterion unreliability, or differing degrees of restriction in the range of ability in the sample studied. They propose that meta-analysis be applied to the accumulated data, thus pooling results from separate studies and arriving at an average value that may be taken as a generally applicable estimate of test validity, one that is closer to the true value than the value obtained from a local sample, usually of quite modest size. Thus, unless the English program in School System X is *radically* different from the program in most schools, the median validity coefficient of .49, based on pooling the results from many schools, will probably be a more appropriate value for School System X to use in thinking about the validity of the verbal reasoning test of DAT for predicting English grades than will be whatever value might be obtained from a limited local study. To this application of meta-analysis, Schmidt and Hunter have attached the name *validity generalization.*

The procedures for meta-analysis and validity generalization are still controversial, but the methods are being applied to an increasingly wide variety of topics in education and occupational psychology. We may anticipate that the next 10 or 20 years will see a more systematic synthesis of the validation research that has accumulated over the past 50 years, leading to stable, generalized estimates of test-criterion relationships. We may hope that these relationships will be accepted by the Equal Employment Opportunity Commission, other government agencies, and the courts as superior replacements for local studies on necessarily small samples and that objective testing procedures will again become a practical procedure for appraising job applicants.

SUMMARY

The most important characteristic for a test to have is validity. But, validity is the responsibility of both the test constructor and the test user because validity refers to the use or interpretation that is made of a test score. In one context, one interpretation of a test score may be appropriate, but in a different context or for a different purpose, the same interpretation might well be invalid.

Three general types of evidence bear on the question of whether a particular test use is a valid use. First, content-related evidence reveals the relationship between the test content and the proposed interpretation. If the correspondence, which is largely a matter of expert judgment, is good, the proposed use is supported. Second, empirical or criterion-related evidence is obtained from the relationships of test scores with other variables of interest, particularly occupational and educational outcomes. Substantial correlations between test scores and measures of performance in the outcome task support the use of the test for prediction, selection, or placement decisions. Finally, construct-related evidence comes from the correspondence of the test scores to deductions from theory. Content- and criterion-related evidence help to determine fit to predictions from theory, but response to experimental interventions and agreement with predicted patterns of relationship with other variables are also important.

QUESTIONS AND EXERCISES

1. If the American College Testing Program were to develop a general survey test in science for high school seniors, what steps might the developers take to establish evidence of the validity of the test?

2. What type of validity evidence is indicated by each of the following statements that might have appeared in a test manual?

    a. Scores on the Attitudes Toward School Inventory correlated +0.43 with teachers' ratings of adjustment.

    b. The objectives to be assessed by XYZ Reading Test were rated for importance by 150 classroom teachers.

    c. Scores on the Wunderkind Programming Aptitude Test correlated +0.57 with supervisors' ratings after 6 months on the job.

    d. The Factors of Brilliance Intelligence Test yields scores that correlate +0.69 with scores on the Wechsler Adult Intelligence Scale.

    e. The Accurate Achievement Battery is based on an analysis of 50 widely used texts and 100 courses of study from all parts of the country.

3. Comment on the following statement: The classroom teacher is the only person who can judge the validity of a standardized achievement test for his or her class.

4. Examine the manuals for two or three tests of different types. What evidence for validity is presented in each? How adequate is the evidence for each test?

5. Using Table 5.4, determine what percentage of those selected would be above average on the job if a selection procedure with a validity of .50 were used and only the top quarter of applicants were accepted for the job. What percentage would be above average if the top three-quarters were selected? What would the two percentages be if the validity were only 0.40? What does a comparison of the four percentages indicate?

6. If personnel psychologists for the navy were doing research on tests for the selection of helicopter maintenance trainees, what might they use as a criterion of success in such a specialty? What are the advantages and disadvantages of each possible measure?

7. What are the advantages of using freshman grade point average as a criterion measure for validating a college admissions test? What are the disadvantages?

8. A test manual contains the following statement: The validity of Test Q is shown by the fact that it correlates .80 with the Stanford-Binet. What additional evidence is needed to evaluate this assertion?

9. You are considering three reading tests for use in your school. As far as you can judge, all three are equally valid, and each reports a reliability of .90. What else would you need to know to make a choice between the tests?

10. Examine several tests of aptitude or of achievement that would be appropriate for a class you might teach. Write up an evaluation of one of these tests, using the guidelines given in the last section of this chapter.

SUGGESTED READINGS

American Psychological Association, American Educational Research Association, & National Council on Measurement in Education. (1985). *Standards for educational and psychological testing.* Washington, DC: American Psychological Association.

Anastasi, A. (1986). Evolving concepts of test validation. *Annual Review of Psychology, 37,* 1-15.

Anghoff, W. H. (1988). Validity: An evolving concept. In H. Wainer & H. Braun (Eds.), *Test validity* (pp. 19-32). Hillsdale, NJ: Erlbaum.

Cook, T. D., & Campbell, D. T. (1979). *Quasi-experimentation: Design and analysis issues for field settings.* Chicago: Rand McNally.

Cronbach, L. J. (1988). Five perspectives on validation argument. In H. Wainer & H. Braun (Eds.), *Test validity* (pp. 3-17). Hillsdale, NJ: Erlbaum.

Ebel, R. L. (1983). The practical validation of tests of ability. *Educational Measurement: Issues and Practices, 2*(2), 7-10.

Embretson (Whitely), S. (1983). Construct validity: Construct representation versus nomothetic span. *Psychological Bulletin, 93,* 179-197.

Fredericksen, N. (1986). Construct validity and construct similarity: Methods for use in test development and test validation. *Multivariate Behavioral Research, 21,* 3-28.

Gardner, E. F. (1983). Intrinsic rational validity: Necessary but not sufficient. *Educational Measurement: Issues and Practices, 2*(2), 13.

Haertel, E. (1985). Construct validity and criterion-referenced testing. *Review of Educational Research, 55,* 23-46.

Hambleton, R. K. (1984). Validating the test scores. In R. A. Berk (Ed.), *A guide to criterion-referenced test construction* (pp. 199-230). Baltimore: Johns Hopkins University Press.

Messick, S. (1989). Validity. In R. L. Linn (Ed.), *Educational measurement* (3rd ed., pp. 13-103). New York: Macmillan.

Schmidt, F. L. (1988). Validity generalization and the future of criterion-related validity. In H. Wainer & H. Braun (Eds.), *Test validity* (pp. 173-189). Hillsdale, NJ: Erlbaum.

Schmidt, F. L., Hunter, J. E., Pearlman, K., & Hirsh, H. R. (1985). Forty questions about validity generalization and meta-analysis. *Personnel Psychology, 32,* 697-798.

Shepard, L. A. (1993). Evaluating test validity. In L. Darling-Hammond (Ed.), *Review of research in education, 19,* 405-450, Washington, DC: American Educational Research Association.

CHAPTER 6

Practical Issues Relating to Testing

FACTORS MAKING FOR PRACTICALITY IN ROUTINE TEST USE

Although validity and reliability may be all-important in measures that are to be used for special purposes, when a test is to be used in classrooms throughout a school or school system or in any large or ongoing testing application, a number of down-to-earth, practical considerations must also be taken into account. It is easy for the administrator to pay too much attention to small financial savings or to economies of time that make it possible to fit a test into a standard class period with no shifting of schedules; nevertheless, these factors of economy and convenience are real considerations. Furthermore, other factors relating to the readiness with which the tests may be given, scored, and interpreted bear importantly on the use that will be made of the tests and the soundness of the conclusions that will be drawn from them.

Economy

The practical significance of dollar savings need not be emphasized in the current environment of tight educational budgets. Dollars are of real significance for any educational or industrial enterprise. Economy in the case of tests depends in part on the cost of test materials and scoring services per examinee and in part on the possibility of reusing the test materials. For example, in the upper elementary grades and beyond, it is feasible to administer a test using separate answer sheets and to use the test booklets for a number of testings. Also, if a test is used in successive years or if testing can be scheduled so that different classes or schools can be tested on different days, an important economy can be effected. Publishers sell test booklets and answer sheets separately for just this reason.

A second aspect of economy is time savings in test administration; however, this economy is often a false one. We saw in Chapter 4 that the reliability of a test depends largely on its length. As far as testing time is concerned, we get about what we give. Some tests may be designed a little more efficiently so that they give a little more reliable measure per minute of testing time, but, by and large, any reduction in testing time will be accomplished at the price of loss in precision or breadth of our appraisal, unless it is possible to use a computer adaptive test (see Chapter 16).

A third, and quite significant, aspect of economy is the ease of scoring. The clerical work of scoring a battery of tests by hand can become either burdensome if it is done by the already busy teacher or psychologist or expensive if it is carried out by clerical help hired especially for the purpose. As a result, test users rely heavily on mechanized scoring, and test publishers are producing tests that can be processed by the increasingly sophisticated equipment being developed. A number of commercially published tests, such as the SAT and the Strong Interest Inventory, can be scored only by the publisher or at special centers licensed by the publisher. Other tests, such as the individually administered Stanford-Binet and Wechsler scales, are scored only by hand. But, for many published tests, test users have the option of hand scoring their own tests, of setting up their own mechanized scoring units, or of sending tests to one of the test scoring services that specialize in test processing.

Several test-scoring services, many run by the test publishers themselves, provide efficient test scoring and reporting, often giving 24-hour turnaround; that is, they will score the tests and put the results in return mail within 24 hours of their receipt of the completed answer sheets. Also, test scoring equipment is becoming so inexpensive and available that many schools or districts maintain their own scoring services. The basic equipment consists of a photoelectric document reader combined with a computer. The document reader responds to marks on an answer sheet or in the test booklet. (At least three companies sell the scanning part of a test scoring system for under $5,000, a cost that is within the means of many school districts and modest-sized companies. There are now even optical scanners, called optical character readers, that will read printed text, but these scanners are considerably more expensive than the equipment just mentioned.)

Using a separate answer sheet is familiar to most American college students, but separate answer sheets are not satisfactory for young children. The complications of finding an answer in the test booklet, keeping the code letter of the chosen answer in mind while locating the proper place on the answer sheet, and then marking the proper spot on the answer sheet are too much for children in the primary grades. However, current equipment makes it possible to use a booklet at the primary level and either to slice the bound edge off the test booklet and run the separate pages through the scanner or to print the test in a fanfold booklet that can be unfolded and run through the scanner as a unit. Modern scanning equipment can handle 50 or more different answer sheet patterns in a single run.

The information from the optical scanner is fed into the computer where it is compared with a key that has been recorded in the computer's memory. One or more scores are determined and printed out on a record form. The computer can also produce various statistics, such as means and standard deviations, as well as local percentiles, for classes, schools, or school systems. Thus, the scoring service, whether it is a commercial agency or a district office, can generally provide not only test scores for individuals, but also the complete range of statistical information about the test results of interest to the local school system. Some of the scoring services will also accumulate results over a period of years, providing a longitudinal picture of the local test results. One advantage to the local school system of having its own scoring and computing equipment is that it is then much easier to carry out item analyses (see Chapter 15) on locally constructed tests, as well as to accumulate local norms and longitudinal results.

A test deemed economical for use in large-scale testing programs will be available in a format for scoring by different types of scanning and scoring equipment. Almost any type of answer sheet can be hand-scored relatively efficiently by using an overlay stencil. Some test publishers supply plastic overlay stencils for this purpose. Others use a special type of answer sheet made up of two sheets fastened together, the back of one being carbon covered or pressure sensitive. The key is printed on the back of the first sheet, and as the examinee marks the front, the carbon-covered or pressure-sensitive material transfers the marks to the back of the sheet, where the number of marks falling in the printed key spaces can be counted.

Potential test purchasers will want to determine what types of answer forms and what scoring services are available for any test under consideration. If scoring is to be done locally, they should know of any restrictions imposed by the available scanner. Test publishers who allow local scoring of their tests will generally have answer sheets that can be scored by the common types of scanners. For several of the popular tests there are also software packages available that will produce score profiles and the various types of reports described in Chapter 3.

Features Facilitating Test Administration

In evaluating the practical usability of a test, one factor to be taken into account is the ease of administration. A test that can be handled adequately by the regular classroom teacher with no more than a session or so of special briefing fits much more readily into a testing program than a test requiring specially trained administrators and large blocks of time for testing. Several factors contribute to the ease of giving and taking a test.

1. *A test is easy to give if it has clear, full instructions.* The instructions for test administration should be written out completely, so that all the examiner must do is read and follow them. Everything the examiner should say to the examinees should be included, verbatim, in the instructions, preferably in contrasting color or bold face type. Instructions for the examinee should also be complete and should provide appropriate practice exercises. The amount of practice that should be provided depends on how novel the test task is likely to be for those being tested. When it is a familiar type of task or a simple and straightforward instruction, no more than a single example may be needed; however, for an unusual item format or a complex test task, more practice will be desirable. The better test publishers make practice tests available so students can get experience with the types of items included on the test.

Familiarity with the types of tasks the test requires is also a possible source of irrelevant differences between examinees. Many underprivileged children are not as familiar with testing situations as are children from more advantaged homes. A plentiful supply of practice items can help reduce the negative effect of task unfamiliarity and yield a more accurate picture of the abilities of disadvantaged children. With the prevalence of tests in society, instruction in how to take tests (through administering a number of practice tests) may even be a reasonable educational activity in the earlier grades because it would reduce "testwiseness" as one irrelevant source of individual differences in scores.

2. *A test is easy to give if there are few separately timed units and if close timing is not crucial.* Timing a number of brief subtests to a fraction of a minute is a bothersome undertaking, and the timing is likely to be inaccurate unless a stopwatch is available for each tester. Some tests have as many as 8 or 10 parts, each taking only 2 or 3 minutes. A test made up of 3 or 4 parts, with time limits of 5, 10, or more minutes for each, will be easier to use. Errors in timing, which can produce inaccurate test scores, are also less likely with fewer and longer parts.

3. *The layout of the test items on the page has a good deal to do with the ease of taking the test.* Items in which the response options all run together on the same line or those with small or illegible pictures or diagrams or which are crowded together or run over from one page to the next all create difficulty for the examinee.

Item difficulty should come from the content and the thought processes required to determine the right answer, not from the test format. Print and pictures should be large and clear. Response options should be well separated from one another. All parts of an item and all items referring to a single figure, problem, or reading passage should appear on the same page or a double-page spread. Also, to the extent that the physical layout of the test is difficult for examinees to follow, scores may be lower than they should be, a fact that would adversely affect the validity of the test and be particularly detrimental for a criterion-referenced test.

Features Facilitating Interpretation And Use of Scores

Although the point is sometimes overlooked, it seems axiomatic that a test is given so that the results can be used. If the score is to be used, it must be interpreted and given meaning. The author and publisher of the test have the responsibility of providing users with information that permits them to make sound appraisals of the test in relation to their needs and to give appropriate meaning to the score of each individual. The authors and publishers do this primarily through the *test manual* and other collateral materials prepared to accompany the test. What may the test user reasonably expect to find in the manual for a test, together with its supporting materials? We have outlined below the aids that the user should expect.

1. *A statement of the functions the test was designed to measure and of the general procedures by which it was developed.* In this statement, the author tells what he or she considers the test to be valid for and provides the evidence that proper steps have been taken to achieve that validity. Particularly for achievement tests, in which the primary concern is that the test measures particular content areas and cognitive processes, the manual should describe the procedures by which the choice of content was made or how the analysis of the functions being measured was carried out. If the author is unwilling to expose his or her thinking to our critical scrutiny, we may perhaps be skeptical of the thoroughness or profundity of that thinking.

Procedures to be reported include not only the rational procedures by which the range of content or types of objectives were selected but also the empirical procedures by which the items were reviewed, tried out, and screened for final inclusion in the test. The validity of the test—the interpretations it supports, caveats regarding these interpretations, and the uses to which it may properly be put—is its most important property. The author's plan and procedures for construction are vital steps in achieving validity and should be explicitly stated so that potential users can judge the quality of these activities.

2. *Detailed instructions for administering the test.* Earlier in this section we discussed the need for this aid to uniform and easy administration by teachers or others who will have to use the test. Of course, proper administration is also vital to achieving scores that are valid for the user's purpose.

3. *Scoring keys and specific instructions for scoring the test.* The problems of scoring have also been discussed. If the test can or must be scored locally, the manual and supporting materials should provide detailed instructions on how the score is

to be computed, how errors are to be treated, and how part scores are to be combined into a total score. Scoring keys and stencils should be planned to facilitate, as much as possible, the onerous task of hand scoring when scoring is to be done by the local user, and instructions should also be given for electronic scoring.

4. *Norms for appropriate reference groups.* These norms, together with information on how the norms were obtained and with instructions for their use, should be included in the test manual or a separate publication devoted to normative information. A full consideration of types of test norms and their uses was presented in Chapter 3. It is therefore sufficient at this time to point out the responsibility of the test producer to develop suitable norms for the groups with which the test is to be used. General norms are a necessity, and norms suitable for special types of communities, special occupational groups, and other more limited subgroups will add to the usefulness of the test in many cases.

5. *Evidence of the reliability of the test.* This evidence should indicate not only the simple reliability statistics but also the operations used to obtain the reliability estimates and the descriptive and statistical characteristics of each group on which reliability data are based. If a test is available in more than one form, it is highly desirable for the producers to report the correlation between the two forms, in addition to any data that were derived from a single testing. If the test yields part scores, and particularly if it is proposed that any use be made of these part scores, reliability data should be reported for the separate part scores. It is good procedure for the author to report standard errors of measurement, as well as reliability coefficients. An author who indicates what the standard error of measurement is at each of a number of score levels should particularly be commended because this information shows the range of scores over which the test retains its accuracy.

6. *Evidence on the intercorrelations of subscores.* If the test provides several subscores, the manual should provide information on the intercorrelations of the subscores. This information is important in guiding the interpretation of the subscores and particularly in judging how much confidence to place in the *differences* between the subscores. If the correlations among the subscores approach their reliabilities, indicating that they measure much the same things, the differences between them will be largely meaningless and uninterpretable. Information on the reliability of the subscores, coupled with knowledge of their correlations, permits an accurate evaluation of the degree to which difference scores add information to the original scores. Some test publishers also provide information on the frequency with which score differences of a particular magnitude occurred in the standardization sample.

Factor analyses (see Chapter 16) of the correlations among subscores should be reported to confirm that any recommended combinations of subscores can reasonably be considered to measure a common dimension. Such analyses support claims of content and construct validity.

7. *Evidence on the relationship of the test to other variables.* Insofar as the test is to be used as a predictive device, correlations with criterion measures constitute the essential evidence on how well it does in fact predict. Full information should be provided on the nature of the criterion variables, the groups for which data are available, and the conditions under which the data were obtained. Only then can the reader fairly judge the validity of the test as a predictor.

It will often be desirable to report correlations with other measures of the same function as collateral evidence bearing on the construct validity of the test. For example, correlations with an individual intelligence test are relevant in the case of a group measure of intelligence.

Finally, indications of the relationship of test scores to age, sex, type of community, socioeconomic level, and similar facts about the individual or group are often helpful. They provide a basis for judging how sensitive the measure is to the background of the group members and to the circumstances of their lives and their education. Evidence of this kind is also useful for judging whether the norm groups used by the publisher are appropriate for the local population.

8. *Guides for using the test and for interpreting results obtained with it.* The developers of a test presumably know how it is reasonable for the test to be used and how the results from it should be evaluated. They are specialists in that test. For the test to be most useful to others, especially the teacher with limited specialized training, suggestions should be given of ways in which the test results may be used for diagnosing individual and group strengths and weaknesses, forming class groupings, organizing remedial instruction, counseling the individual, or whatever other activities may appropriately be based on results from that particular type of instrument.

A Final Word on Quality

A final point to keep in mind is that the care that has gone into preparing the test manual is often itself a good indicator of the care that has been exercised in constructing the test. Test authors who do a careful, thorough job of describing how the test was constructed and how evidence of its reliability and validity was obtained probably cared enough to give their very best. They are likely to have carried out the steps for constructing the test in a thoughtful, professional manner as well.

GUIDE FOR EVALUATING A TEST

As an aid to the potential user, we end this section with a guide for evaluating a test. This guide consists of a series of questions, based in large part on the *Standards for Educational and Psychological Testing* (APA, 1985). Careful study of the complete *Standards* will reward the person who would become a more sophisticated test user. (The most recent edition of the *Standards* differs from its predecessors in that it places more emphasis on the proper interpretation and use of test results. The validity of test scores depends heavily, some would say entirely, on the context of their use, and *it is the responsibility of the test user to guarantee that inferences and decisions based on test scores are supported by appropriate evidence.*)

You will note that many of the questions in this guide relate to the availability and adequacy of information reported about the test. There is an implied, although not explicitly stated, second question as a sequel to many of the sections of the guide, especially those relating to reliability and validity. That question is, given that the information is provided, how satisfactory does the test appear to be, in comparison with others that are available, as well as by absolute standards, for the use I want to make of it? A significant portion of the responsibility for valid testing rests with the test user. You must evaluate the evidence provided by the publisher, as well as what you know about the examinees and the intended uses of the test scores. In light of this information, you must decide whether the evidence justifies using this test for this purpose.

A number of questions in this guide also refer to the adequacy of norms and converted scores. You may wish to review Chapter 3 as you study this portion of the guide.

General Identifying Information

1. What is the name of the test?
2. Who are its authors—by name and position if that information is available? (It should be.)
3. Who publishes the test? And when was it published?
4. Is more than one form of the test available? If so, how many?
5. How much does the test cost?
6. How long does it take to administer the test?

Information About the Test

1. Is there a test manual (or some other similar source of information, such as an article in a journal) that is designed to provide the information a potential user needs to administer the test and interpret the results properly?
2. How recently have there been revisions in the test, the manual, and the norms? (For major commercial tests it is reasonable to expect that both the test and its manual will be revised at least every 10 years and that new norms will accompany the revisions.)

Aids to Interpreting Test Results

1. Does the manual provide a clear statement of the purposes and applications for which the test is intended?
2. Does the manual provide a clear statement of the qualifications needed to administer the test and interpret its results properly?
3. Do the test, manual, record forms, and accompanying materials guide users toward sound and correct interpretation of the test results?
4. Are the manual's statements expressing relationships presented in quantitative terms so that the reader can tell how much confidence to attach to them? (For example, it is much more informative to say that the correlation

with Variable X is .55 than to say that the test correlates substantially with Variable X.)

Validity

1. Does the manual report evidence on the validity of the test for each type of inference for which the test is recommended?
2. Does the manual *avoid* referring to correlations between items and total test score as evidence of validity?
3. If the test is designed to be a sample of a specified domain of behaviors (e.g., an achievement test), does the manual define the domain clearly and indicate the procedures used for sampling from that domain?
4. When criterion-related validity is involved, does the manual describe the criterion variables clearly, comment on their adequacy, and indicate what aspects of the criterion performance are *not* adequately reflected in these criterion measures?
5. Are the samples used for estimating criterion-related validity adequately described? And are they appropriate to the purpose? One way spuriously to inflate apparent validity is to use samples that are much more heterogeneous than those that can be expected in actual use. Are such tricks avoided?
6. Are statistical analyses for criterion-related validity presented in a form that permits the reader to judge the degree of confidence that can be placed in inferences about individuals?
7. If the test is designed to measure a theoretical construct (e.g., trait of ability, temperament, or attitude), is the proposed interpretation clearly stated and differentiated from alternate theoretical interpretations? Is the evidence to support this interpretation clearly stated and fully presented?
8. Are potential threats to valid use of the test scores, such as language handicaps and learning disabilities, identified and appropriate cautions noted? Does the manual consider possible unintended outcomes of using the test?

In summary, to what extent does the available validity evidence justify the uses of the test suggested in the manual or the use that you would want to make of the test results? Remember that *if you intend to use the test for some purpose other than that contemplated by the test developer, the responsibility for demonstrating the validity of the test for that use rests with you.*

Reliability

1. Does the manual present data adequate to permit the reader to judge whether scores are sufficiently dependable for the recommended uses (or for your contemplated uses, if these are different from the recommended ones)?

2. Are the samples on which reliability data were obtained sufficiently well described that the user can judge whether the data apply to his or her situation? As with validity, one way spuriously to inflate apparent reliability is to use samples that are much more heterogeneous than those that can be expected in actual use. Are such tricks avoided?
3. Are the reliability data presented in the conventional statistical form of product-moment correlation coefficients and standard errors of measurement? Are standard errors presented for different levels of performance?
4. If more than one form of the test was produced, are data provided to establish comparability of the forms?
5. If the test purports to measure a generalized homogeneous trait, is evidence reported on the internal consistency (interitem or interpart correlations) of the parts that make up the test?
6. Does the test manual provide data on the stability of test performance over time?

In summary, to what extent do the reliability data provided in the manual justify the uses for the test results suggested by the authors or the uses that you would want to make of the test results?

Administration and Scoring

1. Are the directions for administration sufficiently clear and fully stated so that the administrator will be able to duplicate the conditions under which the norms were established and the reliability and validity data were obtained?
2. If the test is administered by computer or provides computer-assisted administration, are the programs written to run on the equipment you have available? Is adequate documentation and technical support provided?
3. If the test can be scored locally, are the procedures for scoring set forth clearly and in detail, in a way that will maximize scoring efficiency and minimize the likelihood of scoring error? Are the directions for determining subscores clear? If scoring software is available, is adequate documentation and technical support provided?
4. If the test is to be scored by the publisher or a commercial scoring service, does the test scoring service provide for the accumulation of results over time to aid in preparing local norms and local validity evidence?

Scales and Norms

1. Are the scales used for reporting performance clearly and carefully described so that the test interpreter will fully understand them and be able to communicate the interpretation to an examinee?

2. Are norms reported in the manual in appropriate form—usually standard scores or percentile ranks in appropriate reference groups?
3. Are the populations to which the norms refer clearly defined and described? And are they populations with which you can appropriately compare your examinees?
4. If more than one form of the test is available, including revised forms, are tables provided showing equivalent scores on the different forms?
5. Does the manual discuss the possible value of local norms? Does it provide any help in preparing local norms?
6. Is a computer program available to assist with test interpretation and report writing? If so, is the program appropriately interactive; do the interpretations and reports it generates make suggestions about test results and avoid drawing definitive conclusions?

In summary, there are many factors to consider when selecting a test, no one of which is conclusive. It will be your responsibility as a measurement professional to gather evidence related to using a particular test for a particular purpose. No test is perfect, and you will have to weigh the benefits of using each test against the possible costs and consequences. Only when you feel confident that the advantages outweigh the risks should you use the test.

GETTING INFORMATION ABOUT SPECIFIC TESTS

There were 3,009 published tests in English available for sale in 1994. In addition, there are many more than this number that are out of print, were produced locally, or were developed for specific research projects. Many of these are available from one source or another. A single text cannot even begin to list, much less describe, all the instruments developed that might interest you. A few of the best known and most widely used tests will be reviewed in later chapters as illustrations of different types of tests. For the rest, we try in the remainder of this chapter to provide you with some tools to find the tests you need and information about them. We have organized the sections around the questions that you are likely to ask, in the order that you would ordinarily ask them, and we try to give useful ways to find answers to these questions.

What Tests Exist?

What tests of reading comprehension are suitable for fourth graders? What tests of vocational interests exist for high school seniors? What measures of attitude toward nuclear power are available? The first thing we need to know is what already exists. When we have a catalog of possibilities, we can begin to pick and choose. Or, if nothing satisfactory is available, we can undertake to construct something from scratch. Where should we go to assemble a catalog of possibilities?

The first source to turn to is *Tests in Print IV* (Murphy, Conoley, & Impara, 1994). This book (also known as TIP-IV) has been revised about every 10 years and provides an alphabetical listing of the 3,009 instruments that were available from commercial test publishers at the time of its release, with information on when each was published and by whom. A subject matter index is provided to help the reader locate the tests in a given category. *Tests in Print* is a companion volume to the *Mental Measurements Yearbook* series (hereafter referred to as *MMY*), which is described in a later section. *Tests in Print* includes references to entries in the *MMYs* dealing with the test in question, as well as updates of the bibliography of references relating to that test. Each edition of *Tests in Print* replaces the previous one, deleting entries for tests no longer available and adding references to new ones.

Two companion sources to *Tests in Print* are *Tests: A Comprehensive Reference for Assessments in Psychology, Education and Business* (hereafter referred to as *Tests*) (Sweetland & Keyser, 1986) and the *Dictionary of Behavioral Assessment Techniques* (*Dictionary*) (Hersen & Bellack, 1988). The entries in these volumes are alphabetically arranged within topic areas and have the advantage over *Tests in Print* that they provide a brief description of each entry, as well as information about the publisher and price. The descriptions are not evaluative; they closely follow the author's or publisher's statement of what the test measures. The information in *Tests* is somewhat sketchy, in that it does not identify the author, give the date of publication of an instrument, or give any statistical information about it. *Tests* contains about 2,500 entries for current tests and an index of out-of-print tests and their publishers. The *Dictionary* lists 288 clinical rating scales and questionnaires and does give the names and addresses of sources for the instruments.

Tests in Print, the *Dictionary,* and *Tests* are useful for finding tests, but they fall short in two respects. They do not give information on *the most recent tests,* and, except for some entries in the *Dictionary,* they do not give information about *unpublished* instruments. (By unpublished instruments, we mean tests that are not offered for sale. An attitude scale that is given in full in a book or article is, for our purposes, unpublished unless its author offers it for sale.)

To find the most recently published tests, you need to obtain a copy of test publishers' current catalogs. They describe the tests and services that the publisher is currently promoting, and even some expected to be available in the near future. A large number of publishers produce an occasional test, but relatively few are regular and substantial producers of testing instruments. A complete listing of test publishers can be found in *Tests in Print,* and we provide the names and addresses of a number of the major publishers in Appendix 3. (Also, in Appendix 4, we provide an annotated list of tests.) A file of current test catalogs may sometimes be available through the measurement facility of your university or through the testing center in your local school system. If such a resource is not available, write to those publishers who have produced tests like the one you seek and request a copy of their current catalog.

In addition to test catalogs, there is a newsletter, *News on Tests,* which is published quarterly by the Educational Testing Service (ETS). In this newsletter, you may find announcements by test publishers of forthcoming tests and revisions, citations of test reviews, and other up-to-date information about tests and testing practices.

Some journals carry ads from test publishers, as do *The Monitor,* the newsletter of the American Psychological Association, and similar publications from other professional associations.

Locating unpublished instruments that have been locally developed or that have been used only in research studies can be a bit tricky. However, several source books and directories have been prepared since 1975 that provide useful assistance in such an undertaking. Probably the most useful of these sources is the test collection *Tests in Microfiche,* developed by ETS. Beginning in 1975, ETS started distributing not only an index of unpublished tests but also copies of the tests on microfiche. At the end of 1995 the collection included 1,007 instruments and was being expanded at the rate of about 25 tests per year. The most recent additions to the collection, representing a change in practice, were 28 out-of-print tests developed at Purdue University between 1942 and 1960. ETS also accumulates references to publications using these tests.

To supplement its *Tests in Microfiche* service, ETS has begun to list the tests in their Test Collection and their characteristics on the Internet. Because this service is changing so rapidly, it is hard to predict what its eventual characteristics will be, but at this time the service can be accessed by following the instructions given here to get the listed information.

The ETS Test Collection Via the Internet

Thanks to the Internet, it's never been easier to access the ETS Test Collection database. To log on, simply follow these steps:

1. Once you gain access to the Internet, type GOPHER GOPHER.CUA.EDU
2. Arrow down to SPECIAL RESOURCES and press the enter key
3. Arrow down to ERIC CLEARINGHOUSE ON ASSESSMENT AND EVALUATION and press the enter key
4. Arrow down to TEST LOCATOR and press the enter key
5. Arrow down to ERIC/ETS TEST FILE (—/—/—)<?> and press the enter key
6. Type in the keywords you want to search, using the appropriate connector(s) AND, OR, NOT, and hit the enter key
7. You will get a list of tests that meet your search parameters, and in the lower right corner of the screen, you can see how many screens contain the list of titles, e.g., 1/5 means there are five screens containing test titles that match the keywords and you are currently on screen one. To see titles on subsequent screens, use the down arrow key.
8. To see a full description of the test, arrow down to a test title in which you are interested and press the enter key. You will now have a complete record of the test, including the following applicable parts:
    *   CH—accession number (the identification number for that particular test)
    *   UP—the date the test description was entered into the system
    *   *TITLE—the name of the test
    *   *AU—the author(s) of the test—it may be an individual or an organization or institution

- *AVAIL—the name and address of the last known test publisher or distributor or the source where you will find the test items (such as a journal citation)
- PDAT—the publication date of the test
- *DESC—descriptors or subject indexing terms. Those preceded by an * indicate the major focus of the test
- *IDEN—terms, including acronyms, that further describe the test
- ABST—an abstract that gives information on the test, including purpose, skills or knowledge or characteristics assessed, population for which the test is geared, and other information

NOTE: For HELP information on how to search the Test Collection database, in step 5 above, arrow down to ERIC/ETS Test File (—/—/—) (_KB).

Several summaries of the ETS test collection have been published. One of these is the *ETS Test Collection Cumulative Index to Tests in Microfiche, 1975–1987* (hereafter referred to as *Cumulative Index*) (Hepner, 1988), which lists the tests in the collection by title, author's name, and Educational Research Information Center (ERIC) identification number, as well as provides a brief abstract of the test. There is also an annual *Tests in Microfiche Annotated Index* (hereafter referred to as *Annotated Index*) (Educational Testing Service, Test Collection, 1975–1995) which each December updates the information in the *Cumulative Index.*

The ETS collection *Tests in Microfiche* is a service to which many university libraries subscribe. However, the subscription contains the following restriction (printed in the *Annotated Index,* p. iii):

> The materials included in the microfiche may be reproduced by the purchaser for his or her own use. Permission to use these materials in any other manner must be obtained directly from the author. This includes modifying or adapting the materials or selling or distributing them to others.

A number of other sources also provide references to unpublished tests. The *Directory of Unpublished Experimental Mental Measures* (Goldman & Busch, 1978, 1982; Goldman & Mitchell, 1990; Goldman & Osborne, 1985; Goldman & Sanders, 1974) includes over 3,000 entries describing such instruments, while *Tests and Measurements in Child Development: Handbook II* (Johnson, 1976) and *Tests and Measurements in Child Development: A Handbook* (Johnson & Bommarito, 1971) are other sources of unpublished instruments for use with young children. Several volumes cover the field of attitude measurement and reproduce the actual scales used (Robinson, Athanasion, & Head, 1969; Robinson, Rusk, & Head, 1968; Robinson & Shaver, 1973; Shaw & Wright, 1967). More recently, O'Brien (1988) has published a bibliography of selected references on testing, which includes 2,759 sources categorized by the topic or subject covered in the article, and ETS has published a six-volume Test Collection Catalog listing (1) Achievement Tests, (2) Vocational Tests, (3) Tests for Special Populations, (4) Cognitive, Aptitude, and Intelligence Tests, (5) Attitude Tests, and (6) Affective Measures and Personality Tests. In addition to the

---

*The search software is set up to look for the occurrence of keywords in the * fields.

sources already mentioned, the Sources of Test Information list at the end of this chapter presents some references that cover more limited areas.

An additional resource that may be useful in certain circumstances is the *Directory of Selected National Testing Programs* (Educational Testing Service, Test Collection, 1987). This three-volume series gives the names, publishers or producers, addresses, and general descriptions of a wide range of national testing programs. Volume 1 covers selection and admission programs for secondary and postsecondary institutions, government service, graduate and professional schools, and health-related programs. Volume 2 lists academic-credit and advanced-placement testing programs, and Volume 3 gives the testing programs for certification and licensing. The tests covered in this series generally are not available for public review.

Finally, there are computerized data bases that will be described more fully later in the chapter. They represent extended data files that can be searched to locate additional tests, as well as to locate research using a known test or research on a problem of interest.

Exactly What Is Test X Like?

Once you have identified a promising reading test, interest inventory, or attitude measure (called, say, Test X), you will want to find out more about it. Where should you turn?

A certain amount of descriptive information about the test will appear in some of the sources listing tests and in evaluations that appear in the *MMY*s. However, there is really no substitute for examining the test firsthand. So, the first thing to do is to obtain a copy of the test and look at it. A *specimen set,* which usually includes a copy of the test, an answer sheet, and the manual for the test, may be available through your university—in either the library, counseling center, or measurement-area files for published tests. Or, the testing office of your school system may be able to provide one. If not, you may have to order a specimen set from the publisher—the catalog will indicate the price.

A publisher is likely to require some credentials to show that you are an appropriate person to have access to the testing materials. A letter from your instructor or from a supervisor in the school system where you work may suffice. However, some types of instruments that call for special training or skills will have further restrictions on their distribution, and you may have to complete a form to verify that you have the required qualifications. In a few cases, it may be necessary to have a person with the required professional credentials order the test for you and supervise your examination of it.

Many of the unpublished instruments are reproduced in full in some of the compendia listed in Sources of Test Information at the end of this chapter, particularly in the *Tests in Microfiche* collection of ETS. Others are produced in full in articles reporting their development and use. If an unpublished test you wish to examine is not available from one of these sources, you may have to try to get a copy from its author.

Once you have a copy of the test or inventory, what information should you try to get from it? The answer depends on the type of test. If it is a test of school achievement, you should examine the items and ask yourself if the content covered and the processes called for match the objectives you have set for your teaching or that are contained in the school or district curriculum guide. For all kinds of tests, you should ask whether the items are clearly stated and the answer choices plausible. For all types of tests, you should ask whether the directions are clear and the page layouts are attractive and legible. Of course, for unpublished tests, the quality of the test materials may ultimately be up to you because you are likely to have to produce your own copies of the test.

Of equal importance to the test itself are the supporting materials that describe the test's statistical properties, the form in which test results are to be reported, and the aids provided for test use and interpretation. For tests available from commercial publishers, this information should appear in one or more test manuals—possibly in a manual for test administrators or one for counselors or supervisors, and in a technical manual that gives, in considerable detail, the statistical properties of the test. These manuals should be examined thoroughly.

For unpublished tests, the primary sources of technical material about the tests will be in articles or books reporting studies in which the tests were used. The quality of this information is likely to be much lower than that which you will find in the manual for a good commercial test. For relatively new tests or tests that have not been widely used, it is often necessary to contact the author. It is not uncommon to encounter a measuring instrument developed for use in a research study, for which there is no information about reliability or validity except for the findings from that one study. In some cases there may be no evidence at all of instrument quality. When this happens, the test should not be used other than for research purposes, and then only with caution.

Most commercially published tests provide accompanying scoring and reporting services. The services range from simply scoring the test answer sheets and reporting raw scores and percentiles or standard scores to providing extended narrative interpretations of each individual's test results. Examples of some of these reports were given in Chapter 3. The specimen set should describe, and perhaps illustrate, the types of reports that are available, and you should determine how adequately these will serve your needs.

The evidence on reliability and validity should be scrutinized with a particularly critical eye. Remember that the specimen set is primarily a promotional piece. You can expect the publisher to accentuate the positive, so try to cut through the puffery and get down to the basic evidence; be suspicious if evidence is incompletely or vaguely reported. Chapters 4 and 5 and the guide for test evaluation provided earlier in this chapter indicate what evidence you can reasonably expect to find.

What Do Critics Think of Test X?

Because materials from the test publisher focus on selling the test—some do so blatantly; some, subtly—it is highly desirable to get an evaluation by a competent and unbiased reviewer. The one source to automatically turn to for such critical reviews is the series of *Mental Measurements Yearbooks*. This series was initiated by the late Oscar Buros in 1936 and published by him until 1978. Preparation of *The Ninth Mental Measurements Yearbook* (Mitchell, 1985), *The Tenth Mental Measurements Yearbook* (Conoley & Kramer, 1989), *The Eleventh Mental Measurements Yearbook* (Kramer & Conoley, 1992), *The Twelfth Mental Measurements Yearbook* (Conoley & Impara, 1995), and future *MMY*s is in the hands of the Buros Institute of Mental Measurements of the University of Nebraska. The *MMY*s provide reviews, by presumably competent and disinterested people, of each published test of any significance. In recent *MMY*s, the publishers have obtained at least two independent reviews of each new test.

The volumes of this series are cumulative. That is, a test is reviewed when it first comes out, and it is generally not reviewed again unless there has been a significant change in the test or the material supporting it, or unless it is a test of unusually widespread and continuing use. *Tests in Print IV* provides an index giving the volume and page numbers for reviews of tests still in print in the first 11 *MMY* volumes.

In 1988, the Buros Institute of Mental Measurements began a new schedule for producing the *MMY*s. That year saw the publication of a *Supplement to The Ninth Mental Measurements Yearbook* (Conoley, Kramer, & Mitchell, 1988), which gave full *MMY* treatment to 89 new tests that had been published since 1985. *The Tenth Mental Measurements Yearbook* was published in 1989, and its supplement appeared in 1990. The staff of the Buros Institute announced plans to publish a complete volume in alternate years thereafter, with supplements in the intervening years, but *The Eleventh Mental Measurements Yearbook* arrived in 1992, followed by its supplement in 1994. The Twelfth *MMY* was published in 1995, so the Buros Institute may soon achieve its goal. Beginning with the 11th *MMY*, the yearbooks have been available on CD-ROM. This format has the advantage of permitting automated searches, but it is more difficult to flip back and forth between two or more instruments to compare them directly unless you print the reviews you are interested in.

Each of the 12 *MMY*s and the three supplements include tests of all types, but in the mid-1970s, a number of volumes were produced, each bringing together all the reviews of tests in a specific area, such as reading tests or personality inventories. One of these volumes may be an efficient source for the evaluations of interest to you, although many of them are now rather dated. The *MMY*s and *Tests in Print* should be available at the reference desk of any good university library, at many larger public libraries, and at the testing bureau in many school systems. The *MMY*s provide the most important source for evaluative reviews of tests. They also include reviews of books and monographs on testing, a listing of test publishers, and nearly complete bibliographies of published material on each of the tests. Reviews that have been received for upcoming editions of the *MMY* are available in a computer data base described in a later section.

Another source of critical reviews of tests is the seven-volume series *Test Critiques* (Keyser & Sweetland, 1984). Each volume in the series contains a single review of each of several hundred tests. The reviews are often somewhat longer and more detailed than those in the *MMY*s, but lack the contrasting opinions that multiple reviews provide. Unfortunately, the organization of the volumes is less than obvious. Each of the last five volumes contains a subject index to all preceding ones, but within a single volume, the tests are arranged alphabetically by title without regard to topic. This system may cause difficultly in finding a specific test.

Brief reviews of some American tests and a large number of tests published in Great Britain may be found in *Tests in Education: A Book of Critical Reviews* (Levy & Goldstein, 1984). The tests are organized into six general categories: early development, language, mathematics, achievement batteries, general abilities, and personality and counseling.

Reviews of new and important tests will occasionally be found, along with book reviews, in some psychological and educational journals. However, they appear sporadically, and there does not seem to be any journal that has a policy of systematically and regularly reviewing new published tests. At this time, the best source of evaluative information seems to be the *MMY*s and their supplements, particularly now that they are updated more regularly in print and monthly on the computer data base.

A different approach to test evaluation has been taken by Hammill, Brown, and Bryant (1992) in their *A Consumer's Guide to Tests in Print*. This volume contains ratings of seven technical aspects of the quality of a number of published instruments and observations about several nontechnical features of these instruments, as well as an overall rating of quality. The ratings are provided for each subscale of multiscore tests, like the Wechsler scales and the Stanford-Binet, and are presented as: A—highly recommended, B—recommended, and F—not recommended. The tabular form is compact, but the organization of the scales by the function measured results in splitting up the subscales of the multiscore instruments so that one must consult several pages to get an overall impression of a particular test.

What Research Has Been Conducted on Test X?

What studies have been made of the test's reliability? Its validity as a predictor of Z? The influence of coaching on its scores? Its relation to measures of Y?

Of course, some material will appear in the technical manual for the test. Manuals vary widely in the amount of statistical and research information that they report. Some of the better ones become almost a full-length book and report a wide range of analyses of the test's reliability, correlations with other instruments, and predictive validity for academic or job criteria. The manual will also often include a bibliography, providing references to specific research studies. But, for widely used tests, the manual can hardly provide complete information; for example, in the course of its 80-year history, the Stanford-Binet Intelligence Scale has been used to carry out over 6,000 studies, and in only 55 years, almost as many have been carried out with the Minnesota Multiphasic Personality Inventory and the various Wechsler scales. It is also difficult for a manual to be up to date with recent studies. In fact, it is rare for a test publisher to bring out a revision of a test manual that does not correspond to a revision of the test itself, so even the manuals for the best commercially produced tests may be 5 to 10 years old.

As already noted, for published tests, very comprehensive bibliographies appear in the *MMY*s and *Tests in Print*. As is the case with the reviews of the tests themselves, these reference sources include only references to articles and books published since their last editions. Even so, for a number of the popular and widely used tests, the bibliography is *so* extensive, running to thousands of entries, that it becomes almost unusable. However, these bibliographies permit you to scan through titles with the hope of identifying the ones that deal with the specific problem of interest.

The other main avenue for locating research on tests and testing is through the index and abstract services, which appear as monthly journals and are then combined into annual volumes. The ones most likely to be useful for a person interested in testing are *Dissertation Abstracts International,* the *Education Index,* and *Psychological Abstracts.* A useful recent resource is the *Index to Tests Used in Educational Dissertations* (Fabiano, 1989). *Dissertation Abstracts International* has had an online computer search service since 1980, but finding earlier references to tests has been difficult. This reference categorizes over 50,000 tests alphabetically by title. The entries for each test include the type of examinees, the volume and page number of the abstract, and the author's name. Dissertations in psychology are not covered.

A relatively new development in sources of information about testing is the appearance of computerized data bases. There are several data bases that can help you find information about a type of test or a testing problem. One is the computerized update of the *MMY.* Now, it is possible to obtain from the computerized data base of the *MMY*s any reviews or other information that have been assembled in preparing the next edition or supplement.

Two more general data bases that include many references to tests and testing topics are the ERIC and PsychLit collections. ERIC includes information about articles in education and related areas, while PsychLit provides a computerized version of much of the material in *Psychological Abstracts.* Both services are available at many university libraries and contain the complete citation for each article, a set of keywords, and an abstract of the study. They have the advantage that they can search the entire content of each entry for any desired word or phrase. Thus, if you search for a test title, the program will produce a list of all entries that include the name of that test in the title, abstract, or keywords. Searches can also be carried out by author or subject. The half hour or so that it takes to become familiar with these facilities will be time well spent.

Finally, there is the growing world of Internet. There is no way to tell what will be available in a year or two, but it is clear that web pages and data bases in addition to the ETS Test Collection will be available for searching, as will the holdings of many major libraries. Soon the ERIC and PsychLit data bases probably will be available via this avenue. Several psychology and education journals already have web pages, as do all of the major professional organizations. Notices of web page addresses are published frequently in the journals and newsletters of the professional organizations.

In using any data base, the secret of a successful search is a shrewd selection of keywords that serve to guide the computer in identifying relevant entries. In some instances, preparers of the data base provide a glossary of terms that the computer will recognize. It is the responsibility of the user to generate—or to select from the glossary—the entries most likely to elicit relevant items from the data base. Although test titles are unlikely to appear as keywords and may not appear in the abstract, the general traits measured by the instrument may well give access to publications in which the test is referenced.

Generally, a person who wishes to search one of the data bases will find it desirable, and perhaps necessary, to work through the reference division of a university or public library. The library is likely to have a computer terminal with direct access to the data files in question. If not, the reference librarian should be able to help arrange such access. There may be a charge for the search, and you will want to get an estimate of any costs before starting this undertaking.

SUMMARY

In addition to yielding information that is valid for the proposed use, the test must be practical to use. Practicality relates to matters of expense, ease of administration and scoring, and ease with which appropriate inferences can be derived from the test scores, including the adequacy and availability of norm- or criterion-referenced interpretations.

When reviewing a test, it is important to examine all the factors that make for a quality instrument. The test manual or other sources should provide information about the purpose of the test, its reliability and validity, what scales the test provides and what norms are available, and how the test should be administered and scored. When considering which of several tests to use, you will also want to obtain information about what aids are available to assist in score interpretation.

There are several published sources of information about specific tests, including *Tests in Print IV, Tests,* and the *Dictionary of Behavioral Assessment Techniques.* Copies of unpublished tests can be obtained from *Tests in Microfiche,* the *Dictionary of Unpublished Experimental Mental Measures,* and several other more specialized sources. Critical reviews of tests can be found in the *Mental Measurements Yearbooks* and *Test Critiques* as well as in various professional journals and newsletters.

QUESTIONS AND EXERCISES

1. Using the resources listed in the text, prepare as complete a list as you can of currently available standardized tests for a specific purpose (i.e., tests in first-year French, tests of reading achievement, inventories to measure adjustment to college life, etc.).

2. For some characteristic that interests you (e.g., self-concept, attitude toward pollution, creativity, etc.), determine what *research* tests are available in the literature, using the compilations and bibliographic sources referred to in this chapter.

3. Using the volumes of *Mental Measurements Yearbooks,* find out what reviewers think of a particular test that interests you. Do the reviewers agree?

4. To what sources would you go to try to answer each of the following questions? To which would you go first? What would you expect to get from each?

    a. What test should you use to study the progress of two classes in beginning Spanish?

    b. What kinds of norms are available for the Metropolitan Achievement Tests?

    c. Is the Rorschach test of any value as a predictor of academic success in college?

    d. Has a new revision of the Wechsler Intelligence Scale for Children been published yet?

    e. What measures of verbal ability have been published for use with the blind?

    f. What are the significant differences between the Iowa Tests of Basic Skills and the Metropolitan Achievement Tests?

    g. How much does the Cognitive Abilities Test cost?

    h. What do testing people think of the Career Occupational Preference System?

5. Look at two or three publishers' catalogs. Compare the announcements of tests of the same type. How adequate is the information provided? How objective is the presentation of the tests' values and limitations?

SOURCES OF TEST INFORMATION

Of General Interest

Buros, O. K. (Ed.). (1978). *The eighth mental measurements yearbook.* Highland Park, NJ: The Gryphon Press. (This and previous *Mental Measurements Yearbook* volumes are now handled by the Buros Institute of Mental Measurements at the University of Nebraska, Lincoln, NE.)

Conoley, J. C., & Impara, J. C. (Eds.). (1994). *Supplement to the eleventh mental measurements yearbook.* Lincoln, NE: Buros Institute of Mental Measurements.

Conoley, J. C., & Impara, J. C. (Eds.). (1995). *The twelfth mental measurements yearbook.* Lincoln, NE: Buros Institute of Mental Measurements.

Conoley, J. C., & Kramer, J. J. (Eds.). (1989). *The tenth mental measurements yearbook.* Lincoln, NE: Buros Institute of Mental Measurements.

Conoley, J. C., Kramer, J. J., & Mitchell, J. V., Jr. (Eds.). (1988). *Supplement to the ninth mental measurements yearbook.* Lincoln, NE: Buros Institute of Mental Measurements.

Fabiano, E. (1989). *Index to tests used in educational dissertations.* Phoenix, AZ: Oryx Press.

Goldman, B. A., & Busch, J. C. (1978). *Directory of unpublished experimental mental measures: Vol. 2.* New York: Human Sciences Press.

Goldman, B. A., & Busch, J. C. (1982). *Directory of unpublished experimental mental measures: Vol. 3.* New York: Human Sciences Press.

Goldman, B. A., & Mitchell, D. F. (1990). *Directory of unpublished experimental mental measures: Vol. 5.* Dubuque, IA: Wm. C. Brown.

Goldman, B. A., & Osborne, W. L. (1985). *Directory of unpublished experimental mental measures: Vol. 4.* New York: Human Sciences Press.

Goldman, B. A., & Sanders, J. L. (1974). *Directory of unpublished experimental mental measures: Vol. 1.* New York: Behavioral Publications.

Hammill, D. D., Brown, L., & Bryant, B. R. (1992). *A consumer's guide to tests in print* (2nd ed.). Austin, TX: PRO-ED.

Hepner, J. C. (1988). *ETS test collection cumulative index to tests in microfiche, 1975–1987.* Princeton, NJ: Educational Testing Service.

Hersen, M., & Bellack, A. S. (Eds.). (1988). *Dictionary of behavioral assessment techniques.* New York: Pergammon.

Johnson, O. G. (1976). *Tests and measurements in child development: Handbook II.* San Francisco: Jossey-Bass.

Johnson, O. G., & Bommarito, J. W. (1971). *Tests and measurements in child development: A handbook.* San Francisco: Jossey-Bass.

Keyser, D. J., & Sweetland, R. C. (1984). *Test critiques.* Kansas City, MO: Test Corporation of America.

Kramer, J. J., & Conoley, J. C. (Eds.). (1992). *The eleventh mental measurements yearbook.* Lincoln, NE: Buros Institute of Mental Measurements.

Krug, S. E. (Ed.). (1988). *Psychware sourcebook* (3rd ed.). Kansas City, MO: Test Corporation of America.

Lake, D. G., Miles, M. B., & Earle, R. B. (1973). *Measuring human behavior: Tools for the assessment of social functioning.* New York: Teachers College Press.

Levy, P., & Goldstein, H. (1984). *Tests in education: A book of critical reviews.* London: Academic Press.

Mauser, A. J. (1977). *Assessing the learning disabled: Selected instruments* (2nd ed.). Novato, CA: Academic Therapy Publications.

Miller, D. C. (1983). *Handbook of research design and social measurements* (4th ed.). New York: Longman.

Mitchell, J. V., Jr. (Ed.). (1985). *The ninth mental measurements yearbook.* Lincoln, NE: Buros Institute of Mental Measurements.

Murphy, L. L., Conoley, J. C., & Impara, J. C. (1994). *Tests in print* (4th ed.). Lincoln, NE: Buros Institute of Mental Measurements.

O'Brien, N. P. (1988). *Test construction: A bibliography of selected resources.* New York: Greenwood.

Robinson, J. P., Athanasion, R., & Head, K. B. (1969). *Measures of occupational attitudes and occupational characteristics.* Ann Arbor, MI: University of Michigan.

Robinson, J. P., Rusk, J. G., & Head, K. B. (1968). *Measures of political attitudes.* Ann Arbor, MI: University of Michigan.

Robinson, J. P., & Shaver, P. R. (1973). *Measures of social psychological attitudes* (rev. ed.). Ann Arbor, MI: University of Michigan.

Shaw, M. E., & Wright, J. W. (1967). *Scales for the measurement of attitudes.* New York: McGraw-Hill.

Sweetland, R. C., & Keyser, D. J. (Eds.). (1986). *Tests: A comprehensive reference for assessments in psychology, education and business* (2nd ed.). Kansas City, MO: Test Corporation of America.

Publications and Collections Available from the Educational Testing Service.
For information regarding the Test Collection Data Base, *Tests in Microfiche,* the *Tests in Microfiche Annotated Index,* and the Test Collection Bibliographies, write:

Test Collection
Educational Testing Service
Princeton, NJ 08541

Other publications related to the test collection include:

Educational Testing Service Test Collection. (1986). *The ETS test collection catalog* (6 vols.). Phoenix, AZ: Oryx Press.

Educational Testing Service Test Collection. (1987). *Directory of selected national testing programs.* Phoenix, AZ: Oryx Press.

In Specific Subject Areas

Braswell, J. S. (compiler). (1981). *Mathematics tests available in the United States and Canada.* Reston, VA: National Council of Teachers of Mathematics.

Grommon, A. H. (Ed.). (1976). *Reviews of selected published tests in English.* Urbana, IL: National Council of Teachers of English.

Johnson, T. F., & Hess, R. J. (1970). *Tests in the arts.* St. Ann, MO: Central Midwestern Regional Education Laboratory.

Mangen, D. J., & Peterson, W. A. (Eds.). (1982). *Research instruments in social gerontology.* Minneapolis, MN: University of Minnesota Press.

Northwest Regional Educational Laboratory, Center for Bilingual Education. (1978). *Assessment instruments in bilingual education: A descriptive catalog of 342 oral and written tests.* Los Angeles: National Dissemination and Assessment Center.

Savard, J-G. (1969). *Analytical bibliography of language tests.* Quebec: International Center for Research on Bilingualism.

Scholl, G., & Schnur, R. (1976). *Measures of psychological, vocational and educational functioning in the blind and visually handicapped.* New York: American Foundation for the Blind.

Valette, R. M. (1977). *Modern language testing* (2nd ed.). New York: Harcourt Brace Jovanovich.

Wall, J. (1981). *Compendium of standardized science tests.* Washington, DC: National Science Teachers Association.

CHAPTER 7

Assessment and Educational Decisions

INTRODUCTION

You are probably aware by now that a major theme of this book is the relationship between measurement and decision making. In the educational arena, educators, students, and parents are required to make a dizzying number of decisions that impact students' educational experiences. Teachers, for example, must decide not only how to evaluate student progress but also how to best tailor the curriculum to meet the needs of individual students. Students, as they achieve higher levels of education, need to make decisions about their own futures, including selection of courses and vocational planning. Parents, acting in partnership with their child and the schools, also contribute to the decisions that shape a student's educational path.

To make good decisions, every decision maker needs information. More specifically, decision makers must know what information is needed to understand and analyze a problem, where that information can be obtained, how to weigh it, and how to use it effectively to arrive at a course of action. In many instances such information can be obtained, at least in part, through educational testing and measurement.

VALUES AND DECISIONS

Decision making involves values. In education, a decision maker must determine not only what information is relevant to a particular decision, but also which educational goals are most important and what are the most desirable or expedient methods of achieving those goals. Typically, there is no objective way to answer these questions; they are issues of values. Values, both personal and societal, are difficult to quantify. Although it may be possible to measure the degree to which an individual holds a certain value, there is no available assessment procedure that can tell us what values an individual, school, or agency should have or which are most important to consider in making a particular decision. Values may differ markedly across subgroups within a community, and there is often considerable variation in opinion among individuals and agencies regarding which values should take precedence. Many of the controversies surrounding the use of tests and evaluation procedures in decision making, particularly for selection and placement decisions, stem from differences in value systems. In some instances, these conflicts have been resolved by the state and federal courts, which have mandated certain actions designed to promote societal goals for education. In other instances, local school boards or school faculties have reached a consensus on what values should be considered in making decisions. In most cases, however, conflicts about values remain.

PLACEMENT DECISIONS

Classroom teachers frequently divide classes, particularly at the elementary school level, into smaller, within-class groups for instruction. The primary purpose of such grouping is to make instruction more effective by forming small clusters of students who have similar instructional needs. The decision to assign a student to a relatively homogeneous, within-class group is an example of a placement decision that usually is made solely by the teacher. Such decisions typically are based on information about each student's progress in mastering educational objectives.

Sometimes placement decisions must be made for students whose instructional needs differ so markedly from those of other students in the class that the teacher is unable to make the necessary adjustments within the classroom. Typically, these students are of two kinds. At one extreme are gifted students whose level of achievement and speed of learning greatly exceed those of other students in the class, and at the other, are students who are having great difficulty mastering basic educational skills such as reading, are unable to adapt to classroom demands, or are so disruptive that they interfere with the learning of other students in the classroom. A teacher may decide to refer these kinds of students to a school psychologist or counselor for assessment and possible alternative placement.

The primary focus of a placement decision is—or should be—on the individual being placed and on the benefits that would accrue to him or her from a particular placement. However, some placement decisions also benefit the classroom teacher or other students in the class. For example, the decision to remove a particularly disruptive student from the regular classroom and to place him or her in a small class with a teacher trained to handle such students can benefit not only the disruptive student but also others in the regular classroom.

A great deal of controversy exists surrounding placement decisions in educational settings. However, because of the existence of individual differences in achievement among students and the tendency for these differences to become larger, not smaller, as students progress through school, it is likely that such decisions will always be necessary. Students differ markedly in how much they have learned from previous instruction, their motivation to learn, the instructional conditions under which they learn best, their rate of learning, and their ability to apply previous experience to new learning situations. Furthermore, an instructional program that facilitates learning and growth for one student may hinder it for others. Classroom teachers and other educators have long recognized the need to adapt teaching methods, learning materials, and curricula to meet individual differences among students and to place students in the kind of learning environment that will optimize their educational opportunities.

Issues Related to Mainstreaming

In 1975, the passage of the Education for All Handicapped Children Act, otherwise known as Public Law (PL) 94–142 (see Chapter 13), guaranteed students with disabilities the right to be educated with their nondisabled peers. This law requires that public schools educate disabled children in the least restrictive environment conducive to their development. The requirement that a child be educated in the least restrictive environment has been more commonly referred to as *mainstreaming*.

Prior to the passage of PL 94–142, comparisons between regular and special education classrooms yielded a dismal picture. Well-controlled studies comparing the academic achievement of special education students with equivalent students who remained in the regular education classroom found an overall negative effect of being in the special class. Furthermore, in examining special education classrooms, it was found that the teachers were not better trained, that the curricula generally were watered-down versions of regular programs, and that the classes were over-populated with minority children. These findings precipitated the legislation mandating a change in our approach to educating exceptional students.

Currently, approaches to the education of exceptional learners range from full inclusion, in which students spend all day in regular classrooms, to full exclusion where learners spend all of their time outside of regular class. Full exclusion, once the norm, is now a relatively uncommon option reserved for only the most severely handicapped students. Most children with identified disabilities spend at least part of their school day in the regular education classroom and are thus at least partially mainstreamed. The special services typically required by disabled students may be delivered by regular teachers or by special education personnel, depending upon the preference of the school system and the severity of the student's disability.

Each child identified for special services under PL 94–142 must also have an Individualized Educational Plan (IEP) that provides a detailed description of the kinds of services and educational experiences he or she will receive and how the effectiveness of those services will be evaluated. A student's IEP, which must be revised annually, should also include individualized goals and objectives, with timelines, and a description of the child's current level of functioning with respect to these objectives.

Students directly impacted by PL 94–142, typically classified as either mentally retarded, emotionally disturbed, or learning disabled, are an extremely heterogeneous group. Placing each student in the most appropriate category is necessary not only for purposes of funding and allocation of educational services in schools, but also for creating the best match between a student's needs and the type of resources that he or she receives. Recent research has shown that particular qualities of instruction, rather than the classroom setting per se, are more important in predicting academic as well as social outcomes for disabled students (Shepard, 1989).

Mainstreaming clearly presents some challenges for regular education teachers, many of whom are not adequately trained to meet the needs of exceptional students. Because educational funding is limited, political and value questions remain about how financial resources should be allocated within the schools. PL 94–142 reflects the relative importance society has placed on the value of normalizing the educational experiences of disabled students.

How Placement Decisions Are Made

When considering what sort of placement is best for a particular student, recall that the primary goal is to find the best match between the student's instructional needs and the educational experiences to which he or she is exposed. Assignment to Placement A (a particular course, section of the class, or type of special service) rather than to Placement B might seem advantageous either because the two placement options differ, in whole or in part, in the goals toward which they are directed or because they differ in the means used (or route taken) to reach common goals. Thus, the prime goal of a remedial college English section might be to teach correctness and clarity in writing a simple essay, while the prime goal of the creative writing class might be to encourage originality and dramatic effectiveness in writing narrative prose or poetry. Different goals are seen as appropriate for the two groups. On the other hand, the goals of both a regular and an advanced placement mathematics section in a high school might be to progress toward and master a domain designated as "mathematical analysis," but with the expectation that the advanced placement group would pursue topics in greater depth and at a faster rate. In the latter case, a common assessment procedure would indicate how far the members of each group had progressed toward their common goals.

The use of testing to aid with placement decisions is widespread. For decisions about course selection or entry points for instruction, assessment usually involves some test of initial achievement. These tests are most likely to permit constructive placement decisions when (1) they assess specific entry level knowledge and skills for a particular subject area and (2) when the alternative instuctional treatments differ substantially in method, content, or tempo.

Testing for the purpose of securing special services for a student is somewhat different. Whenever a student is identified for special services under PL 94–142, documentation, in the form of test scores, is legally required. The type of test evidence needed to support different classifications varies by state and by classification. For example, assessment of *mental retardation* typically involves administration of an individual intelligence test such as the Stanford-Binet or the age-appropriate Wechsler scale. Because limited intelligence is considered the central feature of mental retardation, comparision of a student's test score to national norms of children of the same age is the primary means of identifying this disability.

A classification of *learning disability* involves more extensive testing. An intelligence test generally is administered to establish that a student's intellectual functioning is normal, not retarded. Standardized achievement tests are also administered to substantiate teacher reports of classroom failure in particular skill areas and to more clearly identify specific deficits. A discrepancy between intellectual capacity, as measured by the intelligence test, and level of academic performance, both in the classroom and on standardized achievement tests, is the key feature of the learning disability construct.

The third major category of disability, *emotional disturbance,* is also assessed through testing. The most common source of evidence for this classification is behavioral assessment. This entails the systematic gathering of behavioral data from numerous sources, including parents, teachers, school psychologists, classmates, and the child in question. In some cases, personality measures may also be used to assess emotional disorders. Those interpreting test data for classification of emotional disturbance should also consider age-appropriate norms and the context of the child's behavior. Since substantial variation is expected among children on any social or maturation dimension, a child generally would only be considered disturbed if he or she consistently scored in the first or second percentile among age-mates.

CLASSROOM INSTRUCTIONAL DECISIONS

One of the most important tasks for classroom teachers is to ensure that students achieve instructional objectives. Teachers must monitor the progress of both the class and of the individual students in order to make good decisions about where to begin teaching, when to move on to the next unit of instruction, whether to reteach the present unit, or whether a particular student or subgroup of students needs special help to master the learning task. The quality of these decisions can strongly influence the effectiveness of the classroom instructional program.

Effective teaching requires that student progress be monitored through a process of both formal and informal assessments. Informal assessments include such techniques as questioning, observing students while they work on tasks, and asking students to read aloud or to verbalize the working through of a mathematics problem. These assessments are useful in gauging student understanding of the material presented and thus in helping teachers to make better decisions in planning instruction. Specifically, teachers need to know whether further review is required or if the students are ready for the introduction of new material. Informal assessment procedures also give teachers immediate feedback about the effectiveness of the teaching methods being employed. If students are not learning as expected, the teacher must decide whether to alter the instructional methods. Assessment techniques that guide the course of instruction are referred to as *formative evaluation.*

"High stakes" decisions about students—such as grades and changes in placement—are usually based on a more formal assessment called *summative evaluation.* Summative evaluation techniques, usually in the form of tests, are used after instruction is completed to summarize what students have learned. This category includes both the teacher-constructed and administered tests typically used to make decisions about grades, and standardized achievement tests used to evaluate instruction and identify exceptionally high or low performing students. Results of these tests may prompt a teacher to refer a student to a school psychologist or counselor for a more in-depth diagnosis, including clarification of the areas in which the student is having particular success or difficulty and identification of possible reasons for any learning problems. Additional testing is routinely done to aid in placement decisions, including placement in special education or gifted classes.

Surveys of teacher behavior (Stiggins, Conklin, & Bridgeford, 1986) have shown that teachers prefer informal methods of assessment and use them more often than they use formal approaches. This pattern of use probably occurs because the informal assessments require less preparation and skill to construct. However, informal assessments should be used in concert with more formal approaches when making decisions about individual students. As test users, teachers must take care to ensure that all assessments used in decision making are reliable and valid for their intended use. When using informal assessments, teachers need to record the results carefully or they may have insufficient information about the performance of their students. Classroom teachers may be reluctant to keep such records because of the time and work involved. However, if this is the case, they should place more reliance on formal techniques, which lend themselves more easily to systematic recordkeeping.

The Use of Objectives

Typically, classroom teachers employ a wide range of instructional objectives for a particular class. Cognitive objectives may include the building of a knowledge base or the development of cognitive skills, such as reading or writing. Affective objectives involve the development of attitudes, values, interests, and personal or social attributes. Depending upon the area of instruction, assessing achievement of these objectives may focus on evaluation of products or performances as well as on acquired cognitive skills and information.

Different methods of assessment are often required to determine if different types of objectives have been achieved by students. However, it is critical, regardless of the approach to assessment, that the information collected be accurate and relevant. If the techniques used to collect information about the achievement of an objective do not yield high-quality information, decisions or actions based on those data are likely to be faulty.

Types of Assessment Instruments

Standardized Achievement Tests.   At the beginning of the school year, when he or she is facing a new class, student scores on standardized achievement tests might help a teacher in planning instruction for that class. For example, knowledge of test scores may aid in the selection of reading materials that are suitable for the students' current level of achievement or in deciding where to start instruction in mathematics or language. However, once instruction has actually begun, the teacher needs information on student achievement of specific instructional objectives, and this information is needed promptly. Standardized achievement tests do not provide this kind of information. Since such tests must focus on objectives that are common to schools throughout the United States, they emphasize general skills and are unlikely to assess objectives related to the specific content emphasized in a particular classroom. Furthermore, they measure only cognitive objectives that can be appraised by paper-and-pencil tests. Affective, procedural, and other objectives requiring skill in oral communication or motor performance are not usually measured by these tests. Standardized tests also are quite expensive and require several hours for administration. Both of these factors make them impractical for frequent use and for certain purposes. In addition, there may be a long wait before teachers receive test results, which means that the results might not be available when instructional decisions need to be made.

Assessment Material Packaged with Curricular Materials.   Some classroom teachers, particularly in the lower grades, use tests accompanying published curricular materials instead of constructing assessments of their own. Most basal reading series and many textbooks include such tests. These instructional materials usually match the test items with the instructional objectives and may also suggest a passing score to be used to classify students as masters or nonmasters of the objectives. Although such materials can reduce the burden of test construction, they should be examined carefully before they are used. In many instances, they are poorly constructed. In addition, the number of items appraising each objective is usually too small to permit judgments about mastery. Despite being labeled as criterion-referenced tests, the domain assessed is seldom defined adequately and the items may not be sufficiently representative for the tests to support this classification. Another important point is that these packaged tests are not standardized tests and, therefore, include no normative information to aid interpretation of test scores.

Teacher-Made Assessment Instruments.   To obtain information for making day-to-day instructional decisions, classroom teachers usually must devise their own tests or assessment procedures. There are five general methods for collecting data on the achievement of instructional objectives:

1. paper-and-pencil tests
2. oral tests
3. product evaluations
4. performance tests
5. affective measures

Each of these methods has advantages and disadvantages, and each is appropriate for appraising the achievement of only certain types of objectives.

1. *Pencil-and-Paper Tests.* Objectives that call for knowledge about a particular subject area, the capacity to use that knowledge to solve problems, or a general educational skill such as reading can be most reliably and validly appraised by teacher-made paper-and-pencil tests. Unfortunately, most teacher-made tests are poor measuring instruments. There are typically two problems with these kinds of tests. First, the items on the tests often do not match the stated goals of the class, and second, the tests tend to have poor psychometric qualities because the items are not well written. Surveys of teachers suggest that they seldom use even minimal data-analysis procedures, such as determining the central tendency or variability on their test results. As a result of these weaknesses, the information obtained from such tests may be of questionable value in making instructional decisions. Some guidelines for writing and improving test items are provided in Chapter 15.

2. *Oral Tests.* Although oral tests are more time-consuming for the teacher, they can be used to assess many of the same types of objectives assessed by pencil-and-paper tests. They have the advantage of providing an opportunity to assess the integration of ideas, while removing the effect of level of skill in written expression. The

major disadvantage to the use of this method is that the evaluation of performance tends to be more subjective.

Another use for individually administered oral tests is the identification of learning problems. For example, a teacher could give a student a series of two-digit addition problems and ask the student to solve them aloud, that is, to talk through the procedures being used to arrive at an answer. These verbalizations can provide clues about the misconceptions that underlie not only errors but also sometimes even correct responses. Oral tests provide fewer clues about a student's underlying difficulty in reading, although the tests might help a teacher identify missing subskills required in the complex process of reading. For students with sensory or motor impairments, oral assessment may provide more accurate information than can be obtained by other methods.

3. *Product Evaluations.* Some instructional objectives, such as those related to penmanship, to constructing a birdhouse in wood shop class, or to typing a business letter, require a student to produce a product that meets certain standards of acceptability. These kinds of objectives cannot be assessed directly by paper-and-pencil tests; it is better to evaluate the product itself. This type of assessment is called *product evaluation.* The major problems with product evaluation stem from the task of identifying the aspects of the product that are relevant to its quality and of establishing standards to measure the aspects that will define different degrees of adequacy or excellence in the product. Product evaluation is discussed in more detail in Chapter 10.

4. *Performance Tests.* Some instructional objectives require a student to carry out a procedure such as giving an oral report, playing a musical instrument, or using a spreadsheet on a computer. As a rule, these kinds of performances do not leave a tangible product that can be judged, or if they do, the actual procedures used by the student to produce the product are as important as the final product. These kinds of objectives can be appraised only by assigning an appropriate task to the student, such as giving an oral report to the class, and then observing and rating the performance as it occurs. This type of evaluation is called *performance assessment.* The major problems with performance assessment are (1) identifying the critical, or salient, aspects of the performance that should be observed and (2) identifying and applying the appropriate criteria for discriminating different degrees of competency in the performance. (Methods for improving performance assessments are presented in Chapter 10.)

5. *Affective Measures.* Almost all instructional programs, particularly at the elementary and secondary school levels, have affective as well as cognitive objectives. Affective objectives deal with personal and social attributes that educators want students to develop, such as values, interests, self-concept, and cooperation with others. Assessing objectives such as these can be quite difficult because they involve the inner feelings or motivations of students, which cannot be measured directly. Currently, the best that we can do is to observe behavior, and from this observation, try to infer what lies behind the behavior, have peers or teachers rate students, or ask students to provide self-reports of their own feelings or motivations. Methods for eliciting these reports are discussed in Chapters 11 and 12. None of these affective assessment measures is entirely satisfactory. However, if teachers and schools

are serious about affective objectives, they need to monitor students' achievement of affective objectives so that adjustments in instruction, or in classroom or school organization, can be made if the level of achievement is not satisfactory, even if the measures are not wholly satisfactory.

DAY-BY-DAY INSTRUCTIONAL DECISIONS

One important role of achievement assessments is to help the classroom teacher make decisions about what is to be taught, studied, and/or practiced by students in the class. The weekly spelling test is a venerable classroom tradition, and quizzes in grammar and mathematics have been prepared and used by teachers for many years to help them make decisions about the next day's lesson or to evaluate a child's progress.

Interest in test use for guiding instructional decisions is on the increase, as is interest in the development of procedures that can provide information about whether a student has mastered a topic or skill. The knowledge provided by such assessments can help the teacher or the student decide whether there is a need for further instruction before the student moves to the next unit. This kind of information is especially relevant for subjects that have a hierarchical structure—that is, when progress on Topic B depends on an adequate understanding of Topic A. While mathematics is the prime example of such a subject, other topic areas show a similar structure. For example, children must know the alphabet and be able to recognize letters before they can learn to spell.

A test used to measure competence in a particular skill will usually be concrete and specific. In using such tests, teachers often set some criterion—usually an arbitrary one—to represent an adequate degree of competence. The use of a criterion has occasionally caused the tests to be incorrectly labeled as criterion-referenced tests. (The qualities that a test must have to be criterion referenced are listed in Chapter 3.) What these tests do have in common with criterion-referenced tests is the presentation of a representative sample of tasks from a narrowly defined domain. Because the domain is relatively narrow, all test items tend to require the same skill, and it is reasonable to expect that a person will either correctly answer all or almost all of the items or perform not much better than at a chance level.

By way of illustration, Figure 7.1 presents two teacher-made tests. The first assesses the students in a fifth-grade class on their knowledge of prime numbers. (For those who have forgotten or may never have known, a prime number is one that cannot be divided evenly by any number other than itself or 1 [unity]. Examples are 11, 13, or 17.) The second test (which also appeared in Chapter 3) assesses skill in capitalization of proper names and is designed to identify students who are having trouble with this skill.

You can see that each little test is quite short; there are 15 numbers from which to choose 6 prime numbers in the first, and 13 words that should be underlined in the second. Setting a criterion level of 90% correct on each test as constituting adequate competence permits the examinee to miss one item on each test but assumes that more frequent mistakes imply inadequate mastery of the concept or skill. These tests illustrate one extreme in specificity and are clearly related to judgments about

Figure 7.1
Teacher-made criterion-referenced tests.

Test of Prime Numbers

Directions: Do you know what a prime number is? Look at the numbers shown below. Six of them are prime numbers. For each one, see if it is a prime number. If it is, draw a circle around it. If it is not, leave it unmarked.

31	47	143
33	49	293
35	51	415
38	59	763
41	97	942

Test of Capitalization

Read the paragraph. The punctuation is correct, and the words that begin a sentence have been capitalized. No other words have been capitalized. Some need to be. Draw a line under each word that should begin with a capital letter.

We saw mary yesterday. She said she had gone to chicago, illinois, to see

her aunt helen. Her aunt took her for a drive along the shore of lake

michigan. On the way they passed the conrad hilton hotel where mary's

uncle joseph works. Mary said that she had enjoyed the trip, but she was

glad to be back home with her own friends.

---

what a pupil has learned. They sample from narrowly and explicitly defined domains of instruction that are relatively easy to specify.

In much of education, the domain represented by a unit of instruction is much fuzzier, and, consequently, the stock of appropriate problems or items is much less clearly defined. Consider, for example, a unit of instruction on the Bill of Rights. We could test an individual's ability to identify or to recall each of the first 10 amendments to the Constitution. But, if we were concerned with the meaning, the significance, and the application of these same 10 amendments to the problems of contemporary America, how could we meaningfully define and sample from that domain? In this instance, the notion of "mastery" slips through our fingers.

When we cannot define the boundaries of a domain, it becomes impossible to determine what constitutes a representative sample of exercises to assess degree of mastery of that domain. Different test makers may produce dissimilar sorts of test exercises to measure what is nominally the same domain. Specifying a criterion level of performance that represents a defined level of "mastery" becomes almost impossible with subject matter that cannot be concretely defined. Therefore, a teacher-made test of knowledge about abstract material may still provide some useful information to guide decisions about further teaching, but the information will not be as concrete as that provided by tests such as those in Figure 7.1.

REPORTING ACADEMIC PROGRESS

It is important to ensure that the student, the parents, and the school know whether a particular student is making satisfactory progress in schoolwork. To the student, evidence of progress and accomplishment is a substantial motivating force, and evidence of specific difficulties should be a signal indicating a need to seek help to overcome the difficulties. Focused tests of the sort found in Figure 7.1 provide an important form of feedback to guide students, as well as teachers, in identifying gaps in knowledge or skills that call for further study or practice.

Most parents are vitally concerned with the progress of their children in school. Of course, families differ in the depth of this concern and differ even more in the resources they provide for coaching in school skills and for supporting their child's efforts to learn. But all parents must be considered partners with the school, and, if they are to be effective partners, they must know how their child is progressing. Parents specifically need to know the level at which their child is functioning in each school subject and be warned promptly of any potential difficulties. All kinds of test results provide a concrete basis for communication from school to parent and for interpretation of the child's progress and difficulties.

As described in Chapter 3, the teacher or school may provide a criterion-referenced interpretation of student progress, which would include a list of competencies that the child has recently developed to a satisfactory level of mastery or of the specific skills with which the child is currently having difficulty. More conventionally, a norm-referenced interpretation is provided that compares the child's general level of performance in a subject area with that of his or her class, other students in the school, or a broader regional or national reference group.

It is necessary, in reporting a child's academic progress to parents, to compare the performance to something. Three approaches to defining the merit of a child's performance are to define

1. performance in relation to perfection
2. performance in relation to par (some expected or average level of accomplishment)
3. performance in relation to potential

Performance in Relation to Perfection

When judging performance in relation to perfection we ask, how close did the student come to exhibiting a perfect score on the quiz? We are likely to interpret a perfect score as "complete mastery," but this interpretation is dangerous even in the case of a narrowly focused test and is completely inappropriate for a test that covers a broad domain. In the latter case, there are always more difficult tasks that could have been set for the examinee, and we never can say that he or she knows everything there is to know about a subject. Even with tasks as specific as identifying prime numbers, some numbers turn out to be a good deal more difficult than others. So "perfection" is displayed only on the specific sample of tasks that is used to represent the domain. Interpreting "80% correct" on the usual teacher-made test as "knows 80% of the subject" is completely absurd, and at most, the interpretation might be "knows 80% of the answers that the teacher thinks a student should be expected to know." On the other hand, this standard of *what the teacher expects* is a very real one and can be important to both pupil and parent.

Performance in Relation to Par

By performance in relation to par, we mean the typical, norm-referenced interpretation of a test score; adequacy of performance is defined by the performance of others. For a teacher-made test, it may be the student's standing relative to others in the class. For the published test, it is a student's standing in relation to a broader reference group, such as all children at this same age or grade level.

In Chapter 3, we discussed various sorts of converted scores, using different scales and reference frames for reporting the score of an individual. We expressed a preference for percentile ranks or standard scores to represent a student's performance in relation to other members of a group to which he or she logically belongs. Of these two types of converted scores, the one that probably conveys the most immediate meaning to a parent or other person not particularly sophisticated about measurement issues is the score reported in terms of relative position—at the 15th percentile, in the second 10th, or in the bottom quarter.

Two aspects of such a report are troubling. One problematic feature of these scales is that it is possible (although perhaps not likely) within a specific class that the differences in performance are so small that the distinction between the top and bottom quarters is of no practical importance. That is, one may be forcing distinctions where no real differences exist. The other troubling aspect is that in using the group as a standard, there must always be 50% of the total group "below the average" and 25% "in the bottom quarter," with the implication that they have somehow "failed" (but see the discussion of the "Lake Wobegone Effect" in Chapter 9). We face a basic problem in our use of language: to the statistician, "average" means "middle of the group," but to most people, it has come to mean "minimally acceptable," so that anything below the average carries the connotation of "unacceptable." Somehow, the two interpretations of "average" must be separated in our thinking, so that the student who falls at the 20th or 30th percentile of the group on some measure is not viewed as a failure.

With a standardized test, the normative data supplied by the publisher permit "par" to refer to some national or regional group, or the school system may develop systemwide norms. The use of national norms may ease the pressure on some fortunately situated schools that draw primarily from an advantaged community in which most children approach or exceed the national average. However, if this par is used, it accentuates the sense of failure in schools from districts or communities that are at the low end of the scale in economic and cultural resources, where a very large proportion of the students will not reach the national or regional average. A blind application of national norms, whether to schools or individuals, is likely to lead to a sense of unreality and frustration.

The same type of problem can occur for individual students of average ability who happen to be in classes primarily composed of unusually talented students. The "normal" students might very well come in at the bottom of the class in every subject no matter how hard they try, with a resulting sense of frustration and failure, simply because the other students are exceptional. A nationally standardized test can provide a welcome reality check for such students by revealing their level of accomplishment relative to a broader sampling of society.

Performance in Relation to Potential

Recognition of the inequity of assessing performance in relation to a uniform and unvarying set of standards has led test users and educational evaluators to try to express performance in relation to potential. This orientation rejects the notion that all people are identical and interchangeable and that the same par is applicable to each person. Those reporting academic progress in terms of potential must establish a standard for each child, which asks, in light of all we know about this child, what level of performance should we reasonably expect?

This question is easy to phrase. When we start to explore it, however, we find that it becomes a tricky one to answer, with a wide range of technical and even ethical overtones. How *do* we determine the expected level of achievement for an individual? For example, we know that it is unreasonable to expect an 8-year-old to jump as far, run as fast, read as well, or do as wide a range of arithmetic problems as a 12-year-old can do. Eight-year-old children also differ in size. Perhaps it is unreasonable to expect an undersized child of this age to jump as far as an oversized one. By the same token, children also differ in their performance on tests designed to measure general intellectual development. Perhaps it is unreasonable to expect the same level of reading or arithmetic performance from the child who obtains a low score on a scholastic aptitude test that we do from the child who obtains a high score.

Statistical analyses of the relationship between aptitude and achievement tests do yield high correlations. Children with low scores on measures of general intellectual functioning tend to get poor scores on measures of reading and mathematics achievement. In one sense, therefore, it might be correct to conclude that they have a lower potential for academic achievement. Because this relationship exists, we are tempted to modify our interpretations of test scores. Unfortunately, what at first seems to be a reasonable course of action turns out to be unworkable in practice. The approach does not work because the difference between the two types of tests is more a function of the way they are used and interpreted than of the underlying capacities assessed. The similarities between the two tests mean that students can be expected to perform the same on both. In the event that scores on the two tests are discrepant, we must first consider measurement error as the most likely cause of the difference. When this explanation has been ruled out, we may entertain a hypothesis of specific learning disability, or an emotional problem if "aptitude" exceeds "achievement."

In addition to the technical problems, there are social consequences that may result from an application of different expectations and standards for different individuals. People tend to adjust their performance to the level of expectation that is set for them. Thus, low expectations may become a partial cause for low achievement. On the other hand, more able students may question the equity of being required to meet a higher level of achievement to receive a particular grade.

Assigning Grades

Many teachers consider assigning grades one of the most unpleasant tasks required of them. It takes up a large amount of time, causes anxieties, and tends to leave a sour taste in their mouths. Few students enjoy being assigned grades, and for teachers, assigning grades is an activity that requires a great deal of time and effort. The payoff to teachers is too often a sizable number of dissatisfied students.

The evaluation of student performance is typically summarized in some condensed and highly abstract symbol. A survey (National Education Association, 1967), supported by another study by Pinchak and Breland (1974), found that a system of numerical or letter grades was used in about 80% of American school systems, except in the first grade, where the percentage was 73, and in kindergarten, where it was 17. Unfortunately, the study of grading has not received much attention in recent literature (Stiggins, Frisbie, & Griswold, 1989).

The use of highly condensed symbols to convey the teacher's evaluation has frequently been criticized for reasons that we shall consider now. The alternatives that have been offered to replace the conventional A, B, C, D, or F system have problems of their own, and no fully satisfactory replacement for this type of grade seems to be at hand.

Importance of Grades

Grades are deeply embedded in the educational culture. They have become the basis, in whole or in part, for a wide range of actions and decisions within educational institutions and between these institutions and the outside world. Eligibility for admission to certain programs or departments, for scholarship aid, for membership on athletic teams, and for continuing in school is often determined by academic standing. Admission to college or graduate school is usually based, at least in part, on grades received at the previous academic level. Thus, there are many points within the educational system where grades interact with the administrative and instructional process to affect the student's progress.

Most learning theorists, from behaviorists to cognitive psychologists, have emphasized the need for feedback in the facilitation of learning. We know that it is difficult for someone to improve unless they know how well they are doing. The process of growing and developing requires the testing of limits, and children need to know how they stand in relation to peers or to some goal. This process is interrupted when the feedback is inaccurate. The natural inclination of teachers is to be helpful and supportive, and they tend to dislike giving feedback that is not positive. Unjustified positive feedback should be avoided, however, because such approaches often backfire resulting in decreased student motivation and stunted academic progress. If students are to improve, they need to know where improvement is needed, but it is also critical that the feedback be presented in such a way that it does not imply an evaluation of the students' worth as individuals.

Parents also need to know how their children are progressing in school. There are a number of possible means of fulfilling this need, including anecdotal records, teacher conferences, and/or lists of objectives mastered or not mastered. Experience has shown that parents know, understand, and respond best to the traditional methods of assigning grades. To institute an alternate system of providing feedback to parents and students would require a tremendous amount of parent education. To date, attempts to substitute alternate methods of reporting student progress have met with strong parental objections. Typical parents, faced with a list of objectives their child has mastered, will ask what grade this implies.

Furthermore, parents have a right to the accurate reporting of their children's progress in school, in terms that they understand. Avoiding the anguish of assigning grades by only giving high grades is a dereliction of duty. Nothing is more damaging to parent-school rapport than to have parents erroneously believe that their child has no academic problems. The school does no one a favor by shielding a child in this manner. In fact, there have recently been successful lawsuits filed against schools for awarding students high school diplomas when they could not do sixth-grade work.

The school also has a responsibility to certify that students have mastered the assigned curriculum, at least at some minimal level, in the courses they have taken. If a student receives a satisfactory grade in a course, it is reasonable for a prospective employer or school to assume that the grade represents a meaningful mastery of subject matter. Clearly, certification is not a school's only responsibility, or even its first responsibility, but it is a responsibility nevertheless, and accurate reporting of student achievement in the form of grades is the form that employers and others outside the education establishment have come to expect.

The traditional grading system has been durable and resistant to change both for the reasons discussed and because no alternative system has been found that better meets the needs of the wide array of consumers of this information.

PLANNING EDUCATIONAL FUTURES

As children progress through the school system, they gradually take on more responsibility for decisions concerning their future educational plans. Past achievement is one type of information that should influence their decisions. Present measured achievement is the best predictor we have of future achievement. General level of achievement may therefore affect the child's future educational decisions, and performance in a particular course may influence his or her decisions about educational specialization.

Grades obtained in school provide one indicator of achievement, but the variability of standards from teacher to teacher within a school and from school to school limits their value as guides to planning academic futures. Grades are personal and local in their significance. For this reason, standardized tests, with broadly representative norms that are comparable from one content area to another, provide a more uniform and universal basis for appraising overall level of achievement, as well as specific strengths and weaknesses.

Two mistakes must be avoided in using test results for planning purposes. One mistake is premature decision making. Individuals change, and present performance predicts the future imperfectly. Counselors should avoid closing out options—such as going to college—prematurely. The other mistake is making a predominately negative use of test results. Test scores are more constructive if they are used to open doors rather than to close them. It is as important for test results to identify talent and encourage its further development as it is for them to redirect individuals for whom the typical college education seems an unrealistic goal. One of the consequences of the widespread use of standardized tests for college admissions—coupled with more extensive financial aid programs—is that educational opportunity based upon ability to learn rather than ability to pay has become a realistic expectation for most of America's youth.

Selection Decisions

Selection decisions represent attempts to choose the individuals who are likely to make the greatest contribution to a particular organization or institution. That is, selection decisions emphasize the welfare of the organization or the society over the welfare of the individual. This type of decision can be contrasted with placement decisions, which are intended to benefit the individual who is being placed in a particular educational setting. Thus, value for an employer hiring a keyboard operator might be expressed (crudely) as number of error-free lines of text entered in an average working day, whereas value for a college might be expressed (perhaps even more crudely and incompletely) as freshman grade point average (GPA). In the simplest terms, the purpose of a system for selection decisions is to hire or admit those individuals who will maximize the total value to the institution—that is, usually those who will have the greatest probability of success.

The notion of value is both fuzzy and complex. Any simple indicator, such as text lines entered or GPA, is at best a rough, pragmatic approximation of a person's true contribution to an organization, be it an employer or an educational institution.

Both past achievements and present performance often have a good deal of validity as predictors of future value. Thus, high school grades consistently have been found to be among the best predictors of future college grades, with correlations typically in the 0.50s and 0.60s, and job skills at the time of hiring provide some of the best indicators of how well those same skills will be performed on the job.

The rationale for using an objective test of achievement in one or more academic subjects to replace or supplement high school grades as a predictor of college success is that such a test would provide a uniform set of tasks for all applicants and, thus, a way of compensating for the differences in grading standards, students' socioeconomic status, and specific content foci of secondary schools. For this reason, the widely used college admission tests, the Scholastic Aptitude Test (SAT) and the American College Testing Program (ACT), have been based on rather general reading, verbal, and quantitative skills.

In the world of work, academic achievement tests appear to be an inappropriate selection device for most jobs. Mental ability tests work reasonably well in situations where the focus is on potential for learning new skills or performing intellectually demanding tasks, but in most situations, proficiency tests that measure specific job skills seem to be the best option. Examples of occupations for which such tests might be appropriate are carpenters, machinists, and electricians, as well as office jobs such as keyboard operator, bookkeeper, or computer programmer. Tests for job skills need to be employed with caution. Although it is possible to measure with some degree of accuracy the most obvious skills related to each job, in most cases the most important characteristics are personal, such as getting along with others and not using drugs, characteristics that are quite difficult to measure.

Whenever using test results to aid in selection decisions, the decision-making institution or organization must be able to document the validity of the test for each particular use (some of the legal requirements and court decisions relating to the use of tests for selection are reviewed in Chapter 14). Consider that when a student submits his or her SAT scores as part of an application to college, these scores, in addition to their being used in the admissions decision, are also often used to award scholarships, to help counsel the student in course and program choices, and to identify the need for remedial classes or tutoring. For each of these additional uses test data validity must be demonstrated in order for use of the data to be appropriate. Just because a test is a good predictor of freshman GPA (and therefore valid for use in the admissions decision), one should not assume that the test scores can also validly be used for other types of decisions.

Curricular Decisions

One function for which measures of achievement are needed is the evaluation of alternative curricular materials or instructional designs. In education, there is a steady flow of proposals for change—change in curricular emphasis, change in instructional materials, and change in instructional procedures. If innovations are to be introduced rationally rather than capriciously and if education is to show any cumulative progress in effectiveness rather than oscillating from one fad to another, systematic evaluation of the outcomes from any change is imperative. Carrying out adequate studies to evaluate any proposed change is admittedly difficult. But without evaluative research studies, decisions to change are made blindly, supported only by the eloquence of their proponents.

A first requirement for any evaluative research is clear specification of what a proposed innovation is designed to achieve. That is, we need a comprehensive statement of the objectives of the program, covering the full range of outcomes sought for both the proposed new program and the program it is designed to replace. If a revised mathematics program is designed to produce improved understanding of the number system, and the program it is replacing is one that has emphasized computational skills, it is important in evaluating the outcomes that the two programs be compared both in terms of furthering understanding of the number system and in terms of computational skills. The identification of the better of the two systems can only rationally be made if we know how well each program achieves not only its own objectives but also other relevant objectives. This information puts us in a position to judge the importance of different aspects of achievement in terms of a specified system of values and comes up with a composite decision about which set of outcomes is preferred.

Once the objectives of an instructional program have been stated with enough detail and explicitness to guide instruction and evaluation, we may ask whether some or all of the objectives can be assessed appropriately using existing published tests. There are, of course, economies of time and effort associated with use of existing tests, as well as some gain in the availability of normative data. The design of most published tests involves a thorough analysis of both the content and objectives of the field that they are meant to cover. For existing tests, these analyses may have been done some years before publication, and will have been done in terms of a curriculum that contains elements common to all school districts. In the case of basic skills such as those encompassed in reading and mathematics curricula, this presents no particular problem because there is considerable agreement among school districts regarding what should be taught. Although this agreement will not always be found in other curricular areas, most of the content of education changes slowly and therefore even programs that differ in form and in specific content may have much in common in terms of their underlying educational objectives. For this reason, there is advantage to examining existing tests before attempting to invest the resources of time, skill, and money to produce a new test specifically for the local evaluation project.

One feature of carrying out curricular evaluations, or any analysis that leads to a decision applied to a whole class, school, or school system, is that it is not necessary that every pupil be assessed with every test exercise. Suppose, for example, there are so many items needed to assess a set of objectives adequately that it would take 4 hours for a student to complete a test made up of these items. If only 30 minutes of testing time were available, it might be possible to divide the material into eight test forms to correspond to the eight 30-minute testing segments needed to accommodate 4 hours of testing material and to have each student take one of the test forms. If a school has, for example, 120 sixth-grade students, approximately 15 children will take each of the eight forms. It would then be possible to determine average level of test performance for the school as a whole, on the complete test, because all of the items would have been used and all of the pupils would have served as examinees. When a large pool of examinees is available, this procedure, which is called *item sampling,* provides a practical way to assess a wide range of curricular objectives, with each examinee spending only a relatively short time being tested. One drawback of item sampling is that it requires the assembly of tests specifically for the current occasion, either through local efforts or from the item files of commercial publishers. Note that with item sampling, we do not get a meaningful or useful score for any single student. The College Basic Academic Skills Examination, a college level achievement test described in Chapter 9, is an example of a commercially available standardized test that uses the item sampling approach.

Public and Political Decisions

Every community is interested in and concerned about its school system. Expenditures for education represent a major budget item of every community and every state, and citizens want to know whether they are getting good value for their money. Citizens are also interested in how their schools compare with other schools in the state and throughout the country, and how well the children in their community are learning the things that they, as parents and citizens, deem important. Citizens do not make decisions about schools very often, but when they do, the decisions frequently are negative. They may vote down a school budget, school bond issue, or school board member, or they may organize a protest against a person, program, or policy. Conversely, of course, they may decide to support the school with money, time, or approbation. The action that they select will depend on how they feel about their schools, and this feeling, in turn, will depend in part on what they know about their schools.

Knowing about schools is, in part, a matter of knowing what is going on in them—available activities, resources for learning, and new ideas. Of greatest importance to most citizens is information about how much children are learning. Thus, in its relationship with the public, each school system faces the problem of presenting to that public some picture of student progress.

One approach to reporting school progress is to report in terms of very specific competencies. Thus, the school might report that 78% of pupils at the end of Grade 3 were able to identify the number of thousands, hundreds, tens, and units in a number such as 7,562. But such a report conveys little meaning to even an informed citizen. The likely response might be, So is that good or bad? What percentage should be expected to do this? How does this compare with last year? How does this compare with the Hohokus school system next door? If specific accomplishments are reported, there are likely to be so many of them that teachers and citizens alike get drowned in a mass of detail.

Some type of summary, then, seems necessary in reporting to the public. By its nature, the summary will involve comparison—comparison with last year's performance, national norms, or some group of similar schools or communities. It is possible for a school system to develop its own set of assessment instruments, to use these in successive years, and to make limited types of comparison, but locally constructed tests with local norms might not satisfy the public. In most cases, there is a need for a way to make comparisons with other communities, states, and the nation as a whole. These comparisons can only be supplied by a test for which normative data are available. In addition, the development of good tests is difficult, expensive, and time consuming. One significant role for standardized achievement tests is to provide the basis for making comparisons with other communities.

The test that forms the most appropriate basis for presenting a school's results to the public is the test that best represents the school's educational objectives. Thus, there are no new or different criteria for selecting a test that is to provide public information; it will be the same test that is most useful for appraising the achievement level of individual students.

Once the test has been administered and scored, it is necessary to assemble the data and present them in a form that will fairly and clearly communicate the results to the public. "Fairly" relates to the proper comparison group; "clearly" relates to the form of presentation. Some of the problems and pitfalls of presenting achievement test results to the public are discussed in Chapter 9.

SUMMARY

A major theme of this book is the examination of the relationship between measurement and decision making. Information gained from tests and other assessment procedures is used to aid many kinds of educational decisions. Whether testing is used to guide decisions about student placement, instruction, or student progress, decision making is an inherently value-laden process.

The nature of the decisions to be made, and hence the type of information needed, determines which approaches to assessment are most appropriate. Whether a teacher chooses achievement tests, the assessment material packaged with instructional materials, oral tests, product evaluations, performance tests, or affective measures is determined by the types of decisions he or she must make. Tests are also used to make placement and selection decisions, to guide day-by-day instructional choices and curriculum evaluation, as well as to report academic progress to parents and the public.

QUESTIONS AND EXERCISES

1. What role do values play in decision making?
2. What is PL 94–142? Discuss the potential implications of this law for schools, students, and teachers.
3. How is testing used to aid in placement decisions? What kind of evidence is necessary to support this use of tests? Why?
4. For a fifth-grade class, give an example of the type of objective that would be assessed by each of the following methods: a pencil-and-paper test, an oral test, a product evaluation, a performance test, and assessment of affective characteristics.

5. Why might a test that is suitable as a measure of past achievement have limited value for a placement decision?

6. What procedures might a community college use to place entering freshmen into sections for a required English course? What would be the objectives of such sectioning? What gains might be expected? What losses?

7. In April of the sixth grade, Helen has a reading grade equivalent of 6.2 (second month of sixth grade) on the Iowa Tests of Basic Skills. How should this be interpreted if her non-verbal standard age score on the Cognitive Abilities Test is 85? If it is 115? If it is 135?

8. How does your answer to the above question change as you shift from *performance in relation to potential* to *performance in relation to par*?

9. What would be involved in preparing a proficiency test for television repairmen? What form might the test take?

10. In what ways might a testing program to evaluate a proposed modified mathematics curriculum differ from a program designed to place students in the appropriate mathematics section?

11. It has been proposed that while the A, B, C, D, F system of grading is relative, a percentage system represents an absolute appraisal. What are the arguments for and against this point of view? Are there any systems of appraisal that are based on an absolute standard? Identify one, and give the evidence to support your position.

12. In what way(s) is the grading system in a school similar to a rating procedure? In what way(s) does it differ? What factors that limit the effectiveness of ratings also limit the effectiveness of a grading system?

13. What should the role of a student's self-appraisal be in evaluating his or her educational progress? What are the limits of such an appraisal?

14. In College Y, there are 10 sections of freshman English. What steps could be taken to ensure uniform grading standards, so that a student would not be penalized by being in a particular section?

15. It has been proposed that schools should abandon grades and report only *pass* or *fail* for students. What would be the gains from such a procedure? What would be the losses? How would the functions now served (admittedly imperfectly) by grades be discharged? How adequate would these alternative procedures be?

16. A school principal remarked to his board of education: "We have higher standards than Mason High. Our passing grade is 70, and theirs is only 65." What assumptions is he making in this statement? How defensible are these assumptions?

SUGGESTED READINGS

Bloom, B. S., Hastings, J. T., & Madaus, C. F. (1971). *Handbook on formative and summative evaluation of student learning.* New York: McGraw-Hill.

Cunningham, G. K. (1986). *Educational and psychological measurement.* New York: Macmillan.

Gronlund, N. E., & Linn, R. L. (1990). *Measurement and evaluation in teaching.* New York: Macmillan.

Gullickson, A. R., & Hopkins, K. D. (1987). The context of educational measurement instruction for preservice teachers: Professor perspectives. *Issues and Practices, 6*(3), 12–16.

Popham, W. J. (1990). *Modern educational measurement: A practitioner's perspective.* Englewood Cliffs, NJ: Prentice-Hall.

Slavin, R. E. (1987). Mastery learning reconsidered. *Review of Educational Research, 57*(2), 175–213.

Slavin, R. E. (1988). *Educational psychology: Theory into practice.* Englewood Cliffs, NJ: Prentice-Hall.

Stiggins, R. J., & Bridgeford, N. J. (1985). The ecology of classroom assessment. *Journal of Educational Measurement, 22*(4), 271–286.

Stiggins, R. J., Frisbie, D. A., & Griswold, P. A. (1989). Inside high school grading practices: Building a research agenda. *Educational Measurement: Issues and Practices, 8*(2), 5–14.

Terwilliger, J. S. (1989). Classroom standard setting and grading practices. *Educational Measurement: Issues and Practices, 8*(2), 15–19.

CHAPTER 8

Aptitude Tests

INTRODUCTION

An aptitude test measures a person's present performance on selected tasks *to provide information that can be used to estimate how the person will perform at some time in the future or in a somewhat different situation.* The situation for which we wish to make a prediction may be school performance, job performance, or some more general adaptation to life's demands. An aptitude test differs somewhat from an achievement test in the tasks that it presents, but the differences are often small and technical. For example, measures of reading comprehension or of arithmetic problem solving may be found both in aptitude and in achievement measures. Generally, aptitude measures depend *more* on general life experiences and *less* on specific instruction than do achievement tests, but the differences in content and process being measured are frequently of degree and not of kind. The one respect in which the two classes of tests *do* clearly differ is in the function that they are designed to serve. An achievement test is typically given to find out how much a student has profited from past instruction or what level of knowledge or skill a person possesses; an aptitude test is given to estimate how the examinee is likely to perform in the future. The key difference is one of purpose and function more than content.

The first aptitude tests were designed to assess broad, general cognitive ability, and much of aptitude testing still is, and probably always will be, conducted with the purpose of appraising general ability to carry out cognitive tasks. Subsequently, emphasis shifted somewhat, and a number of tests of more specialized abilities were developed to identify more specific strengths (and weaknesses) in the examinee.

In this chapter, we will first examine several of the major theories that have been put forward about the nature of cognitive abilities and will also devote our attention to tests that focus on general cognitive ability, those often familiarly labeled "IQ tests." Within the field of general ability tests, we will look first at those that are designed to be given on a one-on-one basis by a trained examiner and then at those designed for group administration. In the next chapter we will turn our attention to some tests of more specialized abilities, in particular those that are the subject of instruction.

THEORIES OF COGNITIVE ABILITIES

For many centuries, people have recognized individual differences in human cognitive abilities. In *The Republic* Plato recommended that people be assigned places in society based on their cognitive abilities, as well as other characteristics. By the late 19th century Herbert Spencer, a British philosopher, was arguing that general cognitive ability, which he called *intelligence,* was the most important human characteristic and a basis for natural selection. As the 20th century dawned, practitioners of the new science of psychology were being called on to apply their methods to problems of social significance related to the schools and to mental deficiency. As we saw in the first chapter, Alfred Binet was one of the first to provide a practical measurement device (see R. M. Thorndike [1990a] or Rogers [1995] for a description of this period).

Binet's Theory

The international movement toward universal compulsory education had created in the minds of many educators a need to be able to identify two groups of children—those who *could not* learn because of low ability and those who *would not* learn because of poor motivation or other causes. The first widely acknowledged instrument to accomplish this separation was produced in France in 1905 by Alfred Binet and Theodore Simon.

Binet did not really have a theory of mental ability. Rather, he reasoned that cognitive ability developed with age, just as physical abilities did. Also, he felt that intelligence was expressed in the performance of complex mental acts. Therefore, the scale he and Simon devised was composed of a series of mental "puzzles" organized by the sequence in which children could successfully answer them. In the second edition of his instrument the tasks he included were grouped into age levels, depending on when the "average" child could accomplish them. The puzzles or tasks at any age level were of several kinds, including two or three short-term memory items, some information items, and some items that required reasoning. Quite different item types might be used at successive ages.

The objective of the Binet-Simon scale was to identify a child's "mental level," or, in modern terminology, age equivalent. Binet, however, was not interested in normative comparisons but in what each child actually could do. Thus, he stuck firmly to his concept of mental level, resisting attempts to change it to "mental age."

Binet died at a relatively young age in 1911. That same year Wilhelm Stern, a German psychologist, introduced the term *intelligence quotient* to represent a child's standing, relative to his or her agemates. Binet certainly would not have approved, but the deed was done. From then on "IQ" increasingly became part of 20th century vernacular. As we saw in our discussion of norms in Chapter 3, the term IQ no longer has any meaning as a description of how the index should be interpreted. For this reason, and because the term has acquired so much surplus meaning over the years, it should be dropped. The term *intelligence,* however, still does have useful meaning, so we will talk about intelligence tests, but not IQ tests. The latter do not exist.

Spearman's g

One of the earliest theories of intelligence was proposed by Charles Spearman, a British psychologist and statistician, in 1904. Spearman noted that all of the correlations between measures of cognitive abilities and academic achievements were positive, and this led him to the conclusion that there was a single global mental ability. He called this ability *general intelligence* and argued that its presence in various measures was the cause of the positive correlations. In a fully developed version of his *two-factor theory,* published in 1927, Spearman asserted that all measures of mental abilities were composed of two factors, general intelligence, which he called simply *g,* and a factor or ability specific to the particular test, which he called *s.* Thus, the reliable variance in a set of test scores could be explained, according to the theory, by the presence of individual differences in *g* and *s.* Spearman characterized *g* as being like a mental engine; it was the energizer of intelligent behavior.

Thurstone's Primary Mental Abilities

In the United States Spearman's theory was viewed as too simplistic. Several psychologists, led by E. L. Thorndike and, later, L. L. Thurstone, argued that there were many different and largely independent dimensions of human intelligence. By the 1930s Thurstone was using a statistical technique he had invented, called *common factor analysis,* to identify these dimensions. This line of research culminated in 1938 in his monograph describing *the primary mental abilities,* of which Thurstone claimed there were at least 12 (Thurstone, 1938).

Factor analysis is a procedure that identifies groups of tests that correlate in such a way that they seem to share a common dimension (see Chapter 16). Thurstone argued that these common dimensions or factors were causal properties of behavior in the same sense that Spearman thought of *g* as a mental engine which energized behavior. Thus, although Thurstone was willing to talk about intelligence, he saw it as multidimensional. A person could be high on one dimension, or ability, and intermediate or low on others. However, Thurstone noted that the factors seemed to be positively correlated, and toward the end of his life he came to accept a hierarchical view of intelligence: Something akin to *g* was the cause of the primary factors being correlated, and the primary factors were the cause of the correlations between the tests.

Spearman and Thurstone defined the basic dichotomy for theories of intelligence; was it one thing or many? Their theories and many that were to follow were derived from an examination of test relations and test content. If a set of tests all correlated positively, there must be a common underlying cause. The nature of the cause was to be found in examining how the tests were similar in their content or process. For example, if we find positive correlations among a set of tests, all of which require rapid performance of relatively simple tasks, we might conclude that there is an ability (a dimension of intelligence) reflected in speed of performance.

One of the problems with approaching the definition of intelligence in this way is that the selection of tests controls the domain of study. This was made clear in the original Spearman/Thorndike debates from before 1920. If the battery being studied includes one test from each of a wide variety of performance domains (Spearman's approach), a single general factor of ability usually will be found. If, on the other hand, several measures from each domain are included (Thorndike's approach) a factor representing each domain will appear. Thus, the early theories based largely on an analysis of test content have not been very fruitful or satisfying.

Theories of Jensen and Wechsler

Two major contemporary theories of intelligence derive more or less directly from the Spearman and Thorndike/Thurstone traditions. One, epitomized in the work of Arthur Jensen, is based on studies of reaction time required to perform acts of varying complexity. It is centered in laboratory research and in studies of the predictive validity of intelligence tests. The other, originating in the work of David Wechsler, derives from a clinical tradition and has focused on the use of patterns of test scores for diagnosis of cognitive difficulties.

Jensen's Theory.   In the 1880s Sir Francis Galton argued that reaction time in performing simple acts should measure a person's intelligence. The fact that such measures did not correlate with school grades and other intelligent behaviors shifted attention to the kinds of test tasks Binet was developing. However, beginning in the 1970s a series of studies by Jensen (1982), Hunt (1987), and others showed that there were stable *negative* correlations between various measures of reaction time and scores on complex cognitive tasks.

Computerized timing devices allowed researchers to record different aspects of the time a subject required to react to a stimulus. A typical study might have the subject seated at a console with a series of reaction buttons arranged in an arc around a "home" button. The subject would keep his or her finger on the home button until a light came on, at which time the subject was to move as quickly as possible to one of the other buttons. The simplest task, involving pure reaction with no decision other than that a stimulus had occurred, would be merely to go from Button A to Button B when the light came on. A more complex task would require the subject to go to different buttons, depending on the color of the light. In this case the subject must not only react but also decide which of several reactions to make. The difference between the time it takes to make the first response and the time it takes to make the second is the time required for the cognitive processing of the decision task. The general trend of results from studies like this has been that people who process information faster (have shorter reaction times) also tend to earn somewhat higher scores on standard tests of intelligence.

What makes results like these interesting, relative to a theory about the nature of intelligence, is the finding Jensen has reported that reaction time measures primarily correlate with what he interprets as *g* in the intelligence tests. That is, in his studies Jensen has found that it is the part of a series of intelligence tests that is common to all of them, which he uses as an approximation to Spearman's *g*, that accounts for the correlation between the tests and reaction time. This has led Jensen to conclude that there is a biological basis for individual differences in intelligence that is very general in nature and can be described as differences in the efficiency of the brain for processing information (Jensen, 1991; 1993).

Further evidence for the presence of a broad cognitive ability that influences performance in a wide variety of areas comes from research on the predictive validity of ability tests. Several authors have reported that almost all of the predictive power of cognitive ability tests for most jobs and training applications is included in the first, or most general, factor of the battery (Ree and Earles, 1992; Schmidt and Hunter, 1992).

This theory is still at the level of basic research and has not resulted in any new practical measures of intelligence. However, it, and reactions to it, have created much public debate about the nature of intelligence and the proper use of intelligence tests. We consider some of these effects in our discussion of the book *The Bell Curve* later in this chapter.

Wechsler's Theory.   In 1939 David Wechsler, then working as a clinical psychologist at Bellevue Hospital in New York, published a test to measure the intelligence of adult patients. The test was really a collection of subtests, most of which had been used as group tests of the Alpha and Beta batteries in the military testing program during World War I. Wechsler adapted them for individual administration and divided them into two scales, one composed of the Form Alpha tests that had required the use of language, the other including the language-free tests from Form Beta. The tests from Form Alpha produced a Verbal Scale whose score reflected Verbal Intelligence. The Form Beta tests yielded a score for Performance Intelligence, and the sum of the two subscales gave Full Scale Intelligence, which Wechsler saw as roughly equivalent to *g*.

Wechsler defined intelligence as "the aggregate or global capacity of the individual to act purposefully, to think rationally and to deal effectively with his environment" (Wechsler, 1944, p. 3). But, his theory was driven by clinical practice. Therefore, patterns in the scores were believed to have clinical significance and could be used to diagnose disorders. The meanings of test scores and patterns of scores evolved over the years to such a degree that the practical theory implied by test use is complex and very applied. Wechsler's theory, which is embodied in the use of the three individual intelligence tests that bear his name, is perhaps the most influential current view on the subject and has given rise to thousands of research studies. It is, however, a clinical theory, a guide to the best or most informative use of test scores, rather than a theory about the scientific nature of intelligence. Kaufman (1990) devotes most of 700 pages of densely packed information to a discussion of the applications of one of the three Wechsler tests.

Cattell-Horn G$_f$-G$_c$ Theory

In 1943 Raymond Cattell first proposed the division of cognitive processes into two broad classes based on their interaction with experience. The theory slept for 20 years while Cattell focused his attention on the study of personality. Then, in 1966, he was joined by John Horn, and the study of intelligence was resumed. The 1966 Horn/Cattell statement identified *Fluid Intelligence* as a problem-solving and information-processing ability that is largely independent of experience. This ability can be invested in various cognitive activities and leads to the development of knowl-edge and skills. These latter abilities, which result from the application of fluid intel-ligence to life experiences, they called *Crystallized Intelligence.* Because both of these abilities are broad based and general in nature, they were given the symbols G_f (general fluid ability) and G_c (general crystallized ability). Capital letters were used to distinguish them from Spearman's *g.*

Over the years, Horn and his colleagues have expanded to nine the number of abilities associated with the theory. Most of these dimensions have been identified by factor analyses of batteries of tests, but they cover a wider variety of tasks and seem more closely attached to biological processes than have previous factorial theories. The nine factors are

G_f —Fluid Intelligence—ability to reason in novel situations

G_c —Crystallized Intelligence—breadth and depth of general knowledge

G_q —Quantitative Ability—ability to comprehend and manipulate numerical sym-bols and concepts

G_v —Visualization Processing—ability to see spatial relationships and patterns

G_a —Auditory Processing—ability to discriminate sounds and detect sound pat-terms and relationships

G_s —Processing Speed—ability to reach quick correct decisions and maintain at-tention

G_{sm}—Short-Term Memory—ability to hold and use a block of information over a short time span

G_{lr} —Long-Term Retrieval—ability to transfer material to permanent storage and retrieve it later

CDS—Correct Decision Speed—ability to reach correct judgments quickly

The Cattell-Horn theory provides the theoretical basis for two of the most popular tests of cognitive abilities, the Stanford-Binet Fourth Edition and the Woodcock-Johnson Tests of Cognitive Ability, which are discussed later in this section.

Carroll's Three-Stratum Theory

In a statistical tour de force, John Carroll (1993) undertook to reanalyze the data from over 400 factor analytic studies of abilities in an effort to find common themes. One of the difficulties in drawing conclusions from studies performed by different investi-gators is that there has been no common agreement on the appropriate way to con-duct a factor analysis. Also, studies seldom shared enough variables to allow reason-able comparisons. Carroll attempted to overcome these problems by going back to the original data and applying a common methodology across all studies. The result was a hierarchical model similar to Thurstone's, with broad cognitive ability, or general intelligence, at the top, a small number of general factors similar to those of the Cattell-Horn model at a second level, and a large number of relatively specific factors describing the abilities required for performance on narrower test classifications at the third stratum.

Sternberg's Triarchic Theory

Beginning in the 1970s, Robert Sternberg conducted a series of studies that have led him to propose a theory which attempts to place intelligence in a unified social, physiological, and psychometric context. He calls his theory a triarchic theory because it is composed of three subtheories (Sternberg, 1985).

The first subtheory is a *contextual* theory which proposes that different behaviors will be considered intelligent in different environments. Traditional views of intelligence, Sternberg argues, have all been developed within an academic environment that values a large fund of information and the ability to reason abstractly and symbolically. However, the behaviors that are valued in nonacademic environments and in other cultures may be quite different. Sternberg has conducted studies of what he calls "street smarts" and other nonacademic adaptive behaviors and has found them to be independent of scores on conventional measures of intelligence. (A small problem with several of these studies is that they have used college students, a group who are relatively homogeneous in intelligence. This would reduce the apparent relationship.)

The second subtheory in Sternberg's system is an *experiential* theory. Sternberg argues that a major aspect of intelligence is the ability to automate or routinize behaviors. When a novel situation is encountered, intelligence is applied to solve the problems posed by the novelty. The more intelligent person solves these problems more quickly, converting the novel into the familiar and freeing the intellect to deal with other problems. For example, a person visiting a new city for the first time has to invest considerable mental capacity in the problems of finding his or her way around. According to Sternberg, the more intelligent person will develop a cognitive map of the area and be able to navigate like a native more quickly than the less intelligent person, thus freeing attention and problem-solving abilities for new experiences.

The third subtheory is called the *componential* theory. This theory is similar to the issues considered by Jensen and Hunt in that it attempts to explain how problems are solved and information is processed.

The componential theory itself has three classes of components. The first of these are *performance components,* which are involved in attending to stimuli, holding information in working memory, retrieving data from long-term storage, and manipulating information. *Knowledge-acquisition components* function to acquire and store new information by selectively applying the performance components to stimuli. *Metacomponents* serve the managerial function of monitoring the application of performance and knowledge-acquisition components to the solution of a problem.

The triarchic theory holds promise as a model to explain how the human mind functions. At this time, however, there are no intelligence assessment procedures that have developed from the theory. Until such instruments become available, the model will have little clinical or diagnostic application.

The Das-Naglieri PASS Model

Another theory that attempts to integrate physiology and information processing is the *PASS theory* of J. P. Das and Jack Naglieri (Das, Naglieri, & Kirby, 1994). Starting from a neurophysiological model of the brain proposed by A. R. Luria, these authors have divided intelligence into four basic processes: *P*lanning, *A*ttention, *S*imultaneous processing, and *S*uccessive processing. The model attempts to relate the four processes to specific neurological structures or areas.

The most basic function is attention. One must be attending to a stimulus in order to process the information it contains or solve the problem it poses. An inability to focus attention is seen as one reason for poor intellectual performance.

Once attention has been directed to a stimulus, the information it contains may require either simultaneous processing or sequential processing. Information that is subject to simultaneous processing "is said to be *surveyable* because the elements are interrelated and accessible to inspection" either directly or from being held in memory (Das et al., 1994, p. 15). Simultaneous processing is involved in language comprehension and other tasks that require perception of the whole problem at once. Successive processing is required whenever the elements of the task must be performed in a particular order. Tasks such as performing skilled movements and serial recall of stimuli are examples of the application of successive processing.

The planning portion of the model is similar to Sternberg's metacomponents in that it is involved in deciding where to focus attention and which type of processing the task requires. The planning process also monitors the success of problem solving and modifies the approach as needed until a solution is achieved.

The four processes operate within an existing *knowledge base.* "This fund of accumulated knowledge can be thought of as the cumulative result of a person's experiences that have been stored in memory. Because all processes operate within the context of knowledge, this base of information influences all cognitive processes and motor programs" (Das et al., 1994, p. 19).

INDIVIDUAL GENERAL-ABILITY TESTS

As we noted earlier, relatively few of the currently popular intelligence tests have been developed from a particular theory. However, most have been influenced by one theory or another. In this section we review five of the most widely used measures of cognitive ability and mention briefly a few others. All of these instruments are designed for individual administration by a trained examiner, and in many cases the clinical observations of the examiner during testing form an important part of the assessment report.

Stanford-Binet Intelligence Scale: Fourth Edition

Early Binet-Type Scales.   At the time of Binet and Simon's work, Charles Spearman proposed a theory of intelligence that has had a directing influence on the development of all tests of ability. Spearman suggested that there is a single global intellectual function, which he called general intelligence, or *g,* underlying each individual's performance on all tests of ability. Many of the early tests were constructed either with this idea as their theoretical base or in an attempt to refute the theory of general intelligence. The scales that Binet created, and those developed in his intellectual tradition, were generally consistent with the theory of general intelligence.

Several adaptations of the Binet-Simon scales were brought out in the United States, but the version that has survived is the one published by Lewis Terman in 1916 and known as the Stanford Revision of the Binet-Simon Scales. It has since come to be called the Stanford-Binet Intelligence Scale, the Stanford-Binet, or simply the Binet. The Stanford-Binet was extensively revised in the 1930s; two forms of the test, Forms L and M, were produced. In 1960, a third edition, Form LM, was released, which included the best items from the 1937 version. New norms were prepared in 1972, but the test itself was not changed. The first real revision of the test in almost 50 years was published in 1986, the Stanford-Binet Intelligence Scale: Fourth Edition (R. L. Thorndike, Hagen, & Sattler, 1986a, b).

As originally developed by Terman, and revised by Terman and Maud Merrill, the Stanford-Binet was organized by age levels and consisted of six quite different tests at each age level. The tests also varied from level to level, but collectively the levels included, among others, tasks involving picture and oral vocabulary; memory for objects, sentences, digits, and visual sequences in the form of bead strings; comprehension of what to do in practical situations; analogies; picture and verbal absurdities; similarities and differences; arithmetical problem solving; and sentence completion. In the fourth edition of the Stanford-Binet, the items are grouped by type so that the examinee attempts vocabulary items as one set of tasks, comprehension items as a second, separate set of tasks, and so forth. Most of the original item types were retained, and some new ones were added.

With the first three versions of the Stanford-Binet, the examiner usually started with tests a year or so below the examinee's current age. If all tests at this level were passed, the examiner continued up to the next age level, and so on, until a "ceiling" was reached—an age level at which all the tasks were failed. If one or more tests were failed at the initial entry level, the examiner dropped back until a "basal" age, the highest age at which all the tasks were passed, was found. The examiner then proceeded with testing to determine the child's ceiling. The result was a single score expressing the general ability of the examinee.

A mental age (MA) was determined by taking the basal age and adding to it months of mental age credit for each test passed beyond the basal level. For tests at the 5-year level and below, each test was worth 1 month because the tests were arranged in half-year increments. From Levels 6 through 14, 2 months were awarded for each success. Above that level, the tests received greater weight "in order to make IQs for the upper levels comparable to IQs for the lower age levels" (Terman & Merrill, 1960, p. 62). To illustrate, suppose a child passed all tests at the 6-year level, three at 7 years, one at 8 years, and none beyond that point. Then the mental age would be determined as follows:

Test Performance	Mental Age Credit	
Basal age	6 years	0 months
Passed three out of six 7-year tests		6 months
Passed one out of six 8-year tests		2 months
Passed zero out of six 9-year tests		0 months
MA =	6 years	8 months

An index of brightness was obtained by relating mental age to chronological age (CA) to yield an intelligence quotient, or IQ. Originally, the procedure was one of division, in which mental age was divided by chronological age. An IQ was obtained using the formula

$$IQ = (MA/CA)\ 100$$

This ratio yielded values with a mean of 100 (hence the origin of the idea that an intelligence quotient of 100 is average) and a standard deviation of about 16 (actual values ranged from about 12 to 20 points). This *ratio IQ* was used with the first two editions of the instrument. However, since the 1960 revision, the Stanford-Binet has reported results as standard scores, adjusted to yield the same population mean (100) and standard deviation (16) that characterized the IQ. The use of standard scores equated the meaning of the index at all ages. (The values of 100 and 16 were chosen for continuity with earlier practice.) These standard scores produce nearly the same numerical scale as the original ratio IQs and have the advantage of uniformity for all ages. They also avoid the problem that we pointed out in Chapter 3, namely, that age equivalents become meaningless when the rate of development changes significantly.

The 1986 Stanford-Binet has largely avoided the terms intelligence quotient and IQ, substituting the phrase "standard age score" (SAS) instead. This term is more descriptive of what the index really is, and it is possible that the change in terminology will eventually eliminate some of the connotations that have grown over the years around the term *IQ*. However, the SAS and IQ numerical scales are essentially identical (mean of 100 and standard deviation of 16). The relationship between the SAS of the Stanford-Binet and the percentile rank within the individual's age group is approximately as follows:

Stanford-Binet SAS	Percentile Rank
130	97
120	89
110	73
100	50
90	27
80	11
70	3

Subtests of the Stanford-Binet.   The 1986 revision of the Stanford-Binet is composed of many of the same item types as the earlier editions, but as already noted, the items are grouped by type into 15 subtests. The items are graded in difficulty from extremely simple items appropriate for below average 2-year-olds up to items of a high level of difficulty. There are two items at each level of difficulty. The 15 types of items included in the current form of the Stanford-Binet are listed and briefly described here. They may be combined to yield four ability scales or an overall measure of ability.

Verbal Reasoning Tests

1. *Vocabulary* (23 levels—test given at all ages). At the seven lowest levels, items are pictures that the examinee is required to name. In the 16 higher levels, words are presented, and the examinee must tell what the word means.

2. *Comprehension* (21 levels—test given at all ages). The three lowest levels require the examinee to point to named parts of a picture of a unisex, ethnically ambiguous child. The higher levels ask the examinee the *why* of things, starting with why people use umbrellas and going up to why it is advantageous to be able to amend a constitution.

3. *Absurdities* (16 levels—test given from age 2 years to about age 14 years). Each item consists of a picture that has something definitely wrong with it (e.g., a bicycle with square wheels or a person with two right hands). The examinee must tell what is wrong—what is silly in the picture.

4. *Verbal Relations* (9 levels—test begun at about age 11 years). This test calls for identification of the basis on which three terms are alike but are different from a fourth term. An easy item might read

cat fox horse but *not* pigeon

Abstract/Visual Reasoning Tests

5. *Pattern Analysis* (21 levels—test given at all ages). The lowest levels of this test use a three-hole form board that looks like this one.

The subject must replace the pieces in the holes. Difficulty is increased by rotating the board and by dividing the three pieces into halves.

Higher levels of analysis are based on adaptation of the classic Kohs Blocks. Each block is a black and white cube with a different design on each face. The six faces are displayed here.

Starting with the task of the examinee matching the face of the block shown by the examiner, the test progresses to assembling from two to nine blocks to produce a design, such as shown here.

6. *Copying* (14 levels—test given from age 2 years to about age 8 years). The lowest levels require matching the arrangements of two or three blocks presented by the examiner. The higher levels call on the child to copy a simple figure, such as the ones displayed here.

7. *Matrices* (13 levels—test begun at about age 6 years). The examinee is presented with an incomplete matrix and is required to select the correct entry to complete the matrix. A relatively simple item is illustrated here.

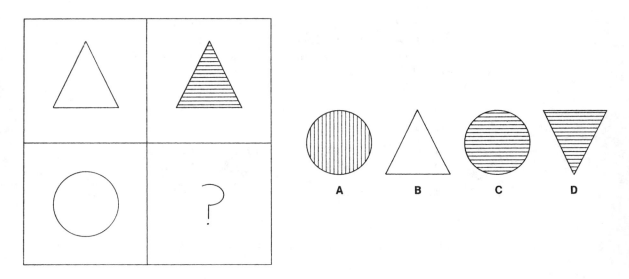

8. *Paper Folding and Cutting* (9 levels—test begun at about age 11 years). The examinee is presented with a demonstration of how a rectangle of paper has been folded and one or more pieces cut out of it. The examinee must indicate how the paper will look when unfolded. A relatively simple item is illustrated here.

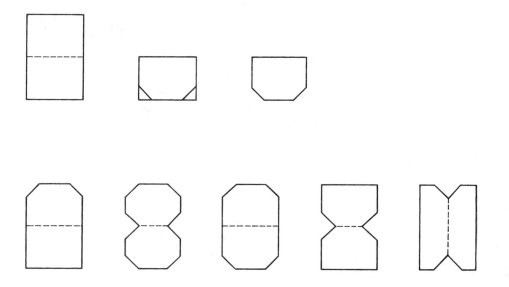

Quantitative Reasoning

9. *Quantitative* (20 levels—test given at all ages). The easiest items involve counting and adding or subtracting the spots on what are essentially dice. From this task, the test goes to a series of pictures, each involving a quantitative question, graded in difficulty. An early item might read, "These are Mary's six marbles. If she gave three to Jane, how many would be left?"

10. *Number Series* (13 levels—test begun at about age 6 years). Sequences of numbers are presented, and the examinee is required to state the two numbers that should come next. A very easy and a more difficult item are shown here.

3 4 5 6 7 _____ _____
4 6 5 8 6 10 _____ _____

11. *Equation Building* (9 levels—test begun at about age 11 years). This test presents the examinee with a set of numerals and operational signs. The examinee is required to rearrange the elements to produce a true number sentence, or equation. Again, a very easy item and a more difficult one are illustrated here.

2 2 4 − =
1/2 1 5 7 − × ( ) =

Short-Term Memory Tests

12. *Memory for Sentences* (21 levels—test given at all ages). The examiner reads a sentence to the examinee, who is instructed to repeat it exactly as it was read. The test starts with two-word sentences, at the lowest level, and progresses to the top-level sentences of more than 20 words.

13. *Bead Memory* (21 levels—test given at all ages). The test involves a stack of beads of four shapes and three colors. At the lowest levels, the examinee is shown a bead for 2 seconds and then must find it on a card showing beads with all the shapes and colors. For most of the test, the examinee has 5 seconds to look at the picture of a stalk with a sequence of beads on it and then must, from memory, correctly reproduce the sequence on his or her own stalk.

14. *Memory for Digits* (7 levels forward, 6 levels reversed—test begun at about age 6 years). The examiner reads a sequence of digits at a rate of approximately one per second. In the first section of the test, the examinee must repeat the digits in the order that they are read. In the second section, the examinee must recite them in reverse order.

15. *Memory for Objects* (7 levels—test begun at about age 6 years). A sequence of pictures of objects is shown to the examinee, one at a time. Then a picture is shown that includes all the objects that were shown in the series, plus several others. The examinee must point to all objects that had been shown to him or her in the order that they were shown.

Organization of the Stanford-Binet.

The current version of the Stanford-Binet represents a marked shift from the theoretical position held by Binet and Terman. Until 1986, the Stanford-Binet yielded only a single global score for general intelligence. The fourth edition is grounded in the much more recent G_f-G_c theory of Cattell and Horn. The tests of the new Stanford-Binet are organized to yield scores in four areas, or dimensions, of ability. The vocabulary, comprehension, absurdities, and verbal relations tests are combined to yield an area score for *verbal reasoning*. Pattern analysis, copying, matrices, and paper folding and cutting are summed to give an *abstract/visual reasoning* area score. A *quantitative reasoning* area score is derived from the combination of the quantitative, number series, and equation-building tests. Finally, the four memory tests yield an area score for *short-term memory*. The verbal-reasoning and quantitative-reasoning scales are intended to represent the crystallized abilities of the Cattell-Horn theory and may be combined to give a score for such abilities, while abstract/visual reasoning is seen as a fluid ability. The short-term memory area score is an indicator of G_{sm}. When all four area scores are combined, the resulting composite score is essentially equivalent to the general intellective dimension proposed by Spearman and measured by earlier forms of the Stanford-Binet.

Administration of the new Stanford-Binet is somewhat more complex than its predecessors. Testing starts with the vocabulary test, and the examiner begins with the items at or just below the examinee's chronological age. (A basal level is defined as the point where the child passes both items at two successive ages.) Then, more difficult items are given until the point is reached where three out of four or all four items at two successive ages are failed, which yields a ceiling. The raw score is determined by giving credit for all items below the basal level and one additional point for each item attempted and passed. The vocabulary score and the child's age are then used to determine a starting point for each of the remaining tests. A basal level and a ceiling are found for each test in the same manner as that used for vocabulary.

A raw score is assigned in each subtest, giving the examinee credit for having passed all the easier items below the basal level. Raw scores on each of the subtests are then converted to normalized standard scores for that age level, using tables in the examiner's manual. The individual subtest standard scores have a mean of 50 and a standard deviation of 8. These can be combined to yield the four area scores and a composite of all of the subtests. The scores for areas and for the total are expressed as SASs—normalized standard scores for that age level—with a mean of 100 and a standard deviation of 16.

The composite standard age score has many of the same properties as the mental age and IQ of the earlier versions of the Stanford-Binet. However, it is also possible to work with the four area scores: verbal reasoning, abstract/visual reasoning, quantitative reasoning, and short-term memory. These area scores are all related to one another and contribute to an overall measure. But, they are sufficiently distinct so that each describes a somewhat different aspect of a person's cognitive functioning.

In the current version of the Stanford-Binet, a major effort has been made to adapt the testing to the ability level of the person being tested, so that the tasks presented are closely matched to his or her ability level. This adaptation is accomplished by using the vocabulary *routing test* to determine, in combination with chronological age, the level at which the examinee is likely to succeed. Thus, the design is to bracket the examinee's ability level as efficiently as possible to minimize time wasted on items that are too easy for the examinee, and frustration on items that are too hard.

Even though the individual tests of the Stanford-Binet are quite short, they are reasonably reliable. Median Kuder-Richardson Formula 20 (KR-20) reliabilities computed within age groups for the individual tests run from 0.73 to 0.94, with all but memory for objects—which has fewer levels than any other subtest—exceeding 0.83. Within-age-group reliabilities for the area scores are higher, and the composite score based on four area scores generally yields a KR-20 reliability in excess of 0.95.

The individual tests show moderate to high correlations with each other. Median within-age-group correlations range from 0.29 between paper folding and cutting and memory for objects, to 0.73 between vocabulary and comprehension, with most of the correlations in the 30s, 40s, and 50s. In general, the tests within an area correlate more highly with other tests in the same area than they do with tests in other areas. The area scores all correlate in the 60s and 70s with each other, indicating that they measure somewhat discrete concepts that share a common core. These correlations are consistent with the theory that guided the development of the instrument. Recent studies of the structure of the Stanford-Binet (Boyle, 1989; R. M. Thorndike, 1990b) have confirmed that the individual tests generally relate to each other in the manner predicted by the theory used in test development.

Wechsler Scales

The other senior series of individually administered tests of general ability is the Wechsler series, the first of which, the Wechsler-Bellevue, was published in 1939. Periodically, the tests have been extended and revised. The series currently is composed of three test levels: the Wechsler Preschool and Primary Scale of Intelligence Revised (WPPSI-R) (Wechsler, 1989), the Wechsler Intelligence Scale for Children III (WISC-III) (Wechsler, 1991), and the Wechsler Adult Intelligence Scale Revised (WAIS-R) (Wechsler, 1981). These are intended for ages 4 to 6 1/2, 6 to 16, and 16 and above, respectively. The scales were developed from the start as sets of subtests, each containing items graded in difficulty. They were also designed from the beginning to produce two subscores (verbal ability and performance ability), as well as an overall ability score. (The Wechsler literature still uses the term IQ, so we will use it also in our discussion of these instruments.) The titles of the subtests from the WISC-III (Wechsler, 1991), together with their subscale arrangement and an illustrative item (similar to those included in the actual test) are shown here. In an actual testing situation more detailed instructions would be given.

Verbal Scale
1.   *General Information.* What day of the year is Independence Day?
2.   *Similarities.* In what way are wool and cotton alike?
3.   *Arithmetic Reasoning.* If eggs cost 60 cents a dozen, what does 1 egg cost?
4.   *Vocabulary.* What does *corrupt* mean?
5.   *Comprehension.* Why do people buy fire insurance?
6.   *Digit Span.* I am going to say some numbers. Listen carefully, and when I am through, say the numbers right after me.

    7 3 4 1 8 6

Now, I am going to say some more numbers, but this time when I stop, I want you to say them backward.

    3 8 4 1 6

Digit Span is an optional subtest on the Verbal scale.

Performance Scale

7. *Picture Completion.* I am going to show you some pictures. In each there is an important part missing. Tell me what is missing.

					1996	
S	M	T	W	T	F	S
		1	2	3	4	5
6	7	8	9	10	11	12
13	14	15	16	17	18	19
20	21	22	23	24	25	26
27	28	29	30	31		

8. *Picture Arrangement.* The pictures below tell a story. Put them in the right order to tell the story.

9. *Block Design.* Using the four blocks that I have given you, make a design just like this one.

10. *Object Assembly.* If these pieces [see next page] are put together correctly, they will make something. Go ahead and put them together as quickly as you can.

11. *Coding.* In the top row, each figure is shown with a number. Fill in the number that goes with each figure in the second row.

Code

△	○	▱	✕	8
1	2	3	4	5

Test

△	8	✕	○	△	▱	8	✕	△	8	etc.

12. *Symbol Search.* See this shape (on the left). Now look at these shapes (on the right). Are any of these shapes the same as this one? If any of them are the same, mark *yes,* if none of them are the same as this shape, mark *no.*

13. *Mazes.* This subtest includes pencil mazes like those found in newspapers.

Symbol Search and Mazes are optional subtests in the Performance Scale.

Each subtest of a scale yields a separate score, which is then converted into a standard score with a mean of 10 and a standard deviation of 3 for that subtest, based on a sample of individuals of the same age as the examinee. The subtest standard scores are combined in three different groupings to yield total scores for verbal, performance, and overall abilities, and from these total scores, three different types of IQ may be read from norm tables. The three IQs are (1) a verbal IQ (VIQ) from subtests 1 through 6, (2) a performance IQ (PIQ) from subtests 7 through 13, and (3) a total IQ (Full Scale IQ, or FSIQ) from the combined subtests.

In addition to the three basic scales, the manual for the WISC-III (but, as of this writing, not the other two Wechsler tests) allows for computing four Index Scores derived from factor analyses of the subtests. These are a *Verbal Comprehension* (VC) score based on Information, Similarities, Vocabulary and Comprehension; a *Perceptual Organization* (PO) score obtained from Picture Completion, Picture Arrangement, Block Design, and Object Assembly; a *Freedom from Distractability* (FD) score from Arithmetic and Digit Span; and a *Processing Speed* (PS) score composed of Coding and Symbol Search. The separate verbal and performance scores may have diagnostic significance in the case of certain individuals with verbal, academic, or cultural handicaps; however, such interpretations should be made only by individuals with extensive clinical training (see Kaufman, [1990] for a thorough discussion of these issues). Studies of the value of such diagnoses have yielded conflicting results. The value of the four index scores is a topic of intense debate in the professional community and remains to be demonstrated. The verbal, performance, and overall IQ scores on the WPPSI-R and WAIS-R are also transformed standard scores. The scale on all the Wechsler instruments is set to make the mean of the normative sample 100 and the standard deviation 15.

The Wechsler scales report internal consistency reliabilities generally in the 90s for the individual subtests. Test-retest reliabilities are somewhat lower, but generally in the 80s. Correlations of the verbal and performance Wechsler IQs with the area standard age scores of the Stanford-Binet are all above 0.60 except for correlations of the WPPSI scales with abstract/visual reasoning. Wechsler full-scale IQs correlate from 0.80 to 0.91 with the Stanford-Binet composite (R. L. Thorndike, Hagen, & Sattler, 1986a). Thus, although the two instruments were independently developed, they yield a consistent assessment of general intellectual ability.

Kaufman Assessment Battery for Children

The first recent addition to the field of individual ability testing, introduced with considerable fanfare in 1982, is the Kaufman Assessment Battery for Children (K-ABC). The battery is composed of three sections, one stated to measure "sequential processing," one to measure "simultaneous processing," and one to measure "achievement."

The sequential processing scale includes three tests of short-term memory for a sequence of unrelated items—hand movements, digits, and unrelated words, respectively. The examinee must simply reproduce these items in the order that they were presented. The tests were selected to measure the successive processing component of the Das-Naglieri model described earlier in this chapter.

The simultaneous processing tests are substantially nonverbal and are intended to measure the simultaneous processing component of the Das-Naglieri model. Of the seven tests, two involve encoding and memory of a visual pattern—faces in one case and spatial arrangement in the other. Two involve perceptual synthesis of incomplete visual material, with the task being to name the object partially displayed. Three require analyzing a pattern or sequence of visual material—a design, matrix, or picture sequence.

The achievement scale includes six tests, two that assess basic reading skills, a general information test requiring the naming of pictures, an "expressive vocabulary" test, a riddles test, and a test of arithmetical skills. For those tests calling for a verbal response, a key is provided for scoring responses given in Spanish.

The 16 tests in the battery yield five scores: sequential and simultaneous processing scores, an achievement score, a mental-processing composite score that is a combination of sequential and simultaneous processing, and a nonverbal score that combines 6 of the 10 processing scales. Each score is scaled to have a mean of 100 and a standard deviation of 15.

The battery is designed to cover the age range from 2 years 6 months (2-6) to 12-6. However, because average performance for age 2-6 in the norm sample is only 3 items passed out of the 40 items on the sequential processing scale and 6 out of 55 on simultaneous processing, the test seems better suited to children 3-6 and over. Test-retest reliabilities over an average interval of 18 days were as follows:

	Ages 2-6 to 4-11	Ages 5-0 to 8-11	Ages 9-0 to 12-5
Sequential processing	.77	.82	.88
Simulataneous processing	.77	.88	.91
Processing composite	.83	.88	.93
Achievement	.95	.95	.97

Correlations between the above scales for the three age groups were

	Ages 2-6 to 4-11	Ages 5-0 to 8-11	Ages 9-0 to 12-5
Sequential/Simultaneous	.41	.49	.52
Sequential/Achievement	.46	.63	.62
Simultaneous/Achievement	.64	.63	.69

The authors (Kaufman & Kaufman, 1983) provide a commendable amount of data on the correlations of the Kaufman scales with other established ability and achievement tests.

Taking account of its correlations with other tests, as well as the correlations between the three sections and 16 subtests, it would seem that the simultaneous processing scale of the K-ABC is primarily a measure of fluid and nonverbal intelligence. The sequential processing scale also to some degree measures this ability but, additionally, provides a measure of short-term memory of a series of disconnected stimuli. The achievement scale seems to measure developed or crystallized intellectual abilities, because its highest correlations are with verbal scales on the WISC-R and the Cognitive Abilities Test (CogAT) (a group test of intellectual ability, discussed in a later section), rather than with scores on school achievement batteries. The K-ABC authors imply that the distinctions between the three scales and, to some extent, the distinctive features of each of the 16 subtests will be useful for educational diagnosis and remediation, but in large part, these values remain to be demonstrated.

Woodcock-Johnson Psycho-Educational Battery—Revised

Another battery of tests that attempts to measure both intelligence and achievement is the Woodcock-Johnson Psycho-Educational Battery—Revised (WJ-R) (Woodcock & Johnson, 1989). This instrument is derived quite directly from the Cattell-Horn model and purports to measure eight of the nine factors listed for that theory, discussed earlier (Correct Decision Speed is omitted). Like the Stanford-Binet, the WJ-R provides a single instrument for use at all ages. The cognitive portion of the battery (WJ-R COG) contains 21 subtests, with varying numbers of tests (as few as 4 and as many as 10) being given at different ages. There are three subtests each for fluid reasoning, comprehension/knowledge, visual processing, auditory processing, processing speed, short-term memory, and long-term retrieval. Quantitative ability is measured by tests from the achievement part of the battery (WJ-R ACH). There are 18 achievement tests measuring skills in oral language, reading, mathematics, written language, and general knowledge.

One of the basic objectives of the WJ-R is to provide a combined set of aptitude and achievement tests normed on a single sample so that discrepancies between aptitude and achievement can be used for diagnosis of educational problems. The tests are normed on large samples, ranging in age from 2 years to over 90 (a total of over 6,300 cases). This is clearly one of the most ambitious efforts at wide-range norms ever undertaken for an individually administered test.

Das-Naglieri Cognitive Assessment System (DN-CAS)

The newest member of the growing family of individually administered intelligence tests is the *Das-Naglieri Cognitive Assessment System (DN-CAS)*. As its name implies, this instrument attempts to operationalize the PASS model of cognitive functioning. Four tests have been developed to measure each of the four elements in the model (16 tests in all). At this time the test battery is in the final stages of standardization.

Abbreviated Individual Test

A major problem in using individually administered tests of aptitude is that they are very costly. A trained examiner must spend at least an hour with each examinee. This costliness has led to three responses: the development of group-administered tests such as those described in the next section, the use of short forms of the Stanford-Binet and Wechsler scales in which only some of the tests are given, and the preparation of some short individual tests.

Various short forms of the Wechsler scales have been proposed. Sattler (1982) provides a table containing estimates of the correlations between various combinations of two to five subtests with the composite IQ on the WPPSI and WISC-R. The two-test combinations generally yield correlations in the 80s, and using more subtests produces higher correlations.

For earlier versions of the Stanford-Binet, several authors provided suggested selections of tests to use as a short form. With the publication of the new edition of the Stanford-Binet, it is also possible to use individual subtests. Based on the median correlations of the individual subtests with the full composite score as reported in the technical manual (R. L. Thorndike, Hagen, & Sattler, 1986a), the best two tests to use to represent the full test are vocabulary (correlation coefficient $[r] = .81$) and quantitative ($r = .82$). An optimum four-test composite sampling all four areas would be Vocabulary, Quantitative, Pattern Analysis ($r = .74$), and Bead Memory ($r = .72$) (R. L. Thorndike, Hagen, & Sattler, 1986b). Each of these tests is used at all age levels. The authors suggest adding Memory for Sentences and Comprehension to these four to give "a reasonably accurate estimate of overall cognitive level and pattern of cognitive abilities" (p. 35). These are the six core tests that are administered at all ages. These reduced batteries should not be used to estimate scores for the four cognitive areas.

The consistent finding that verbal tests show high correlations with broader measures of intellectual ability has led to the development of various short tests based entirely on verbal material. A particularly popular type, because of its inherent interest to children, is the picture vocabulary test, of which the Peabody Picture Vocabulary Test (Dunn & Dunn, 1981) is probably the best known. Each of the two forms of the test has 175 plates, each containing four pictures. The examiner gives a word, and the examinee indicates the picture that relates to the word. The test takes about 15 minutes and provides an indication of general verbal ability.

GROUP GENERAL-ABILITY TESTS

There are certain advantages to having a test administered to a person one-on-one with a trained examiner. No reading need be required on the part of the examinee, so it is possible to test young children and people of limited literacy. And an empathic and perceptive examiner can maintain a continuing high level of motivation on the part of the examinee. Furthermore, the examiner can observe aspects of the examinee's behavior in the testing session that are not reflected in the numerical score but that would assist in diagnosis. There are also disadvantages, however. Examiners may vary in their presentation of tasks and their evaluation of responses, thus introducing measurement error. Some examinees may be self-conscious in a face-to-face situation and block out responses that they really know. But the most critical point is that individual testing is expensive—prohibitively so if information is desired on each child in a school or on each applicant for admission to an educational institution or a training program. Primarily because of cost considerations, most ability testing has become group testing, using paper-and-pencil testing instruments that can be scored objectively.

There are a number of series of group tests on the market. Three relatively widely used series are the Test of Cognitive Skills produced by the California Test Bureau (CTB) and McGraw-Hill, the Otis-Lennon School Ability Test published by the Psychological Corporation, and the School and College Ability Tests prepared by the Educational Testing Service and CTB/McGraw-Hill. However, I will illustrate this category of test with the series with which I am most intimately acquainted—the Cognitive Ability Test, or CogAT. Like many other group-administered tests of general ability, these are multiscore tests providing one score for verbal ability, one for quantitative ability, and one for nonverbal ability. The most recent edition (R. L. Thorndike & Hagen, 1993) of these tests is composed of nine subtests. Sample items like those in each of the subtests are shown in Figures 8.1, 8.2, and 8.3.

Figure 8.1
Sample verbal test items like those used in the Cognitive Abilities Test.

Vocabulary
Impolite:
      A. unhappy   B. angry   C. faithless
         D. <u>rude</u>   E. talkative

Sentence Completion
Mark was very fond of his science teacher, but he did not
_____his mathematics teacher.
A. obey   B. discuss   C. regard   D. desire   E. <u>like</u>

Verbal Classification
Dove   Hawk   Wren   Sparrow
A. moth   B. bat   C. <u>gull</u>   D. bee   E. squirrel

Verbal Analogy
Pea is to **bean** as **peach** is to
A. pit   B. tree   C. eat   D. skin   E. <u>apple</u>

Figure 8.2
Sample quantitative test items like those in the Cognitive Abilities Test.

Quantitative Comparison
  I. **4 dimes**   Mark **A** if I is more money than II.
  II. **5 nickels**   Mark **B** if I is less money than II.
                       Mark **C** if I is the same amount of money as II.

Number Series
18   16   14   12   10
         A. 7   <u>B.</u> 8   C. 9   D. 10   E. 12

Equation Building
1   8   9   +   −
       <u>A.</u> 0   B. 3   C.8   D. 9   E. 18

Figure 8.3
Sample nonverbal items like those in the Cognitive Abilities Test.

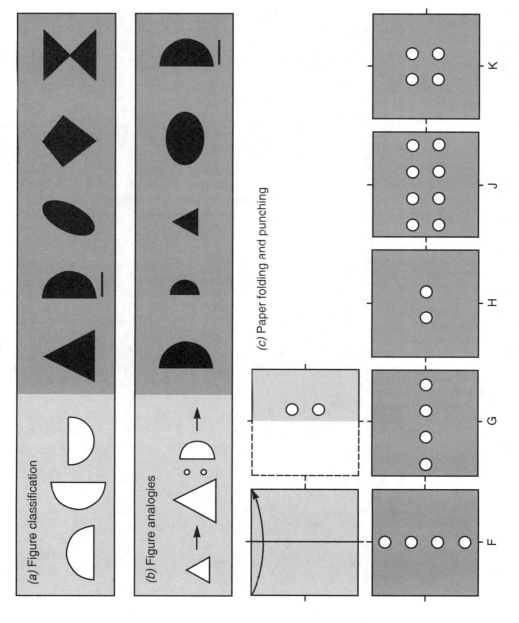

(a) Figure classification

(b) Figure analogies

(c) Paper folding and punching

The tests are organized in a multilevel format and printed in a single booklet that covers the range from Grade 3 to Grade 12. (There are also primary level tests for kindergarten through Grade 3, and the publisher, at a user's request, will provide booklets containing only a single level of the tests.) The multilevel booklet is arranged so that testing can be carried out at any one of eight levels of difficulty, depending on where an examinee is started and stopped. The pattern illustrated here is for the Sentence Completion subtest, and a similar pattern is used for each of the other subtests.

Pattern of Item Ranges for the Sentence Completion Subtest of the CogAT

Level	Start at Item	End at Item	Usual Grade Level
A	1	25	3
B	6	30	4
C	11	35	5
D	16	40	6
E	21	45	7
F	26	50	8–9
G	31	55	10–11
H	36	60	12+

Responses are marked on a separate answer sheet, and a different answer sheet is provided for each level, with spaces for only the items that are to be answered at that level. The test exercises get progressively more difficult, so the format permits a good deal of flexibility in selecting a test level that is appropriate in difficulty for a given class, or even a particular individual. Thus, for a school located in a disadvantaged community, more accurate information about pupils would be likely to result if an easier level of the test were used, so that sixth graders, for example, might be tested with Level C rather than with Level D. More accurate information is obtained from testing when the difficulty of the test tasks closely matches the ability level of the people being tested.

Nonreading group tests can be prepared, as evidenced by the types of tasks represented in Figure 8.3. For very young children, it is, of course, necessary to avoid requiring them to read. It is also desirable to monitor rather closely the progress of children to be sure that they continue to work on the tasks—and to work on the proper tasks. The use of group testing is more questionable with young children, but it is possible after they have been in school for a while and have gotten used to following directions.

Two levels of a primary test have been prepared for the CogAT, to extend downward the range of the multilevel version. These levels are intended for use from late kindergarten to Grade 3. In most instances, directions for each item are read aloud by the examiner, who proceeds at a pace that permits each child to respond by marking the test booklet. At these levels, a separate answer sheet is not used, and the tests are composed of only two verbal, two quantitative, and two nonverbal subtests. Illustrations of some of the types of items are provided in Figure 8.4.

Figure 8.4
Items like those in the Cognitive Abilities Test—Primary Levels.

Verbal

Fill the oval under the <u>refrigerator.</u>

See the slide, the jungle gym and the teeter-totter. Which one belongs with them?

Quantitative

Mark the oval under the <u>biggest</u> piece of pie.

Which one on the right equals the <u>sum</u> of the two boxes on the left?

continued

Figure 8.4
continued

Nonverbal

Which one on the right belongs with the three on the left?

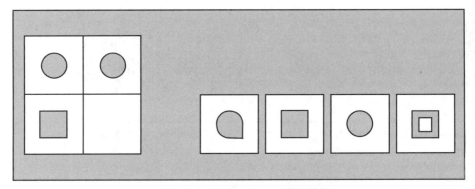

Which one on the right belongs in the empty box on the left?

The CogAT provides three separate scores—verbal, quantitative, and nonverbal. As was the case with the fourth edition of the Stanford-Binet, while these scores represent distinguishable dimensions of individual differences, they are not unrelated. In fact, the correlations among the three scores are quite high, averaging about .70. Thus, although what each measures is somewhat different from what the others measure, all three scores have a good deal in common; this commonality can be thought of as a general cognitive-ability factor.

This point can be brought out more clearly by looking at the results from a factor analysis of the nine subtests that compose the CogAT. Factor analysis is a procedure that undertakes to analyze the relationships between a number of different tests (or other types of measures) to identify a smaller number of more basic, underlying variables that can account for the observed pattern of relationships. The results are shown in Table 8.1.

A factor loading can be interpreted as the correlation of a test with an underlying dimension. In Table 8.1, to simplify the picture, values less than .10 have been omitted because such values can be considered negligible.

The pattern that emerges in this factor analysis is quite clear. For *each one* of the subtests, the predominant loading is on the general factor shared by all of them. In addition, a verbal factor of moderate size appears in all the subtests of the verbal

Table 8.1
Median Factor Loadings of the Multilevel Battery of the Cognitive Abilities Test

Subtest	General	Verbal	Quantitative	Nonverbal
Verbal classification	.71	.48		
Sentence completion	.72	.48		
Verbal analogies	.76	.42		
Quantitative relations	.82		.14	
Number series	.81		.16	
Equation building	.71		.18	
Figure classification	.72			.30
Figure analogies	.77			.34
Figure analysis	.62			.36

Note: Values less than .10 are deleted.

scale and in a somewhat smaller, figural visualization factor in the subtests of the non-verbal scale. The quantitative subtests are not very successful in defining a quantitative factor; they tend to load almost solely on the general-ability factor. In addition, each of the nine subtests involves some elements of ability that are unique to that subtest (specific factors), the nature of which is not made clear by a factor analysis.

The question that you might raise next is, how much of whatever validity is found for the CogAT is to be attributed to the common general ability factor and how much to the less extensive factors, that is, verbal and spatial. A partial answer to this question can be obtained by looking at a set of data available from one large, suburban school district. The CogAT had been given in Grades 5, 7, and 9 of this school system, and it was possible to compare the results with teachers' grades in specific courses and with grade point averages in Grade 9. Selected results based on about 4,300 cases are shown in Table 8.2.

In this table, the higher correlations are generally those for the verbal and quantitative scores, with nonverbal scores tending to be a rather poor third. Such a result might be expected because education relies heavily on the symbol systems of words and numbers. But you should note that the highest correlation is almost universally that for the simple sum of the three scores. Such a simple sum accentuates and is a reliable measure of the general factor that is shared by all three tests.

You might also ask what validity there would be for a *difference* score that brings out what is distinctive to one or another of the three scores. The answer for these data is the following: Across the group as a whole, almost none; the validity of a difference score for predicting relative academic performance in particular subjects is never as much as 0.05. So, in the pure prediction of academic performance, it is almost exclusively the common general-ability factor that forecasts performance.

The value of the three separate scores is primarily in the attention they call to a certain (usually small) number of children who display an uneven pattern of scores on the three tests. For *most* children, SASs on the three tests will be similar, differing by not more than about 10 points, as is indicated by the relatively high correlations among the scores. Differences of this magnitude generally have little predictive or

Table 8.2

Correlations of the Cognitive Abilities Test (CogAT) Scores in Grades 5, 7, and 9
with Class Marks in Grade 9

CogAT Score	Grade 9 Course Grades				
	English	Social Studies	Mathematics	Science	Overall
Grade 5—V	.46	.49	.34	.46	.51
Q	.45	.49	.39	.50	.54
NV	.38	.39	.34	.42	.45
Total	.48	.52	.40	.52	.56
Grade 7—V	.49	.53	.36	.49	.55
Q	.51	.54	.45	.56	.61
NV	.41	.43	.38	.46	.49
Total	.53	.56	.45	.57	.62
Grade 9—V	.52	.56	.39	.52	.58
Q	.52	.57	.48	.59	.63
NV	.42	.45	.41	.48	.52
Total	.55	.59	.48	.60	.65

Note: V = verbal; Q = quantitative; NV = nonverbal.

descriptive value. However, a few individuals will be found who show differences of 20 or even 30 points. Thus, a child may be encountered who has a verbal SAS of 80 but a nonverbal score of 105. One might be moved to ask what produced this dramatic difference. Was English not the language of the home? Some groups of Hispanic students have been found to exhibit this pattern. By contrast, some groups of Asian children have shown much higher performance on the quantitative scale than on the verbal or nonverbal scales. Was the child dyslexic? Or had there been some failure in early teaching of reading skills? And what can be done to help the child's school progress? Would remediating the verbal deficit or exploiting the nonverbal capabilities accomplish the desired goal? One can raise similar questions about other patterns of high and low scores. The key is to use marked discrepancies in scores as a warning light that there may be a nonstandard situation and that developing the best educational program for the child may require further exploration, often in the form of an individually administered test.

One way to judge whether the difference between two scores is large enough to attract attention is to consider the standard errors of measurement of the two scales. The standard error of measurement, you will remember, is an index of the random variation expected in a person's score when that person is retested several times with equivalent tests. Unless the difference between two scores is substantially larger than the standard error of measurement, it should probably be ignored as resulting from random fluctuations in test performance. A reasonable standard to apply is that the difference should be at least three times as large as the larger of the two standard errors. Thus, if the standard errors of measurement for verbal and nonverbal scores are 4.3 and 5.7, respectively, we should probably not interpret a score difference of less than about 18 points as important. The score difference of 20 to 30 points mentioned earlier, exceeds this criterion and may therefore indicate an important inconsistency. However, we should not treat large score differences in a mechanical manner. The presence of an unusually large difference between two scores should be viewed as a signal that there may be something going on that merits closer scrutiny through an individually administered test, a supplementary set of assessment devices, or careful observation.

TESTS OF MULTIPLE ABILITIES

Over the past 50 years, a number of test batteries have been developed that are designed to provide differential predictions of success in specific jobs or training programs. These grew out of job analyses suggesting that different jobs called for quite different abilities. Thus, each of the armed forces developed a classification battery to be used in helping to assign each recruit to a military occupational speciality in which he or she could perform effectively. Because of the large samples that accumulate in military training programs, studies based on these batteries provide some of the most substantial bodies of data that have ever been available on tests as predictors of training success and, to a lesser extent, of job success. We will refer to some of these data in the sections that follow. However, of more practical interest to people in civilian settings are batteries that have been developed for civilian use. We will describe and illustrate two of these: the Differential Aptitude Tests (DAT), designed primarily for use in high school guidance programs and the U.S. Employment Service General Aptitude Test Battery (GATB), designed for vocational counseling services and job placement.

Differential Aptitude Test Battery

The DAT battery was originally published by the Psychological Corporation in 1947 as a guidance battery for use at the secondary school level, and revised and streamlined forms were produced in 1963, 1972, 1982, and 1990. In the design of the battery, some attention was paid to having separate tests with low intercorrelations, but the main focus was on getting measures that would be meaningful to high school counselors. As a result, with the exception of the test of clerical speed and accuracy, intercorrelations are about .50. However, because the reliabilities of the parts are about .90, it is clear that more than one ability is being measured. The eight subtests are briefly described and illustrated here. A ninth score, Scholastic Aptitude, may be obtained from the sum of Verbal Reasoning and Numerical Reasoning.[1]

[1]Differential Aptitude Tests—4th Edition. Copyright © 1982, 1972 by The Psychological Corporation. Reproduced and adapted by permission. All rights reserved.

1. *Verbal Reasoning.* (25 minutes) Items are of the double-analogy type, that is, _____ is to A as B is to _____ .
Five pairs of words are provided to complete the analogy.
_____ is to night as breakfast is to _____ .
A. supper—corner
B. gentle—morning
C. door—corner
D. flow—enjoy
E. supper—morning

2. *Numerical Reasoning.* (30 minutes) This subtest consists of numerical problems emphasizing comprehension rather than simple computational facility.
3 = _____ % of 15
A. 5
B. 10
C. 20
D. 30
E. none of these

3. *Abstract Reasoning.* (20 minutes) A series of problem figures establishes a relationship or sequence, and the examinee must pick the choice that continues the series.

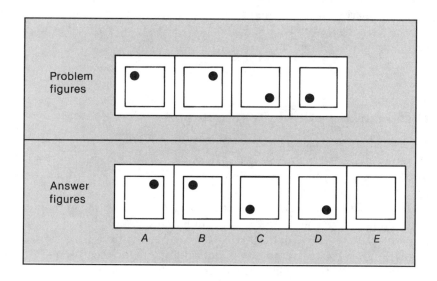

4. *Spatial Relations.* (25 minutes) A diagram of a flat figure is shown. The examinee must visualize and indicate which solid figure could be produced by folding the flat figure, as shown in the example here [on next page].

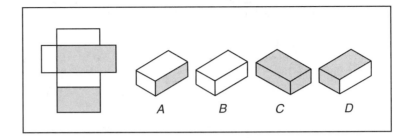

5. *Mechanical Reasoning.* (25 minutes) A diagram of a mechanical device or situation is shown, and the examinee must indicate which choice is correct for the situation.

6. *Perceptual Speed and Accuracy.* (6 minutes) Each item is made up of a number of combinations of symbols, one of which is underlined. The examinee must mark the same combination on his or her answer sheet.

7. *Spelling.* (10 minutes) A list of words is given, some of which are misspelled. The examinee must indicate whether each word is spelled correctly or incorrectly.

	Right	**Wrong**
gurl	‖	‖

8. *Language Usage.* (15 minutes) A sentence is given, divided by marks into four subsections. The examinee must indicate either which section—A, B, C, or D—contains an error or, if there is no error, mark E.

	A	B	C	D	E
1. Ain't we / going to / the office / next week?	‖	‖	‖	‖	‖
A B C D					

The tests of the DAT are essentially power tests, with the exception of the Perceptual Speed and Accuracy test, and time limits in most cases are 20 to 30 minutes. Total testing time for the battery is about 3 hours (2.5 hours working time plus 30 minutes for administrative matters and directions). Percentile ranks, stanines, and scaled scores are available for each grade from Grade 7 through Grade 12. Norms are provided for each of the subtests and also for the sum of verbal reasoning and numerical ability, which is offered as a general appraisal of scholastic aptitude.

General Aptitude Test Battery

The GATB was produced by the Bureau of Employment Security of the U.S. Department of Labor in the early 1940s. It was based on previous work in which experimental test batteries had been prepared for each of a number of different jobs. Analysis of more than 50 different tests prepared for specific jobs indicated that there was a great deal of overlap in some of them and that only about 10 different ability factors were measured by the complete set of tests. The GATB was developed to provide measures of these different factors. In its most recent form, the GATB includes 12 tests and gives scores for nine different factors. One is a factor of general mental ability resulting from scores on three tests (Vocabulary, Arithmetic Reasoning, and Three-Dimensional Space) that are also scored for more specialized factors. The other factors and the tests that contribute to each are described here. Each factor is scaled to yield scores with a mean of 100 and a standard deviation of 20.

1. *Verbal Aptitude.* The score is based on one test, Number 4—Vocabulary. This test requires the examinee to identify the pair of words in a set of four that are either synonyms or antonyms. For example,

a. cautious	b. friendly	c. hostile	d. remote
a. hasten	b. deprive	c. expedite	d. disprove

2. *Numerical Ability.* The appraisal of this aptitude is based on two tests. The first of these, Number 2—Computation, involves speed and accuracy in simple, whole-number computation. For example,

Subtract (−)   256   Multiply (×)   37
                  83   8

The second test comprising the numerical ability score, Number 6—Arithmetic Reasoning, involves verbally stated quantitative problems, such as

John works for $5.20 an hour. How much is his pay for a 35-hour week?

3. *Spatial Aptitude.* One test, Number 3—Three-Dimensional Space, enters into appraisal of this aptitude. The examinee must indicate which of four three-dimensional figures can be produced by folding a flat sheet of a specified shape, with creases at indicated points.

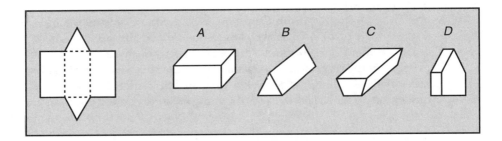

4. *Form Perception.* This aptitude involves rapid and accurate perception of visual forms and patterns. It is appraised in the GATB by two tests, (1) Number 5—Tool Matching and (2) Number 7—Form Matching, which differ in the type of visual stimulus provided. Each requires the examinee to find from among a set of answer choices the one that is identical with the stimulus form.

TOOL MATCHING

FORM MATCHING

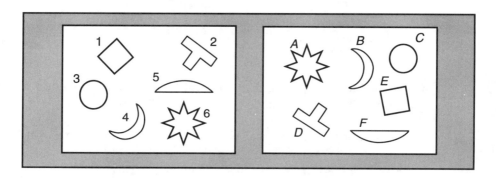

5. *Clerical Perception.* This aptitude also involves rapid and accurate perception, but in this case, the stimulus material is linguistic instead of purely spatial. The test, Number 1—Name Comparison, presents pairs of names and requires the examinee to indicate whether the two members of the pair are identical or whether they differ in some detail.

John Goldstein & Co.—John Goldston & Co.

Pewee Mfg. Co.—Pewee Mfg. Co.

6. *Motor Coordination.* This factor has to do with speed of simple, but fairly precise motor response. It is evaluated by one test, Number 8—Mark Making. The task of the examinee is to make three pencil marks, arranged as shown here, as quickly as possible within each of a series of boxes on the answer sheet.

etc.

The score is the number of boxes correctly filled in a 60-second test period.

7. *Manual Dexterity.* This factor involves speed and accuracy of fairly gross hand movements. It is evaluated by two pegboard tests: (1) Number 9—Place and (2) Number 10—Turn. In the first of these tests, examinees use both hands to move a series of pegs from one set of holes in a pegboard to another. In the second test, examinees use their preferred hand to pick a peg up from the board, rotate it 180°, and reinsert the other end of the peg in the hole. Each task has a short enough time limit

that few examinees are able to move or turn all of the pegs. Three trials are given for each of these tests, and score is the total number of pegs moved or turned.

8. *Finger Dexterity.* This factor represents a finer type of dexterity than that covered by the previous factor, calling for more precise finger manipulation. Two tests, Number 11—Assemble and Number 12—Disassemble, use the same pieces of equipment, a board with 50 holes in each of two sections. Each hole in one section is occupied by a small rivet. A stack of washers is piled on a spindle. During *assemble,* the examinee picks up a rivet with one hand and a washer with the other, puts the washer on the rivet, and places the assembly in the corresponding hole in the unoccupied part of the board. The task is to assemble as many rivets and washers as possible in 90 seconds. During *disassemble,* the examinee removes the assembly and returns the washer to its stack and the rivet to its original place. The score is the number of items assembled or disassembled, as the case may be.

The apparatus tests (non–paper-and-pencil tests)—Motor Coordination, Manual Dexterity, and Finger Dexterity—are all arranged so that at the completion of testing, the equipment has been returned to its original condition and is ready for the testing of another person.

A comparison of the GATB and the DAT reveals that the DAT includes tests of mechanical comprehension and language that the GATB lacks, while the GATB includes form perception and several types of motor tests that are missing in the DAT. Thus, the GATB is more work oriented and less school oriented in its total coverage. Inclusion of the motor tests results in somewhat lower correlations, on the average, among the GATB scales, although the "intellectual" tests correlate about as highly as those of the DAT. The correlations between the different aptitude scores of the GATB for a group of 100 high school seniors are shown in Table 8.3. Excluding the correlations of the verbal, numerical, and spatial scores with the score for the general intelligence scale *(G)* (which is composed of verbal, numerical, and spatial scores), the correlations range from −.06 to .66. The three motor tests show fairly marked correlations, but they are only moderately related to the perception tests and

Table 8.3
Intercorrelations of Aptitude Scores (from the General Aptitude Test Battery) for 100 High School Seniors

	G	V	N	S	P	Q	K	F	M
G—Intelligence	—	.73	.74	.70	.43	.35	−.04	−.05	−.06
V—Verbal		—	.42	.40	.34	.29	.13	−.03	.06
N—Numerical			—	.34	.42	.42	.06	−.03	.01
S—Spatial				—	.48	.26	−.03	.01	−.03
P—Form perception					—	.66	.29	.27	.23
Q—Clerical perception						—	.29	.20	.17
K—Motor coordination							—	.37	.49
F—Finger dexterity								—	.46
M—Manual dexterity									—

are practically unrelated to the tests that make up the general intelligence scale. The perceptual and intellectual scores also relate closely to each other, and there is a strong relationship between the two types of perceptual ability.

There are quite substantial correlations between the corresponding factors of the DAT and the GATB. Representative values from one study (U.S. Employment Service, 1967) are as follows:

Scale	Correlation
Verbal	.74
Numerical	.61
Spatial	.65
Clerical	.57

However, the correlations are low enough so that it is clear that the tests cannot be considered identical. One important difference in the two tests is the fact that the DAT tests are in most cases purely power tests, while the GATB tests are quite highly speeded.

THE ROLE OF GENERAL COGNITIVE ABILITY

The Bell Curve

Every few years a book or monograph is published that attracts wide public attention to various aspects of the data regarding human mental abilities. Such a book, *The Bell Curve,* was published in the fall of 1994 (Herrnstein & Murray, 1994). The basic premise advocated by the authors is that human cognitive ability is extremely important in all aspects of life in a complex society and that differences in this ability are related to a wide variety of both cognitive and social outcomes. The authors point to the use of cognitive ability tests such as the Scholastic Aptitude Tests (SAT) and the Graduate Record Examinations (GRE) by highly selective educational institutions as creating an intellectual elite whose members occupy a disproportionate number of positions of political and economic power. The fact that the children of highly educated parents tend themselves to become highly educated and that the children of economically and socially disadvantaged parents tend to suffer their parents' fate leads the authors to argue that American society in particular, and perhaps other diverse societies in general, may be developing such an extreme social stratification that a permanent underclass will result. While the authors make their basic argument without reference to racial or ethnic groups (their data indicate that their conclusions are independent of race), the fact that racial groups differ in the proportion of their members who are found in the different social strata makes their argument seem racist because it implies that there are racial differences in ability.

The Bell Curve has been attacked from just about every possible direction, sometimes with justification, other times on largely frivolous grounds. Some authors have suggested that the book addresses questions about race and intelligence that should not even be asked, while others have questioned details of the statistical methodology. Although the social-policy implications and recommendations that Herrnstein and Murray have offered may be highly questionable, we may reasonably ask what the data have to say about the value of general cognitive ability and more specific abilities as predictors of academic and job performance. How useful are batteries such as the DAT and the GATB, and how much do they enable us to improve the prediction of educational and occupational success over what is possible from a general measure of cognitive ability?

There have been hundreds, probably thousands, of studies in which test scores have been related to some criterion measure of success on a job. For many years results were found to vary from study to study and from job to job. As a consequence, personnel psychologists tended to emphasize the specificity of jobs in the abilities that they required and the need to carry out local job analyses and specific validation studies, not only for each category of job but even for each local setting in which the job appeared. This call for specific validation studies, given the force of law in the guidelines of the federal Equal Employment Opportunity Commission, becomes a counsel of despair for using tests in vocational selection, placement, and counseling decisions, because relatively few employment situations provide a flow of new employees sufficient in number to generate stable validity data. But more recently, this doctrine of validity specificity has been seriously questioned.

It has been pointed out by Schmidt and Hunter (1981) that much of the variation in results from one study to another can be attributed to a combination of (1) small sample size, (2) differences in degree of curtailment or preselection in the group studied, and (3) differences in the nature and reliability of the criterion measures. Schmidt, Hunter, and their associates (Schmidt & Hunter, 1992; Schmidt, Hunter, Pearlman, & Hirsh, 1985) have carried out a number of *meta-analyses* of existing data. Meta-analyses are reanalyses that pool data from the large number of existing studies to correct for the deficiencies just mentioned and to extract the findings that transcend the individual studies. The following general conclusions emerge from their work.

1. General cognitive ability has significant validity for practically all jobs. The level of validity is related to the complexity of the job, being higher for more complex jobs and lower for simpler jobs.

2. The true validity of general cognitive ability for job performance is quite high, after allowance for the depressing effects of preselection in those studies and for the unreliability of criterion measures.

3. General psychomotor ability also has some validity, its validity tending to be greater for the simpler jobs (such as machine tending or packing and wrapping) in which the demand for cognitive ability is lowest.

4. Measurement of mechanical or technical understanding adds to validity for a range of occupations in which one works with machines or repairs mechanical, electrical, or electronic devices.

5. Beyond the conclusions just listed, there is little evidence for the validity of other and more specific abilities.

These basic findings have been borne out in studies of other contexts by other investigators. Perhaps the best evidence, because of the relatively high quality of the criterion measures and the large sample sizes, has been summarized by Ree and Earles (1992). Using the Armed Services Vocational Aptitude Battery (ASVAB) and samples

Figure 8.5

Mean general intelligence scores (G scores) on the General Aptitude Test Battery for selected occupations. Bar around mean shows ±1 standard deviation range.

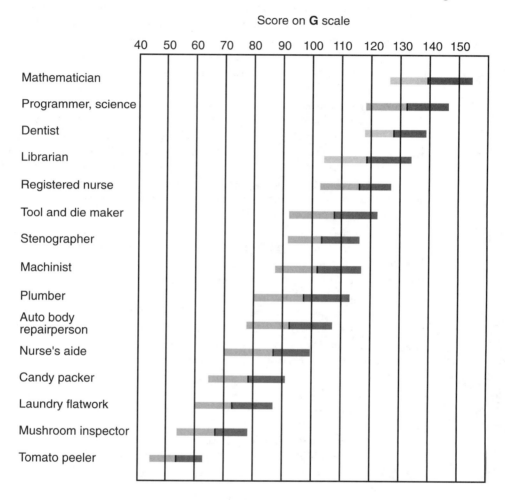

with thousands of subjects in both training and job situations, the authors found a single general cognitive ability composite to be the most effective predictor of performance. In fact, for many of the military jobs these studies investigated, the general cognitive ability factor was the only useful predictor.

The term that Schmidt and Hunter (1981) apply to their approach is *validity generalization*. Although they have been criticized for overstating both the uniformity of validity patterns across a range of jobs and the size of "true" test validity, their work provides a healthy corrective influence to the job specificity doctrine that was prevalent in the period from 1950 to 1980. And one thing that becomes abundantly clear from their work and that of Ree and Earles (1992) is that if data on the distinctive validity patterns for specific educational programs or specific jobs are to be demonstrated at an acceptable level of confidence, groups used in validation studies must be *much* larger than those that have appeared in validation studies in the past.

Schmidt and Hunter have looked at the correlational evidence for ability tests as predictors of educational and vocational success. There is another way to look at the relationship between test scores and occupations; we can ask how and to what extent people in different occupations differ in their test scores. We can designate this a *taxonomic,* as contrasted with a *predictive,* view of test validity. That is, if we give a test to individuals employed in different occupations, will we find that their patterns of abilities differ? Let us look first at the level of general cognitive ability. Though a number of data sets provide such information, U.S. Employment Service data on the GATB have certain advantages in terms of the number and variety of occupations covered, so we will focus on those data. Among the over 400 different occupations that have been studied with the GATB, there were clearly substantial differences in average score on the *G* scale. These ranged from a high of 143 for mathematicians to a low of 55 for tomato peelers. But, before we look at the differences, let us ask how consistent they were from one sample to another in the same job. Among the jobs studied by the U.S. Employment Service, for 48 jobs there were two or more independent samples of 50 or more cases. And across these jobs, the correlation between Sample A and Sample B was .93. Clearly, average *G* score was a very reliable, very stable characteristic of people in a given occupation.

At the same time that we find these quite stable differences *between* occupations, we also find quite a wide range of scores *within* a given occupation. Figure 8.5 shows the average *G* score for a selection of occupations and also the ±1 standard deviation range, the range that includes about two-thirds of all the persons in that occupation. Although the differences in average score are quite dependable, the overlapping is considerable for all but the extreme groups. It is also true that among the occupations studied by the U.S. Employment Service, most fall within a fairly narrow range in average *G* scores. This fact is shown in Table 8.4, where 246 out of the 442 jobs have average *G* scores falling between 90 and 109, or within half a standard

Table 8.4

Frequency Distribution of Average General Intelligence *(G)* Scores in Different Occupations

Score Level	Frequency
140+	1
130–139	6
120–129	23
110–119	57
100–109	107
90–99	139
80–89	89
70–79	18
60–69	1
Below 60	1

Figure 8.6

Profiles of mean scores for pairs of job samples from the General Aptitude Test Battery (GATB). Dashed lines are for Sample 1; solid lines are for Sample 2.

deviation of the overall population mean of 100. A minority of occupations are highly restrictive in the level of *G* score required to enter the particular occupation and then to survive in it. Thus, only 30 of the occupations were characterized by average *G* scores of 120 or over. A person of near average ability can fit into a wide range of occupational niches.

We may ask to what extent occupations display distinct and stable *patterns* of abilities. To what extent do we find occupations in which the members are especially high (or low) in verbal ability? In quantitative ability? In motor coordination or finger dexterity? The GATB data also help to answer these questions. We have taken the 48 jobs with at least duplicate samples and for each job have computed the correlations between the paired samples across the eight primary scores of the GATB (excluding *G*). The 48 correlations ranged from −.02 to +.97; their distribution is shown in Table 8.5, where the median value is .72. Figure 8.6 shows the pattern of

Table 8.5
Profile Correlations for Pairs of Job Samples

Correlation	Frequency
.90–.99	11
.80–.89	9
.70–.79	7
.60–.69	6
.50–.59	6
.40–.49	1
.30–.39	3
.20–.29	1
.10–.19	1
.00–.09	2
Negative	1

scores for duplicate samples for three jobs, one highly consistent, one of average consistency, and one completely lacking in consistency. The conclusion that may be drawn is that questions about consistency of patterning can only be answered on a job-by-job basis. Some jobs do show consistency, but others do not.

SUMMARY

Individual tests of aptitude were first developed near the turn of the century in response to educational problems. The Stanford-Binet soon became the leading test in the United States. The demands of World War I led to the development of group aptitude tests. The Wechsler series of tests was produced first to measure adults and, later, people of all ages. Currently, the fourth edition of the Stanford-Binet, the WPPSI-R, the WISC-III, and the WAIS-R are the most widely used individually administered aptitude tests. Many group tests have descended in one way or another from those of World War I, of which the CogAT is a good example.

Test batteries were introduced in the early 1940s to give better differential prediction of occupational and training potential. Two of the major current batteries are the DAT, which is designed for school counseling, and the GATB, which is used primarily in employment situations. The two batteries are similar, but the GATB places more emphasis on speed and on perceptual and clerical abilities. Recent evidence suggests that it is primarily the general ability measured by each of these batteries that is responsible for their ability to predict scholastic and occupational success.

QUESTIONS AND EXERCISES

1. It has been proposed that all intelligence tests be called scholastic aptitude tests. What are the merits and limitations of this proposal?

2. In what respects is it preferable to rely on a good aptitude test for an estimate of a student's intelligence rather than on ratings by teachers? Are there situations where teacher ratings would be preferable?

3. In each of the following situations, would you elect to use a group intelligence test or an individual intelligence test? Why?

   a. You are studying a boy with a serious speech impediment.

   b. You are selecting students for admission to a nursing program.

   c. You are preparing to counsel a high school senior on educational and vocational plans.

   d. You are studying the academic progress of Hispanic children in a school system in Texas.

   e. You are working with a group of boys, in a state institution, who have been convicted of criminal offenses.

   f. You are trying to identify the sources of difficulty for a child who is a nonreader.

4. Are the usual group intelligence tests more useful for those students who are considering professional occupations or for those considering occupations in the skilled trades? Why?

5. A newspaper article reported that a young woman who had been placed in a mental hospital with an IQ score of 62 had raised her IQ score to 118 during the 3 years she spent there. What is misleading about this statement? What factors could account for the difference between the two IQ scores?

6. In what respects are intelligence tests better than high school grades as predictors of college success? In what respects are they not as good?

7. Why do intelligence tests show higher correlations with standardized achievement tests than they do with school grades?

8. You are a fourth-grade teacher, and you have just received the results for your class from a citywide administration of the Cognitive Abilities Test in all fourth-grade classes. What use might you make of the results? What additional information would you need?

9. An eighth-grade student received the following standard age scores on the Cognitive Abilities Test—Verbal: Grade 4—98, Grade 6—116, Grade 8—104. What would be the best figure to represent the child's *true* scholastic ability level?

10. During the first 2 weeks of school, a school in a well-to-do community gave the Kaufman Assessment Battery for Children to all entering kindergarteners and all first graders who had not been tested in kindergarten. How desirable and useful is this procedure? Why?

11. A school system wanted to set up procedures for identifying students to receive remedial instruction in reading. Students whose reading achievement was seriously behind their potential for learning to read were the target group. What would be a sound procedure for accomplishing this goal?

12. There have been a number of aptitude test batteries developed for use at the secondary school level and with adults but few for use at the elementary school level. Why? Is this a reasonable state of affairs?

13. What are the advantages of using a battery such as the Differential Aptitude Tests instead of tests selected from a number of different sources? What are the limitations?

14. A vocational high school offers programs to train bookkeepers, cosmetologists, dental assistants, and stenographers. Studies with the General Aptitude Test Battery have yielded data on the means (*M*s), standard deviations (*SD*s), and correlations (*r*s), with supervisory

ratings shown here for these four occupations. As a counselor in the school, how would you use this information in helping students to choose among the four programs?

Occupation	Verbal			Numerical			Spatial			Manual Dexterity		
	M	*SD*	*r*	*M*	*SD*	*r*	*M*	*SD*	*r*	*M*	*SD*	*r*
Bookkeeper	106	16	.51	112	15	.37	103	20	.38	105	21	.36
Cosmetologist	96	15	.24	92	13	.31	100	16	.25	98	17	.07
Dental assistant	106	13	.26	102	14	.34	107	16	.30	115	19	.36
Stenographer	105	12	.21	105	14	.24	106	16	.06	103	21	.09

15. How sound is the statement, The best measure of aptitude in any field is a measure of achievement in that field to date? What are the statement's limitations?

16. What are the differences between a reading readiness test and an intelligence test? What are the advantages of using the readiness test rather than the intelligence test for first-grade students?

17. In what ways could a follow-up study of graduates of a high school help in improving the school guidance program?

SUGGESTED READINGS

Anastasi, A. (1988). *Psychological testing* (6th ed.). New York: Macmillan.

Bolton, B. (Ed.). (1987). *Handbook of measurement and evaluation in rehabilitation.* Baltimore: Paul Brookes.

Bond, L. (1989). The effects of special preparation on measures of scholastic ability. In R. L. Linn (Ed.), *Educational measurement* (3rd ed., pp. 429–444). New York: Macmillan.

Carroll, J. B. (1993). *Human cognitive abilities: A survey of factor-analytic studies.* Cambridge, MA: Cambridge University Press.

Das, J. P., Naglieri, J. A., & Kirby, J. R. (1994). *Assessment of cognitive processes: The PASS theory of intelligence.* Boston: Allyn and Bacon.

Eysenck, H. J. (1986). Inspection time and intelligence: A historical perspective. *Personality and Individual Differences, 7,* 603–607.

Eysenck, H. J. (1988). The concept of "intelligence": Useful or useless? *Intelligence, 12,* 1–16.

Garber, H. L. (1988). *The Milwaukee Project: Preventing mental retardation in children at risk.* Washington, DC: American Association on Mental Retardation.

Gregory, R. J. (1987). *Adult intellectual assessment.* Boston: Allyn and Bacon.

Guilford, J. P. (1985). The structure-of-intellect model. In B. B. Wolman (Ed.), *Handbook of intelligence* (pp. 225–266). New York: Wiley.

Herrnstein, R. J., and Murray, C. (1994). *The bell curve: Intelligence and class structure in American life.* New York: The Free Press.

Horn, J. L. (1985). Remodeling old models of intelligence. In B. B. Wolman (Ed.), *Handbook of intelligence* (pp. 267–300). New York: Wiley.

Jensen, A. R. (1991). General mental ability: From psychometrics to biology. *Diagnostique, 16,* 134–144.

Jensen, A. R. (1993). Spearman's hypothesis tested with chronometric information-processing tasks. *Intelligence, 17,* 47–77.

Kaufman, A. S., & Kaufman, N. L. (1983). *Kaufman Assessment Battery for Children. Interpretive manual.* Circle Pines, MN: American Guidance Service.

Newmark, C. S. (Ed.). (1996). *Major psychological assessment instruments (2nd ed.).* Boston: Allyn and Bacon.

Ree, M. J., & Earles, J. A. (1992). Intelligence is the best predictor of job performance. *Current directions in psychological science, 1,* 86–89.

Sattler, J. M. (1988). *Assessment of children's intelligence and special abilities* (3rd ed.). San Diego: Author.

Schmidt, F. L., & Hunter, J. E. (1992). Development of a causal model of processes determining job performance. *Current directions in psychological science, 1,* 89–92.

Snow, R. E., & Lohman, D. F. (1989). Implications of cognitive psychology for educational measurement. In R. L. Linn (Ed.), *Educational measurement* (3rd ed., pp. 263–331). New York: Macmillan.

Sternberg, R. J. (1985). *Beyond IQ: A triarchic theory of intelligence.* Cambridge, MA: Cambridge University Press.

Thorndike, R. L., & Hagen, E. P. (1993). *Cognitive Abilities Test.* Chicago: Riverside Publishing Company.

Thorndike, R. L., Hagen, E. P., & Sattler, J. M. (1986). *The Stanford-Binet Intelligence Scale: Fourth edition. Technical manual.* Chicago: Riverside Publishing Company.

Woodcock, R. W. (1978). *Development and standardization of the Woodcock-Johnson Psycho-Educational Battery.* Hingham, MA: Teaching Resources Corporation.

Standardized Achievement Tests

INTRODUCTION

The Chapter 8 discussion of aptitude tests and achievement tests made a distinction between the two based largely on the inferences that were to be drawn from the scores and the degree to which content validity was a central issue in test design. We described a number of tests of aptitude or general cognitive ability where the cognitive process being assessed was the prime concern. This chapter examines the other side of the coin: tests designed to measure how much individuals have learned, or what their store of information is. Here we focus on centrally produced tests, standardized achievement tests, published commercially or by a state or national testing agency for use in a large number of schools and across school districts. The processes are similar to those an individual teacher might follow in preparing a classroom achievement test; however, there are some important differences between locally prepared achievement tests and those intended for wider distribution.

DISTINCTIVE FEATURES OF STANDARDIZED ACHIEVEMENT TESTS

In anticipation that their tests will achieve widespread acceptance and use over a period of several years, commercial test publishers have shown a willingness to invest substantial amounts of time and money in developing achievement tests and test batteries that will appeal to a broad spectrum of users. State testing agencies must also develop their instruments to cover material common to all school districts that will use the test. The development of such broad-spectrum tests requires that a number of processes be carried out. These include reviewing current curricula for the region where the test is to be used, preparing detailed blueprints of content and skill, writing test exercises, reviewing items to eliminate ambiguous or potentially biased items, completing item analyses to provide objective verification of item quality, and assembling the surviving items into the resulting test. We discussed issues and procedures related to test blueprints and test bias in Chapter 5 under the heading of Content Validity. The general processes of item writing, analysis, and selection are covered in Chapter 15. Here we consider the features unique to achievement tests intended for widespread use, as well as the properties of some example instruments.

Breadth of Objectives.   Because centrally produced tests are designed to be as widely marketable as possible—across districts, states, and the nation as a whole—standardized achievement tests can include only material that every student at the level for which the test is intended would reasonably have had the opportunity to learn. Test authors must examine the objectives for all potential school districts and select only those objectives common to all. As a result, standardized achievement tests do not emphasize the recall of facts, as is commonly believed, because this sort of content is not likely to be similar across curricula. Rather, they tend to include tasks that require information-acquiring skills such as reading comprehension and graph interpretation.

Inclusion of Norms.   The most distinctive feature of centrally produced tests—in contrast to locally produced tests—is the availability of norms. The term *standardized test* implies the availability of normative data (although the term really refers to the use of uniform administration procedures), and publishers of these tests provide a range of normative information to help give meaning to test scores. The types of normative information typically provided with these instruments was described in detail in Chapter 3.

Normative data provide meaning through comparisons with other students at the same grade level. They permit statements about how Tracey is doing in mathematics or social studies in relation to other students of the same age or grade or from the same type of school system. Because all of the tests in a battery are usually normed on the same student sample, the norms also permit statements about how Tracey is doing in mathematics relative to her performance in reading, or how Jason's reading achievement compares with his performance on tests of scholastic aptitude. They may also be used to tell how a particular school compares with schools all over the country, with schools of a particular type, or with schools in a particular type of community, but, as we pointed out in Chapter 3, comparisons of this kind must be made with caution.

The quality of the norm sample is largely a function of how much the publisher is willing to spend; because norm samples may include hundreds of thousands of subjects, they can be expensive. When reading the manual for a standardized achievement test, a reviewer may be easily impressed by the effort and expense that has gone into ensuring a large representative sample. It is, of course, impossible to obtain a truly random sample because test publishers must conduct pilot and standardization testing in those school districts where they can obtain permission to do so. These pilot school districts often turn out to be the districts that already use a particular publisher's tests. However, all of the major test publishers make great efforts to assure that the norm samples for their standardized achievement tests are representative of the population of likely test users in terms of important demographic variables, such as community type and geographic region. It is commercial suicide not to do so.

USES OF STANDARDIZED ACHIEVEMENT TESTS

In considering both the characteristics of standardized achievement tests just mentioned and the information from Chapter 7 on the types of decisions for which achievement test results may be helpful, we come to the following conclusions about the types of decisions for which standardized achievement tests are likely to provide the most useful information:

1. Day-to-day instructional decisions should depend primarily on locally constructed rather than standardized tests.

2. Grading decisions should be based primarily on locally constructed tests covering what has been taught in a given unit or course.

3. Diagnostic and remedial decisions can be based on information both from commercially produced diagnostic tests and from locally produced tests.

4. Placement decisions require a broad appraisal of achievement, and standardized tests with a uniform score scale can be useful in identifying an individual's entry-level performance.

5. Guidance and counseling decisions are usually based on the type of normative comparisons made possible with standardized tests.

6. Selection decisions generally imply comparison with others, and for these comparisons, adequate normative information is often important which implies the use of standardized tests.

7. Curricular decisions between alternative programs imply a broadly based comparison in which standardized measures can play a role, often supplemented by measures developed locally for distinctive special objectives.

8. Like curricular decisions, public policy decisions require a comprehensive view of how well a school is doing. For this the broad survey and comparison that standardized tests permit has significant value.

TYPES OF STANDARDIZED ACHIEVEMENT TESTS

The early objective achievement tests generally measured performance in individual subjects. A school district that wanted to measure the achievement of students in several subjects such as reading, mathematics, and social studies had to administer a different test for each use. The use of so many different tests was expensive and time consuming, and it required that teachers be familiar with the norming and administrative procedures for a number of different instruments. Over the last several decades these separate, uncoordinated tests have gradually been replaced by test batteries which can be administered together using a single test booklet.

These coordinated batteries have several important advantages. Planning is comprehensive, and the test components are designed to provide an integrated coverage of the major academic skills and curricular areas. Each part is planned with an awareness of the other parts so that duplication can be minimized and joint coverage of important material, guaranteed.

More important than these advantages is the fact that all of the subtests of such batteries have been normed on the same sample of students. Comparisons within and between individuals and comparisons within and between groups are more straightforward when norms for all parts of a battery are based on the same group of students; the batteries become much more "iffy" when the reference group changes from test to test. Of course, there are possible drawbacks to using achievement test batteries. Comparing different batteries, we may prefer a mathematics test from one, a language test from another, and a reading test from still another on the basis of the correspondence of each to our local curriculum and objectives. But, for the types of comparisons for which standardized tests are most appropriately used, the gains from unified norms (and test design) seem to outweigh any losses from having to accept a package in which one or two elements are judged to be less than ideal.

GROUP STANDARDIZED ACHIEVEMENT TESTS

There are seven *major,* large-scale achievement test batteries: the California Achievement Test (CAT), published by McGraw-Hill; the Comprehensive Test of Basic Skills (CTBS), also published by McGraw-Hill; the Iowa Tests of Basic Skills (ITBS), published by the Riverside Publishing Company; the Metropolitan Achievement Tests (MAT), published by the Psychological Corporation; the National Achievement Test (NAT), published by American College Testing; the Science Research Associates (SRA) Achievement Series/Survey of Basic Skills published by CTB Macmillan/

McGraw-Hill; and the Stanford Achievement Test (SAT), published by the Psychological Corporation. All of these instruments cover more or less the same skills, but each breaks the pie up into a different number and arrangement of slices, and some begin coverage of a given topic at earlier ages than others. The general content areas covered include reading, language skills, mathematics, science, social studies, study/research skills, and a composite achievement score. The grade ranges for each of the batteries are given in Table 9.1.

With the exception of the National Achievement Test, all of these batteries have been around for many years and have undergone several revisions. In most cases, at least two editions of the tests are available at any one time. The tests are similar in terms of the time and effort that have gone into their development and the time it takes to administer them. Their overall quality is high, and they cover the same range of students and have similar content areas, although the number of separate scores that can be obtained from the different tests varies from as few as 5 to over 20. The test development and norming procedures, generally, are exemplary. The tests differ in terms of specific items, subscales, and techniques of test development, as well as the factor of greatest importance, the specific objectives assessed by each. Anyone involved in making decisions concerning which test to use needs to compare tests carefully to determine which objectives and score reports are most appropriate for the local situation.

To illustrate how the form and content of a test changes from the elementary to advanced levels, Figure 9.1 contains sample items similar to those used in the reading subtest of the ITBS/ITED. As the examinees get older and become more capable of working independently, the presentation shifts from a teacher-paced, oral format to a student-paced, entirely written format. Pictures are used frequently at the lower

Table 9.1
Grade Ranges Covered by Achievement Test Batteries

Level[a]	CAT	CTBS	ITBS	MAT	NAT	SRA	SAT
1	K.0–K.9	K.0–K.9	K.1–1.5	K.0–K.9	K	K.5–1.5	1.5–2.5
2	K.6–2.2	K.6–1.6	K.8–1.9	K.5–1.9	1F	1.5–2.5	2.5–3.5
3	1.6–3.2	1.0–2.2	1.7–2.6	1.5–2.9	1S–2F	2.5–3.5	3.5–4.5
4	2.6–4.2	1.6–3.2	2.5–3.5	2.5–3.9	2	3.5–4.5	4.5–5.5
5	3.6–5.2	2.6–4.2	3	3.5–4.9	3	3.5–4.9	5.5–6.5
6	4.6–6.2	3.6–5.2	4	5.0–6.9	4	6.0–8.5	7.5–8.5
7	5.6–7.2	4.6–6.2	5	7.0–9.9	5	1.0–10.5	8.5–9.9
8	6.6–8.2	5.6–7.2	6	10.0–12.9	6	9.0–12.9	
9	7.6–9.2	6.6–9.2	7		7		
10	8.6–11.2	8.6–11.2	8*		8		
11	10.6–12.9	10.6–12.9	9*		9–10		
12			10*		11–12		
13			11–12*				

[a]Different publishers use different labels for the various levels of their tests. The values given here do not correspond exactly to those of any particular publisher.

*Coverage provided by the Iowa Tests of Educational Development (ITED).

Figure 9.1
Items similar to those used to assess reading on the Iowa Tests of Basic Skills
(ITBS)/Iowa Tests of Educational Development (ITED).

ITBS Level 6 (K.8–1.9) Early Primary Battery
Reading: Words (13 items) 10 minutes

    Teacher reads "Fill in the circle under the word *tell*."

    Take   Tell   Talk   Yell
     O   O   O   O

Reading: Pictures (13 items) 8 minutes

    Teacher reads "Fill in the circle for the word that best tells what is in the picture."

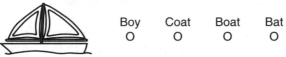

                      Boy   Coat   Boat   Bat
                       O   O   O   O

Reading: Sentences (13 items) 10 minutes

    Child is instructed to choose the word that goes best in the blank.

    Billy walked his _____ .

    Dog   Cat   Mother   Duck
     O   O   O   O

Reading: Word Attack (7 items) 5 minutes

    Child is instructed to fill in the circle under the picture that tells what the last
    word in the sentence is.

    The cat sits in the window.

Reading: Picture Stories (3 pictures, 13 items) 12 minutes

    A picture shows two people interacting in some way. The child answers 4 or 5
    yes-no questions about what is going on in the picture.

Figure 9.1, *continued*

ITBS Level 7 (1.7–2.6) Primary Battery
Reading: Pictures (6 pictures, 23 items) 12 minutes

Same as at Level 6, except three of the pictures have yes-no items (14 items) and the other three have multiple-choice answers.

Reading: Sentences (14 yes-no items) 7 minutes

If your father always cooks dinner, does your mother ever cook it?

Reading: Stories (5 stories, 19 items) 15 minutes

The child reads a four- or five-sentence story and answers three or four multiple-choice items about it. The last story is much longer than the first four.

ITBS Level 8 (2.5–3.5) Primary Battery
Reading: Pictures (6 pictures, 23 questions) 12 minutes

Same as at Level 7. All questions are multiple choice.

Reading: Sentences (14 yes-no questions) 7 minutes

Same as at Level 7.

Reading: Stories (3 stories, 24 items) 15 minutes

Same as at Level 7, but stories are more complex.

ITBS Multilevel Battery (Grades 3–9)
The test booklet contains twenty-four reading passages of increasing complexity and length, including selections of poetry. Questions become increasingly complex and require greater abstraction and interpretation. Tests are arranged so that students at different levels start at different places in the test booklet. For example, students at Level 9 start with the first item and stop at item 44, while students at Level 10 start at item 19 and work through item 68. The groups share items 19–44. The overlapping format makes it possible to test students from different grades as a single group.

Level	Start Item	Stop Item
9	1	44
10	19	68
11	30	83
12	45	100
13	68	124
14	84	141

ITED Reading Comprehension (Grades 9–12)
The reading score is based on 118 comprehension items distributed throughout the Social Studies, Natural Sciences, and Literary Interpretation sections of the Battery.

levels, at the point where basic decoding skills are still being established. Also, emphasis is placed on word analysis and decoding skills at the lower levels, while at the higher levels, more emphasis is on knowledge of word meanings and the reading of continuous text, followed by answering questions that assess reading comprehension.

Two aspects of these changes in the test focus over age ranges are particularly notable. First, to match the capabilities of the maturing students, there is a progressive shift in the nature of what is tested. Second, at the higher levels, the test provides a broad survey of complex skills rather than a specific analysis of sharply defined competencies.

The Comprehensive Test of Basic Skills, Fourth Edition

The fourth edition of the CTBS (CTBS/4) is of interest in this discussion because it illustrates some of the most sophisticated test development and norming techniques. The purpose of the CTBS/4 is to measure basic skills that are developed from exposure to varied curricula. It is intended to be independent of the particular course content taught in any one school district. However, since the test cannot be made entirely independent of the effect of the year in which specific subjects are introduced into each local curriculum its fit to one local curriculum may be better or worse than to another.

Like all other commercially produced batteries intended for widespread use, the CTBS/4 does not endeavor to measure specific knowledge or content directly. The emphasis instead is on more general skills of reading comprehension, mathematics, and reasoning processes in the natural and social sciences. Although modern curricular organizations are considered, items were rejected during test development if students enrolled in traditional programs could not answer them correctly at roughly the same rate as students in other curriculum structures.

The current version of the CTBS, CTBS/4, was first administered in the spring of 1989 in Kentucky and New Mexico and in 1990 in Tennessee. The previous edition, Forms U and V, was originally published in 1981 and is still available for districts and states that want to use the same form of the test over a period of several years. As is the case with every battery, a new edition is produced about every 8 to 10 years, so the total life of a given set of items is about 15 to 20 years.

Three versions of the CTBS/4 are offered: the Complete Battery, the Benchmark, and the Survey test. The Complete Battery provides both norm-referenced and curriculum-referenced scores, the Benchmark test is intended to provide only norm-referenced scores, and the two Survey tests, which make up the halves of the Benchmark test, offer shorter and somewhat less precise estimates of the scores students would obtain on the Benchmark test. The publisher recommends that the Survey tests be used only for groups because these short tests lack sufficient reliability for individual assessment. The norm-referenced portion of the complete battery consists of one of the survey tests, and this is supplemented by curriculum-referenced items to provide instructional diagnosis. A curriculum-referenced-only version of the CTBS/4 is also planned. Table 9.2 lists the grade levels corresponding to the 11 CTBS test levels and the publisher's designations for those levels. With the exception of Level K, each test level can be used in more than one grade. Also, the forms overlap in coverage; for example, both levels 12 and 13 can be used in the second half of grade 2.

Determining the Appropriate Level.   There is always more than one level that can be administered to each grade. For ease of administration and to prevent confusion in scoring, all students in one class or all classes of the same grade are usually given the same level of the test. This practice tends to make the test less reliable for individual students because their ability is not matched with the difficulty of the test as precisely as it might be. A better procedure would be to use the following rules to make decisions concerning which level to administer: For average students, the lower of the two levels should be given during the first half of the year and the higher level, during the second half. Above-average students should be given a higher level test and below-average students, a lower level test.

In addition to producing more precise measurement, this procedure also reduces the frustration students experience when given a test that is too far above or below their level of achievement. Locator tests consisting of 20 vocabulary and 20 mathematics items are available to assist in the selection of the most appropriate test level. Locator, or routing, tests were discussed in the presentation of the fourth edition of the Stanford-Binet Intelligence Scale in Chapter 8.

Content Covered.   The CTBS/4 is divided into seven content areas: reading, spelling, language, mathematics, study skills, social studies, and science. The read-

Table 9.2
Grade Levels and Corresponding Levels of the
Comprehensive Test of Basic Skills (CTBS)

Grade Level	CTBS Level
K.0–K.9	K
K.6–1.6	10
1.0–2.2	11
1.6–3.2	12
2.6–4.2	13
3.6–5.2	14
4.6–7.2	15
5.6–8.2	16
6.6–9.2	17 and 18
8.6–11.2	19 and 20
10.6–12.9	21 and 22

Note: K = kindergarten. Grade-level notations are interpreted as follows: K.0 = beginning of kindergarten; K.9 = ninth month of kindergarten; 1.6 = sixth month of first grade, and so forth.

ing, language, and mathematics content areas, in turn, are further subdivided in various ways at different levels, producing as many as 14 subscores and a composite achievement score. The lowest two levels of the test include only Reading and Mathematics areas, but by Level 11, Language, Science, and Social Studies have been added. Spelling comes in at Level 12 and Study Skills content rounds out the battery at Level 14. The technical manual for the CTBS/4 provides both the objectives associated with each test at each level and the subarea scores reported.

Norming.   The CTBS/4 was developed to provide fall and spring norms, and the norms are intended to be representative of the school population of the entire United States. The total norm sample includes approximately 222,000 students selected from public, parochial, and private schools. A stratified, random-sampling procedure was employed that took into account the geographic region, school size and socio-economic level. Users can select different specialized norm groups, and the publisher will assist states and districts in setting up local norms similar to those described for the ITBS in Chapter 3.

Reporting Results.   The item analysis and scaling of the CTBS/4 are based on item response theory (IRT), a general outline of which is provided in Chapter 16. The methods used represent the state of the art in standardized test development. Because scoring involves not just a count of the number of correct answers a student provides but also the pattern of responses, this technique for interpreting results makes computer analyses essential. (Number-right scoring is available but results in less precise assessment.) The IRT scoring and interpretation must be done either by the test publisher, McGraw-Hill, or by programs leased from that company. The use of a computer for test scoring makes available a wide array of derived scores, such as normal curve equivalents, scaled scores, grade equivalents, and percentiles based on local, state, and national norms.

Reliability.   The technical manual for the CTBS/4 includes both internal consistency-reliability coefficients and standard errors of measurement. The reliabilities are all respectably high for the norm-referenced scores, but no reliability information is reported for the curriculum-referenced scores. Since some of these scores may be based on as few as four items, their reliability may be suspect. The technical manual also provides information that emphasizes that the standard error of measurement is smallest at the midranges of performance and largest at the floor and ceiling of each level of the test. (Standard errors of measurement that are specific to the person's test score range are called *conditional standard errors of measurement,* or *CSEMs.*) The technical material available with the test also illustrates the advantage of IRT techniques over the "number correct" approach to computing scaled scores. The reporting of complete data on standard errors of measurement is useful because it permits estimation of the amount of error associated with scores across the range of student ability. This information demonstrates why we can place more confidence in the scores of students in the midrange of performance than of those in upper or lower levels.

Validity.   The section on validity in the Comprehensive Test of Basic Skills Technical Bulletin (1990) states: "Validity of an achievement test has to do with the degree to which it measures well what it purports to measure." It further states, "Care was taken during the development of CTBS/4 to provide a valid measurement of basic academic skills in the areas of reading, spelling, language, mathematics, and study skills." Nothing more is said about validity except in references to the chapters that deal with test development and item analysis, where detailed information about domain definition and item development procedures is given. Such a limited discussion of validity is typical of most technical manuals for standardized achievement tests, which tend to include numerous tables of reliability data but barely mention validity other than in relation to test content.

Additionally, the definition of validity given in the CTBS/4 manual is quite different from the one found in Chapter 5, and it also is not consistent with the requirements found in the *Standards for Educational and Psychological Testing* (American Psychological Association, American Educational Research Association, & National Council on Measurement in Education, 1985). The *Standards* require that evidence of validity be provided for every suggested *use* of a score, but for the CTBS/4 this information is lacking for instructional planning, evaluation, and placement decisions (Miller, 1992). The simplistic treatment of validity found in the CTBS/4 technical manual contrasts sharply with the otherwise highly sophisticated treatment of the technical aspects of achievement testing found in the rest of the manual.

INDIVIDUALLY ADMINISTERED ACHIEVEMENT TESTS

In the last several years there has been increasing interest in using individually administered tests of academic achievement either as a supplement to measures of cognitive ability or, in some cases, to replace the other measures. This interest springs mainly from a need to diagnose various learning disabilities. One of the primary indicators that a learning disability is present is a larger-than-expected discrepancy between cognitive ability scores and achievement scores. The discrepancy often is first noticed in examining the results from group testing.

When a learning disability is suspected, based on group testing results, the normal procedure usually involves obtaining more precise estimates of the child's cognitive abilities and academic achievement. This means administering an individual cognitive ability test, such as one of those described in Chapter 8, and, increasingly, an individual measure of achievement. Several such measures have recently been developed, and more are on the way.

One of the first individual achievement tests was the Peabody Individual Achievement Test (PIAT-R), published by American Guidance Service. Originally released in 1970, the test was revised in 1989. The PIAT-R can be used with students from kindergarten through Grade 12 and takes about 60 minutes to administer. Scores can be obtained for General Information, Reading Recognition, Reading Comprehension, Total Reading, Mathematics, Spelling, Test Total, Written Expression, and Written Language. Not all scores are available at all ages.

In 1985 the Kaufman Test of Educational Achievement (K-TEA) was published, also by American Guidance Service. This test, produced by the authors of the K-ABC (see Chapter 8), is available in two versions. The Brief version, which takes about 30 minutes to administer, provides scores for Reading, Mathematics, Spelling, and Battery Composite. The Full version, requiring 60 to 75 minutes, subdivides Reading Achievement into Reading Decoding, Reading Comprehension, and Reading Composite. Likewise, the mathematics test produces scores for Mathematics Applications, Mathematics Computation, and Mathematics Composite. Spelling and Battery Composite scores are also given. Either form can be used for students in first through 12th grades.

A third entry in this field is the Woodcock-Johnson Psychoeducational Battery: Achievement, published by Riverside Publishing Company. This test is unique in that it is a companion to the individual cognitive ability test by the same name (see Chapter 8) and was normed on the same sample. The common norm sample makes achievement-ability comparisons more direct than is possible with other instruments. In addition, the norm sample included people ranging from 2 to 90 years of age, allowing the test to be used appropriately with individuals both below and above normal school age. The Standard Battery takes about 50 to 60 minutes to administer and yields scores for Letter-Word Identification, Passage Comprehension, Calculation, Applied Problems, Dictation, Science, Social Studies, Humanities, and a Writing Sample.

SECONDARY-SCHOOL AND COLLEGE-LEVEL ACHIEVEMENT TESTS

At the elementary school level, standardized tests tend to focus on the basic skills of operating with words and numbers. At the secondary school and college levels, the emphasis shifts to the substance of particular curricular areas and even to particular courses. Because the curriculum becomes more differentiated, with the core that is common to all students representing a smaller fraction of the total, there is less need for a uniform comprehensive assessment. However, there are situations where a standardized achievement test battery can appropriately be used.

At the end of World War II, there was a need to evaluate and give credit for educational experiences obtained in the armed forces, so the Iowa Tests of Educational Development were developed. Like all general-ability tests, the ITED battery, which now provides the upper end to the Iowa Tests of Basic Skills for the series of achievement tests produced by Riverside Publishing Company, was designed to be appropriate for individuals who come from varied backgrounds. The test, therefore, tends to emphasize general knowledge and the ability to read and understand material from various fields of knowledge. The present version, the ninth edition of the Iowa Tests of Educational Development (Feldt, Forsyth, Ansley, and Alnot, 1993), has two forms (Forms K and L) and three levels (Level 15 for Grade 9, Level 16 for Grade 10, and Level 17/18 for Grades 11 and 12) and contains the following subtests:

Test E: Correctness and appropriateness of expression
Test Q: Ability to do quantitative thinking

Test SS: Analysis of social studies materials
Test SC: Analysis of natural sciences materials
Test L: Ability to interpret literary materials
Test SI: Use of sources of information

In addition, it provides a composite reading test score. The emphasis on getting, using, and interpreting material of various types and from various sources is apparent in the test titles. Almost all of the subtests make a substantial demand on reading skills, and most of the subtests are highly correlated with each other. As a result, although the entire test provides a good prediction of later academic performance, the subtests are not effective diagnostic tools. They also do not correspond closely enough to what is taught in any specific course to have value in indicating how effective a total school program has been.

More conventional and more representative of other high school batteries is the Tests of Achievement and Proficiency—Forms K and L (Scannell, Haugh, Loyd, & Risinger, 1993). There are eight subtests in the basic battery:

1. Reading Comprehension
2. Vocabulary
3. Written Expression
4. Information Processing
5. Mathematics Concepts and Problem Solving
6. Social Studies
7. Science
8. Math Computation (optional)

The complete battery provides a Reading Total score which combines Vocabulary and Reading Comprehension, a Core Total score which combines Written Expression and Mathematics Concepts with Reading Total, and a Complete Battery score which combines all subtest scores. As you can see from the titles, the battery is a mixture of basic skills (reading, writing, and mathematics) and of content (social studies, science, and literature). However, even in the content areas, there is a fair amount of emphasis on functional knowledge, for example, interpretation of data and of experimental designs in science. Such adaptations bring the tests closer to the common core of secondary education and make them more useful for comparing different schools and curricula and for making guidance decisions relating to a particular student. However, the emphasis on functional knowledge renders the tests less useful as measures of what has been taught in any specific course. A writing assessment can be added to either the ITED or the TAP.

In addition to batteries such as those just described, there are series of tests whose titles correspond rather closely to the names of specific courses. One extensive series was developed by the Cooperative Test Division of the Educational Testing Service. The nature of the tests is suggested by the types of tests in mathematics: structure of the number system; arithmetic; algebra I, II, and III; geometry; trigonometry; analytic geometry; and calculus. Another series is the Evaluation and Adjustment Series published by Harcourt Brace. This series includes tests in chemistry, physics, biology, American history, algebra, geometry, listening comprehension, and other areas. Typically, the tests in these series are designed for students who have completed some specific course—beginning algebra, biology, world history, or the like. Norms usually are based on samples of students who have completed such a course. Therefore, individual factors that influence a student's decision to enroll in a course may affect the integrity of the norming procedures. Little attempt has been made to maintain comparability of the score scale from one field to another, so comparisons across fields are rather questionable. Test content may in some cases match course content well enough that the test can play a role in the end-of-year evaluation of each student, but such a step should be taken with care to ensure that the course objectives correspond to those covered by the test. Alternatively, the standardized test can be used to assess achievement of those objectives it does cover, and locally constructed measures can be used for the rest. Such an approach requires that all of the objectives covered by the test are also objectives for the course.

One role suggested for tests designed to match specific courses is that of exempting particular students from individual course requirements. In part because many young adults have received various kinds of training in the armed forces and in part in recognition of the fact that some individuals may have been educated through media other than formal schooling—for example, through reading, radio and television, and/or work experience—it seems desirable to some educators to provide a channel for accreditation of such experience through examinations. The College Level Examination Program (CLEP) of the Educational Testing Service is such a channel.

The CLEP was established to provide a uniform nationwide procedure for evaluating experience claimed as the equivalent of specific college courses. Examinations have been prepared for 35 areas ranging from accounting and African American history to tests and measurements, trigonometry, and Western civilization. Normative data have been obtained from college students who have completed the designated course, as well as from those who have taken the equivalency test. Scores are presented as standard scores that range from 200 to 800, with 500 representing the average score for the basic reference population (the same metric that ETS uses for its Scholastic Aptitude Test). The way that the results from such a test will be used is determined by the college to which the student is applying and from which he or she wishes to receive equivalency credit. As with any accrediting or licensing examination, the decision on what constitutes a minimum acceptable level is quite arbitrary. Although general normative data may be available for those who have taken the course for which the examination is a substitute, it is likely that no data will be available specifically for the college to which an individual is applying. The score at which the balance shifts in favor of the gain in time saved and away from the risk of misclassifying a student as having mastered a course must be determined intuitively. The use of examinations for licensure and certification of competence is widespread in our society. States use tests for everything from granting driving privileges to deciding who can offer psychological and counseling services, but the system for setting cutoff scores for certification generally falls far short of being rational.

PROBLEMS WITH STATEWIDE ADMINISTRATION OF ACHIEVEMENT TEST BATTERIES—THE "LAKE WOBEGONE EFFECT"

Several years ago, John Cannell, a physician in West Virginia, became concerned when the results of the administration of the CTBS in his state were announced (Cannell, 1988). It seemed that his state was above the national average in all grade levels tested. These results were reported in the face of convincing evidence that West Virginia had serious educational problems. The state had the highest percentage of adults without college degrees, the second lowest per capita income, and the third lowest scores on the tests of the American College Testing (ACT) Program. When Cannell began to check the results of standardized achievement test administrations around the country, what he found was even more disconcerting. He discovered that none of the 50 states were below average at the elementary level. This phenomenon was quickly labeled the "Lake Wobegon Effect" after Garrison Keillor's description of his hometown on the American Public Radio program, A Prairie Home Companion, as a place "where all the women are strong, all the men are good-looking, and all the children are above average."

The discovery that all states are above average should cause the same alarm as the sound of a clock striking 13. There is certainly something wrong; basic rules of statistics dictate that it is impossible for every child or every state to be above average. Test publishers and the school districts that used these tests were quick to defend themselves against charges that they were guilty of any wrongdoing.

The most often heard explanation for these high scores is that the achievement of students has increased since the tests were standardized. With a seven- to eight-year turnaround between revisions, there is a sizable gap between standardization and use. The available evidence, however, fails to support this explanation. ACT and SAT scores have declined (although they have shown some recovery in recent years), National Assessment of Educational Progress scores show little increase nor do Armed Services Vocational Aptitude Battery scores. The hypothesis that overall achievement has increased since the tests were most recently normed would be supported if test results were much lower the first year the test was introduced. The MAT—Form 6, the CAT—Form E, and the ITBS—Forms G and H were all introduced during the 1985–1986 school year, and for each, states that immediately administered the test reported scores that were quite high. The high scores were not the result of teachers teaching to the test because the teachers had not seen the test before the test date. The high scores also could not have resulted from improvement since the last norming because not enough time had passed since that norming.

A second explanation for the high proportion of students who score above average on standardized achievement tests is that the students taking these tests differ from the norm sample. Although the test publishers spend enormous sums norming their tests, including samples that typically exceed 200,000, there is no way to ensure that the sample is truly representative because, as discussed previously, the administration of the test, for norming purposes, can take place only where permission can be obtained. For this reason, these samples may be different in important ways from the students that are assessed when the tests are administered "for real." This problem is exacerbated by the tendency of many school districts to exclude from testing students who might be expected to obtain low scores, such as special education and other special program students. Norming studies usually require that these students be included so that the norms will represent the actual population of students rather than a selected subset. Some school districts or specific teachers within a district might exclude, or at least not encourage, the participation of students who are not expected to do well. When low-performing students are excluded, classroom teachers or districts that engage in such practices can expect their performance to be high, relative to the norming population.

A third explanation for the high proportion of students who score above average relates to changes in the curriculum that are the direct result of the testing process. As more importance is placed on test results, the likelihood that curricula will be altered to fit what is being tested will increase. Some such alterations may be considered legitimate—to the extent that they do not involve teaching to the test. But, even in its most legitimate forms, altering the curriculum to increase the match with test objectives will violate the sampling assumptions of the test, and the resulting standard scores will lose their meaning. To some extent, test publishers may be contributing to the problem by including detailed reports of student and class performance on an item-by-item basis, as described in Chapter 3. There is educational value for the teacher and students in knowing where errors occur most frequently, but to the extent that this knowledge narrows the focus of instruction, the practice may backfire by gradually invalidating the normative data.

If a teacher realizes that a class is consistently failing to answer correctly an item from the test that requires the capitalization of the name of the state of Arizona, it would obviously be inappropriate for the teacher to tell his or her students to always capitalize the word *Arizona*. On the other hand, it seems acceptable for a teacher to alter the lesson plan to emphasize the need to capitalize the names of *all* states. But such a practice can change the meanings of scores derived from norms, because standardized achievement tests are intended to sample student behavior, which permits generalizations about a wide range of behaviors. If the teachers do not know what is included on a test, they have to make sure that they cover everything that could be included. On the other hand, if a teacher knows the general categories included on the test and teaches only these categories, the content sampling of the test will be compromised. Students taking the test under these circumstances will be taught and assessed only over the narrow range of content covered on the test. This narrowing of the curriculum focus occurs, for example, when a teacher, knowing that items assessing this knowledge are on the test, emphasizes the capitalization of states but fails to teach the students to capitalize the names of countries, because this type of item is not assessed by the test.

Another possible explanation for the high proportion of above average students is that teachers could actually be teaching the items from the test or administering the test in a nonstandard way that causes scores to be inflated. For instance, a teacher could provide inappropriate assistance when the test is administered or give students too much time to complete sections of the test that they have trouble completing in the allotted time. At the elementary level, common practice is for teachers to administer the tests in their own classrooms, with no supervision. When undue importance is placed on student performance and there is an absence of supervision of the test administration, the likelihood that cheating will take place increases.

Two public policy factors contribute to this problem. First, there are pressures on teachers to have their students do well on tests, because the teachers may be evaluated on the basis of the test results. A teacher whose class shows below average performance on a state- or districtwide test may have his or her own competence questioned. Second, all the way up the chain of command, those who are responsible for seeing that proper test administration procedures are maintained have a second, and perhaps more important, interest in seeing the scores rise—because they are often evaluated on this basis of the scores. In many states standardized test results are viewed by the public, the media, and the legislature as a report card for the educational system. As a result, the individuals in charge at all levels of the testing program may face a serious conflict of interest and be tempted to overlook inappropriate practices that could lead to inflated scores.

Obviously, a teacher who is giving students too much time to complete a section of a test or actually helping students answer questions is guilty of cheating. Likewise, a teacher who drills students on actual items from a test is involved in a practice that is generally perceived to be inappropriate. On the other hand, a teacher who, because of concern about her students' performance on an achievement test, worked extremely hard to get her students to learn more or who encouraged students to work hard on the test is not engaged in cheating. In fact, such behaviors would probably be viewed as exemplary. But gray areas, such as the following, cause problems: Teachers using items similar to those that appear on a test to be administered, or focusing instruction on those topics that are known to appear on the test. Such practices are generally considered unethical but, unfortunately, are common.

Some school districts have even implemented systemwide programs that involve a curricular emphasis on the specific content of the achievement tests that they use. Test publishers also make available instructional materials that can have a similar impact on student performance. Of course, the relationship between curriculum guides and test content can be a two-way street. If test publishers take their content from an examination of popular curriculum guides, it is equally possible for the tests to influence the curriculum writers.

INTERPRETING STANDARDIZED ACHIEVEMENT TEST BATTERIES

The standardized achievement test is designed to yield a reliable score for each of the skill areas covered. (Reliability coefficients in the high 80s or low 90s would be fairly typical.) Interest tends to focus on the subtest scores and the student's, class's, school's, or district's profile of strengths and weaknesses. We not only want to know how Peter's achievement in mathematics compares with national norms, but how it compares with his achievement in other areas covered by the battery. We may want to know how Ms. Albertson's class is progressing in mastery of mathematics concepts in comparison with their computational skills. There also may be a need to know in what respects schools of the Peterboro district appear better than average and in what respects they show deficiencies. There may be a further interest in knowing whether these differences reflect the desired curricular emphasis; if school administrators, teachers, parents, and the public should be concerned; and if remediation efforts should be initiated.

When it comes to classroom instructional decisions, the subtest scores on a survey achievement battery are of limited value. If Peter's achievement is a full grade below his current grade placement in capitalization skills, what is to be done about it? If Ms. Albertson's class shows an average grade equivalent a half grade lower in mathematics concepts than in mathematics computation, what steps should Ms. Albertson take? What should she teach or reteach? One way to answer these questions is to look at the individual items on the capitalization test that Peter answered incorrectly or the specific mathematics concepts that many of the children in Ms. Albertson's class did not know. This information about individual and collective student performance can be provided by the scoring services made available by test publishers.

Because large-scale testing programs are scored and interpreted by computer, only fairly simple modifications in the scoring program are required to permit more detailed information about the responses of individual children and classes. Report forms can be provided that will indicate which items Peter answered incorrectly on the capitalization subtest. The items can even be grouped by the capitalization rule that they exemplify. Information about the types of mathematics skills with which the class as a whole is experiencing difficulty also can be identified. From this information, Ms. Albertson can determine whether Peter made errors in capitalizing at the beginning of a sentence, at the beginning of a quotation, for names of persons, for names of places, and so forth. She can also see the frequency of errors in various concept and computational mathematical-skill areas for the entire class. This analysis of the test results has the potential for identifying specific difficulties and giving clues for instruction. Through these reports, the test author can assist teachers in what they have always been urged to do, that is, dig beneath the normative test score to identify the specific test exercises with which individuals and the class as a whole are encountering difficulty.

Detailed analysis of successes and failures on specific items can be quite useful for the teacher. However, there are some important cautions about such an approach. First, these tests do not contain enough items to assess each specific skill adequately. Since there may be only one or two items per skill, a child might answer these items correctly and thereby "pass an objective" by making a lucky guess, or answer items incorrectly because of some distraction or reason not relevant to the basic skill the item is testing. One or two items are insufficient to permit a reliable mastery/nonmastery decision about a child, though failure to answer an item correctly can alert the teacher to the need to more fully test the skill being measured, perhaps with a short, teacher-made test focusing specifically on the skill covered by the item answered incorrectly. Similarly, failure on an item by a substantial percentage of students in a class suggests the need to test that skill more thoroughly to determine whether some part of the class lacks mastery of the skill involved in that item.

There is a still more serious problem with the practice of assessing objectives with one or two items. If teachers are familiar with the specific items students are missing and are under pressure to have their students improve their scores, they may be tempted to teach the specific items or at least the specific types of items, a practice that leads to inflated test scores and the "Lake Wobegon Effect."

If the analysis of test results is to be helpful to a teacher, it should be in the teacher's hands as soon after testing as possible. Because modern, computer-based test scoring usually must be done centrally, there inevitably will be a lag between testing and the teacher's receipt of the test-result report. Each added week of delay makes the results less timely for instructional decisions concerning specific children or the whole class. New learning has taken place, previously learned material may have been forgotten, and the details of the descriptive picture will be less accurate. For these reasons, it is important to expedite completion of a testing program, assembly of answer sheets from the participating schools, and shipment of the materials to the processing agency. From that point on, teachers are at the mercy of the U.S. Postal Service and the agency conducting the scoring and report preparation.

Most test scoring services take very seriously the problem of lag between testing and results, and provide a 24-hour turnaround option. With many services it is also possible to transmit test results electronically, so the test papers never leave the school or district. This procedure requires that the necessary scanning and computer equipment be available, but this is now the case in all but the smallest districts. The problem of turnaround time is likely to be particularly serious in statewide testing programs if there is a requirement that returns from all school systems be received before test analysis can be conducted and results, provided. In some cases, processing problems resulting from technical or political issues have delayed reporting beyond the year in which the test results were obtained. By the time these results are in the hands of the teachers, it is too late for any use to be made of them for instructional planning for specific students.

DIAGNOSTIC ACHIEVEMENT TESTS

Diagnosis relates primarily to the single individual. Why does Sarah get a low score on a survey test of reading comprehension? Why does Peter get a low score on the mathematics subtest of the achievement battery? What are the sources of difficulty? Much, probably most, diagnostic testing is conducted with single students after it has been determined from a survey test or from the observations of the teacher that a student is not making satisfactory progress in reading, mathematics, or some other segment of the school program. Although most testing of this kind is done individually, perhaps using one of the individually administered achievement tests described earlier, some standardized tests are available to serve a diagnostic function and to be administered to a group. We will describe one of these, indicating what it undertakes to do and the problems that arise in its use and interpretation.

The third edition of the Stanford Diagnostic Mathematics Test (1984), Forms G and H, is designed for use in Grades 1 through 12. Levels are designated by colors:

The red level is for students at the end of first grade, in the second and third grades, and low performing students in fourth grade. The green level is for fourth-, fifth-, and low performing sixth-grade students. The brown level is for sixth-, seventh-, and low performing eighth-grade students. And the blue level is for 8th through 12th graders. All four levels assess three areas of mathematical competence. Test 1 measures the concepts of the number system and numeration, Test 2 measures computation, and Test 3 measures the application of these concepts and skills. For each test, a series of skills is measured. For example, at the green level of Test 2, computation, the following skills are measured: addition with whole numbers (9 items), subtraction with whole numbers (12 items), multiplication with whole numbers (15 items), and division with whole numbers (9 items).

Raw scores, scaled scores, grade equivalents, percentiles, and a total score are reported for each of the three subtests. Information is also provided on the performance of students on each separate skill measured within each of the three subtests, given in the form of raw scores, and indicating whether the child was above or below a cutoff score.

The test has been normed for both fall and spring administration, but for maximum value it is recommended that the test be administered in the fall so that diagnosis and remediation can be undertaken immediately. In selecting which level to administer, both the grade and the level of functioning of the student should be considered. Little diagnostic information can be derived from a test that is either too easy or too difficult. The test is structured so that either one or two tests can be administered on the same day. If two tests are administered on the same day, a 10-minute rest period between tests is recommended.

Analysis of subtest scores is only the initial step in diagnosis. Performance on the specific skills subsumed within the subtests must also be examined. But even these analyses may not be sufficient. If Peter's scores are compared with the norms for his grade group and it is found that his lowest score is in multiplication of whole numbers, we still do not know what aspect of multiplication is giving him trouble. We have some guidance on where we should focus further scrutiny, but we still need to analyze Peter's errors in multiplication problems to see if we can determine whether his problem is errors in conception or procedure, or a deficit in the mastery of number facts. Upon tentatively identifying an area of weakness, we need to observe the process of Peter's functioning in that area to determine exactly what he does incorrectly and to generate hypotheses on why he does it. A thorough diagnostic study typically requires observation of the process, as well as the product, of student performance.

If a weakness on a particular subtest identifies an individual student in a class, we first look for deficits in that student's acquisition of knowledge. If the class as a whole performs poorly on some subtest, we should ask whether the quality of instruction was as it should have been or whether the introduction of certain topics was delayed in the local curriculum. A discrepancy between local performance and national norms signifies a problem only to the degree that the local curriculum agrees with the assumptions made by the publisher regarding when topics should be introduced. If a topic (such as fractions) has not been taught to a particular class at the time of testing, obviously there is no reason to be concerned if the topic has not been mastered. The group's past instructional history and instructional emphasis must influence interpretation of class-average profiles on such a diagnostic battery.

Because the subtests in a battery provide meaningful diagnostic clues only when the material covered by a subtest has been taught to the students, we may question whether the material on fractions and decimals provides useful diagnostic information for fourth- and fifth-grade groups. We cannot identify deficient performance on a subtest if the average performance is very close to a chance score, which is what we should expect if the students have not received instruction in the skills being measured. In general, the better adapted a test is for displaying a serious deficiency, the poorer it will be for identifying levels of achievement. There is an essential incompatibility between the functions of diagnosing deficiency and assessing all degrees of excellence. The test that is good for one of these purposes is unlikely to be good for the other. Usually, a diagnostic test should be designed more like a criterion-referenced, or mastery, test, so that the expected score for the average examinee is close to a perfect score and so that there is a wide range of possible below-par scores to express degrees of deficiency.

CRITERION-REFERENCED STANDARDIZED ACHIEVEMENT TESTS

The enthusiasm that surrounded the introduction of criterion-referenced approaches to classroom tests generated a parallel interest in the application of this methodology to standardized achievement tests. There are two ways to construct a criterion-referenced standardized achievement test: (1) objectives can be associated with items from existing norm-referenced achievement tests to give them the appearance of a criterion-referenced test, or (2) achievement tests can be constructed from the ground up as criterion-referenced tests. The first approach is widely employed; however, for criterion-referenced tests of the second type, availability is more limited.

Examples of Criterion-Referenced Standardized Achievement Tests

The Psychological Corporation has two reading achievement subtests that are part of the Metropolitan Achievement Test series: (1) the reading survey tests and (2) the reading diagnostic tests. The first subtest is a survey battery similar to other norm-referenced survey achievement batteries, and the second is a criterion-referenced test covering basic reading skills. The SRA Achievement Series has 34 criterion-referenced diagnostic tests available, covering instructional objectives included in the curriculum for children in Grades 1 through 4. Houghton Mifflin, in its School Curriculum Objective-Referenced Evaluation, provides 5,000 items that can be put together in various combinations for constructing criterion-referenced tests to meet the specific needs of teacher and classroom settings.

Steven Osterlind at the University of Missouri has attempted to construct a test to measure achievement of basic academic subjects and skills for the college level. His instrument, the College Basic Academic Subjects Examination (College BASE) can be used for individual or institutional assessment. The test measures student achievement in English, mathematics, science, and social studies. Scores are reported for these four subjects, as well as overall achievement, nine achievement clusters, and 23 specific skills. Scores can also be provided for three reasoning competencies, interpretive, strategic, and adaptive. Individual assessment requires about 3 hours, but institutional assessment for program review, where results are averaged across students, can be accomplished in about 45 minutes, because each student takes only one-fourth of the battery. A writing sample can be added to the subject matter tests to assess writing competence.

Problems with Criterion-Referenced Standardized Achievement Tests

In general, it is not possible for a single test to serve the purposes of both a norm-referenced and a criterion-referenced assessment because criterion-referenced tests need to be tied closely to the specific instructional objectives of the classroom or school district. The publishers of nationally distributed achievement tests must avoid any objectives that are not found in the curricula of most school districts. This need to focus on common objectives works better in the early grades and in reading and mathematics, where school districts have the greatest consensus concerning which objectives should be emphasized. The demand for criterion-referenced achievement tests has led some test publishers to associate instructional objectives with existing items and to claim that these new tests have the properties of, or can be used as, criterion-referenced tests. Such tests are better described as objective-referenced tests and are considered to be poor forms of assessment. Criterion-referenced assessment is attractive because it seems to avoid some of the negative associations that surround testing by avoiding the labeling of students as failures. It is seen as more constructive because it provides specific information about student performance.

Although there are important advantages to using criterion-referenced tests, such as those just cited, the use of criterion-referenced techniques with standardized achievement tests is fraught with logistic problems. It is necessary to administer many items to reliably assess a large number of objectives. For instance, the Metropolitan Reading Diagnostic Test includes over 200 items at most grade levels but assesses some objectives with only three items. The MAT, on the other hand, uses only 60 items to obtain an overall reading score. To measure something, whether it is a skill such as reading comprehension or an objective such as *can add two-digit numbers,* an adequate number of items is required; that is, a test reporting performance on a large number of objectives must be much longer than one reporting seven subtest scores.

SUMMARY

Most standardized testing involves the use of survey test batteries selected from a small number of similar tests. Testing is also conducted using diagnostic and criterion-referenced tests. Survey tests are useful primarily in connection with selection, placement, guidance, curricular, and public policy decisions. Diagnostic tests are used to determine a student's strengths and weaknesses. Diagnostic testing is difficult and time consuming to implement.

At the secondary and college levels, centrally produced achievement tests provide evidence both of outstanding competence—to serve as a basis for advanced placement—and of minimal competence. An important controversy in statewide achievement testing is the existence of the "Lake Wobegone Effect," which, because it inflates scores, makes the interpretation of the results of such tests difficult. Another problem is the tendency by educators to vacillate between attempts to make objective-referenced interpretations of achievement in local schools and attempts to make global appraisals of the effectiveness of different schools and school systems at the state level.

QUESTIONS AND EXERCISES

1. For which of the following purposes would a standardized test be useful? For which purposes should teachers expect to make their own tests? Why?

   a. To determine which students have mastered the addition and subtraction of fractions

   b. To determine which students are below the expected skill level in mathematics computation

   c. To determine the subjects in which each student is strongest and weakest

   d. To determine for a class which punctuation and capitalization skills need to be taught further

   e. To form subgroups in a class for the teaching of reading

2. Obtain a curriculum guide covering the content and objectives of a subject that you are teaching, plan to teach, or someday might want to teach. Examine a standardized achievement test for that subject. Which of the objectives in the curriculum guide are adequately measured by the test? Which ones are not? How adequately is the content covered by the test?

3. Make a critical comparison of two achievement test batteries for the same grade. How do they differ? What are the advantages of each, from your point of view?

4. The manual for a test states that it can be used for diagnostic purposes. What criteria could you use to determine whether it has any real value as a diagnostic tool?

5. Why should we be concerned about the reliability of the scores resulting from a set of diagnostic tests? What implications does the reliability have for using and interpreting such tests?

6. A senior high school that draws from three feeder junior highs has a special accelerated program in mathematics. What are the advantages and disadvantages of selecting students

for this program based on scores of a standardized achievement test in mathematics given at the end of the ninth grade (the last year in junior high)?

7. In October you gave a standardized achievement battery to your fourth-grade class. How might you, as a teacher, use the results?

8. A school using a centralized scoring service buys item analysis data that show the percentage of students answering each item correctly for each grade and each classroom in the school. How could the school as a whole use these results? How could individual teachers use them?

9. Miss Carson, a sixth-grade teacher, says, "I am not as much interested in a student's level of performance as I am in the growth that he or she shows while in my class." In terms of measurement, what problems does this point of view raise?

10. The school system of Centerville is proposing to introduce a revised mathematics curriculum on an experimental basis in selected elementary schools. It wishes to evaluate the effectiveness of the program before introducing it throughout the system. How adequate would a standardized achievement test in elementary school mathematics be for this type of evaluation? What problems are likely to arise? How might these problems be dealt with?

11. A state legislature has passed a law requiring all students to show adequate competency in skills needed for everyday living before they are awarded a high school diploma. What is the first problem that needs to be solved to implement the legislation? What would be the advantages and disadvantages of using the following types of tests to determine adequate competency?

   a. Centrally produced tests by the state education department

   b. Locally constructed tests by each school

   c. A nationally published achievement test

SUGGESTED READINGS

Cannell, J. J. (1988). Nationally normed elementary achievement testing in America's public schools: How all 50 states are above the national average. *Educational Measurement: Issues and Practice, 7*(2), 5–9.

Cunningham, G. K. (1986). *Educational and psychological measurement.* New York: Macmillan.

Hall, B. W. (1985). Survey of the technical characteristics of published educational achievement tests. *Educational Measurement: Issues and Practice, 4*(1), 6–14.

Mehrens, W. A. (1987). *Using standardized tests in education.* New York: Longman.

Miller, M. D. (1992). [Review of *Comprehensive Test of Basic Skills.*] In J. J. Kramer & J. C. Conoley (Eds.), *The eleventh mental measurements yearbook* (pp. 217–220). Lincoln, NE: Buros Institute of Mental Measurements.

Nitko, A. J. (1983). *Educational tests and measurement.* New York: Harcourt Brace Jovanovich.

Sax, G. (1989). *Principles of educational and psychological measurement and evaluation.* Belmont, CA: Wadsworth.

CHAPTER 10

Performance and Product Evaluation

INTRODUCTION

To most people, in and out of education, the word *testing* means the sort of paper-and-pencil assessment methods that are customarily used to assess cognitive objectives. Such tests often employ selected-response item formats in which the examinee chooses an answer from among a set of available alternatives. Experience has shown that clever teachers and test writers can construct cognitive tests for assessing almost any learning outcome, and for many instructional objectives, this is appropriate. However, there are other types of objectives for which a paper-and-pencil assessment is too far removed from the instructional objective that it is intended to measure to be useful.

ARTIFICIALITY OF CONVENTIONAL COGNITIVE TESTS

All testing is to some degree artificial because we seldom directly measure instructional goals. Test standardization exacerbates this problem by increasing the need to use selection type items to facilitate machine scoring and computer analysis. Even with cognitive material, such as reading comprehension, that we think of as most appropriate to be assessed with an objective test format, there can be a problem with matching the assessment task to the instructional goal. Reading comprehension is usually measured by assessing a student's ability to answer multiple-choice items about the meaning of short paragraphs. This method of assessing reading comprehension contrasts with the conventional definition for comprehension, which is based on the capacity of students to understand what they have read, to relate new information to previously learned material, and to critically evaluate long passages of reading. Artificiality also occurs with objective spelling tests that require a student to select the correctly spelled word from among three or four misspelled words, or English usage tests that require the student to distinguish between grammatically correct and grammatically incorrect sentences. The usual process of spelling requires one to generate a correctly spelled word rather than to recognize the correct spelling. Likewise, our interest in assessing knowledge of correct English usage most often calls for the production of a correctly worded sentence. Instruction in English composition classes generally is intended to bring students to the point where they can combine these skills to write grammatically correct paragraphs with a minimum of misspelled words. Achievement of this objective is most directly assessed by evaluating paragraphs that students have written. The mere identification of grammatical errors or misspelled words is not an equivalent form of cognitive functioning. However, despite the indirectness of paper-and-pencil tests, educators are usually willing to accept the artificiality in exchange for objectivity and ease of administration.

CONVENTIONAL COGNITIVE TESTS

There are, however, important instructional objectives and cognitive functions that cannot be appropriately assessed, even to an approximation, by paper-and-pencil tests. These include bahaviors associated with subject matter that calls for a product or a process—for example, the performances required in a music, physical education, speech, or drama class or the projects required in art, industrial arts, and home economics classes.

Evaluating performance in such situations can be quite difficult; as a result, teachers of such courses may avoid assessment altogether. This tendency to deemphasize assessment often is exacerbated by a perception that processes and products are not academic and are therefore less important, an attitude that is sometimes used as a justification for a lack of emphasis on assigning grades in these settings.

The reluctance of teachers to evaluate educational products in the same critical manner that they evaluate more academic activities may partially stem from the belief that performances in areas such as music, art, and physical education are strongly influenced by prior ability. It is widely believed that the quality of the products and the performance of students is to a great degree a function of skills and abilities that the student possessed prior to entering a class and not necessarily the result of instruction. There are art students, for instance, who can produce the best painting in their class on the first day and others who can never paint anything acceptable no matter how much instruction they receive. Of course, this phenomenon might also apply to English composition or the solving of calculus problems, but there is a reluctance to believe that success in these areas is also the result of ability and not just effort. A poor singing voice, therefore, is more likely to be attributed to factors outside of the control of the student than is an inability to solve arithmetic problems.

ASSESSING PRODUCTS

In the past, it was useful to distinguish between assessment situations involving a concrete product, such as a sculpture made in art class, and those performances that left no permanent record, such as a speech or an interpretive dance. The former could be assessed at leisure, while later evaluation had to take place at the time of performance or be based on a potentially faulty memory. However, with the widespread availability of video cameras the distinction no longer applies; performances can be transformed into concrete products.

In most cases, it is the product rather than the process by which it was produced that is the focus of assessment. For example, a teacher is usually more interested in the poem a student has written than the process of its composition. In addition, it is usually easier to evaluate a product than a process. With a product, there is a single object (or performance) that can be compared to others. A process is made up of many parts, each of which probably is transitory, and performance of the parts must be weighted to obtain a summary evaluation. Standards also must be established for each step in the process. However, sometimes the process and the product are not easily distinguishable, such as for a speech or a dance. There are also situations for which the process itself is as important if not more important than the product: (1) when safety is a primary concern, (2) when the student's product itself can be considered transitory, and (3) when it is particularly difficult to evaluate a product. Even in each of these cases, however, modern recording procedures can produce a permanent record of the performance for later evaluation.

Safety.   When the process can be dangerous, there is a necessary emphasis on ensuring that it is carried out correctly. Examples include the procedures used in a chemical experiment, a gymnastic performance, or the use of power tools in a woodworking or machine shop. We may be interested not only in whether the person knows the correct procedural steps or safety measures, but also whether these are carefully followed. Our evaluation of a person in these situations would be influenced to a considerable degree by the person's adherence to the specified procedures.

Transitory Product.   There are circumstances in which the particular product or performance of a student is secondary to the process, because the product is just a step in the direction of better products and performances. An example of this would be a tennis serve. A good athlete might be able to serve more effectively than anyone else in his or her class, despite a lack of correct form. Even if such a serve wins points, a tennis instructor would not give it high marks. A good serve cannot be evaluated in terms of its success alone because improvement in a serve cannot occur without the server's use of the correct form. Most tennis instructors would be happier with a serve that was going into the net but was based on correct form than with a serve that, while winning points, was the product of incorrect form. Computer programming is another area where there may be a need to emphasize proper procedures. Just because a computer program is capable of performing a designated task does not necessarily mean that the program is acceptable. Appropriate procedures and efficiency of programming might also be considered important.

Difficult-to-Evaluate Products.   When the evaluation of a product is subjective, it may be more practical to evaluate the components of the process rather than the product. For example, it is easier to evaluate the process of teaching than to evaluate its products because no satisfactory system of evaluating the effectiveness of teaching has yet been devised. However, there are systems for evaluating the process of teaching—for example, systems based on the results of process-product research. Counseling is another activity for which the process is more easily evaluated than the product, as is management style.

APPLYING PERFORMANCE AND PRODUCT EVALUATION TO COGNITIVE TASKS

Although in the past, cognitive skills typically were not evaluated using performance and product evaluation techniques, there is increasing interest in using these techniques in this context. Some recent calls for educational reform are based on new developments in the role of cognitive psychology in education. These new developments have led to an increased interest in assessing the products and processes of cognitive functioning. The interest in cognitive psychology also stems from criticisms of current educational practice, which relies heavily on objective, paper-and-pencil tests as the sole criterion for measuring educational effectiveness (Nickerson, 1989). As discussed above, selected-response tests are considered artificial because they do not allow students to demonstrate directly their attainment of educational objectives. In addition, the increasing interest in implementing principles of cognitive psychology in the classroom has resulted in a desire to encourage the development of higher-order processing and critical-thinking skills. There is a general belief that these must be evaluated with performance- and product-assessment techniques. Although it may be technically feasible to assess the processes used in meeting educational goals, most of the emphasis in evaluation of cognitive objectives currently involves the assessment of products. The terms *performance test* and *performance assessment* are commonly associated with this practice.

In most cases, evaluation of cognitive objectives by means of performance tests involves the use of constructed-response items. Constructed-response items require that students generate answers in response to questions or prompts rather than choose from a set of available alternatives. Depending upon the educational objective being assessed, students might be asked to write an essay, solve a problem, or in some other way perform a skill. The fundamental characteristic of performance test items is that they simulate actual situations, so that the examinee has the opportunity to demonstrate his or her proficiency at an exemplary task.

Scoring Performance Tests

Scoring of performance test items typically takes one of two forms: keyed response or variable response. Keyed-response formats are quite straightforward in that they involve items with one or more keyed correct responses. A student's response is considered correct if his or her answer matches one of the keyed responses. Variable-response scoring is much more complex than keyed-response scoring. For variable-response items, there is no one correct answer or small set of correct answers. Instead, scores are grounded in a set of scoring criteria called *rubrics*. In most cases, rubrics describe a hierarchy of potential responses and identify the qualities of knowledge and/or skill one would expect at different points along the scale. An example of a performance test item in eighth-grade mathematics and its accompanying scoring rubrics are presented in Figure 10.1.

It is essential in using rubrics for scoring that there be explicit criteria for indicating proficiency in the skills specified in the educational objectives and that scorers have adequate training in applying those criteria. In addition, it is desirable to provide scorers with samples of examinees' responses that are exemplary of different points along the scoring rubric. If either poorly trained scorers or vague scoring criteria are used, performance tests will be substantially less objective and less reliable than their multiple-choice counterparts. However, as Fredericksen and Collins (1989) point out in their discussion of the increasing use of statewide writing assessment, through use of trained scorers and carefully delineated standards, variable-response scoring using rubrics can produce accurate and dependable results.

ASSESSING PROCESSES

A process is always made up of a number of parts or steps, and, therefore, is typically assessed with an emphasis on evaluating each of the steps in the process. Checklists and rating scales are the primary instruments used to assess these steps.

Using Checklists

It is customary when evaluating whether a student has used the appropriate process to use either a checklist or rating scale. In general, the checklist is preferred to the rating scale. With a checklist, the observer is required only to observe the perfor-

Figure 10.1

Example of a performance assessment exercise in mathematics, with scoring rubrics. (Adapted from F. L. Finch (Ed.), (1991) Educational Performance Assessment.)

EXERCISE C

Mr. Ramirez helped four other students make key holders. He gave Rhonda, Sam, Tony, and Uta a board and told them to share it equally.

Rhonda measured and cut one fourth of the board.

Next Sam measured and cut one third of the remaining board.

Then Tony measured and cut one half of the remaining board.

Uta used the piece that was left.

10. Did the four students share the board equally? Draw a picture and explain your answer. Use the Review Check List below to help you write so that your ideas will be understood.

_____
_____
_____
_____
_____
_____
_____
_____

Review Check List

☐ This picture and explanation clearly describe how the students shared the board.
☐ The ideas in this explanation follow a logical order.
☐ This explanation contains correct spelling, capitalization, and punctuation. It is neatly written.

Figure 10.1

Scoring Rubrics

Note: Accept synonymous phrases when appropriate. Evaluation should be on content and evidence of understanding.

Question 4, page 3
If the students continued to measure and cut off one fourth of the length of the remaining board, what would happen? Explain your answer fully. (2 points possible)

Award 2 points to a response explaining that if the students continued to measure and cut off one fourth the length of the remaining board, each succeeding piece would be smaller than the previous one and, theoretically the students would never come to the end of the board, or actually the students would eventually be cutting sawdust.

Award 1 point to a response explaining that the board would eventually be used up but offering no recognition of a pattern.

Question 5, page 3
The students did not clearly understand Mr. Ramirez's directions for cutting the board. What could Mr. Ramirez have said to make his directions clearer? (1 point possible)

He could have told the students each to measure and cut off 16 inches or one fourth of the total length of the 64-inch board. (See note.)

Question 10, page 5
Did the four students share the board equally? Make a drawing and explain your answer. (4 points possible)

Assign score points to student responses that most closely match the characteristics listed. (See note.)

A 4 response
   -contains *both* a picture and an explanation that indicate a clear understanding of the pattern
   -contains a picture showing a whole divided into four equal parts
   -contains an explanation which enhances the picture by comparing the size of each piece using either sentences or computations, or a combination of both

A 3 response
   -contains a picture that indicates a clear understanding of the pattern but only an attempt at an explanation
   -contains an explanation that indicates a clear understanding of the pattern but only an attempt at a picture
   -has limited detail in the picture or the explanation

A 2 response
   -offers an adequate picture only
   -offers an adequate explanation only
   -contains an explanation that does not enhance the picture
   -may be difficult to understand due to errors in language and grammar

A 1 response
   -makes some attempt at a picture *or* an explanation
   -is unclear

A 0 response fails to attempt the question.

An N/S (nonscorable) response is illegible or unreadable.

293

mance and to mark on the observation form whether the desired behavior was present or absent. In contrast, the observer using a rating scale must make decisions about how often the behavior occurs or the quality of the behavior. Also, with a rating scale, judging may be time consuming, which can severely limit the number of behavior classes that are rated.

There are several steps that the person constructing a checklist should follow:

1. Designate the appropriate performance or product
2. List the important behaviors and characteristics
3. Include common errors that the individual being evaluated might make
4. Put the list into an appropriate format

Designate an Appropriate Performance or Product.   The construction of a checklist should always begin with the designation of what the end-product is expected to be. In most cases when the focus is on a checklist to evaluate a process, it may not be possible to precisely define the product itself, but it is necessary to specify it in general terms. The purpose of this step is to provide a focus for delineating the important behaviors and characteristics.

List the Important Behaviors and Characteristics.   Developing a list of behaviors and characteristics that describe a successful performance or product is the critical part of constructing a checklist. A good checklist will include all of the important and relevant behaviors and characteristics necessary to achieve the final product or performance. Behaviors and characteristics that are exhibited by all persons (for example, heart continues to beat) and those that cannot be assessed for any student (such as "has positive cognitive experience") should be excluded because they contribute no useful information and they clutter the checklist. The statements designating the behaviors should be worded to minimize the need for interpretations by the observers. The list should be as inclusive as possible without being so lengthy and detailed that the process of judging becomes unwieldy. Following is an example of a partial list of behaviors that an individual who is able to play tennis effectively should exhibit:

1. Use the correct grip
2. Have his or her feet in the correct position when hitting the ball
3. Keep the elbow straight
4. Hit a forehand to the opposite court
5. Hit a backhand to the opposite court
6. Serve the ball to the correct part of the opponent's court
7. Volley effectively
8. Hit overheads

Of course, each of these behaviors could be broken down even further. There are numerous steps associated with, for example, serving correctly or hitting an overhead. How specific the behaviors in the checklist are depends upon how specific or global the behavior being observed is.

Associated with any such list of behaviors and characteristics, either implicitly or explicitly, are standards. These standards can be as formal as the distance in fractions of an inch that a student's grip can deviate from the ideal grip on a tennis racket or as informal as a consensus among judges about what would be considered a correct grip. The intent of standards is to increase the probability that all judgments have the same basis for determining whether the behavior is present or absent.

Include Common Errors that the Individual Being Evaluated Might Make. It is not sufficient to determine that a student is performing all of the requisite steps in a procedure; it is also important to note the presence of specific behaviors that are considered inappropriate as well. For instance, in observing a teacher, it might be found that he or she exhibits most of the behaviors associated with good teaching but, in addition, responds to student misbehavior with sarcasm. It is important to have such negative behaviors noted along with all of the positive ones.

Put the List into an Appropriate Format. Once the list of desirable and undesirable behaviors and characteristics has been formulated, it should be organized into the sequence that observers are most likely to encounter. The list should be placed on the observation forms in such a way that it is easily readable. Also, space should be provided for the observer to mark a check if the behavior is present. For repeated behaviors such as disruptions, the response form should be organized by time periods. Then the observer can merely place a check mark if the behavior occurred during a designated period of time. Alternative methods can require the observer to indicate the number of times the behavior occurred or to estimate the amount of time that a given activity took. Appropriate space should be provided for the specific type of response.

Once the checklist has been completed, the results must be interpreted. As long as the results are to be used to provide feedback to students about their performance or to help teachers improve their teaching, the components (behaviors and characteristics) can be interpreted separately. If the results of the checklist are to be used to make summative evaluations, the components must be summarized into a total score. This summarizing can be accomplished by summing the items, taking into account, of course, those that refer to behaviors to be avoided. It might also be desirable to weight the items according to their importance.

Using Rating Scales

Rating scales can be used to evaluate a set of behaviors and characteristics in much the same way that checklists are used. Rating scales differ from checklists by having the observer provide a number, or rating, for each behavior to indicate either how often the behavior occurred or to indicate its quality. For purposes of evaluating processes that are ongoing, checklists are usually preferred because of the additional time required to respond to a rating scale. Additional information about how to construct rating scales is included in Chapter 12.

The simplest rating scale would consist of a set of behaviors and characteristics with instructions to the observers to respond to each by selecting a number within a designated range to indicate some quality of the behavior. But, more often the scale is presented in a graphic form, with anchors at either end and numbers designating the points on the scale. Scales can take many forms, including approaches as simple as the following ones:

Uses proper safety procedures in the chemistry laboratory

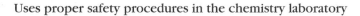

Never   Seldom   Occasionally   Often   Always

or

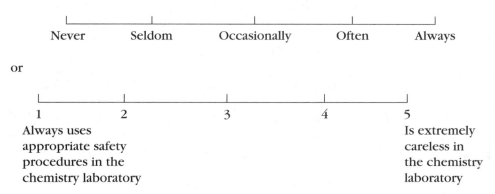

1   2   3   4   5
Always uses   Is extremely
appropriate safety   careless in
procedures in the   the chemistry
chemistry laboratory   laboratory

Another option is to have the observers imagine an individual who was the best possible exemplar of a particular behavior or characteristic and put him or her on one end of the scale and then to imagine the worst possible exemplar and put that individual on the other end. The observer then has the task of indicating where along the continuum the individual being observed should be placed. An example of this approach follows:

Rate the quality of the student's introduction to his or her speech relative to the two examples given.

1   2   3   4   5
Marilyn's superb   Denzil's inept
introduction to   introduction to
her speech   his speech

ASSESSING PRODUCTS AND PERFORMANCES

In a product or performance evaluation, it is preferable to compare a student's work to a predetermined performance standard rather than to the performance of the student's peers. In Chapter 3 we made the distinction between these two approaches to assessment: using a predetermined standard, referred to as criterion-referenced evaluation, and having peers provide the standard, called norm-referenced assessment. As defined by Nitko (1984), criterion-referenced tests are those "deliberately constructed to yield measurements that are directly interpretable in terms of specified performance standards" (p. 12). We have seen that a major goal of product and performance assessment is to obtain an indication of a student's mastery of specific educational objectives. Norm-referenced evaluation indicates a student's relative level of performance compared to peers but tells us nothing about mastery of objectives.

In addition to their being inconsistent with the basic philosophy of performance testing, normative comparisons pose certain problems in evaluating products and performances. In many cases, the products of students are different along many dimensions, which creates difficulties in making legitimate comparisons between the products. Any two products can be different in numerous ways, and each may be superior in some aspects and inferior in others. For instance, in a science project, the teacher or judges must consider originality, scientific contribution, neatness, sturdiness, creativity, extensiveness and quality of narrative explanations, the use of references, and so forth. How do you weight these qualities in making normative comparisons? How do you compare a bold and unusual, yet somewhat awkwardly presented, project with a more conventional, less creative one that is neat, carefully constructed, and meticulously documented? Under these circumstances, it obviously is difficult to compare two such different products. Determining which dimensions are important aspects of the educational objectives being assessed and explicitly delineating mastery criteria makes evaluation of such products much more straightforward.

Advantages of Multiple Observers

A teacher who creates a performance test or checklist will usually be the only person to administer it. However, there are distinct advantages to using multiple observers. First, comparisons can be made among the judges to obtain information about their reliability. If the responses are the same, the indication is that the judgments are reliable. Naturally, when two observers are in disagreement, the suggestion is that there is something wrong with the directions for making the observations, the scoring of observations, or the abilities of the observers. The particular items for which there is disagreement can be examined to decide whether the items or their scoring rubrics need to be defined more clearly. Also, inadequate training of observers is often responsible for lower levels of interrater reliability.

Using more than one observer has other advantages. For example, it is possible to obtain a more accurate score by pooling the responses of several observers than could be obtained from a single observer because the errors of each observer tend to compensate for the errors of others. In fact, pooling ratings can be thought of as having the same effect on reliability that lengthening a test does.

SYSTEMATIC OBSERVATION

Some instructional objectives require neither cognitive behaviors nor a product but instead focus on changes in personality traits and attitudes. One way to obtain information about personality traits and attitudes is by using systematic observations in natural settings.

There are important advantages to observing behavior in the naturally occurring settings of daily life, although these situations are often not uniform from person to person. Avoiding the need to stage special events just for testing purposes makes observation of real life situations appealing and may yield more accurate reflections of behavior.

Of course, as part of our normal lives we observe the people with whom we associate every day, noticing what they do and reacting to their behavior. Our impressions of people are continuously formed and modified by our observations. But these observations are casual, unsystematic, and undirected. If asked to document with specific instances our judgment that Helen is a leader in the group or that Henry is undependable, most of us would find it difficult to provide more than one or two concrete observations of actual behavior to back up our general impressions. In fact, people tend to categorize each other based on a small number of salient observations. On the other hand, observations must be organized, directed, and systematic if they are to yield dependable information about individuals.

It is appropriate at this point to note a distinction between the observational procedures that we are currently discussing and the rating procedures described in Chapter 12. In collecting systematic observations, the observer is required to function as an objective and mechanical recording instrument, whereas in the use of ratings, the rater must synthesize and integrate the evidence presented. With systematic observations, the function of the observer is strictly that of providing an accurate record of the number of social contracts, suggestions, aggressive acts, or whatever the behavioral category of interest is. The observer serves as a camera or recording device with enhanced flexibility and versatility. In ratings, however, the human instrument must judge, weigh, and interpret the information.

Systematic observational procedures have been most fully developed in connection with studies of young children. They seem particularly appropriate in this setting. Young children have not learned to camouflage or conceal their feelings as completely as have older individuals, so there is more to be learned from observing children. They also may be less able to tell us about themselves in words because they have not developed the self-knowledge or the verbal skills required. For these reasons, observational procedures have had their fullest development in the study of infants and young children.

Conducting the Systematic Observation

Extracting a meaningful, dependable, and relatively objective appraisal of some aspect of an individual's personality by observing a sample of behavior is far from easy. First, behavior flows continuously without any clear breaks. A preschooler is at the sand table making a "cake" at one moment, moves on to listen to the teacher talking to a group, and again moves on to build a house with the giant blocks. On the way, the child sits down for a short rest, takes a playful poke at some other child, and shouts to the teacher (or the world in general), "See me! See what I've made." But, this report is only partial. No verbal description can capture the full details of even 5 minutes of the life of an active child. What should be observed? What behaviors represent a personality attribute? When and for how long should observations be made? How should observers be trained? How should the observations be organized? We now turn our attention to these practical questions.

What Should Be Observed? If anything meaningful is to emerge from observing the complex flow of behavior, the observations must have some focus. We must be looking at something or for something—for indications of leadership, insecurity, sociability, emotional strain, energy level, aggressiveness, dependency, or indicators of several such personal attributes—and may have to look for all of them at the same time. The particular research or practical problem specifies what aspect or aspects of behavior should be observed, and the plan for observing follows from a definition of the aspects of behavior that will be relevant to the problem.

What Behaviors Represent a Personality Attribute? Even after an attribute to study has been selected a decision as to what behaviors will be acceptable indicators of that attribute still must be made. Consider the following behaviors:

Sitting alone
Kicking another child
Holding onto a teacher's hand or apparel
Calling attention to a mess on the floor
Tattling on another child
Volunteering information in a discussion

Which of these behaviors should be tallied as indicators of *dependency* in a kindergartener? What behaviors should be added? This type of decision must be made with knowledge of typical childhood behavior and the dynamics underlying it if the observational data are to have real meaning.

When and for How Long Should Observations Be Made? When a program of systematic observations is begun, decisions about where, when, and for how long each person is to be observed must be made. These decisions will reflect a compromise between the cost of extended observations and the need for a representative and reliable picture of the person. Because people and situations vary from day to day, it is generally preferable to have a number of relatively brief periods of observation on different days than to have only one or two long periods of observation. Under these conditions, the sample of the person's behavior will be more representative and the score we obtain will be more reliable. We must be careful not to make the observation too brief a sample of behavior, or it may be difficult to judge what a particular action signifies. Practical considerations such as travel time and the administrative tasks associated with the observation process also may limit the number of observations that we can make on a particular child or group.

To make the decision process more manageable, it might even be useful to break daily, 5-minute observation sessions into still shorter segments of, say, no more than 1 minute or even 30 seconds. The observation made can then consist of an indication of whether the behavior occurred. For instance, each child might be observed for ten 5-minute periods occurring on different days, each 5-minute period might be further subdivided into ten 30-second periods, in which observers would record whether the particular child did or did not exhibit any of a set of defined aggressive behaviors. Assuming that the observers decide to count only the number of observation periods in which children engaged in the target behavior, each child would receive a score, with a possible range from zero to 100, indicating the number of periods in which he or she engaged in aggressive acts. A somewhat different score would result if the number of aggressive acts were recorded in each period. In either case, such scores, based on an adequate number of short samples of observed behavior, have been found to show satisfactory reliability.

The interpretation of the reliability of behavioral observations can be somewhat misleading. Under these circumstances, reliability is often defined in terms of the agreement between two observers, and the size of the coefficient depends on the method used to determine the degree of agreement. The percentage of agreement, which reflects the percentage of times that two observers agree, tends to be inflated when the rate of the behavior is either very high or very low. When a behavior occurs often, it is likely that two observers will both record it and therefore will agree. Likewise, when a behavior hardly ever occurs it is likely that both observers will seldom report it and, again, will agree. Therefore, with a very high or low behavior rate, the reliability will always be high. Statistical techniques can be used to correct for this tendency, but they also have limitations (Foster, Bell-Dolan, & Burge, 1988).

Naturally, it is desirable to plan to make observations in settings where the target behavior is likely to occur. Observations of aggressive acts, for example, are better made during a period devoted to free play than during one devoted to listening to stories or watching television.

How Should Observers Be Trained?   Disagreements among observers can occur even when the behaviors have been carefully defined. In one extreme case, a researcher reported the rate of interobserver agreement on the gender of the teacher in classrooms where the observations were taking place to be 95%. To some extent, discrepancies are unavoidable because of fluctuations in attention and/or legitimate differences of opinion about whether a behavior occurred. Reliability can be increased, however, through training. Training sessions in which two or more observers make records based on the same sample of behavior, compare notes, discuss discrepancies, and reconcile differences provide a good means of increasing uniformity of observations. It can also be useful to have previously trained observers sit in on these sessions to offer suggestions. Such procedures can enhance both the uniformity of interpretation and observation and the placement of subjects into correct observation categories.

How Should Observations Be Organized?   It is of primary importance that the observations be recorded immediately after they are made. Recent research (Hyman & Loftus, in press) on the observations of witnesses recounting events that they have observed has shown that the errors and selectivity of memory can bias the reporting of even outstanding and unusual events. For the rather ordinary and highly repetitive events that are observed in watching a child in preschool, for example, an adequate account of what occurred is possible only if the behaviors are recorded immediately. There is so much to see, and one event is so much like others that relying on memory to provide an accurate after-the-fact account of a child's behavior is likely to lead to serious omissions and distortions of what really happened.

Any program of systematic observation must, therefore, provide a method for immediate and efficient recording of observed events. Many possibilities exist for facilitating recording of behavioral observations. One that has been widely used is a systematic code for the behavioral categories of interest. For example, preliminary observations might be made to define the range of aggressive acts that can be expected from 3- and 4-year-old children. Part of the code might be set up as follows:

h = hits
p = pushes
g = grabs materials from others
c = calls a nasty name

and so forth. A blank observation form can be prepared and divided to represent the time segments of the observations, and code entries can be made quickly while the child is observed almost without interruption.

If it is important for observers to record *who* did *what* to *whom,* a two- or three-part code—with the first symbol designating the actor, the second, the action, and the third, the person acted upon—can represent the information in detail. Obviously, with a recording scheme as complicated as this, it would be essential to train the observers well. Observers skilled in standard shorthand, of course, could take fuller notes of the observations. (Space would have to be provided on the form for such notes.) These notes would then be transcribed and coded or scored later.

Another effective approach is to videotape the scene being observed or make audiotape recordings of the observer's observations. These procedures provide a permanent record of the behaviors in a relatively complete form. The tapes can be analyzed at a later date, and ambiguous behavior can be examined repeatedly to obtain accurate observations.

Laptop computers also have promise for easier, more accurate recording of behavior. They can be programmed to accept a set of codes, or information can be entered on templates. Such a procedure can not only ease the burden on the observer and increase accuracy of the observations, but subsequent data analysis by computer is made much easier.

The most important consideration in organization decisions is to minimize the dependence on memory, to get a record that will preserve as much as possible of the significant detail in the original behavior, and to develop a recording procedure that will interfere as little as possible with the process of observing and the behavior being observed.

Advantages and Disadvantages of Systematic Observation

Systematic observations of behavior have a number of features that make them an attractive method for assessment of personality characteristics, but they have some significant limitations as well. We can summarize some of the advantages and disadvantages of direct observations as follows.

Advantages of Systematic Observation.   The most salient advantages of systematic observations are: (1) They provide a record of actual behavior, (2) they can be used in real-life situations, and (3) they can be used with young children.

1. *A Record of Actual Behavior.* When we observe an individual, we obtain a record of what that person *does* rather than rationalizations and protestations. If observational procedures have been well planned and observers carefully trained, the scores obtained will to a large degree be free from the biases and idiosyncrasies of the observers. A record of the behavior of individuals is not a reflection of what they think they are, or of what others think they are; their actions speak directly. If, as is so often the case, the primary concern is with changes in behavior, observations are the most direct and, in most cases, the most useful way of obtaining information. Also, as has been found with attitudes, what we say about ourselves, our beliefs, and our behavior often bears little relationship to what we will do when faced with a real-life situation. Direct observation of behavior avoids this filter, this source of invalidity.

2. *Useful in Real-Life Situations.* Observational techniques can be applied in the naturally occurring situations of life and are not restricted to laboratory settings. Observations can be carried out in the nursery school, in the classroom, in the cafeteria, on the playground, at camp, in the squadron day room, on the assembly line, or any place where individuals work or play. There are practical difficulties and limitations associated with observations, which we will discuss in a later section, but in spite of some disadvantages, direct observation is a widely applicable approach to studying individual personalities in a natural environment.

3. *Useful with Young Children.* As we have already noted, observational methods can be used with small children, no matter how young, with the youngest being the easiest to observe. Infants are not self-conscious, which makes it easy for the observer to sit and watch what they do without needing special procedures or precautions. Because the presence of the observer may change the social situation with older children and adults, it is sometimes necessary to screen the observer from the person being observed, perhaps by using a one-way vision screen. Of course, using this type of physical arrangement seriously restricts the type of setting in which observations may take place. It may be simpler and more effective to have the observer function unobtrusively and be present long enough for those being observed to ignore him or her, accepting the observer as a natural part of the surroundings.

The value of direct observation is greatest where its application is most feasible—with young children. Young children are limited in their ability to communicate through language, they have little experience or facility in analyzing or reporting their feelings or the reasons for their actions, and they are often shy with strangers.

For this group, systematic observation provides an important method of learning about personality.

Disadvantages of Systematic Observation.   In contrast to the positive aspects of observations as an information gathering technique, there are a number of factors that seriously limit the usefulness of observational methods. These limitations, or disadvantages, range from practical considerations, which we will consider first, to issues of theory.

1. *Cost of Making the Observations.* Observations are costly primarily because of the demands they make on the time of trained observers. In most applications, each individual must be observed for a number of periods, extending in some instances to several hours. When observations are made of a substantial number of individuals or a particular group, the hours rapidly add up. Therefore, systematic observation as well as recording of behavior are usually limited to research projects in which the necessary time commitments can be made. In routine school operations, it is seldom possible for teachers or counselors to find the resources needed to make direct observations of very many students. However, direct observation can provide useful information about single individuals who may be candidates for special services or other exceptional programs.

The cost of direct observation goes beyond the expenditure of time needed to record information. Any need for special settings or recording devices requires additional funds. Furthermore, when the original record is a running diary account or a videotape of an individual's or a group's actions, analysis of the record is likely to be time consuming, and thus costly.

2. *Problems in Fitting the Observer into the Setting.* There is always a concern about whether having an observer present, watching, and taking notes of what happens will actually change what happens. In many of the situations we wish to observe, it is not practical to have the observer hidden from view. We hope, with some justification, that after an initial period in which the presence of the observer is noticeably intrusive, the individuals being observed will gradually begin to ignore the presence of the observer. Getting subjects to ignore the observer may be easier in some situations than in others. When the group is small, when it is necessary for the observer to see the activities closely, or when the group meets for too short a time to get used to being observed, the members may not come to think of the observer as part of the normal environment.

3. *Difficulties in Eliminating Subjectivity and Bias.* It is necessary with observational procedures to take precautions to keep the observer's interpretations and biases out of the observations. The observer should not know much about the study being conducted, the experimental treatment the individual being observed is receiving, or the test scores or other facts about that individual, lest this knowledge affect the observer's perceptions. It is best for the observer to function as a neutral recording instrument that is sensitive to and makes a record of certain categories of behaviors. However, the observer is human. We can minimize subjectivity in the observations by careful training and by keeping the observer blind as to the purposes of the observations, but we cannot eliminate it. We must be aware of the role of the

observer in the final result, especially when the phenomena being studied are complex or involve an element of interpretation.

4. *Difficulties in Determining a Meaningful and Productive Set of Behavior Categories.* Observations are always selective; only certain limited aspects of an individual's behavior can be observed and recorded. Furthermore, if observations are to be treated quantitatively, they must be classified, grouped, and counted. Any system of classification is a somewhat arbitrary framework imposed on the infinitely varied events of life. It is not always easy to set up a framework that well serves the intended purposes. There will never be complete agreement about the categories of behavior used in a particular observation scheme or the types of activities included under a given heading. For one purpose, we might decide to classify aggressive acts in terms of overt behaviors like hitting, pushing, or grabbing. For other purposes, it might be better to note the precipitating event (if we can observe it): aggression in response to conflict over property, as a reaction to verbal disparagement, or after the thwarting of some activity in progress. In any event, scores based on observations of behavior can be no more significant and meaningful than the categories devised for recording and analyzing the behavior.

5. *Difficulties in Determining the Significance of Isolated Behavior.* To make the assessment reliable and objective, systematic observations usually focus on rather small and discrete acts or break the observations and analyses into small parts. There is a real danger here for the meaning of the behavior, the true significance of the action, to be lost. We observe a 3-year-old hugging another 3-year-old. Is this an act of aggression or affection? In isolation, we have no way of telling. Or, suppose that one child hits another. This behavior is obviously an aggressive act, but what does it signify in a child's life? Is it a healthy reaction to earlier domination by another child? Or is it a displaced aggression resulting from events occurring at home? Or does it signify something else? Or nothing? In such cases the meaning attached to the act must be considered tentative, to be confirmed or refuted by other information.

6. *The External Character of Observation.* Observations are external; that is, they focus only on what can be seen. Observations are not intended to inform us about internal states. The "outsideness" is exaggerated when little bits of behavior are analyzed out of context. But the outsideness is a fundamental feature of any observational approach to studying behavior. We always face the problem of determining the meaning of the behavior and must recognize that what we have before us is only what the individual does, not what it signifies.

SUMMARY

Although most instructional objectives and many behaviors of interest in psychological and educational research can be evaluated using conventional cognitive tests, there are circumstances in which other techniques must be used. Alternative methods are particularly important when performances, products, attitudes, or personality traits are assessed. When there is a choice, it is generally easier to assess products than to assess processes, but there are circumstances when the focus of assessment efforts must be on processes. Processes are usually evaluated either with checklists or with rating scales.

Checklists should include the following elements: (1) designation of the appropriate performance or product, (2) listing of the important behaviors and characteristics, (3) inclusion of common errors, and (4) placement of the list into an appropriate format. Rating scales are more effectively used with products than with processes because their use requires more time. With processes, there is usually much to evaluate and little time to do it.

Behavior in naturally occurring situations can best be assessed by systematic observations. To make systematic observation more effective, the following questions must be answered: What should be observed? What behaviors represent a personality attribute? When and for how long should observations be made? How should observers be trained? How should the observations be organized?

Systematic observation has the advantages of (1) representing actual behavior, (2) being applicable to real-life situations, and (3) being usable with young children and others with whom verbal communication is difficult. However, observational procedures present a number of problems and thus have the following disadvantages: (1) cost of making the observations, (2) problems in fitting the observer into the setting, (3) difficulties in eliminating subjectivity and bias, (4) difficulties in determining a meaningful and productive set of behavior categories, (5) difficulties in determining the significance of isolated behavior, and (6) the external character of observation.

QUESTIONS AND EXERCISES

1. Consider the following objectives from a general science class at a junior high school. Specify the most appropriate type of assessment: paper-and-pencil test, process evaluation, or product evaluation. Provide a justification for your selection. Each student will:

   a. prepare a project for the science fair.

   b. demonstrate a knowledge of the taxonomic classification of vertebrates.

   c. conduct a successful titration experiment.

   d. make a presentation on one local threat to the ecology.

2. Construct a checklist that would be appropriate for judging a science fair project.

3. Construct a rating scale that could be used to evaluate performance in a unit on softball in a physical education class.

4. Design a behavior test to measure a personality trait desired of students in music appreciation class.

5. How could a classroom discussion serve as the basis for systematic observation? Make a plan for recording these observations.

6. In a research study, you propose to use systematic observations of school children as a method of studying their social adjustment. What problems would you encounter? What precautions would you need to take in interpreting the results?

7. What advantages do systematic observations have over the observations of everyday life?

SUGGESTED READINGS

Barrios, B. A. (1988). On the changing nature of behavioral assessment. In A. S. Bellack & M. Hershon (Eds.), *Behavioral assessment: A practical handbook* (pp. 3–41). New York: Pergamon.

Berk, R. A. (Ed.). (1986). *Performance assessment: Methods and applications.* Baltimore: Johns Hopkins University Press.

Evertson, C. M. (1986). Observation as inquiry and method. In M. C. Witrock (Ed.), *Handbook of research on teaching* (pp. 162–213). New York: Macmillan.

Finch, F. L. (Ed.). (1991). *Educational performance assessment.* Chicago: Riverside.

Fitzpatrick, R., & Morrison E. J. (1971). Performance and product evaluation. In R. L. Thorndike (Ed.), *Educational measurement* (pp. 237–270). Washington, DC: American Council on Education.

Foster, S. L., Bell-Dolan, D. J., & Burge, D. A. (1988). Behavioral observation. In A. S. Bellack & M. Hershon (Eds.), *Behavioral assessment: A practical handbook* (pp. 119–160). New York: Pergamon.

Hyman, I. E., & Loftus, E. F. (in press). Memory: Modern conceptions of the vicissitudes of early childhood memories. In D. A. Halperin (Ed.), *False memory syndrome: Theraputic and forensic perspectives.* New York: American Psychiatric Press.

Kubiszyn, T., & Borich, G. (1987). *Educational testing and measurement.* Glenview, IL: Scott, Foresman and Company.

Nitko, A. J. (1984). Defining 'criterion-referenced test.' In R. Berk (Ed.), *A guide to criterion-referenced test construction* (pp. 8–28). Baltimore: Johns Hopkins University Press.

Sax, G. (1989). *Principles of educational and psychological measurement and evaluation.* Belmont, CA: Wadsworth.

CHAPTER 11

Interests, Personality, and Adjustment

INTRODUCTION

We turn now to published instruments and procedures that assess interest, personality, and personal adjustment. Our focus shifts from what a person is capable of doing, with best effort, to what that person is likely to do under the day-to-day circumstances of living. Most people have a lot of curiosity about personality and interest tests, because such tests can be used to help them understand themselves and make better decisions. For example, interest tests provide information that can be very valuable to those making career choices, because knowledge about their individual pattern of interests helps them identify career options and opportunities that are most compatible with their lifestyles and goals.

Self-understanding is of such importance to most of us that we can be very uncritical of this type of test. The same person who is very skeptical of tests of cognitive ability—including those instruments that have been developed in accordance with the highest standards of test construction—is often quite willing to accept the results of a personality test that might have been developed without consideration for these standards. For this reason we want to emphasize that while tests of interest and personality can be very useful for their intended purposes, this is only true when the tests have been carefully constructed and standardized and then are used only within the limits prescribed by the test developer.

Interest tests provide information about a person's general pattern of likes and dislikes. People vary considerably in this regard. For example, when two individuals are given choices about how to spend free time, one might choose to sit quietly and read, while the other would choose to be outside engaged in some type of physical activity. What would you choose? Do you prefer to work on projects as part of a team, or do you prefer to work independently? Would you rather visit a flower shop or an amusement park? Would you rather attend the opera or a rock concert? It is easy to see how these preferences might influence career satisfaction. The more we are able to engage in tasks that we like, the greater will be our overall satisfaction with our work situation.

Personality tests are designed to assess the constellation of personal characteristics that are unique to each individual. In some cases, these assessments are quite global and are intended to paint a broad picture of what an individual is like. Other personality tests are designed to measure more specific characteristics, such as the extent to which an individual may be characterized as introverted or extroverted. Measures of adjustment assess the extent to which an individual's personal characteristics may be considered adaptive. Certain personality characteristics, such as the ability to deal effectively with feelings of anger, are associated with psychological health and good adjustment, while other characteristics, such as deeply imbedded feelings of mistrust or suspicion, are associated with psychological disturbance. In this chapter we will discuss three of the major interest tests, as well as several tests of personality and adjustment. We will then examine some of the special problems in the assessment of personality and interest. We will conclude by examining the uses of computerized scoring and interpretation for interest and personality tests.

The various measures of personality and interest are designed to serve different purposes and may be used in very different ways. Three general uses for tests include research, self exploration, and clinical decision-making. Personality tests that are used primarily for research purposes are often designed to provide information on specific personality characteristics, either as a measure of change in response to some experimental manipulation or as a basis for comparison across groups of individuals. Furthermore, in research situations tests often stand alone and are not used in conjunction with other instruments or interviews. Personality tests that are used primarily for self-exploration usually provide information on more global characteristics or interest patterns. While many of the tests used for self-exploration are designed in such a way that they can be scored and interpreted by the examinee alone, they are most effective when combined with an interview and feedback from a trained counselor, skilled in the interpretation of the particular instrument(s) involved. Finally, personality tests play an important role in clinical decision-making and may include both diagnostic and treatment decisions. In such situations, it is extremely important that the tests be utilized in conjunction with a thorough clinical interview and client history. The test then becomes part of the process of clinical assessment that begins with data collection and proceeds through to construction of a treatment plan.

INTEREST MEASUREMENT

Strong Interest Inventory

The Strong Interest Inventory (SII) is the current version of an instrument originally developed by E. K. Strong and first published in 1927 as the Strong Vocational Interest Blank (SVIB). A major revision of the SVIB was published in 1974 under the title Strong-Campbell Interest Inventory (SCII). With the next major revision in 1985, the name was changed to the Strong Interest Inventory. This name was retained for the most recent revision, completed in 1994. The significant revisions of the instruments over the years reflect the belief by Strong that psychological instruments must be updated to retain their quality and usefulness. That point of view is certainly supported, for the Strong remains one of the most respected of all of the available interest inventories.

The underlying principle that has guided the development of all of the Strong instruments is the idea that people who are satisfied within a given occupation share a pattern of interests that differentiates them from individuals in other occupations. Determining how closely an individual's interests match the distinctive pattern of persons in a specific occupation should be a predictor of how content a person would be in that occupation and even, to some extent, whether the person would actually enter and stay in the occupation.

The Strong Interest Inventory, which follows quite closely the design of the original SVIB, is made up of 317 items that are presented in three different formats. Most of the test utilizes a format that requires the examinee to respond to items by selecting *L* (Like), *I* (Indifferent), or *D* (Dislike). Items include occupations (florist, surgeon, editor), school subjects (chemistry, physical education), activities (repairing a clock, meeting and directing people), leisure activities (boxing, skiing, entertaining others), and types of people (ballet dancers, babies, prominent business leaders). In the second format, examinees identify their preferences between two general activities (taking a chance vs. playing it safe), and activities in the world of work (ideas vs. things). In the third format, examinees are asked to indicate whether or not they believe certain personal characteristics are typical of themselves (stimulate the ambitions of my associates or enjoy tinkering with small hand tools).

Considering that the Strong takes only about 30 to 45 minutes to complete, it provides a considerable amount of information for the examinee. Scores are reported in five main forms, including the Occupations Scales, General Occupational Themes,

Basic Interest Scales, Personal Style Scales, and Administrative Indexes. The score report is organized to encourage the examinee to observe overall trends in personal interest and to note how these trends are related to the world of work.

Occupational Scales.   The original type of score developed by Strong is the Occupational Scale (OS). This score has appeared in every version of the Strong and has been updated with each revision. This is the score that provides information about how closely the examinee's pattern of responses matches that of people in a specific occupation. The scoring key for an occupation such as, for example, chemist, was developed by administering the inventory to several hundred employed chemists who met certain standards, including length of employment and stated satisfaction with and success in the occupation. For each item, the percentage of chemists who indicated liking (or disliking) the topic or activity was compared with the percentage making that choice among a large group of *people in general* assembled from many different occupations. If the two percentages differed substantially, the item was scored in the key for chemist. A person's raw score on the chemist scale would be the number of items on which he or she responded the way typical chemists did. The raw score would then be converted to a standard score in which the mean of the occupational group (chemist in this example) was set at 50 and the standard deviation, at 10. For purposes of interpretation, the standard scores are represented on the report form along a range of similarity, with scores of 40 or above indicating that the individual shares the likes and dislikes of persons within the occupation, scores of 30 to 39 indicating that the person shares *some* of the likes or dislikes of persons within the occupation, and scores of 29 or below indicating that the person shares *few* likes and dislikes with persons in the occupation. Persons with scores of 40 or above would probably enjoy the daily activities of the occupation, while those with scores below 29 would probably not enjoy the work of the occupation.

The 1994 Strong contains a total of 211 Occupational Scales. This includes 102 pairs of separate scales for men and women (204 scales). Separate scales for men and women are necessary because it has been determined that men and women within the same occupation do not necessarily display the same pattern of interests. An additional seven scales are included that represent only one gender. These scales represent occupations that are dominated by one gender or the other, such as child care worker (women) and plumber (men). For these occupations it is extremely difficult to obtain adequate samples for both genders. The *Applications and Technical Guide* for the Strong Interest Inventory (Harmon, Hansen, Borgen, & Hammer, 1994) provides detailed information about the nature of the sample for each occupational group.

The occupational scoring keys of the Strong are examples of a strictly empirical, atheoretical approach to interest assessment. The original pool of items was assembled with no clear rationale other than to include a wide range of stimuli that would be likely to elicit "liking" in some people and "disliking" in others. The scoring keys were developed solely on the basis of group differences, with no psychological constructs in mind as to what the specific occupations represented. This method of key development is often referred to as *empirical scale construction*. The sample from each occupation was quite large, typically over 200, so that the scoring keys are unlikely to include many items that just happened to differentiate in that particular sample of cases. Each score tells how similar an individual's interest pattern is to that typical of individuals in a specific occupation. But it is not easy to tell what an individual is like from the fact that she received a 45 on the scale for chemist (female). What sort of individuals' interests are similar to those of female chemists? What are female chemists like anyhow? Of course, the Strong provides a score not just for chemist but also for numerous other occupations. Quite early in the history of the SVIB, the author provided data on the correlations between the scales, finding that some of these correlations were decidedly high. Correlations for one group of science-related scales are shown here.

Job Title	1	2	3	4	5	6
1 Psychologist		.77	.72	.40	.71	.74
2 Mathematician	.77		.91	.66	.80	.72
3 Physicist	.72	.91		.85	.93	.78
4 Engineer	.40	.66	.85		.88	.52
5 Chemist	.71	.80	.93	.88		.73
6 Physician	.74	.72	.78	.52	.73	

The finding of correlations such as these encouraged grouping the scales into clusters and paying attention to the scores of an individual for all the scales in a cluster rather than to those for single, isolated occupations. The cluster "physical scientist" may carry somewhat more breadth of meaning than "chemist" considered by itself, especially since the scales in the "physical scientist" cluster all tend to show negative correlations with scales in the "sales" cluster. The pattern of an individual's high and low values on a scale in relation to the occupational clusters begins to generate a psychological as well as a vocational picture of that individual. However, the correlations between the scales of the Strong inventories are difficult to interpret for two reasons. First, scales in an occupational cluster are likely to include the same items, scored in the same direction. Likewise, scales in different clusters may well include some of the same items but which are scored in opposite directions. This situation is quite a different matter from what we had in the case of a high correlation between two ability tests that included different items. The chemist and physicist scales are alike because, for some reason, the chemist and physicist reference groups responded in a similar way to the rather small set of statements that compose the Strong. The scales for other occupational groups show negative correlations because they include some of the same items, but the items are keyed in opposite directions because the members of one reference group marked "like" and the other marked "dislike."

A second confounding feature of correlations between scales on the Strong is that many people tend to mark "like" to roughly the same number of items. There is no profound meaning to be drawn from this, but it has the consequence, for purely statistical reasons, of making many of the correlations between scales negative. Thus, it would be unwise to attempt to draw substantive conclusions about the nature of interests as constructs from the fact that many of the scales for dissimilar occupations are negatively correlated.

The Occupational Scales are most useful for persons who are relatively close to making a career choice. Persons who are still in the stage of career exploration would likely obtain more valuable information from the next two types of scores provided by the Strong, the General Occupational Themes and Basic Interest Scales.

General Occupational Themes.   The second type of information contained in the Strong is found in the section known as the General Occupational Themes (GOT). The themes represent a focused attempt to give psychological meaning to expressions of like and dislike for occupations and is directly derived from the work of John Holland (1985). Growing out of his experience with the SVIB and reviews of previous factor-analytic studies of interests, Holland concluded that there are six foci, or themes, of vocational interest that represent six different types of individuals and six types of work environments. He labeled them as realistic, investigative, artistic, social, enterprising, and conventional. Holland felt that the salience of one or more of these themes in an individual could be identified through the individual's expressed likes and dislikes for occupations. Starting with his a priori rational analysis, he assembled clusters of occupations to represent each focus. He refined the clusters through analysis of the correlations of single occupations with cluster scores in their own and the other clusters until cluster scores were developed that showed reasonably high reliability, both internal consistency and stability over time, and that were largely unrelated to one another. The foci were visualized as the apexes of a hexagon, as shown in Figure 11.1. The numbers on the hexagon represent the correlations between the occupational themes for the 1994 Strong Interest Inventory. The correlations tend to confirm the hexagonal structure in that the larger correlations tend to be between adjacent foci. Most of the correlations in the table are quite low, indicating that each of the six scores provides new information about an examinee.

Holland viewed his six foci as a way of representing not merely groups of occupations, but also patterns of personality. Support for this view was gathered from an analysis of terms used to describe individuals high on each of the six foci. Some of the frequently mentioned descriptors are listed below.

Realistic	*Investigative*	*Artistic*
robust	task oriented	expressive
rugged	introspective	original
practical	analytical	intuitive
strong	curious	creative
athletic	independent	nonconforming
mechanical	reserved	introspective
direct	unconventional	independent
persistent	intellectual	aggressive

Social	*Enterprising*	*Conventional*
sociable	aggressive	conscientious
responsible	popular	efficient
humanistic	self-confident	obedient
group oriented	cheerful	calm
understanding	sociable	orderly
idealistic	energetic	practical
helpful	verbal	possession and status oriented
	power and status oriented	

Figure 11.1

Holland occupational themes and correlations between themes for 1994 Strong.

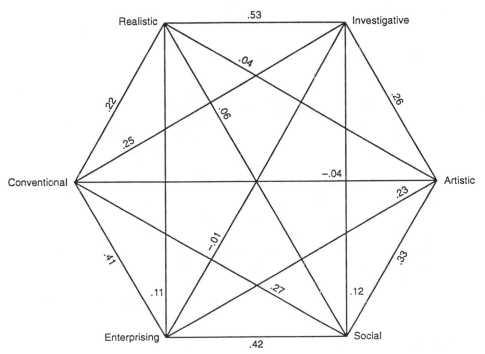

Source: Reproduced by special permission of the distributor, Consulting Psychologists Press, Inc., Palo Alto, CA, for the publisher, Stanford University Press, from the Strong Interest Inventory, Form T317 of the Strong Vocational Interest Blanks. Copyright 1933, 1938, 1945, 1946, 1966, 1968, 1974, 1981, 1985 and 1994 by the Board of Trustees of Leland Stanford Junior University.

Because the themes represent types of people, it is possible to describe individuals in general ways. *Realistic* individuals prefer to be involved in working outdoors and in building and/or repairing. Sample realistic occupations include auto mechanic, gardener, plumber, police officer and rancher. Those who score high on the *investigative* theme enjoy forms of inquiry and like to analyze problems and do research. Sample occupations include college professor, physician, and psychologist. *Artistic* individuals enjoy creative activity including drama, music, writing, and art. Associated occupations include artist, lawyer, librarian, and reporter. Those with high scores on the *social* theme prefer activities that involve care giving and instruction. Occupations include child care provider and public health nurse. The *enterprising* theme is associated with the activities of selling, managing, and persuading. Enterprising occupations include realtor and traveling salesperson. The *conventional* theme incorporates the activities of accounting, organizing, and processing data. These individuals especially like activities that require accuracy and attention to detail, and their occupations include bookkeeper and clerical worker. While the six themes are meant to represent types of people, it is important to emphasize that few individuals represent pure types. That is, most people have interests that reflect two or more of the general themes, and this will be represented in the score profile for each individual. For example, an individual might obtain relatively high scores on both the social and enterprising themes. Examples of associated occupations for the individual with such an interest pattern include high school counselor and parks and recreation coordinator.

In an ambitious tour de force, Gottfredson and Holland (1989) have classified all 12,860 occupations from the *Dictionary of Occupational Titles* (*DOT*) (U.S. Department of Labor, 1977, 1986) according to where each belongs in the Holland system. The classification was developed on the basis of the job analyses that had been carried out by the U.S. Employment Service on the full range of DOT occupations. This represents an impressive attempt to provide an extended catalog of occupations appropriate for individuals who display a certain profile on Holland's general occupational themes.

Because of the great overlap in item content between the older SVIB and subsequent instruments, it was quite easy to incorporate the Holland structure in the scoring and interpretation of the SCII. Scores for the six general occupational themes were first added to the Strong in 1974, supplementing the scores for the specific occupations. Moreover, in the report form provided to counselors and clients, separate occupations are grouped according to the theme or themes considered to be salient for the occupation. Thus, the user is provided with the empirically based occupation scores, arranged according to the general themes, as well as the theme scores themselves.

Basic Interest Scales.   Scores of still a third type are also provided. The Basic Interest Scales (BIS) may be best understood as subdivisions of the General Occupational Themes. First introduced in the 1960s, the scales were significantly revised and updated for the 1994 revision of the Strong. There are 25 Basic Interest Scales, each composed of a set of homogeneous items. The items are homogeneous both in manifest content and in the statistical sense, since the items entering into a given scale all have substantial correlations with each of the other items in that scale. The BISs were derived directly from the items of the Strong, using only statistical criteria and without reference to any theory. They address more specific vocational themes than do the themes of Holland's model, but they are broader in content than the occupational scales and reflect some of the high correlations of those scales. Table 11.1 lists the Basic Interest Scales and shows the association for each to the General Occupation Themes.

Personal Style Scales.   The fourth type of information contained in the Strong score profile is the Personal Style Scales. There are four scales, each of which reflects preferences for broad styles of living and working. New to the Strong in 1994, the scales include Work Style, Learning Environment, Leadership Style, and Risk Taking/Adventure. Scores are reported on the profile form in a similar manner to the occupational themes and interest scales. However, they are constructed as bipolar scales and reported as a preference for both the left and right pole of the scale. Table 11.2 provides summary definitions for the right and left pole of each scale.

Table 11.1
Basic Interest Scales and General Occupational Themes

Realistic	Investigative	Artistic	Social	Enterprising	Conventional
agriculture	science	music/dramatics	teaching	public speaking	data management
nature	mathematics	art	social service	law/politics	computer activities
military activities	medical science	applied arts	medical service	merchandising	office services
athletics		writing	religious activities	sales	
mechanical activities		culinary arts		organizational management	

Administrative Indexes. The fifth type of information provided on the Strong profile sheet is the Administrative Indexes. Of most use to the counselor as an interpretive aid for the profile, these indexes provide statistical information about the examinee's responses, including the total number of responses, percentages of "like," "indifferent," and "dislike" responses, and the total number of infrequent responses. The indexes are most useful as a preliminary check on the validity of the individual test administration and scoring, but also have some interpretive value within the framework of the individual examinee's overall profile of scores.

When interpreting the Strong Interest Inventory, the counselor and the counselee are encouraged to proceed from the quite broad and theory-based occupational themes through the content-based homogeneous basic interest scores to the empirically determined scales for specific occupations. The instrument is now eclectic in the foundations on which its scoring systems have been based and comprehensive in the information that it provides.

A sample page from the Strong profile form is shown in Figure 11.2. The form itself contains several parts, beginning with a "snapshot" (Figure 11.2) that provides summary information on the General Occupational Themes, Basic Interest Scales, and Occupational Scales. The check marks on the form highlight the examinee's performance. Increasing detail is provided on the remaining pages of the form, including

Table 11.2
Brief Definitions of Poles for the Personal Style Scales

Personal Style Scale	Left Pole	Right Pole
Work Style	Works with ideas/data/things	Works with people
Learning Environment	Practical	Academic
Leadership Style	Leads by example	Directs others
Risk Taking/Adventure	Plays it safe	Takes chances

Figure 11.2
Sample profile form for a college student choosing a major—Strong Interest Inventory.

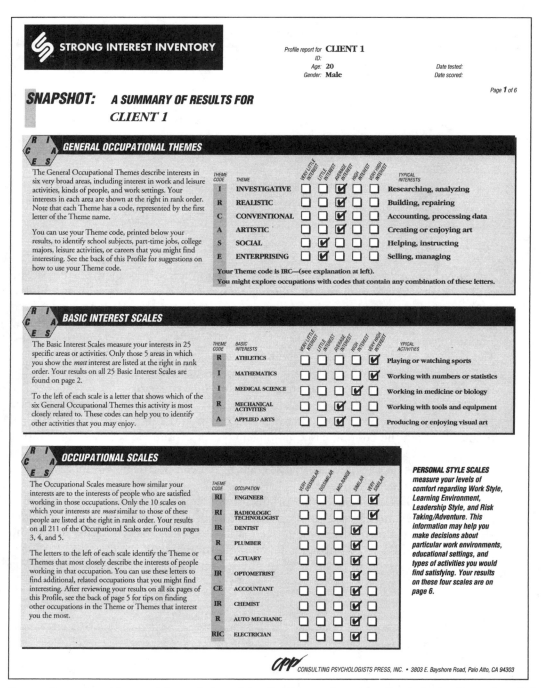

Source: Reproduced by special permission of the distributor, Consulting Psychologists Press, Inc., Palo Alto, CA, for the publisher, Stanford University Press, from the Strong Interest Inventory, Form T317 of the Strong Vocational Interest Blanks. Copyright 1933, 1938, 1945, 1946, 1966, 1968, 1974, 1981, 1985 and 1994 by the Board of Trustees of Leland Stanford Junior University.

316

more information about the General Occupational Themes and Basic Interest Scales. The complete profile also provides results for the Personal Style Scales and Summary of Item Responses.

We turn now to the reliability and validity of Strong Interest Inventory scores. The evidence reported on reliability consists primarily of test-retest correlations over various time intervals. The manual for the 1985 Strong reports average values as shown here for the three types of scores:

	Test-Retest Interval		
Scale	2 Weeks	30 Days	3 Years
GOT	.91	.86	.81
BIS	.91	.88	.82
OS	.91	.89	.87

All three types of scales show reasonable stability, although over the longer time period, the scales for specific occupations (OS) held up somewhat better than the others. Test-retest reliability information that is currently available for the 1994 Strong is limited to periods of 3 months. Comparisons with the data for the 1985 Strong suggest that the instrument has retained its reliability and may have even been slightly improved for some scales. Studies of the original SVIB provide information on stability of the occupational scales over extended periods of time, as well as some indication of the relationship of stability to examinee age at the time of original testing. The data are summarized from the manual (Hansen & Campbell, 1985) in Table 11.3.

The data indicate that interests become increasingly stable during adolescence and early adulthood and that, as one might expect, shifts are more common over longer intervals, though there is still a substantial core of consistency over even the longest intervals.

It is not entirely clear what a prospective user should seek as evidence of the validity of an interest inventory. First, he or she can inquire into the meaningfulness of

Table 11.3
Long-Term Stability of the Strong Interest Inventory

Age at First Testing	Test-Retest Interval					
	2 Weeks	1 Year	2–5 Years	6–10 Years	11–20 Years	20+ Years
17–18		.80	.70	.65	.64	
19–21	.91	.80	.73	.67	.67	.64
22–25			.78	.69	.75	.72
25+			.77	.81	.80	

Note: No data exist for time spaces where cells are blank.

the constructs on which the inventory is based. For the occupational scales, the case has rested in large part on the effectiveness of the scales in differentiating members of a specific occupation from the broad reference group of people in general (concurrent validity). Although the situation varies somewhat from one occupation to another because some occupational groups are more distinctive than others, a rough but reasonably accurate overall summary would be that approximately 10% of people in general would be rated "high" or "very high" on an occupational scale, in comparison with 65% to 70% of those people actually in the occupation.

The meaningfulness of the constructs implied by Holland's six general occupational themes lies in the manner in which each relates to a number of occupational scales, to item content areas expressed in the basic interest scales, and to characterizations of people rated high on each of the six themes. Of special interest in the appraisal of the validity of interest measures is the effectiveness of such measures as predictors of subsequent occupational histories (predictive validity). What percentage of individuals end up in occupations for which their inventory scores indicated high or very high interest? Serious problems arise in estimating congruence between actual occupation entered and interest scale scores, because of the thousands of specific occupations and the limited number of scales of the SVIB and the SII. In spite of these problems, however, studies by different investigators are in reasonably good agreement that about 50% of individuals end up in occupations consistent with their interests expressed at about 20 years of age. This agreement certainly represents a substantial relationship and, in view of the many life factors in addition to interest that can influence an individual's choice of occupation, can be considered evidence of rather good predictive validity for the instrument.

Career Assessment Inventory

A criticism of the Strong inventory concerns the instrument's focus upon primarily professional occupations, making it less useful for individuals who are interested in occupations that do not rely on completion of a college degree. The Career Assessment Inventory (CAI) was developed by Charles Johansson (Johansson, 1991) in order to fill this gap. Frankly modeled on the Strong, the CAI provides scores on Holland's six general occupational themes, 22 basic interest scales, and 91 occupational scales, varying widely in type and level (truck driver, school teacher, tool/die maker, nurse, etc.). A unique feature of the CAI, however, is that scores are not reported separately for males and females. Only items valid for both genders were included in the scale construction, in an effort to encourage freer access of both males and females into desired occupations. While this more gender-neutral perspective is valuable, many of the occupational samples on which the keys are based were relatively small. This is a matter of concern in assessing the validity of the instrument, particularly when judging it against the Strong and its sample sizes. However, the CAI (especially the vocational version) has been demonstrated to be a useful instrument for assessing vocational interest, particularly for non-college-bound high school students or adults who are seeking immediate job entry.

Self-Directed Search

John Holland (1973, 1985) developed the Self-Directed Search (SDS) as a self-scoring tool that individuals could use to classify themselves according to the six personality types or occupational themes (realistic, artistic, investigative, conventional, social, and enterprising) and to assist themselves in career exploration and vocational choice. Most recently revised in 1994, the instrument itself consists of two booklets, the assessment booklet and the occupations finder, and can be completed in approximately 40 to 50 minutes. The assessment booklet provides the individual the opportunity to list occupational daydreams, to consider preferred activities and competencies, and to obtain scores on the six occupational themes. The scores on the three highest themes are used to develop a summary code. For example, an individual who scores highest on the artistic theme, followed by social and investigative, would receive the summary code ASI. Turning to the occupations finder booklet, the person would find a list of occupations associated with that particular code. In the case of the ASI summary code, the list includes artist, instrumental musician, ceramic restorer, and television technician. The finder includes 1,335 occupations, each of which has been classified according to the Holland codes. The individual is then encouraged to further investigate the occupations that align with the particular three-letter summary code.

The unique feature of the SDS, as its name implies, is that it is designed to be used for career exploration without the aid of a career counselor. The booklets are self-explanatory so that individuals can complete, score, and interpret the instrument on their own. While usually completed independently, the SDS can be used in small groups. For example, a high school teacher might choose to use the SDS with a class as part of a curriculum unit on career exploration. While designed to be used independently, the instrument can also provide valuable information for a career counseling interview, and many career counselors incorporate it as part of the career counseling process. Counselor assistance in interpretation of the scores is particularly important for adolescents, who often need to be encouraged to think more broadly about career choices and opportunities.

PERSONALITY ASSESSMENT

We all want to understand the people in our lives. It is not surprising that psychologists and educators also want to identify and measure human characteristics that help predict or explain behavior over time and across situations. Professionals who work in the area of personality assessment try to develop explicit theories about the nature of personality and use formalized measurement instruments in order to make more valid predictions about people. Techniques for personality assessment have become more sophisticated during recent decades, but professionals have not yet arrived at a consensus regarding the nature of personality.

We approach our discussion of instruments to assess personality by examining instruments developed within the context of each of four theoretical approaches to understanding personality. *Dynamic theories* describe components of personality, such as Freud's id, ego, and superego. Dynamic approaches assume that important components of personality are outside of consciousness and, therefore, must be measured in ways that circumvent awareness. *Trait approaches* assume that a finite set of human attributes account for the important differences between people. Traits are most commonly assessed with paper-and-pencil instruments. The test authors select questions and statements they believe to measure the trait or traits of interest. Some trait tests take the process a step further by grouping people who have similar patterns of traits into categories or types. *Humanistic approaches* focus on the manner in which individuals define and evaluate themselves, their self-concept. Self-concept tests invite examinees to rate themselves and their level of self-satisfaction. Finally, *behavioral theories* have challenged our thinking about the very nature of personality by questioning the existence of internal, or intrinsic, characteristics. In these theories, environmental or situational influences are seen as the determinants of behavior, and individual differences are attributed to the learned pattern of behaviors that each person develops to deal with the world.

The assessment of personality is further complicated by the need to distinguish between typical personality development and the development of characteristics or patterns that are associated with social, emotional, and psychological problems. Of course, each approach to personality has a somewhat different take on what constitutes maladjustment and how it might be measured.

Dynamic Approaches

Dynamic approaches to personality measurement rely upon the *projective hypothesis*, the assumption that we cannot help but reveal our core concerns and conflicts with our every perception and action. Our defenses, the strategies that we use to protect ourselves from an awareness of our fears and conflicts, presumably prevent us from seeing the constant trail of clues we leave. Projective techniques have been developed by psychoanalysts in their attempt to read the clues and understand unconscious processes. Test authors thought that more ambiguous tasks or situations would require even more self-projection and, thereby, lead to greater insight into the unconscious.

Rorschach Inkblot Test.   The best known projective technique is Hermann Rorschach's inkblot test. Rorschach constructed a large number of inkblots by placing ink on each piece of paper, folding it in the middle and pressing the two halves together to produce a symmetrical pattern. He selected 10 patterns that he found to be most evocative, based upon informal trials. In Rorschach tests, the examinee, or more likely the patient, is asked to look at each inkblot in sequence and report what the blot might be or what it might represent. The task is not unlike the childhood game of looking at clouds and imagining them as objects, animals, people, or whole scenes or enactments. Look at the sample inkblot shown in Figure 11.3, and list some things that it might represent.

Figure 11.3
An image like those used on the Rorschach.

After completing all 10 cards, the examiner asks the patient about the physical characteristics of the card that stimulated each response. The clinician takes notes that document everything the patient says and does during the administration. Administration of the Rorschach Inkblot Test may take as little as 10 minutes, but the scoring and interpretation of the test is an arduous task that requires extensive training and a protracted period of time for each protocol. Notes for each response are meticulously analyzed. What part of the card (whole? parts?) did the patient focus upon? What physical characteristics of the blot (i.e., shape, shading, color) were important in the formulation of the response? Was the response a typical, original, or unusual perception? How long did it take for the patient to verbalize the response? What kind of content (i.e., human, animal, body parts, geography, architecture, etc.) was included? Look at the sample inkblot again, and analyze your associations. Do you believe they reveal something about your personality? How would you expect someone who is depressed, anxious, or psychotic to respond differently?

In the end a large number of scores and ratios between scores are summarized and analyzed. The analysis and interpretation are guided to some extent by comparing scores to established norms, but a major factor in the final interpretation rests with the clinician.

There are many marvelous stories about skilled Rorschach examiners who diagnosed brain lesions that had been missed by medical tests or insightfully unraveled the dynamics of a perplexing case. Unfortunately, the typical clinician has produced less spectacular results. Clinicians often arrive at discrepant or even contradictory conclusions from the same set of patient responses. The situation is further complicated by a variety of competing systems for scoring the test. The Rorschach was one of the most widely used clinical instruments until the 1970s when psychometric investigations produced such poor results that the popularity of Rorschach's test declined precipitously. A renewed interest in the test is due largely to the efforts of John Exner and his colleagues.

Exner (Exner & Exner, 1972) concluded that the existing scoring systems were so muddled that most clinicians relied primarily upon their subjective impressions to interpret the test. He set out to better standardize the administration process and formalize the scoring system by integrating the best features of the existing systems. Exner culled through the many scores described above and retained only those that achieved a .85 or greater interrater reliability coefficient (Exner, 1974). The product was a new system that has been widely adopted by Rorschach users. However, the Rorschach remains something of a psychometric conundrum. There is no overall score to summarize the large array of subscores and ratios. This fact makes it very difficult to evaluate the overall test-retest consistency of the instrument. Evaluations of the many subscores produce the entire gamut of reliability coefficients depending upon the particular subscore, the interval from first to second administration, and the characteristics of the sample tested (Exner, 1986).

The validity of the Rorschach is even more difficult to assess. The best evidence for validity comes from discriminate studies that use the Rorschach to blindly identify protocols obtained from normal and clinically diagnosed individuals. Parker's (1983) meta-analysis of discriminate studies found validity coefficients in the moderate range. However, the coefficients may be an overestimate of the test's discriminative power in that the responses from very disturbed individuals may be so unusual or bizarre that a test would not really be necessary to identify their condition. Indeed, the scoring system of the Rorschach appears to be best at identifying cases of schizophrenia, in part because individuals with this condition are recognized by their highly unusual responses (Vincent & Harman, 1991). In addition, the Rorschach has not demonstrated good predictive validity. For example, it is not a good indicator of response to treatment or eventual level of functioning (Groth-Marnat, 1990).

Thematic Apperception Test.   The Thematic Apperception Test (TAT) is another popular projective test that was developed by Henry Murray (1943). Murray developed a psychodynamic theory of personality based upon a list of 28 needs, such as dominance, achievement, aggression, nurturance, and sex. He selected a set of black and white drawings and photographs to be used as stimulus cards. The pieces were chosen for their dramatic, yet ambiguous, content. Murray asked examinees to make up stories about the stimulus cards. He believed that the storytellers would reveal their own needs or drives through the stories that they created.

Standardized procedures call for administering 20 cards during each of two sessions on successive days. The instructions present the test as a measure of imagination. Examinees are told that they will be shown a series of pictures and that they are, in turn, to make up a dramatic story about each picture. The story is to include a beginning; a description of what is currently happening in the picture; a description of what the characters in the story might think or feel; and how the story will end. Examine the sample TAT card found in Figure 11.4, and construct a brief story according to those instructions.

Figure 11.4
Sample TAT card.

Murray believed that examinees would unconsciously project their own lives into the characters they created such that ". . . before he knows it, he has said things about an invented character that apply to himself, things which he would have been reluctant to confess in response to a direct question. As a rule the subject leaves the test happily unaware that he has presented the psychologist with what amounts to an X-ray picture of his inner self." (1943, p. 1) Special attention is paid to the hero(ine) of each story. The stories are analyzed to identify the needs and feelings expressed by the hero(ine) (i.e., achievement, jealousy, nurturance, aggression); aspects of the physical and social environment that either frustrate or aid need gratification; the type of endings or outcomes that the stories include (optimistic, pessimistic, realistic, wishful); and common themes that reappear across stories. Analyze your story by identifying the hero(ine) and examining the needs, emotions, environmental forces, outcome, and theme. Does the story provide an X-ray of your personality? Perhaps Murray was a little overly enthusiastic about his technique. More likely, your story does at least remind you of some current events or concerns in your life.

Evaluating the utility of the TAT is a complicated task, in part because the test is seldom administered in a standardized manner. Examiners typically administer fewer than the prescribed 20 cards, often change the order of presentation, and seldom use more than one session to conduct the administration. Some examiners use a consistent set of their favorite cards in a fixed order of presentation; others select cards and modify order based upon the assessment situation. Examiners also routinely modify the test instructions so as to avoid misleading examinees about the actual purpose of the test and often ask detailed questions in order to explore or clarify certain issues. Modifications in the administration procedures can have a profound effect upon the nature of the stories people relate. Seemingly minor changes in instructions or context of administration can seriously alter the validity of the test (Lundy, 1988). Finally, there is great variation in the way stories are interpreted. Some clinicians use formalized scoring systems with specific criteria to rate the expression of needs. Others form diagnostic impressions based upon clinical experience.

Overall, the psychometric evaluations of the TAT have tended to be discouraging. However, the research is difficult to interpret because of the great variability in the way the test is administered. Keiser and Prather (1990) reviewed administrative procedures used in published evaluations of the test and found that most studies used five or fewer cards. They concluded that "The research on the TAT is highly variable, with stimulus cards so varied that generalization from one study to another or to clinical practice is hardly possible. A large part of this appears to be due to the lack of consistency and specificity of materials and procedures. It has become commonplace to use cards other than Murray's (1943) and few people follow his instructions. However, in most cases, not only were the specific cards or administrative procedures not mentioned, but often Murray's cards were not used" (pp. 801–802). Estimates of test reliability and validity change dramatically when the test is administered in a consistent manner and scored using a well defined system. The best examples come from research on motivation using the TAT spanning 5 decades. Spangler (1992) conducted a meta-analysis of this research and concluded that when properly administered and scored, the TAT provides adequate test-retest reliability, high interrater reliabilities, and that it predicts long-term "real world" outcomes such as grades, income, occupational success, and leadership better than do questionnaires that have been designed and validated to specifically predict these outcomes.

Trait Approaches

Trait approaches to describing personality evolved from the everyday characterizations we use to describe people. Gordon Allport (1937), a pioneer in the study of traits, believed that behind the deluge of everyday descriptors are a number of real neuropsychological structures or traits that account for consistency in behavior. Allport and Odbert (1936) used a dictionary to identify over 18,000 words describing personality. They were able to reduce the list to approximately 4,500 descriptors by collapsing synonyms and retaining descriptors that implied consistent and stable modes of adjustment. Allport (1955) favored intensive, long-term individual case studies as the best method for investigating these structures. Despite his preferences, the study of personality traits quickly became a highly technical enterprise. Since the 1950s researchers have usually administered paper-and-pencil tests to large samples of people and analyzed the resulting mountains of data, using some of the most sophisticated statistical procedures available. These efforts have produced literally hundreds of different tests, each purporting to measure one or more traits.

Factor-Analytic Explorations of Traits

16 Personality Factor Questionnaire (16PF). Raymond Cattell was convinced that the proliferating list of traits and trait tests could be reduced to a more manageable number by employing factor analysis. Factor analysis provides a way of analyzing correlation patterns derived from many measures to identify a smaller number of more basic components, or factors, that can explain the relationships among the original measures (see Chapter 16). Cattell (1950) edited Allport and Odbert's list of 4,500 traits and selected approximately 200 descriptors, which he referred to as *surface traits*. He arranged to have a large number of people rated on the 200 surface traits. When he correlated the ratings, Cattell found that many of the surface traits were indeed highly related to one another. Factor analysis of the correlations between the 200 surface traits identified 12 underlying factors, or *source traits*. Cattell carried out a series of studies using similar peer ratings, as well as self-report inventories and behavioral measures. He arrived at a set of 16 dimensions or source traits that he felt were needed to fully describe an individual's personality:

Emotional Stability
Self-Assured
Relaxed
Trusting
Controlled
Conscientious
Outgoing
Group Dependent
Happy-Go-Lucky
Venturesome
Assertive
Artless
Radical
Imaginative
Tender Minded
Intelligent

The list of source traits is condensed because some of the surface traits were so highly correlated that they appeared to be the same trait called by different names (e.g., self-assured = confident = poised). Other surface traits seemed to be combinations of source traits (e.g., compulsive = conscientious + controlled). Cattell developed the Sixteen Personality Factor Questionnaire (16PF), a self-report inventory designed to measure the identified source traits. Items used to measure each dimension, to be most useful, should measure only that dimension, and each dimension should be relatively independent from every other dimension. While Cattell was successful in achieving reasonable homogeneity among the items used to assess each dimension, the 16 dimensions are not independent of one another. Does the overlap between the 16 dimensions suggest that the number of dimensions could be further reduced and still provide a comprehensive description of personality?

Cattell was only one of many researchers trying to identify the underlying dimensions of personality. Other trait researchers followed much the same path. They began with a large number of descriptors or test items and factor analyzed them to generate lists of 10 to 20 interrelated factors. In the last decade, a number of researchers began to note similarities across the dimensions identified from a wide variety of studies that used very different populations and measurement techniques. Five relatively independent *higher order factors* seem to emerge when the different lists of factors are combined and the interrelationships among the various factors are considered (Digman, 1990). The five higher order factors are commonly referred to as the *Big Five*. The Big Five are: Neuroticism, Extroversion, Openness, Agreeableness, and Conscientiousness.

Revised NEO Personality Inventory (NEO PI-R).   Costa and McCrae (1992) approached the task of test construction from a different direction. Rather than factor analyzing items or descriptions to identify factors, they began at the top with the five higher order factors, or *domains,* as they called them "and then analyz(ed) each domain to identify the most important and useful traits, or facets, to measure" (p. 39). Items were selected or written to measure each of the five higher order domains and administered to large numbers of people. Items that tapped one and only one domain were retained. The items for each domain were then factor analyzed in order to identify the subtraits or *facets* that make up the domain. The latest result of their efforts is the Revised NEO Personality Inventory (NEO PI-R). The *NEO* portion of the test name refers to the first three Big Five Factors: Neuroticism, Extroversion, and Openness (PI = personality inventory). Earlier versions of the test measured only three of the five factors. The current version measures all five factors, but the original acronym has been retained.

The NEO PI-R is a 240-item test intended to measure normal adult personality. The test comes in two forms, one for self-report (Form S) and the other for observer ratings (Form R). Form R items are parallel to those on Form S but are stated in third person. The self and observer ratings can be plotted on the same profile sheet in order to provide a comparison of a person from two perspectives. The assumption of a hierarchical structure of personality traits is evident in the computed scores. The test yields 35 different scores, as shown in Figure 11.5, five for the domains of Neuroticism, Extroversion, Openness, Agreeableness, and Conscientiousness and six facet scores for each domain ($5 \times 6 = 30$). Each facet score is the sum of responses to eight items and each domain score is the sum of 6 facet scores.

The meaning of the correlated domain and facet scores is illustrated by a test-manual table reporting correlations between test scores and a list of 300 descriptors (Table 11.4). A minus sign in front of a descriptor indicates a strong negative correlation, an indication that the descriptor is an antonym for the scale.

NEO PI-R Form S (self-report) was developed using data from three different research projects including approximately 2,200 people. A norming sample of 1,000 (500 men and 500 women) was selected from the larger group. Selection was manipulated so that the age, gender, and race of the norming sample were congruent with demographic data from the latest census projections. However, the educational level of the sample is suspect in that almost all of the participants attained at least a high school

Figure 11.5
NEO PI-R profile sheet.

Reproduced by special permission of the Publisher, Psychological Assessment Resources, Inc., 16204 North Florida Avenue, Lutz, Florida 33549, from the NEO Personality Inventory– Revised, by Paul Costa, and Robert McCrae, Copyright 1978, 1985, 1989, 1992 by PAR, Inc. Further reproduction is prohibited without permission of PAR, Inc.

327

Table 11.4
Adjective Checklist Correlates

NEO PI-R facet	Adjective Check List items
Neuroticism facets	
N1: Anxiety	anxious, fearful, worrying, tense, nervous, − confident, −optimistic
N2: Angry Hostility	anxious, irritable, impatient, excitable, moody, −gentle, tense
N3: Depression	worrying, −contented, −confident, −self-confident, pessimistic, moody, anxious
N4: Self-Consciousness	shy, −self-confident, timid, − confident, defensive, inhibited, anxious
N5: Impulsiveness	moody, irritable, sarcastic, self-centered, loud, hasty, excitable
N6: Vulnerability	−clear-thinking, −self-confident, − confident, anxious, −efficient, −alert, careless
Extraversion facets	
E1: Warmth	friendly, warm, sociable, cheerful, −aloof, affectionate, outgoing
E2: Gregariousness	sociable, outgoing, pleasure-seeking, − aloof, talkative, spontaneous, −withdrawn
E3: Assertiveness	aggressive, −shy, assertive, self-confident, forceful, enthusiastic, confident
E4: Activity	energetic, hurried, quick, determined, enthusiastic, aggressive, active
E5: Excitement-Seeking	pleasure-seeking, daring, adventurous, charming, handsome, spunky, clever
E6: Positive Emotions	enthusiastic, humorous, praising, spontaneous, pleasure-seeking, optimistic, jolly
Openness facets	
O1: Fantasy	dreamy, imaginative, humorous, mischievous, idealistic, artistic, complicated
O2: Aesthetics	imaginative, artistic, original, enthusiastic, inventive, idealistic, versatile
O3: Feelings	excitable, spontaneous, insightful, imaginative, affectionate, talkative, outgoing
O4: Actions	interests wide, imaginative, adventurous, optimistic, −mild, talkative, versatile
O5: Ideas	idealistic, interests wide, inventive, curious, original, imaginative, insightful
O6: Values	−conservative, unconventional, −cautious, flirtatious

education. The difficulty with educational level may have been compounded by the test authors' attempt to compensate by eliminating individuals with high levels of educational attainment in order to keep the sample mean near the mean for the population. The NEO PI-R Form R (observer rating) was normed on a much smaller subsample using spouse and peer ratings for 142 members of the Form S sample.

The psychometric properties of the NEO PI-R are quite impressive. Internal consistency analyses for the self-report domain scores produced alpha coefficients that varied from .86 for Agreeableness to .92 for Neuroticism. Observer ratings were even more consistent, with alpha coefficients ranging from .89 for Openness to .95 for Agreeableness. Self-report facet score reliabilities vary from .56 to .81, and those for observer ratings range from .60 to .90. Some of the facet reliabilities are particularly high, considering that each facet score is calculated from only eight items.

Table 11.4

NEO PI-R facet	Adjective Check List items
Agreeableness facets	
A1: Trust	forgiving, trusting, −suspicious, −wary, − pessimistic, peaceable, −hard-hearted
A2: Straightforwardness	−complicated, −demanding, −clever, −flirtatious, −charming, −shrewd, −autocratic
A3: Altruism	warm, soft-hearted, gentle, generous, kind, tolerant, −selfish
A4: Compliance	−stubborn, −demanding, −headstrong, − impatient, −intolerant, −outspoken, −hard-hearted
A5: Modesty	−show-off, −clever, −assertive, −argumentative, − self-confident, −aggressive, −idealistic
A6: Tender-Mindedness	friendly, warm, sympathetic, soft-hearted, gentle, −unstable, kind
Conscientiousness facets	
C1: Competence	efficient, self-confident, thorough, resourceful, confident, −confused, intelligent
C2: Order	organized, thorough, efficient, precise, methodical, −absent-minded, −careless
C3: Dutifulness	−defensive, −distractible, −careless, −lazy, thorough, −absent-minded, −fault-finding
C4: Achievement Striving	thorough, ambitious, industrious, enterprising, determined, confident, persistent
C5: Self-Discipline	organized, −lazy, efficient, −absent-minded, energetic, thorough, industrious
C6: Deliberation	−hasty, −impulsive, −careless, −impatient, − immature, thorough, −moody

Source: Reproduced by special permission of the Publisher, Psychological Assessment Resources, Inc., 16204 North Florida Avenue, Lutz, Florida 33549, from the NEO Personality Inventory–Revised, by Paul Costa, and Robert McCrae, Copyright 1978, 1985, 1989, 1992 by PAR, Inc. Further reproduction is prohibited without permission of PAR Inc.

Note. Correlates are given in descending order of absolute magnitude; all are significant at $p < .001$, $N = 305$. Minus signs before adjectives indicate negative correlations with the facet scale. Adapted from McCrae & Costa, in press-b.

Good retest reliability should be obtained from tests purporting to measure stable personality traits. Unfortunately, most personality measures do not fare well when long-term temporal reliability is assessed. A relative strength of the NEO PI-R self and observer ratings is their stability over extended retest intervals. For example, a six-year interval study of self and observer ratings found temporal stability coefficients in the .68 to .83 range for the domain scores.

Costa and McCrae (1992) have accumulated considerable evidence for some types of test validity. Factor analyses of the NEO PI-R consistently reproduce the hierarchical structure that the authors intended to create. The domain and facet scores also have been shown to have good convergent validity (correlate well with other tests purporting to measure the same traits and subtraits) and discriminant validity (low or near zero correlations with measures of unrelated traits and subtraits). Correlations between self (Form S) and other (Form R) ratings demonstrate moderate to high levels of association between self ratings and observer ratings for both the domains and the facets. The correlations between spouse and self ratings are considerably higher than the correlations between peer and self ratings, indicating that more knowledgeable and intimate judges provide ratings that are more consistent with self-perceptions.

A 60-item, self-report, short form of the test, the NEO Five-Factor Inventory (NEO-FFI), is also available. The short form provides only domain scores. Alternate-form domain scores for the NEO-FFI and the NEO PI-R are all in the .90 range, except for a coefficient of .77 for the Agreeableness domain. An observer-rating short form is not currently available.

The main criticism that can be leveled against the NEO PI-R is that despite its psychometric elegance, it has not yet been shown to have wide practical application. Dimensions derived from factor analysis are statistical abstractions distilled from patterns of correlation. Names given to these abstractions—such as "openness" or "neuroticism"—are only verbal labels intended to symbolize the underlying statistical relationships. It is sometimes easier to compare statistically derived factors with other abstractions, such as scores or factors from other tests, than it is to apply them to real world predictions and decision making. While the NEO PI-R holds promise for practical applications, these applications have not yet been fully explored or confirmed. The weight of validity evidence still rests on correlations with other tests, many of which were used to develop the original five-factor model of personality. A second concern is that the test, like all self-report measures, relies upon the honesty and forthrightness of the person providing the ratings. Respondents are asked to report whether they have answered honestly, answered all of the questions, and marked answers in the correct spaces. The authors' faith in the forthrightness and competence of respondents in completing the test is based upon a review of data from the test development samples. This faith may be severely tested in assessment situations where an examinee may have motivation to minimize or exaggerate personal difficulties (e.g., disability evaluation or personnel screening).

Earlier in this section, we asked whether Cattell's 16 factors could be reduced to an even smaller number of traits. Recent research (Gerbing & Tuley, 1991) on the relationship between the 16PF and an earlier version of Costa and McCrae's test, the NEO PI, suggests that the NEO and 16PF scales measure essentially the same personality traits. Even though the names of the scales may be quite different, there is a strong correspondence between Cattell's 16 factors and corresponding facet scores on the NEO PI. In addition, Cattell's 16 factors can themselves be factor analyzed to produce a smaller number of higher-order factors that correlate quite well with the domain scores on the NEO PI.

Personality Typologies.   Trait approaches hold the possibility of sorting individuals into clusters or *types* by their status on two or more traits. A number of theorists have developed models that identify a set of personality dimensions and use them to classify people into personality types. One prominent model based on the first two Big Five dimensions was developed by Hans Eysenck (Eysenck & Rachman, 1965).

Eysenck suggested that Neuroticism and Extroversion are the primary dimensions of personality and that a person's status on the combination of these two dimensions can identify four basic personality types. People who are high on neuroticism and low on extroversion will tend to be pessimistic and sober. He refers to this somewhat depressive type as Melancholic. Other combinations of high and low scores on the two primary dimensions lead to three other personality types as shown in Figure 11.6.

Identifying Traits Using Empirical Scale Construction.   There is a basic limitation inherent in the factor analytic approach to scale construction and associated typologies. The scales and personality descriptions that result depend upon the investigator identifying the most useful trait dimensions in the inventory. A factor analysis cannot reveal traits that are not present in the set of items. Instruments developed using *empirical scale construction* strategies, however, do not require a priori knowledge of the important dimensions. Rather, a large number of items is given to a group of people and the items are keyed into scales based on their ability to differentiate between intact and naturally occurring groups. You have already been introduced to these strategies in the section on interest testing. Different occupational groups were given a questionnaire to measure their patterns of liking. The liking patterns of subsequent examinees were then compared with those of different occupational groups in order to identify occupational interests. Many theorists consider the liking patterns to be an expression of underlying traits. They argue that examinees are really being matched with occupations based upon their personality types. The same strategy has been used to develop empirically keyed instruments to assess personality characteristics.

Minnesota Multiphasic Personality Inventory (MMPI).   The MMPI was developed in order to provide objective scales that could be used to diagnose people with specific psychological disorders. The authors of the original version of the MMPI (Hathaway & McKinley, 1940) approached the assessment of pathology with an empirical scaling strategy modeled after those used in the development of interest tests. Exist-

Figure 11.6
Eysenck Model of
Personality Types

Adapted from Eysenck, H.I., & Rachman, S. (1965). *The causes and cures of neurosis: An introduction to the modern behavior therapy based on learning theory and principles of conditioning.* San Diego: Knapp.

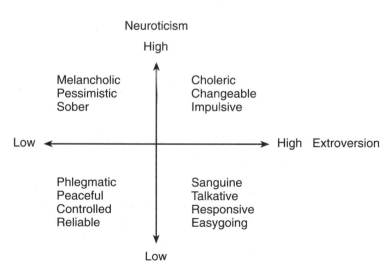

ing tests, research, and texts addressing traits associated with pathology were used to construct a large pool of test items that could be answered with a *yes* or *no* response. Instead of the occupational groups used in interest test development, Hathaway and McKinley identified and tested small groups of individuals who were thought to be clear exemplars of particular psychological disorders. They began with a group of neurotic patients who presented somatic concerns for which physicians could find no organic basis. The test items were administered to the identified patients and to a comparison group of presumably normal individuals who were visitors at the hospital. Items that differentiated the two groups were retained and used to construct the Hypochondriasis scale of the MMPI. The scale was also administered to a second group of hypochondriacal patients to ensure that it would also differentiate them from the "normal" group. The test developers proceeded in a like manner to develop *clinical scales* for nine additional groups.

Clinical Scales of the Minnesota Multiphasic Personality Inventory. The 10 basic scores established on this empirical basis carry the labels shown here. The labels are followed by a characterization of the group on which the scale was based.

1. *Hypochondriasis (Hs)*. Individuals showing excessive worry about health, often accompanied by reports of obscure pains and disorders, but with no organic basis for the symptoms (32 items).
2. *Depression (D)*. Individuals suffering from chronic depression, feelings of uselessness, and inability to face the future. The items on this scale also reflect high personal standards and self-punitiveness (57 items).
3. *Conversion Hysteria (Hy)*. Individuals who have reacted to personal problems by developing physical symptoms such as paralysis, cramps, gastric complaints, or cardiac symptoms or who show denial of problems (60 items).
4. *Psychopathic Deviate (Pd)*. Individuals showing irresponsibility, disregard of social norms or concern for others, and lack of deep emotional response (50 items).
5. *Masculinity-Femininity (Mf)*. Individuals, particularly males, tending to diverge from culturally prescribed gender roles. Low scores also identify individuals with stereotypical sex-role perceptions. At the time the test was developed, homosexuality was considered a disorder and the scale was initially intended to identify homosexual individuals. It has not been a good indicator of sexual orientation. The subsequent focus on gender-role interests and behavior actually foreshadowed later psychological research that resulted in professional organizations recognizing homosexuality as normal. Conflict over sexual orientation or gender role remains a clinical concern (56 items).
6. *Paranoia (Pa)*. Individuals tending to be excessively suspicious of others and their motives. High scores reflect interpersonal sensitivity and the idea that one is being persecuted (40 items).
7. *Psychasthenia (Pt)*. Individuals troubled by excessive fears (phobias) and compulsions to repeatedly perform certain acts. Item content reflects high moral standards, self-blame, and rigid impulse control (48 items).

8. *Schizophrenia (Sc)*. Individuals characterized by bizarre and unusual thoughts or behavior and subjective experiences out of step with reality (78 items).
9. *Hypomania (Ma)*. Individuals tending to be physically and mentally overactive, with rapid shifts in ideas or actions (46 items).
10. *Social Introversion (SI)*. High scores characterize individuals who tend to keep to themselves and avoid social gatherings. Low scores indicate extroversion and ascendance (69 items).

The test developers did not have a priori ideas about which characteristics would differentiate the normal and diagnosed groups. Instead, they administered the entire array of test items and used statistical procedures to select the items that would be used to classify individuals. One problem that has plagued the MMPI through its current revision is the "normal" group that was used to develop the scales. There is good reason to believe that the hospital visitors did not represent the general population on either demographic or personality variables. Even if they did, the fact that they were visiting patients at a medical facility strongly suggests that many in the group were experiencing psychological duress at the time they completed the test items. Selection of good target and comparison groups is extremely important in empirical test construction, because sampling errors will affect the items chosen for the scale.

Use of the MMPI for over 50 years has accumulated experiential data. In the 1980s, the body of research served as a basis for a revision of the instrument (Hathaway & McKinley, 1989), a revision that was intended to correct some of the deficiencies that had been noted in the original instrument. For example, new norms have been developed, based on a national sample of 1,138 males and 1,462 females. The sample now includes suitable representation of ethnic and minority group members. Unfortunately, the educational level attained by the new sample is much higher than the national average, raising questions about use of the test with less educated individuals. While the renorming was helpful in adjusting scores to fit current population characteristics, it did not rectify the original problem of using a nonrepresentative group for item selection. The original items were, nevertheless, culled and edited to correct items with outdated or offensive content, and 154 new items were tried out. The revised instrument (MMPI-2) contains 567 items, although the "basic scales are scored from the first 370 items" (Hathaway & McKinley, 1989, p. 15). A sample profile form is found in Figure 11.7

Like the Strong and many other tests using empirical scale construction, the MMPI-2 has considerable item overlap among the various scales. A *yes* response on one item may add to the elevation of two scales and lower the elevation on a third. As a result the scales are not independent of one another. While this is a serious measurement concern, it also reflects a reality behind the construction of the test: People with different psychological disorders may exhibit common as well as group-specific symptoms or characteristics that make them different from the general population. As a consequence, the identification of individuals with psychological disorders is not as simple as the test developers would like. Clinical diagnosis usually is not accomplished merely by obtaining a high score on just one of the scales. Instead, interpretation of an MMPI-2 profile is based on the pattern formed by scores on several

Figure 11.7
Profile Form—Minnesota Multiphasic Personality Inventory-2.

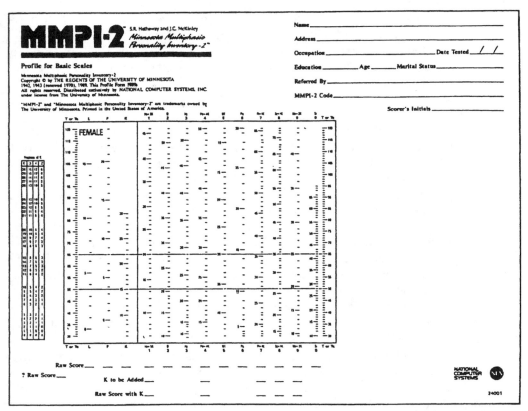

Source: Copyright © by The Regents of The University of Minnesota 1942, 1943 (renewed 1970), 1989. This Profile Form 1989. All rights reserved. Distributed exclusively by National Computer Systems, Inc. under license from The University of Minnesota.

scales. For example, individuals with diagnosed personality disorders often obtain patterns that include high scores on both the Pd and Ma scales, indicating a combination of disregard for social norms and a high level of impulsivity. Individuals with high D scores often obtain low Ma scores, because depressed mood is often accompanied by low levels of activity. The MMPI manual (Hathaway & McKinley, 1989) contains extensive directions on how to yield a profile by coding the scores by their elevation. Generally, interpreting test results requires comparing the pattern of the highest two or three scales with the 426 recognized clinical profiles.

Researchers responsible for the MMPI-2 maintain that their very conservative revision of the test allows for the possibility of using research on MMPI profiles in order to interpret MMPI-2 profiles (Butcher & Williams, 1992). However, direct comparisons between MMPI and MMPI-2 profiles obtained from the same examinees often reveal important differences that can alter interpretation and classification (Dahlstrom, 1992).

The item pool and the empirical keying technique of the MMPI have appealed to psychologists interested in a wide variety of specialized problems, and over 200 additional scoring keys have been developed for all kinds of special groups ranging from alcoholics to underachievers. The MMPI is alleged to be the most extensively used self-descriptive instrument in clinical practice and has been applied in a wide range of other settings. For example, the MMPI-2 is often used in personnel selection for jobs that involve a high degree of responsibility or stress, such as a police officer.

The MMPI item pool is a somewhat unusual mixture of items, some of clearly pathological import and some that sound neutral or innocent. The two types of statements are referred to as obvious and subtle items. Most MMPI scales have a mixture of both, even though the two types tend to be almost completely uncorrelated. The resulting scale scores are often composed of two unrelated scores combined into one. Cross validation studies have shown that the subtle items contribute little to the identification of pathological groups (Duff, 1965). It appears that most of the power of the scales lies in the obvious items, and this makes the MMPI subject to distorted responding by individuals who have reasons to exaggerate or minimize their difficulties. The test authors quickly recognized this problem and developed *validity* scales designed to identify and correct for respondent misrepresentations. Four *validity scales* are regularly used:

1. *?* The number of items which an individual does not mark. A large number of blank items is seen as an indication of defensiveness and withdrawal from the task.

2. *L* The number of obviously "good" but extremely improbable behaviors that the examinee claims, seen as an indication of rather naive defensiveness or attempt to portray virtuosity. (15 items)

3. *F* The number of very rare and unusual responses that the individual makes, items that even seriously disturbed individuals seldom endorse. A high score may indicate that the respondent did not understand or follow the directions or that the respondent may be exaggerating symptoms. (60 items)

4. *K* The number of items endorsed by the examinee that were also frequently chosen by seriously disturbed individuals who obtained normal scores on the test. High scores are seen as a sign of a sophisticated, defensive style and the tendency to describe oneself in a "socially desirable" manner. (30 items)

The most interesting and controversial validity scale is the *K* scale. It is unclear how well this scale measures defensiveness as opposed to a genuine and legitimate positive self-image. Moderately elevated scores on the *K* scale are common among groups of successful individuals who appear to be getting on well in life, as well as among certain clinical populations. To correct for this defensiveness, the authors of the MMPI suggest adding a portion of the *K*-scale score to the raw scores of five of the clinical scales.

Both test-retest and internal consistency reliability information are given for clinical scales of the MMPI-2. Retest reliabilities over an average interval of 1 week ranged from .67 to .92 for a sample of 82 males and from .58 to .91 for 111 females. Coefficient alpha reliabilities from .33 to .85 were reported for males, while the female sample yielded values from .36 to .87. Most of the item content of the MMPI-2 is essentially unchanged from its predecessor. Consequently, the validity evidence collected from a half century of research on the original MMPI, as well as some of the old reservations about its quality as a psychometric instrument, still apply.

The Minnesota Multiphasic Personality Inventory—Adolescent (MMPI-A) has also been published recently in order to address well documented difficulties in interpreting MMPI profiles obtained from adolescents (Butcher & Williams, 1992). As with the MMPI-2, a conservative approach to test revision was used in order to update existing MMPI test items. In addition, many items were rewritten or replaced in order to provide content appropriate for adolescents. The MMPI-A offers the same array of clinical and validity scales as the adult version. Scales were normed using an age-appropriate sample. The MMPI-A scales tend to produce lower test-retest reliability coefficients and higher internal consistency coefficients than do the MMPI-2 scales. Validity evidence from the original MMPI may not apply well to the MMPI-A. First, the test developers justify use of the adolescent form because the original MMPI did not always work well for adolescent evaluations. There is reason to believe that personality structure, both normal and abnormal, is different for adolescents and adults. Second, the MMPI-A is less similar to the original MMPI than is the MMPI-2, because MMPI-A items were both updated *and* adjusted for developmental level. Little validity research has yet been accumulated to evaluate this relatively new test.

In spite of its psychometric limitations, the MMPI has had wide acceptance and use, especially by clinical psychologists. In a sense it can be thought of as a standardized and comprehensive, although impersonal, psychiatric interview. Thus, in addition to use of the scores and overall profile, the clinician may look at the responses to specific questions or groups of questions as part of the search for insights about and understanding of a client. However, such use should be limited to individuals with extensive clinical training and should serve only as the starting point for diagnosis. The test authors set completion of graduate courses in testing and in psychopathology as minimum educational standards for using the MMPI, but we would suggest higher standards unless you are working under the direct supervision of a trained clinician.

California Psychological Inventory (CPI).   Empirical test construction techniques are also used to develop measures of normal personality. The California Psychological Inventory is a well-known and widely used test of 20 common personality traits: dominance, capacity for status, sociability, social presence, self-acceptance, independence, empathy, responsibility, socialization, self-control, good impression, communality, well-being, tolerance, achievement via conformance, achievement via independence, intellectual efficiency, psychological mindedness, flexibility and masculinity/femininity. Scale items were selected based upon their ability to identify individuals who were known to possess a high level of a particular trait. For example, the Sociability index was developed by identifying people who were involved in many social organizations and activities. A large number of items were administered to a socially active group and to a comparison group that exhibited more typical levels of social behavior. Items that differentiated between the groups were retained for the scale. The CPI provides scores for all 20 traits.

Humanistic Approaches—Personality as Self-Perception

Even though the earliest American social scientists used the term *self-concept*, it is Carl Rogers who is responsible for making the construct a part of popular culture. Rogers (1951) believed in self-determination. He believed that we are constantly creating ourselves and that the product of our self-creation is the *self-concept*, an integrated set of self-perceptions and evaluations that are the core of personality. He argued that the person best equipped to assess self-conceptions is the person who holds them. Rogers proposed the novel idea that the person should simultaneously function as examiner and examinee. He called his earliest formal measure of self-concept the *Q-sort*, a self-rating method that utilizes a set of cards with brief, self-descriptive statements. A person is first asked to rank the cards from least to most descriptive of herself. She is then asked to rank the same statements to describe the person that she would like to become. The self-ratings provide a measure of self-concept and the difference between self and ideal ratings yields a measure of self-satisfaction. The person is then encouraged to interpret and explore the meaning of the descriptions and the discrepancies between self and ideal ratings. The parallel between Rogers' and Allport's emphasis on in-depth case studies may be apparent. The difference is that Rogers encouraged the person to be both the subject and the investigator.

Subsequent Measures of Self-Concept. A number of self-concept measures were soon developed by other authors. Paper-and-pencil formats displaced the Q-sort technique, and modern test technology was applied to the development and analysis of the tests that followed. The qualitative self-interpretation of the early instruments was replaced by normative comparisons of test scores. The format for contemporary self-concept measures has become almost indistinguishable from that of trait tests. The differentiating characteristic of self-concept tests is that they provide a measure of self-perception and/or self-satisfaction for the evaluation of individuals within the normal range of human behavior. The resulting scores, whether referred to as self-concept or self-esteem scores, tend to be highly intercorrelated measures of self-perceived adjustment (Bracken, 1991).

In recent years there has been a renewed interest in self-concept measurement, particularly regarding children and adolescents. Self-concept scores have been shown to correlate with a wide variety of indicators of development and social adjustment. The causal relationship between self-concept and advancement or adjustment is not clear. A positive view of oneself may, for example, be either the cause or the result of good adjustment. Nevertheless, many educators advocate teaching children to view themselves more positively, in the hope that better adjustment and higher achievement will follow.

Multidimensional Self-Concept Scale (MSCS).   The MSCS is a 150-item test developed by Bracken (1992) to assess self-concept among children and adolescents ages 9 to 19. Two decades of factor-analytic studies using a number of different self-concept measures indicated that self-concept is not unidimensional. Self ratings vary depending upon the aspect of ourselves that we rate and the social context in which we picture ourselves. For example, someone may have a positive image of himself in relationship to his family, yet be uncomfortable about himself in social situations. Or someone may see herself as a very competent person but be embarrassed about her body. The MSCS recognizes the complex nature of self-concept by providing a total score and six subscores for the domains of social, competence, affect, academic, family, and physical self-concepts as shown in Figure 11.8.

Bracken views these domains as highly interrelated subdivisions of the global self-concept. The test was normed on a school age sample of 5th to 12th graders selected to be representative of the U.S. population within each age bracket. Rotatori (1994) points out that while the sample is representative for sex and race, some regions of the country are overrepresented, and data on socioeconomic status are not included.

The test has very good internal consistency, producing alpha coefficients in the high 90s for the total score at every age level. Domain scores are only slightly lower with alphas ranging from .85 for ninth graders on the Competence subscale up to .97 for several grade levels on the Family subscale. The test shows strong temporal stability, yielding a .90 test-retest coefficient for the total score over a 4-week test-retest interval. Temporal stability coefficients for the domain scores ranged from .73 for the Affect to .81 for Academic and Physical subscales. The author argues for the test's content validity, based upon the match between the domains measured on the test and the self-concept factors identified by previous research.

Evidence for concurrent validity is found in the high correlations obtained when comparing MSCS scores with scores from other self-concept tests. The test manual also cites research indicating that the test was a good discriminator for identifying children who were rated as low in self-esteem or who obtained poor scores on a test of emotional disturbance.

Figure 11.8
Self-concept model—
Bracken. (Source: B.A.
Bracken, *Multidimensional
Self-Concept Scale Manual.*
Austin, TX: PRO-ED, 1992,
p.5. Reprinted by permission.)

Behavioral Approaches

Traditional behaviorism is the antithesis of conventional ideas about personality. John B. Watson and later B. F. Skinner adamantly opposed the use of constructs which could not be directly observed. Dynamic forces, traits, and self-conceptions are all examples of the class of constructs which traditional behaviorists wished to abolish. The advancement of cognitive psychology has had a profound effect upon behaviorism. Of particular import is the work of theorists such as Albert Bandura, who came to realize learning social behaviors involved both overt actions and "internal" behaviors such as representing events through images and words, making judgments, or experiencing emotion. The scope of behaviorism was greatly expanded once internal behaviors, particularly cognitions, were accepted as legitimate foci for study.

Traditional behaviorists do not believe that it is necessary to infer internal structures in order to explain consistency in behavior across time and situation. Rather, similar behavior in different contexts is explained as learned responses that are regulated by similarities in the different environments. Individual differences can be accounted for by one's previous learning history. People seek different situations or behave differently in the same situation because they have learned to associate different stimuli and behaviors with different consequences.

Initially, behavior patterns were assessed primarily by direct observation. An observer might record a specific behavior, the environmental stimuli that preceded the behavior, and the consequences that followed. Situational tests have also been used in which behavior patterns are assessed by placing a person in an actual situation in order to predict performance. For example, a job applicant's ability to manage work stressors could be evaluated by placing him or her in a stressful environment. The process was later abridged by the use of self-report forms that allowed respondents to recall or rate important stimuli, behavior patterns, and consequences. Eventually, paper-and-pencil self-report forms began to include accounts of cognitions, judgments, and emotions. Modern testing technology has also been applied to these self-report forms, such that the format is very similar to traditional trait inventories. Nevertheless, authors of these instruments assert that they are directly measuring behavior or behavior patterns and not internal structures (e.g., ego, trait, or self-concept) that control or direct behavior.

Millon Clinical Multiaxial Inventory-III (MCMI-III).   Theodore Millon (Millon, Millon, & Davis, 1994) has created a very innovative, behaviorally based test that has gained considerable popularity among clinicians. The test is a direct competitor with the MMPI-2 because it is also used to identify and classify people who have serious psychological problems. However, Millon used a theoretical approach to test development as opposed to the empirical scale construction used by Hathaway and McKinley. The MCMI-III is the latest revision of the test based upon Millon's theory of personality and psychopathology (Millon, 1990). The 175-item test provides scores for 24 clinical scales, which are organized into four groups: clinical personality disorders (11 scales), severe personality disorders (3 scales), clinical syndromes (7 scales), and severe clinical syndromes (3 scales).

Clinical Personality Disorders Scales.   Millon believes that people with clinical personality disorders can be classified using two dimensions of behavior: pattern of reinforcement and style of coping behavior. Millon initially identified 10 clinical personality disorders based upon five patterns of reinforcement and two styles of coping ($2 \times 5 = 10$). The 10 basic disorders, which are called Clinical Personality Patterns, are listed in Table 11.5. The behavioral characteristics associated with each personality pattern are summarized in Table 11.6. An 11th personality pattern and an associated scale, Depressive, shows characteristics similar to the Schizoid and Avoidant personality. This pattern was added to the basic 10 to account for people who show the added coping style of simply not coping, of giving up. These individuals exhibit a loss of hope and a despair about the future. Thus, 11 clinical personality pattern scales are reported in the complete instrument.

Severe Personality Disorders Scales.   The Severe Personality Disorders Scales assess personality disturbances that are marked by extremely dysfunctional coping styles and occasional loss of contact with reality. The three scales for these disorders are

Schizotypal: Detached, autistic, confused individuals who are perceived by others as being very strange. Their very dysfunctional coping style may include both active or passive features such as hypersensitivity or lack of emotional responding

Borderline: Dependent individuals experiencing intense mood swings that are often triggered by perceived acceptance or rejection from another person. The dysfunctional coping style often includes suicidal behavior and/or self-mutilation in reaction to perceived rejection

Paranoid: Independent individuals who engender anger and exasperation in others in reaction to their distrustful, deceptive, and defensive style, which projects blame onto other people. Their dysfunctional coping style is marked by vigorous resistance to input or direction from others

Clinical Syndromes Scales.   The Clinical Syndromes Scales describe relatively distinct patterns of symptoms that may develop as an extension of one's personality

Table 11.5
Millon Clinical Personality Patterns

Reinforcement Pattern	Coping Style	
	Passive	Active
Detached	Schizoid	Avoidant
Dependent	Dependent	Histrionic
Independent	Narcissistic	Antisocial
Discordant	Self-Defeating	Aggressive
Ambivalent	Compulsive	Negativistic

Table 11.6
Millon Clinical Personality Disorders Behavioral Characteristics

Clinical Personality Disorder	Reinforcement Pattern	Coping Style
Schizoid	Detached: Few rewards for pleasures in life	Passive: Apathetic, resigned
Avoidant	Detached	Active: Actively avoid pain
Dependent	Dependent: Pleasure or pain derived from how others feel about them	Passive: Wait for others to direct or reach out to them
Histrionic	Dependent	Active: Manipulate in order to gain attention or favors
Narcissistic	Independent: Selfish gratification of own needs and wants	Passive: Bask in self-approval
Antisocial	Independent	Active: Exploit and use others
Self-Defeating	Discordant: Substitute pain for pleasure	Passive: Allow themselves to be used and abused
Aggressive	Discordant	Active: Seek pleasure through the abuse of others
Compulsive	Ambivalent: Conflict over seeking approval vs. expressing anger (independent vs. dependent)	Passive: Suppress resentment and are overconforming
Negativistic	Ambivalent	Active: Express resentment and feel guilt

style. For example, compulsive types have a vulnerability to developing anxiety related symptoms. The Clinical Syndromes Scales cover the following:

Anxiety: Symptoms of worry, apprehension, and/or fearfulness

Somatoform: Symptoms related to health and bodily functions including aches, pains, health related fears, fatigue, dizziness, and so on

Bipolar-Manic: Periods of elation, inflated self-esteem, hyperactivity, distractability, and unrealistic optimism.

Dysthymia: Extended periods of low to moderate levels of depression, periods which are not a core part of personality and which do not make one incapable of continued functioning

Alcohol Dependence: Alcohol abuse that interferes with social adjustment and functioning

Drug Dependence: Drug abuse that interferes with social adjustment and functioning

Post-Traumatic Stress Disorder: Involuntary and intrusive memories or reexperiencing of a traumatic event, accompanied by hypersensitivity to and avoidance of reminders of the trauma

Severe Syndromes Scales. The Severe Syndromes Scales describe symptom patterns that are extreme enough to cause severe disorientation and/or loss of the ability to function and cope. These include:

Thought Disorder: Psychotic thought patterns that include confused thinking, disorientation, hallucinations, delusions, and/or fragmented and peculiar ideas. Usually accompanied by bizarre behavior

Major Depression: Depressive symptoms so severe that the person is not able to continue in a functional manner

Delusional Disorder: Suspicions and delusions so extreme that the person loses contact with reality

Each of the 24 clinical scales was developed to operationally measure personality types or syndromes described by Millon's theory (Millon, Millon, & Davis, 1994). The scales were then compared to the diagnostic manual developed by the American Psychiatric Association, a list of the currently recognized mental disorders and their symptoms. Scale items were added or modified in an attempt to simultaneously satisfy the demands of both Millon's theory and the diagnostic manual. The resulting 325-item pool was administered to 600 psychiatric patients. Various combinations of scale items were statistically evaluated in order to select items that best described each diagnostic category while decreasing the number of items necessary to identify individuals with particular disorders. It is important to note that scale items were selected based upon their ability to allow differentiation between different diagnostic groups, and not diagnostic versus normal groups, as with the MMPI scales. Another primary difference between the two tests is that the initial item selection for the MCMI-III was guided by theory and was subsequently checked using statistical methods. The MMPI scales were derived on a purely empirical basis.

In addition to the 24 clinical scales, Millon developed four scales that are similar to the MMPI validity scales. These include:

Validity: Items that describe extremely unlikely experiences
Disclosure: Tendency to be open and revealing versus closed or secretive
Desirability: Desire to present oneself as virtuous or socially attractive
Debasement: Tendency to belittle or deprecate oneself

The Disclosure, Desirability, and Debasement scales can be used to adjust clinical scale scores, as is done with the K scale of the MMPI.

Figure 11.9 is a sample profile summarizing the scores obtained from a hypothetical client. The Modifying Indices section of the profile contains information about the client's approach to the test. Scores for the Disclosure, Desirability, and Debasement scales are coded respectively as *X, Y,* and *Z*. The Clinical Personality Patterns section of the profile uses the codes of *1* to *8B* to report the scores for the Schizoid(1), Avoidant(2A), Depressive(2B), Dependent(3), Histrionic(4), Narcissistic(5), Antisocial(6A), Aggressive(6B), Compulsive(7), Passive-Aggressive(8A), and Self-Defeating(8B) clinical personality disorder scales. The Severe Personality section reports scores for the three severe personality disorders: Schizotypal(S), Border-

Figure 11.9
MCMI-III Profile Sheet. (Used by permission of National Computer Systems, Minneapolis, MN.)

343

line(C), and Paranoid(P). The Clinical Syndromes section reports scores for the scales of Anxiety Disorder(A), Somatoform Disorder(H), Bipolar-Manic Disorder(N), Dysthymic Disorder(D), Alcohol Dependence(B), Drug Dependence(T), and Post-Traumatic Stress Disorder(R). Finally, the Severe Syndromes section reports scores for the Thought Disorder(SS), Major Depression(CC), and Delusional Disorder(PP) scales.

An additional innovation in the MCMI-III is the manner in which the scores are reported. Millon decided that the use of normally distributed scores would be inappropriate, because scales intended to measure pathology should not produce a bell shaped distribution. Instead, the test reports *base rate* (BR) scores, which are anchored to the prevalence of each disorder in the norming sample. The BR scores have a range of 0 to 115. A BR score of 75 to 85 indicates that characteristics of a particular disorder or syndrome are present, with a score of 85 or more indicating that the characteristics are very pronounced.

Internal consistency for the MCMI-III scales is adequate. Alpha coefficients range from .66 for Compulsive to .90 for Major Depression, with most coefficients falling in the .80 to .85 range. Test-retest coefficients for a 5 to 14 day interval range from .84 for Anxiety to .96 for Somatoform. Most coefficients are in the .89 to .93 range.

Millon investigated the concurrent validity of the MCMI-III by correlating scale scores with a wide variety of collateral instruments and with clinician ratings. The MCMI-III demonstrates moderate to strong convergent validity with a variety of instruments that purport to measure similar types of psychopathology. For example, the MMPI-2 Depression scale correlates with the MCMI-III Dysthymic ($r = .68$), Major Depression, ($r = .71$) and Depressive (.59) scales. Unfortunately, the MCMI-III scales do not always demonstrate good discriminant validity from other clinical measures. For example, the MMPI-2 Depression scale also correlates solidly with many other MCMI-III scales (Schizoid .46; Avoidant .46; Dependent .53; Histrionic $-.52$; Narcissistic $-.52$; Self-Defeating .49; Schizotypal .45; Borderline .47; Anxiety .52; Somatoform .65; Post-Traumatic Stress Disorder .50; and Thought Disorder .58). The situation is not surprising because the MCMI-III scales correlate highly with one another. The manual does not report a factor analysis of the component scores, but inspection of the correlation matrix for the scales suggests that the scales are not as distinctive as the test developer intended. The high correlations between many of the scales (rs in the .70+ range are very common) strongly suggest that the reporting of 24 different clinical scores may not be justified because of the overlap in scales. Despite the lack of scale purity, the test is fairly efficient in matching diagnoses assigned by clinicians. However, a part of the efficiency derives from using the same clinical ratings to both set and evaluate BR scores.

PROBLEMS WITH PERSONALITY AND INTEREST MEASURES

Paper-and-pencil interest and personality tests are subject to a number of problems and criticisms. One possible source of error has been called *response sets,* a tendency on the part of the examinee to approach the test in a manner that distorts the test results. For example, a person may have a tendency to *acquiesce,* or "yea-say." This response set is simply a propensity for accepting or agreeing to statements. In the context of the Strong Interest Inventory, a person with an acquiescent response set would mark too many of the items "like." The scores on a personality or adjustment test could be distorted by the examinee's willingness to conclude, "Yes, in some ways or at some times that might be true of me." Related response sets include favoring either midpoints or extremes when asked to respond on an item asking for degree of agreement/disagreement with a statement.

A second category of response sets involves approaching the test in a certain frame of mind or with the intent of creating a certain impression. For example, some examinees base their responses on *social desirability,* the tendency to choose responses that they believe are most socially approved of, or accepted. Interest statements are relatively neutral in value, so social desirability is not likely to become a serious problem with them. However, this social responsibility response set can become a problem in personality and adjustment measures where many items have high or low desirability or when examinees attempt to present themselves in a negative light. Care must be taken in interpreting test results when an examinee might gain from appearing troubled. Suppose you were claiming psychological damage in a lawsuit, taking a test as a part of a disability assessment that could result in support payments, or were claiming psychological impairment in relationship to a criminal charge. How might you approach the test differently than if you were taking the same test either in a research study, in the context of seeking counseling, or as a part of an employment screening?

Test results from self-report personality and adjustment measures can also be distorted by several other problems. The examinee may be unable or unwilling to read and understand an extensive list of items. Some people may not have the ability to stand back and view their own behavior and decide whether a particular statement applies. Others may be either too self-critical or too willing to admit to personal frailties. Validity indicators such as those on the MMPI-2 and the MCMI-III help to identify and adjust for these problems, but the validity scales are far from perfect. For example, it is often difficult to tell whether a person is truly confident or is trying to present him- or herself as such.

Of additional concern are ethical issues relating to testing situations that could involve the invasion of privacy, the requirement that individuals give information that may be against their own interests, or that certain "undesirable" personality or adjustment scores could limit someone's opportunities. Consequently, these personality and interest instruments should be used only when the results are to benefit the examinee and will be interpreted by a person with adequate clinical training and experience.

Interest and personality measures are notably different from cognitive ability measures. Scales on cognitive ability tests usually show positive correlations, often fairly substantial ones that allow test results to be summarized with a single score. The result is that most of the ability to predict academic and job success is carried by the common general-ability factor. The simplicity of the factor structure makes the tests relatively easy to understand and interpret. Interest and personality measures are rather different. The tests reviewed here include a number of different scores or scales that cannot be summarized in a single score. Thus, each score should provide new and distinct information about an individual's interests or personality. Factorially complex tests make assessing validity and interpreting results more challenging, simply by the multifaceted nature of the instrument. Tests such as the NEO PI-R, which come closer to achieving scale independence, present enough challenge. Others, such as the MMPI-2 and the MCMI-III have scales that should ideally be fairly independent but are actually highly correlated, a fact that further complicates the interpretation and validation of the test scores.

Perhaps the strongest criticism of objective personality tests was outlined by Walter Mischel (1968). Mischel was familiar with a large body of research that had accumulated from studies in social psychology. The studies demonstrated that experimenters can create both laboratory and real world situations that will largely determine behavior, irrespective of "personality differences." Social environments can be manipulated to almost completely determine whether people will act with honesty or dishonesty, altruism or apathy, conformity or independence, aggression or passivity, and so on. Mischel initially argued that the idea of personality is an illusion. People do not behave in a consistent manner over time and situations but instead are controlled by their social environments. He pointed out that personality tests are often consistent with themselves and with other tests, but that they do a very poor job of predicting actual behavior. His review of research concluded that personality tests almost always produce coefficients in the .20 to .30 range when correlated with external measures of behavior.

A number of researchers have criticized Mischel's conclusions on both logical and methodological grounds. They argued that a single behavior or situation is not an adequate measure of individual differences. Suppose you consider yourself to be a generous person. Are you generous all of the time in every situation? Would you consider one randomly selected incident on one randomly selected day to be a good indicator of your generosity? Critics argued that an adequate behavioral measure of a personality dimension should include ratings for a number of different behaviors associated with the characteristic, collected from several observers, in a variety of situations, across a reasonable time span. Epstein (1983) demonstrated that the correlations between personality measures and behavior do increase substantially when data from multiple observations are aggregated to provide a better behavior sample. Mischel (1993) has acknowledged limitations in his original conclusions due to the inadequacy of the behavioral samples. He now concedes that there is a stronger correspondence between tests and classes of behavior than he originally thought. However, he believes that individuals are not as consistent as we suppose. Mischel now believes that behavior is best understood as an interaction between individual characteristics and the social situation, with situational variables often having the greater influence.

COMPUTERIZED SCORING AND INTERPRETATION

Scoring and interpretation of interest and personality tests is often complicated and time consuming because of the complex nature of the various scales. For example, in some cases, scoring requires differential weighting of the items, making hand scoring very laborious. Computer scoring for such instruments has been a boon to clinicians, as has the development of software programs that allow the instrument to be administered on a computer, making scoring almost instantaneous. Another important development has been the proliferation of organizations that produce computer generated interpretive reports. A vast array of scoring services and computerized interpretive reports are available to the clinician, ranging from services that provide scores on specific scales, to elaborate narrative reports that appear as though they have been written by a clinician and may even include predictive statements about performance or behavior (Herman & Samuels, 1985). Computer technology has revolutionized the process of interest and personality testing; however, it is important to be aware that there are both advantages and disadvantages to the use of these automated systems.

Advantages

1. *Time savings and convenience.* Scoring and feedback can be provided in a much more timely manner, particularly when test administration is completed on the computer.

2. *Efficiency for clinician.* Use of computerized scoring systems frees the clinician to devote more time to the direct service of the client. Furthermore, the newer software systems for generating reports produce many alternative statements, allowing the clinician to pick and choose text that is most appropriate for the client and assessment question.

3. *Standardization.* The highly standardized nature of these reports helps to eliminate the variations and potential biases that follow from individual interpretations. The same scores will always generate the same narrative comments.

4. *Empirical predictions.* Computer generated reports have the potential for being more directly tied to actuarial data because of the large data base of case and client histories that can be built into the system.

Disadvantages

1. *Loss of individualization.* Reports generated by a computer may not be adequately individualized to capture the highly personal nature of the client's situation. Such generic descriptors often produce statements that may apply to anyone. They can also have a more mechanical tone and will miss subtlety and nuance in description.

2. *Documentation.* Scoring services do not necessarily provide documentation for the various narrative statements that are produced in the report. This makes it impossible to evaluate the quality of the report or the scoring service.

3. *Questions of validity.* While computer generated reports may be based upon a great many client cases, the number of clients who are similar to the particular

client in question may actually be quite small. This can significantly affect the validity of predictions. While the best scoring services are working to expand and strengthen the data bases upon which such predictions are made, this information is still not always available. Without adequate evidence of validity for any predictive statement, there is no reason to believe that a computer generated prediction has any more validity than a prediction made by an experienced clinician.

SUMMARY

Tests designed to assess interests, personality, and adjustment are typically used for one of three purposes: research, self-understanding, or clinical assessment and diagnosis. While many of these tests are primarily of use to the clinician or academic psychologist, others do have much wider utility. Interest tests in particular have application to a variety of contexts. Because an individual's pattern of interests may have such impact upon career choice and work satisfaction, career counselors often make use of these instruments. Furthermore, counselors may use interest tests and some personality inventories to help clients achieve greater self-understanding and to make better choices regarding work, relationships, and so on. Educators are increasingly interested in the applications of self-concept scales to the study of various learning situations and the academic performance of children and adolescents.

QUESTIONS AND EXERCISES

1. Consider the following interest inventories: (1) the Strong Interest Inventory; (2) the Career Assessment Inventory; and (3) the Self-Directed Search. Which one(s) would you recommend in each of the following situations? Give reasons for your choices.

   a. A college sophomore seeks counseling concerning his or her choice of major and occupation.

   b. A counseling program is being set up for students entering a vocational high school that has several different trade programs.

   c. An inventory is needed for a course for 10th graders exploring careers and the process of occupational choice.

2. How do you explain the lack of stability in the scores on interest inventories administered prior to adulthood?

3. Consider going to the career center on your campus and completing one or more interest inventories. Ask to have a counselor meet with you to discuss the instrument and its interpretation.

4. What is meant by the term *response set?* What are some potentially important response sets? How might they affect the results on an interest inventory, a personality inventory, and an adjustment inventory?

5. What conditions must be met if a self-report inventory is to be filled out accurately and give meaningful results?

6. What are the *Big Five* and how do they relate to personality measurement?

7. What important differences did you notice between the MMPI-2 and MCMI-III? What are the relative strengths and weaknesses of each test?

8. Why are personality, adjustment, and interest tests usually more difficult to understand and interpret than are tests of cognitive abilities?

9. What benefits are to be derived from computerized interpretations of personality inventories? What are the disadvantages of these automated systems?

SUGGESTED READINGS

Gottfredson, G. D., & Holland, J. L. (1989). *Dictionary of Holland occupational codes* (2nd ed.). Odessa, FL: Psychological Assessment Resources.

Groth-Marnat, G. (1990). *Handbook of psychological assessment* (2nd ed.). New York: Wiley.

Harmon, L. W., Hansen, J. C., Borgen, F. H., & Hammer, A. L. (1994). *Strong Interest Inventory, applications and technical guide.* Stanford, CA: Stanford University Press.

Holland, J. L. (1985). *Making vocational choices: A theory of vocational personalities and work environments* (2nd ed.). Englewood Cliffs, NJ: Prentice Hall.

Holland, J. L., Powell, A. B., & Fritzsche, B. A. (1994). *Self-Directed Search Professional User's Guide.* Odessa, FL: Psychological Assessment Resources.

Jackson, D. N., Holden, R. R., Locklin, R. H., & Marks, E. (1984). Taxonomy of vocational interests of academic major areas. *Journal of Educational Measurement, 21,* 261–275.

Millon, T. (1990). *Toward a new personology.* New York: Wiley.

Moreland, K. L. (1985). Validation of computer-based test interpretations: Problems and prospects. *Journal of Consulting and Clinical Psychology, 53,* 816–825.

Walsh, W. B., & Osipow, S. H. (Eds.) (1986). *Advances in vocational psychology: Vol. 1. The assessment of interests.* Hillsdale, NJ: Erlbaum.

CHAPTER 12

Attitudes and Rating Scales

INTRODUCTION

As we discussed in Chapter 10, there are important educational decisions that require information that cannot be obtained with conventional cognitive tests. Some of these decisions involve objectives that refer to processes and products of instruction, and others require information about personality traits and attitudes. For example, the teacher of a music appreciation class may be concerned with the attitudes and feelings students have toward music, as well as their cognitive knowledge about the subject. Instructional objectives for social studies classes may emphasize both the development of good citizenship and positive attitudes toward the culturally different, as well as knowledge of how government works. It is always more difficult to gain knowledge about personality traits and attitudes than about cognitive characteristics, because with cognitive tests we are measuring maximum performance, or how much the person can do. When assessing personality and attitudes, we are measuring typical performance, personal preferences, and dispositions. It is much easier to structure a test to elicit an accurate representation of maximum performance than one of typical performance.

We can learn about the characteristics of people in three main ways: (1) by observing for ourselves the behavior of the individual, using methods discussed in Chapter 10, (2) by obtaining information indirectly through another person—in the form of references and ratings, or (3) by gaining information directly from the individual—that is, with some form of self-report. Self-report measures of maximum performance (that is, cognitive tests) were covered in Chapters 8 and 9, and self-report assessments of personality characteristics and interests were discussed in Chapter 11. This chapter introduces methods for soliciting information about a person through use of reports from other individuals. In addition, we cover ways to elicit self-report statements of attitudes or beliefs about persons or objects.

LEARNING ABOUT PERSONALITY FROM OTHERS

One important way in which an individual's personality is manifested is through the impression he or she makes on others. The second person can then serve as a source of information about the personality of the first. We can ask teachers to provide information on the degree to which their students have learned to appreciate music or the degree of their opposition to drug use. Or, we could ask students to make this evaluation about each other. The first situation is an application of ratings by a superior or supervisor; the second illustrates ratings by peers.

These techniques for learning about the personality of others have proved useful in many situations. We might want answers to any of the following questions: How well does Person A like Person B? Does Person A consider Person B to be a pleasing individual to have around? An effective worker? A good job risk? Does Person A consider Person B to be conscientious? Trustworthy? Emotionally stable? Questions of this sort are regularly asked of teachers, supervisors, former employers, ministers, and even friends of individuals being rated.

Rating scales also can be used to learn about an individual's cognitive characteristics, abilities, and achievements. Usually such information is obtained directly with paper-and-pencil tests completed by the examinee, but rating scales can provide useful supplementary information about the impression a person's cognitive functioning makes. Under some circumstances, particularly for very young children or people who are unable to respond for themselves, rating scales may even replace paper-and-pencil tests. Of course, we need to be sure that these ratings provide accurate estimates if they are to be used to make important decisions.

Letters of Recommendation

Information from letters of recommendation can be used for many different purposes, but letters are most commonly used to evaluate a candidate for something: admission to a school or for awarding a scholarship or fellowship, a job, membership in a club, or a security clearance. How useful and how informative is the material that is included in free, unstructured communications describing a person? Actually, in spite of the vast number of such letters written every year (a recent review [Knouse, 1989] suggests that 90% of companies use such letters and virtually all graduate schools also use them), relatively little is known about the adequacy of letters of recommendation or their effectiveness. Opinions about their value vary widely, and factual studies are inconclusive as to the reliability and validity of information obtained from letters of recommendation or the extent to which such information influences actions taken with respect to the applicant.

A large portion of the research currently being done on letters of recommendation is specific to admission to graduate schools. In one early study of this kind, an analysis of 67 letters written for 33 psychology internship applicants (Siskind, 1966) found 958 statements distributed as follows:

Type of Statement	Number	Percentage
Positive statements	838	87
"Don't know" statements about a characteristic	17	2
Statements referring to natural shortcomings, the result of inexperience or youth	44	5
Other statements indicative of shortcomings	59	6

Reviewers do use such letters, and there is a moderate degree of consistency (reliability = .40) among letters written about a given person. One clue as to why this relationship occurs comes from a classic study of adjectives used in a series of letters written in support of applicants for engineering jobs (Peres & Garcia, 1962). Of 170 different adjectives extracted from the letters, almost all were positive in tone, but when the "best" employees were compared with the "worst" employees, the adjectives differed enormously in the degree to which they differentiated these groups. An applicant might be called "congenial," "helpful," and "open" or he or she might be called "ingenious," "informed," and "productive." The first three adjectives were applied about equally often to the best and to the poorest workers, while the last three adjectives were used only to describe the best workers. Apparently, the validity of the inferences drawn from a letter of recommendation depends to a considerable extent on the degree to which the reviewer has learned to "read between the lines" and to weigh the nice things that are said using an appropriate *discrimination factor* that identifies virtues mentioned as job relevant or tangential. Similar findings were obtained by Baxter, Brock, Hill, and Rozelle (1981) in a study of letters of recommendation for graduate school applicants, and Knouse (1989) reviews what is known about how to make letters particularly effective. Aamodt, Bryan, and Whitcomb (1993) found that if explicit scoring criteria were used, letters of recommendation were valid predictors of performance in graduate school.

In addition, writers of letters of recommendation are free to write whatever they choose, so there is no core of content common to letters about a single person or to the letters dealing with different people being considered for the same position. One letter may deal with a person's social charm; a second, integrity; and a third, originality. Furthermore, writers of recommendations differ profoundly in their propensity for using superlatives. Some employers and schools attempt to solve this problem by offering suggestions for specific traits that the letter writer should address.

An additional consideration is that the applicant usually is free to select the people who will write the letters. Certainly, we can expect all but the most naive applicants to select people who will be supportive.

The extent to which a letter of recommendation provides a valid appraisal of an individual and the extent to which it is accurately diagnostic of outstanding points, strengths, or weaknesses are almost completely unknown. However, there is little reason for optimism in terms of their validity. The lack of a common frame of reference for such information makes interpretation particularly difficult and hazardous.

Rating Scales

The extreme subjectivity of the unstructured statement, the lack of a common core of content or standard of reference from person to person, and the extraordinary difficulty in attempting to quantify unstructured materials gave impetus to the development of rating scales. Rating scales were developed to obtain appraisals on a common set of attributes for all raters and all individuals being rated and to have the attributes expressed on a common quantitative scale.

We have all had experience with ratings, either in the capacity of rating others or being rated ourselves. Rating scales appear on many report cards, particularly in sections reporting nonacademic performance. We often find a section phrased somewhat as follows:

Characteristic	First Period	Second Period	Third Period	Fourth Period
Effort	_____	_____	_____	_____
Conduct	_____	_____	_____	_____
Citizenship	_____	_____	_____	_____
Adjustment	_____	_____	_____	_____

H = superior   S = satisfactory   U = unsatisfactory

Many civil service agencies and industrial firms send rating forms out to people listed as references by job applicants, asking for evaluations of the individual's "initiative," "originality," "enthusiasm," and "ability to get along with others." These same companies or agencies often require supervisors to give merit ratings of their employees, classifying them as "superior," "excellent," "very good," "good," "satisfactory," or "unsatisfactory" on a variety of traits or on overall performance. Colleges, medical schools, fellowship programs, and government agencies require ratings as a part of their selection procedures. Beyond these practical uses, ratings are used in many research projects; vast numbers of ratings are completed, often reluctantly, every day.

Most frequently ratings are retrospective, summarizing the impressions developed by the rater over an extended period of contact with the person being rated. Sometimes ratings are concurrent, arising out of an interview or a period of observation. Almost universally, a rating involves an evaluative summary of past or present experiences in which the "internal computer" of the rater processes the data in complex and unspecified ways to arrive at the final assessment.

The most common rating procedures involve presenting the rater with a set of traits and a range of numbers, adjectives, or descriptions that represent levels or degrees of the traits. The rater is asked to evaluate one or more people on the trait or traits by assigning a number, letter, adjective, or description to the trait. Figure 12.1 contains examples of two rating scales similar to ones that have been used by a company to evaluate middle level managers. The first, which is one dimension from a set of eight addressed by the original instrument, assesses the trait of leadership; a general description of the trait is provided along with definitions of various levels of

Figure 12.1
Two forms of rating scales.

Consider this person's ability to inspire confidence. How much respect does he (she) command as an individual, not just because of his (her) position? Do people look to him (her) for decisions? Is he (she) afraid to "stick his(her) neck out" for what he (she) believes? Does he (she) inspire teamwork?

_____ Completely lacking. Definitely a follower with equals. Does not try to convince others that his (her) way is best.

_____ Tries to lead with some success, but has never achieved a strong position. Is passive in directing subordinates.

_____ Good leader. Other people wait to hear what this person has to say. Respected by colleagues. People call for this person's opinion.

_____ Exceptional leader. Able to take over and pull things into shape. People seem to enjoy going along with this person's ideas. Is respected by subordinates and colleagues.

Please place a mark on the scale to show the overall rating of this person in their present position.

Not meeting the require- ments	Fair, but needs to improve	Satis- factory	Doing good work	Excel- lent job

leadership. The second example requires an overall evaluation of how well an employee has carried out the responsibilities of a particular position.

These are illustrations of the wide range of rating instrument formats. We shall turn shortly to some of the major variations in rating patterns, but now let us consider some of the problems that arise when one tries to get a group of judges to make such appraisals.

Problems in Obtaining Sound Ratings

There are two general classes of problems that make it difficult to obtain accurate and valid ratings. First, there are factors that limit the rater's *willingness* to rate honestly and conscientiously, in accordance with the instructions for rating. Second, there are factors that limit a person's *ability* to rate consistently and correctly, even with the best of intentions. We shall consider each of these problem areas in turn.

Factors Affecting the Rater's Willingness to Rate Conscientiously. When ratings are collected, we commonly assume that each rater is trying to follow the instructions that have been given and that any shortcomings in the ratings are due entirely to chance and human fallibility. However, this is not necessarily true. There are at least two sets of circumstances that may impair the validity of a set of ratings: (1) The rater may be unwilling to take the time and trouble that is called for by the appraisal procedure; and (2) the rater may identify with the person being rated to such an extent as to be unwilling to give a rating that will hurt the other person.

Unwillingness to Put Forth Sufficient Effort. Ratings are a nuisance under the best of circumstances. The careful and thoughtful rating of an individual requires considerable effort. In an attempt to provide a uniform frame of reference, the authors of some rating procedures have developed extensive lists of traits and elaborate descriptions of the behaviors that exemplify each trait. This practice can result in excellent ratings, but if the rating form is long and the number of individuals to be rated is large, the task may be so overwhelming that it seems not worth the effort. When ratings are carried out in a perfunctory manner, the rating process is less effective. Unless raters are really "sold" on the importance of the ratings, the judgments are likely to be hurried and superficial, with more emphasis on finishing the task than on making accurate analytical judgments.

Identification with the Person Being Rated. Ratings are often requested by distant administrators and impersonal agencies. The Civil Service Commission, the Military Personnel Division of a commanding general's headquarters, the personnel director of a large company, or the central administrative staff of a school system are all quite far removed from the first-line supervisor, the squadron commander, or the classroom teacher—the people who must do the ratings. The rater usually feels greater connection to the people being rated—the workers in the office, the junior officers in the outfit, or the pupils in the class—than to the agency requesting the ratings. One of the first principles of supervision or leadership is that "the good officer looks out for his/her people." The state of morale in an organization depends on the conviction that the leader of the organization takes care of its members. When ratings come along, "taking care of" becomes a matter of seeing to it that one's own people fare as well as—or a little better than—those in competing groups.

As a result, in too many situations, the rater is more interested in ensuring that those with whom he or she works closely get high ratings than in providing accurate information. This situation is made even worse by the common policies of making the ratings public and requiring the rater to discuss with the person being rated any unfavorable material in the ratings. Administrative rulings that specify the minimum rating necessary for promotion or a pay increase aggravate the situation further. It should come as no surprise that ratings tend to climb or to pile up at a single scale point. There is a tendency for the typical rating, accounting for a very large proportion of all ratings given, to be "excellent." "Very good" almost becomes an expression of dissatisfaction, while a rating of "satisfactory" is reserved for the person the rater would like to get rid of at the earliest opportunity.

In some cases, the reverse effect can also occur. If a supervisor has recently had an unpleasant interaction with a subordinate, one way to retaliate is to give a rating that is lower than justified. When subordinates are rating their supervisor, as is the case when students rate the performance of their instructor, the opportunity for this form of payback is even greater, because the ratings generally are anonymous and may provide the only way for disgruntled subordinates to vent their hostile feelings.

It is important to be aware that a rater cannot always be depended on to work wholeheartedly at giving valid ratings for the benefit of the requesting agency, that making ratings is usually a nuisance to the rater, and that there is likely to be more of a commitment to the rater's own subordinates than to an outside agency. A rating program must be continuously "sold" and policed if it is to remain effective. However, there are limits to the extent to which even an active campaign can overcome a rater's natural inertia and interest in the group with which he or she identifies.

Factors Affecting the Rater's Ability to Rate Accurately. Even when raters are well motivated and try to do their best to provide valid judgments, a number of factors still operate to limit the validity of their judgments. These factors center on the lack of opportunity to observe the person to be rated, the covertness of the trait to be rated, ambiguity in the meaning of the dimension to be rated, lack of a uniform standard of reference, and specific rater biases and idiosyncrasies.

Lack of Opportunity to Observe. Raters often have limited opportunities to observe the person being rated. For example, a high school teacher with five classes of 30 students each may be required to judge the "initiative" or "flexibility" of all 150 students. A college professor who has taught a particular class of 100 students may receive rating forms from an employment agency or from the college administration asking for similar judgments on some of the students. Under such circumstances, there usually has been insufficient contact with individual students to provide an adequate basis for the judgments being requested. The person being rated may physically have been in the presence of the rater for many hours, possibly several hundred, but these were very busy hours in which the rater, as well as the person being rated, was concerned with more pressing matters than observing and forming judgments about the traits for which ratings have been requested.

In a civil service or industrial setting, the same problems arise. The primary concern is getting the job done. Even though, in theory, a supervisor may have a good deal of time to observe each worker, in practice, he or she is busy with other things. We may be able to "sell" supervisors on the idea of devoting more of their energy to observing and evaluating the people working for them, but there are very real limits on the amount of effort—thus time—that most supervisors can withdraw from their other functions and apply to this one.

The problem may not only be a lack of opportunity to observe but also a lack of opportunity to observe the particular characteristic in the person to be rated. Any person sees another only in certain limited contexts, and these contexts reveal only some aspects of behavior. The teacher sees a child primarily in the classroom, the foreman sees a worker primarily on the production line, and so forth. In a *conventional* classroom it is doubtful whether the teacher has seen a child under circumstances that might be expected to elicit much "initiative" or "originality." The college professor who teaches mainly through lectures is not well situated to rate a student's "presence" or "ability to work with individuals." The supervisor of a clerk doing routine work is not in a position to appraise "judgment." Whenever ratings are proposed, either for research purposes or as a basis for administrative actions, we should ask whether the rater has had an adequate opportunity to observe the people to be rated in enough situations for the ratings to be meaningful. If the answer is *no,* we would be well advised to abandon rating the trait in question.

Each rater sees a person in a different role and is therefore likely to focus on quite different aspects of the person. Students see a teacher from a different vantage point than does the principal. Classmates in officer candidate school have a different view of other potential officers than does their tactical officer. For those deciding who should be the rater, it is appropriate to ask who has had the best opportunity to see the relevant behavior displayed. Normally, that person should be the one from whom we request the ratings.

Covertness of the Trait.   If a trait is to be appraised by someone other than the person being rated, its existence must produce observable behavior. Such characteristics as appearing to be at ease at social gatherings, having a pleasant speaking voice, and participating actively in group projects are characteristics that are essentially social. They appear in interactions with other people and are directly observable. By contrast, attributes such as "feelings of insecurity," "self-sufficiency," "tension," or "loneliness" are inner personal qualities. They are private aspects of personality and can be inferred only crudely from what the person does. We refer to these as covert characteristics.

An attribute that is largely covert can be judged by an outsider only with great difficulty. Inner conflict, or tension, may not show on the surface, and when it does, it may reveal itself indirectly. Furthermore, it is unlikely to manifest itself in the same way for each person. For example, deep insecurity may express itself as aggression against other students in one child or as withdrawal into an inner world in another. Insecurity is not a simple dimension of overt behavior. It is instead an underlying trait that may be manifested in different ways by different people or in different ways by the same person at different times or in different circumstances. Only with a thorough knowledge of the person, combined with psychological insight, is it possible to infer from overt behavior the nature of a person's underlying covert dynamics.

For these reasons, rating procedures for covert aspects of personality are generally unsatisfactory except in special circumstances where highly trained observers are rating people they know very well. Qualities that depend both on a thorough understanding of a person and on the generation of inferences from behavior are measured with low reliability and poor validity in most common rating contexts. Ratings are more accurate for those qualities that show outwardly as a person interacts with other people, the overt ones. Experience has shown that these overt qualities can be rated more reliably and one feels confident that they are rated with more validity than can covert ones. The validity lies in part in the fact that these social aspects of behavior have their meaning and definition primarily in the effects one person has on others.

Ambiguity in the Meaning of the Dimension.   Many rating forms require ratings of broad and abstract traits. For example, the rating scale presented earlier included "citizenship" and "adjustment." These are neither more nor less vague and general than the traits included in many rating forms. Agreement among raters regarding the meanings of these terms is unlikely. What do we mean by "citizenship" in an elementary school student? How is "good citizenship" shown? Does "good citizenship" mean not marking on the walls? Or not spitting on the floor? Or not pulling little girls' hair? Or does it mean bringing newspaper clippings to class? Or joining the Junior Red Cross? Or staying after school to help the teacher clean up the room? What *does* it mean? No two raters are likely to have exactly the same things in mind when they rate a group of students on "citizenship."

Or consider "initiative," "personality," "supervisory aptitude," "mental flexibility," "executive influence," or "adaptability." These are all examples drawn from rating scales in actual use. Although there is certainly some core of uniformity in the meaning that each of these terms will have for different raters, there is a great deal of variability in meaning from one rater to another. The more abstract a term, the more variable its meaning from person to person, and such qualities as those just listed are conspicuously abstract.

The rating that a given child receives for citizenship will depend on what citizenship means to the rater. If to one teacher citizenship is indicated by a child conforming to school regulations, he or she will certainly rate high those children who conform. If to a different teacher citizenship is indicated by a child taking an active role in school projects, that teacher may give high ratings to quite different children. The first step in getting consistent ratings is to establish a minimal level of agreement among raters about the meanings of the qualities being rated. One way to accomplish this task is to provide the desired definition on the rating form. If a good citizen is defined as a "child who follows the school rules," then a common understanding of the term will be fostered if the definition is made explicit in the directions for the rating scale.

Lack of Uniform Standard of Reference.   Many rating scales call for judgments of the people being rated in sets of categories such as the following:

Outstanding, above average, average, below average, unsatisfactory
Superior, good, fair, poor
Excellent, good, average, fair, poor
Outstanding, superior, better than satisfactory, satisfactory, unsatisfactory
Superior, excellent, very good, good, satisfactory, unsatisfactory

How good is "good"? Is a person who is "good" in "judgment" in the top 10% in judgment for the group with whom he or she is being compared? The top 25%? The top 50%? Or is this person just not one of the bottom 10%? And, what is the composition of the group with which this person is being compared? Are all members the same age? Are they all employees of the same company? Are they all persons in a particular job? Are all employees in the same job with the same length of service? If the latter, how is the rater supposed to know the level of judgment that is typical for people in a particular job with a given amount of experience?

The problem that all these questions bring up is the need for a standard against which to appraise the person being rated. Variations in interpretation of terms and labels, in definition of the reference population, and in experience with the members of that background population all contribute to rater-to-rater variability in the standards of rating. The phenomenon is familiar to those involved in academic grading. There are enormous variations among faculty members in the percentages of As, Bs, and Cs awarded in comparable courses. The same situation holds for any set of categories, numbers, letters, or adjectives that may be used. Standards are highly subjective interpretations, and they can therefore be expected to vary widely from one rater to another. (You can easily illustrate this problem for yourself. Take a set of words like *frequently, usually,* and *seldom,* and ask several of your friends what each word implies in terms of a percentage. In one group of 160 college freshmen I found the meaning inferred from the word *frequently* ranged from 50% up to 95%. Some people thought *usually* might mean as little as 50% of the time, while others thought *seldom* might imply as often as 65% of the time.)

Raters differ not only in the level of ratings that they assign but also in how much they spread out their ratings. Some raters are conservative and rarely rate anyone very high or very low; others tend to go to both extremes. Differences in variability in ratings reduce their comparability from one rater to another. These differences among raters appear not to be a chance matter but to be a reflection of the personal characteristics and value structures of individual raters.

One attempt to overcome the problem of a uniform frame of reference is to attach specific percentages to the verbal descriptions. For example, many college and graduate school reference forms will ask for ratings of "general academic ability," "knowledge of the discipline," and so forth on a scale such as

Outstanding, Superior, Above Average, Average, Below Average

and define "outstanding" as "being in the top 5% of the reference group." The other categories are given similar specific definitions, such as "top 10%," "top 25%," "top 50%," and "bottom half." The scale is given additional definition by asking the rater to specify the reference group, for example, "college seniors" or "first year graduate students." Unfortunately, one sometimes finds that 25% of college seniors are in the top 5% of college seniors!

Specific Rater Biases and Idiosyncrasies.   Raters not only differ in general toughness or softness but may be characterized by other idiosyncrasies as well. Life experiences have provided each of us with likes and dislikes and an assortment of individualized interpretations of the characteristics of other people. You may distrust people who do not look at you when they are talking to you. Your teenage son may consider anyone who listens to classical music to be "not with it." Your boss may consider a firm handshake to be a guarantee of strong character. Your tennis partner may be convinced that people with small eyes are not trustworthy. The behaviors people believe indicate the presence of these traits are concrete, and the descriptions of these behaviors can be clearly verbalized by the person making judgments, regardless of the validity of the stereotype.

But there are myriad other more vague and less tangible biases that we each have and that can influence our ratings. These biases help to form our impressions of other people and influence all aspects of our reactions to them, and they can enter into our ratings too. In some cases, our rating of one or two traits may be affected. But often the bias is one of a general liking for or an aversion to the person, and this generalized reaction influences all of our ratings. Ratings, therefore, reflect not only the general subjective rating standard of the rater but also any biases about the characteristics of the person being rated.

A different type of idiosyncrasy that is likely to influence overall judgments of effectiveness on a job (or in an educational program) is individual differences in the types of behavior considered desirable. Supervisors of employees in closely similar jobs have been found to differ widely in the attributes they considered important. For example, some raters may consider "solving problems on one's own initiative" among the most important traits a subordinate could have, and others may consider it among the least important. To the extent that such differences in values prevail, it is inevitable that supervisors will fail to agree on who are their more effective subordinates.

The Outcome of Factors Limiting Rating Effectiveness.   The effects of factors limiting rating effectiveness are manifested in systematic distortions of the ratings, in relatively low reliabilities, and in questionable validity of rating procedures. We summarize these problems under four headings: the generosity error, the halo effect, low reliability, and questionable validity.

The Generosity Error.   We have already noted that raters often identify more with the people they are rating than with the agency for which ratings are being prepared. Over and above this, there also seems to be a widespread unwillingness, at least in the United States, to damn a fellow human with a low rating. The net result is that ratings tend generally to pile up at the high end of any scale. The unspoken philosophy of the rater seems to be that every person is as good as the next, if not better, so that the term *average* in practice is not the midpoint of a set of ratings but instead a point at the lower end of the group. It is a little like the commercial classification of olives, where the tiniest ones are called "medium," and the classification continues from there through "large" and "extra large" to "jumbo" and "colossal." I have occasionally quipped to my students that a good set of anchor points for a rating scale might be "poor," "average," "above average," "superior," and "godlike."

If the generosity error operated uniformly for all raters, it would not be particularly disturbing; we would merely have to remember that ratings cannot be interpreted in terms of their verbal labels and that "average" means "low" and "very good" means "average." Makers of rating scales have even countered this humane tendency with some success by having several extra steps on their scale on the plus side of average, so that there is room for differentiation without the rater having to be negative by labeling a person or trait as "average." The differences between raters in their degrees of "generosity error" are more troublesome than the fact that there is a generosity error. Corrections for such differences are difficult to implement.

The Halo Effect.   Limitations in experience with the person being rated, lack of opportunity to observe the specific qualities that are called for in the rating instrument, and the influence of personal biases that affect general liking for the person all conspire to produce another type of error in ratings. This is the tendency of raters to evaluate in terms of an overall impression, without differentiating specific aspects of personality, to allow the total reaction to the person to color judgment of each specific trait. E. L. Thorndike in 1920 gave this type of rating error the name *halo effect.*

Of course, a relationship between desirable traits is to be expected. We find positive correlations between different abilities when these abilities are assessed by objective tests, and we do not speak of a halo effect that produces a spurious correlation between verbal and mechanical ability. Just how much of the relationship between the different qualities on which we get ratings is genuine and how much is a spurious consequence of halo is hard to determine, but when correlations between traits exceed the interrater agreement in ratings of the traits, there is cause for concern. Landy, Shankster, and Kohler (1994) note that a consensus seems to be emerging that while the halo effect is a real phenomenon, its apparent presence is not a good index of the quality of a rating scale.

Low Reliability.   The reliability between raters using conventional rating procedures has generally been found to be low. When two ratings are uncontaminated, which means the raters have not discussed the people being rated, and when the usual type of numerical or graphic rating is used, the resulting appraisals can be expected to have a low correlation, often in the 50s. However, evidence suggests that when great care is taken in structuring rating scales through a careful delineation of the endpoints, or anchors, on the scale, and when the raters are well trained and have had ample opportunity to observe those being rated, the reliability of ratings can be improved (Landy et al., 1994).

If it is possible to pool the ratings of a number of independent raters who know the people being rated about equally well, the reliability of the appraisal can be substantially increased. Pooling ratings has the same effect as lengthening a test, and the Spearman-Brown Prophecy Formula (discussed in Chapter 4) can legitimately be applied in estimating the reliability of pooled independent ratings. Thus, if the reliability of a single rater is represented by a correlation of .55, we have the following estimates for the reliability of pooled ratings:

.71 for 2 raters
.79 for 3 raters
.86 for 5 raters
.92 for 10 raters

Unfortunately, in many situations, obtaining additional equally qualified raters is impractical, if not impossible. An elementary school student has only one regular classroom teacher; a worker has only one immediate supervisor. Adding other raters who have more limited acquaintance with the person being rated may weaken rather than strengthen the ratings.

Questionable Validity. All the limiting and distorting factors that we have considered—in particular, rater biases and low reliability—tend to suppress the validity of rating instruments. However, it is seldom possible to empirically determine the validity of ratings. The very fact that we are using ratings suggests that no better measure of the characteristic in question is to be had. Usually there is nothing else available with which we can verify the accuracy of ratings.

In one sense, the validity of ratings is axiomatic. If we are interested in appraising how a person is perceived by other people, that is, whether a child is well liked by his classmates, or a foreman, by her work crew, ratings *are* the reactions of these other people and are directly relevant to the trait or behavior in question.

When ratings are being studied as predictors, it is sometimes possible to obtain statistical data that can be used to quantify the accuracy of the prediction. This is something that must be determined in each setting and for each criterion that is being predicted. In some cases, ratings may be the most valid available predictors. One example comes from studies of the ratings of aptitude for military service that were given at the U.S. Military Academy at West Point (Adjutant General's Office, Personal Research Section, 1953). These ratings by tactical officers and fellow cadets were shown to correlate better with later ratings of combat effectiveness than any other aspect of the candidate's record at West Point. This criterion is again a rating, but it is probably as close to the real "payoff" as we are likely to get in this kind of situation. In other situations, of course, ratings may turn out to have no validity at all. Each case must be studied for its own sake.

Ratings usually are used as a criterion measure. When this is the case, everything possible should be done to ensure the accuracy and reliability of the ratings, because they represent the standard against which other procedures will be judged. It behooves us, therefore, to examine ways that ratings can be improved.

Improving the Effectiveness of Ratings

Thus far we have painted a rather gloomy picture of rating techniques as measurement devices. It is certainly true that there are many hazards and pitfalls in rating procedures. But, in spite of all the limitations of ratings, they are and will continue to be the means of appraisal for a host of situations in which we have to rely on the judgments of other people. The sincerity and integrity of a potential medical student, the social skills of a would-be salesperson, the maturity of a sixth grader, or the conscientiousness of a private secretary can probably be evaluated only through the judgment that someone makes of these qualities in the people in question. On the positive side, Landy et al. (1994) note that when the best methods of scale construction are combined with adequate training procedures for the raters, the weight of evidence indicates that ratings can give accurate and valid appraisals of individual characteristics. What can be done, then, to mitigate the defects of rating procedures and achieve the conditions Landy et al. describe? We shall first consider the design of the rating instrument and then the planning and conduct of the ratings.

Refinements in the Rating Instrument.   The usual rating instrument has two main components: (1) a set of *stimulus variables* (the qualities to be rated) and (2) a pattern of *response options* (the ratings that can be given). In the simplest and most conventional forms, the stimulus variables consist of trait names, and the response options consist of numerical or adjectival categories. Such a form was illustrated earlier. This type of format appears to encourage most of the shortcomings discussed in the preceding section; consequently, many format variations and refinements have been tried in an attempt to overcome or at least to minimize these shortcomings. In the variations, the stimulus variables, the response options, or both have been manipulated. Some of the main variations are described next.

Refinements in Presenting the Stimulus Variables.   Simple trait names represent unsatisfactory stimuli, for two reasons. In the first place, the words mean different things to different people. The child who shows "initiative" to Ms. Johnson may show "insubordination" to Mr. Cordero, whereas Mr. Cordero's "good citizen" may seem to Ms. Johnson to be a "docile conformist." In the second place, trait names often are quite abstract and far removed from the realm of observable behavior. Consider "adjustment," for example. We cannot directly observe a child's adjustment. Instead, we can observe only the reactions of the child to situations and people. Some of these reactions may be symptomatic of poor adjustment. But the judgment about the child's adjustment is an inference based on what we have a chance to observe.

Users of ratings have striven to obtain greater uniformity in the meaning of traits to be rated by basing the ratings more closely on observable behavior. These attempts have modified the stimulus aspect of rating instruments in three ways.

1. *Trait names can be explicitly defined.* "Social adjustment" is a rather nebulous label. It can be given somewhat more substance by elaborating on what the label is intended to mean, as in the following example.

> *Social adjustment.* Interest in and skills of interacting with both children and adults in work and play situations. Willingness both to give and to take in interpersonal situations. Conformity to basic social norms of behavior.

The elaboration attaches more substance to an intangible concept and should provide greater uniformity of meaning among different raters and between the raters and the designer of the rating form.

There is no question that an expanded definition of each attribute to be appraised is a desirable first step in improving rating procedures. However, it is doubtful that a brief verbal definition will do very much to overcome the raters' individual differences in the meanings that they attach to terms, and, consequently, to the rating task.

2. *Trait names can be replaced by several more limited and concrete descriptive phrases.* For example, the abstract and inclusive term "social adjustment" might be broken down into several components, each relating to a more limited aspect of behavior. Thus, in place of the one term, we might have:

Works in groups with other children
Plays with other children
Interacts with teacher and other adults
Obeys school rules

A judgment would now be called for with respect to each of these more restricted and more tangible aspects of student behavior.

3. *Each trait can be replaced with a number of descriptions of specific behaviors.* This practice carries the move toward concreteness and specificity one step further. Thus, the general descriptor "works in groups with other children" might be elaborated with something like:

Works in groups with other children
Takes an active part in group enterprises
Makes and defends suggestions
Accepts majority decisions
Does his or her share of the work
Helps others with their work

A similar subdivision would be carried out for each of the three other components listed in the previous step. The descriptions used to define "works in groups with other children" make the behavior still more tangible and specific. There should be much less ambiguity as to what it is that is to be observed and reported, but there is still an element of interpretation in deciding, for example, what level of involvement constitutes "takes an active part."

Replacing one general term with many specific behaviors gives promise of more uniformity in meaning from one rater to another. It may also bring the ratings in closer touch with actual observations the rater has had an opportunity to make of the behavior of the person being rated. If it is the case that the trait to be rated involves behaviors that the rater has had no opportunity to observe, replacing trait names with specific observable behaviors may make this fact painfully apparent and force the designer of the instrument to reexamine the problem of relating the instrument to observations the raters really have had an opportunity to make.

The gains that a list of specific behaviors achieves in uniformity of meaning and concreteness of behavior judged are not without cost. The cost lies in the greatly increased length and complexity of the rating instrument. There are limits to the number of different judgments that a rater can be asked to make. Furthermore, a lengthy, analytical report of behavior may be confusing to the person who tries to use and interpret it. The lengthy list of specific behaviors will probably prove most effective when (1) judgments are in very simple terms, such as "present" or "absent" and (2) there are provisions for organizing and summarizing the specific judgments into one or more *scores* for broad areas.

Refinements in Response Categories.   Expressing judgments about a person being rated by selecting some one of a set of numbers, letters, or adjectives is still common on school report cards and in civil service and industrial merit rating systems; however, these procedures have little to commend them except simplicity. As we discussed earlier, often the categories are arbitrary and undefined. No two raters interpret them in exactly the same way. A rating of "superior" may be given to 5% of employees by one supervisor and to 25% by another. One teacher's A is another teacher's B. Subjective standards reign supreme.

Attempts to achieve a more meaningful scale or greater uniformity from rater to rater have included use of the following:

1. percentages
2. graphic scales
3. behavioral statements
4. person-to-person scales
5. present or absent scales
6. frequency of occurrence or degree of resemblance judgments

1. Percentages.   In an attempt to produce greater uniformity from rater to rater and better discrimination among the ratings given by a particular rater, procedures sometimes call for raters to make judgments in terms of percentages of a particular defined group. Thus, a professor rating an applicant for a fellowship might be instructed to rate each candidate according to the following scale:

In the top 2% of students at this level of training
In top 10%, but not in top 2%
In top 25%, but not in top 10%
In top 50%, but not in top 25%
In lower 50% of students at this level of training

Presumably, the specified percentages of a defined group provide a uniform standard of quality for different raters and the asymmetric set of categories maximizes discrimination where it is most desired, among the top candidates. However, the stratagem is usually only partially successful. Individual differences in generosity are not that easily suppressed, and we may still find 25% of the people being rated placed in the top 10% category.

2. Graphic scales. Our second variation is more a matter of form than clarity of definition. Rating scales are often prepared so that judgments can be recorded by making a check mark at some appropriate point on a line instead of choosing a number, letter, or adjective that approximates the level of the trait. These instruments are called *graphic scales* and have the following general form.

Responsibility for completing work

The use of graphic scales results in an attractive page layout, can be compact and economical of space, and may seem somewhat less forbidding than a form that is all print. However, although the simplicity of graphic presentation may help newer raters to visualize the construct as being on a continuum, for sophisticated users, a graphic presentation seems to make little difference.

3. Behavioral statements. We have seen that the stimuli may be in the form of relatively specific behavioral statements. Statements of this sort may also be combined with the graphic layout to present the rating alternatives. Thus, we might have an item of the following type:

Participation in School Projects

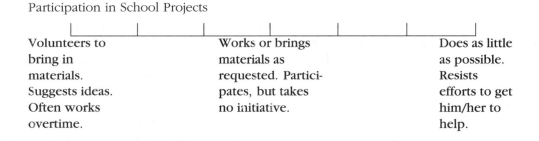

Here, three sets of statements describing behavior are listed on a graphic scale; they are used to define three points on the scale. The descriptions can be expected to make the task more concrete and the scale steps more uniform. However, the use of behavioral statements does not ensure that all raters will see things the same way, because raters must still make subjective decisions on how to interpret these behavioral statements.

A whimsical development of a rating form that provides a fairly clear illustration of behavioral statements is shown in Figure 12.2.

4. Person-to-Person Scales.   An early attempt to add uniformity of meaning to the response scale, developed as far back as World War I, uses persons instead of numbers, adjectives, or descriptions to represent the scale points. The rater is asked to think of someone he or she has known well who is very high on the quality being rated. That person's name is entered on the rating form to define the "very high" point on the scale. In the same way, the names of other people known well by the rater are entered in spaces to define "high," "average," "low," and "very low." The five stimulus persons then define levels for the trait. The rater is instructed to compare the individual to be rated with the five stimulus people defining the levels of the trait. The rater then judges which stimulus person the individual being rated most closely resembles on the trait in question the related value becomes assigned to the person being rated.

The developers thought that the person-to-person scale would lend concreteness to the comparisons and overcome the tendency of some raters to be consistently generous. When all raters have a wide range of acquaintances, so that their stimulus people may be expected to be fairly comparable, the procedure may add more uniformity from rater to rater. Unfortunately, raters seldom have both broad and similar ranges of acquaintances. Ratings almost always involve implicit comparisons with other people, but explicit use of particular people to define the steps on a rating scale has not been widely adopted.

5. Present or Absent Scales.   When a large number of specific behavioral statements are used as the stimuli, the response that is required could just be a series of checks to indicate which statements apply to the individual being rated. The rating scale then becomes a behavior checklist. An example of such a rating form, adapted from the *Checklist of Adaptive Living Skills* (Morreau & Bruininks, 1991), is shown in Figure 12.3.

If this type of appraisal procedure is to yield a score on a trait, rather than a long list of behaviors, the statements must be scaled or assigned score values in some way. The simplest way is to score each statement $+1$, -1, or 0, depending on whether it is favorable, unfavorable, or neutral, with respect to a particular attribute (e.g., perseverance, integrity, or reliability) or a particular criterion (such as, success in academic work, success on a job, or responsiveness to therapy). A person's score can then be the sum of the scores for the items checked. We shall consider checklists in more detail when we discuss adaptive behavior scales.

6. Frequency of Occurrence or Degree of Resemblance Judgments.   Instead of having to react in an all-or-none fashion to an item, as with checklists, the rater can be given choices such as "always," "usually," "sometimes," "seldom," or "never." (In formulating items to be responded to with these categories, you must take care that no term expressing frequency is included in the statement of the item. Otherwise, you might commit the syntactic atrocity of judging that Johnny "always" "usually accepts majority decisions.") Another approach is to have the person being rated characterized as "very much like," "a good deal like," "somewhat like," "slightly like," or "not at all like" the behavior described in the statement. The terms indicating frequency or resemblance may vary; the ones given here are only suggestive. Also, an

Figure 12.2
Employee performance appraisal.

Area of Performance	Degree of Performance				
	Far exceeds job requirements	Exceeds job requirements	Meets job requirements	Needs improvement	Does not meet minimum requirements
Quality of Work	Leaps tall buildings in a single bound	Leaps tall buildings with a running start	Can leap short buildings with prodding	Climbs stairs effectively	Trips entering buildings
Promptness	Is faster than a speeding bullet	Is as fast as a speeding bullet	Would you believe a slow bullet?	Misfires frequently	Wounds self when handling guns
Adaptability	Walks on water	Swims well	Washes with water	Drinks water	Chronically waterlogged
Communication	Talks with God	Talks with the angels	Talks to others	Talks to self	Argues with self

Figure 12.3

Items from the *Checklist of Adaptive Living Skills.*

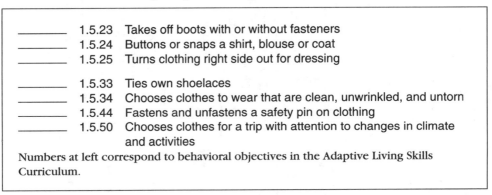

_____	1.5.23	Takes off boots with or without fasteners
_____	1.5.24	Buttons or snaps a shirt, blouse or coat
_____	1.5.25	Turns clothing right side out for dressing
_____	1.5.33	Ties own shoelaces
_____	1.5.34	Chooses clothes to wear that are clean, unwrinkled, and untorn
_____	1.5.44	Fastens and unfastens a safety pin on clothing
_____	1.5.50	Chooses clothes for a trip with attention to changes in climate and activities

Numbers at left correspond to behavioral objectives in the Adaptive Living Skills Curriculum.

Source: Copyright © 1993 by The University of Iowa. Reproduced from *Checklist of Adaptive Living Skills.* Reproduced by permission of the publisher, The Riverside Publishing Company.

individual's score could take account of both the significance and the frequency of the behavior in question. That is, an important attribute could receive more credit than a minor one, and a check that the behavior "always" occurred could be given more credit than "usually."

As we noted earlier, indefinite designations of frequency or degree of the sort suggested here will not be interpreted the same way by all raters, so the old problem of differences in rater biases and idiosyncrasies reappears. When asked to indicate what percentage of the time was implied by each of several terms, a class of introductory psychology students gave a wide range of answers. For some students *always* meant more than 80% of the time, while for others it meant *every* time. Words like *usually* and *frequently* were taken to mean somewhere between 50% and 95% of the time. Similar variation has been found for other frequency terms. Moreover, when the number of specific behaviors being checked is substantial, a simple checking of presence or absence correlates quite highly with the more elaborate form.

Improving the Accuracy of Ratings

The best designed instrument cannot give good results if it is used under unsatisfactory rating conditions. Raters cannot give information they do not have, and they cannot be made to give information they are unwilling to give. We must, therefore, try to select raters who have had close contact with the people being rated and ask them for judgments on attributes they have had an opportunity to observe. We also should give raters guidance and training in the type of judgment expected from them and, if possible, they should observe the people to be rated *after* they have been educated in the use of the rating form. When there are several people who know equally well the individuals to be rated, ratings should be gathered from each person and then pooled. Every effort should be made to motivate the raters to do an honest and conscientious job. Let us consider each of these issues in more detail.

Selecting Raters. For most purposes, the ideal rater is the person who has had the most extensive opportunity to observe the person being rated in those situations likely to elicit the qualities being rated. (Occasionally, it may be desirable to get a rating of the impression that a person makes on brief contact or in a limited experimental situation, but this is not the usual case.) It is also desirable that the rater maintain an impartial attitude toward the person being rated. The desirability of these two qualities, thorough acquaintance and impartiality, is generally recognized in the abstract. However, the goals may be only partially realized in practice, because knowing someone well and being impartial may be mutually exclusive.

Administrative considerations usually dictate that the rating and evaluation function be assigned to the teacher in a school setting and to the supervisor in a work setting. Since the relationship in each case is one of direct supervision, there is generally a continuing and fairly close personal relationship. But the relationship is a one-directional and partial one. The teacher or supervisor sees only one aspect of the student or worker, the side that is turned toward the boss.

Those qualities that the boss has a good chance to see, primarily qualities of work performance, can probably be rated adequately by a teacher or supervisor. We would expect ratings of job or subject-matter knowledge to correlate fairly highly across supervisors or teachers. However, those qualities that show themselves primarily in relationships with peers or subordinates probably would be evaluated more soundly by those peers or subordinates, and in such cases, they should be the ones to do the rating.

Deciding Who Should Choose the Raters. The selection of persons to rate applicants for a job or admission to a college requires consideration of another issue. The applicant usually is asked to supply a specific number of references or to submit evaluation forms filled out by a predetermined number of individuals. The choice of the raters is usually left up to the applicant, and we may anticipate that he or she will select people who will furnish favorable ratings. It might be more satisfactory if the applicant were asked to supply the names and addresses of people with whom there is a particular relationship and who could therefore be requested to supply relevant information, rather than leaving the applicant free to select the referees. A job applicant might be asked to give the names of immediate supervisors in recently held jobs; a fellowship applicant might be asked to list the names of major advisors and of any instructors from whom two or more courses have been taken. This action would shift the responsibility of determining who provides the ratings from the applicant to the agency using them. Such a shift should reduce the amount of positive bias for the applicant.

Providing Education for Raters. Good ratings do not just happen, even with motivated raters and good instruments for recording the ratings. Raters must be "sold" on the importance of making good ratings and taught how to use the rating instrument. However, this is often easier said than done. As was indicated earlier, unwillingness to put forth the necessary effort, on the one hand, and identification with the person being rated, on the other, are powerful competing motives. These problems can only be overcome by education and indoctrination to convince the raters that their tasks are important, and the "selling job" must continue if raters are to maintain thoughtfulness and integrity in their appraisals over a period of time.

Raters should have practice with the specific rating instrument that they will use. A training session, in which the instrument is used under supervision, is often desirable. This enables raters to discuss meanings of the attributes, prepare sample rating sheets, and review the resulting ratings. Also, the prevailing generosity error can be noted, and raters can be cautioned to avoid it. Additional practice for raters may generate a more symmetrical distribution of ratings. Training sessions will not eliminate all the shortcomings of ratings, but they should reduce the more common distortions.

Selecting Qualities to Be Rated.   Two principles appear to apply in determining the types of information to be sought through rating procedures. First, it is undesirable to use rating procedures to get information that can be provided by a more objective and reliable indicator. A score on a well-constructed aptitude test is a better indicator of cognitive ability than is a supervisor's rating of intellect. When accurate production records exist, they should be preferred over a supervisor's rating for productivity. We resort to ratings when we do not have better indicators available.

Second, we should limit ratings to relatively overt qualities—ones that can be expressed in terms of actual observable behavior. We cannot expect the rater to peer inside the person being rated and tell us what is going on. Furthermore, we must bear in mind the extent and nature of the contact between the rater and the person being rated. For example, a set of ratings to be used after a single interview should be limited to the qualities that can be observed in an interview. The interviewee's neatness, composure, manner of speech, and fluency in answering questions are qualities that should be observable in a single interview. Industry, integrity, initiative, and ingenuity are not directly observable in such a limited encounter, although these qualities might be appraised with some accuracy by a person who has worked with the interviewee for a time. Ratings should be of behavior observable in the setting in which the rater has known the person being rated.

Pooling Independent Ratings from Several Raters.   One of the limitations of ratings is low reliability. If several people have had a reasonably good chance to observe the person being rated, reliability can be improved by pooling their independent ratings. Unfortunately, the number of persons well placed to observe a person in a particular setting—school, job, camp, and so forth—is usually limited. Often, only one person has been in close contact in a particular relationship with the person being rated. A student has had only one homeroom teacher; a worker, only one foreman; and a camper, only one tent counselor. Others have had some contact with the person, but the contact may have been so much more limited that pooling their judgments adds little to the information of the rater most intimately involved.

Note that we specified the pooling of *independent* ratings. If the ratings are independently made, the error components will be independent and will tend to cancel out. If, however, the judgments are combined through some sort of conference procedure, we do not know what will happen. Errors may cancel out, wisdom may win, or the prejudices of the most dogmatic and forceful rater may prevail. Pooling independent ratings is the only sure way to cancel out individual errors.

Constructing Rating Scales Based on Input from Raters.   A method that has become popular for developing instruments to evaluate performance is based on involving raters in developing the rating scales that they will eventually use. Development of such instruments proceeds in three stages.

1. A group of future raters agrees on the dimensions that can be distinguished as the important aspects of performance on a given job. For example, the following broad categories might be suggested as important qualities for first-line supervisors to have in a large company.

Knowledge and judgment
Conscientiousness
Skill in human relations
Organizational ability
Objectivity
Skill at observing situations

2. The potential users then generate a pool of *critical incidents,* or examples of actually observed behavior, to illustrate superior, average, and inferior performance in each of the selected dimensions. (The term *critical incidents* comes from the idea that these behaviors should be critical to success or failure in the position.) Raters in a second independent group are then called on to assign each incident to the appropriate dimension. Only when the second group of raters agrees on the assignment of critical incidents to a dimension are these incidents retained in the final instrument.

3. Each person in the second group of raters indicates where on a scale of excellence each statement falls. The average level and the consistency of these judgments are scrutinized, and a subset of items is retained that shows good agreement among raters and for which the complete set shows a wide range of average scale values. The following items were taken from a scale entitled Interpersonal Relations with Students that has been used to evaluate college faculty (Harari & Zedeck, 1973). The scores on the scale range from 1 (low) to 7 (high).

Scale Value	Statement
6.8	When a class doesn't understand a certain concept or feels "lost," this professor could be expected to sense it and act to correct the situation.
3.9	During lectures, this professor could often be expected to tell students with questions to see him during his office hours.
1.3	This professor could be expected to embarrass or humiliate students who disagree with him.

To apply this methodology, the rater, having been provided with the set of statements for each dimension, indicates which statement comes closest to describing the person being rated. Users have reported that this procedure yielded less method variance, less halo error, and less leniency error than more conventional rating procedures (Campbell, Dunnette, Arvey, & Hellervik, 1973).

Focusing Raters on Behaviors Prior to Ratings.   One objection to ratings is that they are usually made after the fact and are based on general, unanalyzed impressions about the person being rated. We can attempt to get away from a dependence on use of memory in ratings by introducing the rating program well in advance of the time at which the final ratings are to be made. Then, a record form can be developed in which critical areas of performance are identified, as described in the previous section, and a space provided for recording instances of desirable—as well as undesirable—actions of the person being rated.

The procedures for this type of scale development are quite time consuming, and the resulting instrument tends to be a little cumbersome. More experience is needed with developing rating scales using input from raters before we can judge whether gains from prior use of the scales are maintained in later use and whether the gains made are sufficient to justify the additional effort required in developing the scales. But an advantage of scales constructed in this way is that they result in specific behavioral descriptions, which often are more reliably rated and more valid than other methods (Landy et al., 1994).

Rating Procedures for Special Situations

Several rating procedures have been developed for special situations. In this section we discuss four of them: (1) adaptive behavior scales, (2) ranking procedures, (3) the forced-choice format, and (4) nominating procedures.

Adaptive Behavior Scales.   Work with very young children and with handicapped individuals with severely limited abilities has led to the development of assessment procedures that combine some of the characteristics of rating procedures with those of ability tests. These instruments are designed to be completed by informants (parents, teachers, care givers, and so forth) about the person being assessed. Examples of such instruments are the AAMR Adaptive Behavior Scales—Residential and Community Edition (ABS-RC:2) of the American Association of Mental Retardation (AAMR) (Nihira, Leland, & Lambert, 1993), the AAMR Adaptive Behavior Scale—School Edition (ABS-S:2) (Lambert, Leland, & Nihira, 1993), the Checklist of Adaptive Living Skills (Morreau & Bruininks, 1991), and the Vineland Adaptive Behavior Scale (Sparrow, Balla, & Cicchetti, 1984).

These instruments all have similar formats—a set of items that are based on either developmental tasks typical of children at different ages or skills needed for independent living. The informant is then asked to indicate whether the person can accomplish the task. The items can be scored either "yes/no" or rated along a range indicating how typical the behavior is. The responses are summed, and the total scores are compared to normative standards to indicate the child's developmental age or the person's level of impairment. The following items might be found on such a scale:

Uses toilet
Uses knife and fork
Throws ball
Stacks three blocks
Uses irregular verbs
Makes friends

Clearly, the number of potential items is enormous. The items can also be subdivided into categories such as motor, self-grooming, social, language, and school-related skills, with separate scores given for each area of functioning.

Adaptive behavior scales are most appropriately used when there is a need to obtain information about a person's level of functioning, either to supplement what can be learned from mental ability tests or to substitute for them. These instruments are most frequently used to assess children with learning problems, and they are particularly appropriate for trainable and young, educable mentally retarded children.

Concern about the disproportionate numbers of minority children enrolled in special education classes has increased interest in using adaptive behavior scales. There is concern that standardized intelligence tests may be unfairly labeling some minority children as mentally retarded. The unfairness stems from the ability of many of these students to function normally in nonschool settings. Adaptive behavior scales can be used to understand better the functioning of students in a wide range of settings and to help diagnostic teams make better decisions about placement.

Although the administration of one of these instruments can be a useful part of the overall diagnosis of a child with learning or developmental problems, the instruments share important limitations. A major deficiency of these instruments is their dependence on the ability or willingness of the informants to provide accurate information. Parents in particular are prone to see their children in the best possible light and to be hesitant to admit shortcomings in their offspring.

A related problem concerns the intrusive nature of some of the items and the appropriateness of asking informants to give the information to individuals who are, in many cases, strangers. The use of these adaptive behavior scales as substitutes for standardized measures of cognitive ability has not proved successful, because the scores from these instruments tend not to be strongly related to performance in school. They may, however, give valuable supplementary information about ability to function in nonacademic settings.

Ranking Procedures.   When each rater knows a substantial number of people being rated, raters may be asked to rank the ratees with respect to each attribute being assessed. Thus, a teacher might be asked to indicate the child who is most outstanding for contributing to class projects and activities "above and beyond the call of duty," the one who is second, and so on. Usually, the rater is instructed to start at the extremes and work toward the middle because the extreme cases are usually easier to discriminate than the large group of average ones in the middle. This feature is sometimes formalized as *alternation ranking,* that is, picking the highest and then the lowest, the next highest and then the next lowest, and so on. Tied ranks (where people being rated seem equal) may be permitted, to ease the task of the rater. If tied ranks are not permitted, the person doing the ranking may feel that the task is an unreasonable one, especially for a large group.

Ranking is an arduous task, but it does achieve two important objectives. First, it forces the person doing the evaluation to discriminate among those being evaluated. The rater is not permitted to place all or most of the people being rated in a single category, as may happen with other rating systems. Second, ranking washes out individual differences in generosity or leniency among raters. No matter how generous the rater is, someone must be last and no matter how demanding he or she is, someone must come first. Individual differences in standards of judgment are eliminated from the final score.

If scores based on rankings by different judges are to be combined, there is one assumption introduced in ranking that may be as troublesome as the individual judging-standard differences that have been removed. If we are to treat rankings by different judges as comparable scores, we must assume that the quality of the group ranked by each judge is the same. That is, we must assume that being second in a group of 20 represents the same level on the trait being appraised in all groups of 20. Usually, there is no direct way to compare the subgroups, so we have to assume that they are comparable. If the subgroups are fairly large (e.g., 30 people) and are chosen more or less at random from the same sort of population, this assumption may be reasonable. But, with small groups or groups selected in different ways, failure to meet the assumption of comparability may introduce substantial errors into scores based on ranking. Of course, when two raters rank the same people, this issue does not arise.

Ranks in their raw form do not provide a very useful type of score, because their meaning depends on the size of the group; being third in a group of three is quite different from being third in a group of 30. Furthermore, steps of rank do not represent equal units of a trait. As we saw in our discussion of percentile norms (Chapter 3), with a normal distribution, one or two places in the rank at the extremes of a group represents much more of a difference than the same number of places in rank near the middle of the group. For this reason, it is common practice to convert ranks into normalized standard scores to obtain a type of score that has uniform meaning regardless of the size of the group, and has uniform units throughout the score range.

The Forced-Choice Format.   All the variations considered so far operate on the same basic pattern. The rater considers one attribute at a time and assigns the person being rated to one of a set of categories or places him or her in a position relative to others on the particular attribute. Now, we will consider a major departure from that pattern. The essence of this procedure is that the rater must choose from a *set* of attributes and decide which one (or ones) most accurately represents the person being rated. For example, an instrument for evaluating instructors might include sets of items such as the following:

a. Is patient with slow learners
b. Lectures with confidence
c. Keeps interest and attention of class
d. Acquaints classes with objectives for each lesson

The rater's assignment would be to select the one or two items from the set that are *most descriptive* of the person being rated.

Note that all of the statements in this set are positive; they are nice things to say about an instructor. They were selected to be about equally positive in their description of an instructor. They do differ, however, in the extent to which they distinguish between people who have been identified, on other evidence, as good or poor instructors. In this case, the most discriminating statement is Statement *a,* and the least discriminating one is Statement *b.* That is, good instructors were identified as being patient with slow learners and poor instructors were not. Both good and poor instructors were equally likely to be identified as lecturing with confidence. Good instructors were somewhat more likely to be judged as keeping the interest and attention of the class and acquainting the class with lesson objectives. Thus, a score value of 2 could be assigned to Statement *a,* 1 to Statements *c* and *d,* and zero to Statement *b.* An instructor's score for the set would be the sum of the scores for the two items marked as most descriptive of him or her. The score for the whole instrument would be the sum of the scores for 25 or 30 such blocks of four statements. Scores of this type have been found to have good split-half reliability (often .85 to .90), so this type of instrument can provide a reliable score, at least in the eyes of individual raters. Of course, this score does not tell us anything about the agreement or lack of agreement that might be found between different raters.

By casting the evaluation instrument into a forced-choice format, the scale maker hopes to accomplish three things.

1. *To eliminate variation in rater standards of generosity or kindness.* Because the items in a set include equally favorable statements about a person, those who prefer to be positive in their evaluations of others will not be inclined to choose any particular statement over the others. Thus, a more accurate picture of the person being rated should emerge because the true nature of the ratee should determine which statements are selected.

2. *To minimize the possibility of a rater intentionally biasing the score.* With most rating scales, the raters control the process. They can rate a person high or low as they please. In a forced-choice instrument, the rater should be unable to easily identify positive and negative statements and should therefore be unable to raise or lower a score at will. The success of this approach will depend on the skill of the scale constructor in equating the attractiveness of the grouped items. Although there are some indications that a forced-choice format is less susceptible to intentional biasing than other rating scales are, it is still far from tamper proof in the hands of a determined rater.

3. *To produce a better spread of scores and a more nearly normal distribution of ratings.* Making all options equally attractive minimizes the effect of the generosity error, which results in a better spread of scores.

A variation on the forced-choice format is the *Q-sort.* This rating format provides the rater with a large number of statements that may be descriptive of the people to be rated. The rater places each item in one of several (often about seven) categories ranging from highly descriptive to not at all descriptive of the ratee. The unique feature of this approach, however, is that the rater is required to produce a particular distribution of placements. A simple example might be, if there were 50 statements and five categories, the task would require that five statements be placed in the two most extreme categories, 10 statements be placed in the next two categories, and the remaining 20 statements would, by default, be assigned to the middle category. As with most of the forced-choice formats, the Q-sort has more often been used for personality description than for performance rating.

Disadvantages of the Forced-Choice Format.   The most important disadvantage of the forced-choice format is that raters dislike using this approach, largely because it takes control away from them. They cannot easily rate an individual high or low depending on their overall feelings, which leads to frustration often manifested in an unwillingness to work diligently at the task of rating.

The forced-choice format also requires that the scale constructor exercise considerable skill in designing option choices that appear to be equally desirable but which differ in the extent to which they characterize more successful individuals. The method demands that the items go through extensive tryout prior to actual use, in order to determine which items differentiate between successful and unsuccessful people.

Forced-choice formats generated a good deal of interest, some research, and a certain amount of practical use during the period from 1945 to 1965, but the burden of preparing them and the negative reactions to them by raters have resulted in a gradual decline in interest in them in recent years. They continue to be used, however, in some personality and attitude scales and in some measures of vocational interests and preferences.

Nominating Techniques.   Up to this point we have considered methods that are most frequently used when the person doing the rating is in a superior position to the person being rated. We now turn our attention to a method for collecting information about individuals through their peers, other members of their social group. Such procedures can be particularly valuable to a teacher or to a supervisor whose subordinates interact with each other extensively. Our discussion will focus on the classroom, but the principles apply to other social settings.

To understand the students in the class, a teacher must have an awareness of the roles and social relationships of the class members—the peer group. The standards and values of a student's peers provide the sanctions and rewards that are very influential in determining how a person will act in the group setting. Acceptance or rejection by the peer group can be one of the most important determinants of the person's behavior and outlook on life.

In general, teachers have a fairly good sense of which students are and which are not accepted by their peers. A correlation of about .60 between teacher rankings and the pooled choices of peer group members seems to be fairly typical. But an improved picture of group dynamics can often be obtained by the *nominating technique.* This procedure is most often applied to social choice patterns, but can also be used for more general trait ratings.

In the classroom a teacher can use the simple expedient of asking students to name their choices of best friends or work partners to solicit such ratings. For example, the teacher might say to the class: "For our unit on Canada we are going to need some committees who will work together on parts of the project. I would like to know which classmates you would like to have on a committee to work with you. Put your name at the top of the piece of paper I give you. Then under your name put the names of the other students you would most like to have on your committee."

Such a procedure produces a set of nominations or choices for work partners. These choices can then be shown pictorially in a diagram such as the one in Figure 12.4. A diagram like this is called a *sociogram,* and the procedure for constructing it is called *sociometry.*

From the sociogram in Figure 12.4 we can see that students A and B are the "stars," the most sought after members of the class. Each forms the nucleus of his or her own group or clique. Students J and O did not choose anyone and were not chosen by any other students; they are isolates. Students H and I chose each other but were not chosen by any other students. Except for the mutual friendship between them, they too are isolates. Students P, Q, M, and N are fringe members; they do not really belong to any of the groups, but they do express a desire to affiliate.

The sociogram in Figure 12.4 indicates that this is not a closely knit group. The rather large number of isolates and fringe members and the linkages across from one clique to the other suggest an unstable pattern that is in the process of changing. This sociogram might represent a class at the beginning of the school year in which the residue of last year's friendships is mixed with new currents as students from other classes and perhaps other schools begin to be integrated into the group.

Figure 12.4
Sociogram of fourth grade class.

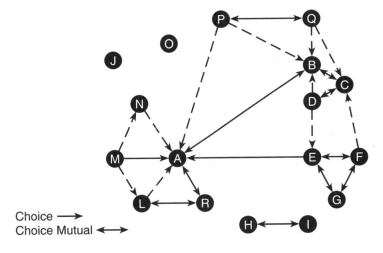

Choice ⟶
Choice Mutual ⟷

Nominations can be used at any age level and may be made with respect to any characteristic. For example, they have frequently been used in the armed services in officer candidate school, where each member of the class may be asked to nominate a specified number of individuals in the unit who have shown the greatest evidence of "leadership" during the course. Candidates may also be asked to nominate those who have shown the *least* indication of leadership. Taking all nominations for the group as a whole, it is possible to arrive at a score for each individual by giving a plus for each favorable nomination and a minus for each unfavorable one.

A variation of the nominating technique that has been used with school children has usually been referred to as the "Guess Who" technique. In this procedure the children might be instructed somewhat as follows.

Suppose we were going to put on a class play. The characters in the play are described below. For each character you are to put down the name of one or more members of the class who would be good for the part because the person is just like that anyway.

"This person is always cheerful and happy—never grouchy or cross."

"This person is always butting in and telling other people how to do things—cannot mind own business."

"This person is very quiet and doesn't get into games or do things with other children."

The number of characters can be increased as needed. Each "character" is a description in fairly concrete terms of a quality of behavior in which the investigator is interested. Descriptions at opposite ends of the scale can be included—that is, friendly versus unfriendly, dominant versus submissive, and so on—and can be treated as positive and negative ends on a single scale. Each child receives a score for each character based on the number of nominations received.

The attractive feature of nomination procedures is their simplicity, which makes them rather painless to administer and usable with young children or groups with little sophistication or experience in making ratings. They work because the large number of raters makes it possible to use a simple count of nominations in place of the usual quantitative rating. However, nomination procedures can generate resistance. Parent groups sometimes have reacted violently when children were asked to make negative nominations of rejection or separation from their classmates. It is important to be aware of these sensibilities in students and the community.

MEASURING ATTITUDES

In the previous sections, we discussed methods of learning about people—their abilities, as well as their personality traits and attitudes—by obtaining information from others who know them well in terms of the type of information sought. It is also possible to obtain this kind of information directly from the individuals being appraised.

The assessment of abilities and personality traits has been discussed in Chapters 8 through 11. In attitude measurement, we are interested in obtaining a reliable score that can represent the intensity of an individual's sentiments toward or against something. Like other self-report measures, attitude assessments are limited by what the individuals know and are willing to communicate about themselves.

Most people have similar perceptions about the social desirability of the items measuring personality traits, so there is a tendency for everyone to respond to items on such instruments in a similar fashion—generally, in a way that makes them look good; this tendency is a limitation inherent in such instruments. Because the social desirability of many attitudes differs from one person to another (that is, there is less agreement about what the "right" response is), these measures are less affected by this response bias. When we seek the overall attitude level of a group and do not need to know about the attitudes of individuals, it is possible to keep responses anonymous. This practice increases the probability that responses will represent a more genuine reflection of attitudes.

A major problem with attitude assessment instruments is the apparent ease with which they can be constructed. Just because items can be collected quickly and an instrument put together easily does not mean that the instrument will measure the constructs it is intended to measure in a reliable and valid manner. Unless attitude scales are created in a systematic fashion, using what is known about good scale construction, the results probably will be meaningless.

The construction of an attitude rating scale usually begins with a catalog of statements covering possible views on the target concept, drawn from readings, associates, and the recesses of the author's consciousness. The goal of this process is to select a broad range of statements that is representative of all the possible items that could be used to measure the attitude under investigation. These items should range from the most positive and favorable statements to the most negative and unfavorable and should cover all aspects of the attitude. Each statement should be clear and brief, present a single idea, and be focused on a feeling rather than on a fact, that is, an attitude rather than an item of information. The following list of suggestions for selecting statements to include in an attitude rating scale, adapted from Edwards' (1957) classic work, has been found to improve attitude scale construction.

1. Do not use statements that refer to the past rather than to the present.
2. Avoid statements that are factual or could be interpreted as factual.
3. Make sure no statement can be interpreted in more than one way.
4. Do not use filler statements that are irrelevant to the psychological construct being investigated.
5. Avoid statements that would be endorsed by almost anyone or by almost no one.
6. Be sure to include statements that cover the entire range of the construct of interest.
7. Keep the wording of the statements simple, clear, and direct.
8. Keep the statements short (rarely exceed 20 words).
9. Be sure each statement contains only one complete thought.
10. Avoid universals such as *all, always, none,* and *never* because they often introduce ambiguity (are they meant to be absolute?).
11. Words such as *only, just, merely,* and others of a similar evaluative nature should be used with care and moderation.
12. Statements should be written in simple sentences rather than compound or complex sentences unless this cannot be avoided.

13.   Avoid using words that may not be understood by those who are to be given the completed scale. Make the reading level appropriate to the intended audience.

14.   Do not use double negatives (p. 14).

Summative Attitude Scales

Attitude scales usually require the subjects to respond to the statements by using a numerical indication of the strength of their feeling toward the object or position described in the statement. The responses are summed to estimate the strength of the attitude. The most frequently used technique for obtaining such a numerical indication is to have respondents indicate their level of feeling toward a number of statements, often in terms of the degree to which they agree or disagree with the statements. This technique is called a *summative rating,* because the person's attitude is then reflected by the sum of the responses to the individual statements. It is also called a *Likert scale* after Rensis Likert, who first introduced the technique in the 1930s. The following key is an example of the options that might be provided to an individual responding to the scale.

5—Strongly agree
4—Mildly agree
3—Don't know
2—Mildly disagree
1—Strongly disagree

If you wanted to measure the attitudes of teachers in a school toward grouping students, you might include statements such as the following:

1.   Grouping students in classes by ability inhibits social development.
2.   Students achieve more when they attend class with other students of similar ability.
3.   Gifted students should be taught in classes made up of other gifted students.
4.   Special education students should be assigned to regular classes.

Statements 1 and 4 express an attitude generally opposed to ability grouping, while Statements 2 and 3 are supportive of the practice. The teachers would respond by placing a number adjacent to each statement, indicating their degree of agreement with the statement. The scale should include statements that would be endorsed by people at both the positive and negative ends of the attitude continuum, to correct for the tendency of respondents to agree with most statements presented to them, a tendency called "acquiescence." Those people who strongly agree with Statements 1 and 4 should disagree with Statements 2 and 3. If they do not, then we must question whether they are taking the task seriously. It is often extremely difficult to reverse statements without substantially changing the meaning, but it is essential to have both ends of the spectrum of sentiments represented.

In the process of summing across items to obtain an attitude score for each person, the scoring of negatively stated items is reversed, so that people who express disagreement with the negative statements receive a positive score. Strongly disagreeing with a negative statement is treated in the scoring like strongly agreeing with a positive one. This is accomplished by subtracting the subject's value assigned to an item from one point more than the highest value that can be assigned. For example, on the five-point scale described above, if the instrument is being scored so that high scores reflect a positive attitude toward ability grouping, a response of strongly agree (5) to Item 4 would be given a score of $6 - 5 = 1$. Thus, a person who strongly agreed with Statements 2 and 3 and strongly disagreed with Statements 1 and 4 would receive the maximum score of 20, while someone with exactly the reverse pattern would receive the minimum score of 4.

Number of Steps. The number of steps in the scale is important. The more steps, the greater the reliability of the scale, because the range available for expressing a position increases (we saw the effect of restriction of range on reliability in Chapter 4). The increase is noticeable up to about seven steps. Items with more than seven steps are seldom used, because the increase in reliability resulting from the additional steps is slight, and it is often difficult to write meaningful anchors. It is easier to increase reliability by adding more items.

Types of Anchors. The five-point scale described earlier certainly is the most popular one to use for measuring attitudes. But even though the agree-disagree anchors are particularly flexible, other anchors should be used when they fit the meaning of the statements. For instance, anchors on a continuum such as "effective—ineffective," "important—unimportant," or "like me— not like me" have been used successfully when appropriate to the context.

An Odd or an Even Number of Steps. When constructing a scale you must also decide whether to use an odd or an even number of steps. Most respondents seem to prefer an odd number, so that they have an appropriate response when they feel neutral toward a statement. With an even number of steps, they might feel as if they are being forced to take sides in an issue where they truly feel neutral. On the other hand, repeated selection of the neutral position can be an easy way out for the person unwilling to devote an appropriate amount of time to the task of responding to all items.

One drawback to using an even number of steps and denying the individual responding the opportunity to make a neutral response is a possible increase in the number of statements not responded to because some respondents may refuse to give any response if they cannot pick the midpoint. In general, there would seem to be more to be gained in good will with respondents by including a neutral point than would be lost by forcing them to choose sides.

Single-Item Scales

When interest is focused on the attitudes of a group of people rather than on single individuals, it is common practice to use a single questionnaire to assess attitudes toward each of several objects or points of view. Often, each issue under consideration is represented by a single statement. Although the response of a single individual lacks sufficient reliability to provide a useful assessment of the person's attitude, the trend in a group can be accurately determined in this way, because the response error tends to average out over the group and produce a reliable indication of the sentiments of the group. This is the basis for opinion polling.

Although single-item scales are common, they have some inherent problems. The single item prevents the assessment of internal consistency, so reliability is expressed as a margin of error in the proportion. If the one item is misunderstood by a respondent, the results of the assessment become invalid for that person. There is also the danger that the single item may be written in a way that systematically biases the results. Consider the following two statements:

1. Parents should be forced to bus their children long distances for the purpose of achieving school desegregation.
2. The courts should use any reasonable means for achieving school desegregation.

It is likely that in the mind of the author both statements reflect a positive attitude toward the use of busing as a means of achieving school desegregation. But used as single items, the statements could be expected to yield quite different results. Even people who strongly support desegregation might respond negatively to the first statement. Instability of meaning due to subtle differences in the wording of single-item scales is often a problem in opinion polls and is the reason that proponents of two opposing positions can both claim that they enjoy the support of most of the public. This type of bias could occur to some degree with any attitude scale, but with use of a large number of items, the likelihood exists that the positive and negative items will cancel each other out.

Example of an Attitude Rating Scale

The first task in developing an attitude scale on a topic such as women's liberation and equality would be to gather a large number of items representing the full range of topics and views on the subject. For women's liberation, the topics would cover equal employment opportunities, child care, sexual freedom, personal independence, degree of role differentiation, and so forth. Each statement should be clear and brief, present a single idea, and focus on a feeling rather than on a fact, that is, an attitude rather than information.

Item Selection.   The total pool of items initially generated is usually much too large to use as a measuring instrument. Also, the ideal is to use only items that we can be confident measure the trait, so it is necessary to select the best subset of items. This subset is selected by having the items reviewed and rated by judges. The judges' function is not to indicate agreement or disagreement with any item but rather to assess where the statement falls on a "for to against" scale in relation to the target concept. Judges should also be asked to indicate any statements that seem irrelevant to the attitude dimension and to offer suggestions for aspects of the trait for which statements have not been provided. The scale points might range from nine, indicating a very strongly favorable statement about women's liberation and status, through five, or neutral, to one, indicating a statement very strongly hostile toward women's liberation and status.

The purpose of the judges' ratings is to find (1) where on the "for to against" dimension each statement falls and (2) how well a group of judges agree on the statement's meaning. The goal is eventually to select a set of statements that represent all degrees of favorableness and unfavorableness and have statements that convey nearly the same meaning to everyone.

The position of any item on the scale of "favorableness-unfavorableness" is indicated by the median rating that it receives from the judges, and its ambiguity, by the spread of ratings as indicated by the interquartile range. Consider the following two statements where judges used a nine-point scale:

	Median	**Interquartile Range**
A wife's job and career are just as important as her husband's.	8.1	1.5
Feminine fashions are a device to hold women in an inferior role.	7.0	5.1

The first statement seems to be promising for inclusion in the final attitude scale. It is a strongly "pro" statement, and judges are in good agreement about where it falls on the attitude dimension. The second statement is a poor choice for the scale. Although on the average it is rated as implying a moderately favorable position toward women's liberation, there is great disagreement among judges on what the statement signifies. It was assigned by different judges to each step position from one to nine. Furthermore, about 10% of the judges marked this statement as irrelevant to the dimension under study. Statements which elicit this level of disagreement should be eliminated from the scale.

Given the judges' ratings, we can select a reasonably brief set of statements that have clear meanings, that represent all degrees of intensity of views, and that cover the main facets of the domain being studied. The statements can usually best be presented to subjects in a format such as the one shown in Figure 12.5, on which the respondent indicates the degree of acceptance of each statement. Responses can be scored 4, 3, 2, 1, 0, with AA getting a score of 4 and DD, a 0. The item responses would all be entered into the computer in this way, and the nine negative items (3, 5, 8, 9, 14, 16, 17, 18, 19) would be reversed by the computer in obtaining total scores for the scale. The possible score for the 20 items would thus range from 80 (most strongly in favor of women's liberation) to 0 (most hostile). A score of 40 would be considered neutral.

Figure 12.5

Sample of an attitude scale.

ATTITUDE TOWARD WOMEN'S LIBERATION

Read each statement. Then circle the symbol that best represents your reaction to the statement, according to the following scale:

AA — strongly agree with the statement.
a — tend to agree with the statement.
? — undecided. Neither agree nor disagree.
d — tend to disagree with the statement.
DD — strongly disagree with the statement.

AA a ? d DD	1.	Men and women should receive the same pay for the same work.
AA a ? d DD	2.	No woman should have to bear a child unless she chooses to.
AA a ? d DD	3.	Most women are unsuited by temperament for supervisory or administrative jobs.
AA a ? d DD	4.	There should be no clubs or public places that are restricted to a single sex.
AA a ? d DD	5.	A woman's place is in the home.
AA a ? d DD	6.	Standards for promotion should be the same for men and women.
AA a ? d DD	7.	A woman's job and career are just as important as her husband's.
AA a ? d DD	8.	Men and women are basically different in their makeup and are suited to fill different roles.
AA a ? d DD	9.	A woman who follows a career can seldom expect to have a satisfactory home life.
AA a ? d DD	10.	There are no inborn psychological differences between men and women.
AA a ? d DD	11.	Men should share equally in housework—getting meals, cleaning, etc.
AA a ? d DD	12.	Every woman should have an independent career if she wants one.
AA a ? d DD	13.	In matters of sex, there should be a single standard for men and for women.
AA a ? d DD	14.	The workers for women's liberation are frustrated female failures.
AA a ? d DD	15.	Except for physical strength, anything a man can do, women can do equally well.
AA a ? d DD	16.	Women's liberation is of interest only to a few women on the lunatic fringe.
AA a ? d DD	17.	It doesn't make sense to make a large investment in a woman's education, because she is likely to marry and not use her advanced training.
AA a ? d DD	18.	By nature, women are submissive and men are dominant.
AA a ? d DD	19.	The natural role for a woman is a secondary, supporting one.
AA a ? d DD	20.	In all respects, men and women should receive the same treatment.

A sample of the results obtained from administering the scale to 133 students in measurement classes is shown in Table 12.1. The scale shows quite satisfactory reliability. In general, these students tended to endorse statements favorable to women's rights, and the more strongly favorable positions (above the median) appeared most often among women, students under 30, unmarried respondents, and non-Catholics.

Item Analysis. Once a set of statements is collected and assembled into an instrument, using the preceding suggestions, it should be administered to a pilot group. Ideally, responses should be made on a machine-scorable answer sheet, which facilitates entering the responses into a computer where they are accessible to the statistical analysis program being used. The responses should be summed, making sure that any negative items are reversed. The responses to each item are then correlated with the total score, and the coefficient obtained indicates how much each item contributes to the overall reliability of the test. The higher the correlation, the better the item. The size of the correlation necessary for a good item depends on the subject matter and test length. A negative correlation may indicate an error in scoring or that the item needs to be revised. By deleting, replacing, or revising bad items, the reliability of the test can be greatly improved.

Reliability. It is important to determine the internal consistency reliability of attitude rating scales using coefficient alpha. As is true with other measures of reliability, the size of coefficient alpha is affected by the variability in the dimension being measured within the sample. Therefore, it is important for the scale to be administered to a sample that shows a reasonable amount of variability in the trait being measured. For instance, if you are assessing attitudes toward the value of higher education among a group of highly educated people, you are likely to find little variability and, consequently, low internal consistency reliability. Internal consistency is an indication that we can make discriminations in the sample and is also evidence that we are

Table 12.1

Selected Results for an Attitude Scale on Women's Liberation

Scores for Selected Percentiles		Percentages by Demographic Variables	
Score	Percentile	Group	Percentage Above the Median
75	90th	Women	61
		Men	29
68	75th	30 and over	41
		Under 30	57
61	50th	Single	55
		Other	46
51	25th	Catholic	39
		Other	57
40	10th		

measuring a one-dimensional trait. If several traits are measured on a single scale and only one score is reported, the traits will tend to cancel each other out and the scale will have low variability and low reliability.

Alternative Formats

Attitude measures sometimes use formats other than the summative one we have considered so far. One simple alternative is to present a set of statements such as those shown in Figure 12.5, being careful to include some neutral statements (neutral statements are not essential and often are not desirable in a summative scale), and to instruct the respondents to mark either (1) *all* statements that they agree with or (2) the statements—possibly a specified number—that *best* represent their views. With this format it is important to have accurately determined a scale value for each item because the score for an individual is the average of the scale values of the statements that person endorsed. This approach to attitude measurement was originally proposed by L. L. Thurstone in 1928 and is known as *Thurstone scaling*.

A slightly different approach is to select a short set of statements (usually five or six) that are very homogeneous in content, differing only in degree of some specific attitude. An example relating to the acceptability of abortion might take the following form:

1. Abortion should be available to any woman who wishes one.
2. Abortion should be legal if a doctor recommends it.
3. Abortion should be legal whenever the pregnancy is the result of rape or incest.
4. Abortion should be legal whenever the health or well-being of the mother is endangered.
5. Abortion should be legal whenever the life of the mother is endangered.

These five statements presumably represent a gradient of permissiveness. A person who agrees with Statement 1 would presumably agree with Statements 2 through 5 (if the statements are in correct order), a person who agrees with Statement 2 but not 1 would probably endorse Statements 3 through 5, and so forth. The person's position on the continuum is defined by the highest statement accepted. Scales of this type (called *Guttman scales,* after the psychologist who first proposed them) have some logical advantages but have proven very difficult to construct.

Semantic Differential.   One other approach to attitude measurement has seen fairly wide use. This is the so-called *semantic differential,* which grew out of the work of Osgood and others on the structure of the domain of meaning represented by adjectives (Osgood, Suci, & Tannenbaum, 1957). Through factor analytic studies, these investigators found that most of the variations in meaning that are expressed by different adjectives can be represented by three main dimensions designated *evalua-*

tive, potency, and *activity.* Adjective pairs that represent the extremes of each dimension are shown below.

Evaluative

good	bad
nice	nasty
fair	unfair

Potency

strong	weak
capable	helpless
dominant	submissive

Activity

energetic	lazy
busy	idle
active	passive

A set of adjectives such as these can be used to get at a person's perception of any target. The target can be a general concept such as women's liberation or abortion, or it can be a specific person such as one's teacher or oneself. Usually the order of the adjectives is scrambled, and the positive and negative poles of some pairs are reversed on the page, to reduce thoughtless, stereotyped responding. A scale with five to nine steps is presented, and respondents are asked to indicate how the target concept or person appears to them by making a mark at the appropriate point between the two adjectives. For example, a respondent reacting to the concept of women's liberation as very good would make a check in the space nearest to "good"; someone perceiving women's liberation as neither good nor bad would check halfway between the two extremes, and so forth.

The semantic differential method provides a quick and easy way to collect impressions on one or several target objects or concepts. However, the set of adjective pairs can often seem inappropriate for the target, and it may stretch a person's imagination to respond. One suspects that in these circumstances the responses may be rather superficial and at a purely verbal level.

One limitation of *all* the attitude assessment procedures we have described is that they involve solely a verbal response. They communicate what people are willing to say they feel or believe, but the respondents may not be entirely open and forthright. More important, people's actions may not correspond to their verbally endorsed beliefs and feelings. A child who verbally subscribes to statements of good will toward members of another ethnic group may still avoid members of that group when picking playmates or friends to invite to a birthday party—or may not. The verbal statements of attitude must be recognized as just that. Although it may be of interest in its own right to learn that after a particular college course or television program students have changed in the verbally stated attitudes that they endorse, it must not be assumed automatically that other aspects of their behavior toward the target object or group will have changed.

SUMMARY

To gain insight into the personality and attitudes of others, you can obtain information directly from individuals, observe their behavior, or obtain information from someone who is in a position to provide it. Personality and attitude assessments are usually accomplished either informally through letters of recommendation or formally, in a structured manner, using rating scales. Both methods have similar limitations centered on the raters' willingness and/or inability to provide accurate assessments. In spite of the limitations of ratings, evaluations of an individual through ratings will undoubtedly continue to be widely used for administrative evaluations in schools, civil service, and industry, as well as in educational and psychological research. Every attempt should be made to minimize the limitations.

The limitations of rating procedures result from the following characteristics of the assessment technique:

1. Raters' unwillingness to make unfavorable judgments about others (generosity error), which is particularly pronounced when the raters identify with the person being rated.
2. Wide individual differences in "humaneness" among raters (differences in rater standards) or in leniency or severity of rating.
3. Raters' tendency to respond to another person as a whole in terms of general liking or aversion, and difficulty in differentiating among specific aspects of the individual personality (halo error).
4. Limited contact between the rater and person being rated—limited both in amount of time and in type of situation in which the person being rated is seen.
5. Ambiguity in meaning of the attributes to be appraised.
6. The covert and unobservable nature of many of the inner aspects of personality dynamics.
7. Instability and unreliability of human judgment.

In view of these limitations, the ratings will provide a more accurate picture of the person being rated when the following criteria are met:

1. Appraisal is limited to those qualities that appear overtly in interpersonal relations.
2. The qualities to be appraised are analyzed into concrete and relatively specific aspects of behavior, and judgments are made of these aspects of behavior.
3. The rating form forces the rater to discriminate, and/or it provides controls for rater differences in judging standards.
4. Raters selected are those who have had the greatest opportunity to observe the person being rated in situations in which the qualities to be rated are displayed.
5. Raters are "sold" on the value of the ratings and are trained in using the rating instrument.

6. Independent ratings of several raters are pooled when there are several people qualified to conduct ratings.

Evaluation procedures in which the significance of the ratings is concealed to some extent from the rater also present an interesting possibility for civil service and industrial use, particularly when controls on rater bias are introduced through forced-choice techniques.

Attitude scales have been developed to score the intensity of favorable or unfavorable reactions to a group, institution, or issue. Although these reactions represent only verbal expressions of attitude and may be inconsistent with actual behavior, such expressions may presage behavioral changes.

QUESTIONS AND EXERCISES

1. If you were writing to someone who had been given as a reference by an applicant for a job in your company or for admission to your school, what should you include in your letter, to obtain the most useful evaluation of the applicant?

2. Make a complete list of the different ratings used in the school that you are attending or the school in which you teach. What type of a rating scale or form is used in each case?

3. How effective are the ratings that you identified in the previous question? How adequate is the ratings spread obtained? How consistently is the scale employed by different users? What is your impression of the reliability of the ratings? What is your impression of their freedom from the halo effect and other errors?

4. What factors influence a rater's willingness to rate conscientiously? How serious is this issue? What can be done about it?

5. Why would three independent ratings from separate raters ordinarily be preferable to a rating prepared by the three raters working together as a committee?

6. In the personnel office of a large company, employment interviewers are required to rate job applicants at the end of the interview. Which of the following characteristics would you expect to be rated most reliably? Why?

    a. Initiative

    b. Appearance

    c. Work background

    d. Dependability

    e. Emotional balance

7. In a small survey of the report cards used in a number of communities, the following four traits were most frequently mentioned on the cards: (a) courteous, (b) cooperative, (c) good health habits, (d) works with others. How might these traits be broken down or revised so that the classroom teacher could evaluate them better?

8. What advantages do ratings by peers have over ratings by superiors? What disadvantages?

9. What are the advantages of ranking, in comparison with rating scales? What are the disadvantages?

10. Suppose a forced-choice rating scale is developed to use in evaluating teacher effectiveness in a city school system. What advantages will this rating procedure have over other types of ratings? What problems will be likely to arise in using it?

11. Suppose you are placed in charge of a merit rating plan being introduced in your company. What steps will you take to try to get the best possible ratings?

12. What factors limit the usefulness of paper-and-pencil attitude scales? What other methods might a teacher use to evaluate attitudes?

13. Prepare a rough draft for a brief attitude scale to measure a teacher's attitudes toward objective tests.

SUGGESTED READINGS

Aamodt, M. G., Bryan, D. A., & Whitcomb, A. J. (1993). Predicting performance with letters of recommendation. *Public Personnel Management, 22,* 81–90.

Egan, O., & Archer, P. (1985). The accuracy of teachers' ratings of ability: A regression model. *American Educational Research Journal, 22*(1), 25–34.

Knouse, S. B. (1989). Impression management and the letter of recommendation. In R. C. Giacalone & P. Rosenfeld (Eds.), *Impression management in the organization.* Hillsdale, NJ: Erlbaum.

Lambert, N., Leland, H., & Nihira, K. (1993). *AAMR Adaptive Behavior Scale—School Edition (2nd ed.).* Austin, TX: PRO-ED.

Landy, F. J., Shankster, L. J., & Kohler, S. S. (1994). Personnel selection and placement. In L. W. Porter and M. R. Rosenzweig (Eds.), *Annual Review of Psychology, 45,* 261–296.

Morreau, L. E., & Bruininks, R. H. (1991). *Checklist of adaptive living skills.* Chicago: Riverside.

Morrison, R. L. (1988). Structured interviews and rating scales. In A. S. Bellack & M. Hershon (Eds.), *Behavioral assessment: A practical handbook* (pp. 252–278). New York: Pergamon.

Nihira, K., Leland, H., & Lambert, N. (1993). *AAMR Adaptive Behavior Scales—Residential and Community* (2nd ed.). Austin, TX: PRO-ED.

Saal, F. E., Downey, R. G., & Lahey, M. A. (1980). Rating the ratings: Assessing the psychometric quality of rating data. *Psychological Bulletin, 88*(2), 413–428.

Sax, G. (1989). *Principles of educational and psychological measurement and evaluation.* Belmont, CA: Wadsworth.

Sparrow, S. S., Balla, D. A., & Cicchetti, D. V. (1984). *Vineland Adaptive Behavior Scales.* Circle Pines, MN: American Guidance Service.

CHAPTER 13

Assessment and Exceptional Children

INTRODUCTION

The notion that test results represent an underlying reality appears throughout history. While testing today bears little resemblance to its historical predecessors, there does appear to be relative agreement among professionals and lay persons alike as to the need for testing in certain situations and with certain populations. Children with exceptionalities are one such example. For many if not most of these children, the route to special services generally begins with some component of standardized testing, a component that has a profound impact on the rest of the service delivery sequence.

Decisions to provide special services to certain groups of people are generally based on the priorities of the broader population. For children with disabilities, the handicapping condition begins with the realization that children have no control over the circumstances of their birth and very little control over the circumstances of their care (Safford & Safford, 1996). Prior to the 18th century, the general level of care for children with disabilities was anything but humane. Archeological evidence suggests that while some early societies were very accepting of persons with disabilities, others were not. Early Greek and Roman legal documents contained provisions for the abandonment, isolation, and extermination of infants and children with deformities (Boswell, 1988).

During the Middle Ages, the care and treatment of persons with disabilities was typically done by relatives, others serving as stand-ins for relatives, or members of religious orders who lived in monasteries. The early role of monasteries is a historically important one for persons with disabilities, in that the medieval abbeys offered physical protection in times of turmoil; they also offered information on educational, medical, and spiritual matters and were, in many locales, the organizational center of community life. Because the monasteries offered their inhabitants a broad-based level of care and nurturance in an accepting, compassionate, Christian-based atmosphere, many parents who were unable to care for their children at home turned them over to the clergy in the monasteries. It was not long, however, before the notion of congregate care facilities gave rise to large-group living facilities for more secular, less virtuous reasons. These asylums, as they came to be known, sprung up throughout Europe to separate the most confused, disorganized, and violent members of society from the rest of the general population (Gallatin, 1982, p. 19).

According to Safford and Safford (1996), pre-Revolutionary thought in France represented a watershed of new developments in the care and treatment of persons with disabilities. Inherent in the Renaissance-era principle of humanism was a heightened level of respect for the worth and dignity of the person, and a new commitment to freedom of thought and spirit. Were it not for a few very active advocates who were willing to challenge the status quo and work to extend the precepts of humanism to the disenfranchised, the community integration movement of the late 20th century might never have occurred. Jean Etienne Esquirol's (1772–1840) work with people with epilepsy, Philippe Pinel's (1745–1826) work with those with mental illness, and Edouard Seguin's (1812–1880) work with people with mental retardation all serve as early examples of person-centered, practical approaches to early educational and psychological service delivery. In fact, Seguin's (1866) methods were considered by educators to be so impressive that they served as early models for many teachers in special—as well as nonspecial—education service settings.

In the post-Renaissance era, care evolved into diagnosis, treatment, and intervention. It became obvious that instructional methodology offered only a partial solution when it came to designing educational treatment strategies for persons with disabilities. The issue of the learner's ability level also had to be dealt with. That information would have to come from the newly developing science of psychology. In the span of only a few decades, the young and somewhat esoteric science of psychology moved from the psychophysical laboratory of its founder, Wilhelm Wundt (1832–1920) to the applied service delivery setting of Lightner Witmer (1867–1956).

Lightner Witmer made many contributions to the young discipline of psychology. One of his most important achievements for students of measurement and evaluation to appreciate was his role in the founding in 1896 of America's first child guidance clinic at the University of Pennsylvania (Schultz & Schultz, 1996). A second major achievement was his founding of two of psychology's core subspecialties, clinical psychology and school psychology. Most important, Lightner Witmer had demonstrated that science and service could be brought together to solve immediate, practical, and pressing problems of an applied nature. Through his many contributions and the contributions of those who came after him, he was able to formally begin the process of offering psychoeducational services to one of America's most vulnerable populations: children with learning difficulties.

The purpose of the present chapter is to identify and explain important components of assessment as they relate to children with exceptionalities. The chapter begins with an overview of legislation and litigation affecting testing practices with children today. Following a discussion of the assessment process, an introduction to major domains of involvement, and an overview of traditional academic functioning, attention is turned to current and emerging issues for this highly protected segment of the general population.

SUMMARY OF MAJOR LEGISLATION AND LITIGATION

Few activities conducted by educational and psychological service providers are as closely monitored by the legal system as those of standardized testing (Bersoff, 1981). The practice of psychoeducational assessment today stems from a number of different influences, many of which have emanated from judicial and legislative mandates to protect traditionally underserved segments of the population. Children and youth with disabilities are one such example. According to the most recent federal guidelines, children and youth with disabilities are students, preschool through 12th grade, who have

> mental retardation, hearing impairments including deafness, speech or language impairments, visual impairments including blindness, serious emotional disturbance, orthopedic impairments, autism, traumatic brain injury, other health impairments, or specific learning disabilities; and who, by reason thereof, need special education and related services. (Education of the Handicapped Act Amendments, § 101(a), 104 Stat. 1103 [1990])

Several laws and judicial decisions have affected the testing practices of educational and psychological service delivery to persons with disabilities. We summarize the most important here.

Influential Legislation

Four major pieces of legislation and their related amendments have particular import for the use of psychological tests with special populations. The Education of the Handicapped Act Amendments of 1990 (P.L. 101–476, 20 U.S.C. § 1400), commonly known as the Individuals with Disabilities Education Act (IDEA), is actually an amendment to an earlier piece of legislation known as the All Handicapped Children's Act of 1975 (P.L. 94–142). While the parent legislation is generally considered by educators to be the most far-reaching piece of legislation to affect the lives of children with disabilities, IDEA updates the earlier legislation and brings it more in line with contemporary thought and social policy. In its simplest form, IDEA provides children and youth with two broad-based legislative guarantees, the assurance of a free, appropriate, public education and the guarantee that special education services will be provided in the least restrictive environment possible. Major changes to the 1975 law include such things as: people-first language, where the emphasis is on the word *people* instead of the disability (e.g., people *with* mental retardation rather than the mentally retarded); the addition of two more categories of disabilities: autism and traumatic brain injury; and the addition of transition services for young adults moving from school to work.

The Civil Rights Act of 1964 (P.L. 88–352, 42 U.S.C. § 2000e *et seq.*) and its most recent amendments are credited with initiating the breakdown of the use of employment testing and hiring practices based solely on factors such as age, ethnicity, gender, race, and religion. While the original Civil Rights Act did not directly address the needs of persons with disabilities, it was responsible for setting the tone by which legislation could be useful in ameliorating some of the inadequacies of modern American society, particularly in regard to social service delivery. According to Rogers (1995), the major thrust of Title VII of the Civil Rights Act is to protect the test taker against unlawful and discriminatory use of tests. Examples of such discrimination include using tests that inappropriately differentiate between subgroups on an irrelevant variable such as race or ethnicity, and using test scores to hire persons when the scores themselves do not predict on-the-job performance.

A second major piece of civil rights legislation that pertains to persons with disabilities is the Americans with Disabilities Act of 1990 (ADA) (P.L. 101–336, 42 U.S.C. § 12101). This particular piece of legislation builds on other legislation, including the Civil Rights Act of 1964, and offers specific protection for individuals with disabilities. ADA covers both public and nonpublic settings and includes areas such as employment and public services, transportation, telecommunications, and accommodations (e.g., libraries, office buildings, restaurants, shopping centers). While not directly tied to assessment-related practices, ADA is important because it legally elevates people with disabilities to a status alongside other segments of the population who have previously been underserved and who are now offered special protections under the law. The Civil Rights Act of 1964 defined classes of individuals who are protected from discrimination on the basis of race, religion, or other personal characteristics; the ADA adds persons with disabilities to the list of protected segments of the population.

The Family Educational Rights and Privacy Act of 1974 and its most recent amendments (FERPA)(P.L. 93–380, 20 U.S.C. § 241) have done more to shape the means by which educational and psychological records are handled than any other single piece of legislation. FERPA offers such guarantees as (1) the rights of parents or guardians to view all records pertaining to their children's education, (2) the rights of parents or guardians to challenge any information in the records, and (3) the securing of written consent prior to release of information from anyone's official records. In addition, educational and psychological service providers must not only protect the privacy of a person's records but must also facilitate the person's understanding of their records and transfer of the records in a professionally responsible manner.

Influential Litigation

Of all the major court cases presented in the name of public education, none stands out as more dramatic or foundational than *Brown v. Board of Education* (1954). This court case was built on the premise that all children are members of a broader *class* of citizenry (i.e., students) and, therefore, must all be treated equally when it comes to educational services and opportunities. While the U.S. Supreme Court's 1954 decision was initially designed to protect children who were Black against unfair discrimination in the provision of such services, the Court's decision has been used as a precedent for similar practices involving children with disabilities. For children with disabilities, just as with children of color, educational services may not be denied on the basis of an enduring and unalterable trait that is beyond their control.

As most professionals and lay persons alike can attest, there have been a number of well documented court cases that have offered highly publicized decisions one way or the other on the issue of test bias. The first such case was *Hobson v. Hansen* (1967) and is noteworthy in two major respects; first, it called into question the notion of using a group test as the sole instrument for placing children into ability tracks, and, second, for the first time, the court condemned tests as racially biased when disproportionately high numbers of children who were poor and Black were found in lower ability tracks.

In *Guadalupe Organization v. Tempe Elementary School District* (1972), it was determined that a child's primary language must be determined prior to assessment and that formal provisions to assure accurate assessment must be made when the primary language is not English. Examples of provisions mentioned in this case were: the administration of instruments by psychologists who are fluent in both the child's primary language and in English, the presence of an interpreter to assist with the assessment, the use of instruments that do not stress spoken language, and an assurance that the test results will be explained to parents or guardians in their primary language.

Finally, there are two court cases that have targeted intelligence tests. *Larry P. v. Riles* (1984) is the court case known to most educational and psychological service providers as the case in which the validity of intelligence tests was called into question for Black children. In that decision, the presiding judge ruled in favor of the minority plaintiffs, finding that standardized, individually administered tests of intelligence were biased against children who were culturally different from those on whom the test was normed. Shortly thereafter, in a similar court case in Illinois, *Parents in Action on Special Education v. Hannon* (PASE v. Hannon, 1980), a very different decision was reached: that standardized measures of intelligence such as the WISC-R and Stanford-Binet, when taken in the context of a broader assessment system, were found not to be biased against children from culturally different backgrounds.

Sociopolitical Context of Assessment

Few will argue with the need to provide services to children with exceptionalities. Additionally, most will acknowledge a need to provide services within the context of a broad range of service delivery options. For many people inside and outside of special education, the difficulty stems from how the special segments of the population are defined and how the various goods and services are made available within the context of limited economic resources.

The distinction, it seems, is a philosophical one. Differences in opinion do exist, and they seem to come down to a system in which the most intellectually capable people are allowed to ascend to the top of the civil hierarchy based on something as seemingly objective as an IQ test, versus a system that allows for more social equivalence, where the wishes and preferences of all the people are pursued with equal freedom. Plato (c. 428–348 B.C.) was a proponent of the former. He believed in a natural aristocracy in which the most capable should be responsible for the rest of society, with absolute [intellectual] competence the main criterion for civil authority. Political philosophy notwithstanding, Plato's own version of intellectual Darwinism bears on a discussion of psychological testing in that Plato clearly separated ability level from other predisposing factors such as political power and economic wealth, a position that was as much at odds with the spirit of the times then as it sometimes seems to be today.

John Locke's (A.D. 1632–1704) position was very different from Plato's. As the theoretical architect of democracy and the philosophical force behind many of America's constitutional tenets, Locke believed that for optimal decision making there was value in people uniting together to transfer power from the individual to the state. For Locke, the majority ruled not through force but, rather, through discovery of natural laws made available through revelation, human autonomy, universal principles, or conformity to moral law (Stumpf, 1994). Examples of this point are the aforementioned civil rights laws in which individual liberties are protected within the rights of the state.

Although the philosophical rationales for testing may be centuries old, a more immediate issue has to do with the provision of services to children with exceptionalities. Proponents of testing contend that while the educational service delivery system is not perfect, it represents the best that a pluralistic society has to offer. Opponents argue, instead, that the bureaucratic maze of methods and procedures, unofficially known as "red tape," is precisely what is wrong with the educational system today. They argue further that if children and their families were left alone to pursue their own form of education, uninhibited by state and federal restraint, all would be better off. Opponents of standardized testing contend that testing is often the first step toward a special education program that relegates a child to a life of limited options and negative social stereotypes.

Even under the best circumstances, the problems of providing services to children with complex disabilities place serious demands on everyone involved: the child, the child's family, and the organizations providing special services. The best instrument in the best of hands is only a guarantee of honest efforts. The best instrument in poorly trained hands or a poorly designed test in the best diagnostic hands are both recipes for disaster. When either of the latter two scenarios result, the child, the system providing services, and equally important, the reputations of education and psychology proper all suffer. Messick (1995) offers a timely and insightful perspective on the role of value-based implications and social consequences in psychometric validity. For Messick, psychometric validity is more than just testing an instrument's ability to perform under known conditions; it is the recognition of a relationship between a construct and the social policies that undergird it, a recognition that many service providers would do well to consider.

ASSESSMENT PROCESSES

Clinical Versus Educational Models

People training to be educational and psychological service providers—whether they be teachers, counselors, or school psychologists—enter their respective programs from a number of different disciplines and with a variety of expectations. When children with special needs are referred for services within a school-based service delivery system, they often encounter an assessment process very different from the one that would greet them in a community mental health center or clinic. The difference usually stems from the theoretical orientation of the staff, the service delivery system itself, and the training of the service providers.

Professionals espousing the more clinical, medically based models of intervention often see intra- and interindividual differences from a deficit-based point of view. A deficit-based model is one in which a pathology or disability is assumed to be present and require fixing. The solution, then, is most often outside of the person and inside the service delivery system. A developmentally based model of intervention, on the other hand, assumes that difficulties are transitional and perhaps even situation specific, and are experienced by many persons moving through the life stage or situation. The solution for remediation in this case may be within the person, the community, the service delivery system, or some combination of the three.

A model of assessment implies much more than simply an orientation to intra- and interindividual differences. A true model of assessment suggests an overarching plan for evaluating a child's problem or disability. In the educational community, that usually means following the mandates of Pub. L. No. 101–476 (IDEA) and employing multidimensional methods of assessment, using service providers from several disciplines (e.g., counselor, nurse, psychologist, social worker, teachers) across the primary and related areas where the child has difficulty functioning. In a clinical setting, the model may be more restricted in that it may start and stop with one person, the psychologist or counselor, and move to include other health professionals only on an as-needed basis. That is, in an educational setting the first steps in assessment are multifaceted, and intervention becomes more focused as the situation is clarified. In the clinical setting the first steps involve the client and clinician/counselor, and the others are brought in only as the need for them is encountered.

For many children, perhaps the majority of children, services begin and end with school personnel. For others, services received may represent a composite of the two models. Parents of children who are receiving special services from school personnel but who are also seeing health service providers outside of the school (e.g., occupational therapist, psychologist, social worker) must not only reconcile the different recommendations but must also work to integrate them in a practical and complementary manner. For the child with an active and involved case manager who readily stays on top of assessment and intervention, the outcomes can be most rewarding. However, for the parent who is forced into the informal role of case manager, the task can be both frustrating and disconcerting.

Referral to Placement Sequence

Referring a child for special services is generally not done without a great deal of concern and sometimes even anguish on the part of those who care most for the child. Despite the fact that special education services are used by nearly 10% of the children in the public schools, and that they really form a system designed to provide extra care and attention to the children who are most in need, many family members are understandably hesitant about placing their children in such services. Fear is usually allayed once they see the procedural safeguards that are in place to protect the children against unwarranted and invasive psychoeducational procedures. Following is a brief overview of the stages typically associated with the referral to placement sequence. The process typically follows a sequence of steps beginning with referral and culminating with placement in one or more supportive educational settings.

Screening.   Virtually all school districts have a mechanism for identifying children three years of age or older who are at-risk for school failure. Usually, the screening includes a brief health history and basic medical evaluation to rule out such things as vision, hearing, speech, and other obvious health impairments. Additional evaluations are also conducted by school personnel using age-appropriate batteries to assess intellectual, social, and motor functioning. Screening evaluations are different from other, more in-depth evaluations in that they are generally conducted with all children in a grade, school, district, or community and are designed to identify only those children whose scores place them in the high-risk category, which means that school personnel are alerted that problems may occur. This precaution is taken so that intervention can begin before problems become serious and more difficult to deal with.

Prereferral Intervention.   Prereferral intervention teams consist of school personnel assembled to respond to the needs of children identified as being in the early stages of academic difficulty. The goal of a prereferral team is to work with the teachers of a child who is showing signs of difficulty in the regular classroom. About 10% of children are identified as needing this level of support. The prereferral team works on the assumption that many students can, with the aid of additional in-class supports and instruction, avoid placement in the special education program. After a period of prereferral intervention, evidence supplied by the traditional classroom teacher is then used to recommend one of three options: (1) termination of the in-class supports, (2) continued or altered in-class supports, or (3) referral for more in-depth psychoeducational evaluations.

Referral for Special Education Services.   Referral for special education services can come from any person involved with a child experiencing academic, socioemotional, or motor difficulties. In most cases the referral comes from either the parent or the classroom teacher, with input from the prereferral team. The referral is usually accompanied by a well-developed file of evidence compiled by school personnel, containing a record of the reasons for the referral and the outcomes of strategies tried by the prereferral intervention team. Up to this point, the child is not yet in the special education service delivery system. However, once the child is assigned a case manager and parental permission for diagnostic testing is requested by the special education staff, the child enters the special education system.

If permission to evaluate is received, then a multidisciplinary evaluation team composed of teachers, parents, parental advocates, and academic support personnel prepares a formal assessment plan covering the child's primary and related areas of difficulty. Assessments are typically carried out by the support personnel (e.g., counselors, physicians, psychologists, social workers, speech pathologists). The rationale behind a multidisciplinary evaluation is twofold: first, it may take professionals from different disciplines to provide a perspective on a given disability; and, second, a group of persons typically provides a better overall opinion with better procedural safeguards than any single person can. Figure 13.1 provides a diagram of the steps in the special education referral process.

Eligibility meeting.   Once the assessment information has been gathered and synthesized by the child's case manager, the manager schedules an eligibility meeting to determine if the child qualifies for special education. If the child qualifies, then the multidisciplinary evaluation team prepares an Individualized Education Plan (IEP) that outlines such things as the educational curriculum, learning objectives for the curriculum, criteria for achievement, length of time services are to be utilized, and

Figure 13.1
Nondiscriminatory special education referral model.

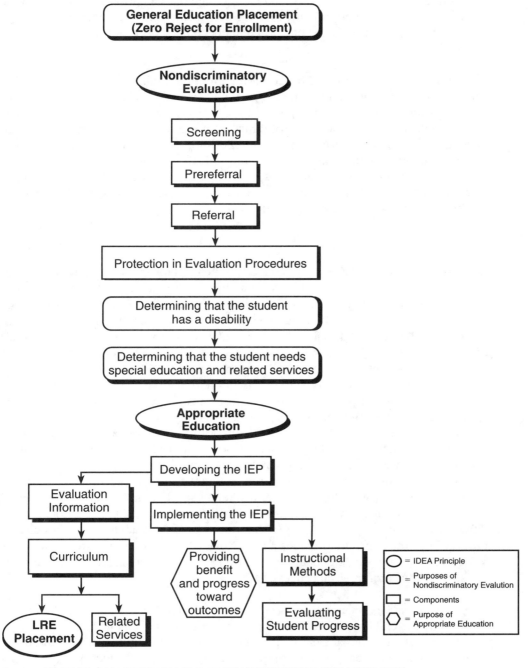

Source: EXCEPTIONAL LIVES: SPECIAL EDUCATION IN TODAY'S SCHOOLS by
Turnbull/Turnbull/Shank/Leal, © 1995. Reprinted by permission of Prentice-Hall, Inc.,
Upper Saddle River, NJ.

the actual place of service delivery. Since IEPs are written annually, length of time is generally considered to be for the remainder of the school year unless otherwise specified. IDEA mandates that services will be provided in the child's regular education classroom whenever possible.

Follow-up Evaluations.   One of the procedural safeguards provided by IDEA to children enrolled in special education programs and their families is the requirement that every child receiving special education services will be reevaluated at a minimum of every 3 years. Case managers must make out new IEPs each year for each child, but the added expectation of a complete psychoeducational evaluation every three years is intended to protect the child against malfeasance. That is, children who no longer need special education services are to be released from its added assistance as soon as is recognizable. That is not to say that evaluations are not required along the way, prior to the three-year interval—they are, just as with all children in the regular education track. It just means that the IEP evaluations and the 3-year reevaluations are routinely conducted to assure parents and school personnel that the child still requires the extra attention and services necessary to perform adequately in school.

Parents or legal guardians are not required by law to attend their child's special education program meetings. School personnel are, however, required to invite them to the meetings (Turnbull, Turnbull, Shank, & Leal, 1995). Simpson (1990) has identified a number of dimensions along which parents and family members may become involved in the educational interventions of their children. Foremost among the information that should be provided to parents is accurate, direct, informative feedback from diagnostic testing. In a world that is at times based more on numbers, norms, and nomenclature than readily accessible information, parents who have never been exposed to the assessment process can be very intimidated. Assistance in child and family advocacy, IEP planning, and home tutoring are some of the many areas in which parents can strengthen their involvement with their child's education.

MAJOR DOMAINS OF INVOLVEMENT

Intelligence and Cognitive Functioning

It is difficult to present any meaningful discussion of assessment of special abilities without giving attention, first and foremost, to the construct of intelligence. Whether interested in the more cognitive reasons for difficulty or the more practical side of assessment, those involved must consider the nature and impact of intelligence on academic performance and programming.

In almost all cases, state and local guidelines require that the assessment battery include a measure of intellectual functioning when a child is referred for special services. The reason for this is fairly straightforward. Intelligence tests are typically the strongest, broadest, and most stable instruments used in the evaluation. The instruments are used as diagnostic tools to gather a wide range of information, from simple recall of information to complex processing of new and nontraditional stimuli (see

Chapter 8). Disorders and disabilities manifesting themselves through various psychomotor channels can also be picked up. Even when these instruments are used more for clinical than intellectual applications, there is evidence to suggest that thought and personality disorders manifest themselves through deficits in cognition, as revealed by intelligence tests.

For children with speech and language disabilities—the largest group of children receiving special education services today—intellectual assessment is less important than for other high-frequency disability categories (e.g., learning disabilities and mental retardation). The main reason is that it is entirely possible for a child to have difficulty in expressive ability, either oral or written, without affecting other, higher-order processing skills. However, for children in other high-frequency categories, such as specific learning disabilities and mental retardation, basic psychological processes are implicated at such a deep, ubiquitous level that multiple information processing pathways are undoubtedly involved.

Children with low-frequency disabilities, such as visual, aural (hearing), or orthopedic problems, often have difficulty with the assessment process, particularly when the instruments with which they are being evaluated do not have provisions for children with nontraditional types of disabilities. One of many obvious examples is a child without arms who is expected to complete fine motor tasks. When intellectual assessments are conducted with children with exceptionalities, the testing must often be conducted using modified formats, due to the nature of the test items and the very real limitations of the child not being able to see, hear, or physically manipulate the test stimuli. The difficulty with individually derived adaptations to standardized instruments is that they are frequently not the adaptations used during standardization and, worse, they are often generated *on the spot* by examiners who mean well but do not see enough children with any particular disability to develop a familiarity with appropriate instruments.

An often cited exception to the limitations mentioned above pertains to children with gifts and talents. Gifted and talented children are those whose level of performance in the classroom places them among the highest percentiles on most standardized measures of intelligence. But for these students, other criteria such as measures of creativity must frequently be used to understand their unique blend of skills and abilities. Creativity cannot be easily assessed with standardized tests because they tend to emphasize convergent thinking, which by definition is not a creative act. The goal of convergent thinking is the identification of an established correct answer. Creativity, on the other hand, is related to divergent thinking, the goal of which is the generation of answers that differ from the expected or the generation of many solutions to a problem. Creativity tests tend not to be reliable, and it is difficult to demonstrate their validity. Therefore, some students are placed in such programs despite not being gifted, while other students who could benefit from such programs may be ruled ineligible.

Two major intelligence tests seem to stand above the rest when it comes to historical precedence and name recognition, the Stanford-Binet Intelligence Scale: Fourth Edition (Thorndike, Hagen, & Sattler, 1986a), and the Wechsler Intelligence Scales, which actually constitute a set of related and highly similar batteries that span the age range from early childhood (Wechsler Preschool and Primary Scale of

Intelligence—Revised; Wechsler, 1989), through childhood (Wechsler Intelligence Scale for Children—Third Edition; Wechsler, 1991), to adulthood (Wechsler Adult Intelligence Scale—Revised; Wechsler, 1981). Within the scope of school-based assessments, a third instrument, the Kaufman Assessment Battery for Children (Kaufman & Kaufman, 1983) is used with near-equal frequency to that of the Stanford-Binet. A number of other standardized instruments are available but are used to a much lesser degree than either the Binet or the Wechsler scales. All of these instruments and the theories of cognitive ability on which they were based were described in Chapter 8.

Adaptive Behavior and Self-Help Skills

The concept of adaptive behavior has undergone substantial revision in recent years. From its formal beginning as a component of social maturity to its status today as an independent, multifaceted construct, adaptive behavior has moved from a simple system of behavioral observations to one of relative psychometric complexity (McGrew, Ittenbach, Bruininks, & Hill, 1991). Until recently, adaptive behavior was considered to be a person's ability to function effectively in his or her own environment. Since 1992, however, the American Association on Mental Retardation (1992) has attempted to redirect the focus and responsibility of adaptation away from the person with disabilities and onto the community, by way of supports needed for community living. Adaptive behavior is now considered to be a very important part of many assessment systems, especially those evaluating children and youth with disabilities.

The construct of adaptive behavior has, until very recently, been atheoretical and has evolved in a very inductive way based on the presence or absence of behaviors considered important for daily living. From the observations have come items, from items have come scales, from scales have come instruments and, finally, from instruments have come the beginnings of identifiable theories. One such theory is Greenspan and Granfield's (1992) theory of General Competence. The theory postulates that general competence consists of two broad subdomains, Environmental Competence and Social Competence, which serve as third stratum factors. Both of these have intellectual and nonintellectual components which arise from more narrowly defined competences (see Figure 13.2). Empirical validation of these and other dimensions has not been quite as supportive. While content analyses of published scales have suggested as many as ten different content areas (cf. Bruininks, Thurlow, & Gillman, 1987), factor analytic results have tended to indicate a single underlying factor.

Adaptive behavior assessment is most often associated with mental retardation. By law, a diagnosis of mental retardation cannot be made without a finding of significantly subaverage performance on a measure of intelligence and corresponding deficits in two or more adaptive skill areas. A definition such as this guards against a child being labeled as mentally retarded on the basis of intelligence alone, and is intended to preclude a classification of mental retardation for children who happen to

Figure 13.2
Comprehensive model of general competence.

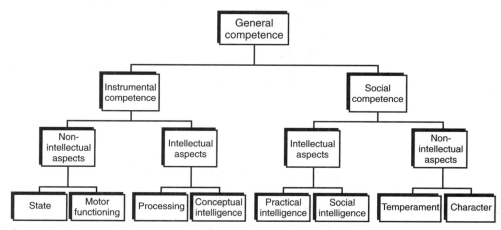

Source: Greenspan, S. R., & Granfield, J. M. (1992). Reconsidering the construct of mental retardation: Implications of a model of social competence. *American Journal of Mental Retardation, 96*(4), 447.

do poorly on standardized measures of intelligence but perform well in nonschool settings—at home and in the community. The term typically used for such children is the *six-hour retarded child,* a term that derives from the title of the report generated by the President's Committee on Mental Retardation (1970).

Adaptive behavior received its most important impetus from the court cases of the mid-1970s and early 1980s which forced examiners to rely less on single measures of intelligence and more on multiple measures of aptitude and ability prior to placement in special education programs. The reason for the decision then and the reason for its widespread appeal now is that adaptive behavior offers a much more practical perspective on what a child can do with the more immediate, pressing problems of everyday life than that offered by most intelligence tests. Four popular measures of adaptive behavior are the AAMR Adaptive Behavior Scales ([Residential and Community] Nihira, Leland, & Lambert, 1993; [School] Lambert, Nihira, & Leland, 1993), the Scales of Independent Behavior (Bruininks, Woodcock, Weatherman, & Hill, 1985), and the Vineland Adaptive Behavior Scales (Sparrow, Balla, & Cicchetti, 1984a, 1984b, 1985). These instruments are described in greater detail in Chapter 12.

Personality and Socioemotional Functioning

Problems associated with personality and socioemotional assessment are even more daunting than the problems encountered in intellectual and adaptive behavior assessment. As will be discussed in Chapter 14, decisions about emotional and behavioral disorders are often based on clinical judgments, judgments that most often stem from the rather subjective nature of the construct itself. When we talk about the construct of personality, what we are really talking about is one's general psychosocial constitution and their likelihood for appropriate intra- and interpersonal functioning across a range of settings and conditions. According to IDEA, children who are considered to have disabilities that are socially or emotionally based exhibit one or more of the following characteristics to a marked degree over an extended period of time (Turnbull et al., 1995):

- an inability to learn that cannot be explained by intellectual, sensory, or other health factors
- an inability to build or maintain satisfactory interpersonal relationships with peers and teachers
- inappropriate types of behavior or feelings under normal circumstances
- a general pervasive mood of unhappiness or depression
- a tendency to develop physical symptoms or fears associated with personal or school problems

Theories of personality and social functioning abound, with descriptions of various orientations ranging from the highly controversial psychodynamic models of Freud to the much heralded, highly behavioristic orientations of Skinner (see Chapter 11 for a discussion of theories and assessment instruments). Such wide disparity in orientations introduces problems with terminology. A frequently used term is *emotionally disturbed,* but many behaviorists reject the emphasis on the unobservable psyche and, instead, prefer the term *behaviorally disordered.* To the average person, the terms mean essentially the same thing and are often used interchangeably. There are some in the field, however, who prefer to combine the two terms into the broader, seemingly less poignant classification of *behaviorally disturbed.* These children simply tend to get into trouble more often than others and have tendencies toward maladjustment that are considered to be socially induced—in other words, they just misbehave.

Children who simply misbehave are not eligible for special services in the school or community. The term *emotionally disturbed* will be reserved for those children whose behavioral response patterns are symptoms of a deeper emotional problem. Such children are eligible for special education service delivery. For these children, assessment of the disorder typically takes one of four routes: informal observations, systematic behavioral observations, interpretation of standardized test scores, or responses on projective tests. There are also examples in the professional literature of clinicians making inferences of emotional disturbance based on the profiles of established cognitive ability tests such as the Stanford-Binet or the Wechsler scales. Shepard (1989) asserts that when diagnoses of clinical syndromes are made on the basis of unusual or bizarre responses to aptitude test questions, it is highly likely that behavioral observations alone would be sufficient for identification. Consequently, she advocates diagnosing clinical syndromes on the basis of behavioral observations, a conclusion that many special education service providers also seem to be coming to in increasing numbers.

If a special education service provider is interested in the more social components of a child's functioning, it is likely that a behavioral instrument such as the Behavioral Evaluation Scale–II (McCarney & Leigh, 1990) or the Burks Behavioral Rating Scales (Burks, 1977) will be sufficient for gathering the needed information. However, if the concern pertains more to emotional functioning, with heightened concerns about deeper psychopathology, then the Child Behavior Checklist (Achenbach & Edelbrock, 1983) or the Minnesota Multiphasic Personality Inventory–Adolescent (Butcher & Williams, 1992) may be more useful.

For reasons mentioned previously, measurement of personality and socioemotional functioning is much more difficult than for other disability categories. One very obvious reason pertains to the stability of the human personality. Manifestations of personality, like any other construct, may actually vary from hour to hour or day to day. Additionally, examinees' responses and the ratings of those responses also introduce a great deal of subjectivity. Even examiners' own preferences as to whether the behavioral manifestations are indicators of a deeply rooted trait or just a sign that an adjustment disorder is present and needs to be addressed is an important area that can affect one's scores and diagnosis. There are also the problems of honesty in responding and degree of personal insight, as described in Chapter 11.

Neuropsychological Functioning

Assessment of neuropsychological functioning represents a relatively new area of assessment for psychoeducational service providers. As a subdiscipline of psychology, neuropsychology builds upon many of the new advances in clinical, cognitive, and school psychology, with shared contributions from medicine and neurology. Despite the equivocal results of early research in perceptual-motor abilities, much of the new research in neuropsychology continues to draw heavily upon the perceptual-motor research of decades past.

The persistence and commitment of educational and psychological service providers to this all-important domain of human functioning is as much a testament to the importance of perceptual-motor and sensorimotor functioning as it is to the need for new developments in the psychodiagnostics of integrative functioning. According to Weeks and Ewer-Jones (1991), failure to perceive information correctly threatens one's ability to attach meaning to stimuli in a worthwhile manner. When meaning becomes distorted, responses to those meanings are often produced in unusual or atypical ways. This is the reason that basic avenues of sensory operations such as vision, hearing, and simple motor functioning are included in the first stage of assessment for children suspected of requiring special educational assistance.

Sometimes providing such simple devices as glasses or a hearing aid is all that is needed for problem resolution. Very frequently, though, assessment and intervention require much more than can be gleaned from a Snellin reading chart or a tone audiometer. Efforts to take perceptual-motor-skill development beyond simple sensory input have also met with mixed reviews. Whereas educational and psychological service providers formerly used tests of visual and auditory processing, integration, and discrimination, now assessments of brain-behavior relationships include everything from computerized tomography to magnetic resonance imaging to positron emission tomography. Consequently, the ability to diagnose and treat neuropsychological and sensorimotor disorders is much improved from that of even 20 years ago.

Gilandas, Touyz, Beumont, and Greenberg (1984) suggest that the field of neuropsychology is still evolving and in search of an agreed-upon model of organization and assessment. Two broad-based, paper-and-pencil batteries have been used with greatest frequency: the Halstead-Reitan Neuropsychological Test Battery (Reitan & Wolfson, 1993), and the Luria-Nebraska Neuropsychological Battery (Golden, Purisch, & Hammeke, 1991). Both tests are composed of tasks that tap basic psychological processes and higher-order integrative skills.

TRADITIONAL ACADEMIC FUNCTIONING

Reading, Math, and Written-Language Assessment

Any child can have difficulty in school. In fact, most children have difficulty at one time or another during their educational years. However, children who receive special education services typically experience a level of difficulty that requires intervention well beyond what the regular curriculum can realistically provide. As indicated in Chapter 9, measures of academic achievement are often used to estimate a child's level of content mastery in a given academic area. Measures of academic aptitude, on the other hand, are used to estimate how a child should be performing relative to same-age and same-grade peers. When taken together, standardized measures of academic achievement and aptitude can provide evaluators with a reasonably good picture of potential disparity between actual and expected performances in traditional academic skill areas. For most children in special education, that disparity usually translates into deficits in the basics of reading, writing, or arithmetic. For older children it can easily include other content areas such as science or social studies but will, in all likelihood, still involve the fundamental skills of reading, writing (written language), or arithmetic.

Of the three areas mentioned, McLoughlin and Lewis (1990) indicate that more children are evaluated for reading disabilities than for any other single area of academics. Perhaps it is because reading pervades the general curriculum to a far greater degree than any other skill. A disability in reading will manifest itself across the curriculum because it interferes with the basic acquisition of written information. Mathematics ability represents the second most frequent area of referral for children with exceptionalities. Although mathematics is absolutely essential for quantitative thinking in a modern world, its contribution to the rest of the curriculum is more limited than that of reading and, as a result, is less often implicated. Of the three areas, written language constitutes the least frequently evaluated area of disability. Though sound writing ability is critical for successful functioning throughout life, it is an area in which the diagnostic and intervention research has lagged behind other areas, and school district personnel are hesitant to place children in special education only on the basis of a disability in written language.

Assessment of basic academic skills has tended to take one of two paths. When a referral for evaluation is for general academic difficulty, that is, for trouble in more than one content area, a standardized measure of achievement that incorporates all three of the aforementioned areas is frequently used. When a referral is for a single academic area, such as math or written language, but does not appear to implicate other areas, for example, reading, a specialized diagnostic instrument may be used. Although both sets of instruments can provide an index of how a child compares with other children nationally, only in-depth, diagnostic instruments in specific content areas have the capacity to offer insight into the source or nuances of a specific disability.

A number of different measures are available for information about a child's general and relative levels of academic functioning. Group administered tests such as the Iowa Tests of Basic Skills (Riverside Publishing Company, 1993), the Metropolitan Achievement Tests (Harcourt Brace, 1992), and the Stanford Achievement Test Series (Harcourt Brace, 1996) are well-recognized batteries. Many school districts encourage or even require their children with disabilities to take these exams. But not all children are able to take group administered tests and many who do take these tests do poorly and must also take individually administered tests of achievement. The Kaufman Test of Educational Achievement (Kaufman & Kaufman, 1985), the Peabody Individual Achievement Test–Revised (Markwardt, 1989), and the Woodcock-Johnson Tests of Achievement (Woodcock & Mather, 1989) are examples of the latter. See Chapter 9 for a more detailed description of these and other standardized achievement tests.

In addition to these test batteries, a number of individually administered batteries exist for diagnostic and program planning purposes. As one might expect, there are more reading instruments than anything else. The Gray Oral Reading Test (Wiederholt & Bryant, 1992), the Stanford Diagnostic Reading Test (The Psychological Corporation, 1995), and the Woodcock-Johnson Reading Mastery Tests (Woodcock, 1987) are examples of such instruments. In the area of mathematics assessment, the Enright Diagnostic Inventory of Basic Arithmetic Skills (Enright, 1983), the Keymath–Revised (Connolly, 1988), and the Test of Mathematical Abilities (Brown, Cronin, & McEntire, 1994) tend to be used with greatest frequency. Finally, in the area of written-language assessment, the Test of Written Language–2 (Hammill & Larsen, 1988), and the Woodcock Language Proficiency Battery–Revised (Woodcock, 1991) are instruments with well-known track records.

Curriculum-Based Assessment

Curriculum-based assessment (CBA), or, as it is often called, curriculum-based measurement, represents a wide range of activities. The broadest interpretation of the term includes any techniques that are directly tied to a given curriculum. A more narrow definition, but one that many educational and psychological service providers now adopt, tends to restrict the definition to include only informal measures of student achievement.

The difference between these two definitions lies in the scope and breadth of what is included. In the first definition, all tests, even the very large, nationally-normed, group-administered tests such as the Metropolitan and Stanford Achievement Tests administered throughout the elementary curriculum are included right alongside the specific daily or weekly measures of basic skill development. In the second definition, only the small-scale, teacher-designed, and individually administered measures of basic skill development are included. The curricula that serve as the criteria of choice, not surprisingly, can be very different. In the first definition, test items are intended to reflect a national curriculum or, at least, the curricular elements that all students should have been exposed to, irrespective of their region of the country. In the second definition, the criterion of choice is most likely the curriculum that is being taught by a given teacher in a given school on a given day or week. Both perspectives are valid and are important measures of student progress, just with different comparative criteria.

Curriculum-based measures represent an alternative assessment model for many psychologists practicing inside and outside of educational settings. Most traditional training programs tend to emphasize the individually administered, norm-referenced tests of intelligence with more recent attention given to measures of personality, adaptive behavior, and general development. In curriculum-based measurement, microlevel skills such as the ability to read, write, or spell words from a given list for a given week are the targets of choice. For children with specific learning disabilities, mental retardation, or even speech and language disabilities, the teacher is able to identify an objective for a day, test whether or not it was achieved, and then chart the child's progress in a way that the progress can be compared with the progress made on other days or weeks. The frame of reference is explicitly ipsative or self-referenced (Chapter 3). For children with more severe disabilities—or more extensive support needs—the criteria for success may be less academic and more behavioral. Here are some examples of curriculum-based measures adapted from Marston (1989).

- count the number of words a student reads correctly from a word list, in a 1-minute interval
- count the number of words written during a 3-minute interval, given a story starter
- count the number of letter sequences spelled correctly during a 2-minute interval, given words dictated every 7 seconds

The fact that CBA is an alternative assessment model for many educational and psychological service providers brings with it a number of assumptions for best practice. The first expectation is that the service providers are willing to learn new skills of assessment that may have a quicker route to intervention. A second assumption lies in the direct, repeated nature of the evaluations. It is assumed that the child is evaluated on a constant and recurring basis so that actual trends in performance can be identified and used for further programming. A third assumption is that the teacher and psychological service provider will be responsible for determining the degree to which the local measures (e.g., weekly spelling tests or weekly math tests) are reliable and valid measures of the skills. It does little good for a teacher to design a series of tests that does not accurately reflect progress for a given semester (Marston, 1989).

An often unintended byproduct of such measurement practices lies in the generation of local norms. Educational and psychological service providers can gauge the progress a student is making relative to other children in the school or school district. Many CBA proponents will quickly state that the purpose of CBA lies more with the tests' representativeness for a given child's day-to-day skill development than with person-group comparisons. However, for the teacher or psychological service provider who is also interested in person-group comparisons, CBA allows for that possibility.

Ecological Assessment

Just as curriculum-based assessment represents an alternative model of assessment for most educational and psychological service providers, so too does ecological assessment. In ecological assessment, the focus of assessment is shifted away from content and onto the entire psychoeducational service delivery system. The purpose of ecological assessment is to evaluate all factors influencing the learning process. Although the model works for children without disabilities just as well as it does for children with disabilities, many of the ecological models have emanated from use with special populations, since children with disabilities are usually exposed to a wider range of assessment activities.

As with other educational and psychological phenomena, the ecological models are more casual than formal and are frequently based on the individual perspectives of the investigators. Most models, however, emphasize the importance of the interaction between the child and others in the environment and have, in part, stemmed from mental health models that have incorporated community- and socially-based interventions (cf. Kelly, 1966, 1986). For children with disabilities, Witt, Elliott, Kramer, and Gresham (1994) contend that ecological assessment must also involve the classroom teacher. The assessment plan must include the teacher's expectations for the child, the physical environment of the classroom, and the learning tasks at hand. Hiltonsmith and Keller (1983) offer a framework for gathering data in both home and school settings. Their model appears simple on the surface, in that it concentrates on such setting factors as appearance and content, operations, and opportunities, but the model is actually complex in that evaluation of how basic cognitive and social-emotional stimulants are fostered and encouraged in each setting is difficult.

The advantages of using an ecological model are as positive as they are complex. First, ecological assessment widens the scope of the responsibility for ameliorating the disability to other forces in the environment, similar in many ways to the movement in adaptive behavior assessment. Second, it takes assessment beyond single entities such as the child, the family, or even academic expectations to include interactions between all parts of the environment. Third, it allows for new and innovative approaches to assessment much more so than traditional measures currently do. It includes everything from standardized measures to the most subjective, qualitatively based outcomes of day-to-day operations.

An obvious limitation to using ecological models in routine evaluations is the amount of time and energy it takes to gather the necessary information. There are very few instruments on the market today built to handle, in any meaningful way, the broad-based interactions that are involved in the ecological models presented here and elsewhere. Those that tend to focus on one aspect of a child's learning environment often overlook other equally important components. For example, Ysseldyke and Christenson (1993) have designed a fairly comprehensive ecological assessment instrument, The Instructional Environment Scale–II, that measures 17 key factors influencing a child's academic performance, 12 associated with the school setting, and 5 associated with home supports. Following is a listing of the 17 factors surveyed by the Instructional Environment System–II.

Instructional Environment Components

Instructional Match	Teacher Expectations
Classroom Environment	Instructional Presentation
Cognitive Emphasis	Motivational Strategies
Relevant Practice	Informed Feedback
Academic Engaged Time	Adaptive Instruction
Progressive Evaluation	Student Understanding

Home-Support-for-Learning Components

Expectations and Attributions	Discipline Orientation
Effective Home Environment	Parent Participation
Structure for Learning	

While this instrument is strong on classroom-based inferences, it deemphasizes some of the more social aspects of classroom climate. Conversely, Flanders' (1970) interaction scale, while several decades old, still retains good name recognition. It emphasizes adult-child interactions while minimizing child-peer interactions and traditional academic outcomes.

CURRENT AND EMERGING ISSUES

Minimum Competency Testing

An important aspect of the educational reform movement of the 1970s was minimum competency testing. Performance at an unacceptable level mandated remediation or retention and, at times, even denial of a diploma. These competency testing programs have three main purposes: (1) to identify students in need of remediation, (2) to ensure that graduates and/or those who are promoted to the next grade have reached some minimum level of competency, and (3) to provide additional motivation to students to increase their academic achievement. This approach has had great appeal to politicians and the general public because of its rather direct means of dealing with some of the perceived inadequacies of public instruction. Interest in minimum competency testing seems to have touched nearly every state. How the process is actually manifested in each state varies due to uncertainties related to implementation. Many groups of individuals are at work designing minimum competency guidelines, and testing programs range from those centralized at the state level to those directed and implemented by local school districts. Some states have created their own tests, while others have contracted with outside agencies; most states, however, use what they, in the broadest sense of the definition, describe as criterion-referenced tests but which may not actually satisfy the definition of criterion-referenced testing as described in Chapter 3.

Questions as to the legality of minimum competency tests abound. The problem is not simply with implementing the tests or even with establishing minimum guidelines for promotion or graduation. Instead, difficulty lies with the absolute nature of decisions pertaining to length of time for remediation or, more important, who actually receives a diploma. Currently, most of the legal issues have been resolved, generally in favor of minimum competency testing programs, but more are sure to be introduced. Disparate racial impact and the higher failure rates of minority students are areas of great concern. The courts have ruled that it is not necessary to prove discriminatory intent when the differential test scores were the result of past discriminatory policies of school segregation, corrected only a few years earlier.

Debra P. v. Turlington (1979) reaffirmed the mandate of fair warning and the requirement that minimum competency testing not carry forward the effects of racial segregation. The court of appeals also added one further condition, that the test had to have content validity. According to McClung (1979), content validity for minimum competency testing consists of two types: *curricular validity,* which refers to the match between the competency test and the curriculum, and *instructional validity,* which is the establishment of a match between what is assessed on the minimum competency test and what actually happens in the classroom. While this type of judgment represented a controversial decision to school personnel, in the sense that it pertained to all types of tests, the courts have traditionally left such judgments in the hands of professional educators.

When minimum competency testing was first introduced, there was a widely held view that a successful legal challenge to this form of testing would come from critics who believed that such programs were unfair to special education students. However, the courts have consistently ruled that school systems can require special education students to take such a test and deny them a diploma if they do not pass. According to Jaeger (1989), the courts have also ruled that it is not necessary for those requiring such a test for students in special education programs to themselves establish curricular and instructional validity. These school systems also have not been required to defend the existence of disparate impact on special education students, which stands in sharp contrast to the judicial response to testing students from minority backgrounds.

Designing minimum competency tests presents no special problems once definitions of the domain and level have been determined. Yet, such tests need to be different from usual ability tests. These tests should be designed in such a way as to be maximally sensitive at one specific ability level, the level chosen to represent minimum competence. The test items, then, should be targeted at a narrow band of difficulty and allow for differentiating between those falling just below and those just above the minimum passing score. It is impossible to determine this point with complete precision, and inevitably the test will differentiate over a fairly wide range of competence. The better job a minimum competency test does in allowing for differentiating the minimally competent from those who fall just below this point, the less effective it will be in allowing differentiating among students across the full range of abilities.

A major problem with minimum competency testing programs is that they do not seem to focus as much on educating students as they do on ensuring that students below a certain level do not obtain degrees. Interest in minimum competency testing has begun to fade as it has become apparent that the tests have failed to do what was initially intended. Under these circumstances, an interplay might be expected between those who want to have higher standards, and therefore a higher cutoff score, and those who want fewer students to fail. The resulting criteria should fall between the goals of the two groups. Nearly all the interest groups favor a very low failure rate, and thus no interplay occurs. Ultimately, the most salient criticism of minimum competency testing is its irrelevance to the educational process and student competency.

Outcomes-Based Assessment

Outcomes-based assessment represents a new title for a time-honored notion of quality and productivity. Whether one is considering the American educational system or an assembly line in one of North America's most prestigious industries, the concept of outcomes-based assessment begins with what is needed most and then works backward to design a system that can provide that product.

The key to success in industry is research and development. The key to success in education is also research and development, but the task becomes a bit more complicated in that it involves members of a protected population, children and youth. Modernizing the American educational system means modernizing its products and redefining its mission in accord with contemporary public policy. Confidence in the American educational system, for reasons mentioned previously, has waned and is now in need of renewed energy and vigor, an energy and vigor that are capable of bringing about a commitment to new educational standards for success. The public's thrust for new standards has been validated by two recent, highly publicized reports entitled *A Nation at Risk: The Imperative for Educational Reform* (U.S. Department of Education, 1983) and *National Goals for Education* (White House, 1991).

Special education, like general education, has begun to embrace the notion of outcomes-based education and outcomes-based assessment at the local, state, and national levels (Ysseldyke, Algozzine, & Thurlow, 1992). Evaluating the success of special education for teachers and policymakers at all levels means much more than

Figure 13.3
Conceptual model of educational outcomes for school completion.

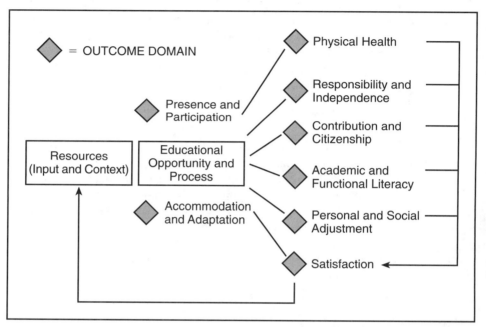

Source: Copyright 1994, The Haworth Press, Inc., Binghamton, NY. Ysseldyke, J. E., & Thurlow, M. L. (1994). What results should be measured to decide whether instruction is working for students with disabilities? *Special Services in the Schools, 9*(2), 49.

simply evaluating the progress of a child as she or he moves through the special education system; rather, it means documenting the success of the entire service delivery system and of all the children and youth in its charge—in a multitude of ways and across a multitude of settings. According to Salvia and Ysseldyke (1995), there are four main reasons why people have an interest in outcomes-based assessment: improvement of instructional programs, accountability, public information, and policy formulation.

Just as state and local policymakers need information on the quality and productivity of their schools, teachers also need information on the progress of their respective students. Researchers at the University of Minnesota's National Center on Educational Outcomes (Ysseldyke, Thurlow, & Erickson 1994) have developed a conceptual model by which special educators may organize their assessment processes using the domains of relevance, intended outcomes, indicators of outcome quality, and sources of information (see Figure 13.3). Although the model is still in development and the extent to which educational leaders are embracing this or similar models varies from state to state, one point is abundantly clear, to overlook the potential importance and long-range impact of outcomes-based principles would be to overlook a new and rather innovative means of assessing student, school, and system-wide outcomes within the context of a single, unified frame-work.

SUMMARY

Testing, as it is currently practiced, bears little resemblance to its historical prede-cessors. Yet, the mission remains much the same: to identify and serve people in need, whether that means providing service delivery in the schools or in community mental health centers. In either case, children with exceptionalities are exposed to a wide range of assessment practices representing many different educational and psy-chological domains. While standardized measures of intelligence, personality, adap-tive behavior, neuropsychological functioning, and achievement are essential to the assessment process, a new wave of assessment practices is flowing into special edu-cation service delivery. Curriculum-based assessment, ecological assessment, mini-mum competency testing, and outcomes-based assessment all represent new and in-novative ways of conceptualizing the manner in which children with exceptionalities are evaluated and served by educational and psychological service providers. The fu-ture is a bright one, but only to the extent that those charged with the responsibility of providing such services are willing to combine the best instruments with their best efforts to produce the best results possible.

QUESTIONS AND EXERCISES

1. How do the care and treatment of people with disabilities today differ from that of several hundred years ago? How does it differ from that of even fifteen to twenty years ago?

2. Identify and briefly describe the four most important pieces of legislation affecting the lives of people with disabilities presented in this chapter. Of the four, which is considered to be the most important for people who routinely assess children and youth with disabilities?

3. Two very well-known court cases constitute the center of the debate over the legality of standardized testing with cultural minorities, *Larry P. v. Riles* and *PASE v. Hannon*. What makes these two court cases so important and how were the outcomes different?

4. Briefly identify and explain the simple five-step referral to placement sequence used for serving children and youth with disabilities. Where does assessment fit into this sequence?

5. What role do standardized intelligence tests play in most multidimensional assessment sys-tems? Can you identify the two IQ tests most frequently used in the schools today?

6. For children who are referred for possible emotional disturbances, how might the multidi-mensional assessment battery differ from that traditionally used for academic difficulties only?

7. Identify and describe the three most frequently cited areas in which children encounter dif-ficulty in academic achievement. Of the three discussed in this chapter, which single area accounts for more referrals than any other? Why do you believe this is the case?

8. What makes curriculum-based assessment plans different from other, more traditional as-sessment plans? How might curriculum-based assessment devices be used to complement the results of norm-referenced instruments?

SUGGESTED READINGS

ETS Trustees' Colloquy. (1995). *Performance assessment: Different needs different answers.* Princeton, NJ: Educational Testing Service.

Flanagan, D. P., Andrews, T., & Genshaft, J. L. (in press). The utility of intelligence tests with special education populations. In D. P. Flanagan, J. L. Genshaft, & P. L. Harrison (Eds.), *Beyond traditional intellectual assessment: Contemporary and emerging theories, tests, and issues.* New York: Guilford.

Huebner, E. S. (1989). Errors in decision making: A comparison of school psychologists' interpretation of grade equivalents, percentiles, and deviation IQs. *School Psychology Review, 18*(1), 51–55.

Marston, D. B. (1989). A curriculum-based measurement approach to assessing academic performance: What it is and why do it? In M. R. Shinn (ed.), *Curriculum-based measurement: Assessing special children* (pp. 18–78). New York: Guilford.

Safford, P. L., & Safford, E. J. (1996). *A history of childhood and disability.* New York: Columbia University, Teachers' College Press.

Salvia J., & Ysseldyke, J. E. (1995). *Assessment* (6th ed.). Boston, MA: Houghton Mifflin.

Taylor, R. L., & Tindal, G. (Eds.). (1994/1995). *Trends in assessment* [Whole monograph]. *Diagnostique, 20*(1–4).

Turnbull, A. P., Turnbull, H. R., Shank, M., & Leal, D. (1995). *Exceptional lives: Special education in today's schools.* Upper Saddle River, NJ: Merrill/Prentice Hall.

CHAPTER 14

Ethics and Issues in Assessment

INTRODUCTION

According to one scholar writing in the area of legal and ethical issues, psychological tests represent one of the highest technical advancements in the field of psychology (Swenson, 1993). Others have placed intelligence tests among the 20 most important discoveries of the 20th century, right alongside other major discoveries such as atomic fission, the computer, Einstein's theory of relativity, and Watson and Crick's model of the double-helix (Miller, 1984). Irrespective of testing's relative rank among other major advancements of our time, it is safe to assume that most people's lives have in some way been influenced by tests of one sort or another.

Ethics can be viewed as a set of conduct rules that defines and synthesizes socially valued elements of right and wrong, and that specifies guidelines for professional duties and moral obligations. Most professional organizations have published codes of ethics to assist their members with the more difficult decisions of day-to-day responsibilities. The most important enforcement mode for ethical violations of members is typically group pressure applied by organization members. Although the ethics of testing are imprecisely defined and open to individual interpretation, there is general consensus among educational and psychological service providers that ethical guidelines are foundational components of effective service delivery.

The purpose of the present chapter is to identify and explain many of the ethical issues faced by educational and psychological service providers using some of education's and psychology's most valued tools—their tests. The discussion will be organized around several of the general ethical principles put forth by the American Counseling Association (1995) and the American Psychological Association [APA] (1992). The four principal areas of focus are: professional training and competence, professional and scientific responsibility, respect for the rights and dignity of others, and social responsibility.

PROFESSIONAL TRAINING AND COMPETENCE

Professional Training

Educational and psychological service providers must, out of necessity, develop skills in assessment and intervention. But one cannot become proficient at these tasks without first developing a depth of understanding in such areas of knowledge as cognition and learning, human growth and development, developmental abnormalities and psychopathology, and general human relations. In other words, assessment information obtained by a human service provider must stand in the context of other equally important information and must be interpreted within the context of the science of psychology. The notion that assessment as a viable skill can stand alone without the assessor having foundational skills in other related areas of human functioning and psychoeducational service delivery is a fallacy.

Proficiency in psychodiagnostic procedures depends in large part upon how well the individual has been able to integrate the aforementioned areas and successfully blend that broad-based foundation of human functioning with principles of measurement and assessment. This is the major reason most licensure boards require that their applicants have graduated from a college or university having an accredited program with an integrated set of course work. Graduate training programs accredited by the American Psychological Association (for psychologists) and the Council on Accreditation of Counseling and Related Educational Programs (for counselors) both require courses and contact hours in assessment, diagnosis, and treatment intervention across a wide range of disorders and disabilities.

As with any profession, being well trained during graduate education is far different from staying abreast of new developments in a given field throughout one's career. Many, if not most educational and psychological service providers leave school well trained and well prepared to offer assessment and intervention services. As time slips by and a professional routine sets in, however, a conscientious and dedicated service provider must work at staying on top of new developments in the field's theory and practice. The subfield of assessment is no different. The broader the provider's practice, the more difficult it is to stay on top of the many new tests published each year, let alone the research that serves as their conceptual foundation and documents their validity for the decisions for which they are used. Perhaps many service providers would be surprised to find out that staying current in one's field and with one's tools of inquiry means more than simply maintaining the standards learned in graduate school; constant retraining and professional growth are standards for best practice. According to the American Counseling Association's *Code of Ethics and Standards of Practice* (1995): "counselors must not base their assessment or intervention decisions or recommendations on data or test results that are obsolete or outdated for the current purpose" (p. 23).

The problem with testing lies not so much with the characteristics of the tests, but, rather, with the ways in which they are often used (Moreland, Eyde, Robertson, Primoff, & Most, 1995). One way that leaders within the disciplines of education and psychology have responded to this phenomenon is through the creation of a Joint Committee on Testing Practices (JCTP) in 1984. A primary goal of this group was to develop "an empirical approach to test user qualification that would be helpful to those interested in improving how tests are used" (Moreland et al., 1995). The group identified a list of 12 minimum competencies for proper use of tests. A list of areas in which misuses are likely to occur is shown in Figure 14.1.

There are a number of areas in which misuse is likely to occur. Comprehensive assessment systems offer one such example. Any time an examiner is asked to record and integrate information from assessment batteries with clinical observations of behaviors that suggest serious psychological disturbance, the potential for error is great, particularly for those who do not keep up with new developments in their field. A second area of likely misuse is in the area of psychometric knowledge. Examiners who fail to understand such basics of psychometric theory as reliability and validity may overstate the accuracy of their information and instill in their examinees an inappropriately high level of confidence in their scores and profiles. A third example pertains to the appropriate use of norms. Testers who fail to examine the normative bases of their instruments may find that the tests they are using are not appropriate for all examinees. For example, asking an undergraduate student from Taiwan who reports difficulty adjusting to college and to the American culture to take a standardized measure of adjustment may result in very misleading information (if no persons from Taiwan were included in the normative sample the test has not been shown to provide accurate information for such persons). Simply stated, college students from Taiwan or any other non-Western culture may be completely unfamiliar with the culture and contexts in which questions are presented. If

Figure 14.1
Twelve minimum competencies for proper use of tests.

Item No.	Competency
1.	Avoiding errors in scoring and recording
2.	Refraining from labeling people with personally derogatory terms like *dishonest* on the basis of a test score that lacks perfect validity
3.	Keeping scoring keys and test materials secure
4.	Seeing that every examinee follows directions so that test scores are accurate
5.	Using settings for testing that allow for optimum performance by test takers (e.g., adequate room)
6.	Refraining from coaching or training individuals or groups on test items, which results in misrepresentation of the person's abilities and competencies
7.	Willingness to give interpretation and guidance to test takers in counseling situations
8.	Not making photocopies of copyrighted materials
9.	Refraining from using homemade answer sheets that do not align properly with scoring keys
10.	Establishing rapport with examinees to obtain accurate scores
11.	Refraining from answering questions from test takers in greater detail than the test manual permits
12.	Not assuming that a norm for one job applies to a different job (and not assuming that norms for one group automatically apply to other groups)

Source: Moreland, K. L., Eyde, L. D., Robertson, G. J., Primoff, E. S., & Most, R. B. (1995). Assessment of test user qualifications: A research-based measurement procedure. *American Psychologist, 50*(1), 16.

life experiences relevant to an individual are not fairly represented on an instrument, then that instrument should not be used to make diagnostic evaluations of any importance (cf. Moreland et al., 1995).

Professional Competence

Professional training is only one of many broad areas of importance that bear directly on the ethics of testing and service delivery. Once a person leaves school and enters the world as a trained human service provider, it is assumed that the person is providing services that are in concert with sound ethical and legal standards, that the instruments used are based on sound scientific principles, and that the test-related decisions represent an integration of science, law, and ethics.

As you might imagine, there is a wide range of services available to people who are in need of educational and psychological assistance. Unfortunately, there is an equally wide range of competency levels among the professionals providing such services. People who are in need of educational and psychological services should not have to feel as if they must be vigilant or responsible for evaluating the services received, but such often seems to be the case in the highly competitive ways of the modern era. The notion of caveat emptor, "let the buyer beware," may now be as relevant for social science service delivery as it is in business and industry. Consequently, it is important for people to be protected from those who cannot perform the service competently. Because services are provided to the most vulnerable segments of the population (e.g., children, older adults, persons with disabilities), extra care and attention to the regulation of these services is absolutely essential.

The challenge to being a competent human service provider necessitates that the professional adhere to a number of broad-based expectations, but the tenets supporting the role of tester are relatively straightforward. For example, both the American Counseling Association (1995) and the American Psychological Association (1992) have sections of their ethical standards manuals devoted entirely to evaluation and assessment. First and foremost among the two associations' assessment standards is the issue of professional competence. More specifically, practicing professionals must respect the boundaries of their training and not administer or interpret tests for which they have not been trained. Further, it is understood that all assessments occur only within the context of a professionally defined relationship.

Second, and as alluded to previously, service providers who conduct evaluations, and certainly those who design instruments that serve as the basis for those evaluations, are required to be sufficiently well grounded in the basics of psychometrics, from simple reliability and validity issues to more complex theories of measurement, that they can interpret test results in a competent, professional manner. Examiners who are unable to intepret the technical portions of the manuals for the tests they use are generally unable to differentiate good tests from bad tests. Additionally, those who overlook the research underpinnings of their instruments greatly devalue the scientific merits of both their efforts and the results of their evaluations.

Interpretation of assessment results represents a third important area of ethical emphasis. The competent evaluator is one who can readily blend the principles of psychometrics with other situational factors affecting the testing process. That is, competent professionals must recognize the "limits to the certainty with which diagnoses, judgments, or predictions can be made" (APA Standard 2.04[b], 1992). When the examinee's characteristics are such that the examiner's ability to interpret test results fairly and without reservation is compromised, then the examiner should withdraw from the evaluative process and refer the client to someone else for whom interpretation and service delivery is not compromised. There is a rapidly growing body of literature on diverse and cross-cultural strategies for assessment that professionals may consult if interested (Dana, 1990; Lonner, 1985).

A fourth issue very much related to assessment and evaluation lies within test scoring and interpretation services. Professionals sometimes contract with outside agencies to score their protocols, often the very test companies they bought the instruments from in the first place. Despite the fact that someone else, in this case, the test scoring service, is performing the scoring part of the evaluation, the test examiner remains responsible for the quality and efficacy of the entire testing operation, including the interpretation of the results. Examiners who defer to computer-generated recommendations of a test profile without verifying the appropriateness for their clients are clearly at odds with most organizations' codes of ethics, and even more important are at odds with best practices in the respective disciplines of education and psychology.

Validity of Clinical Opinion

The notion that validity is a function of a test, only, is dying slowly. With test publishers being more conscientious than ever about putting a wealth of validity information in their test manuals, it may indeed seem as if the validity of the testing process resides primarily in the instrument—but such is not the case. Increasingly, clinicians are being held accountable for their decisions, decisions that relate *in part* to the instrument but also in a very large part, to their own clinical acumen.

According to Matarazzo (1990), society now wants firmer evidence of the validity of opinions offered by psychologists. In support of this, he notes that "attorneys, juries, and judges are asking psychologists in the courtroom for considerably more evidence than our clinic or hospital colleagues have requested [in the past] to demonstrate that the instruments and techniques used, in part, in forming their clinical opinions are valid ones" (p. 1002). Despite the sobering and challenging tone of Matarazzo's position, he also provides evidence to suggest that the diagnostic consistency of clinicians' evaluations has increased substantially over the past several decades, from little to no interclinician reliability in the 1950s to the very high indices of the 1980s.

A major reason for the increase in estimated reliability over the years has to do with improvements in diagnosis and classification of disorders and disabilities. Brodsky (1991) contends that clinicians' ability to diagnose, classify, and treat a person in need of psychological services stems directly from their depth of understanding about the theoretical and scientific foundations of their opinions. In short, if they have a broader conceptual understanding of what they are doing they can answer the question, How do you know what you know?

Is it possible that the science of psychology has advanced to the point that clinical opinions, if properly measured, are as accurate and useful as other, less subjective methods? Meehl (1986) and his colleagues (Dawes, Faust, & Meehl, 1989) don't believe so. For them, the subjectivity of clinical opinion causes them to fall far short of other, more data based approaches. They provide several reasons for their conclusion.

- overconfidence in one's clinical judgment
- difficulty in separating valid from invalid variables of influence
- tendency to overattend to factors that support one's hypothesis and to underattend to contradictory ones
- influence of situational factors on the decision-making process (e.g., fatigue, experience, ordering of relevant variables)

In the opinion of Dawes et al. (1989) formula-based decision rules have proven to be far more reliable and valid than clinical opinions alone. Data based equations for predicting human behaviors and outcomes not only have their place in psychological service delivery but can and should be used to improve the human condition. To do otherwise is unprofessional, unethical, and theoretically questionable (Meehl, 1986). Simply stated, clinicians should allow more science into the practice of the science of the mind, and this means, in part, more sophisticated use of the results of assessment devices.

PROFESSIONAL AND SCIENTIFIC RESPONSIBILITY
Standards for Educational and Psychological Testing

Educational and psychological testing occurs in a variety of contexts and across a broad range of settings. Because of the great disparity in the origin, design, construction, and use of tests, three large governing bodies in education and psychology have jointly composed a set of standards to provide "criteria for the [formal] evaluation of tests, testing practices, and the effects of test use" (American Educational Research Association [AERA], American Psychological Association [APA], National Council on Measurement in Education [NCME], 1985, p. 2). This document, officially known as the *Standards for Educational and Psychological Testing,* which we will refer to as the standards manual, represents the fifth in a series of publications that originated in 1954 to provide developers and users of tests with assistance in evaluating the technical adequacy of their instruments for educational and psychological assessment. The authors of the manual have classified the standards into two broad levels: primary standards, those standards considered to be applicable to *all* tests used by educational and psychological service providers; and secondary standards, those standards that require the test user or publisher to go beyond the basic obligations of sound testing practice. A third classification, conditional standards, is less formally defined than the first two and refers to standards that may actually be considered a primary standard in some cases and a secondary standard in others, depending upon the situation and the consequences of meeting or failing to meet the respective standards.

The standards are divided into four broad but related areas: technical standards for test construction and evaluation, professional standards for test use, standards for particular applications, and standards for administrative procedures. It should be noted that at the time this text went to press, the sixth edition of the standards manual was in development, but was not yet ready for distribution. We recommend that anyone who routinely engages in any form of testing—from test design and implementation to assessment and evaluation—obtain a copy of the new standards when they are published and become familiar with the guidelines as soon as possible.

Technical Standards for Test Construction and Evaluation. The technical standards provide the scientific basis and foundation for all of the other standards. According to the standards manual, "validity is the most important consideration in test evaluation" (AERA et al., 1985, p. 9). As such, the standards manual addresses the different types of validity evidence needed to support test use. Reliability and measurement error represent a second key component. Standards for the development and revision of formal, published instruments, an often overlooked area of importance, describe criteria important for scale construction. Even the process of creating scales and scores has standards guiding its development. Finally, there are specific standards that pertain to the development of the test manuals that accompany the instruments.

Professional Standards for Test Use.   Professional standards represent another major component of the standards manual. Whereas the prior section dealt primarily with test development and the burden to provide evidence to support any recommended test use, the section on professional standards pertains to their use in applied settings. Less statistical and more practical than the previous section, the principles of test use allow for greater flexibility in professional testing but, at the same time, require more in the way of professional judgment. For example, Standard 6.1 states that: "Test users should evaluate the available written documentation on the validity and reliability of tests *for the specific use intended*" (AERA et al., 1985, p. 41; italics added). The authors of the manual acknowledge that there are times and instruments for which validity information is lacking. Consequently, the standards allow the test user to take into consideration the conditions and contexts of assessment, and distinctions are made between the various types of testing situations (e.g., clinical, school, employment, licensure, and program evaluation).

Standards for Particular Applications.   This section applies mainly to guidelines for testing people who are members of special populations. As indicated in Chapter 13, children, youth, and persons of minority backgrounds are afforded special protections under the law, protections that encompass educational and psychological testing practices. Although the standards were written to reflect the special needs of two broad classes of persons—linguistic minorities and people with disabilities—the changing nature of educational and psychological service delivery, combined with a greater emphasis on cross-cultural assessment, mandates more and better instruments for traditionally underserved segments of the population. Very young children with severe handicaps and older adults with disabling conditions are examples of two groups being introduced with greater frequency into the human service delivery system. Future standards should reflect the needs of these and other segments of the broader population, as well.

Standards for Administrative Procedures.   This fourth and final section applies to the acquisition of test scores, that is, the administration, scoring, and reporting of one's test data. The authors of the manual make it clear that formal testing is very similar to experimentation in that the results are most reliable when testing is conducted under standardized, highly controlled conditions. Standards for protecting the rights of examinees, including such things as informed consent, test security, and placement into special programs, are also included and will be discussed later in this chapter.

Test Bias

One of the most prevalent themes in popular discussions of testing is that tests are unfair to certain groups. The term used is *bias*. It is often asserted that standardized tests are used to deprive certain groups of access to educational and employment opportunities. To the extent that tests are used mechanically as selection and placement devices, and to the extent that some groups in our society have historically performed less well on tests, tests *do* become instruments through which access to education and employment is disproportionately barred to members of these groups. The question that must be addressed is whether individuals are unjustly barred and, more generally, what constitutes fair and equitable use of tests for the selection, placement, and classification of individuals.

The issue of bias in testing has probably been the most hotly debated topic relating to educational and psychological measurement over the past few decades. When Congress passed the Civil Rights Act of 1964 (Pub. L. No. 88-352, 42 U.S.C. §2000e *et seq.*), Title VII of the Act expressly prohibited the use of tests for the purpose of employment discrimination based on race, creed, color, sex, or national origin. However, the framers of the Act expressly permitted the use of tests for job-related decisions, when test scores could be shown to be related to an individual's level of job performance. Thus, the Act required that the test be a valid predictor of job performance for all classes of individuals with whom it was to be used, and a test would be considered unbiased if it gave equally accurate predictions for members from any racial, ethnic, or gender group. Due to the random nature of errors present in any one individual's test scores and the fact that test validity for any particular decision is based on group data, the test score for any individual may be inaccurate, and hence the decision based on that score may be wrong. Assuming that decisions must be made, we may view a test as unbiased if it leads to the same decision accuracy for the members of all groups with which it is used.

The situation changed dramatically for the use of tests in employment in 1971 when the U.S. Supreme Court, in the case of *Griggs v. Duke Power Company,* held that a test could be *presumed to be* biased if it gave differential predictions *for various groups.* This decision, subsequent amendments to the Civil Rights Act of 1964, and various federal administrative directives led to the development of the Uniform Guidelines for Employee Selection Procedures (Equal Employment Opportunity Commission, 1978), which hold that if the members of one group tend to score lower on a particular scale than members of another group, it becomes the responsibility of the employer to demonstrate that the test is a valid predictor of job performance. The principle developed by the Supreme Court in *Griggs* is called *adverse impact;* a demonstration of adverse impact by the plaintiff shifts the burden of proof to the employer to show that discrimination did not occur.

A 1976 suit in Illinois by the Golden Rule Insurance Company against the Educational Testing Service led to one solution to the test bias issue. Golden Rule alleged that differential passing rates for Blacks (52%) and Whites (77%) on the Illinois Insurance Licensure Examination was proof that the test was racially biased. In an out-of-court agreement in 1984, the parties agreed to a revised criterion for selecting items for the examination. The Educational Testing Service agreed to use items for which the success rate for Blacks and Whites differed by no more than 15%. The principle adopted in the Golden Rule case has been used in several other situations, in an effort to equate passing rates on various employment selection tests.

Simply barring the use of tests of aptitude or ability may have unintended consequences. W. B. Allen (1988), a California member of the U.S. Commission on Civil Rights, has described such a situation:

> In the case of Mary Amaya, a California mother, the state refuses to her son [sic] an IQ test on the grounds that it is *protecting* him from bias inherent in the test. . . .
>
> Consider the irony: Mrs. Amaya's son has been recommended for assignment to remedial courses. She believes that he may not require them. In an earlier, less enlightened era, an older son of hers had a similar experience. In that case the IQ test refuted the psychologist's subjective evaluation and the lad was spared a potentially damaging assignment. Mrs. Amaya would like to have such an opportunity for her youngest son, as well. It has been denied. . . . Thus, a family of at best modest means is placed in a position of having to fight off the entire legal edifice of its state and federal courts in order to guarantee an opportunity for its son. (pp. 368–369)

Quoting the Superintendent of Public Instruction, Allen (1988) notes further that, in California:

> there is no fundamental civil right to be able to take an IQ test. Where such a test may be a means to establish one's eligibility for an opportunity, therefore, it may nevertheless be denied to a black child by the state. (p. 368)

Thus, protection can be a mixed blessing.

There have been a number of other court challenges to the use of tests and other objective measures to aid in decision making in education and employment. The challenged procedures have included everything from aptitude and achievement tests to height and strength requirements. Until recently, the courts have tended to find in favor of the plaintiffs and against the tests and objective decision rules. Following is a summary of a 1988 U.S. Supreme Court decision that may indicate a change in direction *(Watson v. Fort Worth Bank and Trust)*:

> Seven justices agreed that a statistical disparity is not always sufficient to make out a prima facie case [of discrimination]. . . . In addition, a majority of the justices would require a plaintiff to identify the *specific* decision-making practice being challenged and then prove that this practice *caused* the exclusion of applicants for jobs or promotions because of their membership in a protected group [minority or female]. (Sharf, 1988, p. 242)

Challenges to the use of tests have had the beneficial effect of encouraging test developers to be much more careful in both the selection of test items and in the composition of norm groups. For example, in the preparation of the fourth edition of the Stanford-Binet, the authors used a panel of judges that included members of the larger minority groups to screen items for content that might be gender or race biased before the items were ever tried out. A second panel reviewed the items and item statistics from the initial tryouts to eliminate any items that were clearly biased. Other test developers use similar procedures. However, even with elaborate precautions taken to eliminate bias, differences often remain between the average test performances of different ethnic groups. Consequently, the question of test bias is inextricably bound to test validity. Remember that validity relates to the use that will be made of a test score. A test may be valid for one purpose and not for another. The notion of test bias is really a statement that a particular test is not appropriate for making certain decisions with a given group of individuals.

Truth in Testing

According to Rogers (1995), the criticisms of testing are greatest when information from tests constitutes the major driving force in the decision-making process. Where testing seems to have its greatest impact—and criticism is minimized—is when testing serves as an alternative to other forms of decision making. That is, when the testing process helps reduce the subjectivity of a decision-making process already in place. Instruments used at the beginning of a lengthy decision-making process and considered to be economical, nonintrusive, and yield a high probability of useful information are considered to be good candidates for public acceptance. One such example is the use of preschool screening instruments in community-based child-find programs. These evaluations are generally quick, performed free or at a minimal cost to parents, and usually yield important information about a child's level of development. Consequently, most parents are glad to avail themselves of the testing opportunity, and their use is typically not controversial.

Controversy usually enters when the costs are high and results, open to misinterpretation. In cases where the use of an instrument does not improve the decisions reached by other methods or, worse, when a test complicates the decision-making process, then it is time to reevaluate the rationale for testing in the first place. Consequently, professionals administering tests should be familiar with the basics of decision theory. In decision theory, the predictive accuracy of a decision-making process using a published instrument is formally analyzed on the basis of *hits* (correct decisions) and *misses* (incorrect decisions), with special attention given to the particular pattern of misses. Incorrect decisions can result in two ways:

False positives. People who perform sufficiently well on a test to give the impression that they have the necessary skills for a specific activity. In actuality, they do *not* have the necessary skills.

False negatives. People who perform sufficiently poorly on a test to give the impression that they do not have the skills necessary for a specific activity. In actuality, they do have the necessary skills.

Although Anastasi (1988) credits Wald (1950) with formally developing decision theory, and Cronbach and Gleser (1965) with its application to psychological tests, it was actually Taylor and Russell (1939) who laid out the basics of the theory well enough to be mathematically modeled by later researchers. Taylor and Russell were able to demonstrate the interrelationships between rates of selection without the instrument's information *(base rate),* ratio of people surpassing the cutoff score as compared with those who do not surpass the cutoff score *(selection ratio),* ratio of correct decisions to incorrect decisions *(hit rate),* and the instruments' validity coefficients. Similar to the situation with validity of clinical opinion, generally only the largest and most progressive testing companies provide validity information from studies that use some aspect of decision theory.

In light of the less than perfect reliability of test scores; the occasional day when for irrelevant reasons an individual performs poorly; or the rare occurrence of errors in scoring, score conversion, or score handling, the possibility that a person may be condemned by an erroneous or flawed score is sufficiently real for the counselor or psychologist to wish to give the examinee (or a parent or guardian) an opportunity to see and respond to the score. The response might take the form of a description of mitigating circumstances, a request for a retest, or presentation of other compensating information. In any event, making results available to and perhaps discussing them with the concerned person, avoids the impression of star chamber proceedings in which a person is forced to provide information that is otherwise secret or seems to be used in secretive ways—and may also avoid some decision errors that result from errors of measurement or errors in score processing.

Implementing these requirements, as specified in the Family Educational Rights and Privacy Act of 1974 (Pub. L. No. 93-380, 20 U.S.C. §241), has generated some practical problems for schools, yet it does provide a safeguard against the types of faulty test results just mentioned. Another reaction to the secrecy that has surrounded testing in education is the New York state law regarding truth in testing, which was enacted in 1979 in response to the aptitude testing programs of the Educational Testing Service. This law required companies that publish tests administered in the state of New York to do three things:

- disclose the results of all test validity studies
- notify all students as to how their scores were calculated (any item weights used and the types of transformations applied) and what the scores mean (what norm groups were used)
- provide a copy of test questions, the answer key, and the participant's answers to an examinee who requests them

One objective of this law was to enable people who felt that their test scores might be inaccurate to check one potential source of error and to rebut their test scores if errors were indeed found. This is a laudable purpose; however, in terms of the quality and economy of measurement, the law has had several adverse consequences. The New York law has resulted in an increase in test development costs; because examinees may have the tests, new items must be written each time a test is given. Hence, because they can be used only once, the validity of a particular set of items is less well established than was the case prior to enactment of the law. The cost of assessment for test users has increased accordingly. Further, it is much more difficult to equate the meaning of scores over a period of years because of the changing nature of the items and scales. It remains to be seen whether the law's potential benefits to individuals will offset the increased costs and losses to the educational system. Preliminary reports indicate that there have been very few requests for copies of the tests, suggesting that the law may have been unnecessary.

RESPECT FOR THE RIGHTS AND DIGNITY OF OTHERS
Privacy and Confidentiality

Concerns about individual privacy have increased steadily over the past few years. The widespread and sometimes irresponsible use of data bases in which information about individuals can be stored and quickly accessed, combined with the growing belief that people's lives are their own business, have sensitized people to procedures that constitute unwarranted invasions into the private lives of others.

It is important for educational and psychological service providers to distinguish between *privacy,* which refers to the degree of access others have to one's body or behavior, and *confidentiality,* which refers to the degree of access others have to information given voluntarily from one person to another (U.S. Department of Health and Human Services, 1993). From an evaluator's standpoint, when is it reasonable to demand such information? Additionally, under what circumstances may a societal need to know override individuals' rights to keep their own secrets, that is, their rights to privacy?

Presenting oneself for educational or psychological evaluation can be a most humbling experience, at times even intimidating. Answering questions about highly personal aspects of one's life is never done in a light-hearted or superficial manner. Consequently, highly personal questions should never be asked in anything other than an equally serious and humane way. It is well to ask under what circumstances and to whom such revelations should be made. While the personal exposure of information on an achievement test may be less revealing than that called for on a personality measure, both types of measures call for information that most people would probably rather not share with others. A number of questions are pertinent to any discussion of ethics in assessment.

Who Will Benefit from the Information Collected?   When assessment data are collected to provide specific help to an individual, objections will likely be minimal, particularly when the testing occurs at the request of the individual or parent. Examples of this arise when classroom tests are given and used to identify children in need of further academic assistance or when diagnostic tests are given as a prelude to program planning. The objective of the testing may be to provide instruction targeted at the level at which these children function, and in such a case, the children should benefit from a program that proceeds at their pace. But, children may also be identified as "second class" in some way if they do not make it into the top group. In such cases, the educational benefits for the children should be made clear to them and their parents before the testing is undertaken.

A second relevant example arises when a student goes to a counselor for help with personal or career concerns, and inventories are used to provide both the counselor *and* the client with information. In each of these cases the individual being evaluated is considered to be the direct beneficiary of the testing. There are, however, times when the benefits of the assessment flow indirectly back to the examinee, such as when the person being evaluated is a member of a class of persons on whom aggregate data are needed. The collection of achievement test data either to help guide school district personnel in the allocation of their resources or to help school personnel better understand their student body are examples of situations in which the examinees are the secondary beneficiaries of test data collected.

Licensure exams for practicing professionals (e.g., counselors, physicians, psychologists, teachers) constitute a third example. While information contained on most licensure exams does not benefit the test taker specifically, it is a gauge of general professional competence and a measure of likelihood for effective service delivery on the part of the service provider. Professionals taking such exams are direct beneficiaries only in the sense that they gain access to a professional practice; the primary beneficiary in this case is considered to be the people who request the professional's services and society in general.

How Will the Information Be Used?   Relevance of the information must be established prior to any formal assessment. Once relevance has been demonstrated, there must be compelling evidence that the test scores will provide information that will lead to correct decisions regarding service delivery. Even when the goal of assessment is worthwhile, there is little point to gathering evidence for which the likelihood for impact is questionable or small, with little hope for improvement in the decision-making process. Conversely, the more relevant the assessment information, the more justification there is in calling upon the individual to provide it.

If a parent suspects the presence of attention-deficit disorder and takes the child to a counselor or school psychologist for evaluation, then the service provider gathers only the data needed to confirm or disconfirm this hypothesis. If secondary concerns emerge during the course of the evaluation, as may be the case for some children with emotional disorders or other learning disabilities, then additional evaluations may also be required. In either case, however, psychologists gather only the information deemed "sufficient to provide appropriate substantiation for their findings" (APA Standard 2.01[b], 1992). Gathering additional information to shed light on other unofficial hunches or because someone is already taking other tests should never occur.

A question very much related to proper use may be, What will happen to the assessment data once they are collected? The issue here pertains to physical storage and handling of assessment-related information. If there is a risk of revealing confidential information to others, there is also a risk of having assessment information stored in such a way that others, whose interests are less direct or less noble, may also have access to it. An example from the contemporary press would be the disclosure of someone's personal medical history and records to insurance companies who, unknown to the person, disseminate the information to other organizations for managed-care decisions and cost-benefit analyses. The American Psychological Association's Code of

Conduct requires that when client information is included in data bases that are available to others for whom recipient consent has not been given by the receiver of the psychological services, "coding [should] be used to avoid the inclusion of personal identifiers" (APA Standard 5.07[a], 1992). Within the areas of education and psychology, a similar case can be made for information that is archived for research purposes.

How Personal Is the Information Being Sought?   Some questions are perceived as much more invasive than others. In a study about privacy and personnel selection, Rosenbaum (1971) asked which items people felt were an invasion of their privacy. Five broad factors were identified from among a total item pool of 66 items: family background and influences, personal history, interests and values, financial management, and social adjustment. Two areas in particular, family background and influences, and financial management, were viewed as the most invasive by 49% and 52% of the respondents, respectively.

As long as information is general and ambiguous, or when information is anonymous, as is the case in many public surveys, people are not overly concerned about others' access to their information. However, when anonymity is not assured, for example, when personally identifiable information is available with written answers to certain questions, and particularly when the test or inventory contains highly sensitive information, people are justified in having concern about the confidentiality of their information. It is quite common for personality inventories to request information about attitudes, interests, and preferences in the areas of politics, religion, finances, and other personal matters. Consider the following questions:

- Do you have trouble making new friends?
- Did you ever want to run away from home?
- Do you sometimes have thoughts that are too bad to talk about?

These questions certainly ask the individual to make public—to whomever may have access to the responses—some quite personal aspects of his or her inner life. Although information on these topics can be very revealing, more dramatic examples are those questions pertaining to highly sensitive areas such as sexual behavior, illicit drug use, and matters of the law. Adequate provision for the security of this information is absolutely essential. Data should be available only to those who need it for legitimate decision-making purposes.

Autonomy and Self-Determination

Respecting a person's right to autonomy and self-determination means respecting their right to self-governance and independent decision making. Additionally, it means respecting the person's right to deal effectively with the ambiguities of everyday living, particularly as it relates to actions on their own behalf. One way to minimize the offensiveness of any invasion of privacy is to conduct an assessment only after obtaining the *informed consent* of the person for whom an evaluation is needed.

Informed consent implies that the person to be tested has been told what information will be collected, why it is being collected, and how it will be used. It also implies that the consenter is competent to understand what information is being sought and that the person has the right to decide whether to participate or not. According to Porter (1995), informed consent is more of a process than a one-time occurrence. It is a means of keeping an examinee informed of what is going on throughout the entire evaluation and perhaps even after the evaluation has been completed. The whole notion of informed consent rests on three premises:

- the information provided to the examinee is complete and allows for a fully informed decision,
- the individual has the ability to comprehend the information presented, and
- the decision to participate is made voluntarily and without duress or undue influence.

Meeting these conditions may be difficult when the consenter is of limited ability or is from a background different from that of the person soliciting the information. All persons who present themselves for testing and psychodiagnostic evaluation should be presumed competent unless otherwise demonstrated. The term *informed consent* is generally reserved for those who are of legal age and have no mental disability that precludes them from understanding what is being requested and for giving truly informed consent. For persons who do not meet these criteria, such as children and adults with mental disabilities, consent is requested from the parents or legal guardians (ACA Standard G.2[e], 1995, p. 17). Even in these cases, though, permission to evaluate should also be sought from the minor or person with disabilities—out of respect for the person and for the sheer practicality of trying to gather information from someone who has not consented. In this case, however, the term *assent* is used. A third term, *coconsenter,* is used when a person has the legal right to consent to evaluation but for one reason or another the consent of another adult is deemed important to the decision-making process.

Informed consent raises problems for both the person seeking the information and for the person providing it. For the person being tested, the right to agree to formal evaluation must be made without undue influence. That is, unless there are extenuating circumstances requiring others' participation, such as a court ordered evaluation or an impending medical emergency, consent must be completely voluntary. College students who want to earn extra credit in a given course, job applicants who desperately want to be viewed positively on preemployment testing, and prisoners who believe that their privileges may depend upon their willingness to cooperate are examples of three groups of people who may be under considerable pressure to consent to whatever evaluation procedures are requested and for whom true consent may actually be compromised.

Two problems with informed consent often emerge in educational and psychological testing. The first pertains to the need for informed consent within the context of *deception,* that is, the need to mask the true intent of an evaluation to get accurate results. Deception occurs when fully informed consent is likely to result in an alteration of behaviors or responses to questions during testing. In such cases, it is essential that the purpose of the assessment is fully justified and that the participants are informed of the true purpose, generally referred to as *debriefing,* as soon after participation as possible. In the case of a research study, review of the study design by other researchers is usually required, to verify the need for the deception. The second problem stems from the reality that requiring active, signed consent invites the possibility of *dissent,* a refusal that might never have been contemplated if acquiescence had been taken for granted. In projects where sample characteristics of experimentally accessible populations are so important (e.g., norming tests, surveying of abilities or attitudes), refusals and dropouts are a serious problem and often threaten the validity of the entire project.

A third concern, which is related to the prior two but retains a sense of importance all its own, is that of subjecting the person to physical or psychological risk. Testing in the social sciences does not usually pose much of a risk to test takers; however, formal testing does induce some level of anxiety in most persons. The greater the consequences, the greater the probability of anxiety. Personality inventories may pose another type of risk, that of requiring people to respond to questions that describe important yet highly revealing aspects of themselves. Therefore, if some extra anxiety is indicative of a psychological hazard, examiners must acknowledge that for test takers, taking tests and receiving their results may at times constitute hazards that go beyond those of everyday living. The problem for examiners is to judge the severity of the hazard and to balance it against the countervailing benefits to the person tested.

A somewhat different type of risk is that which may result from classifying individuals. In an effort to simplify the highly complex behaviors and personalities of others, some people resort to using labels. This labeling carries with it implications which may influence how people are viewed and treated in the educational and social-service systems (e.g., mentally retarded, emotionally disturbed). When people are responded to as if they are representatives of a broader class of people, and particularly if the traits have little or no basis in reality, these labels deprive the person and other members of the class of their individuality and worth as individuals.

Beneficence

Treating people in an ethical, professional manner means more than simply protecting them from unnecessary risks; it means taking the necessary steps to secure their well-being (ACA Standard A.1[a], 1995, p. 2). As indicated previously, the notion of educational and psychological service providers protecting the rights, dignity, and well-being of those in their charge is an ethical mandate; however, in today's world of automated assessments, profile analyses, and computer generated reports, the well-being of the client sometimes seems to be less important than completion of the task or schedule.

According to The National Commission for the Protection of Human Subjects of Biomedical and Behavioral Research (1979), a commission established jointly by the National Institutes of Health, the Public Health Service, and the Department of

Health and Human Services to specifically codify standards for the ethical treatment of human subjects involved in such research, the well-being of others extends far beyond common courtesy and thoughtfulness to that of a moral, ethical, and professional obligation. Built into this obligation is a twofold expression: Do no harm, and maximize the benefits while minimizing the risks. The difficulty for behavioral and biomedical scientists today lies in the need to expose people to some degree of risk to avoid a greater harm at a later date.

Not all persons needing educational and psychological services are capable of understanding the risks and benefits associated with an evaluation or an experimental treatment program. Of those who are capable of understanding the risks and benefits involved, not all are capable of acting on their own behalf. For these reasons, the government has identified several groups of people who are considered to be particularly vulnerable and for whom special protections are afforded: children, prisoners, pregnant women, persons with mental disabilities, and persons who are believed to be economically or educationally disadvantaged (Federal Policy for the Protection of Human Subjects, 45 C.F.R. 46 [1991]). In work involving individuals in any of these categories, the benefits of the evaluations must be direct and the risks immediately justifiable in light of all possible alternatives.

SOCIAL RESPONSIBILITY

Test use takes place in a social context and has particular social consequences. As Cole and Moss (1989) and Messick (1989) point out, testing is also a matter of social policy. There is relatively little question that tests can improve efficiency and productivity in educational and occupational contexts, but at what cost and using which criteria? The formula for determining social worth varies from person to person and group to group, based on a number of complicated factors. Psychometric research alone cannot determine whether the cost in relation to one type of value is justified by the gain in another. That judgment must be made by society, its members, and the people responsible for establishing social policy. Irrespective of the approach or resolution, however, two questions remain to be answered in every social policy question pertaining to testing: Is testing fair? and Is testing good for society?

Distributive Justice

Let's first address the issue of fairness in regard to testing. Those who construct tests or teach about tests generally believe that the use of tests will permit, though certainly not guarantee, better, wiser, and more socially appropriate decisions. Despite the fact that testing is most often carried out to achieve positive outcomes both for the individual and for the larger society, it is sometimes difficult for members of the general public to appreciate how a system built on discrimination (i.e., discrimination between individuals of differing ability levels) can assure egalitarian principles. In this section, we will consider those positive outcomes. In a later section we will present some of the more subtle factors influencing the sociopolitical context within which testing occurs.

The notion of distributive social justice, in this case, implies the principle of fairness in that the benefits of educational and psychological services to people, for people, and by people are distributed in an equitable and impartial way. As many members of our educational and social service delivery systems are so keenly aware, social injustices occur across a wide range of possibilities, from no or limited access to current service delivery systems to an undue burden imposed within the respective service delivery systems (The National Commission, 1979).

One commonly held view of how tests can advance egalitarian principles by using instruments known for their discriminative abilities is through objective standards of performance. People generally rise to meet the standards that are set for them. When standards such as minimum proficiency criteria are maintained for all students, those who are initially unable to reach the preestablished levels of proficiency soon raise their achievement levels to meet the standards for success, particularly if their efforts are supported by the larger society. One example is from the minimum competency testing movement in the state of Florida. When passing an objective test of academic skills became a requirement for graduation from a community college, the failure rate was initially much higher among minority students than among majority students. However, with instruction focused on the skills measured by the tests, the minority students soon raised their achievement levels to those required by the tests, improving the success rates dramatically (Gottfredson & Sharf, 1988).

Social Benefits of Testing

The second question, Is testing good? remains equally difficult to answer in a manner that would be applicable to all people and under all conditions. To those who construct the tests, the most immediate response is *yes*—but only in qualified hands and only for designated purposes. Consequently, there are a number of social problems at the individual, civic, and national levels for which testing can—and frequently does—play a constructive role. According to Messick (1993), and under the rubric of *unified validity*, the worthiness of a test cannot be separated from its use and the inferences that result; that is, the testing process and the people who direct it must offer their community appropriate, meaningful, and useful score-based inferences.

Medical training is an example of a scarce and heavily subsidized social resource that is helped by standardized testing. Providing the necessary faculty and laboratories for training medical students places a costly demand on society. It becomes important to society that those who are given the opportunity to receive this training be people who are likely to learn the skills and, thus, succeed in the specialty for which they are being trained. The field of medicine has seen some very interesting developments in examinations; these examinations involve assessing not only the individual's mastery of the content but also his or her ability to demonstrate mastery in diagnosing individual cases and in prescribing proper treatments. In one such examination, a computer is used to simulate a patient. The medical student taking the examination can ask initial questions, call for various tests, and ask more questions based on the results of answers to previous questions before diagnosing the case (Fredericksen, 1986). Obviously, no test can provide a perfect assessment of performance in a professional or occupational specialty, but a test can provide one important safeguard against the individual who is uninformed, incompetent, or inept. The health of society depends upon it.

A markedly different example of the importance of efficient use of social resources lies in the production of durable goods. If a worker is ineffective in using expensive equipment for industrial production, this inefficiency represents a social cost, one that is perhaps less recognized as a general concern to society than is the allocation of positions in medical schools. However, over the years, improved efficiency in operating our whole production establishment has been one of the goals of personnel testing. The economic gains from applying selection procedures, even ones with modest validity, can be substantial; Schmidt (1988b) cites estimates that run into the tens of billions of dollars annually. Production losses of such a magnitude would seriously affect the prices and competitiveness of U.S. products in world markets.

Education is an expensive enterprise, and its productivity is not easy to assess. While performance on achievement measures provides an indication of the *yield* from an educational investment, this performance is a partial indication at best. Attention in recent years has been centered on educational standards and accountability, but good assessments of the educational system's more general output (e.g., socialization and critical thinking) are lacking. Thus, it becomes increasingly important to guide the educational enterprise so that it can be as effective as possible. Testing can assist with this function.

As indicated in Chapter 7, testing has a role in appraising the outcomes of education, particularly in evaluating curricular innovations at the individual, school, and district levels. For example, over the past few decades, there has been much research directed toward the notion of *learning styles*, implying that information about a specific individual can help to provide an educational treatment that is appropriate and even beneficial for a specific child. To date, the amount of verifiable information on the relationship between learning styles and educational treatment is disappointingly limited. The basic premise does, however, remain attractive. With the increasing availability of microcomputers in classrooms and recent advances in computer assisted evaluation and instruction, truly individualized learning programs may actually become possible.

One beneficial characteristic of tests is that they do not prejudge the abilities of any of their respondents; that is, they characterize the work of each person as an individual, not as a member of any particular group. The test has no preconceptions about who should do well or who should do poorly. Although total reliance on objective measures in most educational and psychological contexts is neither possible nor desirable, objective evidence can temper the natural human tendency to prefer members of one's own social or ethnic group and result in fairer treatment for all (see Ryanen, 1988). In this case, tests may actually be a liberating force that can help open up opportunities to talented individuals who, because of their group membership, might otherwise have been denied such possibilities.

Another benefit to which testing can contribute is the store of potentially useful knowledge about individuals. The sciences of psychology and education, in as much as education can be considered a science, depend on knowing how human beings develop and the factors that influence the critically important growth processes. If we wish to study the conditions that favor human growth and development, we must be able to measure the product of that development—often by some type of test. If we wish to map the factors that foster hostility of one group toward another group in society, we must also be able to measure that hostility—probably with some type of test or scale. With all of their shortcomings, tests of one sort or another will continue to play a central role in research on human growth, development, and learning.

Maximizing the Positive

We have tried to make it clear in the previous sections that although there are legitimate concerns about the uses of tests and test results, there are significant advantages to be gained from the practice of educational and psychological testing. Regrettably, not all of the decisions that emanate from evaluations will be the correct ones. Yet, choices have to be made and actions have to be taken on the best available evidence. The decision to pursue one option generally implies a decision to disregard another, less appealing alternative. The best information available at the time should be weighed in light of all relevant factors. To do otherwise would diminish the importance of the testing process. Following are a number of maxims that subtly influence the decisions to use tests in a productive, beneficial way.

Examine and Be Clear About All Values Involved. Most decisions, whether they relate to one individual or to a whole class or category of individuals, involve a complex of interacting and competing values. The decision to place a student in a special class might mean more efficient learning for that child and a higher ultimate level of achievement, but the decision might also result, to a degree, in the student's social isolation from the mainstream of the school. The decision of a student to apply for admission to a particular law school might involve such satisfying consequences as personal prestige and future economic benefits, if admitted, but might result in such costs as the loss of self-esteem or missed opportunities at other institutions if the candidate is rejected or fails to meet the demands of the program. A personnel selection system may achieve benefits for the employer, such as money saved through shorter training programs, reduced personnel turnover, and higher worker productivity, but at a cost to the larger society in reduced employment opportunities for young persons from the inner city. Choices would exist for individuals and society whether tests had been invented or not, and the decision to ignore the possibility of alternatives is itself a decision. Only as the competing values are recognized and weighed can society decide how tests can contribute to better decisions.

Recognize That Test Scores Are Only Indicators or Signs.   A score on a mathematics test is an indicator of mathematics ability, not the mathematics ability itself. A score on a scholastic aptitude test is one partial indicator of readiness to undertake school learning. The sign is at best an imperfect representation of reality, but the underlying reality is only accessible through the signs that it gives. We become aware that a person has a fever through a thermometer, or more crudely, through a hot and flushed face, but neither the thermometer nor the person's physical appearance is itself the fever. All measurement is more or less indirect, but when distorting physical, cultural, or social factors intervene, the significance of the indicator may become modified or blurred. Proper interpretation of the measurement requires a sensitivity to possible distortions.

Recognize Test Results As Only One Type of Descriptive Information.   The key words in this statement are *one* and *descriptive*. In any type of decision, many other types of information are relevant, in addition to test scores. A score for the Stanford-Binet or the WISC-III may provide one item of information useful for prescribing a learning program for a poor reader, but an assessment of visual abilities, information about home circumstances, or knowledge about interests and hobbies may provide other equally relevant data. And, the ability test score can do no more than describe one aspect of the person's current functioning. Alone, it does not tell why the person performs in a particular way, nor does it reveal what causal relationships that performance has, for example, to the difficulties the person is having with reading. Test users must always guard against inferring more than is warranted from a test score.

Relate Test Results to Whatever Else Is Known About the Person or Group.   Test scores do not exist in a vacuum. A score only gains maximum meaning when it is fitted into a complete and comprehensive constellation of information about the person. This constellation includes information about the cultural context of the individual, family background, personal history, physical and health status, and much, much more. Computers are being programmed to handle and summarize some portions of this information, but even so, there is a very real question of how fully and soundly the human mind can synthesize such a system of information about an individual case. The problem becomes more complex in dealing with substantial numbers of individuals, for example, as is the case with school and employment personnel. Yet, decisions must be made, and the wisest decisions will result when all the available evidence can be weighed, digested, and applied to the problem at hand.

Recognize the Possibilities of Error in All Types of Descriptive Information.   We have discussed the measurement error in test scores. We have even pointed out the possibility of gross errors in test administration, scoring, or reporting. The users of test results need continuously to be aware of the approximate nature of any score and to bracket the score, at least mentally, with a band of uncertainty. But it is also true, although perhaps less explicitly recognized, that all the other kinds of information that we have about a person are also subject to error. The teacher's impression of how well Joyce reads, how popular she is with her classmates, or how interested her parents are in her school success are all rough and fallible judgments. The physician's appraisal of Joyce's health or the social worker's characterization of her home environment are both subjective, approximate, and fallible. We always arrive at decisions on the basis of partial and imperfect information, with test scores being imperfect along with everything else. They have the advantage, however, that they are usually more objective than other information and their fallibility has often been carefully studied and quantified.

Acknowledge the Limits of Human Wisdom, and Maintain Tentativeness About the Basis for Decisions.   We must make decisions, even though we have to make them on the basis of partial and fallible data. We make them as best we can with what wisdom is given to us. Some are tactical day-to-day decisions, such as those made while instructing or guiding a specific child, and the possibility exists of promptly changing direction, on the basis of new information from a continuous monitoring of progress. Other decisions are instrumental decisions that only partially commit one to the future, such as the decision to take mathematics courses because of a tentative commitment to enter an engineering program in college. The tentative nature of such decisions should be recognized; redirection can readily be undertaken in light of future evidence. With some decisions, though, redirection is more difficult than it is for a given student taking mathematics courses, and the decision may have permanent consequences. But for all decisions, no matter what role test results had in guiding them, we should always remember that a given decision might be wrong. The conscientious test user will always strive to minimize this possibility.

SUMMARY

The use of tests in education and psychology has faced a number of challenges in recent years. Tests have been viewed as invading the privacy of the people who take them, as forcing people to reveal information about themselves that proves detrimental, and as exposing people to unnecessary psychological risks. The most strident criticism of tests has been that they are biased against minority groups and women. Both the courts and government agencies have taken an active role in controlling the use and abuse of tests. The psychological profession in general and testing companies in particular have attempted to reduce possible harmful side effects of testing programs, both by setting standards for appropriate test use and by reducing bias in the scores. Because tests can help to achieve many individual and social benefits, in the form of better decisions, it is important that tests be used wisely and carefully. When tests are used properly for their intended purposes, they can be a powerful ally in improving the human condition.

QUESTIONS AND EXERCISES

1. Why do professional organizations such as the American Counseling Association and the American Psychological Association have published codes of ethics? Why do both of these codes have entire subsections devoted specifically to testing?

2. The Joint Committee on Testing recently identified the most likely areas for misuse in the administration of standardized tests. Identify and explain the three most likely areas of misuse presented in this chapter.

3. What is meant by the phrase *validity of clinical opinion?*

4. Truth in testing laws have had a profound impact upon the manner in which standardized tests are developed and administered. What is the major objective of such legislation? How has this legislation changed the ways in which tests are administered today?

5. Briefly distinguish between privacy and confidentiality? How serious is the problem of invasion to one's privacy? What controls are in place to assure test takers' right to privacy?

6. Examiners who routinely test people afforded special protections under the law (e.g., children and youth, cultural minorities, people with disabilities) must be able to distinguish among several related terms: consent, co-consent, assent. Briefly explain how these three terms are similar and how they are different.

7. What is meant by the term *unified validity?* How does the definition of this term differ from that of other types of validity used previously in this book?

8. There are potential situations involving the use of tests where the rights of one individual or group come into conflict with the rights of another individual or group. Identify two such situations and list the factors that support the claims of each side in the argument.

SUGGESTED READINGS

Dawes, R. M., Faust, D., & Meehl, P. E. (1989). Clinical versus actuarial judgement. *Science, 243*(4899), 1668–1674.

Eyde, L. D., Robertson, G. J., Krug, S. E., Moreland, K. L., Robertson, A. G., Shewan, C. M, Harrison, P. L., Porch, B. E., Hammer, A. L., & Primoff, E. S. (1993). *Responsible test use: Case studies for assessing human behavior.* Washington, DC: American Psychological Association.

Grodin, M. A., & Glantz, L. H. (1994). *Children as research subjects: Science, ethics, and law.* New York: Oxford University Press.

Impara, J. C., & Plake, B. S. (1995). Comparing counselors', school administrators', and teachers' knowledge in student assessment. *Measurement and Evaluation in Counseling and Development, 28*(2), 78–87.

Keith-Spiegel, P., & Koocher, G. P. (Ed.). (1995). *Ethics in psychology: Professional standards and cases.* Hillsdale, NJ: Erlbaum.

Matarazzo, J. D. (1990). Psychological assessment versus psychological testing. *American Psychologist, 45*(9), 999–1017.

Messick, S. (Ed.). (1995). Values and standards in performance assessment: Issues, findings, and viewpoints [Special issue]. *Educational Measurement: Issues and Practice, 14*(3).

The National Commission for the Protection of Human Subjects of Biomedical and Behavioral Research. (1979). *The Belmont report: Ethical principles and guidelines for the protection of human subjects of research.* Washington, DC: National Institutes of Health.

Principles of Objective Test Development

INTRODUCTION

In the earlier chapters in this book we discussed the properties that a good test should have. But how are those properties achieved? How does one write the items that go into good tests of achievement or of cognitive ability? Chapters 10, 11, and 12 offered some suggestions for preparing performance assessments; measures of interest, personality and adjustment; and measures of attitudes and opinions. In this chapter we will look at some of the principles that lead to good test items for measures of achievement and ability. The principles we discuss apply both to tests that an individual teacher might prepare to assess student achievement and to standardized tests.

The only real difference between the two applications is in the resources that are available.

In the section of Chapter 5 on content validity we examined the definition of the domain that the test should cover. In this chapter we assume that the task of preparing the test blueprint has already been accomplished and that we know what types of items we will need and how many of each type should be prepared. Our presentation will focus on achievement testing of the objectives from the test blueprint given in Chapter 5, but the same general principles apply to cognitive-ability items. Because objective tests are the most widely used forms in standardized testing programs and are popular with teachers, we will focus on writing and analyzing items for these tests, those in which the examinees select the best answer from among a set of alternatives.

SUGGESTIONS FOR WRITING TEST ITEMS

General Principles for Objective Items

In this section we will discuss suggestions and recommendations that apply to writing all types of objective test items. Many of these principles also apply to essay questions and other forms of test items.

1. *Keep the reading difficulty and vocabulary level of the test item as simple as possible.* It is best to avoid complex sentence structure or unnecessarily difficult words that can prevent students from showing what they know about the content the item is intended to assess. When technical vocabulary has been emphasized in a course and knowledge of that vocabulary is one of the objectives of instruction, it may appropriately be used, but obscure general vocabulary should be avoided. In the example given here, which was written for eighth graders, the sentence posing the item is unnecessarily wordy and complex, and the words *promiscuous, pernicious,* and *deleterious* are unnecessarily difficult for this grade level. (For each example, the correct answer is underlined. For true-false items, T indicates true and F indicates false.)

EXAMPLE

Poor: The promiscuous use of sprays, oils, and antiseptics in the nose during acute colds is a pernicious practice because it may have a deleterious effect on:

A. the sinuses.
B. red blood cells.
C. white blood cells.
D. the olfactory nerve.

Better: Frequent use of sprays, oils, and antiseptics in the nose during a bad cold may result in:

A. the spreading of the infection to the sinuses.
B. damage to the olfactory nerve.
C. destruction of white blood cells.
D. congestion of the mucous membranes in the nose.

2. *Be sure each item has a correct or best answer on which experts would agree.* Ordinarily, statements of a controversial nature do not make good objective items, although there are instances when knowledge of different viewpoints on controversial issues may be important. When this is the case, the item should clearly state whose opinion or what authority is to be used as the basis for the answer. The student should not be placed in the position of having to endorse a particular opinion or viewpoint as an indisputable fact. When the objective requires that the student marshal evidence for or against a controversial topic, the appropriate approach is to use an essay question.

EXAMPLE

Poor: T F   Alcoholism is a disease.

Better: T F   According to your textbook, alcoholism is a disease.

3. *Be sure each item deals with an important aspect of the content area, and not with trivia.* Sometimes teachers and other test constructors try to increase the difficulty of an item by basing it on obscure or trivial details, such as the content of a footnote or an isolated fact from a table. The first example that follows, written for the eighth-grade health test, asks for a trivial detail, the knowledge of which could not possibly make any difference in an eighth grader's level of competence in health. Example 2 consists of a statement of little importance, lifted from the textbook. Any student would know that it was true whether or not they were familiar with the course content. The only way that someone would get this item incorrect would be from thinking it was so obvious that it must be a trick question.

EXAMPLE 1

Poor: In 1995, the death rate from accidents of all types per 100,000 population in the 15–24 age group was:

A. 59.0.

B. 59.1

C. 59.2.

D. 59.3.

Better: In 1995, the leading cause of death in the 15–24 age group was from:

A. respiratory diseases.

B. cancer.

C. accidents.

D. rheumatic heart disease.

EXAMPLE 2

Poor: T F   The manufacture of prescription drugs is a highly scientific industry.

4. *Be sure each item is independent.* The answer to one item should not be required as a condition for solving the next item. Every student should have a fair

chance at each item on its own. In the example shown next, the person who does not know the answer to the first item is unlikely to get the second one correct.

EXAMPLE

Poor:

1. Scurvy is caused by the lack of:
   A. vitamin A.
   B. vitamin B_1.
   C. vitamin B_{12}.
   D. vitamin C.
2. A good source of this vitamin is:
   A. orange juice.
   B. cod-liver oil.
   C. liver.
   D. whole rice.

It is also important to make sure that the statement of one question does not provide the answer to another question. For example, if the stem of the second item had been "A good source of vitamin C is," and the order of the two items had been reversed, it is quite likely that many more students would have correctly identified the cause of scurvy. When it is necessary to include both items in the test, the effect of one item on the other can be minimized by putting the items on different pages.

5. *Avoid the use of trick questions.* Objective items tend to be trick items when the student has to pick one word or number out of a sentence that appears to be focusing on an entirely different point. In the poor example that follows, the item is keyed *false* because the immunizing agent for diphtheria is either a toxoid or an antitoxin, not a vaccine. However, the statement conveys the idea that the student is to react to the effectiveness of immunization procedures against diphtheria. If the purpose of the item is to test whether a student knows the correct use of the word *vaccine,* it would be better to rephrase the item as indicated in the first better alternative. However, if the purpose of the item is to test knowledge that the death rate from diphtheria has dropped during the century, the second better alternative would be a preferred rewording. Trick questions are likely to mislead the better student who attempts to focus on the meaning of the statement rather than to check each word.

EXAMPLE

Poor: T   F   The use of diphtheria vaccine has contributed to the decline in death rate from this disease between 1900 and the present.

Better: T   F   The immunizing material used to prevent diphtheria is called a vaccine.

Better: T   F   Immunization has caused the death rate from diphtheria to decline from 1900 to the present.

6. *Be sure the problem posed is clear and unambiguous.* This is a general admonition, somewhat like Go forth and sin no more! and it may be just as ineffective. However, it is certainly true that ambiguity of statement and meaning is the most pervasive fault in objective test items. Let us look at two examples of this problem.

EXAMPLE 1

Poor: T̲ F   Diabetes develops after 40.

The statement is keyed *true.* But what does it mean? Does it mean *only after 40 years of age* or does it mean *more frequently after 40?* What does *develop* mean in this context? You can obtain data on the relative frequency of diagnosis of diabetes in people of different ages, but the time of diagnosis and the time of development are not the same. To which type of diabetes is the item writer referring, diabetes mellitus, diabetes insipidous, or some other form? Items such as this one are likely to trouble the student who knows the most, and not the less informed student. The item cannot be revised to make it an adequate item and should not be included in the test.

EXAMPLE 2

Poor: Which of the following substances is most essential to human life?

   A. protein
   B̲. water
   C. vitamins
   D. minerals

The keyed answer to the question is B, but all of the substances are essential to human life. To answer the question, the examinee has to guess what the item writer meant by "most essential." In this question, the item writer was trying to determine whether the students knew that healthy people could survive for a fairly long period of time without food but could survive for only a few days without replenishing water lost from the body. The revised question tests for this knowledge with greater clarity.

EXAMPLE 2, REVISED

Better: A healthy person is marooned on a deserted island. To survive, the person needs almost immediately to find a source of:

   A. protein to maintain body cells.
   B̲. water to drink.
   C. vitamins to maintain body metabolism.
   D. carbohydrates or fats to supply energy.

With these six general points in mind, we turn our attention to guidelines for writing items in the various formats commonly used for objective tests.

Writing True-False Items

True-false tests owe much of their popularity to objectivity in scoring and ease of construction. Their use also permits the inclusion of a larger number of items on a test than do other item formats. Despite these advantages, the true-false test is not considered to be a sound method of assessing student performance, because it is hard to write items that are neither too difficult nor too easy or items that are not so ambiguous or tricky that they provide a poor assessment of knowledge. This approach is appropriate for only a limited range of objectives, and in many fields there are no statements, except for the trivial, that can be said to be unambiguously true or false.

The true-false item is best suited to knowledge that is categorical—for example, bacteria are either pathogenic or nonpathogenic and diseases are either communicable or noncommunicable. It is possible to write reasonable true-false items around this type of knowledge. But only a small fraction of the knowledge in any field is of this type, and much that fits the pattern is relatively unimportant. Because the statement that constitutes an item typically appears in isolation, with no frame of reference, judgments about truth or falsity are difficult.

Another problem with true-false items is that a student has a 50% chance of getting the item correct by guessing. For this reason, this format yields less accurate information per item about a student's performance than do other forms of items. As a result, a large number of items are needed to provide a precise appraisal of each student's competence.

Suggestions for Writing Better True-False Items.   Though the true-false item format has serious limitations and its use is not recommended, there are rules that, when applied, can result in better true-false items for people who insist on using them. True-false items are rarely found on professionally developed tests (however, note the exception to this statement for the lower levels of the ITBS Reading test described in Chapter 9).

1. *Ensure that the item is unequivocally true or false.* Each statement should be true enough or false enough that experts would unanimously agree on the answer. Many statements cause problems because the well-informed student can build a case for why any statement is true or why it is false. Consider the following:

EXAMPLE

Poor: T F   Penicillin is an effective drug for the treatment of pneumonia.
Better: T F   Penicillin is an effective drug for the treatment of streptococcal pneumonia.

Although the item in the first alternative is keyed *true,* the student with the most knowledge about penicillin will know that this antibiotic is more effective against certain types of pneumonia than others. Such a student might mark the statement false because it is not equally true in all cases. The revised statement removes the ambiguity.

2. *Avoid the use of specific determiners or qualified statements.* Statements that include such words as *all, never, no, always,* and other all-inclusive terms represent such broad generalizations that they are likely to be false. Qualified statements involving such terms as *usually, sometimes, under certain conditions,* and *may be* are likely to be true. Testwise examinees know this and will use such cues to get credit for knowledge they do not possess.

EXAMPLE

Poor: T   <u>F</u>   All bacteria cause disease.
Better: <u>T</u>   F   Pathogenic bacteria are parasites.

3. *Avoid ambiguous and indefinite terms of degree or amount.* Expressions such as *frequently, greatly, to a considerable degree,* and *in most cases* are not interpreted in the same way by everyone who reads them. When the student is left to guess what the item writer had in mind, the result is likely to be frustration and poor measurement. In the poor example that follows, the students may be troubled by the word *frequently* because drying as a method of preserving food is used extensively today only for fruits.

EXAMPLE

Poor: <u>T</u>   F   Drying is frequently used to preserve foods.
Better: <u>T</u>   F   Fruits can be preserved by drying.

4. *Avoid the use of negative statements, and particularly double negatives.* It has been known for years (Wason, 1961; Zern, 1967) that the time needed to answer a negatively stated item is greater than that needed for an equivalent positively stated item. Furthermore, more errors are made in response to negatively phrased items. That is, students tended to miss items because they had trouble with the wording rather than because they did not possess the information required to answer correctly.

Both Wason and Zern used pairs of statements such as "36 is not an even number" and "36 is an odd number." The negative statement requires an involved, reverse process of reasoning to untangle its meaning and is semantically more difficult. In addition, students under the time pressure of the examination can easily overlook the negative. Double negatives present even greater problems of interpretation.

EXAMPLE 1

Poor: T   <u>F</u>   Resistance to smallpox obtained through the use of smallpox vaccine is not called active immunity.
Better: T   <u>F</u>   Resistance to smallpox obtained through the use of smallpox vaccine is called passive immunity.

EXAMPLE 2

Poor: <u>T</u>   F   Tuberculosis is not a noncommunicable disease.
Better: <u>T</u>   F   Tuberculosis is a communicable disease.

5. *Limit true-false statements to a single idea.* Complex statements that include more than one idea are difficult to read and understand. A statement that contains one true idea and one false idea is usually inappropriate because it is likely to be more a measure of test-taking skills than of true knowledge of the target subject matter. Complex statements may be used if the student's attention is directed toward the one part of the statement that he or she is to judge to be true or false.

EXAMPLE

Poor: T   F   Bleeding of the gums is associated with gingivitis, which can be cured by the sufferer by daily brushing of teeth.

Better: T   F   Daily brushing of the teeth will cure gingivitis.

---

6. *Make true and false statements approximately equal in length.* There is a tendency for true statements to be longer than false ones. Generally, the greater length of true statements results from the need to include qualifications and limitations to make the statement unequivocally true. An occasional long, true statement will not cause a problem if it is matched by an occasional long, false one, if there is no generally consistent difference in length between the two categories of statements.

7. *Include approximately the same number of true statements as false ones.* Teachers are sometimes tempted to include more true statements than false ones because of their concern that students will remember false statements and therefore be learning course content that is wrong. A problem arises when students discover this tendency and learn to answer *true* to statements they are in doubt about.

Variations in the Format of True-False Items.   Several variations in the format of true-false items have been suggested as ways of improving them. Most of these variations endeavor to accomplish one or more of the following: (1) reduction in the ambiguity of the items, (2) reduction of the effects of guessing on the scores, and/or (3) providing more specific information about how much a student knows. The four most frequently used variations are described below.

1. *Underlining a word or clause in the statement.* This variation is the simplest one, and it is used to reduce ambiguity by focusing the attention of the examinee on the most important part of the statement.

EXAMPLES

---

1. T   F   Malaria is transmitted by the <u>Anopheles</u> mosquito.
2. T   F   If foods are frozen, harmful bacteria in them will be <u>killed</u>.

The instructions for such items should clearly indicate that the student is to judge the truth or falsity of the underlined portion in relation to the rest of the statement. Underlining also permits the use of more complex statements.

2. *Requiring students to correct false statements.* A student who correctly marks a statement *false* may have made a lucky guess or may have chosen the answer

on the basis of misinformation. For example, for the item "Insulin is secreted by the pituitary gland," a student could indicate that it is false, thinking that insulin is secreted by the adrenal glands. In this case, incorrect information leads to a correct answer. To make sure that the student knows the facts underlying a false statement—and to reduce guessing—give the student instructions to correct all statements that are marked false. The above example can be corrected by changing "insulin" to one of the pituitary hormones, by changing "is secreted" to "is not secreted," or by changing "the pituitary gland" to "an endocrine gland" or "the pancreas." Because there may be many ways to make the statement correct, it is advisable to underline the key word or words in all statements, both true and false, when this variation is used. The part of the statement that is underlined should be the specific content that the teacher is trying to appraise. Thus, in the example, a teacher trying to determine whether students knew the name of a hormone secreted by the pituitary gland should underline the word "insulin." Likewise, a teacher interested in determining whether students knew the name of the gland that secretes insulin should underline "the pituitary gland."

3. *Basing true-false items on specific stimulus material provided for the student.* True-false items tend to be most effective and most useful when they are based on specific stimulus material such as a chart, map, graph, table, or reading passage. In this situation, the examinees are instructed to respond to the item only in terms of the given material, providing them with a frame of reference that is better defined. This type of true-false item can be effectively used to appraise comprehension, interpretation, extrapolation, and logical reasoning, if appropriate stimulus material is used and the items are written to elicit these abilities. An example of this item type is given here.

EXAMPLE

Directions: The pie graph below shows how each dollar is spent for medical care. Look at the graph carefully. Statements are given following the graph.

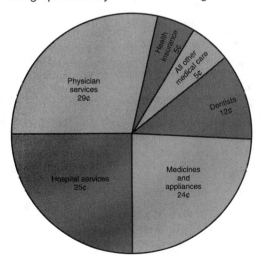

Read each statement carefully.

Mark T, if the data in the graph support the statement.

Mark F, if the data in the graph contradict the statement or no data are provided in the graph to either support or contradict the statement.

(T) 1. More of the medical-care dollar is spent for physicians' services than for any other single category of the expense.

(F) 2. Few Americans have health insurance.

(F) 3. Americans spend 24 cents out of every dollar they make on medicines and appliances.

(T) 4. Hospital and physicians' services together account for slightly more than half of the money spent for medical care.

(T) 5. Less money is spent on dental care than on physicians' services.

(T) 6. About 25% of the medical-care dollar is spent on hospital services.

This form of item is sometimes made more complex by requiring the student to answer in four or five categories such as *definitely true, probably true, insufficient data to determine whether it is true or false, probably false,* and *definitely false.* In this format, the item becomes a multiple-choice item rather than a true-false item.

4. Grouping short, true-false items under a common question or statement heading. Two examples of this variation are given here.

EXAMPLES

Directions: Place a T in front of each choice that is a correct answer to the question. Put an F in front of each choice that is NOT a correct answer to the question.

A. Which of the following diseases are caused by viruses?

   (T) 1. chicken pox   (T) 5. measles

   (F) 2. diphtheria   (T) 6. mumps

   (T) 3. influenza   (F) 7. tuberculosis

   (F) 4. malaria   (F) 8. typhoid fever

B. A 14-year-old girl ate the following food during a 24-hour period:

Breakfast	**Lunch**	**Dinner**
Cup of black coffee	Glass of Coca-Cola (8 oz)	Roast Beef (9 oz)
	Hamburger (4 oz) with bun	Mashed Potatoes (1/2 cup)
	French fried potatoes	Glass of milk (8 oz)
	(20 pieces)	Apple pie (1 piece)

In which of the following was her diet deficient?

   (T) 1. calcium   (F) 5. niacin

   (F) 2. calories   (F) 6. protein

   (F) 3. carbohydrates   (T) 7. vitamin A

   (T) 4. iron   (T) 8. vitamin C

The format of this variation looks like a multiple-choice item, but the task for the student is to judge whether each choice is true or false in relation to the original question; therefore, it is basically a series of true-false items. The variation can be an efficient way to test for simple applications and for knowledge of categories, classifications, or characteristics. It is particularly effective for in-depth testing of a specific part of a topic. The format reduces the reading load for the student, and the question serves as a frame of reference for judging truth or falsity and removes some of the ambiguity of true-false statements. An alternative to this approach is to have the students place a check mark next to the statements that are true and to leave the others unmarked.

Writing Multiple-Choice Items

The multiple-choice item is the most flexible of the objective item types. It can be used to appraise the achievement of any of the educational objectives that can be measured by a paper-and-pencil test, except those relating to skill in written expression, originality, and the ability to organize a response. An ingenious and talented item writer can construct multiple-choice items that require not only the recall of knowledge but also the use of skills of comprehension, interpretation, application, analysis, or synthesis to arrive at the correct answer.

Unfortunately, not all multiple-choice items are of high quality, as it takes a great deal of time and skill to write good items. One of the important characteristics of the multiple-choice item is that single options can be altered or replaced. The test author, by changing distractors, has flexibility in adjusting the difficulty of the test item. Tests can then be constructed for optimum difficulty level, thus maximizing the capacity to differentiate between those taking the test.

The multiple-choice item consists of two parts: the stem, which presents the problem, and the list of possible answers or options. In the standard form of the item, one of the options is the correct or best answer and the others are foils or distractors. The stem of the item may be presented either as a question or as an incomplete statement. The form of the stem seems to make no difference in the overall effectiveness of the item, as long as the stem presents a clear and specific problem to the examinee.

The number of options used in the multiple-choice item differs from test to test, and there is no real reason why it cannot vary for items in the same test. An item must have at least three answer choices, or options, to be classified as a multiple-choice item, and the typical pattern is to have four or five answer choices, to reduce the probability of guessing the answer. A distinction should be made between the number of options presented for a multiple-choice item and the number of *effective*, or *functioning*, options that the item has. In the poor example that follows, written for the eighth-grade test on health that provided our example for content validity, the item will really function as a two-choice item because no one is likely to choose option A or D. The revised item still presents four answer choices but is now more likely to function as a four-option item because options A and D have been made more reasonable.

EXAMPLE

Poor: About how many calories are recommended daily for a 14-year-old girl who is 62 in. tall, weighs 103 lb, and is moderately active?

A. 0

B. 2,000

C. 2,500

D. 30,000

Better: About how many calories are recommended daily for a 14-year-old girl who is 62 in. tall, weighs 103 lb, and is moderately active?

A. 1,500

B. 2,000

C. 2,500

D. 3,000

The revised item will probably be more difficult than the original one because the options are closer in value, so those who do not know the answer will be guessing among four choices rather than two.

The difficulty of a multiple-choice item depends on the cognitive processes required by the item, as well as the closeness of the options. Consider the set of three items shown in the next example, all relating to the meaning of the term *fortified food.* We can predict that Version 1 will be relatively easy, Version 2 somewhat more difficult, and Version 3 still more difficult. In Version 1, the stem is a direct copy of the textbook definition of fortified food, and the distractors are not terms used to indicate the addition of nutrients to foods. The difference between Versions 1 and 2 is that the stem of Version 2 recasts the textbook definition into a novel form and calls for a different mental process than Version 1 does. The difference between Versions 2 and 3 is in the closeness of the options.

EXAMPLES

1. When a nutrient has been added that is not present in natural food, the food is said to be:

    A. fortified.

    B. processed.

    C. pasteurized.

    D. refined.

2. When milk processed for sale has had vitamin D concentrate added to provide at least 400 U.S.P. units per quart, the carton can then legally state that the milk is:

    A. fortified.

    B. processed.

    C. pasteurized.

    D. refined.

3. When milk processed for sale has had vitamin D concentrate added to provide at least 400 U.S.P. units per quart, the carton can then legally state that the milk is:

  A. fortified.
  B. enriched.
  C. irradiated.
  D. restored.

Suggestions for Writing Better Multiple-Choice Items. The construction of good tests requires the allocation of an adequate amount of time, proper planning, adherence to a set of well-recognized rules for item construction, and practice. Commercial test publishers retain groups of experienced item writers who generate large numbers of high quality items for use in tests such as the ACT Assessment and the SAT. But individual teachers and researchers often need to prepare their own multiple-choice items. We can do nothing about your timeliness or planning for writing test items, but if you use the following rules for writing better multiple-choice items, the tests you prepare will be improved.

1. *Be sure the stem of the item clearly formulates a problem.* The stem should be worded so that the examinee clearly understands what problem or question is being asked before reading the answer choices. Look at the poor example that follows. When you finish reading the stem, you know only that the item is related to a part of the pancreas. You have no idea what the problem is until you read each of the options. The answer choices that are provided are heterogeneous in content; that is, one relates to structure, one to function, one to permanence, and one to location. The poor item is really nothing more than four true-false items with the words "The cell islets of the pancreas" in common. The revised item provides both a clearly formulated problem in the stem and a more homogeneous set of answer choices.

EXAMPLES

Poor: The cell islets of the pancreas:

  A. contain ducts.
  B. produce insulin.
  C. disappear as one grows older.
  D. are located around the edge of the pancreas.

Better: The cell islets of the pancreas secrete the substance called:

  A. trypsin.
  B. insulin.
  C. tryptophan.
  D. adrenaline.

2. *Include as much of the item as possible in the stem, and keep options as short as possible.* In the interests of economies of space and reading time and of having a clear statement of the problem, try to word and arrange the item so that the answer choices can be kept relatively short. If the same words or phrases are repeated in all or most of the options, as in the poor example given next, rewrite the stem to include the repetitious material. Answer choices that are long in relation to the stem frequently occur because of failure to formulate a problem clearly in the stem.

EXAMPLE

Poor: The term "empty-calorie" food designates:
A. a food that has few essential nutrients but high caloric value.
B. a food that has neither essential nutrients nor caloric value.
C. a food that has both high nutritive value and high caloric value.
D. a food that has high nutritive value but low caloric value.

Better: The term "empty-calorie" applies to foods that are:
A. low in nutrients and high in calories.
B. low in both nutrients and calories.
C. high in both nutrients and calories.
D. high in nutrients and low in calories.

3. *Include in the stem only the material needed to make the problem clear and specific.* Items with long, wordy stems containing material that is irrelevant to the problem are likely to reduce the effectiveness and efficiency of the test. First, the unnecessary material increases the amount of reading needed for an item; it is then more difficult to separate generalized skill in reading from knowledge of the subject matter. Second, superfluous material increases reading time at the expense of answering time, making the test inefficient because fewer items can be included on the test for a given amount of testing time. The first three sentences in the following example clearly are unnecessary for defining the problem for the examinee.

EXAMPLE

Poor: Cells of one kind belong to a particular group performing a specialized duty. We call this group of cells a tissue. All of us have different kinds of tissues in our bodies. Which of the following would be classified as epithelial tissue?
A. tendons
B. adenoids and tonsils
C. mucous membranes
D. cartilage

Better: Which of the following would be classified as epithelial tissue?

    A. tendons

    B. adenoids and tonsils

    C. mucous membranes

    D. cartilage

If the purpose of the test is to appraise whether the examinee can differentiate those data necessary to solve the problem or support an argument from those that are either unnecessary or irrelevant, then one would have to include extra data in posing the problem. In such an instance, though, the extra material would be central to the process being measured and, therefore, would not be irrelevant.

4. *Use the negative only sparingly in an item.* Just as was true for true-false items, negatively stated multiple-choice items increase the reading difficulty of an item and require the student to perform more difficult reasoning tasks. Negative items also provide little information about exactly what the examinee knows.

There are times when it is important to test whether the examinee knows the exception to a general rule or can detect errors. For these purposes, a few items with the words *not* or *except* in the stem may be justified, particularly when overinclusion is a common error. When a negative word is included in a stem, it should be underlined and/or capitalized to call the examinee's attention to it.

The poor example that follows was written to measure whether students knew the function of the semicircular canals, but the item as written does not measure this aspect of the students' knowledge. The revised example measures the objective more directly. There are two reasons why the second better example shows a more appropriate use of the negative stem: (1) The most common error made by students about the duties of the Food and Drug Administration is the inclusion of meat inspection, a duty of the Department of Agriculture, and (2) it would be difficult to get three plausible misleads if the item were stated in a positive form.

EXAMPLES

Poor: Which of the following structures of the ear is NOT concerned with hearing?

    A. eardrum

    B. oval window

    C. semicircular canals

    D. cochlea

Better:

    1. Which one of the following structures of the ear helps to maintain balance?

        A. eardrum

        B. oval window

        C. semicircular canals

        D. cochlea

2. Which of the following activities is NOT the responsibility of the U.S. Food and Drug Administration?

   A. inspection of warehouses storing food for interstate shipment

   B. inspection of slaughter houses that ship meat across state lines

   C. initiation of court action to remove unhealthful food from the market

   D. testing samples of foods for interstate sale

5. *Use novel material in formulating problems that measure understanding or ability to apply principles.* Most locally constructed tests place too much emphasis on rote memory and neglect measurement of the ability to use information. The multiple-choice item is well adapted to measuring simple recall, but a novel situation must be presented to the examinee if more than rote memory is to be required to answer the question. The second and third examples of items assessing knowledge of fortified foods on page 455 illustrate how you can move away from the form in which the material was originally presented to test comprehension rather than recall. Two examples are given here to illustrate how an item can be structured to appraise the ability to use information.

EXAMPLES

Rote memory 1: Which of the following foods will yield the largest number of calories when metabolized in the body?

   A. 1 gram of fat

   B. 1 gram of sugar

   C. 1 gram of starch

   D. 1 gram of protein

Application: Which of the following would result in the greatest reduction of calories if it were eliminated from the daily diet?

   A. 1 tablespoon of butter

   B. 1 tablespoon of granulated sugar

   C. 1 slice of white, enriched bread

   D. 1 boiled egg

Rote memory 2: Death from pneumonia and influenza is most frequent among:

   A. infants and aged people.

   B. infants and elementary school children.

   C. teenagers and aged people.

   D. teenagers and young adults.

Interpretation: Look at the graph below, which shows, by age group, the death rate from Disease X.

Which of the following diseases could be Disease X?

    A. pneumonia
    B. cancer
    C. tuberculosis
    D. heart disease

Note that it is important to refer to the disease by a letter that is not used for any of the response alternatives.

6. *Be sure that there is one and only one correct or clearly best answer.* In the typical multiple-choice item, the examinee is instructed to choose one and only one answer. Having instructed the examinee to choose *the* answer that is best, the test maker is obligated to provide one and only one best answer for each item. Although this provision may seem obvious, many items on locally constructed tests either have two or more equally good answers or no good answer. In the following example, option B is keyed as the correct answer but there is also a large element of correctness for options C and E. The revised version eliminates this fault, but the item may now be too easy.

EXAMPLE

Poor: A color-blind boy inherits the trait from a:

    A. male parent.

    B. female parent.

    C. maternal grandparent.

    D. paternal grandparent.

    E. remote ancestor.

Better: A color-blind boy most probably inherited the trait from his:

    A. father.

    B. mother.

    C. paternal grandfather.

    D. paternal grandmother.

       In addition to making sure that there is only one correct answer, the item writer should make sure that the keyed answer is unequivocally the best. It is the item writer's responsibility to use the very best scholarship, as well as his or her skill in phrasing the stem and answer choices, to produce a problem and answer with which experts in the field will agree.

       7. *Be sure wrong answers are plausible.* One of the major advantages of the multiple-choice item is its capacity to require the examinees to select the correct answer from among three, four, or five choices, thus reducing the chance of their guessing the correct answer. However, the wrong alternatives must be attractive to examinees who are lacking in knowledge about the material the item is intended to assess. Therefore, the incorrect answer choices should be logically consistent with the stem and should represent common errors made by students in a particular grade or at a particular ability level.

       In the first poor example that follows, Options A and C are compounds, not elements, and are thus inconsistent with the stem. In the second poor example, Options C and D are very implausible.

EXAMPLES

Poor: Which of the following elements is found in proteins but not in carbohydrates or fats?

    A. carbon dioxide

    B. oxygen

    C. water

    D. nitrogen

Poor: The gas formed in the cells after the oxidation of food, and taken to the lungs and expelled is:

    A. oxygen.

    B. carbon dioxide.

    C. helium.

    D. chlorine.

One good way to develop plausible distractors, particularly with items that measure quantitative concepts and skills, is to determine what answer a student would get by making a particular error at some point in analyzing or solving the problem. It is sometimes possible to identify specific informational or procedural deficiencies in this way.

    8. *Be sure no unintentional clues to the correct answer are given.* Inexperienced test constructors frequently give away the correct answer to an item or give clues that permit the examinee to eliminate one or more of the incorrect answer choices from consideration. Items that contain irrelevant clues or specific determiners, correct answers that are consistently longer than incorrect answers, or grammatical inconsistencies between the stem and the wrong alternatives tend to be easier than items without these faults. To the extent that there are differences among examinees in their awareness of these clues, what is being measured by the items changes and the validity of the test is compromised.

    Examples of items containing some types of unintentional clues are given here. Item 1 is an example of a clang association, that is, a repetition of a word, phrase, or sound in the keyed answer and in the stem. Item 2 contains specific determiners that have the same effect in multiple-choice options as in true-false statements. In Item 3, the keyed answer is much longer than the other options. Item 4 is an example of a grammatical inconsistency; the word "a" in the stem implies a singular word, but Options A and C are both plural. The revised items show how each of these faults can be corrected to make the items more effective in measuring knowledge rather than test-wiseness.

EXAMPLES

Clang Association

Poor:

    1. The function of the platelets in the blood is to help in:

        A. carrying oxygen to the cells.

        B. carrying food to the cells.

        C. clotting of the blood.

        D. fighting disease.

Better:

1. Which of the following structures in the blood helps in forming blood clots?
    A. red blood cells
    B. lymphocytes
    C. platelets
    D. monocytes

Specific Determiners
Poor:

2. Which of the following is characteristic of anaerobic bacteria?
    A. They never live in soil.
    B. They can live without molecular oxygen.
    C. They always cause disease.
    D. They can carry on photosynthesis.

Better:

2. The one characteristic that distinguishes all anaerobic bacteria is their ability to:
    A. withstand extreme variation in air temperature.
    B. live without molecular oxygen.
    C. live as either saprophytes or parasites.
    D. reproduce either in living cells or nonliving culture media.

Length Clues
Poor:

3. The term *side effect* of a drug refers to:
    A. additional benefits from the drug.
    B. the chain effect of drug action.
    C. the influence of drugs on crime.
    D. any action of the drug in the body other than the one the doctor wanted the drug to have.

Better:

3. Which of the following, if it occurred, would be a side effect of aspirin for a man who had been taking two aspirin tablets every 3 hours for a heavy cold and slight fever?
    A. normal body temperature
    B. reduction in frequency of coughing
    C. easier breathing
    D. ringing in the ears

Grammatical Inconsistency
Poor:

    4. Penicillin is obtained from a:

        A. bacteria.

        B. mold.

        C. coal tars.

        D. tropical tree.

Better:

    4. Penicillin is obtained from:

        A. bacteria.

        B. molds.

        C. coal tars.

        D. tropical trees.

    9. *Use the option "none of these" or "none of the above" only when the keyed answer can be classified unequivocally as correct or incorrect.* This option can be appropriately used by experienced test writers on tests of spelling, mathematics, and study skills. In these types of tests an absolutely correct answer can be given. On other types of tests, where the student is to choose the best answer and where the keyed answer is the best answer, but not necessarily absolutely correct, the use of "none of these" or "none of the above" is inappropriate.

    The option "none of the above," if used, works better when the stem is stated as a question rather than a sentence to be completed. An incomplete sentence seldom works because "none of the above" seldom completes the stem grammatically. An example of this is illustrated in the following item, which appeared on a tenth-grade biology test.

EXAMPLE

Poor: Of the following, the one that is *never* a function of the stem of plants is:

    A. conduction.

    B. photosynthesis.

    C. support.

    D. food storage.

    E. none of the above.

    Not only is the option "none of the above" grammatically inconsistent with the stem, but it is also logically inconsistent with the stem. Option E does not name a function of the plant, and the double negative effect of the option and the "never" in the stem makes comprehension of the meaning of the item difficult. There is no way of revising the item to make it better because any function of a plant is performed by the stem in some plants.

If "none of these" or its equivalent is used as an option in items requiring quantitative solutions or in spelling tests, it should be used as frequently for the correct option as any other answer choice and the stem of the item should be phrased as a question. On such tests, the option functions best if it is used as the correct answer on some of the easier items at the beginning of the test to reinforce the instruction that "none of the above" is sometimes the correct answer.

The example given next represents a poor use of the "none of the above" option in an item calling for a numerical answer, because only approximations are given rather than exact quantities. Option B is keyed as the correct answer, but Option E is better because the estimates of the blood volume for an average adult range from a low of 10 pints to a high of 16 pints. In addition, this item may be assessing knowledge that in most cases would be judged trivial.

EXAMPLE

Poor: How many pints of blood does a normal human adult of average weight have?

   A. 3 pints

   B. 13 pints

   C. 30 pints

   D. 50 pints

   E. none of the above

Better: Approximately what percentage of the body weight of a healthy human adult is blood?

   A. 3% to 5%

   B. 8% to 9%

   C. 12% to 15%

   D. 20% to 25%

10. *Avoid the use of "all of the above" in the multiple-choice item.* This type of item is used either when only three options can easily be generated and a fourth option is needed or when there is an easily obtained list of characteristics or traits of something and it is difficult to come up with three incorrect distractors. In this latter case, it is easy to list three of the characteristics along with an "all of the above" statement. Usually, when the option "all of the above" is used on teacher-made tests, it is the correct answer. Items using this option tend to be easy because the examinees will be led to the correct answer even though they have only partial information. Look at the poor example that follows. Assume that the examinees have been instructed to mark only one answer and that John knows that both age and weight are used to compute basal energy requirements but does not know that height is also part of the computation. He will certainly mark D for his answer; thus, he gets credit for having complete information even though he does not. In the revised version, the examinee must have full information to arrive at the keyed answer. The option "all of the above" is much more effective if it is used in a variation of the standard form, the complex multiple-choice item, described in the next section.

EXAMPLE

Poor: Which of the following factors must be considered in computing basal energy requirements?

A. age

B. height

C. weight

<u>D.</u> all of the above

Better: Which of the following factors must be considered in computing basal energy requirements?

A. weight only

B. age only

C. height and weight only

D. age and weight only

<u>E.</u> age, height, and weight

Variations in the Format of Multiple-Choice Items.   A number of variations of the standard multiple-choice item have been suggested. One commonly used variation is the matching item, discussed in a separate section. In this section, we discuss two other variations that are sometimes used.

1. *Complex multiple-choice items.* This variation, which is sometimes called the multiple-multiple-choice item, gets its name from the format and the combinations of options used as answer choices. It is most effective when it is used to appraise knowledge of or ability to apply or interpret multiple causes, effects, functions, or uses. The following example illustrates a poor use of the complex multiple-choice item, and several faults of item construction. Although there are multiple signs of impaired circulation, the options are short; therefore, the knowledge could be tested more efficiently in the usual multiple-choice format. The technical problems with the item are as follows: (1) No specific problem is presented to the examinee; (2) Signs 1, 2, and 3 are used in all the answer choices so that the student is required only to determine whether Signs 4 and 5 are correct; (3) the method of presenting choices (contrast between Option C and Options B and D) is varied, which creates unnecessary difficulty for the student; and (4) Options B and C are identical.

EXAMPLE

Poor: If a bandage or cast on the arm is too tight, it might interfere with the circulation in the arm. Signs of interference with circulation include:

1. cold.   3. numbness.   5. loss of motion.

2. blanching.   4. swelling.

<u>A.</u> all of these

B. 1, 2, 3, and 4

C. all except 5

D. 1, 2, 3, and 5

The following example illustrates an effective use of the item type, because it requires the examinee to discriminate between both the kind of food and the kind of commerce that come under the jurisdiction of the Food and Drug Administration. This type of item is both more difficult and more discriminating than the typical form of multiple-choice item that tests for the same knowledge. It is also more difficult to write good items in this format.

EXAMPLE

Effective: Look at each of the food processing or producing activities below.

1. A housewife makes jellies and sells them in her home town.
2. A butcher makes scrapple and pork sausage and sells them only in the state of Maryland.
3. A food processor makes jellies in California and sells them in New York.
4. A slaughterhouse in Chicago ships meats in all 50 states.
5. A citrus grower produces oranges in Florida and ships them to all eastern states.

Which of the activities would be subject to the regulations and supervision of the U.S. Food and Drug Administration?

  A. 2 and 4 only
  B. 3 and 5 only
  C. 3, 4, and 5 only
  D. 1, 3, and 5 only
  E. all of them

2. *Paired statements as stimuli.* This format is an efficient and effective way of measuring judgment of relative amounts or quantities, relative effects of changing conditions, or relative chronology. It preferably should be used for content having established quantitative values. For example, the use of the pair of statements, (I) *The number of hours of sleep needed by a 14-year-old boy* and (II) *The number of hours of sleep needed by a 30-year-old man* would be undesirable, because there is no empirically determined value for the number of hours of sleep required for any age group.

EXAMPLE

Directions: Items 1 through 3 are based on pairs of statements. Read each statement carefully. On your answer sheet, mark:

  A. if the amount in Statement I is greater than that in Statement II.
  B. if the amount in Statement II is greater than that in Statement I.
  C. if the amount in Statement I is equal to that in Statement II.
  D. if there is not sufficient information to determine which amount is greater.

    (B) 1. I: Caloric value of 1 tablespoon of cane sugar.
          II: Caloric value of 1 tablespoon of butter.

(A) 2. I: The daily requirement of calories for a 25-year-old male lumberjack who is 73 in. tall and weighs 190 lb.

II: The daily requirement of calories for a 25-year-old male office clerk who is 73 in. tall and weighs 190 lb.

(A) 3. I: The daily requirement of iron for a 16-year-old girl.

II: The daily requirement of iron for a 16-year-old boy.

Writing Matching Items

The characteristic that distinguishes the matching item from the ordinary multiple-choice item is that there are several problems whose answers must be drawn from a single list of possible answers. The matching item can best be thought of as a series of multiple-choice items presented in a more efficient manner. For example, a series of stimuli is listed down the left-hand column of the test paper and a series of options is listed down the right-hand column. The student picks the option that goes with each stimulus. The matching item has most frequently been used to measure factual information such as meanings of terms, dates of events, achievements of people, symbols for chemical elements, and authors of books. Effective matching items can be constructed by basing the set of items on a chart, map, diagram, or drawing. Features of the figure can be numbered and the examinee can be asked to match names, functions, and so on with the numbers on the figure. This type of item is useful in tests dealing with study skills, science, or technology; for example, such items might require biology students to identify cell structures.

When there is a need to assess a student's ability to make associations, matching items are more efficient than a series of multiple-choice items. The major disadvantage of this approach is that it is suitable only for measuring associations and not for assessing higher levels of understanding. Another disadvantage of this method is that such a test cannot easily be machine scored, because the number of options often exceeds the five spaces allocated to each item on standard, machine-scorable answer sheets. Of course, answer sheets can be customized for this type of item.

To be useful, matching items, like other types of test items, must be carefully constructed. Poorly constructed matching items can be superficial measurement devices and can present the examinee with a task that makes significant demands on skills that are not part of the domain the test is designed to measure. Look at the following matching exercise, which appeared on a test in health and hygiene for an eighth-grade class.

The example illustrates some of the most common mistakes made in preparing matching items. First, the directions are vague and fail to specify the basis for matching. Second, the set of stimuli is too heterogeneous for a good matching exercise. How many answer choices in Column II are logically possible answers for the first statement in Column I? For the second? The statements in Column I have very little in common except that they relate to teeth and dental health, in general.

Third, the set is too long, and the answer choices in Column II are not arranged in any systematic order. Even examinees who know the answer to a statement have to search through the entire list in Column II to find it, which is time consuming. Fourth, some of the entries are vague, for example, entries 9, 11, and 12 in Column I and entries i, l, and m in Column II. The vagueness makes it difficult to justify the answer keyed as correct; furthermore, the accuracy of number 12 can be questioned. Fifth, there are 16 statements in Column I and 16 answer choices in Column II. If the student knows 15, he or she automatically gets the 16th correct.

EXAMPLE

Poor: *Directions:* Place the correct letter to the left of each number. Use each letter only once.

Column I		Columh II	
(p)	1. Number of permanent teeth	a.	Malocclusion
(i)	2. Vitamin D	b.	Tear and rip food
(n)	3. Vitamin C	c.	Trench mouth
(k)	4. Enamel	d.	Straightening teeth
(o)	5. Bleeding gums	e.	Jawbone socket
(c)	6. Vincent's angina	f.	Contains nerves and blood vessels
(d)	7. Orthodontia	g.	Grind food
(e)	8. Alveolus	h.	Crown
(a)	9. Lower jaw protruding	i.	Sunshine
(f)	10. Pulp	j.	Cleaning device
(m)	11. Acid	k.	Hardest substance
(l)	12. Low percentage of decay	l.	Primitives
(b)	13. Cuspids	m.	Decay
(g)	14. Molars	n.	Citrus fruits
(h)	15. Visible part of tooth	o.	Gingivitis
(j)	16. Dental floss	p.	Thirty-two

Note: The "correct" answers are those designated by the person who constructed the exercise.

Suggestions for Writing Better Matching Items.   Since matching items can be thought of as a condensed series of multiple-choice items, many of the same rules for writing better items apply to both. In this section, we discuss the specific rules for writing matching items.

1. *Keep the set of statements in a single matching exercise homogeneous.* The example would have been better if all of the choices were parts of a tooth, diseases of the teeth and gums, or methods of promoting oral hygiene. Homogeneous choices force the student to make genuine discriminations to arrive at correct answers. If you need to test several diverse areas of content, use a separate set of stimuli and responses for each area.

2. *Keep the set of items relatively short.* Limiting the number of items to five or six makes it easier to keep the content homogeneous. Also, short sets of items put less of a clerical burden and reading load on the examinee.

3. *Have the students choose answers from the column with the shorter statements.* The reason for this suggestion is that the answer column will be read several times by the student and it takes less time to read short statements than long ones. Having the student select from the column of shorter statements helps to minimize the already important influence of reading ability on test performance.

4. *Use a heading for each column that accurately describes its content.* A descriptive heading helps to define the task for the examinee. If the test maker is unable to identify a heading that specifically defines the content, the entries are probably too heterogeneous.

5. *Have more answer choices than the number of entries to be matched, unless answer choices can be used more than once.* The larger number of answer choices reduces the influence of guessing on test scores. It also prevents students from arriving at correct answers through a process of elimination that does not require the student always to know the correct association.

6. *Arrange the answer choices in a logical order, if one exists.* Students who know the answers should be able to find them easily. Arranging names in alphabetical order or dates in chronological order reduces the time required to find the answer.

7. *Specify in the directions both the basis for matching and whether answer choices can be used more than once.* This practice will tend to reduce ambiguity and make the task more uniform for all examinees.

A variation in the matching-item format is the classification or master list. This variation can be used quite effectively to appraise application, comprehension, or interpretation. It is an efficient way of exploring the range of mastery of a concept or a related set of concepts. An illustration of this type of item is given here.

EXAMPLE

Master Matching
Instructions: Four kinds of appeals that advertisers of health and beauty products make are given below.

    A. Appeal to fear or a sense of insecurity

    B. Appeal to snobbery or identification with a particular small group or individual

    C. Appeal to a desire to be like others, that is, to join the "bandwagon"

    D. Appeal to authority

Statements 1 through 6 are advertisements of imaginary products. Read each statement carefully. For each statement, mark the letter of the appeal that is being used. Answer choices may be used more than once.

    (A) 1. Don't let iron-tired blood get you down. Keep your verve and vivacity. Take Infantol.

(D) 2. Research shows Lucy's Little Lethal Pills are 10 times more effective than ordinary pain killers.

(B) 3. Duchess Poorhouse, the international beauty, bathes her face twice a day with Myrtle's Turtle Oil.

(B) 4. Men, are you tired of a woman's deodorant? Be a man. Use No-Sweat. Leave the weaker stuff to the weaker sex.

(B) 5. At $1,629.21, the Inside Jogger is not for everyone. Only a select few can be proud owners of one! Are you one of these?

(C) 6. Be one of the crowd. Drink and serve Popsie's Cola.

PREPARING THE OBJECTIVE TEST FOR USE

Effective assessment requires that irrelevant sources of variation in test scores be minimized. In commercially published tests we expect the quality of work, both the organization and layout of the test and the printing, to be high; that is part of what we are paying for. When tests or other assessment devices are prepared locally, the burden for assuring quality falls on the users themselves. The most important points to consider in arranging the items of the test will be discussed in the paragraphs that follow. Although these features are presented in reference to objective tests, many of the same principles apply to rating scales, attitude surveys, and other forms of assessment.

1. *Prepare more items than you will need.* Unlikely though it may seem, not every item you write will be a good one. Following the guidelines in the preceeding sections will help, but even professional item writers fail to hit the mark with about 30% of their items. Therefore, it is essential to have about half again as many items for tryout as you expect to use in the final test, which is then constructed from the best items.

2. *Proofread the items.* After the items have been written, it is a good idea to set them aside for a week or two, then go back and proofread them. You will be amazed that the items which appeared so clear and straightforward when you wrote them will seem obscure a few days later. Better yet, have a colleague read the items for clarity. If someone who is knowledgeable in the subject and in testing has difficulty making sense out of the item, so will the intended examinees.

After the items have been selected, it is necessary to prepare the test itself. The following suggestions will help you achieve reliable and valid measurement by eliminating extraneous influences on test scores that may arise from the physical features of the test.

3. *Arrange items on the test so that they are easy to read.* In the interest of those taking the test, items should not be crowded together on the test paper, because spreading out the items makes them more easily read and understood. Multiple-choice items also are easier to read if each response is on a separate line. Furthermore, items should not be split between pages, because such an arrangement may confuse the examinees. If several items all refer to a single diagram or chart, try to arrange the test so

that the diagram or chart and all of the items are on the same page or on facing pages, so the examinees do not have to turn pages to go from the stimulus material to the items. An alternative when it is impossible to fit the stimulus material (chart, diagram, etc.) and the questions on a single page or facing pages is to put the stimulus material on a separate sheet that is not stapled with the rest of the test. On the downside, optimum arrangement of items to facilitate an examinee's ability to read and understand the items can add to the cost of reproducing copies of the test, because more pages will be needed for each test. (It goes without saying that the print should be large enough that it is easy to read.)

4. *Plan the layout of the test so that a separate answer sheet can be used to record answers.* The use of a separate answer sheet may make the test-taking process a bit more difficult, but there is a considerable gain in ease and accuracy of test scoring. Most standardized tests require separate answer sheets at all but the lowest levels of the test, and by the third grade, most students can easily learn to use one. The ability to use a separate answer sheet is a test-taking skill that should be taught to students, and practice in the skill should be provided early. Although test scoring equipment can be expensive, the use of a machine scorer is highly recommended. Not only does machine scoring save time, it also reduces the chance of scoring errors. Even the simplest machines will score the answer sheets and capture the data and store it on a disk. This type of equipment can greatly facilitate item-analysis procedures and further analyses of the data. In Chapter 16 we discuss the use of computers for test score interpretation and report writing.

5. *Group items of the same format (true-false, multiple-choice, or matching) together.* Each different kind of objective item requires a different set of directions. Grouping items of the same format together makes it possible to write a concise and clear set of directions that will apply throughout that part of the test. Each item type also requires a different response set or approach on the part of the examinee. The examinee will be better able to maintain an appropriate response set if the items of the same type are grouped together.

6. *Within item type, group together items dealing with the same content.* This practice makes the test more coherent and provides a reasonable context for the examinee. It can also help both the student and the teacher to see the student's strong and weak points.

7. *Arrange items so that difficulty progresses from easy to hard.* This practice is of particular importance on a test for which testing time is limited and some items on the test will not be attempted by all students. Those unattempted items should be the more difficult ones that examinees would have been less likely to answer correctly even if they had reached them. On a power test on which most students answer all of the items, this arrangement can encourage students, particularly young children and less able students, by ensuring some early success. This practice may motivate them to attempt all of the items on the test rather than to give up. However, this recommendation is supported more by professional judgment than by empirical evidence.

8. *Write a set of specific directions for each item type.* A good set of directions will provide information about how the examinees are to record their answers, the basis on which they are to select their answers, and the scoring procedures that will

be used. For a test made up of multiple-choice items that will not be corrected for guessing and for which separate answer sheets are used, one might use the following set of directions.

EXAMPLE

Directions: Read each item, and decide which choice best completes the statement or answers the question.

Mark your answers on the separate answer sheet. Do not mark them on the test itself. Indicate your answer by darkening the space next to the letter on the answer sheet that corresponds to your choice; that is, if you think that Choice B is the best answer to Item 1, darken the space next to B in the row after item 1 on your answer sheet.

Your score will be the number of correct items, so it is to your advantage to respond to every item, even if you are not sure of the correct response.

Be sure your name is on your answer sheet.

The following set of directions could be used for a test made up of true-false items in which answers are to be recorded on the test paper and the total score will be corrected for guessing.

EXAMPLE

Directions: Read each of the following statements carefully.

If all or any part of the statement is false, circle the F in front of the statement.

If the statement is completely true, circle the T in front of the statement.

Your score will be the number of correct answers minus the number of incorrect answers, so do not guess blindly. If you are not reasonably sure of an answer, omit the item.

Be sure your name is on your test.

These instructions would have to be revised if a separate answer sheet was being used. Commercially produced answer sheets for optical scanning usually are set up so that the first answer space (A) is equated to *true* and the second space (B) represents *false.* Also, if several types of items are being used on the test, examinees should be warned at the beginning of the test that additional directions will be provided later and that they should read those instructions carefully. With inexperienced examinees, such as young children, and with novel item forms, it is often helpful to put one or two examples of how to answer the questions immediately following the directions.

9. *Be sure that one item does not provide clues to the answer of another item or items.* Unless one is very careful in assembling items for a test, the answer to an item may be given away by a previous item. All of the items that are finally selected should be carefully checked, because it is possible for a true-false or completion item to give clues to the answer of a multiple-choice item or vice versa. For example, in the example that follows, the true-false item provides a clue to the answer to the objective item.

EXAMPLE

1. T F The spores of the bacteria causing botulism are present in soil and air.
2. Which of the following bacteria form spores?
    A. Staphylococcus causing food poisoning
    B. Bacillus causing botulism
    C. Bacillus causing typhoid fever
    D. Pneumococcus causing pneumonia

10. *Be sure that the correct responses form an essentially random pattern.* Some test constructors attempt to make the job of scoring easier by establishing a regular pattern of correct answers. For example, on a true-false test, they use a repetitive pattern such as T, T, F, F, F, or on a multiple-choice test, they use a pattern such as A, C, B, D. When a pattern is used, some testwise examinees may discover the pattern and use it as a means of answering items that they really do not know. On four-option, multiple-choice tests, there is a tendency for the correct answers to appear more frequently in the second and third positions than in the first and last positions. On a multiple-choice test the correct answer should appear in each of the possible response positions about the same percentage of the time. For example, on a four-option, multiple-choice test of 50 items, the constructor might check to see that each response position contains the keyed answer in not less than 10 and not more than 15 items. With word processing equipment the task of rearranging response alternatives is easy enough that this requirement is not hard to meet. If the test is to be machine scored, there is nothing to be gained from patterning the correct answers.

SCORING THE OBJECTIVE TEST

Once the test has been constructed, typed, reproduced, and administered, the assessment procedure is still not complete. The test must be scored, and the scores must be interpreted. The interpretation of scores in normative- and criterion-referenced frameworks was discussed in Chapter 3. However, scores can also be influenced by the errors caused by guessing. A decision needs to be made before the test is given whether scores will be corrected for guessing. Examinees should be told whether a correction will be used, because it may influence their strategy for taking the test. Measurement experts are not in complete agreement about the usefulness of the correction for guessing, but it seems to slightly improve the accuracy of measurement. The correction also is more important on item types where chance can play a larger part, such as in true-false items.

Correction for Guessing

It is well known that there are differences among examinees in their tendencies to guess on an objective test when they are not sure of the answer. These differences in willingness to guess introduce score variations that are not related to real individual differences in achievement. The more examinees guess, the less reliable the scores will be because getting an answer right by guessing is, by definition, introducing chance or random measurement error into the scores. Differences in willingness to guess are particularly important when tests are speeded, because not everyone has enough time to finish. Under these conditions, people who guess on items when there is not enough time to answer carefully will obtain higher scores than those who leave the items blank. One reason for instructing examinees not to guess and for imposing a penalty for incorrect answers is to try to make the guessing behavior more alike for all examinees.

A Formula for Correcting for Guessing.   One approach to dealing with the problem of guessing is to adjust scores with a correction-for-guessing formula. The most commonly used formula is based on the assumption that all incorrect responses result from guessing. Examinees are expected either to get an item correct or to omit it. The correction-for-guessing adjustment is found by subtracting from the examinee's score the number of points equal to the gain that would be expected from guessing. On a multiple-choice test with four alternatives, a person responding at random can be expected, by chance alone, to get one out of four answers correct. Therefore, for every three questions answered incorrectly, a person can be expected to get one correct by guessing. To put this logic into mathematical terms, the following equation is used:

$$\text{Corrected score} = R - \frac{W}{n - 1}$$

where
  R is the number of items answered correctly,
  W is the number of items answered incorrectly, and
  n is the number of answer choices for an item.
  Items for which examinees do not give an answer, that is, items they omit, do not count in this formula for guessing. On a true-false test (where there are only two possible answers), $n - 1$ in the formula becomes $2 - 1$, or 1, and the correction for guessing reduces to the number of correct answers minus the number of incorrect answers.
  The two examples that follow, the first based on a true-false test and the second, on a five-alternative, multiple-choice test, illustrate how the equation works. Note that the effect of guessing is assumed to be much larger on the true-false test, so the correction causes a much larger change in the person's score.

EXAMPLE 1

Student Performance

Type of Test	n	R	W	Omits
True-false	2	48	20	7

Corrected score = 48 − 20/(2 − 1) = 48 − 20/1 = 28

EXAMPLE 2

Student Performance

Type of Test	n	R	W	Omits
Multiple-choice	5	48	20	7

Corrected score = 48 − 20/(5 − 1) = 48 − 20/4 = 43

Criticisms of the Correction-for-Guessing Equation. The correction-for-guessing formula has been criticized both because its assumptions are difficult to meet and because it generally fails to do what it purports to do, which is to correct for guessing. The formula is based on the following two assumptions: (1) that all guesses are blind, with each response having an equal probability of being chosen, and (2) that every incorrect answer results from guessing—that is, the person never responds on the basis of misinformation. The first assumption rejects the possibility that a student might make an educated guess based on partial information or might eliminate some options. If this happens, the probabilities in the formula change. On a four-option multiple-choice test, the probability that a student will obtain a correct answer becomes greater than one in four. Only in a highly speeded test, where it is not possible to give a reasoned response to all questions, will examinees engage in truly blind guessing. The second assumption precludes the possibility that a person might make an incorrect response based on faulty or misunderstood knowledge. But a good item writer will construct misleads so as to attract those with partial or incorrect information.

Undercorrection. On a four-option, multiple-choice test, the formula will undercorrect to the extent that an examinee can eliminate some alternatives and then guess between the smaller number of remaining responses. Examinees are well advised to guess under these circumstances because the penalty for guessing is less than the expected increase in score that would accrue from guessing. If even one alternative can be eliminated, guessing will help the individual's score. On the other hand, persons who are not testwise are likely to be intimidated by the knowledge that the correction-for-guessing formula is being employed, and for this reason they may refrain from guessing.

Technical Factors. Another feature of the correction formula is that it does not change the rank order of students if no questions are omitted. Under these circumstances, there is a perfect correlation between raw scores and corrected scores. Only when there are omitted responses does the correlation become less than 1.0, and even then it remains in the 90s (Ebel, 1979) unless there is a great deal of variability in the number of items omitted.

Reliability and validity are only increased by correcting for guessing if there is a positive correlation between omitted responses and the raw score (Ebel, 1979). Of course, this circumstance would not normally be expected to occur because the person who works most quickly and answers the most questions is usually the more knowledgeable. Additionally, the more testwise examinees are likely both to answer more questions and also do better on the test overall.

Why the Correction-for-Guessing Equation Is Used.   You might, at this point, ask why, given the previous discussion, the correction-for-guessing equation is ever employed. The motivations of those using this formula may be more related to discouraging guessing than to correcting for it. Because guessing contributes directly to error variance, it is believed that the use of this equation might increase reliability. Reliability coefficients are the most easily obtainable and objective evidence of the quality of a test, so a great deal of emphasis is placed on these indices, and even a slight increase in reliability is hailed as improvement in a test.

Guessing on a test presents the most serious problem for tests that are highly speeded or that have items with only two answer choices. The scores obtained from such tests will probably be more dependable if they are corrected for guessing. In multiple-choice tests that have four or five answer choices (or options) and liberal enough time limits to permit all or most examinees to attempt every item, a score that is simply the number of correct answers is quite satisfactory, and there is little or no gain made from correcting for guessing.

USING ITEM ANALYSIS TO IMPROVE OBJECTIVE TESTS

Commercial test publishers do not rely on judgment and the skills of item writers to make final decisions about which items to include on their tests. Rather, they conduct pilot studies called *item tryouts* to get empirical evidence concerning item quality. If a test is to contain 100 items, the publisher may try out 150 to 200 items in order to be sure the final test will have the desired properties. For the tryout, several forms of the test are prepared with different subsets of items, so each item appears with every other item. Each form may be given to several hundred examinees. Although it is not necessary that the tryout sample be representative of the target population for which the test is intended, it should include individuals who span the range and have about the same average ability as the target population. Final item selection is then based on the kind of analysis described here. Although locally produced tests seldom are pretested in this elaborate way, item analysis of the data from one administration of the test can be employed to help improve items that may be used another time.

There are several different methods of conducting an item analysis. In terms of sophistication, the methods range from those based on complex item-response theory to fairly simple ones that can easily be employed by a teacher or researcher with minimal training and without access to a computer. With the appropriate equipment and software, it is possible to set up procedures that can easily provide a wealth of item analysis information to the test constructor, with minimal effort on his or her part. Most universities and larger school districts have test scoring equipment that can perform item analyses.

Simplified Procedures for Conducting Item Analyses

The first step in performing an item analysis is the tabulation of the responses that have been made to each item of the test—that is, how many individuals got each item correct, how many chose each of the possible incorrect answers, and how many skipped the item. You must have this information for the upper and lower sections of the group, based on the total test score. From this type of tabulation, you will be able to answer the following questions about each item:

1. How difficult is the item?
2. Does the item distinguish between the higher and lower scoring examinees?
3. Do some examinees select all the options? Or are there some options that no examinees choose?

In the following discussion, intended to illustrate the type of information provided by an item analysis, four items from a social studies test are presented, along with the analysis of responses for each item. This test was given to 100 high school seniors enrolled in a course called Current American Problems. There were 95 multiple-choice items on the test, each with four options. The highest score on the test was 85, and the lowest score was 14. The test papers were arranged in order, by the total score, starting with the score of 85 and ending with the score of 14. The top 25 papers were selected to represent the upper group (scores ranged from 59 to 85) and the last 25 papers were selected to represent the lower group (scores ranged from 14 to 34). The item analysis is based only on those in the upper and lower groups. The responses made to each item by each student in the upper and lower groups were tallied to give the frequency of choosing each option. These frequencies are shown in the columns on the right. The correct option is underlined. Each item is followed by a brief discussion of the item data.

The first thing we can learn about the test comes from the total score distribution. The test was quite difficult. The 3rd quartile (Q_3) is located at the point where the median should be, 62% correct [(59/95) = .62]. A second indication that the test is too hard is that at least one student scored 10 points below the chance level of 24. When this happens, it is necessary to inspect the score distribution to determine whether this was an isolated case or if several other students scored well below chance. Such poor scores could result from misinformation, serious problems with several of the items, or a motivation to do poorly. When below-chance scores are encountered, the test administrator should talk to the low-scoring examinees and try to determine the cause of the poor performance. If people are taking the test with an intent to miss items, then the value of an item analysis of these responses is highly questionable. The test also shows a wide range of scores. The range is 72 points out of a possible 95, and the interquartile range is 25; therefore, the test has been successful in spreading out the students.

The difficulty of an item is defined as the proportion of examinees who answered the item correctly. The item in our first example is an easy item because everyone in the upper group and 20 students in the lower group got it correct. Since 45 of the 50 students in the analysis got the item right, the item has a difficulty of .90 (45/50). (Note that the difficulty index is really an easiness index; high values of the index mean low difficulty.)

EXAMPLE 1

"Everyone's Switching to Breath of Spring Cigarettes!" is an example of the propaganda technique called:

	Upper	Lower
A. glittering generality.	0	2
B. bandwagon.	25	20
C. testimonial.	0	2
D. plain folk.	0	1
Item omitted	0	0

Although it is quite easy, the item does differentiate in the desired direction because the incorrect answers that occurred fall in the lower group. That is, students who earned higher scores on the total test were more likely to get the item correct. The item is also good in that all of the incorrect options are functioning; that is, each incorrect answer was chosen by at least one student in the lower group. Two or three easy items like this one would be good icebreakers with which to start a test.

Our second example is a difficult but effective item, difficult because only 13 out of 50 students got it correct, and effective because all 13 students getting the item correct were in the upper group. All of the incorrect options attracted some students in the lower group, and all of the incorrect options attracted more members of the lower group than of the higher group. Incidentally, an item such as this one illustrates that blind guessing may have less effect on scores than is often supposed. When a wrong alternative is provided that is highly attractive to people who do not have the knowledge or skill required, the effect of guessing is reduced.

EXAMPLE 2

There were no federal income taxes before 1913 because prior to 1913:

	Upper	Lower
A. the federal budget was balanced.	3	5
B. regular property taxes provided enough revenue to run the government.	9	15
C. a tax on income was unconstitutional.	13	0
D. the income of the average worker in the U.S. was too low to be taxed.	0	5
Item omitted	0	0

The next example turned out to be a poor item. First, the item is very difficult; only 8 out of the 50, or 16% of the students, got it correct. Second, the item is negatively discriminating; that is, correct answers were more frequent in the lower group than in the upper group. There are two possible explanations for these results: (1) The item was ambiguous, especially for students who knew the most, or (2) the students have not learned the provisions of the Corrupt Practices Act. There are two pieces of evidence that point to the second as the more likely explanation. The concentration of responses of the upper group at Option A suggests misinformation, and the essentially uniform distribution of responses of the lower group indicates random guessing. To arrive at the correct answer to the item, the student would have to know (1) the limit placed on contributions to the national committee of a political party, (2) who is forbidden to make contributions, and (3) what kind of organization the National Association of Manufacturers is. One might guess that it is points one and three that are causing difficulty for the upper group.

EXAMPLE 3

Under the Corrupt Practices Act the national committee of a political party would be permitted to accept a contribution of:

	Upper	Lower
A. $10,000 from Mr. Jones.	15	6
B. $1,000 from the ABC Hat Corporation.	4	6
C. $5,000 from the National Association of Manufacturers.	2	6
D. $500 from union funds of a local labor union.	4	7
Item omitted	0	0

Our last item is of reasonable difficulty (38/50 = .76) and shows some discrimination in the desired direction (21 versus 17), but the differentiation is not very sharp. The response pattern is one that is quite common. Only two of the four choices are functioning at all. Nobody selected either Option B or C. If we wished to improve this item, we might try substituting "wages paid for easy work" for Option B and "money paid to people on welfare" for Option C. The use of the adjective "easy" in Option B (it is also in the stem) and the idea of getting money for not working in Option C might make the item more difficult and, therefore, more discriminating. (Note that a clang association, while not acceptable in the correct answer, is appropriate in a distractor because it will tend to attract examinees who do not have the information or skill being tested by the item, which should make the item more discriminating.)

EXAMPLE 4

The term "easy money," as used in economics, means:

	Upper	Lower
A. the ability to borrow money at low interest rates.	21	17
B. dividends that are paid on common stocks.	0	0
C. money that is won in contests.	0	0
D. money paid for unemployment.	4	8
Item omitted	0	0

More Formal Item Analysis Procedures

The informal, straightforward approach to conducting an item analysis, discussed in the previous section, has the virtue of conceptual simplicity. We discussed item difficulty as the percent of examinees who answered the item correctly, and this definition of difficulty is fully sufficient for classical item analysis. A more abstract definition is required by item response theory, which we present in Chapter 16.

The lack of a concrete discrimination index is the most important limitation of the informal procedures. We spoke of an item having a positive discrimination in the sense that more people who scored high on the test got that item right than was the case for low scorers. But for more formal situations, such as in commercial test development, it is desirable to be able to quantify an item's ability to discriminate those who possess the information from those who do not. Two methods of indicating the discriminating power of an item are often used.

The Discrimination Index. One commonly used procedure, which we will label the *discrimination index,* is readily computed from the same data layout that we used to study the functioning of our distractors. For technical reasons, this type of analysis is usually carried out on the top and bottom 27% of examinees (that is, the extreme 54% rather than the extreme 50%, as we described earlier); however, the principles are identical, regardless of the split used. When the number of examinees is small, the upper and lower groups often are defined as above and below the median. This increases the number of people participating in the analysis but may systematically reduce the discrimination index values, because the groups are less different when the middle of the distribution has not been excluded.

The discrimination index (D) is computed by subtracting the number of students who got the item correct in the lower group (N_L) from the number who got it correct in the upper group (N_U) and dividing the difference by the number in one group. The discrimination index equation is as follows:

$$D = \frac{N_U - N_L}{N_U}$$

Applying this formula to the data from our four examples produces the following values for the discrimination index:

Example 1 $D = (25 - 20)/25 = .20$
Example 2 $D = (13 - 0)/25 = .52$
Example 3 $D = (2 - 6)/25 = -.16$
Example 4 $D = (21 - 17)/25 = .16$

These results reveal several important aspects of item discrimination. First, items that are very hard (3) or very easy (1 and 4) cannot discriminate very well. In the limiting case where everyone passes the item or everyone fails it, the value of D will be exactly zero, indicating no discrimination. While having a few very easy items that do not discriminate well may be acceptable, because of their beneficial motivational properties, we would seldom want extremely hard items unless they measured achievement of a particularly critical objective. For most purposes our test will differentiate best when it contains a majority of items of moderate difficulty, because these are the items that show the best discrimination. For example, maximum discrimination of 1.00 occurs when all of the members of the upper group got the item right and all of the members of the lower group missed it.

The second point that becomes clear from our examples is that when more people in the lower group pass the item than in the upper group, the value of D will be negative. This is what we mean by a negatively discriminating item. Items like this are never desirable in a test because they are measuring something other than what the rest of the test is measuring. They may be measuring nothing at all, or they may be poorly stated and confusing or misleading to the more able examinees. If an item is intended to measure an important objective and is a negative discriminator, the test constructor must either correct the problems with the item or find another way to assess that objective.

In addition to having items that are positively discriminating (that is, more people in the upper group get the item right), it is also desirable to have the distractors function in a comparable way. A distractor is functioning properly (sometimes called a positively discriminating distractor) when more members of the lower group than the upper group choose it. This is the case in example items 1 and 2 above. More people in the lower group selected each distractor. The performance of the distractors is not as critical to the quality of the test, but the best test items will have this property.

Item-Total Score Correlations.   When the tests have been machine scored and computer facilities are available, an alternative way to assess the discriminating power of the items is to compute the correlation of each item with the total score. One advantage of this method is that items may be scored right/wrong, or scores may be awarded on degree of correctness when certain complex item formats are used or there is a bonus for rapid responding. (Both of these scoring procedures are used on the Wechsler scales, for example, although the instrument is not formally an objective test.) The item-total correlation uses all of the data rather than just the extreme cases, and the resulting correlations have the same general properties as the D index.

Many of the programs that control optical scanning equipment also have item analysis options that will produce output very similar to what we have examined, but they are more likely to use the item-total score correlation than the D-index.

Using Discrimination Indexes.   The simplest way to use the discrimination index for test development is to retain the items with the highest values (e.g., over .50), to eliminate the ones with the lowest (e.g., below .20), and to consider for modification those items between these two points. Items with negative discrimination values should, of course, be rejected. In trying to determine why an item has a low index, look first at item difficulty. Items that are too easy or too hard are almost always poor discriminators. Sometimes an item is a poor discriminator even though the computed difficulty might be in an acceptable range, such as when two of four distractors are completely implausible, leaving the correct answer and one functioning distractor. Even if the item is so difficult that only a few students know the correct answer, many more students will get the correct answer by guessing, because they need only to guess between the two plausible responses. Of course, the test maker also needs to determine whether the item is flawed in some other way and if its construction violates the rules of good item writing. It is also important to see that all of the distractors are functioning effectively. Distractors that are not plausible make items too easy, and those that are too closely related to the correct answer make an item too difficult. This possibility of manipulating item difficulty by modifying the distractors is an advantage of multiple-choice tests.

SUMMARY

Writing good test items is a learnable skill. In this chapter we have reviewed the principles that apply to all good objective test items. These include (1) keeping reading level and vocabulary appropriate to the purpose of the test, (2) making sure each item has one best answer, (3) making sure the content is important, (4) keeping items independent, (5) avoiding trick questions, and (6) making sure the item poses a clear problem.

Although they are of limited value, true-false questions are popular. Special points to keep in mind in writing true-false items include (1) ensure that each statement is unequivocally true or false, (2) avoid specific determiners, (3) avoid ambiguous terms of amount, (4) avoid negative statements, (5) limit each item to a single idea, (6) make true and false statements of approximately equal length, and (7) have about the same number of true statements as false ones. Four modifications of the general true-false format include (1) underlining the important concept in the statement—to reduce ambiguity, (2) requiring examinees to correct false statements, (3) basing several statements on a single set of stimulus material, and (4) grouping several short statements under a common heading.

Multiple-choice items provide much more flexibility in the objectives that can be measured. Items in this format generally require examinees to read a stem that poses a problem and select the best answer from among three to five alternatives. Principles to be followed in writing good multiple-choice items include (1) be sure the stem formulates a clear problem, (2) include as much of the item in the stem as possible to reduce reading load, (3) include only necessary material in the item, (4) avoid negatively worded items, (5) use novel material to assess comprehension and application objectives, (6) be sure there is only one correct answer, (7) be sure wrong answers are plausible, (8) avoid unintentional clues to the correct answer, and (9) use sparingly the "none of these" and "all of these" response alternatives. The complex multiple-choice item and the paired statements format are alternative forms of the multiple-choice item.

Matching items are a special case of the multiple-choice format in which several item stems share a set of response alternatives. Good matching items should involve homogeneous sets of statements and relatively short answers. Examinees should choose their answers from the shorter statements, and each column should have a heading that clearly identifies its content. There should be more response alternatives than statements, the responses should be arranged in a logical order, and directions should include the basis for matching.

When preparing a test, you should (1) write more items than you intend to use, (2) proofread the items carefully, (3) arrange the items in a readable form, (4) plan a layout that enables you to use separate answer sheets, (5) group items by format and by content, (6) arrange items by difficulty, (7) prepare specific directions for each type of item, (8) make sure one item does not give away the answer to another, and (9) make sure there is no systematic pattern to the correct answers.

One feature of all select-response tests is that some examinees will get some items correct by guessing. Guessing reduces the reliability of measurement because it introduces random error into the scores. A correction for guessing sometimes is applied to test scores by subtracting an estimate of how many answers examinees got right by guessing from their total score. The value of a correction for guessing is questionable.

Commercial test publishers evaluate their items before a test is released for public use. This is done with item analysis, a procedure that involves checking the difficulties of the items to assure that they are in the desired range and examining the ability of items to discriminate between higher scoring and lower scoring examinees. For most purposes, a good test item will be moderately difficult and have a discrimination index value of about .50 or higher. Item analysis is also used to make sure all of the distractors are functioning as they should.

QUESTIONS AND EXERCISES

1. Why do people who construct tests for their own local use so often use poor test development procedures?

2. What are the requirements for good test construction?

3. Under what circumstance would a criterion-referenced test be more appropriate than a norm-referenced test?

4. A teacher writes 10 objectives for a biology class and for each objective, writes five items. An objective is considered mastered if a student correctly answers four out of five items. What is the most appropriate label for this approach to testing?

5. Present arguments both for using criterion-referenced tests and for not using them.

6. In a junior high school, one teacher takes complete responsibility for preparing the common final examination for all the classes in general science. This teacher develops the examination without consulting the other teachers. What advantages and disadvantages do you see in this procedure? How could it be improved?

7. One objective that is often proposed for the social studies program in secondary schools is to increase the students' *critical reaction to the news in different news media*. How could the formulation of this objective be improved so that progress toward it could be measured?

8. Look at the blueprint for the examination on a unit on health that appears under Preparing the Test Blueprint in Chapter 5. For which of the cells in this blueprint would it be appropriate to use either recall or selection exercises? What factors influenced your decisions?

9. Construct four multiple-choice items designed to measure understanding or application in some subject area with which you are familiar.

10. Write a series of true-false items to assess the same outcomes used in Problem 9. Which approach seemed to assess student knowledge most effectively?

11. Prepare a short, objective test for a small unit that you are teaching or taking. Indicate the objectives that you are trying to evaluate with each item.

12. For which of the following tests would correcting scores for guessing be justified? Give the reason or reasons for your decision.

    a. A 100-item, true-false test. All students answered all questions.

    b. A 70-item, multiple-choice test of spatial relations. Each item has five answer choices. For each item, one or more answer choices may be correct. All students answered all questions.

    c. A 50-item, multiple-choice test with four answer choices for each item, one of which is the keyed answer. Only 40% of the examinees completed all items.

    d. A 60-item, multiple-choice test with four answer choices for each item, one of which is the keyed answer. Ninety percent of the students answered all items.

13. A college professor has given an objective test to a large class, scored the papers, and entered the scores in the class record book. What additional steps might the professor take before returning the papers to the students? Why?

14. Collect five examples of poor items you have seen on tests. Indicate what is wrong with each item.

SUGGESTED READINGS

Albanese, M. A. (1988). The projected impact of the correction for guessing on individual scores. *Journal of Educational Measurement, 25,* 149–157.

Albanese, M. A., & Sabers, D. L. (1988). Multiple true-false items: A study of interitem correlations, scoring alternatives, and reliability estimation. *Journal of Educational Measurement, 25,* 111–123.

Berk, R. A. (Ed.). (1984). *A guide to criterion-referenced test construction.* Baltimore: Johns Hopkins University Press.

Gronlund, N. E. (1982). *Constructing achievement tests.* Englewood Cliffs, NJ: Prentice Hall.

Gronlund, N. E., & Linn, R. L. (1990). *Measurement and evaluation in teaching* (6th ed.). New York: Macmillan.

Harper, A. E., Jr., & Harper, E. S. (1990). *Preparing objective examinations.* New Delhi: Prentice Hall of India.

Hopkins, K. D., Stanley, J. C., & Hopkins, B. R. (1990). *Educational and psychological measurement and evaluation* (7th ed.). Englewood Cliffs, NJ: Prentice Hall.

Mager, R. F. (1975). *Preparing instructional objectives* (2nd ed.). Belmont, CA: Fearon.

Nitko, A. J. (1983). *Educational tests and measurement.* New York: Harcourt Brace Jovanovich.

Osterlind, S. J. (1989). *Constructing test items.* Boston: Kluwer.

Sax, G. (1989). *Principles of educational and psychological measurement and evaluation.* Belmont, CA: Wadsworth.

Thissen, D., Steinberg, L., & Fitzpatrick, A. R. (1989). Multiple-choice models: The distractors are also part of the item. *Journal of Educational Measurement, 26,* 161–176.

Wainer, H. (1989). The future of item analysis. *Journal of Educational Measurement, 26,* 191–208.

CHAPTER 16

Special Topics in Test Development and Use

INTRODUCTION

From 1900 to about 1950, the rates of development and of increase in use of tests and testing procedures were dramatic. Starting from practically nothing, standardized tests were developed to appraise a wide variety of educational skills, to assess generalized intellectual ability and specialized aptitudes, and to evaluate many aspects of interest and temperament. By midcentury, almost all of the patterns for objective test items had been developed and were being widely used. The basic statistical procedures for analyzing test reliability and validity and for developing test norms were also generally available. With a few exceptions, a general reader would find it difficult to distinguish between a test (or test manual) published in 1950 and one published in 1995. As Linn (1989) observes,

> . . . on inspection of three versions of a well-established, standardized achievement test battery, one published around the time of each of the three editions of this book [*Educational Measurement,* 1951, 1971, 1989] one might easily wonder if there had been any progress in the field of educational measurement since the early 1950s. The multiple-choice items, grade-equivalent scores, and percentile ranks would give quite a sense of constancy. (p. 1)

Developments during the past 45 years have primarily involved (1) an increased interaction between testing and the general field of cognitive psychology, (2) new models of test performance based on item response theory, (3) the pervasive impact of computers on all aspects of test preparation and use, (4) the application of Bayesian statistics to the analysis and interpretation of test results, and (5) the application of concepts of meta-analysis to the accumulated body of test validation research. Some of these developments are likely to continue to influence testing procedures over the next 10 or 20 years, so we will discuss them in this final chapter. The chapter concludes with an introduction to a procedure for analyzing patterns of test scores, that of factor analysis, which has had a major impact on theories of abilities and personality, as well as on test construction.

TESTING AND COGNITIVE PSYCHOLOGY

Educational and psychological measurement historically have developed rather separately from the general course of psychological research. Testing was concerned primarily with the *products* that people produced rather than the mental *processes* by which these products were achieved. Furthermore, emphasis was on *differences* between people in their abilities to produce these products, rather than on the common principles of human learning and behavior that concerned researchers in the psychology of learning and problem solving. More recently, at least at the frontiers of research, this separation has started to break down. Cognitive psychologists have started to investigate individual differences in cognitive processes, and psychometricians have begun to analyze the processes underlying the solutions to the problems on their tests.

Underlying this trend, at least in part, is a common focus on *information processing,* fostered by the spread of computers and by research with computers in simulating human problem solving. A whole branch of computer science has grown up, to which the label *artificial intelligence* has been attached, in which the possibility of modeling human problem solving with a computer has been investigated. Following the steps in processing information through a computer has suggested analogous stages in human problem solving, and this line of research has suggested processes that might be studied by test makers to provide them with a better understanding of individual differences in ability and achievement.

Encoding Information

Just as the computer receives inputs of data through its keyboard or from magnetic tape or disk, a CD-ROM, or a network, humans also receive and encode sensory inputs. When we attempt to measure the effectiveness of an individual's encoding processes, we can do so only by recording that individual's *responses.* This restriction introduces one of the dilemmas of measures that try to isolate for study one element of the information processing sequence. We can only observe the outcomes in behavior, making it difficult to determine where in the sequence failures were generated. Thus, given the task, *Find one that is just like this one* (pointing),

does the child fail because of (1) the inability to understand the directions, (2) imperfect encoding of

(3) the inability to remember the sample while looking for its match, (4) noncooperation in the task, or some other reason. To test for one process component, the dif-

ficulties of the other components must be held to the lowest possible level. Then, if the encoding part of the task is made progressively more difficult by using the same task but with more abstract figures, such as

the investigator may hope that failures on such items represent encoding deficiencies. Encoding tasks involving matching single letters, combinations, and short words appear in reading tests at the preprimer level, such as with the Metropolitan Achievement Tests.

Encoding capabilities develop rapidly during the preschool and initial school years and have been assessed as an aspect of readiness for schooling. One recent line of research (Hunt, 1987; Jensen, 1982) suggests that speed of encoding (and responding to) quite simple stimuli may be an indicator of the effectiveness of the information processing sequence for even quite difficult tasks and may be predictive of the individual's level of performance in the higher level cognitive tasks that appear in general ability tests. This line of investigation, which tries to relate speed of simple information processing to the limit of ability in complex tasks, is one that is likely to be pursued actively in the years ahead. Snow and Lohman (1989) provide a review of developments in this area.

Processing in Short-Term Memory

A limited amount of the material that has been entered into a computer may be held in what is called a *memory buffer*, ready for immediate use in whatever processing the computer has been programmed to carry out. Similarly, a small amount of encoded material may be stored in human short-term memory for immediate use in a task, such as calling someone to repair the telephone. Unfortunately, in comparison with the memory buffer of a computer, the capacity of human short-term memory is sharply restricted. Research suggests that about six to eight discrete units of information is as much as can be held in human short-term memory at any one time. If more is loaded in, much of the input may be lost. So one practical limit on human information processing is the meager storage capacity of short-term memory.

Test tasks, such as digit span or verbatim memory of a series of disconnected words or of a sentence, have been designed primarily to reflect the capacity of short-term memory. On such tests, we find both individual differences and an increase in average score with age during childhood. Furthermore, these tests show moderate correlations with other measures of cognitive functioning, leading researchers to suspect that failures and errors in solving complex problems arise in some cases from failure to keep alive in working memory one or more components of the problem. This cause of failure is not readily isolated in problem solutions but might be identified if the efforts to solve the problem were verbalized in detail.

Long-Term Memory Storage and Retrieval

Computers are built with outstanding resources for storing information in auxiliary memory devices, tapes, and especially disks, from which the information can be recalled on demand. Similarly, long-term memory storage is a prominent feature of human memory, although the details of human memory appear to differ in significant ways from computer memory. On the one hand, human memory is not 100% dependable; we all have had the experience of being unable to retrieve an elusive item at one moment that pops up spontaneously a little later. Furthermore, human memories are linked in a complex network, so that the memory of a given fact or event may be elicited by any one of a variety of other mental events, in contrast to the specificity of the memory organization of a computer. But, whether by computer or human processes, retrieval of material from long-term memory and processing it together with current inputs in working memory is central to information processing and to problem solving.

Past and present ability tests have given undue emphasis to assessing what material can be retrieved from long-term memory. A test of factual knowledge is, after all, one of the easiest tests to prepare. Such a test does not, of course, determine what is *in* the memory storage bank, but only what can be retrieved on demand. Although sheer information can easily be overemphasized in a test, factual knowledge should not be derogated. To think, one must have something to think about, so factual knowledge in any subject is a basic requirement. But it is retrievable knowledge that is valuable, so perhaps future testing should probe the linkages within the memory store—what is related to what—rather than just the elements of knowledge per se. One attribute of an expert in any field appears to be not just that the person has more knowledge about the field than others do but also that the knowledge is more complexly and logically organized. An instructive exercise for exploring, at a relatively simple level, the nature of long-term memory structures and the process of retrieval might be to ask of someone, "Tell me everything you can about the number *nine*." Try this exercise—on yourself, a friend, or a student. The diversity of responses should give you some sense of the complexity of long-term memory structures.

Various types of free- and controlled-association tests have been used in the past as research tools to study the structure of human memories and human knowledge. Somewhat related are the fluency and flexibility tests that have been designed to assess "creativity" or "divergent thinking." These tests can be thought of as attempts to tease out some of the complex linkages in long-term memory.

Information Processing

Executive Processes.   At the heart of the information processing capabilities of a computer are the programs that tell it what to do with its information inputs, what information to retrieve from its memory storage, and how to combine the old and the new information to arrive at the required answer. In the same way, executive processes represent the heart of human information processing and problem solving activities. (Sternberg, 1985, has called these processes *meta-components* in his theory of intelligence.) They can be thought of as strategies that guide the attack on the problem and the search for a solution. At a simple level, in arithmetic problem solving, an explicit or implicit strategy might start with the following questions: What is given? What do I know? What is required to be found out? What model does the required answer fit into? What relationships do I know of between the "givens" and the "required?"

Effective problem solving, as well as effective learning, depend on using good strategies for (1) organizing what is known, (2) seeking information, either in your own memory store or in external sources, and (3) applying information in new contexts. Gross deficiency in these processes or strategies is one of the most apparent limitations of those with mental retardation. To the degree that test tasks present novel and problematic situations, their answers require strategies of search and synthesis rather than of simple recall. But, the strategies are usually implicit in the solution rather than clearly displayed.

Sometimes, defective strategies can be identified by analyzing errors that an examinee makes. Thus, a pupil who adds the following numbers:

$$
\begin{array}{r}
17 \\
25 \\
+19
\end{array}
$$

and arrives at the answer 421 is presumably using a strategy of adding the right-hand column and writing down the sum on the right and then adding the left-hand column and writing down that sum on the left. Or, a pupil who gives 4 as an answer to 8/½ appears to be using the strategy that *divide means make smaller.* When individuals are tested individually, they can be asked to "think out loud"; that activity can provide further evidence of ineffective strategies. The hope is that additional testing procedures can be developed that will enable professionals to focus more directly on the nature and effectiveness of the strategies employed by examinees in attacking a variety of problems. (See Snow & Lohman, 1989, for a review of recent studies of problem-solving strategies and Frederiksen, Mislevy, and Bejar, 1993, for a series of essays on attempts to blend cognitive psychology and measurement theory. You may also see that the Das-Naglieri [Das, Naglieri, & Kirby, 1994] approach to assessing cognitive ability uses similar information-processing concepts.)

Output.   The end product of computer information processing is some sort of output. Likewise, the end product of human information processing is output in the form of behavior. Sometimes the motor aspects of this output are of interest in their own right, as performance on a copying test may depend in part on the accuracy of encoding the form to be copied and in part on the motor coordination that permits accurate copying. Or, as in evaluating handwriting, the motor skill is the primary skill being assessed.

More often, the cognitive structure of the output is of primary interest. Thus, the completeness and precision of a definition, the accuracy and idiomatic appropriateness of a translation, or the coherence and clarity of an exposition may be of concern. Multiple-choice questions are poorly suited to appraising the output side of an individual's information processing. The behavior involved almost never permits an assessment of the process of interest. Here, open-ended tasks requiring a constructed response come most clearly into their own. Some of the steps taken to improve reliability and to eliminate biases from the appraisal of performances and products were described in Chapter 10.

Of course, the adequacy of the output as a solution to a substantive problem depends on the effective execution of all the prior stages of information processing. It is far from easy to judge to what extent a deficient end product reflects inadequate encoding of the task, a meager working memory span that is inadequate to keep all aspects of the task in mind, a meager and poorly organized stock of information in long-term memory, a lack of effective strategies for seeking and organizing the relevant material, or poor skills for producing the appropriate response. The most challenging task facing designers of tests is to develop effective and efficient measures that permit the localization of the reasons for poor performance, so remedial measures can be undertaken.

IMPACT OF COMPUTERS ON TESTING

One of the most significant influences on testing over the past 20 years has been the rapid spread of personal computers, as well as the increase in their information processing capabilities and the decrease in their cost. Computerization has had an impact on all phases of assessment: test construction, test scoring and reporting, procedures for test administration, and the presentation and interpretation of test results.

There is little doubt that computers will occupy an even more prominent place in educational and psychological measurement in the years to come. Computing power is becoming so inexpensive and so readily available that it is easy to imagine a time when every classroom and office will have a computer to assist in all sorts of record keeping and administrative tasks. Some of these uses will relate to testing and evaluation.

Computers and Test Development

In the course of producing a well-designed standardized test, the test maker generates masses of data. After items have been written, they must be tried out on adequate samples, and the results must be analyzed to verify that the items are of appropriate difficulty and that they do differentiate between more and less capable individuals with respect to the domain that the items represent. Statistical routines and item analysis software are central to these processes.

After items have been assembled into a test and scored, the scores must be converted into a continuous scale, often extending over several levels of a test, that is expressed in equal units of the ability in question. Norms must be developed that are applicable to the groups with which the test is to be used. Reliability estimates must also be calculated, and correlations of the test with other measures or with background variables, determined. All of these analyses are facilitated by computers, and some, such as the more elegant procedures for item analysis and test scaling, become feasible only when adequately powerful computers are available. The computer has both expedited and changed the nature of testing and item analysis.

Commercial programs are now available that allow the teacher to employ similar analyses on locally developed tests. Although it is unrealistic to expect local tests to undergo the rigorous development and analysis to which commercially produced tests are subjected (or should be subjected), because computers and optical scanning equipment are likely to become sufficiently widely available, classroom teachers will be able to get item analyses on their tests at little cost in time or effort. These analyses will allow teachers to improve the tests and their test-writing skills as a result of feedback received from the analyses.

Computers and Test Scoring and Reporting

Test scoring services have been operating for so many years that few people even remember when all test processing was done by hand. Even the IBM test-scoring machines of the 1940s are only a dim memory. Optical scanners that read the marks on an answer sheet are taken for granted, together with the computers that receive and analyze the electrical inputs from the scanners. The variety of these analyses continuously increases, so that the computer is programmed to generate not only raw and converted scores for individuals but also, as indicated in Chapter 3, summary statistics for class groups, schools, and school systems. Results are provided not only for tests and subtests but also for individual items.

Computerized test processing was originally limited to large, centralized computer installations. In recent years, with the proliferation of microcomputers, systems have been developed that combine optical scanning and a microcomputer, thus bringing the capability of preparing computerized scoring reports within the reach of local school systems and individual counselors and researchers. Many large schools and school districts also process their enrollment and attendance information using scanner and computer hardware. There is every reason to believe that test and information processing equipment will become more compact, more affordable, and more powerful in the years to come.

Perhaps one of the least expected developments in test processing software has been the development of programs that score essay tests (Page, 1994) using scoring rubrics similar to those described in Chapter 10. Page and his associates report that their program produces results that are as reliable as the average of up to six human judges. Of course, the quality of the output depends critically on the adequacy of the scoring rubric, but as more experience is accumulated with computerized scoring of produce-response tasks, we may see a move toward increased use of items of this type in standardized tests.

Computers and Test Administration

Computers are also used for the actual administration of tests. Computerized testing was a natural adjunct to computer-assisted instruction, in which formative testing occurred as an integral part of the instructional program. But use of a computer terminal as the medium for test administration has other advantages as well. Whenever pupils are individually working on a subject at different rates and at different levels, it is advantageous to be able to have a specific pupil take a specific test at just the time when she or he is ready for it. If the library of tests is stored on a disk ready to be called up when needed, the pupil can be seated at the terminal, call up the specified test, be tested, and receive immediate feedback of the test results. The pupil and the teacher can use this feedback to guide the next phase of instruction.

The type of testing for which the computer is uniquely well suited is computer-adaptive testing (CAT). In this assessment technique, tests are specially tailored to the individual examinees on the basis of their prior responses, to provide the maximum amount of information about each examinee. The basis for designing CAT is considered in more detail later in this chapter.

As computers become commonplace implements in society, it will be possible for test administrators to bring them into the assessment situation as a part of the normal testing environment. Examinees will not find it strange that a computer is in the room and will not be distracted if the examiner refers to it from time to time. Some individually administered tests are quite complex to administer and require very careful attention on the part of the examiner, if errors are to be avoided. Under these conditions, the computer can be used to help the examiner record exact responses, determine their correctness, and then select the next item, depending on the examinee's recent performance. The clinical setting will continue to require the judgment of a trained examiner, but the computer will be useful in eliminating errors in test administration and scoring, errors which, unfortunately, are now quite common (Kaufman, 1990, pp 101–105.)

Computers and Test Interpretation

Test authors and publishers have increasingly relied on computers to generate narrative reports of test results that interpret the numerical scores for the user. A catalog of statements is stored in computer memory, and the computer is programmed so that a score falling in a given range, a particular combination of two or more scores, or even a combination of responses to specific questions triggers the production of one or more of these statements. The elements in the narrative may be as simple and as directly related to a particular score as "Henry is somewhat below the average in arithmetic problem solving" or as extended as the interpretive personality picture provided in Chapter 11. The report may focus solely and very specifically on one examinee's scores, or it may include an extended general discussion of the conceptual basis for the instrument. For example, National Computer Systems produces a report for the Strong Interest Inventory that is 20 pages long and provides, as a basis for interpreting the examinee's scores, a full exposition of the general nature of the instrument and of the rationale for the different types of scores that it produces, together with suggested sources for further information about occupations that appear congruent with the examinee's pattern of interests.

Narrative computer printouts can be no better than the wisdom and clinical experience on which they are based. However, they do permit the distillation of that experience as it has accumulated in the professional literature and in the pooled background of a number of experts. Computer-generated printouts protect the examinee from possible bias or inexperience of a local practitioner, while also expediting what can be a time-consuming and tedious chore of report writing. Their use guarantees that aspects of the record dealt with by the narrative will not be inadvertently overlooked by a current interpreter and also ensures uniformity and consistency in interpretation. The narrative *does* need to be evaluated by a counselor or clinician who knows other facts about the client, but it can serve as a useful foundation for such an evaluation.

BAYESIAN THINKING IN TEST INTERPRETATION AND USE

Most people would agree that how we interpret a person's performance on some presently administered test task or testing instrument should be influenced by other things that we already know about that person. Thus, if a child has been doing acceptable work in the fifth grade and then receives a deviation intelligence quotient (IQ) of 80 on a verbal ability test, the teacher should suspect that some extraneous influence has lowered the child's score on the test. The teacher has a *prior estimate* that the child is of at least average ability, and when the test results fail to confirm this prior estimate, the result should become suspect.

During the past 20 years, considerable attention has been directed toward systematizing the use of prior and collateral information in arriving at the most reasonable belief about a person's true status on some trait. *Bayes' theorem* (a theorem about probability, developed by the British theologian Thomas Bayes in the 18th century) provides a basis for arriving at a final estimate of a person's status *(posterior estimate),* based on an initial estimate *(prior estimate)* and additional information. For example, suppose an ability test given 2 years ago in the third grade yielded an IQ equivalent of 100 for Joe, while one just given in the fifth grade shows an IQ of 80. What is our best estimate of Joe's true current IQ? It seems reasonable that we should not *completely* ignore the result from the earlier test, but how much weight should we give it? The answer depends on two variances: (1) the variance error of *estimate* of the fifth-grade test from the third-grade test, which is the square of the standard error of estimate for predicting fifth-grade scores from third-grade scores (see Chapter 5), and (2) the variance error of *measurement* of the fifth-grade test, which is the square of the standard error of measurement of the fifth-grade test (see Chapter 4). Suppose the correlation of the third-grade test with the fifth-grade test is .80, the reliability of the fifth-grade test is .90, and the standard deviation of the fifth-grade test is 16 points. The variance error of estimate then is $(16^2) (1 - .80^2) = 92.16$, and the variance error of measurement is $(16^2) (1 - .90) = 25.60$. The two items of information should be weighted in proportion to the reciprocals of these error variances, thus giving not quite four times as much weight to the current as to the earlier test. The weighted average gives 84.35 as our best estimate of Joe's true current IQ. This value has a variance error of 20.04, in comparison with 25.60 for the current test taken alone. So we gain some precision by also considering the earlier test. (For an introduction to Bayes' theorem and Bayesian thinking, see R. L. Thorndike, 1982, pp. 288–299.)

One important application of Bayesian thinking is to *adaptive testing,* which is described in a later section. Here, we start with a prior estimate of the individual's ability level and present a test task selected to match that prior estimate. If the examinee passes the item, our posterior estimate is raised somewhat to reflect this success. This posterior estimate after Item A becomes the prior estimate for Item B, and so on through the test, with the estimate of ability level adjusted to take account at each point of the information obtained from the earlier test items. As more information accumulates, the posterior estimate stabilizes, and the examinee's ability level is determined within narrow limits. Clearly, a fully adaptive testing strategy can only be used when the test is administered by computer, because of the need for rapid calculation of the revised ability estimates.

Bayesian procedures can become somewhat involved, but Bayesian thinking is basically simple. What it says is that we should frequently—possibly always—take account of what we already know when interpreting new information about an individual or about a group. What we already know may be the results of an earlier test; it may be information stemming from other sources, such as a teacher's day-to-day contacts; or it may at times be information about the performance of *other* individuals either in the same group or receiving the same treatment. This inclusion of prior data, of course, is what counselors, clinicians, and, sometimes, teachers have done for years when using test information. The difference here is twofold: first, Bayesian procedures require that the prior information be in quantitative form, even if that quantification is only a rough estimate, and second, use of them ensures an objective process of assigning relative importance to the prior information. The question is *how much* weight to give to this prior or collateral evidence; results obtained from Bayes' theorem help to answer that question. The need to use this other information, and procedures for doing so, are likely to become more widely known and accepted in the years ahead. Although it has not happened yet, we may look forward to the day when test interpretation software will incorporate Bayesian methods, at least as an option.

TESTING AND ITEM RESPONSE THEORY

Many of the recent developments in testing stem from what has come to be called *item response theory,* or *latent trait theory.* The practical application of this theory has depended on the availability of computers and has in turn shaped the ways in which computers are used in testing. Let us look at a set of interlocking developments that stem from the interactions of theoretical models and the availability of computers to implement them.

Latent trait theory assumes the existence of a relatively unified underlying trait, or characteristic, that determines an individual's ability to succeed with some particular type of cognitive task. Possible attributes might be *knowledge of word meanings, arithmetical reasoning,* or *spatial visualizing.* We can represent the trait as a linear scale (as shown in Figure 16.1) on which both tasks and people can be placed. The tasks in this example are words to be defined, and the trait is knowledge of word meanings.

For the *tasks,* the scale can be thought of as a scale of difficulty, so the words in the illustration go from very easy on the left to quite difficult on the right. The difficulty of an item is defined as the ability level at which half of the examinees will get the item correct. For *people,* the scale can be thought of as a scale of ability. A person's ability level is defined by the tasks that a person can just about do—that is, the difficulty level at which the examinee would get half of the items correct. Thus, Joe can most likely define *borrow* because his ability exceeds the difficulty of the item, but he is unlikely to be able to define incision because its difficulty exceeds his ability. The likelihood that Billy can correctly define *borrow* is relatively low.

It is important to note that in this model, a person's ability level is subject to change over time. That is, if Billy is 6 years old, we can expect that his position on the scale of ability will change as he matures. Conversely, we would expect the relative difficulty of the words to remain nearly constant for long periods of time. The stability of the difficulty scale is what gives meaning to the ability scale.

The ability/difficulty scale is an arbitrary one, just as the Fahrenheit scale of temperature is. You could use a scale with different-sized units (for example, Celsius) or a different zero point (for example, Celsius or Kelvin). But, for a given scale, the units are presumably equal throughout the scale and the *relative* position of a person or task does not depend either on the size of the units or on the placement of the zero point. As an example of our temperature-scale analogy, consider that a summer day may be warmer than a winter day, and this fact does not depend on whether the summer temperature is expressed as 20°C or 68°F and the win-

Figure 16.1
Scale of world knowledge.

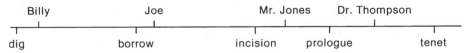

ter temperature is 0° C or 32° F. The relative positions of the two days are the same in either scale, and a spring day of 10° C or 50° F would be halfway between them on the scale. Likewise, a heat greater than 100° C (212° F) has the ability to cause water to boil (at standard atmospheric pressure) and a heat below this point does not.

The relationship between ability level and passing an item of a given difficulty is not an all-or-none matter but, instead, is a question of probability. The form of the relationship between ability and probability of passing an item is shown in Figure 16.2. The graph in this figure is called the *item characteristic curve,* or *item trace line,* and there is one such curve for every item. Thus, if we include the word *incision* on a test given to a group of people at Joe's level of ability, about 25% would know the meaning, while among those at Mr. Jones' level, about 85% would be able to provide a definition. Turning things around, Joe could define 25% of the words whose difficulty was the same as incision's, while Mr. Jones could provide definitions for about 85% of them.

As we see from Figure 16.2, the probability of a person's passing an item as a function of ability level is expressed by a curve that is quite flat at the two extremes but rises steeply around the level that matches the difficulty of the item. The test item differentiates effectively between those whose abilities are somewhat above and those whose abilities are somewhat below the difficulty level of the task but provides very little differentiation among those whose abilities are very high or very low. Dr. Thompson and other people at her ability level would pass almost all the items at the difficulty level represented by *incision,* and we would know that she had very high verbal ability, but we would not know *how* high. We would need words in the

Figure 16.2
Item characteristic curve for the meaning of the word *incision.*

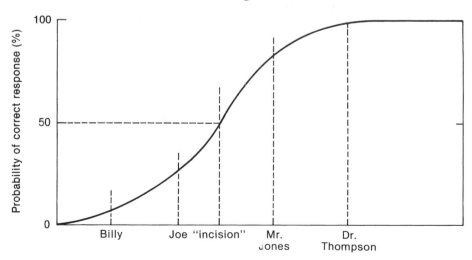

difficulty range from *prologue* to *tenet* in order to locate Dr. Thompson's ability with any precision, because these words are sufficiently difficult that she would not get all of them correct.

The trace line of an item is a characteristic of the item that does not depend on the people taking the test, but our ability to reveal the entire curve depends on applying the item to a sufficiently heterogeneous group that people over the full range of ability are represented. If we gave items like *incision* only to people like Joe and Mr. Jones, we could only see that part of the curve that falls between them. Because this range covers the difficulty level of the item, the result would not be too serious, but if only people like Billy or like Dr. Thompson were included, we would be able to tell very little about the item.

Each item has its own characteristic curve that is defined by its difficulty level (the 50% point) and its discrimination. Discrimination was discussed in Chapter 15, but here it takes on a slightly different meaning. The ability of an item to allow for discrimination of different levels of ability is a function of the rate at which the probability of getting the item correct changes with ability. Graphically, this rate of change can be seen as the slope of the item-characteristic curve. Figure 16.3 shows curves representing two items that differ in difficulty but are equal in discrimination. The shapes of the two curves are the same, but their difficulties, the ability levels required to have a 50% chance of getting the item correct, are different.

Figure 16.4 shows two items that are of the same difficulty but differ in discrimination. The slope, or rate of change in the probability of getting the item correct, is much steeper for Item 1 than for Item 2. More discriminating items are more sensitive to differences in the ability levels of examinees.

Figure 16.3
Item characteristic curves for items that differ in difficulty.

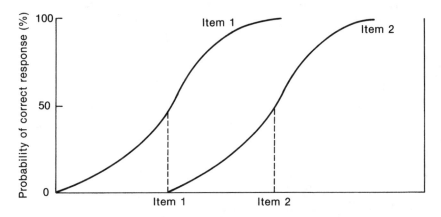

Two items of equal discrimination that differ in difficulty

Figure 16.4
Item characteristic curves for two items of equal difficulty but differing in discrimination.

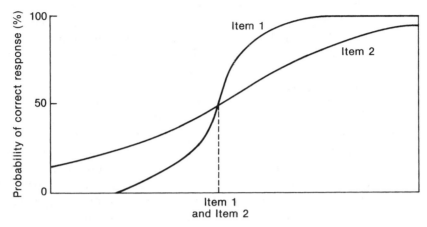

Two items of equal difficulty that differ in discrimination

For items of the multiple-choice or selected response variety, the curve has a third feature, the probability of getting the item correct by chance, or guessing. This effect is seen when the curve flattens out at some probability greater than zero. Figure 16.5 provides an example of such a curve. This is different from the situation for Item 2 in Figure 16.4. In the latter case, although the graph does not go down far enough for the trace line to reach zero, the curve is still descending. If people of extremely low ability had been included in the sample, we should find an ability level where examinees have zero chance of getting the item correct. Item trace lines for produce-response items can always reach zero; those for select response items never can.

If we have determined the difficulty values on a common scale for a sufficient pool of items, we can use items from that pool to do a number of useful and interesting things. We outline some of them here.

1. *Estimating ability level from any set of items.* If the difficulty scale values are available for a large pool of items measuring a common trait, an unbiased estimate

Figure 16.5
Effect of guessing on the item-characteristic curve.

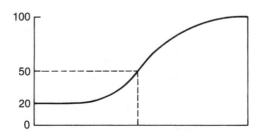

(unbiased in a statistical sense, not in the social policy sense discussed in Chapter 14) of a person's ability level on that trait can be obtained from *any* set of items drawn from that pool. The precision of the estimate will depend on the number of items, increasing in precision as the number increases. It will also depend on how closely the difficulty of the items matches the ability level of the person, with accuracy increasing with the closeness of the match. But there will be no systematic error in the estimate in any case, assuming the probability of a correct response is not zero (chance level for selected response items) or 1.0. In these two cases, the item gives no information about the person's ability.

2. *Preparing equivalent test forms.* By drawing from the pool sets of items having the same average difficulty value, the same spread of difficulty values, and the same average discrimination, we can prepare test forms that are equivalent in the sense that any given raw score signifies the same level of examinee ability, irrespective of the test form on which it is based. We could use the test forms to measure gains from instruction, giving one form before some instructional period, and another after. Or, in situations in which test security or pupil copying is likely to be a problem, different forms could be given to pupils in alternating seats. If, for some reason, one test were invalidated for a person, an alternate, equivalent form could be administered.

3. *Matrix sampling in testing.* At times, a researcher may wish to very completely cover some domain of content and may not be interested in making decisions about specific pupils but, instead, in assessing the performance level of a class, a school, or a school system. It is then not necessary that every test item be administered to every person. Each person can be given a fraction of the items, as long as each item has been given to some of the people. The investigator can then think of the class or school or school system as a composite "person." Upon determining the proportion of items passed at known difficulty scale values, the researcher can estimate an ability level for the group, either with respect to the complete domain or with respect to specific limited segments of that domain. This approach makes it possible to hold testing time within reasonable limits and yet to cover completely the domain of content in which the investigator is interested.

Computer-Adaptive Testing

The rapid development and widespread availability of computers has combined with item response theory and the Bayesian approach to probability to lead to the development of computer-adaptive testing. By adaptive testing, we mean the rapid adjustment of the difficulty level of the test tasks to the ability level of the person being tested. As we indicated earlier, tasks that are much too difficult or much too easy give little new information about the ability level of an examinee. For example, our knowing that an examinee who is an applicant for college admission knew the meaning of the word *dig* would tell us essentially nothing about whether the applicant was a promising candidate. Dig is a word that *any* high school senior could be expected to know. We would also learn relatively little if the examinee failed on *fracedinous.* Probably not one high school senior in 100,000 would know the meaning of the word. (*Webster's Unabridged Dictionary* defines it as "producing heat by putrefaction [obsolete].") We gain useful information by testing with tasks on which we *do not* know in advance whether the examinee will succeed.

Ideally, in adaptive testing, we start at a difficulty level at which we are *most uncertain* whether the examinee can pass the item. This point would usually be at an item of about 50% difficulty for that age or grade group, because in the absence of any special information, this is our best prior probability of the person's ability level. Each correct item raises the posterior estimate of the person's ability level somewhat and makes it appropriate to present next a somewhat more difficult item. As long as the examinee continues to get items correct, we continue to raise our estimate of the ability level and to raise the difficulty level of the next item presented. If our prior information was accurate, and thus our starting level was close to the examinee's ability level, the examinee should quickly get an item incorrect, and we would lower our posterior estimate slightly and drop back to a slightly easier item. With a sequence of passes and failures, we would soon zero in with items near the examinee's ability level, and the record of passes and failures would give a good final estimate of this ability.

Any given level of precision in the estimate can be achieved by well-designed adaptive testing, using perhaps half as many test items as would be required in a conventional test designed for use with a complete age or grade group. This is because in conventional tests, in order to include items that are appropriate for people of differing abilities, it is necessary to include items that are too easy or too hard for a given examinee.

A truly effective procedure for adaptive testing must entail searching the pool of items and finding one that is of appropriate difficulty, given the current estimate of the examinee's ability level. This searching is something that only a computer can do efficiently. The complete pool of items can be stored on a disk in the computer memory, coded by difficulty level and, if need be, by discrimination level and content category. The computer can be programmed to adjust its estimate of the examinee's ability level by an appropriate amount after each pass or failure and to seek out the yet unused item that best matches that new estimate. An ongoing record is maintained of the examinee's estimated ability level and of the precision of that estimate. The computer can be programmed to terminate testing either after a specified number of items has been administered or when a specified precision of estimate has been reached.

One feature of adaptive testing is that within any given group, no two individuals are likely to take exactly the same test, because each unique pattern of right and wrong answers produces a different test. A person with very consistent performance would take a short test because the process would focus in on the ability level quite quickly. On the other hand, a person showing variable performance, that is, passing some quite hard items while missing some relatively easy ones, would require a much longer test for the same level of precision in the ability estimate.

Early developmental work on adaptive testing was conducted for organizations such as the U.S. Navy and the U.S. Civil Service Commission with the expectation that testing would be carried out at local terminals connected to a massive mainframe computer. However, this type of adaptive testing is now well within the capability of the better microcomputers that are becoming widely available in local school systems. Where testing time is at a premium, as when it is important to assess several different aspects of a person's ability, the possibility of using a shorter test without losing precision can be very attractive. Organizations such as the College Board are now making computer adaptive tests in various subjects available for college placement, and it seems highly likely that publishers of curricular materials for use in the public schools will soon follow suit.

Two-Stage Testing.   A rougher approximation to fully adaptive testing can be achieved by what may be called two-stage testing. In this procedure, a short test is given, probably one that takes no more than 10 minutes. This test is scored, and on the basis of the score, the examinee is routed to one of two, three, or possibly more levels for the main testing. Those examinees with the highest scores on the short test are routed to the most difficult form of the main test; those in the middle range, to the test of average difficulty; and those with lowest scores, to the easiest form. Such a procedure would be useful if you were working with a heterogeneous group about whom you knew very little in advance, such as, for example, a group of refugees from Southeast Asia or a miscellaneous group of job applicants. The intent to make the test as appropriate as possible to the persons being tested was the basis of our suggestion in Chapter 9 that where different levels of the test are available, more advanced students be given the harder form of the test and less advanced students, the easier form.

One of the interesting potential applications of item response theory and adaptive testing is the linking of grading procedures between classes or sections of a course. One of the motivating forces that led to the creation of standardized tests such as the Scholastic Aptitude Test was the desire for comparable information for students from different schools. If some items that had been calibrated by item response methods were included in locally developed tests in different schools or in different sections of a course where, for example, ability grouping had been used, the tests could be equated and the relative performance of pupils in different classes assessed on a common scale. The different levels of the Cognitive Abilities Test use item response theory to achieve a common scale, called a universal scale score, for the different levels of the test. The American College Testing Program also uses the theory to create a common scale for several different tests that have no items in common but have been given to a common group of examinees.

As computers become generally available, we can anticipate development of a wide range of tests in one or another of the adaptive formats. The development is likely to proceed slowly at first because both users and regulating bodies (courts, legislatures, and the like) must be persuaded of the essential soundness of the procedures, but we anticipate that these developments will be one of the major changes in testing during the coming years.

META-ANALYSIS AND VALIDITY GENERALIZATION

In psychology and education, studies are often carried out with rather small samples of cases, and, partly as a consequence of this fact, different studies have often given quite inconsistent results. In the past two decades, researchers have sought better ways of distilling an essence of truth from a mass of seemingly contradictory results. The term *meta-analysis* was coined (Glass, 1977) to apply to the systematic pooling and integration of results from many different studies of the same phenomenon.

A specific example of meta-analysis is the integration of test validity data for different groups and from different sources. As soon as ability tests became available, researchers started to collect data on the validity of those tests for both educational and vocational criteria. Validity coefficients were found, for any given test or type of test, to vary rather substantially for the same school subject or for what appeared to be the same job. For example, the validity coefficients for English grades on the verbal reasoning test of the Differential Aptitude Tests (DAT) ranged, in different groups, from .07 to .76.

People came to accept the doctrine, especially in relation to vocational prediction, that validity must be established in each specific location. However, more recently, Frank Schmidt and his associates (Schmidt, 1988a, 1988b; Schmidt & Hunter, 1981, 1992; Schmidt, Hunter, Pearlman, & Hirsh, 1985) have demonstrated that much of the variation in results from one study to another can be attributed to a variety of statistical artifacts—sampling error in small samples, criterion unreliability, or differing degrees of restriction in the range of ability in the sample studied. They propose that meta-analysis be applied to the accumulated data, thus pooling results from separate studies and arriving at an average value that may be taken as a generally applicable estimate of test validity, one that is closer to the "true" value than the value obtained from a local sample, usually of quite modest size. Thus, unless the English program in School System X is *radically* different from the program in most schools, the median validity coefficient of .49, based on pooling the results from many schools, will probably be a more appropriate value for School System X to use in thinking about the validity of the verbal reasoning test of DAT for predicting English grades than will be the value obtained from a limited local study. To this application of meta-analysis, Schmidt and Hunter have attached the name *validity generalization.*

The procedures for meta-analysis and validity generalization are still controversial (see Landy, Shankster, & Kohler, 1994, for a critical review), but the methods are being applied to an increasingly wide variety of topics in education and occupational psychology. We may anticipate that the next 10 or 20 years will see a more systematic synthesis of the validation research that has accumulated over the past 50 years, leading to stable generalized estimates of test-criterion relationships. We may hope that these relationships will be accepted by the Equal Employment Opportunity Commission, other government agencies, and the courts as superior replacements for local studies from necessarily small samples and that objective testing procedures will again become a practical procedure for appraising job applicants.

FACTOR ANALYSIS

Since its introduction by Charles Spearman in 1904, factor analysis has grown to be one of the most widely used data-analytic procedures in education and psychology. A reader of the school or clinical psychology literature is certain to encounter articles that apply factor analysis. Most test manuals and many studies of test validity report factor analyses either of the items that make up the test or of the test in combination with other tests. For these reasons, it is important that a would-be user of tests have at least familiarity with both the vocabulary and purposes of factor analysis.

Spearman introduced factor analysis as part of his theory of intelligence. He argued that a single dimension of individual differences, which he called general intelligence, or *g*, underlay performance on measures of cognitive ability and caused these variables to be positively correlated. A person who was above average on *g* would also be above average on tests of mental abilities, while those who were below average on *g* would occupy the below average places in the distribution of test scores, thus causing all tests of such abilities to be positively correlated. Mathematical developments by Truman Kelley, L. L. Thurstone, and others from the 1920s through the 1940s produced the sophisticated set of procedures that are now incorporated in all the major statistical packages, under the heading of factor analysis.

At its most fundamental level, factor analysis is nothing more than a way to search out the order in the correlations among a set of variables. Suppose, for example, that we have four variables, two tests of vocabulary (call them V_1 and V_2) and two of mathematics computation (M_1 and M_2). Suppose also that we find correlations among these tests as shown in Table 16.1. The correlations arranged in this way produce what is called a *correlation matrix*. The values are the correlations of each row variable with each column variable. Thus, the correlation between the two vocabulary tests is +.77, while that between the first vocabulary test and the first mathematics test is +.36. The values of 1.00 in the diagonal of the matrix merely show that each test correlates perfectly with itself.

If we study the pattern of correlation values, we see, as we should expect, that the two tests of the same function correlate more highly with each other than they do with the tests of the other function. In an example as simple as this one, the pattern jumps out at us and we hardly need factor analysis to see it, but we will carry through with this example to illustrate the parts of the analysis. In more complex problems, such as the example with which we close this chapter, the analysis is more revealing.

Factor analysis involves some very complex mathematics, but fortunately all that can be left to the computer. What we see when the computer is done is a set of correlations between the observed variables, our four tests, and the underlying latent variables, the factors. The printout (or computer screen) would contain information

Table 16.1
Matrix of Correlations Between 2 Vocabulary Tests and 2 Mathematics Tests

	V_1	V_2	M_1	M_2
V_1	1.00	.77	.36	.41
V_2	.77	1.00	.33	.39
M_1	.36	.33	1.00	.81
M_2	.41	.39	.81	1.00

Table 16.2
Factor-Loading Matrix

	Factor 1	Factor 2	Communality
V_1	.79	.50	.88
V_2	.78	.53	.89
M_1	.79	−.54	.91
M_2	.82	−.47	.90
Variance	2.54	1.05	

like that shown in Table 16.2.[1] The values in the body of the table are called *factor loadings.* They are the correlations of the four observed variables with the two factors. The values in the last column, the *communalities,* are the sums of squares of the loadings in each row, for example,

$$.79^2 + .50^2 = .88$$

The communalities show how much of each variable's variance is explained by the set of factors. The values at the bottom of the table are the *factor variances.* They are the sums of squares of the columns, for example,

$$.79^2 + .78^2 + .79^2 + .82^2 = 2.54$$

and show how much of the variance of the set of variables is explained by each factor.

These results show that all four variables correlate quite highly with the first factor and that the vocabulary tests correlate positively with the second factor, while the mathematics computation tests correlate negatively with it. This is a very common pattern for the initial results of a factor analysis to take, and it is what led Spearman to postulate a general factor of intelligence.

To other investigators of tests, however, particularly L. L. Thurstone, factors like the second one did not seem to make psychological sense. Thurstone argued that a proper factor solution should make good scientific sense and should exhibit a property he called *simple structure.* He believed in scientific parsimony—that our observations could be explained by a relatively small number of relatively simple constructs—and he felt that it should be possible to explain each observed variable in terms of one or two underlying factors. This principle he called simple structure. In the finally developed concept (Thurstone, 1947), a set of factors obtained from a group of variables showed simple structure if each variable had high loadings on one or two factors and near zero loadings on all others. Also, each factor should

[1] There are several types of factor analysis, each with certain strengths and weaknesses. In this example we are using the procedure known as principal components analysis because of its relative simplicity. If you wish to learn more about factor analysis, you should read Comrey (1992) or Gorsuch and Harlow (1997).

contribute to a relatively small number of variables. (Thurstone had other criteria as well, but these are sufficient for our purpose.)

Graphic Presentation and Factor Rotation

It is said that a picture is worth a thousand words. This can be very true in understanding factor analysis and the concept of simple structure. For example, it is possible to depict the correlation between two variables as the angle between two lines, where the lines represent the variables. The formal relationship is that the correlation between two variables is equal to the cosine of the angle between them. The cosine (or cos as it may appear on the keyboard of your calculator) is a trigonometric function which equals 0.00 for an angle of 90°, .707 for an angle of 45°, and 1.00 for an angle of 0°, as shown in Figure 16.6.

Figure 16.6
Relationship between the cosine of an angle and the correlation coefficient.

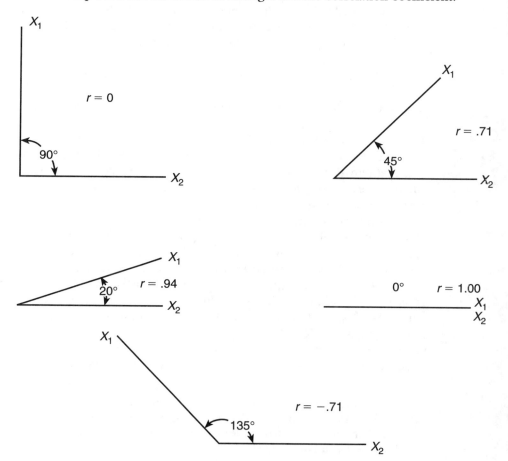

The relationships in this figure correspond reasonably well to mental images we might have of what a correlation means. Two variables that correlate perfectly ($r = 1.00$) can be thought of as being identical, and an angle of zero means that the lines representing them coincide. Two variables with zero correlation are completely independent or unrelated, and a right angle seems to represent this independence quite well. Of course, intermediate values of the correlation produce intermediate angles, with smaller angles implying larger correlations. To make our picture complete, negative correlations and their negative cosine values are associated with angles greater than 90 degrees, which again makes sense because lines that go in opposite directions imply variables that contrast with each other. The bottom illustration in Figure 16.6, an angle of 135° (45° more than 90°), corresponds to a correlation $-.71$

Thurstone used these geometric relationships to produce graphical representations of his factor analyses. If we let the factors represent the axes of a graph, as shown in Figure 16.7, we can plot each variable as a line in the graph going from the

Figure 16.7
Plot of four variables on two factors from Table 16.2.

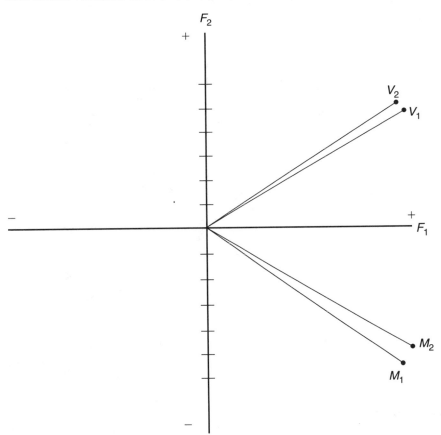

origin to a point that has as its coordinates the loadings of the variable on the factors. When this process is complete for the loadings in Table 16.2, we get the results in the figure. For example, the line representing V_1 has the coordinates +.79 and +.50. Figure 16.7 shows quite clearly what our intuition told us would happen and what we found in the table of factor loadings; there are two groupings of variables, one of vocabulary tests and another of mathematics tests. Each pair of variables forms a tight cluster that is quite far removed from the other.

Rotation.   After he plotted the factors and variables as we have done, Thurstone realized that he could move the factors without changing the variables and that by doing so he could make each factor correspond quite closely to one of the groupings of variables. He called the process *rotation* because it involves holding the variables in place and rotating the factors around the origin. By shifting the factors about 45° (the actual amount is 44.4°) in a clockwise direction, the structures are made much simpler, as is shown in Figure 16.8. The new factor loadings, shown in Table 16.3, reveal that each test now has a high loading on one factor and a small positive loading

Figure 16.8
Plot of four variables on two rotated factors.

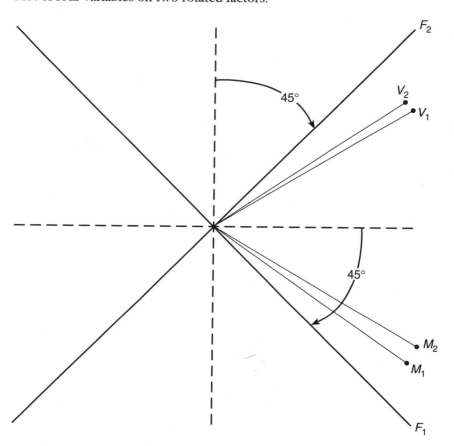

Table 16.3
Factor-Loading Matrix—Orthogonal Rotation

	Factor 1	Factor 2	Communality
V_1	.22	.91	.88
V_2	.18	.92	.89
M_1	.94	.17	.91
M_2	.92	.24	.90
Variance	1.81	1.76	

on the other. The factor variances in the bottom row show that the rotation has equalized the contributions of the two factors.

Analytic Rotation. Early factor analysts actually plotted the factors and variables as we have done, but this procedure was open to the criticism that the amount of rotation was subjective. Therefore, as computers became available in the 1950s, factor analysts sought ways to make the rotation process mathematically rigorous. Several proposals were offered, but the one that has gained the widest acceptance, largely because it generally gives the best simple structure, is known as Varimax (Kaiser, 1958). Varimax is so universally applied that it is the default method on most computer programs. If you do a factor analysis and do not specify some other method, this is the one you will get. The results in Table 16.3 actually were obtained by Varimax. It is an artifact of the data in our example that the graphic rotation of 45° corresponded so closely to the Varimax value of 44.4°.

Orthogonal and Oblique Rotation. The two rotations we have examined so far, our graphic solution and the Varimax one, are both examples of what is known as *orthogonal rotation.* What this means is that the factors are maintained rigidly at 90° to each other during the rotation process. Orthogonal means "at right angles" or "uncorrelated." Both factors are rotated by exactly the same amount.

Orthogonal rotation has the advantage that it is fairly simple to do and to understand, but as scientists we must question whether it does a good job of representing reality. If the factors assume the role of scientific constructs (such as intelligence) that are viewed as playing a causal role in determining people's scores on the observed variables (this is what Spearman, for example, believed), then we must ask whether it is reasonable to assume that these constructs are uncorrelated in nature. In our example we have found one factor that we might consider to correspond to the construct "verbal ability" or, more narrowly, "word knowledge," and another that we might call "mathematical ability," or "computational facility." But, the vocabulary tests have positive correlations with the mathematics tests. How could this happen? Two alternatives present themselves: Either the mathematics tests require verbal ability (a possibility) and the vocabulary tests require mathematical ability (highly unlikely), or the underlying abilities are themselves correlated. It is this latter possibility that Thurstone considered when he proposed that factors could be rotated to positions where they were correlated, that is, where they were no longer at right angles to each other. He called this procedure *oblique rotation.* In oblique rotation each factor is rotated independently to a position that produces simple structure and a meaningful solution. (A third possibility is that both types of tests also measure test-taking skills and that it is this third factor that causes the apparent correlation between what are two uncorrelated abilities. Identifying this factor would necessitate including measures of test-taking skills in the analysis, along with the four primary tests.)

Just as there are several alternative computer-driven orthogonal rotation procedures, there are alternative ways to carry out an oblique rotation. One popular method, known as Direct Oblimin, yielded the results shown in Table 16.4 and Figure 16.9. In this analysis Factor 1 was rotated about 32° to a position at the center of the mathematics tests and Factor 2 was rotated about 56° to a similar position with respect to the vocabulary tests. The values in Table 16.4 show that each test is related to only one factor (coefficients below 0.10 are generally considered negligible) and the factors have a correlation of +.41. That is, this analysis suggests that each

Figure 16.9
Plot of four variables on two factors rotated by Direct Oblimin to oblique simple structure.

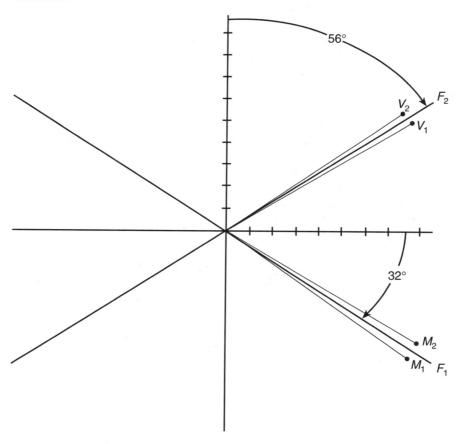

Table 16.4
Factor-Loading Matrix—Oblique Rotation

	Factor 1	Factor 2
V_1	.02	.93
V_2	−.02	.95
M_1	.97	−.04
M_2	.93	.04

factor contributes to only one type of test and that the underlying abilities are moderately correlated. A result such as this may correspond more closely to scientific reality than does the orthogonal one.

One of the drawbacks of oblique rotation is that it is somewhat more complicated than the orthogonal variety. Part of the complication arises from the fact that when the factors are correlated, the contributions to the variables cannot be viewed as equivalent to correlations. Therefore, the sums of squares of the row entries in Table 16.4 no longer give the communalities, and the sums of squares down the columns do not give the factor variances. The entries in the table, properly called *pattern coefficients,* represent the direct influence of each factor on each variable, but because the factors are correlated, they also exert indirect influences through the other factors. If you wish to pursue this topic in more detail, you should consult Comrey (1992), Gorsuch and Harlow (1997) or Loehlin (1992).

A Real Example

The example we have considered so far was concocted to illustrate the basic features of factor analysis in a simple way. Any problem of scientific interest will involve at least 10 to 20 variables, maybe many more. For mathematical reasons that need not concern us, each factor must have at least three variables that have substantial loadings on it in order to yield a defined solution. We will use a factor analysis of the Stanford-Binet—Fourth Edition standardization data, which involves 15 variables and four factors, to illustrate the kinds of results that you might encounter in a study in the education or psychology literature. This example is adapted from a paper written several years ago (R. M. Thorndike, 1990b).

The first question you must ask after you have selected a set of variables to investigate is how many factors to look for. There are several ways to answer this question, and these are reviewed in detail by Comrey (1992) and Gorsuch and Harlow (1997), but the way we will choose to answer the question is to ask how many factors we would expect on the basis of the theory that gave rise to the test; that is, we will use our factor analysis to determine whether the data collected during the standardization of the Stanford-Binet produce results that are consistent with the theory that was used in test development, a theory that calls for four factors (see Chapter 8). A positive outcome from this analysis lends support to the test authors' claims for construct validity of the test.

Once we have decided on four factors, we must choose a method of factor analysis. There are several alternatives, each of which is described in detail by Comrey (1992) and by Gorsuch and Harlow (1997). We will use the method that is called Principal Axis Factor Analysis, or PAF, in the SPSS statistical system. Other methods give essentially comparable results, and if this were not the case, we should worry that our factors might be artifacts of the method we used. The PAF method is similar to the Principal Components method we used in our earlier 4-variable example. The only difference is that the 1.00s in the diagonal of the correlation matrix are replaced by estimates of the communalities. This is very common practice in performing factor analyses because the analysis then is performed only on the variance that is contributed by the factors.

The correlation matrix that we submit for analysis is shown in Table 16.5 (only the lower half of the matrix is shown because the upper half is a mirror image of the lower half). The computer will substitute communalities for the 1.00s that are in the input correlation matrix. The lines mark off groups of tests that are assumed to measure the same underlying factor of ability.

An examination of the correlation matrix does not make the structure of these data at all obvious. The only feature that is clear is that all the correlations are positive, which is what we would expect of tests of cognitive abilities. There is also some tendency for the tests of a given factor to have higher correlations with other tests of the same factor, but the case is not nearly so clear as it was in our simple example.

The results of the initial factor analysis are shown in Table 16.6. Once again, all of the tests have substantial positive loadings on the first factor and the other factors present no clear picture of a structure to the data. In most reports of research, this table would not even be presented because rotation is so universal that no one tries to interpret unrotated factors.

We present a Varimax rotation of the factors in Table 16.7. Although a meaningful structure does not leap out of the table, we can get a clearer picture if we attend only to those loadings that are greater than .30. It is common practice in reporting Varimax rotations to delete all loadings less than .30 because they are considered too small to be meaningful, but we have chosen to present the larger loadings in boldface so you can see that many of the loadings produced by Varimax are in the range .20 to .30, which may not be trivial. The first factor has high loadings for the Verbal Reasoning tests plus Memory for Sentences and, to a lesser extent, Quantitative. The second factor includes the Abstract/Visual Reasoning tests plus Absurdities, Quantitative, Number Series, and Bead Memory. The third factor represents the Quantitative Reasoning tests, Paper Folding and Cutting, Matrices, and some of the Verbal Relations test. Finally, the last factor accounts for the Short Term Memory tests with small additional loadings by Quantitative and Number Series. Notice that the factors are roughly equal in size as shown by their variances.

Finally, Table 16.8 shows the Direct Oblimin pattern coefficients from an oblique rotation. Once again, we have retained small coefficients that probably would be omitted from most published reports and have used bold-face for those values above .30. The pattern is quite a bit clearer now. The first factor includes only the four Verbal Reasoning tests and Memory for Sentences (which we might expect to load on this factor because it includes verbal material). The second factor has high

Table 16.5
Correlations Among Subtests of the Stanford-Binet

	Voc	Com	Abs	VR	Pat	Cop	Mat	PF	Qua	NS	EqB	BM	MS	MD	MO
Vocabulary	1.00														
Comprehension	.73	1.00													
Absurdities	.62	.59	1.00												
Verbal Relations	.71	.63	.43	1.00											
Pattern Analysis	.47	.47	.51	.42	1.00										
Copying	.44	.41	.44	.38	.50	1.00									
Matrices	.57	.50	.50	.47	.55	.41	1.00								
Paper Folding and Cutting	.49	.47	.43	.50	.60	.45	.55	1.00							
Quantitative	.59	.57	.47	.56	.52	.45	.58	.57	1.00						
Number Series	.57	.56	.51	.46	.55	.43	.66	.61	.67	1.00					
Equation Building	.47	.42	.30	.48	.42	.28	.53	.53	.61	.64	1.00				
Bead Memory	.51	.47	.47	.41	.51	.46	.52	.49	.52	.54	.41	1.00			
Memory for Sentences	.64	.58	.46	.51	.40	.40	.44	.35	.52	.48	.38	.47	1.00		
Memory for Digits	.45	.42	.34	.36	.35	.33	.44	.37	.48	.52	.40	.44	.56	1.00	
Memory for Objects	.40	.38	.33	.32	.36	.34	.40	.29	.40	.43	.30	.44	.42	.44	1.00

Table 16.6

Initial Factor Matrix for the Stanford-Binet

	Factor				
	1	2	3	4	Communality
Vocabulary	.82	−.36	−.01	−.19	.84
Comprehension	.76	−.28	−.04	−.13	.67
Absurdities	.67	−.16	−.25	.04	.54
Verbal Relations	.70	−.20	.02	−.29	.62
Pattern Analysis	.69	.19	−.31	.09	.62
Copying	.59	.01	−.27	.16	.42
Matrices	.74	.16	−.02	.01	.57
Paper Folding and Cutting	.70	.28	−.16	−.11	.61
Quantitative	.78	.12	.10	−.07	.64
Number Series	.80	.25	.09	.01	.71
Equation Building	.66	.33	.28	−.26	.69
Bead Memory	.68	.06	−.07	.20	.51
Memory for Sentences	.69	−.30	.17	.15	.63
Memory for Digits	.61	−.03	.31	.29	.56
Memory for Objects	.53	−.04	.10	.27	.37
Variance	7.34	.70	.48	.48	

Table 16.7

Varimax-Rotated Factor Matrix for the Stanford-Binet

	Factor				
	1	2	3	4	Communality
Vocabulary	**.78**	.29	.25	.29	.84
Comprehension	**.67**	**.32**	.23	.28	.67
Absurdities	**.46**	**.51**	.10	.23	.54
Verbal Relations	**.65**	.21	**.35**	.16	.62
Pattern Analysis	.21	**.67**	.30	.18	.62
Copying	.24	**.53**	.13	.25	42
Matrices	.29	**.45**	**.45**	.30	57
Paper Folding and Cutting	.24	**.53**	**.51**	.10	.61
Quantitative	**.36**	.35	**.53**	**.33**	.64
Number Series	.24	**.42**	**.58**	**.37**	.71
Equation Building	.22	.15	**.76**	.21	.69
Bead Memory	.24	**.48**	.25	**.40**	.51
Memory for Sentences	**.49**	.19	.15	**.57**	.63
Memory for Digits	.19	.16	.27	**.65**	.56
Memory for Objects	.18	.28	.15	**.49**	.37
Variance	2.53	2.40	2.18	1.88	

Table 16.8
Pattern Coefficients for Matrix of Median Correlations
for All Samples

Test	Factor			
	1	2	3	4
Vocabulary	**.86**	.03	.06	.00
Comprehension	**.70**	.11	.07	−.00
Absurdities	**.40**	**.45**	.03	−.03
Verbal Relations	**.74**	−.01	−.07	.18
Pattern Analysis	.00	**.74**	.00	.08
Copying	.09	**.54**	.13	−.08
Matrices	.12	**.39**	.16	.27
Paper Folding and Cutting	.09	**.55**	.09	**.35**
Quantitative	.25	.21	.20	**.37**
Number Series	.05	**.33**	.26	**.42**
Equation Building	.13	.01	.11	**.71**
Bead Memory	.04	**.44**	**.31**	.05
Memory for Sentences	**.44**	−.07	**.52**	−.06
Memory for Digits	.01	−.02	**.70**	.13
Memory for Objects	.00	.18	**.50**	.00

	Matrix of Factor Correlations			
Factor 1	1.00			
Factor 2	.64	1.00		
Factor 3	.55	.60	1.00	
Factor 4	.44	.41	.35	1.00

coefficients for the four Abstract/Visual Reasoning tests, Absurdities, Number Series, and Bead Memory. When we consider the content of the Absurdities and Bead Memory tests, there is good reason to expect that they might involve visual abilities because both contain visual material. The task in Absurdities is to detect what is wrong with a picture, and Bead Memory requires holding visual sequences in short-term memory. The only nonobvious loading is the one for Number Series, and even this is a visual sequencing task. The third factor is composed entirely of the Short-Term memory tests, although Number Series is threatening to get into the act. Finally, the three Quantitative Reasoning tests define the fourth factor, although Paper Folding and Cutting and Matrices also show up here.

The results in Table 16.8 provide an example of a reasonably good oblique simple structure. They also give evidence supporting the construct validity of the Stanford-Binet as it was conceived by its authors. The factors that we should expect on the basis of the theory that motivated this form of the test did actually appear, although perhaps not as cleanly as the authors would have wished. Each test is defined by one or two factors, and each factor contributes to a relatively small number of tests. Several of the exceptions seem quite reasonable, from what we know of the tasks the tests present. The one problem test is Quantitative. It seems to load about equally on all the factors, which may mean that this test more nearly measures what is common to the whole battery than does any other test.

At the bottom of the table is a section labeled Matrix of Factor Correlations. This table shows that the factors all correlate moderately with each other, a fact that we would expect from the moderate positive correlations among all the tests, as shown in Table 16.5. These correlations also give support for the practice of combining the four Stanford-Binet area scores into a single composite that is claimed to provide an index of general cognitive ability.

Exploration and Confirmation

The example that we have just considered illustrates the use of factor analysis to test the Stanford-Binet as a measure of a set of theoretical constructs. That is, we entered the analysis with some clear expectations of what we would find and the fact that we found more or less what we expected is support for the claim that the theory underlying the test is a reasonable representation of human behavior. It also supports the claim that the test is a measure of those theoretical constructs. The use of factor analysis in this way is called *confirmatory factor analysis.* Many studies that use factor analysis begin with a much less well structured idea of what will be found. It is not uncommon for authors to have no clear notion of the structure in a set of data. They are using factor analysis to explore the data and to try to find a structure that makes sense. We could almost say that they are using factor analysis for theory generation rather than theory testing. Analyses of this kind are called *exploratory factor analyses.*

These are quite different philosophical approaches, and an exploration of their implications would require that we undertake another book. A discussion of the use of factor analysis for data exploration versus theory confirmation is provided by Nunnally and Bernstein (1994). Our purpose here is to give you a working vocabulary and conceptual foundation that will allow you to read factor-analytic studies with a critical and understanding eye.

SUMMARY

In Chapter 1, we suggested that the pace of development in psychological and educational measurement has been uneven. In the first third of the 20th century, there was rapid progress in the development of new measurement instruments and techniques. Most features of human behavior were exposed to tests, and there was great enthusiasm for testing as a key to the social millennium.

By contrast, the middle third of this century was a period of relative stagnation. Few real advances were made in either techniques or instruments, and some of the innovations of the period, such as ability batteries, have generally failed to live up to their original promise.

As this chapter suggests, the last third of this century seems to have been a period of renewed activity and achievement in testing, coupled with greater sensitivity by test developers and users to the impact that tests can have. It is probably impossible to eliminate all bias in all test items, but both concern about the problem of bias in tests and the development of techniques of item response theory should help to minimize its impact. There is now a much more sophisticated view of tests and of the cognitive processes that underlie test behavior. Computers are making possible new kinds of testing and the rapid interpretation and reporting of test results. And factor analysis is being used to generate theories and to test them against data. The trends seem decidedly positive, and we may look forward to more progress in the coming decades.

SUGGESTED READINGS

Baker, F. B. (1985). *The basics of item response theory.* Portsmouth, NH: Heinemann.

Baker, F. B. (1989). Computer technology in test construction and processing. In R. L. Linn (Ed.), *Educational measurement* (3rd ed., pp. 409–428). New York: Macmillan.

Bunderson, C. V., Inouye, D. K., & Olsen, J. B. (1989). Four generations of computerized educational measurement. In R. L. Linn (Ed.), *Educational measurement* (3rd ed., pp. 367–408). New York: Macmillan.

Cook, L. L., & Eignor, D. R. (1983). Practical considerations regarding the use of item response theory to equate tests. In R. K. Hambleton (Ed.), *Applications of item response theory* (pp. 175–195). Vancouver: Educational Research Institute of British Columbia.

Green, B. F. (1988). Critical problems in computer-based psychological measurement. *Measurement in Education, 1,* 223–231.

Green, B. F., Bock, R. D., Humphreys, L. G., Linn, R. L., & Reckase, M. D. (1984). Technical guidelines for assessing computerized adaptive tests. *Journal of Educational Measurement, 21,* 347–360.

Hambleton, R. K. (1989). Principles and selected applications of item response theory. In R. L. Linn (Ed.), *Educational measurement* (3rd ed., pp. 147–200). New York: Macmillan.

Hedges, L. V., & Olkin, I. (1985). *Statistical methods for meta-analysis.* New York: Academic Press

Page, E. B. (1994). Computer grading of student prose, using modern concepts and software. *Journal of Experimental Education, 62,* 127–142.

Page, E. B., & Petersen, N. S. (1995). The computer moves into essay grading: Updating the ancient test. *Phi Delta Kappan, 76,* 561–565.

Ronning, R. R., Glover, J. A., & Conoley, J. C. (1987). The influence of cognitive psychology on psychological testing. Hillsdale, NJ: Erlbaum.

Skaggs, G., & Lissitz, R. W. (1986). IRT test equating: Relevant issues and a review of recent research. *Review of Educational Research, 56,* 495–529.

Wresch, W. (1993). The imminence of grading essays by computer—25 years later. *Computers and Composition, 10,* 45–58.

Wright, B. D., & Bell, S. R. (1984). Item banks: What, why, how. *Journal of Educational Measurement, 21,* 331–345.

References

Aamodt, M. G., Bryan, D. A., & Whitcomb, A. J. (1993). Predicting performance with letters of recommendation. *Public Personnel Management, 22,* 81–100.

Achenbach, T. M., & Edelbrock, C. (1983). *The child behavior checklist.* Burlington, VT: University of Vermont, Department of Psychiatry.

Adjutant General's Office, Personnel Research Section. (1952). *A study of officer rating methodology, validity and reliability of ratings by single raters and multiple raters* (PRS Report No. 904). Washington, DC: Author.

Adjutant General's Office, Personnel Research Section. (1953). *Survey of the aptitude for service rating system at the U.S. Military Academy, West Point, New York.* Washington, DC: Author.

Allen, W. B. (1988). Rhodes handicapping, or slowing the pace of integration. *Journal of Vocational Behavior, 33,* 365–378.

Allport, G. W. (1937). *Personality: A psychological interpretation.* New York: Holt, Rinehart and Winston.

Allport, G. W. (1955). *Becoming.* New Haven, CT: Yale University Press.

Allport, G. W. & Odbert, H. S. (1936). Trait-names, a psycholexical study. *Psychological Monographs, 47,* (Whole No. 211).

American Association on Mental Retardation. (1992). *Mental retardation: Definition, classification, and systems of supports* (9th ed.). Washington, DC: Author.

American Counseling Association. (1995). *Code of ethics and standards of practice.* Alexandria, VA: Author.

American Educational Research Association, American Psychological Association, & National Council on Measurement in Education. (1985). *Standards for educational and psychological testing.* Washington, DC: American Psychological Association.

American Psychological Association. (1954). *Technical recommendations for psychological tests and diagnostic techniques.* Washington, DC: Author.

American Psychological Association. (1992). *Ethical principles of psychologists and code of conduct.* Washington, DC: Author.

Americans with Disabilities Act, 42 U.S.C.12101 (1990).

Baxter, J. C., Brock, B., Hill, P. C., & Rozelle, R. M. (1981). Letters of recommendation: A question of value. *Journal of Applied Psychology, 66,* 296–301.

Berk, R. A. (1980). A consumer's guide to criterion-referenced test reliability. *Journal of Educational Measurement, 17,* 323–349.

Bersoff, D. N. (1981). Testing and the law. *American Psychologist, 36*(10), 1047–1056.

Birns, B. (1965). Individual differences in human neonates' responses to stimulation. *Child Development, 36,* 249–256.

Bloom, B. S. (Ed.) (1956). *Taxonomy of educational objectives, Handbook I: Cognitive domain.* New York: Longman, Green and Company.

Boswell, J. (1988). *The kindness of strangers: The abondonment of children in western Europe from late antiquity to the Renaissance.* New York: Pantheon.

Boyle, G. J. (1989). Confirmation of the structural dimensionality of the Stanford-Binet Intelligence Scale (Fourth Edition). *Personality and Individual Differences, 10,* 709–715.

Bracken, B. A. (1991). Multidimensional self concept validation: A three instrument investigation. *Journal of Psychoeducational Assessment, 9,* 319–328.

Brennan, R. L. (1984). Estimating the dependability of the scores. In R. A. Berk (Ed.), *A guide to criterion-referenced test construction* (pp. 292–334). Baltimore: Johns Hopkins University Press.

Brodsky, S. L. (1991). *Testifying in court: Guidelines and maxims for the expert witness.* Washington, DC: American Psychological Association.

Brown v. Board of Education of Topeka, Kansas, 347 U.S. 483 (1954).

Brown, V. L., Cronin, M. E., & McEntire, E. (1994). *Test of Mathematical Abilities (2nd ed.).* Austin, TX: PRO-ED.

Bruininks, R. H., Thurlow, M. L., & Gillman, C. J. (1987). Adaptive behavior and mental retardation. *The Journal of Special Education, 21*(1), 69–88.

Bruininks, R. H., Woodcock, R. W., Weatherman, R. F., & Hill, B. K. (1985). *Scales of Independent Behavior.* Chicago: Riverside.

Buhler, R. A. (1953). *Flicker fusion threshold and anxiety level.* Unpublished doctoral dissertation, Columbia University, New York.

Burks, H. F. (1977). *Burks Behavioral Rating Scales: Preschool and Kindergarten Edition.* Los Angeles: Western Psychological Services.

Butcher, J., & Williams, C. L. (1992). *The Minnesota Multiphasic Personality Inventory— Adolescent.* Minneapolis: University of Minnesota Press.

Butcher, J. N. & Williams, C. L. (1992). *Essentials of MMPI-2 and MMPI-A Interpretation.* Minneapolis: University of Minnesota Press.

Campbell, J. P., Dunnette, M. D., Arvey, R. D., & Hellervik, L. V. (1973). The development and evaluation of behaviorally based rating scales. *Journal of Applied Psychology, 57,* 15–22.

Campbell, D. T., & Fiske, D. W. (1959). Convergent and discriminant validation by the multitrait-multimethod matrix. *Psychological Bulletin,56,* 81–105.

Cannell, J. J. (1988). Nationally normed elementary achievement testing in America's public schools: How all 50 states are above the national average. *Educational Measurement: Issues and Practice, 7*(2), 5–9.

Cattell, R. B. (1950). *Personality: A systematic, theoretical, and factual study.* New York: McGraw-Hill.

Civil Rights Act, 42 U.S.C. 2000e *et seq.* (1964).

Cohen, J., & Cohen, P. (1983). *Applied multiple regression for the behavioral sciences* (2nd ed.). Hillsdale, NJ: Erlbaum.

Cole, N. S., & Moss, P. A. (1989). Bias in test use. In R. L. Linn (Ed.), *Educational measurement* (3rd ed., pp. 201–220). New York: Macmillan.

Comprehensive Test of Basic Skills technical bulletin. (1990). Monterey, CA: McGraw-Hill.

Comrey, A. L., & Lee, H. B. (1992). *A first course in factor analysis.* Hillsdale, NJ: Erlbaum.

Connolly, A. J. (1988). *KeyMath-Revised: A diagnostic inventory of essential mathematics.* Circle Pines, MN: American Guidance Services.

Conoley, J. C. & Impara, J. C. (Eds.). (1995). *The twelfth mental measurements yearbook.* Lincoln, NB: Buros Institute of Mental Measurements.

Conoley, J. C., & Kramer, J. J. (1989). *The tenth mental measurements yearbook.* Lincoln, NE: Buros Institute of Mental Measurements.

Conoley, J. C., Kramer, J. J., & Mitchell, J. V., Jr. (Eds.). (1988). *Supplement to the ninth mental measurements yearbook.* Lincoln, NE: Buros Institute of Mental Measurements.

Costa, P. T. & McCrae, R. R. (1992). *Professional Manual: Revised NEO Personality Inventory (NEO PI-R) and NEO Five-Factor Inventory (NEO-FFI).* Odessa FL: Psychological Assessment Resources Inc.

Cronbach, L. J., & Gleser, G. C. (1965). *Psychological tests and personnel decisions.* Champaign: University of Illinois Press.

Dahlstrom, W. G. (1992). Comparability of two-point high-point code patterns from original MMPI norms to MMPI-2 norms for the restandardization sample. *Journal of Personality Assessment, 59,* 153-164.

Dana, R. H. (1990). Cross-cultural and multi-ethnic assessment. In J. N. Butcher & C. D. Spielberger (Eds.), *Recent advances in personality assessment* (vol. 8; pp. 1-26). Hillsdale, NJ: Erlbaum.

Darlington, R. B. (1990). *Regression and linear models.* New York: McGraw-Hill.

Das, J. P., Naglieri, J. A., & Kirby, J. R. (1994). *Asessment of cognitive processes: The PASS theory of intelligence.* Boston: Allyn and Bacon.

Dawes, R. M., Faust, D., & Meehl, P. E. (1989). Clinical versus actuarial judgement. *Science, 243*(4899), 1668-1674.

Debra P. v. Turlington, 78-892 Civ. T-C (M.D. Fla. July 12, 1979) at 2380.

Digman, J. M. (1990). Personality structure: Emergence of the five-factor model. *Annual Review of Psychology, 41,* 417-440.

DuBois, P. H. (1970). *A history of psychological testing.* Boston: Allyn and Bacon.

Duff, F. L. (1965). Item subtlety in personality inventory scales. *Journal of Consulting Psychology, 29,* 565-570.

Dunn, L. M. & Dunn, L. M. (1981). *Peabody Picture Vocabulary Test—Revised: Manual for Forms L and M.* Circle Pines, MN: American Guidance Services.

Ebel, R. L. (1979). *Essentials of educational measurement* (3rd ed.). Englewood Cliffs, NJ: Prentice Hall.

Education of the Handicapped Act Amendments, 20 U.S.C. 1400 (1900).

Educational Testing Service, Test Collection. (1975-1995). *Tests in Microfiche Annotated Bibliography* (Set A-Set U). Princeton, NJ: Author.

Educational Testing Service, Test Collection. (1987). *Directory of selected national testing programs.* Phoenix, AZ: Oryx Press.

Edwards, A. L. (1957). *Techniques of attitude scale construction.* New York: Appleton.

Enright, B. E. (1983). *Enright Diagnostic Inventory of Basic Arithmetic Skills.* North Billerica, MA: Curriculum Associates.

Epstein, S. (1983). Aggregation and beyond: Some basic issues on the prediction of behavior. *Journal of Personality, 51,* 360-392.

Equal Employment Opportunity Commission, U.S. Civil Service Commission, U.S. Department of Labor, & U.S. Department of Justice. (August, 1978). Uniform Guidelines on Employee Selection Procedures. 43 Fed. Reg. 166, 38290-38309. Washington, DC: U.S. Government Printing Office.

Exner, J. E. (1986). *The Rorschach: A comprehensive system: Volume 1. Basic foundations* (2nd ed.). New York: Wiley.

Exner, J. E., & Exner, D. E. (1972). How clinicians use the Rorschach. *Journal of Personality Assessment, 36,* 403-408.

Eysenck, H. J., & Rachman, S. (1965). *The causes and cures of neurosis: An introduction to the modern behavior therapy based on learning theory and principles of conditioning.* San Diego: Knapp.

Fabiano, E. (1989). *Index to tests used in educational dissertations.* Phoenix, AZ: Oryx Press.

Family Educational Rights and Privacy Act, 20 U.S.C. 241 (1974).

Federal Policy for the Protection of Human Subjects: Notices and Rules, 45 C.F.R. 46 (1991).

Feldt, L. S., & Brennan, R. L. (1989). Reliability. In R. L. Linn (Ed.), *Educational measurement* (3rd ed., pp. 105–146). New York: Macmillan.

Feldt, L. S., Forsyth, R. A., Ansley, T. N., & Alnot, S. D. (1993). *Iowa Tests of Educational Development*, Forms K and L. Chicago: Riverside.

Flanders, N. (1970). *Analyzing teacher behavior.* Menlo Park, CA: Addison-Wesley.

Flynn, J. R. (1984). The mean IQ of Americans: Massive gains 1932 to 1978. *Psychological Bulletin, 95,* 29–51.

Foster, S. L., Bell-Dolan, D. J., & Burge, D. A. (1988). Behavioral observation. In A. S. Bellack & M. Hershon (Eds.), *Behavioral assessment: A practical handbook* (pp. 119–160). New York: Pergamon.

Fredericksen, J. R., & Collins, A. (1989). A systems approach to educational testing. *Educational Researcher, 18*(9), 27–32.

Fredericksen, N. (1986). Construct validity and construct similarity: Methods for use in test development and test validation. *Journal of Multivariate Behavioral Research, 21,* 3–28.

Fredericksen, N., Mislevy, R. J., & Bejar, I. I. (1993). *Test theory for a new generation of tests.* Hillsdale, NJ: Erlbaum.

Gallatin, J. (1982). *Abnormal psychology: Concepts, issues, trends.* New York: Macmillan.

Gerbing, D. W. & Tuley, M. R. (1991). The 16PF related to the Five-Factor Model of Personality: Multiple-indicator measurement versus the a priori scales. *Multivariate Behavioral Research, 26,* 271–289.

Gilandas, A., Touyz, S., Beumont, P. J., & Greenberg, H. P. (1984). *Handbook of neuropsychological assessment.* Orlando, FL: Grune & Stratton.

Glass, G. V. (1977). Integrating findings: The meta-analysis of research. *Review of Research in Education, 5,* 351–379.

Golden, C. J., Purisch, A. D., & Hammeke, T. A. (1991). *Luria-Nebraska Neuropsychological Battery* (LNNB). Los Angeles: Western Psychological Services.

Goldman, B. A., & Busch, J. C. (1978). *Directory of unpublished experimental mental measures: Vol. 2.* New York: Human Sciences Press.

Goldman, B. A., & Busch, J. C. (1982). *Directory of unpublished experimental mental measures: Vol. 3.* New York: Human Sciences Press.

Goldman, B. A., & Mitchell, D. F. (1990). *Directory of unpublished experimental mental measures: Vol. 5.* Dubuque, IA: Wm. C. Brown.

Goldman, B. A., & Osborne, W. L. (1985). *Directory of unpublished experimental mental measures: Vol. 4.* New York: Human Sciences Press.

Goldman, B. A., & Sanders, J. L. (1974). *Directory of unpublished experimental mental measures: Vol. 1.* New York: Behavioral Publications.

Gorsuch, R., & Harlow, L. (1997). *Factor Analysis* (3rd. ed.). Hillsdale, NJ: Erlbaum.

Gottfredson, G. D., & Holland, J. L. (1989). *Dictionary of Holland occupational codes* (2nd ed.). Odessa, FL: Psychological Assessment Resources.

Gottfredson, L. S., & Sharf, J. C. (1988). Fairness in employment testing [Special issue]. *Journal of Vocational Behavior, 33*(3), 225–477.

Greenspan, S. R., & Granfield, J. M. (1992). Reconsidering the construct of mental retardation: Implications of a model of social competence. *American Journal of Mental Retardation, 96*(4), 442–453.

Griggs v. Duke Power Company, 401 U.S. 424 (1971).

Groth-Marnat, G. (1990). *Handbook of psychological assessment* (2nd ed). New York: Wiley.

Guadalupe Organization v. Tempe Elementary School District, E.D. Ariz. (1972).

Guilford, J. P. (1985). The structure-of-intellect model. In B. B. Wolman (Ed.), *Handbook of intelligence* (pp. 225–266). New York: Wiley.

Hammill, D. D., & Larsen, S. C. (1988). *Test of Written Language—2.* Austin, TX: PRO-ED.

Hammill, D. D., Brown, L., & Bryant, B. R. (1992). *A consumer's guide to tests in print* (2nd ed.). Austin, TX: PRO-ED.

Hansen, J. C., & Campbell, D. P. (1985). *The Strong manual* (4th ed.). Palo Alto, CA: Consulting Psychologists Press.

Harari, O., & Zedeck, S. (1973). Development of behaviorally anchored scales for the evaluation of faculty teaching. *Journal of Applied Psychology, 58,* 261–265.

Harcourt Brace. (1992). *Metropolitan Achievement Tests* (7th ed.). Orlando, FL: Author.

Harcourt Brace. (1996). *Stanford Achievement Test Series* (9th ed.). Orlando FL: Author.

Hathaway, S. R. & McKinley, J. C. (1940). A multiphasic personality schedule (Minnesota): I. Construction of the schedule. *Journal of Psychology, 10,* 249–254.

Hathaway, S. R., & McKinley, J. C. (1989). *The Minnesota Multiphasic Personality Inventory II.* Minneapolis: University of Minnesota Press.

Hepner, J. C. (1988). *ETS test collection cumulative index to tests in microfiche, 1975–1987.* Princeton, NJ: Educational Testing Service.

Herman, K., & Samuels, R. (1985). *Computers: An extension of the clinician's mind—A sourcebook.* Norwood, NJ: ABLEX.

Herrnstein, R. J., & Murray, C. (1994). *The bell curve: Intelligence and class structure in American life.* New York: The Free Press.

Hersen, M., & Bellack, A. S. (Eds.). (1988). *Dictionary of behavioral assessment techniques.* New York: Pergamon.

Hiltonsmith, R. W., & Keller, H. R. (1983). What happened to the setting in person-setting assessment? *Professional Psychology: Research and Practice, 14,* 419–434.

Hobson v. Hansen, 269 F. Supp. 401 (D. D.C. 1967) *aff'd* sub nom. *Smuck v. Hobson,* 408 F.2d 175 (D.C. Cir. 1969).

Holland, J. L. (1973). *Making vocational choices: A theory of vocational personalities and work environments.* Englewood Cliffs, NJ: Prentice Hall.

Holland, J. L. (1985). *Making vocational choices: A theory of vocational personalities and work environments* (2nd ed.). Englewood Cliffs, NJ: Prentice Hall.

Hunt, E. (1987). Science, technology, and intelligence. In R. R. Ronning, J. A. Glover, J. C. Conoley, & J. C. Witt (Eds.), *The influence of cognitive psychology on testing and measurement: The Buros-Nebraska symposium on measurement and testing* (Vol. 3, pp. 11–40). Hillsdale, NJ: Erlbaum.

Hyman, I. E., & Loftus, E. F. (in press). In D. A. Halperin (Ed.), *False memory syndrome: Theraputic and forensic perspectives.* New York: American Psychiatric Press.

Jaeger, R. M. (1989). Certification of student competence. In R. L. Linn (Ed.), *Educational measurement* (3rd ed., pp. 545–572). New York: Macmillan.

Jensen, A. R. (1982). The chronometry of intelligence. In H. J. Eysenck (Ed.), *A model for intelligence.* New York: Springer.

Jensen, A. R. (1991). General mental ability: From psychometrics to biology. *Diagnostique, 16,* 134–144.

Jensen, A. R. (1993). Spearman's hypothesis tested with chronometric information-processing tasks. *Intelligence, 17,* 47–77.

Johansson, C. B. (1991). *Career Assessment Inventory—vocational version.* Minneapolis: National Computer Systems.

Johnson, O. G. (1976). *Tests and measurements in child development: Handbook II.* San Francisco: Jossey-Bass.

Johnson, O. G., & Bommarito, J. W. (1971). *Tests and measurements in child development: A handbook.* San Francisco: Jossey-Bass.

Kaiser, H. F. (1958). The varimax criterion for analytic rotation in factor analysis. *Psychometrika, 23,* 187-200.

Kaufman, A. S. (1990). *Assessing adolescent and adult intelligence.* Boston: Allyn and Bacon. p. 73

Kaufman, A. S., & Kaufman, N. L. (1983). *Kaufman Assessment Battery for Children. Interpretive Manual.* Circle Pines, MN: American Guidance Services.

Kaufman, A. S., & Kaufman, N. L. (1985). *Kaufman Test of Educational Achievement* (K-TEA). Circle Pines, MN: American Guidance Services.

Keiser, R. E. & Prather, E. N. (1990). What is the TAT? A review of ten years of research. *Journal of Personality Assessment, 52,* 309-320.

Kelly, J. G. (1966). Ecological constraints on mental health services. *American Psychologist, 21,* 535-539.

Kelly, J. G. (1986). Context and process: An ecological view of the interdependence of practice and research. *American Journal of Community Psychology, 14,* 581-590.

Kentucky Department of Education, Office of Education for Exceptional Children. (1990). *The manual of local education requirements related to exceptional children.* Frankfort, KY: Author.

Keyser, D. J., & Sweetland, R. C. (1984). *Test critiques.* Kansas City, MO: Test Corporation of America.

Knouse, S. B. (1989). Impression management and the letter of recommendation. In R. C. Giacalone & P. Rosenfeld (Eds.), *Impression management in the organization.* Hillsdale, NJ: Erlbaum.

Kramer, J. J., & Conoley, J. C. (Eds.). (1992). *The eleventh mental measurements yearbook.* Lincoln, NE: Buros Institute of Mental Measurements.

Lambert, N., Leland, H., & Nihira, K. (1993). *AAMR Adaptive Behavior Scale—School Edition (Revised).* Austin, TX: PRO-ED.

Landy, F. J., Shankster, L. J., & Kohler, S. S. (1994). Personnel selection and placement. In L. W. Porter & M. R. Rosenzweig (Eds.), *Annual Review of Psychology, 45,* 261-269.

Larry P. v. Nelson Riles. 343 F. Supp. 1306 (N.D. Cal. 1972), affirmed 502 F.2d 963 (9th Cir. 1979).

Larry P. et al. v. Wilson Riles et al. No. C 71-2270. United States District Court for the Northern District of California,m San Francisco, October 1979, slip opinion.

Levy, P., & Goldstein, H. (1984). *Tests in education: A book of critical reviews.* London: Academic Press.

Loehlin, J. C. (1992). *Latent variable analysis.* Hillsdale, NJ: Erlbaum.

Lonner, W. J. (1985). Issues in testing and assessment in cross-cultural counseling. *The Counseling Psychologist, 13*(4), 599-614.

Lundy, A. (1988). Instructional set and thematic apperception test validity. *Journal of Personality Assessment, 52,* 309-320.

Markwardt, F. C. (1989). *Peabody Individual Achievement Test—Revised.* Circle Pines, MN: American Guidance Services.

Marston, D. B. (1989). A curriculum-based measurement approach to assessing academic performance: What it is and why do it? In M. R. Shinn (Ed.), *Curriculum-based measurement: Assessing special children* (pp. 18-78). New York: Guilford.

Matarazzo, J. D. (1990). Psychological assessment versus psychological testing. *American Psychologist, 45*(9), 999-1017.

McCarney, S. B., & Leigh, J. (1990). *Behavioral Evaluation Scale—II* (BES—II). Columbia, MO: Hawthorne Educational Services.

McClelland, D. C., Atkinson, J. W., Clark, R. A., & Lowell, E. L. (1953). *The achievement motive.* New York: Appleton-Century-Crofts.

McClendon, M. J. (1994). *Multiple tregression and causal analysis.* Itasca, IL: Peacock.

McClung, M. S. (1979). Competency testing programs: Legal and educational issues. *Fordham Law Review, 47,* 652.

McGrew, K. S., Ittenbach, R. F., Bruininks, R. H., & Hill, B. K. (1991). Factor structure of maladaptive behavior across the lifespan of persons with mental retardation. *Research in Developmental Disabilities, 12,* 181–199.

McLoughlin, J. A., & Lewis, R. B. (1990). *Assessing special students* (3rd ed.). Upper Saddle River, NJ: Merrill/Prentice Hall.

Meehl, P. E. (1986). Causes and effects of my disturbing little book. *Journal of Personality Assessment, 50*(3), 370–375.

Messick, S. (1989). Validity. In R. L. Linn (Ed.), *Educational measurement* (3rd ed., pp. 13–103). New York: Macmillan.

Messick, S. (1993). *Foundations of validity: Meaning and consequences in psychological assessment.* Princeton, NJ: Educational Testing Service.

Messick, S. (1995). Validity of psychological assessment: Validation of inferences from persons' responses and performances as scientific inquiry into score meaning. *American Psychologist, 50*(9), 741–749.

Miller, G. A. (1984). The test. *Science 84: Fifth Anniversary Issue, 5*(9), 55–60.

Miller, M. D. (1992). [Review of *Comprehensive Test of Basic Skills.*] In J. J. Kramer & J. C. Conoley (Eds.), *The eleventh mental measurements yearbook* (pp. 217–220). Lincoln, NE: Buros Institute of Mental Measurements.

Millon, T. (1990). *Toward a new personology.* New York: John Wiley.

Millon, T., Millon, C., & Davis, R. (1994). *Millon Clinical Multiaxial Inventory—III Manual.* Minneapolis, MN: National Computer Systems, Inc.

Mischel, W. (1968). *Personality and assessment.* New York: Wiley.

Mischel, W. (1993). *Introduction to personality (5th ed.).* New York: Harcourt Brace Jovanovich.

Mitchell, J. V., Jr. (Ed.). (1985). *The ninth mental measurements yearbook.* Lincoln, NE: Buros Institute of Mental Measurements.

Moreland, K. L., Eyde, L. D., Robertson, G. J., Primoff, E. S., & Most, R. B. (1995). Assessment of test user qualifications: A research-based measurement procedure. *American Psychologist, 50*(1), 14–23.

Morreau, L. E., & Bruininks, R. H. (1991). *Checklist of Adaptive Learning Skills.* Chicago: Riverside.

Murphy, L. L., Conoley, J. C., & Impara, J. C. (1994). *Tests in print* (4th ed.). Lincoln, NE: Buros Institute of Mental Measurements.

Murray, H. A. (1943). *Thematic Apperception Test manual.* Cambridge, MA: Harvard University Press.

The National Commission for the Protection of Human Subjects of Biomedical and Behavioral Research. (1979). *The Belmont report: Ethical principles and guidelines for the protection of human subjects of research.* Washington, DC: National Institutes of Health.

Nickerson, R. S. (1989). New directions in educational assessment. *Educational Researcher, 18*(9), 3–7.

Nihira, K., Leland, H., & Lambert, N. (1993). *AAMR Adaptive Behavior Scales—Residential and Community* (2nd ed.). Austin, TX: PRO-ED.

Nitko, A. J. (1984). Defining "criterion-referenced test." In R. A. Berk (Ed.), *A guide to criterion-referenced test construction* (pp. 8–28). Baltimore: Johns Hopkins University Press.

Nunnally, J. C., & Bernstein, I. H. (1994). *Psychometric theory.* New York: McGraw-Hill.

O'Brien, N. P. (1988). *Test construction: A bibliography of selected resources.* New York: Greenwood.

Osgood, C. E., Suci, G. J., & Tannenbaum, P. H. (1957). *The measurement of meaning.* Urbana: University of Illinois Press.

Page, E. B. (1994). Computer grading of student prose, using modern concepts and software. *Journal of Experimental Education, 62,* 127–142.

Parker, K. (1983). A meta-analysis of the reliability and validity of the Rorschach. *Journal of Personality Assessment, 47,* 227–231.

PASE v. Hannon, 506 F. Supp. 831 (N.D. Ill., 1980).

Peres, S. H., & Garcia, J. R. (1962). Validity and dimensions of descriptive adjectives used in reference letters for engineering applicants. *Personnel Psychology, 15,* 279–286.

Porter, T. B. (1995). Basic considerations in informed consent in research. *Clinical Research and Regulatory Affairs, 12*(2), 95–109.

President's Committee on Mental Retardation (PCMR). (1970). *The six-hour retarded child.* Washington, DC: U.S. Government Printing Office.

The Psychological Corporation. (1995). *Stanford Diagnostic Reading Test* (4th ed.). San Antonio, TX: Author.

Reitan, R. M., & Wolfson, D. (1993). *The Halstead-Reitan Neuropsychological Test Battery: Theory and clinical interpretation* (2nd ed.). South Tucson, AZ: Neuropsychology Press.

Riverside Publishing Company. (1993). *Iowa Tests of Basic Skills.* Chicago: Author.

Robinson, J. P., Athanasion, R., & Head, K. B. (1969). *Measures of occupational attitudes and occupational characteristics.* Ann Arbor: University of Michigan.

Robinson, J. P., Rusk, J. G., & Head, K. B. (1968). *Measures of political attitudes.* Ann Arbor: University of Michigan.

Robinson, J. P., & Shaver, P. R. (1973). *Measures of social psychological attitudes* (rev. ed.). Ann Arbor: University of Michigan.

Rogers, C. R. (1951). *Client centered therapy: Its current practice, implications and theory.* Boston: Houghton Mifflin.

Rogers, T. B. (1995). *An Introduction. The psychological testing enterprise.* Pacific Grove, CA: Brooks/Cole.

Rosenbaum, B. L. (1971). *An empirical study of attitude toward invasion of privacy as it relates to personnel selection.* Unpublished doctoral dissertation, Columbia University, Teachers College, New York.

Rotatori, A. F. (1994). Test review: Multidimensional Self Concept Scale. *Measurement and Evaluation in Counseling and Development, 26,* 265–267.

Ryanen, I. A. (1988). Commentary of a minor bureaucrat. *Journal of Vocational Behavior, 33,* 379–387.

Safford, P. L., & Safford, E. J. (1996). *A history of childhood and disability.* New York: Columbia University, Teachers' College Press.

Salvia, J., & Ysseldyke, J. E. (1995). *Assessment* (6th ed.). Boston: Houghton Mifflin.

Sattler, J. M. (1982). *Assessment of children's intelligence and special abilities* (2nd ed.). Boston: Allyn and Bacon.

Scannell, D. P., Haugh, O. M., Loyd, B. H., & Risinger, C. F. (1993). *Tests of achievement and proficiency,* Forms K and L. Chicago: Riverside.

Schmidt, F. L. (1988a). The problem of group differences in ability test scores in employment selection. *Journal of Vocational Behavior, 33,* 272–292.

Schmidt, F. L. (1988b). Validity generalization and the future of criterion-related validity. In H. Wainer & H. Braun (Eds.), *Test validity* (pp. 173–189). Hillsdale, NJ: Erlbaum.

Schmidt, F. L., & Hunter, J. E. (1981). Employment testing: Old theories and new research findings. *American Psychologist, 36,* 1128–1137.

Schmidt, F. L., & Hunter, J. E. (1992). Development of a causal model of processes determining job performance. *Current Directions in Psychological Science, 1,* 89–92.

Schmidt, F. L., Hunter, J. E., Pearlman, K., & Hirsh, H. R. (1985). Forty questions about validity generalization and meta- analysis. *Personnel Psychology, 32,* 697-798.

Schultz, D. P., & Schultz, S. E. (1996). *A history of modern psychology* (6th ed.). Fort Worth, TX: Harcourt Brace Jovanovich.

Seguin, E. O. (1966). *Idiocy and its treatment by the physiological method.* New York: Wood.

Sharf, J. C. (1988). Litigating personnel management policy. *Journal of Vocational Behavior, 33,* 235-271.

Shaw, M. E., & Wright, J. W. (1967). *Scales for the measurement of attitudes.* New York: McGraw-Hill.

Shepard, L. A. (1989). Identification of mild handicaps. In R. L. Linn (Ed.), *Educational measurement* (3rd ed., pp. 545-572). New York: Macmillan.

Shepard, L. A. (1993). Evaluating test validity. In L. Darling-Hammond (Ed.), *Review of research in education,* (Vol. 19, pp. 405-450). Washington, DC: American Educational Research Association.

Simpson, R. L. (1990). *Conferencing parents of exceptional children* (2nd ed.). Austin, TX: PRO-ED.

Siskind, G. (1966). "Mine eyes have seen a host of angels." *American Psychologist, 21,* 804-806.

Snow, R. E., & Lohman, D. F. (1989). Implications of cognitive psychology for educational measurement. In R. L. Linn (Ed.), *Educational measurement* (3rd ed., pp. 263-331). New York: Macmillan.

Sparrow, S. S., Balla, D. A., & Cicchetti, D. V. (1984). *Vineland Adaptive Behavior Scales.* Circle Pines, MN: American Guidance Services.

Sparrow, S. S., Balla, D. A., & Cicchetti, D. V. (1984a). *Vineland Adaptive Behavior Scales: Interview Edition, Expanded Form.* Circle Pines, MN: American Guidance Services.

Sparrow, S. S., Balla, D. A., & Cicchetti, D. V. (1984b). *Vineland Adaptive Behavior Scales: Survey Form.* Circle Pines, MN: American Guidance Services.

Sparrow, S. S., Balla, D. A., & Cicchetti, D. V. (1985). *Vineland Adaptive Behavior Scales: Classroom Edition Form.* Circle Pines, MN: American Guidance Services.

Stanford Diagnostic Mathematics Test (3rd ed.). (1984). San Antonio, TX: Psychological Corporation.

Sternbeg, R. J. (1985). *Beyond IQ: A triarchic theory of intelligence.* Cambridge, England: Cambridge University Press.

Stumpf, S. E. (1994). *Philosophy: History & problems* (5th ed.). New York McGraw-Hill.

Subkoviak, M. J. (1984). Estimating the reliability of mastery—Non-mastery classifications. In R. A. Berk (Ed.), *A guide to criterion-referenced test construction* (pp. 267-291). Baltimore: Johns Hopkins University Press.

Sweetland, R. C., & Keyser, D. J. (Eds.). (1986). *Tests: A comprehensive reference for assessments in psychology, education and business* (2nd ed.). Kansas City, MO: Test Corporaton of America.

Swenson, L. C. (1993). *Psychology and law for the helping professions.* Pacific Grove, CA: Brooks/Cole.

Taylor, H. C., & Russell, J. T. (1939). The relationship of validity coefficients to the practical effectiveness of tests in selection: Discussion and tables. *Journal of Applied Psychology, 23,* 565-578.

Thorndike, R. L. (1982). *Applied psychometrics.* Boston: Houghton Mifflin.

Thorndike, R. L., Hagen, E. P., & Sattler, J. M. (1986a). *Guide for administering and scoring the Stanford-Binet Intelligence Scale: Fourth edition.* Chicago: Riverside Publishing Company.

Thorndike, R. L., Hagen, E. P., & Sattler, J. M. (1986a). *Stanford-Binet Intelligence Scale: Fourth Edition.* Chicago: Riverside.

Thorndike, R. L., Hagen, E. P., & Sattler, J. M. (1986b). *The Stanford-Binet Intelligence Scale: Fourth edition. Technical manual.* Chicago: Riverside.

Thorndike, R. M. (1990a). *A century of ability testing.* Chicago: Riverside.

Thorndike, R. M. (1990b). Would the real factors of the Stanford-Binet (fourth edition) please come forward? *Journal of Psychoeducational Assessment, 8,* 412–435.

Thurstone, L. L. (1938). Primary mental abilities. *Psychometric Monographs,* No. 1.

Thurstone, L. L. (1947). *Multiple factor analysis.* Chicago: University of Chicago Press.

Turnbull, A. P., Turnbull, H. R., Shank, M., & Leal, D. (1995). *Exceptional lives: Special education in today's schools.* Upper Saddle River, NJ: Merrill/Prentice Hall.

U.S. Department of Education. (1983). *A nation at risk: The imperative for school reform.* Washington, DC: Author.

U.S. Department of Health and Human Services. (1993). *Protecting human research subjects: Institutional Review Board guidebook.* Washington, DC: U.S. Government Printing Office.

U.S. Department of Labor. (1986). *Dictionary of occupational titles: Fourth edition supplement.* Washington, DC: U.S. Government Printing Office.

U.S. Employment Service. (1967). *Manual for the General Aptitude Test Battery, Section III: Development.* Washington, DC: U.S. Department of Labor.

Vincent, K. R., & Harman, M. J. (1991). The Exner Rorschach: An analysis of its clinical validity. *Journal of Clinical Psychology, 47,* 596–599.

Wald, A. (1950). *Statistical decision function.* New York: Wiley.

Wason, P. (1961). Response to affirmative and negative binary statements. *British Journal of Psychology, 52,* 133–142.

Watson v. Fort Worth Bank and Trust, U.S. Sup. Ct., No. 86-6139 (June, 1988).

Wechsler, D. (1944). *The measurement of adult intelligence.* Baltimore, MD: Williams & Wilkens.

Wechsler, D. (1981). *WAIS-R manual.* San Antonio, TX: Psychological Corporation.

Wechsler, D. (1981). *Wechsler Adult Intelligence Scale—Revised.* San Antonio, TX: Psychological Corporation.

Wechsler, D. (1989). *Wechsler Preschool and Primary Scale of Intelligence—Revised.* San Antonio, TX: Psychological Corporation.

Wechsler, D. (1991). *Wechsler Intelligence Scale for Children—Third Edition.* San Antonio, TX: Psychological Corporation.

Wechsler, D. (1989). *WIPPS-R manual.* San Antonio, TX: Psychological Corporation.

Wechsler, D. (1991). *WISC-III manual.* San Antonio, TX: Psychological Corporation.

Weeks, Z. R., & Ewer-Jones, B. (1991). *The psychoeducational assessment of children* (2nd ed.). Boston, MA: Allyn and Bacon.

White House. (1991, February 4). *The national education goals: A second report to the nation's governors.* Washington, DC: Author.

Wiederholt, J. L., & Bryant, B. R. (1992). *Gray oral reading test (3rd ed.).* Austin, TX: PRO-ED.

Willett, J. B. (1988). Questions and answers in the measurement of change. In E. Z. Rothkopf (Ed.), *Review of research in education* (Vol. 15, pp. 345–422). Washington, DC: American Educational Research Association.

Witt, J. C., Elliott, S. N., Kramer, J. J., & Gresham, F. M. (1994). *Assessment of children: Fundamental methods and practices.* Madison, WI: Brown & Benchmark.

Woodcock, R. W. (1991). *Woodcock language proficiency battery—Revised, English form.* Chicago, IL: Riverside.

Woodcock, R. W. (1987). *Woodcock reading mastery tests—Revised.* Circle Pines, MN: American Guidance Service.

Woodcock, R. W., & Mather, N. (1989). *Woodcock-Johnson tests of achievement: Standard and supplemental batteries.* Chicago, IL: Riverside.

Ysseldyke, J. E., Algozzine, B., & Thurlow, M. L. (1992). *Critical issues in special education.* Boston, MA: Houghton Mifflin.

Ysseldyke, J. E., & Christenson, S. L. (1993). *The Instructional Environment System—II.* Longmont, CO: Sopris West.

Ysseldyke, J. E., Christenson, S. L., & Kovaleski, J. F. (1994). Identifying students' instructional needs in the context of classroom and home environments. *Teaching Exceptional Children, 26,* 37–41.

Ysseldyke, M. E., Thurlow, M. L., & Erickson, R. N. (1994). *Possible sources of data for post-school level indicators.* Minneapolis, MN: University of Minnesota, College of Education and Human Development, National Center on Educational Outcomes.

Zern, D. (1967). Effects of variations in question phrasing on true-false answers by grade-school children. *Psychological Reports, 20,* 527–533.

Calculating the Mean, Standard Deviation, and Correlation Coefficient

---

THE MEAN FOR GROUPED DATA

In Chapter 2, we described the procedures for calculating the mean—from the original set of scores, the raw data. When the scores have been placed in a frequency distribution, we can use a shortcut to calculate the mean. If the data have not been assembled into groups, the following procedure will yield exactly the same answer that would be obtained from the original scores; however, if the scores have been summarized in a grouped frequency distribution, the results may be slightly different because of the inaccuracies introduced by grouping.

Suppose we have the following small frequency distribution of scores on a five-item test. The values in the X column are the possible scores, and the values in the f column are the frequencies.

X	f
5	6
4	12
3	30
2	8
1	3
0	1

The values in the f column, of course, represent the number of people who got each score. Six people answered all items correctly, 12 people missed only one item, and so on. If we add the scores of the people who scored 5, we would have $5 + 5 + 5 + 5 + 5 + 5 = 30$. If we multiplied the score 5 by the number of people who earned that score (5×6), we would get the same answer. The same is true for every score value. Adding twelve 4s is the same as multiplying 4 by 12, and so forth. We can therefore get the sum of all 60 scores by multiplying each score by the number of people who earned it and adding these products. In symbols, for individual score totals, that is

$$\Sigma X = \Sigma f X$$

For our problem, we add $(6 \times 5) + (12 \times 4) + (30 \times 3) + (8 \times 2) + (3 \times 1) + (1 \times 0) = 187$. We would have gotten the same answer if we had been working with the original 60 scores, but then we would have had to add a column of 60 numbers. We get the mean by dividing ΣX by the number of individuals, represented by Σf or N. The mean is

$$M = \frac{\Sigma X}{N} = \frac{187}{60} = 3.12$$

Not suppose the same 60 people had taken a 50-item test and that the results had been entered into a grouped frequency distribution with an interval of three. In working with a grouped frequency distribution, we use the midpoint (X in the tabulation that follows) of each interval to stand for all scores in the interval (see Chapter 2). The results might look like this:

Interval	Midpoint (X)	f	fX
48–50	49	3	147
45–47	46	7	322
42–44	43	13	559
39–41	40	20	800
36–38	37	11	407
33–35	34	6	204
			$\Sigma f X = 2,439$

Because the midpoint of each interval stands for all scores in the interval, regardless of what these scores actually are, we use the midpoint just like we used the score values above. That is, instead of adding $49 + 49 + 49$ to get the sum of scores for the three people in the top interval, we use $3 \times 49 = 147$. The sum for the seven people in the next interval is found to be $7 \times 46 = 322$. Each of the other products of f and X is found in the same way. These values have been placed in the last column. The sum of these entries gives a value of 2,439 for $\Sigma f X$ that, when divided by the number of individuals (60), yields a mean of 40.65. Note that the equation used here is identical to the one used earlier except that X stands for the midpoint of an interval rather than for a single score value.

THE STANDARD DEVIATION FOR GROUPED DATA

We can approach the computation of the standard deviation *(SD)* for grouped data in the same way that we approached the computation of the mean. Recall from Chapter 2 that we needed the sum of squared scores to find the standard deviation. We can square each score individually and add them, or we can place them in a frequency distribution as we did in the previous section. Here, we have the same distribution just used for our five-item test, but the third column contains the square of each score value, and the last column contains X^2 multiplied by its frequency.

X	f	X^2	fX^2
5	6	25	150
4	12	16	192
3	30	9	270
2	8	4	32
1	3	1	3
0	1	0	0
			$\Sigma fX^2 = \overline{647}$

The sum of the values in the last column, 647, is the same value we would obtain if we squared each of the 60 scores individually. Putting this value into the equation for the standard deviation, we get

$$SD = \sqrt{\frac{\Sigma fX^2}{N} - M^2}$$

$$= \sqrt{\frac{647}{60} - 3.12^2}$$

$$= \sqrt{1.05} = 1.02$$

We can carry out the same procedure for computing the SD on the second set of data used as an example for computing the mean if we substitute the interval midpoints for the scores, as shown here.

Interval	Midpoint (X)	f	X^2	fX^2
48–50	49	3	2,401	7,203
45–47	46	7	2,116	14,812
42–44	43	13	1,849	24,037
39–41	40	20	1,600	32,000
36–38	37	11	1,369	15,059
33–35	34	6	1,156	6,936
				$\Sigma fX^2 = \overline{100,047}$

The value of ΣfX^2 is 100,047. Using this value in the equation for standard deviation gives the following:

$$SD = \sqrt{\frac{100,047}{60} - 40.65^2} = \sqrt{15.03} = 3.88$$

Many calculators allow for grouped-data entry. The procedure usually works in the following way. You enter a score value on the keyboard and then push a special key, often having a capital sigma on it, to enter the value. Next, you enter the frequency for that score and push a second key, often the "equal" key. The calculator computes and stores fX and fX^2. This sequence is repeated for each score value and its frequency, and at each step, the calculator adds the new values to those already in memory. When all the data have been entered, you can either recall the sums or, on most calculators, simply press a key for the mean and a second one for the standard deviation.

COMPUTING THE CORRELATION COEFFICIENT

The correlation coefficient (r) was introduced in Chapter 2 as an index that expresses the extent to which two variables (say, X and Y) go together, or correlate. It indicates the extent to which high X scores go with high Y scores and vice versa. But "high" and "low" must be expressed in some uniform terms from one set of data to another if the index is to have the same meaning for different sets of data. Standard scores (z scores) provide just such a framework because they express position as so many standard deviations above or below the mean of the distribution of scores.

The correlation coefficient between X and Y (or, more precisely, the *Pearson product-moment* correlation coefficient—there are other kinds of correlations) is defined as the mean product of standard scores. if each person's X and Y are expressed as so many standard deviations above or below its mean, the product of the standard scores for each individual is found, and the mean of these products is found, the result is the correlation between X and Y. Expressed as an equation,

$$r = \frac{\Sigma z_X z_Y}{N}$$

whether r is the correlation coefficient, z_x and z_Y are standard scores on X and Y, and N is the number of individuals.

This is the *definition* of the correlation coefficient. However, it does not provide an efficient or convenient routine for calculation. If we substitute the raw score definitions of the z scores in the equation just given, we get something that looks harder but is really much easier to work with.

In most cases, we would already have computed the mean and standard deviation of both X and Y. The only additional step then is to find the sum of the products of X and Y across all individuals. Once we find this quantity, ΣXY, we can use the following equation for r.

$$r = \frac{\frac{\Sigma XY}{N} - M_X M_Y}{SD_X SD_Y}$$

That is, to find the correlation coefficient, follow these steps:

1. Find the product X times Y for each individual.
2. Find the sum of these products.

3. Divide this sum by the number of individuals.
4. Find the product of the means of the two variables.
5. Subtract the quantity in Step 4 from the quantity in Step 3.
6. Find the product of the standard deviations of the two variables.
7. Divide the quantity in Step 5 by the quantity in Step 6.

The result is the correlation between X and Y.

The procedures for computing the correlation coefficient can be illustrated with the following small set of data. Each row gives X, Y, X^2, Y^2, and XY for a different individual. The values in the last row are the sums.

Individual	X	Y	X^2	Y^2	XY
1	10	12	100	144	120
2	8	6	164	36	48
3	13	10	169	100	130
4	11	11	121	121	121
5	14	11	196	121	154
6	12	14	144	196	168
Sums	68	64	794	718	741

The column sums are used to compute the various quantities required to calculate the correlation coefficient as follows:

$$M_x = 68/6 = 11.33$$
$$M_y = 64/6 = 10.67$$
$$SD_x = \sqrt{(794/6) - 11.33^2} = 1.99$$
$$SD_y = \sqrt{(718/6)} = 10.67^2 = 2.41$$
$$r = \frac{(741/6) - (11.33)(10.67)}{(1.99)(2.41)} = \frac{123.5 - 120.89}{4.80}$$
$$= 0.54$$

Again, many calculators have a program that will compute the correlation with the press of a single key, once you have entered the data. Ordinarily, they will accumulate the five required quantities—XY, X, Y, X^2, and Y^2—in particular memory locations (which are listed in the user's manual). These quantities can be recalled, one at a time, to compute the means and standard deviations of the two variables and the correlation between them while entering the data into the calculator only once. It is also likely that the calculators will have keys that can be used to compute each of these statistics automatically.

APPENDIX 2

Percent of Cases Falling Below Selected Values on the Normal Curve

Deviation in Standard Deviation Units	Cases Falling Below (%)	Deviation in Standard Deviation Units	Cases Falling Below (%)	Deviation in Standard Deviation Units	Cases Falling Below (%)
+3.50	99.98	2.05	97.98	.85	80.23
3.40	99.97	2.00	97.72	.80	78.81
3.30	99.95	1.95	97.44	.75	77.34
3.20	99.93	1.90	97.13	.70	75.80
3.10	99.90	1.85	96.78	.65	74.22
3.00	99.87	1.80	96.41	.60	72.57
2.95	99.84	1.75	95.99	.55	70.88
2.90	99.81	1.70	95.54	.50	69.15
2.85	99.78	1.65	95.05	.45	67.36
2.80	99.74	1.60	94.52	.40	65.54
2.75	99.70	1.55	93.94	.35	63.68
2.70	99.65	1.50	93.32	.30	61.79
2.65	99.60	1.45	92.65	.25	59.87
2.60	99.53	1.40	91.92	.20	57.93
2.55	99.46	1.35	91.15	.15	55.96
2.50	99.38	1.30	90.30	.10	53.98
2.45	99.29	1.25	89.44	.05	51.99
2.40	99.18	1.20	88.49	0.00	50.00
2.35	99.06	1.15	87.49	−.05	48.01
2.30	98.93	1.10	86.43	−.10	46.02
2.25	98.78	1.05	85.31	−.15	44.04
2.20	98.61	1.00	84.13	−.20	42.07
2.15	98.42	.95	82.89	−.25	40.13
2.10	98.21	.90	81.59	−.30	38.21

continued

Deviation in Standard Deviation Units	Cases Falling Below (%)	Deviation in Standard Deviation Units	Cases Falling Below (%)	Deviation in Standard Deviation Units	Cases Falling Below (%)
−.35	36.32	−1.65	4.95	−2.85	0.22
−.40	34.46	−1.70	4.46	−2.90	0.19
−.45	32.64	−1.75	4.01	−2.95	0.16
−.50	30.85	−1.80	3.59	−3.00	0.13
−.55	29.12	−1.85	3.22	−3.10	0.10
−.60	27.43	−1.90	2.87	−3.20	0.07
−.65	25.78	−1.95	2.56	−3.30	0.05
−.70	24.20	−2.00	2.88	−3.40	0.03
−.75	22.66	−2.05	2.02	−3.50	0.02
−.80	21.19	−2.10	1.79		
−.85	19.77	−2.15	1.58		
−.90	18.41	−2.20	1.39		
−.95	17.11	−2.25	1.22		
−1.00	15.87	−2.30	1.07		
−1.05	14.69	−2.35	0.94		
−1.10	13.57	−2.40	0.82		
−1.15	12.51	−2.45	0.71		
−1.20	11.51	−2.50	0.62		
−1.25	10.56	−2.55	0.54		
−1.30	9.68	−2.60	0.47		
−1.35	8.85	−2.65	0.40		
−1.40	8.08	−2.70	0.35		
−1.45	7.35	−2.80	0.26		
−1.50	6.68				
−1.55	6.06				
−1.60	5.48				

APPENDIX 3

Sources for Educational and Psychological Tests

Many agencies publish one or two tests, questionnaires, or other measurement instruments; however, most of the widely used tests are handled by a relatively small group of publishers. The list that follows includes publishers of the tests described in Appendix 4 and a few other publishers that have a substantial list of titles.

Academic Therapy Publications
20 Commercial Blvd
Novato, CA 94949-6191

American College Testing Program
P.O. Box 168
Iowa City, IA 52243

American Guidance Services, Inc.
Publishers Buildings
Circle Pines, MN 55014

Clinical Psychology Publishing
4 Conant Square
Brandon, VT 05733

Consulting Psychologists Press
3803 East Bayshore Road
P. O. Box 10096
Palo Alto, CA 94306

CTB Macmillan/McGraw-Hill
20 Ryan Ranch Road
Monterey, CA 93940

Educational Testing Service
P. O. Box 6736
Princeton, NJ 08541-6736

Educators Publishing Service
31 Smith Place
Cambridge, MA 02138-1100

Hawthorne Educational Services
800 Gray Oak Drive
Columbia, MO 65201

Institute for Personality and Ability Testing
P. O. Box 188
Champaign, IL 61824

Jastak Associates, Inc.
P.O. Box 3410
Wilmington, DE 19807

National Occupational Competency Testing Institute
409 Bishop Hall
Ferris State University
Big Rapids, MI 49307

NCS Assessments
P. O. Box 1416
Minneapolis, MN 55440

PRO-ED
8700 Shoal Creek Blvd
Austin, TX 78757

Psychological Assessment Resources
P.O. Box 998
Odessa, FL 33556

Psychological Corporation
555 Academic Court
San Antonio, TX 78204

Psychometric Affiliates
P.O. Box 807
Murfreesboro, TN 37133

Riverside Publishing Company
425 Springlake Drive
Itasca, IL 60143

Scholastic Testing Service
480 Meyer Road
Bensenville, IL 60106

Science Research Associates/London House (also SRA/London House)
9701 West Higgins Road
Rosemont, IL 60018

Sigma Assessment Systems
Research Psychologists Press Division
P. O. Box 610984
Port Huron, MI 48061-0984

Slosson Educational Publications
P. O. Box 280
East Aurora, NY 14052

Stoelting Company
1350 South Kostner Avenue
Chicago, IL 60623

Teachers College Press
Teachers College, Columbia University
525 West 120th Street
New York, NY 10027

Teleometrics International
1755 Woodstead Court
Woodlands, TX 77380

University of Minnesota Press
111 Third Avenue
Suite 290
Minneapolis, MN 55401

Western Psychological Services
12031 Wilshire Boulevard
Los Angeles, CA 90025

Commercially Available Psychological and Educational Tests and Inventories

INTRODUCTION

In this appendix, we present lists and brief descriptions of some of the commercially available psychological and educational tests and inventories. The appendix is organized by topic, and the tests within a topic are arranged alphabetically. Each entry contains the test title, publisher, intended age range or grade of test takers, testing time, a notation of the most recent review of the test in the *Mental Measurements Yearbook (MMY),* and a brief review of the test. Of course, there are thousands of tests that we have not included here.

SECTION A—TESTS OF GENERAL ABILITY

Several measures of general cognitive ability are distributed only under programs controlled by their publishers, including the Scholastic Aptitide Test of the College Board and the American College Testing (ACT) Program's ACT Assessment. The latter is described as an achievement test, but it is used for making college admissions decisions. These instruments are revised for every administration and are of uniformly high quality. However, their restricted distribution makes them of limited value for use with any but their narrow target group. We note the existence of these instruments, but do not include them for review.

Cognitive Abilities Test (CogAT)—Form 5
Riverside Publishing Company
Grades: Primary battery, Kindergarten–Grade 3; Multilevel, Grades 3–13
Testing time: Primary, 2 sessions of about 30 minutes each; Multilevel, 30 minutes for each of 3 sections
Last MMY *review:* 10th (of the 4th Edition)

The Nonreading primary battery has two levels; the multilevel battery is composed of eight overlapping levels of difficulty. The multilevel battery provides separate scores for verbal, quantitative, and nonverbal sections. These batteries are jointly normed with the Iowa Tests of Basic Skills and the Tests of Achievement and Proficiency. Results are reported as standard age scores (mean = 100 and standard deviation (SD) = 16), percentile rank by age and grade, and stanine by age and grade. (See Chapter 8 for a detailed discussion.)

Culture Fair Intelligence Tests
Institute for Personality and Ability Testing
Ages: Scale 1, 4–8 and older learning disabled; Scale 2, 8–14 and average adults; Scale 3, Grades 9–16 and superior adults
Testing time: Scale 1, 22 minutes; Scales 2 and 3, 15 minutes
Last MMY *review:* 6th

Scale 1 consists of eight subtests, four of which must be administered individually. Scales 2 and 3 contain four subtests involving different perceptual tasks: completing progressive series, classifying, solving incomplete designs, and evaluating conditions. Raw scores on Scale 1 are converted into mental ages and IQ scores; on Scales 2 and 3, they are converted into percentile ranks by ages and IQ scores. The stimulus materials were revised in 1977, but the test manuals were last revised in 1973. A Spanish language version of Scales 2 and 3 is available.

Goodenough-Harris Drawing Test
Psychological Corporation
Ages: 3–15
Testing time: Untimed (usually 10–15 minutes)
Last MMY *review:* 7th

This is a nonverbal test of mental ability, suitable as either a group or an individual test. The current version of the test is the 1963 revision of the original Draw-a-Man test. The examinee is required to draw a picture of a man, a woman, and himself or herself. Prospective users of the test should have a copy of Dale B. Harris's *Children's Drawings as Measures of Intellectual Maturity* in addition to the examiner's kit. The test was standardized on 2,975 children from families representative of the occupational distribution of the United States in 1950. Raw scores are converted to standard scores (mean = 100 and *SD* = 15), and these scores may be converted into percentile ranks. Reliability and validity information is extremely dated.

Henmon-Nelson Tests of Mental Ability
Riverside Publishing Company
Grades: Kindergarten–Grade 2, and Grades 3–6, 6–9, 9–12
Testing time: Kindergarten–Grade 2 untimed (approximately 25– 30 minutes); Grades 3–12, 30 minutes
Last MMY *review:* 8th (Canadian Edition, 12th)

This test provides a quick measure of general intellectual ability at a modest cost. Scores are reported as age and grade percentiles and stanines as well as deviation IQ scores. The last standardization was 1973. Scores correlate well with other group tests of intelligence, with teachers' grades, and with achievement test results. Reliabilities are in the range of 0.85–0.95.

Kaufman Adolescent and Adult Intelligence Test (KAIT)
American Guidance Service
Ages: 11 to 85+
Testing time: 58–102 minutes, depending on age and test form
Last MMY *review:* 12th

Introduced as a competitior with the WAIS-R and Stanford-Binet, the KAIT is an individually administered test of intelligence for use with adolescents and adults. The test provides three broad cognitive measures, a Crystallized Scale (combination of scores on Definitions, Auditory Comprehension, and Double Meanings subtests [Famous Faces is an alternate subtest]), a Fluid Scale (combination of Rebus Learning, Logical Steps, and Mystery Codes [Memory for Block Designs is an alternate subtest]), and Total. In addition, the optional Rebus Delayed Recall and Auditory Delayed Recall subtests can provide a measure of Delayed Recall and there is a Mental Status subtest.

Kaufman Assessment Battery for Children (K-ABC)
American Guidance Service
Ages: 2 1/2–12 1/2
Testing time: 35–85 minutes (longer for older examinees)
Last MMY *review:* 9th

This test was first published in 1983 to answer some of the deficiencies ascribed at that time to older instruments such as the Stanford-Binet Intelligence Scale and the Wechsler scales. There are 10 "mental processing" subtests and 6 "achievement" subtests, with different combinations given at different ages. A particular child may take as many as 13 of the tests. Special scales are included to enable the assessment of children with hearing impairment or speech or language disorders or non-English-speaking children. (See Chapter 8.)

Kuhlmann-Anderson Intelligence Tests, (KA) Eighth Edition
Scholastic Testing Service, Inc.
Grades: Kindergarten and Grades 1, 2–3, 3–4, 5–6, 7–9, 9–12
Testing time: 25–60 minutes
Last MMY *review:* 9th

The KA consists of eight subtests at all levels. The lower levels yield a single overall score; the higher levels produce three scores: verbal, quantitative, and total. Percentile ranks and deviation IQ scores within age are reported. Reliability coefficients are generally satisfactory. The difference score between verbal and quantitative subtests does not appear to have high enough reliability to be useful. Data on concurrent validity are satisfactory, but few predictive validity coefficients are reported in the technical manual. The subtests have very short time limits, making this a highly speeded test and placing heavy demands on examinees for fast work and on examiners for accurate timing.

McCarthy Scales of Children's Abilities
Psychological Corporation
Ages: 2 1/2–8 1/2
Testing time: Varies with age
Last MMY review: 9th

The instrument consists of 18 tests grouped into six overlapping scales: general cognitive, verbal, perceptual performance, quantitative, memory, and motor. The scores for the latter five scales are reported as normalized standard scores with a mean of 50 and an *SD* of 10. The general cognitive scale, based on 15 of the 18 tests, is reported as a general cognitive index (GCI), a normalized standard score with a mean of 100 and an *SD* of 16. The standardization sample was carefully designed to include equal numbers of males and females and proportional representation by race, geographical region, father's occupational level, and urban or rural residence. The median split-half reliability for the GCI is about 0.93 within age levels. Split-half reliabilities for the other five scales range from 0.79 to 0.88. Retest reliabilities over a 1-month interval for 125 children in three age groups were about 0.90 for the GCI and ranged from 0.69 to 0.89 for the other scales. Factor analyses support the usefulness of reporting six separate scores, and GCIs show reasonable agreement with scores from other instruments.

Otis-Lennon School Ability Test, Seventh Edition (OLSAT7)
Psychological Corporation
Grades: K–12
Testing time: 60–75 minutes depending on level
Last MMY review: 11th (of the OLSAT6)

This test is a revision of the Otis-Lennon Mental Ability Tests. There are two editions currently available, each with seven levels. The OLSAT6 (1988) (2 forms) was standardized concurrently with the Metropolitan Achievement Tests (Seventh Edition) and the Stanford Achievement Tests (Eighth Edition) and the OLSAT7 (1995) (1 form) was standardized concurrently with the Stanford Achievement Test (Ninth Edition). The instrument yields Total score, called the School Ability Index, which is a normalized standard score with a mean of 100 and *SD* of 16, and subscores for Verbal and Nonverbal ability. Internal consistency reliabilities range from 0.88 to 0.96. Six-month test-retest reliabilities were 0.84–0.92. A 3- to 4-year retest interval yielded values of 0.75–0.78. Equivalent form correlations were in the 0.82–0.92 range, depending on test level. Standard errors of measurement are reported to be about four points. (Scores are also reported in stanines and percentiles.) Correlations with other measures of scholastic aptitude are in the 0.50s and 0.60s.

Peabody Picture Vocabulary Test Revised (PPVT-R)
American Guidance Service, Inc.
Ages: 2 1/2 to adults
Testing time: 15–20 minutes
Last MMY *review:* 9th

The PPVT-R is an individually administered test of vocabulary consisting of a graduated series of 175 plates, each containing four pictures. The examiner gives an oral stimulus word and the examinee points to, or otherwise indicates, the picture on the plate that best illustrates the meaning of the stimulus word. The PPVT-R is frequently used as an abbreviated test of general ability. Norms are based on 4,200 children, ages 2–18 years, and 828 adults. Raw scores can be converted to age equivalents, standard scores with a mean of 100 and an *SD* of 15, and percentile ranks. Alternate form reliabilities range from 0.71 to 0.91, with a median of 0.82, while internal consistency coefficients run from 0.61 to 0.88. Correlations of the PPVT-R with various measures of intellectual ability range from about 0.40 to 0.60.

Raven's Progressive Matrices
Psychological Corporation
Ages: 5 and over
Testing time: Untimed (approximately 15–45 minutes, depending on form)
Last MMY *review:* 6th

This test has three forms: Standard (in black and white for 6-year-olds to adult), Advanced (in black and white for ages 11 and over of superior ability), and Coloured (in color for ages 5– 11, mental patients, and the elderly). It represents an attempt to appraise the general ability factor, Spearman's *g*. The tasks consist of abstract designs with missing parts. The examinee chooses from the given options the design that best fits. Although the test is claimed by some to be "culture fair," there is little evidence to support this claim. The test is untimed. Evidence on reliability and validity is limited and inconsistent. The manual for the test is inadequate, and normative data are sketchy at best. Most of the norms are based on British samples.

Schaie-Thurstone Adult Mental Abilities Test
Consulting Psychologists Press
Ages: 22–84
Testing time: 50–60 minutes
Last MMY *review:* 10th

This instrument was published in 1985 as a revision and updating of the Primary Mental Abilities Test (PMA). There are two forms, one essentially equivalent to the PMA and one for older adults. There are seven scales. Long-term stability data are impressive, with 7-year retest coefficients of about 0.80 for all scales. Validity is assessed in terms of conformity of the scales to Thurstone's theory of mental abilities. Scale scores are reported as *T* scores (normalized standard scores with a mean of 50 and an *SD* of 10), and there is a composite IQ with a mean of 100 and an *SD* of 15.

Slosson Intelligence Test
Slosson Educational Publications
Ages: 2 weeks–27 years
Testing time: Untimed (approximately 10–30 minutes)
Last MMY *review:* 12th

This is a quick screening test of general mental ability for use primarily with younger children. Reliability and validity information is sketchy and inconsistent. The test was originally designed as a short form of the 1960 Stanford-Binet, but was revised to provide a "quick estimate of general verbal cognitive ability" in 1991.

Stanford-Binet Intelligence Scale, Fourth Edition
Riverside Publishing Company
Ages: 2 to adults
Testing time: Varies with level
Last MMY *review:* 10th

See the discussion of this instrument in Chapter 8.

Wechsler Adult Intelligence Scale Revised (WAIS-R)
Psychological Corporation
Ages: 16 and over
Testing time: 50–75 minutes
Last MMY *review:* 9th

See the discussion of the instrument in Chapter 8. The publisher is currently preparing a revision.

Wechsler Intelligence Scale for Children, Third Edition (WISC-III)
Psychological Corporation
Ages: 6–16
Testing time: 50–75 minutes
Last MMY *review:* 12th

See the discussion of this instrument in Chapter 8. A special monograph supplement of the *Journal of Psychoeducational Assessment* provides a series of reviews and studies with the WISC-III.

Wechsler Preschool and Primary Scale of Intelligence Revised (WPPSI-R)
Psychological Corporation
Ages: 4–6 1/2
Testing time: 50–75 minutes
Last MMY *review:* 11th

See the discussion of this instrument in Chapter 8.

Woodcock-Johnson Psycho-Educational Battery-Revised (WJ-R)
Riverside Publishing Company
Ages: 3–80
Testing time: Part 1, 60–90 minutes; Part 2, 30–45 minutes; Part 3, 15–30 minutes
Last MMY review: 12th

Published in 1989, the Woodcock-Johnson battery is composed of three parts: Part 1—cognitive ability, 12 scores; Part 2— achievement, 10 scores; Part 3—scholastic interest, 5 scores. There are 13 derived scores: 4 scholastic aptitude clusters, 4 cognitive factor clusters, 4 achievement clusters, and a broad cognitive ability score. It is administered individually and is the only instrument to assess ability, achievement, and interests. Reliabilities are generally in the high 0.80s and 0.90s for the cluster scores, and a median reliability of 0.97 was found for broad cognitive ability. Correlations with other measures of general ability are in the 0.70s and 0.80s. See discussion in Chapter 8.

SECTION B—APTITUDE TEST BATTERIES

Armed Services Vocational Aptitude Battery (ASVAB)
U.S. Military Enlistment Processing Command
Grade level: High school
Testing time: 135 minutes
Last MMY review: 9th

This aptitude battery is designed for use in high school vocational guidance programs and in armed services recruitment centers. The battery has 12 subtests and provides 6 composite scores: verbal, mathematics, perceptual speed, mechanical, trade technical, and academic ability. Median Kuder-Richardson Formula 20 reliabilities are 0.82 for the subtests and 0.92 for the composites. Validity correlations are reported for various military training programs and for high school grades. The test is given and scored without charge by personnel from the U.S. Department of Defense.

Structure of Intellect Learning Abilities Test (SOI)
Western Psychological Services
Level: Preschool to adult, 7 forms
Testing time: Forms A and B, 150–180 minutes; Forms G, M, P, R, and RR, 60–90 minutes
Last MMY review: 10th

Forms A and B are alternate forms, each with 26 tests that assess the five cognitive operations of Guilford's Structure of Intellect model: cognition, memory, evaluation, convergent production, and divergent production. Scores include the five cognitive dimensions; the figural, symbolic, and semantic contents, and the units, classes, relations, systems, transformations; and implication products from the SOI model. The other five forms (G, M, P, R, and RR) contain selected tests from Form A or similar tests intended for lower levels. Median reliability for the individual subtests is 0.57 (the range is 0.35-0.88). Reliabilities for general ability scores range from 0.65 to 0.90, with most in the 70s. Validity of the battery depends on the validity of the SOI model, which has been questioned. Norms are not as complete as for most batteries, but the tests cover a wider age range.

U.S. Employment Service General Aptitude Test Battery (GATB), 1986 Edition
U.S. Employment Service
Grades: 12 and above and adults
Testing time: 120–150 minutes for group tests
Last MMY *review:* 9th

See Chapter 8 for a discussion of this battery. It is only available for use by state employment offices.

U.S. Employment Service Nonreading Aptitude Test Battery (NATB), 1982 Edition
U.S. Employment Service
Level: Educationally limited students in Grades 9–12 and adults
Testing time: 107 minutes
Last MMY *review:* 9th

This battery is an adaptation of the GATB designed for use with high school students and adults with limited reading ability.

SECTION C—INTEREST INVENTORIES

Kuder General Interest Survey—Form E
Science Research Associates, Inc.
Grades: 6–12
Testing time: Untimed (approximately 30–40 minutes)
Last MMY *review:* 12th

A revision and downward extension of the Kuder Preference Record—Vocational, this instrument measures the individual's relative preference for activities in 10 job categories: outdoor, mechanical, scientific, computational, persuasive, artistic, literary, musical, social service, and clerical. Percentile scores are available for four norm groups: (1) males and (2) females in grades 6-8 and (3) males and (4) females in grades 9-12 (revised, 1991).

Kuder Occupational Interest Survey (KOIS) Revised—Form DD
Science Research Associates, Inc.
Grades: 10–12 and adults

Testing time: Untimed (approximately 30–40 minutes)
Last MMY *review:* 10th

The instrument consists of 100 triads. In each triad, the examinee selects one activity that is most liked and one that is least liked. The instrument yields 119 occupational scores (79 with male norms and 40 with female norms), 48 college major scores (29 with male norms and 19 with female norms), 10 vocational interest estimates (preferences for different kinds of activities), and a dependability (verification) score. Twenty occupations and 12 majors have norms for both males and females. Scores are reported in terms of the relationship between the examinee's responses and those of successful and satisfied groups in the occupations and college majors. A new supplement allows conversion of interest scores to Holland codes. Answer sheets must be machine scored, but scoring services are quick and efficient. Evidence of reliability and validity is accumulating.

Kuder Preference Record—Vocational (KPR-V)
Science Research Associates, Inc.
Grades: 9–12 and adults
Testing time: Untimed (approximately 40–50 minutes)
Last MMY *review:* 8th

The KPR-V yields 10 interest area scores: outdoor, mechanical, computational, scientific, persuasive, artistic, literary, musical, social service, and clerical. In addition, there is a verification score.

Ohio Vocational Interest Survey, Second Edition (OVIS-II)
Psychological Corporation
Grades: 7 to college and adults
Testing time: Untimed (approximately 60 minutes)
Last MMY *review:* 9th

The instrument is divided into two sections, a student information questionnaire and an interest inventory. The student information questionnaire gathers information about the examinee's occupational plans, school subject preferences, curricular plans, post-high school plans, and vocational course interests. The interest inventory consists of 253 work activity items. Scores are given for 23 occupational area scales that are linked to the *Dictionary of Occupational Titles.* There is also a score called a scale clarity index, which is supposed to reflect the carefulness and consistency of the examinee's answer choices. Raw scores are converted to percentile ranks and stanines by grade and gender.

Self-Directed Search (SDS), 1985 Revision
Psychological Assessment Resources
Level: High school, college, and adults
Testing time: Untimed (approximately 40–60 minutes)
Last MMY *review:* 10th

The SDS was developed to simulate a vocational counseling experience. It is designed to be self-administered, self-scored, and self-interpreted. Scores are provided for the six personality/interest types of Holland's model (realistic, investigative, artistic, social, enterprising, and conventional) on each of three scales (activities, competencies, and occupations). The SDS can be administered and scored by microcomputer. Scores are linked to the *Dictionary of Occupational Titles* codes through the Holland codes. Internal consistency reliabilities for the scales are in the 80s and 90s. Validity evidence is derived primarily from association with Holland's model. See Chapter 11 for further discussion.

Strong Interest Inventory of the Strong Vocational Interest Blank (SII-SVIB)
Consulting Psychologists Press
Grades: 11–12, college, and adults
Testing time: Untimed (approximately 40–60 minutes)
Last MMY *review:* 12th

See the discussion of this instrument in Chapter 11.

Vocational Preference Inventory (VPI), 1985 Revision
Consulting Psychologists Press
Grades: 12–16 and adults
Testing time: Untimed (approximately 30 minutes)
Last MMY *review:* 10th

The VPI consists of 160 occupational titles to which the examinee indicates "like" or "dislike." The inventory yields 11 scores, 6 of which are the Holland types and can be used as vocational interest scales: realistic, investigative, artistic, social, enterprising, and conventional. The remaining 5 scales are personality scales for self-control, masculinity, status, infrequency, and acquiescence. The inventory is probably most useful as a vocational interest inventory. Many reviewers consider the VPI to be a good instrument for vocational counseling or research. It can be administered and scored by Apple or IBM computers. Vocational scales can be linked to Holland's *Occupations Finder* and the *Dictionary of Holland Occupational Codes.*

SECTION D—READING TESTS

Gates-MacGintie Reading Test, Third Edition
Riverside Publishing Company
Grades: K.6–12
Testing time: Varies by level
Last MMY *review:* 11th

This test has nine levels: PRE for grades K.6-1.2, R for grades 1.0-1.9, Level 1 for grades 1.3-1.9, Level 2 for grade 2, Level 3 for grade 3, Level 4 for grade 4, Level 5/6 for grades 5-6, Level 7/9 for grades 7-9, and Level 10/12 for grades 10-12.

For many years, this instrument has been the most often administered reading test. It was first published in 1926. It provides only three scores: vocabulary, comprehension, and total, except at the lowest two levels, where five and four scores are available respectively. Unlike rival reading tests, it does not provide information about separate skills. It is intended to provide an overall estimate of reading level and does not aspire to be diagnostic. Reliability is quite satisfactory ranging from the high 0.80s to the mid 0.90s.

Metropolitan Readiness Test (MRT), Fifth Edition
Harcourt Brace Jovanovich
Grades: Prekindergarten–Grade 1
Testing time: 80–100 minutes
Last MMY *review:* 12th

This test is intended to asses the underlying or enabling skills that are necessary for early school learning, in particular, reading; to determine readiness for instruction; and to identify instructional needs. The test has two levels. Level 1 is intended for use with 4-year-olds prior to their entry into kindergarten and with students already in kindergarten. Level 1 includes auditory memory, beginning consonants, letter recognition, visual matching, school language, listening, and quantitative language. Level 2 is intended for use with students in the second half of kindergarten and the beginning of first grade. Assessed in this level are beginning consonants, sound-letter correspondence, visual matching, finding patterns, school language, listening, quantitative concepts, and quantitative operations. A full range of standard scores and norms are provided.

Nelson-Denny Reading Test—Forms G and H
Riverside Publishing Company
Grades: 9 to adults
Testing time: 35–50 minutes
Last MMY *review:* 9th

This test provides four scores: vocabulary, comprehension, total, and rate. It is intended for use with high school, college, and adult students as a means of obtaining summary norm-referenced survey scores. There are two subtests: vocabulary with 100 items and comprehension with 36 items. The test is intended to be used to screen students, to predict college success, and to diagnose reading difficulties. There is little evidence provided in the manual to support the validity of the test for these purposes, however. The test has the high reliability one expects of tests of this type. This instrument is a valuable and useful test because it is one of the few reading tests appropriate for use with older students.

Stanford Diagnostic Reading Test (SDRT), Third Edition
Psychological Corporation
Grades: 1.5–12
Testing time: Varies with level
Last MMY *review:* 9th

This test is intended to provide diagnostic-prescriptive information to teachers both to help individual students and to assist in decision making about grouping students who have the same instructional needs. There are four levels. Red level (Forms A and B), for Grades 1.6–3.5, has six scores: auditory vocabulary, auditory discrimination, phonetic analysis, and three comprehension scores (word reading, reading comprehension, and total). Green level (Forms A and B), for Grades 2.6–5.5, has seven scores: auditory vocabulary, auditory discrimination, phonetic analysis, structural analysis, and three comprehension scores (literal, inferential, and total). Brown level (Forms A and B), for Grades 4.6–9.5, has seven scores, which are the same as those of the green level except that reading rate replaces auditory discrimination. Blue level (Forms A and B), for Grades 9.0–13.0, has 12 scores: three for comprehension (literal, inferential, and total), three for vocabulary (word meaning, word parts, and total), three for decoding (phonetic analysis, structural analysis, and total), and three for rate (fast reading, scanning and skimming, and total). A wide range of normative scores are available along with an impressive array of computer scoring and interpretation services. Extensive use of intraindividual differences are emphasized, but these should be interpreted with caution because of the unreliability inherent in such comparisons.

SECTION E–ACHIEVEMENT TEST BATTERIES

California Achievement Tests (CAT) (Forms E and F)
CTB Macmillan/McGraw-Hill
Grades: Kindergarten–Grade 12
Testing time: Varies with level
Last MMY *review:* 10th

This achievement test battery has been available and used extensively for over 50 years. Forms E and F of the 1985 version are intended to replace Forms C and D. Form E consists of 11 levels (Levels 10–20) covering kindergarten through Grade 12, while Form F contains 8 levels (Levels 13–20) and ranges from the second half of Grade 2 to Grade 12. The two forms can be used together for fall and spring testing. The test covers the usual topics for an achievement test battery: word analysis, vocabulary, comprehension, language expression, mathematics computation, concepts, and applications. Test development including item selection, norming, and scaling represents the state of the art in test development. Extensive use is made of item response theory. Particularly useful are standard error of measurement curves, which make it possible to evaluate the capacity of a test to make discriminations anywhere along the ability scale.

Comprehensive Tests of Basic Skills, Fourth Edition (CTBS/4)
CTB Macmillan/McGraw-Hill
Grades: Kindergarten–Grade 12
Testing time: Varies with age
Last MMY *review:* 11th

There are currently three options available to the schools choosing to adopt the CTBS/4. (1) Complete battery tests are similar to the previous editions, Forms U and V. The complete battery provides norm-referenced and curriculum-referenced information. (2) Benchmark tests are intended to provide the most reliable and valid norm-referenced scores. This option is most suitable for schools that do not need curriculum-referenced information. (3) There are two survey tests, each half as long as the benchmark tests; they are intended to provide a quicker measure of the achievement level of students than the benchmark tests do. Of course, because the survey tests are shorter, their item coverage and statistical characteristics are inferior to those obtained from the benchmark tests. A curriculum-referenced version of the CTBS/4 has also been planned.

Scales included in CTBS/4 are visual recognition (kindergarten), word analysis (Grades 1–3), vocabulary (kindergarten through Grade 12), comprehension (kindergarten through Grade 12), language mechanics and language expression (Grades 1–12), spelling (Grades 2–12), study skills (Grades 4–12), mathematics computation and mathematics concepts and applications (kindergarten through Grade 12), science (Grades 1–12), and social studies (Grades 1–12). The CTBS/4 differs from earlier editions by placing greater emphasis on the assessment of higher order thinking skills. Item selection, norming, and scaling represent the state of the art in test development, effectively employing item response theory techniques. The CTBS/4 is similar in its psychometric properties to the California Achievement Tests, which is not surprising because they share the same publisher and the same test development staff.

Iowa Tests of Basic Skills (ITBS) Form J

Riverside Publishing Company
Grades: Kindergarten–Grade 9
Testing time: Varies with level
Last MMY *review:* 11th

This test is a highly regarded achievement test battery that uses all of the most accepted techniques of test development that might be expected of such a venerable test. It differs from the other two most often used achievement test batteries, the Comprehensive Tests of Basic Skills and the California Achievement Tests, in eschewing the use of item response theory. The early primary battery is available for Form G only and has two levels: Level 5 for Grades K.1–1.5 and Level 6 for Grades K.8–1.9. The primary battery has two levels: Level 7 for Grades 1.7–2.6 and Level 8 for Grades 2.5–3.5. For Grades 3–9, there are multilevel and separate level editions. The basic battery has 6 tests, and the complete battery has 11 tests. In addition, there are supplemental science and social studies tests that use an essay format.

Iowa Tests of Educational Development (ITED) (8th Edition)

Riverside Publishing Company
Grades: 10–12
Testing time: Level I, 250 minutes; Level II, 280 minutes
Last MMY *review:* 10th

This test has two forms, Forms X8 and Y8, and two levels, Level I for Grades 9 and 10 and Level II for Grades 11 and 12. There are nine tests and therefore nine scores provided:

Test E—Correctness and appropriateness of expression
Test Q—Ability to do quantitative thinking
Test SS—Analysis of social studies materials
Test NS—Analysis of natural sciences materials
Test L—Ability to interpret literary materials
Test V—Vocabulary
Test SI—Uses of sources of information
Composite
Reading total

Unlike other achievement batteries, the ITED assesses secondary school students differently than elementary school students. The ITED focus is on neither basic skills nor the specific course content found in high school curricula. The focus is instead on long-term educational goals and higher-order thinking skills. The reliability of the separate tests ranges from the mid-0.80s to the high 0.90s. Strong evidence that the test is unspeeded is provided. Completion rates are in the .90s and all items are answered by 95% of the students who take the test.

Metropolitan Achievement Tests, Seventh Edition (MAT7)
Psychological Corporation
Grades: Kindergarten–Grade 12
Testing time: 90–230 minutes, varies with level
Last MMY *review:* 12th

This test focuses on eight basic skills: vocabulary, reading, mathematics, spelling, language, science, social studies, and writing. It has fourteen levels:

Preprimer, K.0–K.5
Primer—K.5–1.5
Primary 1, 1.5–2.5
Primary 2, 2.5–3.5
Elementary 1, 3.5–4.5
Elementary 2, 4.5–5.5
Intermediate 1, 5.5–6.5
Intermediate 2, 6.5–7.5
Intermediate 3, 7.5–8.5
Intermediate 4, 8.5–9.5
Secondary 1, 9.0
Secondary 2, 10.0
Secondary 3, 11.0
Secondary 4, 12.0
A writing test is also available for grades 1.5–12.

The MAT7, like its predecessors, is a high-quality instrument that is available only to school districts for use in standardized testing programs. The first two levels provide scores for prereading, mathematics, language and a composite. Levels primary 1 through intermediate 4 offer 12 scores: four for reading; three for mathematics; one each for language, science, and social studies; a basic battery score for reading, mathematics, and language; and a total score. Reliabilities are generally in the .80s and above. Validity evidence offered is in the form of correlations with previous editions and a review of current textbooks.

Stanford Achievement Tests (8th Edition)
Psychological Corporation
Grades: 1.5–9.9
Testing time: Varies with level
Last MMY *review:* 11th

This test has eight levels. Primary 1, for Grades 1.5–2.5, yields 14 scores: four reading scores (word reading, reading comprehension, word study skills, and total reading), four mathematics scores (concepts of number, computation, applications, and total mathematics), a listening score, a language score, a spelling score, an environment score, and scores for the basic and total batteries. Primary 2, for Grades 2.5–3.5, yields 14 scores: the same scores provided by Level 1 except that reading vocabulary is substituted for word reading. Primary level 3, for grades 3.5–4.5, provides 20 scores: the same 8 scores for reading and mathematics as the 2 lower levels, 3 scores for language (mechanics, expression and total), and scores for spelling, study skills, science, social science, listening, using information, thinking skills, and basic and complete batteries. The 3 Intermediate and the 2 Advanced levels yield 19 scores: three reading scores (comprehension, vocabulary, and total reading), four mathematics scores (concepts of number, computation, applications, and total mathematics), three language scores (mechanics, expression, and total language), and the same additional scales as the Primary 3 battery. Like the other major achievement test batteries, the Stanford Achievement Test Series employs sophisticated test development procedures. A brief edition of this test was published in 1992 and is reviewed in *MMY* 12.

SECTION F—INDIVIDUALLY ADMINISTERED TESTS OF ACHIEVEMENT

Gates-McKillup-Horowitz Reading Diagnostic Test, Second Edition
Teachers College Press
Grades: 1–6
Testing time: Untimed (highly variable depending on tests used)
Last MMY *review:* 9th

The purpose of this test is to identify strengths and weaknesses within the individual student and not to provide normative comparisons. Twenty-three scores are provided: omissions, additions, repetitions, mispronunciations (directional errors, wrong beginning, wrong middle, wrong ending, wrong in several parts, accent errors, and total), reading sentences, words flash, words untimed, word attack (syllabication, recognizing and blending common word parts, reading words, giving letter sounds, naming capital letters, and naming lowercase letters), vowels, auditory blending, auditory discrimination, and spelling. The use of the test is predicated on the assumption that reading can be analyzed from a reductionistic framework and that oral phonic skills are of primary importance: both assertions are dubious.

KeyMath Revised
American Guidance Service
Grades: Kindergarten–Grade 9
Testing time: 35–50 minutes
Last MMY *review:* 11th

This test is an individually administered diagnostic mathematics test that can be administered quickly and easily and that is used quite often in conjunction with special education assessment. This test includes three domains with different subtests subsumed under each: basic concept (numeration, rational numbers, and geometry), operations (addition, subtraction, multiplication, division, and mental computation), and applications (measurement, time and money, estimation, interpreting data, and problem solving). Four types of scores are available: (1) total test, the student's performance on all subtests combined; (2) area, the student's performance in each area; (3) subtest, performance on each subtest; and (4) domain, performance in each domain. A variety of scores are provided, including standard scores, percentiles, normal curve equivalents, age and grade equivalents, and stanines. Confidence intervals are also provided. This revision is a major improvement over the previous version, which provided only grade equivalents and an insufficient amount of additional information to compute any other type of score. With the exception of the kindergarten level, where some of the reliabilities are very low, the reliabilities are within an acceptable range, 0.80s and 0.90s for the upper grades.

Peabody Individual Achievement Test Revised (PIAT-R)
American Guidance Service, Inc.
Grades: Kindergarten–Grade 12
Testing time: Untimed, power test (The only timed test is the written expression subtest, which takes 20 minutes.)
Last MMY *review:* 11th

The PIAT-R includes the following subscales: general information, reading recognition, reading comprehension, mathematics, spelling, total reading, total test, and written expression. It is individually administered with user-friendly materials such as easels, making this test an easy one to administer. Scores that reflect overall student performance on subscales are provided, but this test is not intended to be diagnostic or used as the sole criterion for high stakes decisions about students. The PIAT-R, like the Wide Range Achievement Test (WRAT), is a good screening test for use in circumstances where a quick estimate of academic functioning is needed.

Wide Range Achievement Test 3 (WRAT-3)
Jastak Associates, Inc.
Grades: Kindergarten to adults
Testing time: 15–30 minutes
Last MMY *review:* 12th

This test, which covers reading, spelling, and arithmetic, is frequently used because it can be easily and quickly administered. Its psychometric characteristics have often been criticized. The weakest of the three scales is reading, which is assessed by having the student read aloud a list of words that have been placed in ascending order of difficulty. The revised version of this test does little to allay these concerns because, except for changes in format and the manner of presentation, there is little difference between this test and the previous edition.

Woodcock-Johnson Psycho-Educational Battery-Revised (WJ-R) Tests
    of Achievement
Riverside Publishing Company
Ages: 2–90
Testing time: 50–60 minutes
Last MMY *review:* 12th

The achievement portion of this comprehensive battery provides 9 Standard Battery scores relating to reading comprehension, mathematics, science, social studies, humanities, and written and oral communication; 5 Standard Battery cluster scores derived from combinations of the basic 9 scales; 9 Supplemental Battery scores dealing primarily with more fine-grained aspects of reading and language; and 6 Supplementary cluster scores. The fact that this instrument is coordinated with the cognitive ability portion of the WJ-R into a complete aptitude-achievement package makes it quite attractive. (See Chapter 8.)

Woodcock Reading Mastery Test—Revised
American Guidance Service, Inc.
Grades: Kindergarten to adults
Testing time: 40–45 minutes for the entire battery
Last MMY *review:* 10th

This test consists of six individually administered reading tests all contained in an easel kit. Six test scores are provided, four of which are reading achievement scores (word identification, word attack, word comprehension, and passage comprehension) and two of which are readiness scores (letter identification and visual auditory learning). There is also a supplementary letter checklist. Five derived scores are provided from clusters: readiness, basic skills, reading comprehension, total reading (full scale), and total reading (short scale). Two forms, G and H, are available. A software package called ASSIST is available to aid in the complex process of converting raw scores to standard scores. Split-half reliabilities are provided, and they range from 0.34 to 0.98.

SECTION G—PERSONALITY INVENTORIES

Adjective Checklist (ACL)
Consulting Psychologists Press
Grades: 9–16 and adults
Testing time: Untimed (approximately 15–20 minutes)
Last MMY review: 9th

The ACL is an alphabetic list of 300 adjectives from "absent-mined" to "zany." The examinee responds by marking the adjectives that are self-descriptive. The instrument can be scored for 3 control scales and 34 variables that include 15 needs (from Murray's system), measures of personal adjustment, counseling readiness, self-confidence, self-control, lability, and the types associated with transactional analysis. Scoring is complicated because different norm tables are required depending on the number of adjectives checked. Median scale alpha coefficients were 0.76 for males and 0.75 for females. Retest correlations were lower. Validity data are rather meager; therefore, the instrument is most appropriate for research.

California Psychological Inventory—Revised (CPI)
Consulting Psychologists Press
Ages: 13 and over
Testing time: Untimed (approximately 45–60 minutes)
Last MMY review: 11th

The CPI was developed as a personality assessment instrument for use with normal populations. It consists of 480 items to be answered "true" or "false." About half of the items on the CPI were taken from the Minnesota Multiphasic Personality Inventory. The CPI yields 18 scores, three of which are check scales to determine test-taking attitudes. Items on 11 of the 15 scales were selected for their ability to discriminate among contrasting groups. Retest reliabilities for high school groups over a 1-year interval averaged 0.65 for males and 0.68 for females. Retest reliabilities for an adult group over a 1- to 3-week interval averaged about 0.80. Correlations among the scales tend to be moderate to high. Current development efforts are focusing on the interpretation of patterns of scale scores. Separate norms are provided by gender for high school and college samples. Some of the validity data based on differences between extreme groups are questionable.

Comrey Personality Scales (CPS)
Educational and Industrial Testing Service
Ages: 16 and over
Testing time: Untimed (approximately 30–50 minutes)
Last MMY review: 8th

Eight personality scales are reported for this inventory (trust, orderliness, social conformity, activity, emotional stability, extroversion, masculinity, and empathy) as well as scales for validity of responding and response bias. The scales were developed to be homogeneous using factor analysis. Median scale internal consistency was 0.93. Correlations among the scales are generally modest. Evidence for the validity of the scales as measures of personality dimensions for normal individuals is increasing.

Eysenck Personality Inventory (EPI)
Educational and Industrial Testing Service
Grades: 9–16 and adults
Testing time: Untimed (approximately 10–15 minutes)
Last MMY *review:* 8th

The EPI yields three scores: extroversion, neuroticism, and lie. Two forms are available, and the author recommends administration of both forms to obtain adequate reliability for individual measurement. The items require a "yes" or "no" response. Each form consists of a 24-item extroversion (e) scale, a 24-item neuroticism (n) scale, and a 9-item lie scale. Normative information is weak.

Fundamental Interpersonal Relations Orientation (FIRO) Scales (FIRO Awareness Scales)
Consulting Psychologists Press
Grades: 9–16 and adults
Testing time: Untimed (approximately 120 minutes for combined scales)
Last MMY *review:* 9th

The FIRO Scales are self-report questionnaires designed to assess a person's need for inclusion, control, and affection in various aspects of interpersonal situations. There are six subscales, each of which focuses on a different interpersonal situation: behavior toward others (FIRO-B), feelings toward others, retrospective childhood relationships with parents, coping operations preference enquiry (COPE), marital attitudes evaluation, and educational values. A downward extension of the behavior scale for Grades 4–8 is available. Except the COPE, all subscales contain nine single-statement items, each of which is answered on a six-point scale. In the COPE subscale, the examinee rank orders the defense mechanisms that he or she uses for each interpersonal situation. Only the FIRO-B subscale is well enough developed to be used for other than exploratory studies.

Gordon Personal Profile (GPP)
Psychological Corporation
Grades: 9–16 and adults
Testing time: Untimed (approximately 15–20 minutes)
Last MMY *review:* 10th

The items in this instrument are arranged in sets of four statements, two favorable and two unfavorable, from which the examinee is to select the statement that is "most" like him or her and the one that is "least" like him or her. The GPP yields five scores: ascendancy (A), responsibility (R), emotional stability (E), sociability (S), and self-esteem (SE). Although the five traits were selected as being independent, the correlations between the A and S scales and between the R and E scales are 0.60 or higher. Reliability is adequate. Validity data reported in the manual include correlations between scores and peer ratings and counselors' ratings for college groups. Additional validity data are presented for groups in industrial and training situations. Percentile norms are provided for high school and college students, low- and middle-level employees, managers, salespeople, and supervisors.

Gordon Personal Profile Inventory (GPP-I)
Psychological Corporation
Grades: 9–16 and adults
Testing time: Untimed (approximately 20–25 minutes)
Last MMY *review:* 10th

This inventory uses the same format as the GPP. It produces four scores: cautiousness, original thinking, personal relations, and vigor. Internal consistency reliability coefficients (split-half) of the four scales range from 0.77 to 0.84. Validity data consist primarily of correlations between scores on the subtests and performance criteria. However, because there is no theoretical basis for predicting either the magnitude or direction of the correlations, these data must be viewed somewhat skeptically unless they appear for several groups. Most of the validity information comes from studies conducted in the 1960s and is therefore quite dated. Percentile norms are provided by gender for high school and college groups.

Guilford-Zimmerman Temperament Survey (GZTS)
Consulting Psychologists Press
Grades: 9–16 and adults
Testing time: Untimed (approximately 45 minutes)
Last MMY *review:* 8th

This inventory provides 10 scores: general activity, restraint, ascendance, sociability, emotional stability, objectivity, friendliness, thoughtfulness, personal relations, and masculinity. There are 300 items, with 30 items per scale. All items are affirmative statements to which the respondent answers "yes, "no," or "?." Scales have reasonable internal consistency (80s) and temporal stabilities. There are over 500 studies contributing to the interpretation of GZTS scores. It is one of the better inventories for describing aspects of the normal personality. Experience is needed to determine whether the dimensions are of practical importance for personal or vocational counseling.

IPAT Anxiety Scale Questionnaire (ASQ)
Institute for Personality and Ability Testing
Ages: 14 and over
Testing time: Untimed (approximately 5–10 minutes)
Last MMY *review:* 8th

The ASQ consists of 40 items that yield five part scores and a total score. In addition, the 40 items yield separate "covert" and "overt" anxiety scores. Construction of the scale was based on extensive factor analytic studies. Empirical validity of the scale is based on (1) correlations of total scores with psychiatric ratings (range of 0.30–0.40 uncorrected for attenuation), (2) differences in mean scores between anxiety neurotics and the standardization population, and (3) differences in mean scores among other clinically diagnosed groups. Reliability coefficients for the part scores, based on subtests with as few as 4 and as many as 12 items, are too low to justify the use of the part scores with individuals. The ASQ is probably most useful as a quick screening device for literate adults and as a research instrument.

Millon Clinical Multiaxial Inventory II (MCMI-II)

National Computer Systems
Population: "Adults receiving mental health services"
Testing time: 25–30 minutes
Last MMY *review:* 11th

See Chapter 11 for a detailed discussion of this instrument.

Minnesota Multiphasic Personality Inventory Revised (MMPI-II)

University of Minnesota Press
Ages: 16 and over
Testing time: Untimed (approximately 30–90 minutes)
Last MMY *review:* 11th

This instrument is oriented toward abnormal rather than normal groups. It was designed to differentiate between clinical groups, but there is some question on how well it does this. It is too long to be used as a screening test, but the profile based on the separate scale scores provides a good deal of material for interpretation by the sophisticated clinical psychologist. It is the most widely used and cited objective personality measure. A Spanish translation is available. An adolescent version, published in 1992, was reviewed in the 12th *MMY.* See Chapter 11 for further discussion.

Myers-Briggs Type Indicator (MBTI), 1985 Revision

Consulting Psychologists Press
Grades: 9–16 and adults
Testing time: Untimed (approximately 50–60 minutes)
Last MMY *review:* 10th

The MBTI is a forced-choice self-report inventory that is based on a modification of the Jungian theory of types. It yields four bipolar scores: extraversion versus introversion; sensation versus intuition; thinking versus feeling; judgment versus perception. The universe of all combinations of types yields 16 possibilities. The instrument was originally published in 1943 and has undergone a number of revisions. There are currently three forms available, all of which can be administered by computer. The MBTI has been extensively used in counseling and research.

Personality Research Form (PRF), Third Edition
Research Psychologists Press
Grades: 6–16 and adults
Testing time: Untimed (approximately 35–70 minutes, depending on form)
Last MMY *review:* 10th

There are six forms of the PRF. Forms A and B are alternate forms that yield 15 scores for individuals 16 years and older (30–45 minutes). Forms AA and BB are alternate forms that yield 22 scores for college students (40–70 minutes). Form E yields 22 scores for Grades 6–16 and adults (40–70 minutes) and is available in French and Spanish. Form G is for use in business and industry and yields 20 scores (40–70 minutes). Scales correspond to needs from Murray's theory of personality. Scores are expressed as *T* scores. Norms are available by gender for college students and normal adults. Additional norms are given for juvenile offenders. The inventory has superior technical sophistication, and reviewers consider it a promising inventory, although they note the lack of clinical interpretive data.

Sixteen Personality Factor (16PF) Questionnaire (5th Edition)
Institute for Personality and Ability Testing
Ages: 6 and over (depending on form)
Testing time: Untimed (approximately 45–60 minutes)
Last MMY *review:* 12th

Construction of the 16PF was based on extensive factor analytic studies and research. There are forms for children 6–8, 8–12, and 12–18 and people 16 and over. The inventory yields 16 scores on primary factors as well as scores on four second-order factors. Split-half reliabilities for individual scales from a single form tend to be low, but pooling scores from alternate forms yields scores of adequate reliability. Norms are provided for each level of the instrument and are based on up to 15,000 cases.

Study of Values (or AVL Study of Values), Third Edition
Riverside Publishing Company
Grades: 10–16 and adults
Testing time: Untimed (approximately 20 minutes)
Last MMY *review:* 7th

The Study of Values, originally published in 1931, was designed to measure Spranger's six "value types": theoretical, economic, aesthetic, social, political, and religious. The second edition, published in 1951, redefined the social value type and added more discriminating items. The third edition, published in 1960, differs from the second only in providing more normative data. The median reliability coefficients for the different subscales are 0.82 (split-half) and 0.88 (test-retest with a 1-month interval). Validity data presented in the manual consist primarily of demonstrations of value patterns of various educational and occupational groups that differ in predicted ways. Norms are provided for college groups and for occupational groups that usually require some college education. Most material is quite dated.

Survey of Personal Values (SPV)
Science Research Associates, Inc.
Grades: 9–16 and adults
Testing time: Untimed (approximately 15 minutes)
Last MMY *review:* 10th

The SPV yields six scores: practical mindedness, achievement, variety, decisiveness, orderliness, and goal orientation. The instrument consists of 30 triads of statements; the respondent must select the statement from each triad that is most important and the statement that is least important to him or her. Raw scores are converted into percentile ranks. Norms are available for ninth-grade vocational students by gender (over 1,000 males and over 1,000 females), high school students by gender (over 1,300 males and over 1,300 females), vocational junior college students by gender (2,300 males and 587 females), college students by gender (984 males and 1,080 females), workers in routine jobs (1,461), and workers in managerial jobs (1,089). Alpha reliability coefficients ranged from 0.77 to 0.87. Retest reliabilities were 0.74–0.92 (one week) and 0.38–0.74 (one year). Validity evidence is accumulating, but the instrument is still best used for research.

Tennessee Self-Concept Scale (Revised) (TSCS)
Western Psychological Services
Ages: 12 and over
Testing time: Untimed (approximately 20 minutes)
Last MMY *review:* 11th

The TSCS is a self-administering instrument consisting of 100 statements with five response options ranging from "completely false" to "completely true." Two forms, the counseling form and the clinical and research form, are available, but the two forms contain the same items and differ only in the method of scoring. The counseling form yields 14 scores, and the clinical and research form yields 29 scores. Items were constructed to appraise the following aspects of the self: identity, self-satisfaction, behavior, physical self, social self, moral-ethical self, personal self, family self. In addition, three derived scores are provided: total positive score, reflecting overall level of self-esteem; variability score, reflecting amount of consistency among areas of the self; and distribution score, reflecting a tendency to use extreme response ratings. Scoring by hand is tedious, but computer scoring is available. The manual for the test is incomplete and lacks essential information. At its present stage of development, this test is most suitable for research.

Name Index

Subject Index